The Musorgsky Reader

Da Capo Press Music Reprint Series

GENERAL EDITOR

FREDERICK FREEDMAN

VASSAR COLLEGE

THE
Musorgsky Reader

A Life of
Modeste Petrovich Musorgsky
in
Letters and Documents

EDITED AND TRANSLATED BY

Jay Leyda and Sergei Bertensson

𝓢 DA CAPO PRESS • NEW YORK • 1970

A Da Capo Press Reprint Edition

This Da Capo Press edition of *The Musorgsky Reader* is an unabridged republication of the first edition published in New York in 1947. It is reprinted by special arrangement with the author.

Library of Congress Catalog Card Number 70-87393
SBN 306-71534-1

THE
Musorgsky Reader

Modeste Petrovich Musorgsky
A photograph presented in 1876 to Ludmila Shestakova

THE
Musorgsky Reader

A Life of
Modeste Petrovich Musorgsky
in
Letters and Documents

EDITED AND TRANSLATED BY

Jay Leyda and Sergei Bertensson

W · W · NORTON & COMPANY · INC · *New York*

PRINTED IN THE UNITED STATES OF AMERICA
FOR THE PUBLISHERS BY THE VAIL-BALLOU PRESS

Contents

Illustrations

An Impersonal Note

FOR NO very obvious reason there is less responsibility exercised in writing about Musorgsky than about any other Russian composer, even including that victim of fiction, Tchaikovsky. Our popularizing writers have surpassed even Musorgsky's contemporaries in factual carelessness and misguided opinion. As late as 1944 a program note for a metropolitan American orchestra packed this amount of misstatement into a brief space:

> Moussorgsky worked on "Boris Godunoff" for more than 12 years. The score remained in part fragmentary and Rimsky-Korsakoff, as musical executor, completed missing portions and orchestrations from sketches left by the composer.

As editors of Musorgsky's documents, we were determined to be unusually cautious in gathering and arranging in chronological order all the known nonmusical facts of his life. These facts, many of them familiar to music students, have been gathered from their original sources, whether these be personal documents or the testimony of Musorgsky's friends and acquaintances. This variety of voices—Balakirev, Cui, Stasov, Rimsky-Korsakov, Borodin, Tchaikovsky—not only gives body to a vital period of Russian musical thought, but gives, as well, a third dimension to the familiar flattened figure of Musorgsky. His is no simple nor easily defined personality. If one is eager and willing to learn the motivations and workings of his character, one will have to go beyond the complexities of Musorgsky's music, into the complexities of Musorgsky's letters. None of his contemporaries, alone, can adequately sum up this character for the reader; for example, Madame Rimskaya-Korsakova, whose acquaintance with Musorgsky extended over his last fifteen years, tells us little more than this:

> Musorgsky was an enemy of every sort of routine and commonplace, not only in music but in every phase of life, even in trifles. He disliked using ordinary simple words. He always contrived to alter and distort

ix

even surnames. The style of his letters was unusually individual and piquant; they glittered with wit, humor and bull's-eye-hitting epithets. In the last years of his life this individual style became an affectation, particularly noticeable in his letters to V. V. Stasov. However, this affectation and unnaturalness sometimes showed itself not only in his letters but in the whole of his behavior.

Gerald Abraham goes on to say, "That is very true. Musorgsky's fantastic letters—sometimes exasperatingly fantastic, with their puns and roundabout phrases and distortions of names—defy adequate translation." [1]

It is true that most of Musorgsky's letters have frightened translators, although Mr. Abraham, along with S. W. Pring and Paul Swan, could justly boast that they have been conscientious and intelligent in rendering those fragments of his correspondence which they have made available for English and American readers. In preparing our translation, such good models as theirs were unfortunately rare. We learned that "free adaptation" had been considered as legitimate a practice with Musorgsky's documents as with his scores. "Distasteful" elements have been skirted with no more respect for his intention than have the "crude" elements in his musical manuscripts. Difficult passages were usually omitted with no indication that Musorgsky had something more to say— Although I must confess that total omission is preferable to the pale paraphrase of Musorgsky's ideas and speech given by a disgusted translator of the "kitchen" paragraph in Letter 89.[2] No, Musorgsky does not submit to translation without a struggle, and I speak for both translators of this volume in saying that neither of us, without the other, could have attempted or completed this work. It takes two, at least, to cope with a mind like Musorgsky's.

We have preferred to sacrifice all secondary values, such as smoothness and neatness, to our main aim: the communication of Musorgsky's written thought in as exact an English equivalent as it was in our

---

[1] M. D. Calvocoressi and Gerald Abraham, *Masters of Russian Music* (New York, A. A. Knopf, 1936), p. 209. Mr. Abraham has not only contributed the admirable biography of Musorgsky in that volume but has also edited, with scrupulous care, Calvocoressi's biography, left unfinished at his death: *Mussorgsky* (London, J. M. Dent; New York, E. P. Dutton, 1946).

[2] The exact text on p. 192 may be compared with this version: "Admitting that I shun technique, does it mean that I am no good at it? When I eat a good pie, do I want to behold how much butter, how many eggs, cabbages and fishes went to the making of it? The proof of it is in the eating . . ." (*The Musical Quarterly*, July 1923).

joined powers to find. We have also tried to be sensitive to the dominant atmosphere of certain letters—whether this was an atmosphere of gaiety, oppression, or hysteria. Our efforts were guided by the tremendous editorial task achieved by Dr. Pavel Lamm on Musorgsky's musical manuscripts, and for motto we used Lyadov's honest comment on his own efforts to bring order to the manuscripts of *Fair. at Sorochintzi:*

> It seems so easy to correct Musorgsky's alleged shortcomings. Yet, when it is done, one feels at once that the result is no longer Musorgsky. Certainly it would be easy merely to delete one or another of the voice doublings, to do away with some of the parallel voices, to smooth over a modulation—but the fault in this method lies in fact that something quite different from Musorgsky is the result. The characteristic quality, the peculiarity of his workmanship are lost. Truly, one does not know how to begin. If one allows the music to remain as Musorgsky wrote it down, it is often crude, faulty, and unbeautiful; if one brings order therein, it is no longer Musorgsky. In the editing of his works, therefore, one is forced either to violate all rules, or to forfeit the composer's original character.

Although we have done our best to narrow down the quantity of obscure passages in Musorgsky's letters, there are still far too many remaining, we know. But we considered it wiser to leave these in, for someone else to work out their obscurities, than to hide them from some possible future solution.

No element in these letters, no matter how strange it may sound at first reading, is completely foreign to the non-Russian reader. We have Charles Ives to show us another musician determined to find words for his ideas, no matter how laborious the process, nor how turgid the result.[3] We've seen men as remote (and as near) as Charles Lamb and Franz Kafka, choked by forced office work, in perpetual conflict with their responsibilities as artists. We have Poe's morbidity and dipsomania to remind us that an artist need not be Russian to seek refuge from spiritual pain in alcohol. Not even Musorgsky's fascinating letter-writing masks are unique with him; Dickens wrote letters (to Stanfield) in the character of an old sea-dog, and Oliver Wendell Holmes

---

[3] In Ives' *Essays before a Sonata* (New York, 1920) there is the following "Musorgskian" wrestling with stubborn words: "They [the images] do often arouse something that has not yet passed the border line between subconsciousness and consciousness—an artistic intuition (well named, but)—object and cause unknown!—here is a program!—conscious or subconscious, what does it matter?" (p. 8)

wrote (to James T. Fields) in the character of a schoolmistress, producing documents that will some day give Russian translators, readers and analysts as much trouble and pleasure as Musorgsky's masks of an old peasant woman and of an eighteenth-century police clerk have given us.

The letters written in these particular masks (Nos. 40 and 44 to Shestakova, Musorgsky's contribution to the collective letter [41] written to Balakirev, and No. 143 to Golenishchev-Kutuzov) have all been published only in recent years, but Lapshin's remarks [4] on this masking tendency are still valid:

> . . . in the letters to Stasov, in addition to the usual language of an intellectual of the '70's, we find an imitation of the writing style of the clerks and scribes that Musorgsky portrayed in *Boris Godunov* and *Khovanshchina,* and one notices a certain intentional compression of pseudo-archaism and pseudo-slavisms [No. 74 and others]. There is also an ironic imitation of the bookish language of the XVIII century . . . If the charming humor of Borodin's letters to his wife reminds us, in style, of Pushkin's letters to his wife; if Rimsky-Korsakov's humor in his letters reminds us of Gogol, and Tchaikovsky's humor— of Chekhov,—then Musorgsky's humor in his letters to Stasov reminds one in its language at times of Dostoyevsky and some Dostoyevsky figures—Lebyadkin (in *Demons*) and Ferdyshchenko (in *The Idiot*), —there is at once something jesting and macabre in Musorgsky's exaggerations . . . Thus Musorgsky loved to appear in his letters, for a joke, as a masquer . . . Loving to put on masks himself, he also loves to put masks on others with nicknames that either caricature or underline some external peculiarity in them. Shcherbachov becomes "Flagon" because he loved to use scent; Tchaikovsky becomes "Sadyk-Pasha" because of the impression he made on Musorgsky of a luxurious autocrat . . . In the humor, caricature, and grotesquerie of Musorgsky's letters, there is also something in common with the style of the letters and feuilletons of Berlioz, with his tendency towards mystifications, parodies—often brilliant, but occasionally in the same dubious taste we often find in Musorgsky.[5]

Musorgsky's colorful masks, however, serve to reveal him more fully to his friends and to us, rather than to hide the writer behind a mask of artificial naturalness, such as Tchaikovsky confessed to using:

> Regardless to whom or why I write, I always worry about what impression the letter will produce not only on the correspondent but even

---

[4] In the special Musorgsky number of *Muzikalnyi Sovremennik,* January-February 1917. Lyadov's comment, above, is taken from Karatygin's article in the same issue.

[5] How concerned everyone is with Musorgsky's "bad taste!"

on the casual reader. Therefore, I pose. Sometimes, I *try* to make the tone of the letter simple and sincere, that is, to make it *seem* so. (*Diaries*, 27 June, 1888) [6]

Elsewhere in his diaries Tchaikovsky speaks contemptuously of an artist's search for "truth," but it is this very search that inspires most of Musorgsky's letters (as it does Katherine Mansfield's personal documents), and Musorgsky employs masks in this search in much the same way that imagery assists the surrealists. How significant it is that one of his most enlightening statements wears the police-clerk mask (No. 143):

> This latter [Musorgsky], in fraudulent dreams, maliciously repudiating the codified mussical laws, established throughout the centuries by the activity and labors of highly honorable and respected men and, furthermore, regulated by the centuries, opines that any kind of human speech can be brought into mussical harmony and by that, bearing malice in his obvious impotence of mussicianship, snares people for the sake of his evil and most dangerous purposes, and what is mournful is that: he has caught a great number of gullible and ignorant souls in mussical matters and worst of all—he continues to ensnare them.

Musorgsky's complete correspondence must have been far more extensive than is indicated by known letters. Although a large and important series of letters, to Golenishchev-Kutuzov, has only recently been discovered, we fear that the most conspicuous gap in our information will never be filled. The absence of all family letters may be linked to the disappearance of Modeste's brother, Philarète, from the circle of Musorgsky's acquaintances and from history.[7] Nor are there any love letters—at least not in the accepted sense of this term; of these all we have is the legend of a packet of letters buried with Musorgsky's first sweetheart. There seems little likelihood that the "female involved" in Letter 23 or the "strong, burning and loving woman" of Letter 93 will ever be identified. These doors seem closed to research, except for the several hints scattered through the documents in this volume. It would be dangerous to read too much into the fondness and intimacy often expressed in Musorgsky's letters to Shestakova, Stasov

---

[6] *The Diaries of Tchaikovsky*, translated by Wladimir Lakond (New York, W. W. Norton & Company, Inc., 1945).

[7] Stasov's last communication with Philarète was in the year of Modeste's death, to obtain information for his memorial monograph. Karatygin, however, saw Philarète in the nineties, but neither his death-date nor the whereabouts of his descendants (a son in the Navy and two spinster daughters) is known.

and Golenishchev-Kutuzov—one must constantly remind oneself of an extra-warm heart (who would be surprised to find one in Musorgsky?) that learned to function in a period of romantic, Byronic self-revelation (the disproportionate passion of Delacroix's letters still worries his editors and biographers). However, the quantity of Russian diminutives (Musoryanin, Musinka, Korsinka, Dyainka) and endearments (I kiss your dear little hands, little dove) derive from no affectation on Musorgsky's part, but from genuine affection.

The letters written to Musorgsky are even more rare than those written by him. We have brought into this volume all but two brief notes from this slim file. Much of this correspondence may have been in that careless bonfire at Bobrovo—and in how many other bonfires! It is almost as if some watchful agency took care that the questions Musorgsky preferred not to answer were left forever unanswered.

Only brief notes of small interest (appointments, dinner arrangements, etc.[8]) have been omitted from this volume; these omissions are indicated in the complete list of known Musorgsky correspondence compiled in the appendix. We have, however, felt justified in an occasional alteration of the dating determined by the Russian editors of the two volumes of published letters. These alterations have been made on the basis of internal evidence, and our reasoning will be followed in future Russian editions of the letters. From Andrei Rimsky-Korsakov's edition we have brought up his No. 147 from 1874 to 1875, and placed his No. 212, dated 1878, back in 1874. No. XXIV in the Golenishchev-Kutuzov volume has been altered from 1879 to 1878.

All Musorgsky letters that have been included are translated intact —with one qualification: at the risk of joining Musorgsky's editorial "cleansers" we have omitted violently chauvinist phrases directed against Jews and Catholics as groups. Musorgsky's anti-Semitism and anti-Catholicism derived from his unthinking adherence to the nationalist program laid down by Balakirev and Stasov. Balakirev's private thoughts are not well known enough to compare with his public statements, but we do know enough about the personal relationships of both Stasov and Musorgsky to group these two men among those illogi-

---

[8] It has been pointed out that not only these casual messages but most of Musorgsky's letters (sent by mail or messenger from one St. Petersburg address to another) would not have been written if the telephone had been in use at that time.

cal acquaintances that we all have who draw a distinction between the Jews they know ("some of my best friends") and those they don't ("but *they* are *Jews!*"). Though the son of a Jewish tailor, Mark Antokolsky was one of Stasov's most intimate and respected friends, and was numbered in the Stasov "troika" alongside Repin and Musorgsky. And Musorgsky's anti-Semitic remarks are made eternally absurd by the living contradiction of his music, which contains some of the most moving tributes to Hebrew history, tradition, and character that any composer has given us: the choruses of *The Destruction of Sennacherib* and *Jesus Navinus (Joshua)*, the ballad of *King Saul* and *Hebraic Song*, and the Jewish portraits in *Pictures at an Exhibition*. As if to point out this contradiction, Musorgsky's letters from his tour of southern Russia contain one of his most virulent anti-Semitic comments (omitted from No. 204) as well as the following (in No. 207):

> On the steamer from Odessa to Sevastopol . . . I wrote down Greek and Jewish songs, as sung by some women, and I sang the latter with them myself, and they were very pleased and among themselves they referred to me as *meister*.—By the way, in Odessa, I went to holy services at two synagogues, and was in raptures. I have clearly remembered two Israelite themes: one sung by the cantor, the other by the temple choir—the latter in unison; I shall never forget these!

Yuri Keldysh has written of Musorgsky's chauvinism (in the Andrei Rimsky-Korsakov edition of the letters, pages 543–546), but a thorough study of this subject must be placed on the already long list of Musorgsky projects for the future.

Musorgsky's relation to the whole social and political environment of the sixties and seventies in Russia also awaits more than the schematic treatment that this subject has been given. Curiously, the development of Musorgsky as man and artist exactly coincides with the reign of Alexander II—who was assassinated three days before Musorgsky's death, and who came to the throne in the same Crimean War that turned the thoughts of a young guards officer from military to musical ambitions.

When the eighteen-year-old Musorgsky first met the twenty-year-old Mili Alexeyevich Balakirev in the spring of 1857, there was an immediate novice-professional relationship established, in spite of the slight difference in their ages. While Musorgsky spent his spare time, as an officer in the Preobrazhensky Guards, in light, amateur musical occupations—piano pieces and opera dreams—Mili Balakirev was fully launched in Russia's musical world with a number of published and performed compositions, a career as a public concert artist, and, last but not least, the farewell benediction of Russia's first musical genius, Mikhail Glinka. Glinka's sister, Ludmila Shestakova, quotes Glinka as saying, as he left Russia in April 1856, never to see it again,

> If I am no longer there to take charge of the musical education of our Olya [Shestakova's daughter Olga], promise me that you will allow no one but Balakirev to teach her music. He is the first man in whom I have found views on the art corresponding to my own. You can fully trust him; and believe me, in time he will become a second Glinka.

When Glinka died in Berlin the year Musorgsky met Balakirev, the latter's position as leader of the Russian nationalist tendency in music was unchallenged. Fiery, energetic, commanding, chauvinist, Balakirev mustered together dazzled but talented youngsters, to form the Balakirev Circle.

Musorgsky was the second recruit to the Circle; Cesar Cui had joined the year before, and had achieved one opera with Balakirev's assistance. Of the Circle's future members, the twenty-four-year-old Borodin was still a research scientist who composed music as a hobby, attached to his enjoyments as an amateur musician, and the thirteen-year-old Rimsky-Korsakov had already spent one year in the Naval Cadets School. Of the Russian composers who were to remain outside the circle, seventeen-year-old Tchaikovsky was still in the College of Jurisprudence, and Serov was more productive of musical criticism than of music. When Glinka died in Berlin, the only other Russian composer of his generation who can stand beside him in music history, Alexander Dargomizhsky, then forty-four years old, had completed all his operas except his last, *The Stone Guest*, that awaited the encouragement of the young men in the Circle.

The documents with which this book begins relate to the ideas of Balakirev, the first powerful influence on the composer Musorgsky.

JAY LEYDA

A Personal Note

IN THE spring of 1940 I wrote to my mother, then living in Reval, asking her how she and my father had first met Musorgsky. She replied:

> Your father first met him at the home of the poet, Count Golen-ishchev-Kutuzov, with whom Musorgsky was very friendly. Before my marriage he visited me only once. It was after my debut at the Marinsky Opera, when I was living with my mother by the Yekaterinsky Canal. He arrived, introduced himself, and after a while asked me to sing some Dargomizhsky songs. He accompanied me in "Charm Me" and several others. As I was to sing these songs at a concert shortly afterwards, I asked him for suggestions and criticism, but evidently he approved, for he had nothing but praise for me. I thanked him and he left. I seem to remember that he was living in great seclusion at that time, and visited no one very often but Ludmila Ivanovna . . .

Ludmila Ivanovna Shestakova was a dear friend to both my parents before their marriage, and they often met Musorgsky in the Shestakova apartment. My mother's operatic career as Olga Skalkovskaya was cut short two years after her debut by her marriage with Dr. Lev Bertensson, but this was by no means the end of her musical activity. Her love for music and my father's admiration for it (he was the only doctor to join the board of directors of the Imperial Russian Musical Society) made music the life-blood of the literary and theatrical salon that the Bertenssons maintained.

But it was the drawing-room of Shestakova that was the center of St. Petersburg's musical life, by virtue of its hostess's authoritative charm and her dead brother, Glinka. Here were the mild Rimsky-Korsakov, the even more gentle Borodin, Cui of the sharp tongue, Stasov of the loud voice, and Napravnik who spoke eternally about rhythm as if it were some sort of medicine.

Musorgsky was this group's first tragedy. Shestakova had called upon

xvii

my father previously when Musorgsky was ill [1], but it was in the great man's final helplessness that my father was able to help him most. His and other documents at the end of this volume portray those last weeks and days of Musorgsky. When the music journalist, Ivanov, published his melodramatic and distorted account of this end, Borodin, Cui, and Rimsky-Korsakov at once addressed a letter to the newspaper, *Golos,* publicly thanking Dr. Bertensson and his assistants for their help in easing Musorgsky's last moments, but apparently not even this could offset the wide publicity (till this day) given Ivanov's more theatrical version.

I was not born till four years after Musorgsky's death, but I grew up in the midst of his friends and companions. His name was so familiar that it seemed unnecessary to make special inquiries about him. "Modeste Petrovich often said . . . " was a phrase often used by my father and mother. Uncle Vasili Bertensson, the family humorist, loved to tell the tragicomic anecdote of Musorgsky's assistance at a benefit concert, printed in our Chapter VII. In visiting our good friends, the Molas or Vanlyarsky families, the name of Musorgsky was often pronounced with a melancholy ring.

My first visits to Shestakova were made with my mother, and later, as a high-school and college student, I was a frequent guest in her cozy apartment on Gagarinskaya Street. Although she was then the victim of a stroke that left her half-paralyzed and a permanent armchair invalid, I cannot remember her as anything but cheerful, lively, and blessed with wit and memory. Everything she told me about her beloved brother and about *Ruslan and Ludmila,* which had been my first experience of opera, thrilled me. But it never occurred to me to make one inquiry about the man whose most lasting friend she was, and whom she knew and understood better than did anyone else.

During those last years of Ludmila Ivanovna's precious life, Musorgsky's operas were not produced in St. Petersburg, and his other works appeared infrequently on concert programs. It was only in 1909 and 1910, when *Boris Godunov* and *Khovanshchina* were given brilliant productions at the Marinsky Theatre, that I became fully

---

[1] Letter 200 in this volume is the only one of Musorgsky's many letters written to Shestakova in his last six years to be preserved—for Shestakova presented this souvenir of Dr. Bertensson's treatment of Musorgsky's illness to the doctor, and he in turn deposited it in the Pushkin House in January 1916. Her other letters exist only in transcription. Another souvenir of the doctor's acquaintance is a print of the 1874 (Lorens) photographic portrait, autographed to Lev Bertensson.

aware of Musorgsky's greatness as a composer. By that time Ludmila Ivanovna had joined her brother. How bitterly I regretted that while she was still alive I never thought to ask her all she knew and remembered about her beloved Musinka. How she would have loved this, for there must have been much more to tell than she told of him in her brief memoirs.

Without the support of this friend I was ready to accept the popular notion of Musorgsky: a great artist but, unfortunately, a drunkard. Like so many others, even at present, I never bothered to analyze this easy formula. Another of my father's patients, Lev Tolstoy, once dismissed the whole Musorgsky question in a conversation with the doctor, "I like neither talented drunks nor drunken talents." If this volume of Musorgsky documents supplies a long-overdo answer to Tolstoy's, and the world's, mistaken simplification of this man's struggle, my conscience will be quieted for all the questions I didn't ask Ludmila Ivanovna.

SERGEI BERTENSSON

An Acknowledgment

THE PREPARATION of this volume has been generously assisted by everyone to whom we applied for help—Dr. Pavel Lamm in Moscow, Dr. Avrahm Yarmolinsky at the New York Public Library, Dr. Michael Karpovich, Dr. Alfred Einstein, Mr. Alfred J. Swan, and Miss Gladys Caldwell and the staff of the Music Department at the Los Angeles Public Library. The University of California at Los Angeles and the Library of Congress made it possible for us to consult books and periodicals locally unavailable. Mr. Alfred Frankenstein has broken into his unique collection of Musorgskiana to aid our illustrations, and Mrs. Sina Fosdick of the American Russian Cultural Association established our contact with Mrs. Nicholas Roerich in India. The most onerous task was cheerfully assumed by Mr. Ben Maddow and Dr. Paul Lang, who read the first translation and editing of the documents, and brought to them a great deal of their present order and sense.

J. L. and S. B.

Note to the Reader

ALL THE letters and documents presented in this book appear, as far as can be determined, in chronological order. The system of numbering these materials is as follows: All letters and other items from Musorgsky's pen are numbered consecutively throughout the volume; letters by others are given the number of the last preceding Musorgsky item, plus the differentiating letters *a, b,* etc.; contemporary documents are inserted in their chronological order without numbers.

The dates used in the letters and contemporary documents are those of the Julian calendar, which continued to be used in Russia until after the 1917 revolution, although the Gregorian calendar had long since been adopted by most of Europe.

Marks of elision in Musorgsky's letters are his own, with the exception of those enclosed in brackets. These latter indicate omissions by the editors.

Words enclosed between carets (< >) were crossed out in the original letters.

I

The Balakirev Circle
1857 — 1863

In 1820, Piotr Alexeyevich Musorgsky, the illegitimate son of an officer of the Preobrazhensky Guards and a serf woman, was legitimized by decree of the Senate, and inherited his father's estate of some 10,000 desyatins in the province of Pskov, 150 desyatins in the province of Yaroslav, and an unknown quantity of serfs. In 1832 [?] Piotr Alexeyevich married Yulia Ivanovna Chirikova, the daughter of a landowner in modest circumstances, and the family settled on their Pskov estate, near the village of Karevo, Toropetz County, by the two lakes of Zhistza and Dvina.

On March 9, 1839, their fourth son was born—Modeste Petrovich Musorgsky. When he was ten, the entire family moved to St. Petersburg for the purpose of entering Modeste and his only surviving brother Philarète (born in 1836) in the secondary school of SS. Peter and Paul. From the start of the regular curriculum, Modeste's father also arranged for his younger son's piano lessons with an excellent pianist and teacher, Anton Herke, a pupil of Adolf von Henselt. These lessons continued throughout Modeste's schooling.

After two years at the secondary school Modeste was transferred to an army preparatory school, and in August 1852 he entered the School of Guards Ensigns.

The Ensigns School

. . . Here Musorgsky was still surrounded by the same atmosphere of serfdom [as on the country estate, where his childhood had been spent]. Each ensign had his own valet-serf, who was flogged by the authorities if he should fail to humor his young master. There was also a serf-master relationship between the junior and senior cadets, a relationship of blind obedience to military superiors. The senior cadets called themselves "Messrs. cornets," and bore themselves haughtily in the presence of their junior comrades, whom they called "vandals." Each cornet had a vandal as well as a valet-serf for his services, and bullied him in various ways by the right of the strong; for example, the vandal was obliged to carry his cornet on his shoulders to the washroom. Messrs. cornets considered it humiliating to

1

prepare their lessons. This opinion was also shared by the school director, General Sutgof.

All the Messrs. cornets' dreams were concentrated on the grandeur and honor of a Guards uniform . . . All free time after drilling was dedicated by the cadets to dancing, amours, and drink. General Sutgof was strictly watchful that drunken cadets shouldn't return to school on foot, and that they shouldn't drink common vodka, and in defense of the school's honor he was proud when a cadet came back from leave drunk with champagne, sprawled in an open carriage drawn by his own trotters. This was the sort of institution in which . . . the young Musorgsky was educated; he studied German philosophy enthusiastically, read historical works and translated foreign books, for all of which General Sutgof, who took a personal interest in him, scolded him, saying: "What sort of an officer will you make, *mon cher?*"

. . . His piano lessons continued throughout the several years of Musorgsky's stay in the Guards school. Herke introduced the young Russian virtuoso to German piano literature exclusively. The virtuoso loved to improvise, guided only by his ear and his imagination, without the slightest idea of how to put down his thoughts on paper or of the most elementary rules of music. In the School of Guards Ensigns the young pianist was always compelled to bang out dances endlessly to humor the cadets, varying his repertoire with his own improvisations.

. . . While yet in school Musorgsky sang Italian opera arias with a fresh baritone. As for Russian composers, especially Glinka and Dargomizhsky, this well-mannered youth had not the faintest notion of them. Musorgsky never suspected the existence of any sort of musical theory or science . . . —NIKOLAI KOMPANEISKY [1]

On October 8, 1856, Musorgsky was enrolled as an officer in the regiment of the Preobrazhensky Guards.

Guards Officer

[In the Preobrazhensky Regiment] training, marching, equestrian drill, making formal calls, dancing, cards, drinking, purposeful amours in search of a rich countess or, if it came to the worst, a merchant's daughter with a fat wallet. Musorgsky fully mastered the external qualities of a Preobrazhensky officer: he had elegant manners, walked cockily on tiptoe, dressed like a dandy, spoke French beautifully, danced even better, played the piano splendidly and sang wonderfully, even learned how to get drunk, abandoned his reprehensible study of German philosophy—in short, the future smiled upon him . . .

But he didn't have the chance to scatter as much money as did his

---

[1] For the source of this and all other evidence by Musorgsky's contemporaries, see the list of sources in the Appendix.

comrades. He took part in sprees, he would hammer out polkas for whole nights at a time, and his comrades valued these merits, but this wasn't enough to support the honor of a guardsman's uniform—one had to scatter riches . . . These unsuitable conditions eventually forced Musorgsky to resign. But the three years in the milieu of a Guards officer had a destructive influence on all his subsequent life . . . —NIKOLAI KOMPANEISKY

My first encounter with Modeste Petrovich Musorgsky was in 1856 (I think in the fall, in September or October). I was a freshly baked military doctor, a staff physician in the Second Military Hospital; M.P. was an officer of the Preobrazhensky regiment, only just hatched out of the egg (he was then seventeen years old). Our first encounter was in the orderly room of the hospital. I was the doctor on duty; he was the officer on duty. We shared the same room; it was boring to be on duty for both of us; we were both expansive; it is understandable that we struck up a conversation and very quickly got along together. That day we were both invited for the evening to the home of the chief medical officer of the hospital, Popov, who had a grown daughter; for her sake he often arranged parties, to which were regularly invited the doctor and officer on duty that day. This was the courtesy of the chief surgeon. M.P. was at that time quite boyish, very elegant, the very picture of an officer: brand-new, close-fitting uniform, poised feet, sleek, pomaded hair, nails as if carved, immaculate, altogether gentlemanly hands. Refined, aristocratic manners, conversation the same, speaking somewhat through his teeth; sprinkled with French phrases, rather affected. Some traces of foppishness, but very moderate. Extraordinarily polite and well-bred. The ladies made a fuss over him. He sat at the piano and, coquettishly throwing up his hands, played excerpts from *Trovatore, Traviata,* etc., very sweetly and gracefully, while the circle around him buzzed in chorus: *"charmant, delicieux!"* and so on. It was in such circumstances that I met M.P. three or four times at Popov's and on duty at the hospital. For some time after this I did not meet M.P., as Popov left the hospital and his parties stopped, and I was no longer on duty at the hospital, as I had joined the chemical staff as assistant professor.—ALEXANDER BORODIN

1.   *To MILI BALAKIREV* [2]

[Postmarked: 16 December 1857
St. Petersburg]

MOST PRECIOUS MILI ALEXEYEVICH,

I don't know how to thank you for selecting the piano; I am sure in

---

[2] It was in the autumn of 1857 that young Musorgsky was transformed from dilettante to earnest disciple, as he began regular lessons with Balakirev. Balakirev's own explanation of these lessons, given long afterward to Stasov, was: "As I am no theorist, I could not give Musorgsky instruction in harmony . . . so I confined myself to explaining the different forms of composition; with this object

advance that it's a good one. With God's help, I will take it away from Becker's at the first opportunity.—In spite of all my wishes to spend an evening with you in musical pursuits, I must tell you in advance that I can't make it on Tuesday; I have to go to my relatives. They're really very cross with me, saying that I've "completely forgotten them."—If you wish, set a date for the lesson yourself, and just let me know a couple of days ahead, so I can confirm it.

At your service,

MODESTE MUSORSKY [8]

2. To MILI BALAKIREV

17 December [1857]

MOST EXCELLENT MILI ALEXEYEVICH,

The culprit is forgiven and impatiently awaits you on Thursday. Today, thank God, the fate of the long-hoped-for piano has been settled. Tomorrow the most worthy Becker is delivering it to us.—I am a thousand times grateful to you for the excellent choice. *La machine est parfaitement solide.* Today I pounded so on this machine that the tips of my fingers began to smart painfully as if ants were racing through them, but nothing happened to the machine itself except that one string jangled. The tone is excellent, the bass very good, and I am entirely satisfied with the instrument.—I've stored away Beethoven's 2nd Symphony for the inauguration of the new instrument on Thursday.—Thank you again, Mili Al., and I'll expect you on

---

we played through all Beethoven's symphonies and many of the works of Schumann, Schubert, Glinka, and others, as piano duets. I pointed out the technical structure of these compositions as we went through them, and got him to analyze the various musical forms. As far as I remember, there were few actual professional lessons; these came to an end, for one reason or another, and were succeeded by friendly exchange of opinions." The only extant work by Musorgsky of this period is the piano piece, *Souvenir d'enfance* (dated October 16, 1857). There was, however, an earlier piano work, *Porte-Enseigne Polka*, of 1852, of which Musorgsky was too ashamed to show it to his new friends.

[8] Musorgsky uses this spelling of his family name consistently, both in signatures and on envelopes, until his thirty-sixth letter to Balakirev (undated, 1861—omitted in this volume), and thereafter he restores the g of his family name. It may also be mentioned here that throughout his life Musorgsky did not use the common pronunciation of his name (Musorg'sky) but preferred to accent the first syllable. Both altered spelling and altered pronunciation may have been chosen for the sake of the greater elegance which he affected in his youth.

Thursday positively. My brother [4] sends you his profoundest respects . . .

Yours,

MODESTE MUSORSKY

3. To MILI BALAKIREV

[Postmarked: 7 January, 1858]

MOST EXCELLENT MILI ALEXEYEVICH,

For God's sake bring him,[5] I shall be very glad to become friends with him, the more so as those works which I heard from you come quite close to my heart.—By all means bring him.

Yours,

MODESTE MUSORSKY

P.S. Excuse this incoherent scribble, my head is whirling, I've just come from the review at the palace.[6]

4. To MILI BALAKIREV

[Postmarked: 24 January, 1858]

MOST EXCELLENT MILI ALEXEYEVICH,

You can't imagine how disappointed I am that our music lesson could not be arranged for tonight. This is how it happened: we received your note long after you had left it, for by seven o'clock this evening my brother and I had gone off to the opera.[7]—I am terribly disappointed and ashamed, particularly since it is so far from your

---

[4] Philarète Petrovich Musorgsky, three years older than Modeste Petrovich. He is referred to in Modeste's letters by various nicknames: Kito, Kitosha, Kitinka. The two sons were now living with their widowed mother: their father, Piotr Alexeyevich, had died in 1853.

[5] Another addition to the Balakirev Circle, Apollon Seliverstovich Gussakovsky, who will be referred to in the correspondence variously as Gusak, Gusachok, Gusinke, Gusikovsky.

[6] A lengthy annual ceremony on Twelfth Night attended by the sovereign and court in which the water of the Neva is blessed by the metropolitan. Musorgsky's regiment, the Preobrazhensky Guards, being the most traditional of all Russian military units, played an important role in the military ceremony which followed. Further references to military duties in the following letter indicate a dissatisfaction with the complicated double life of a soldier-composer, a dissatisfaction that soon required a decisive conclusion. The charming uniformed pianist had already receded into the past.

[7] The opera performed that night was Auber's *Fra Diavolo*.

place to ours on Razyezhaya Street and, besides, you're not feeling very well . . . however, I appeal to your indulgence and kindness and I hope you won't be angry and will love Razyezhaya Street as ever.—My brother asks me to convey to you his most respectful compliments.

Yours,

MODESTE MUSORSKY

P.S. I am on duty tomorrow; this is terribly disappointing, for I have been wishing so to see you.

5. *To MILI BALAKIREV*

MOST PRECIOUS MILI,
[Postmarked: 25 February, 1858]

To my very great shame I must confess that the allegro [8] is not yet ready—so, annoying as it may be, I comply with your request: to write you in case I do not finish it—this allegro that's boring me sick. However, I am not desperate; I hope to see you this week, in order to test my labor as your pupil on your piano. Incidentally I am lately so lazy and languorous that I don't know how to get rid of the feeling; never, now that this is finished, not for anything will I again write oriental music, it's all snares.[9] Till we meet. I started this letter sadly and end it stupidly.

Devoted to you from the soul,

MODESTE MUSORSKY

Soldier or Artist

. . . I told him that Lermontov could remain a hussar officer and be a great poet, regardless of all sorts of guard duty in the regiment and in the guardroom, regardless of all sorts of reviews and parades. Musorgsky answered that "that was Lermontov and this is I; he, perhaps, was able to fit one into the other, but I—I can't; the service interferes with my working as I must!" The final occasion, deciding the matter, was basically this situation: that they transferred him to a sharp-shooters' battalion and, therefore, beginning with the summer of 1859, he would have to be moved out to permanent residence in Tzarskaya Slavyanka, and this he definitely could not agree to: to

---

[8] This allegro may be the first movement of the sonata in E-flat major referred to in Letter 6.

[9] This early distaste for "oriental" music toward which Balakirev was so attracted, may be the first indication of Musorgsky's lifelong search for "real" sources.

leave Petersburg—this meant not only deserting his mother, with whom he had lived without a separation since birth, but also to desert Dargomizhsky, Balakirev, Cui, and his musical studies . . . —VLADIMIR STASOV

On July 5, 1858, Musorgsky resigned his commission, giving as his reason the impossibility of separation from friends and family, and left almost immediately with his brother for Tikhvin, to take a cure.

5a. *MILI BALAKIREV to VLADIMIR STASOV,*[10] *St. Petersburg [Extracts]*

Jericho, 5th July, Saturday, 1858

DEAR BRETHREN!

With great pain I've come to *Jericho.*[11] On the train, with a little string pulling, I landed in the mail car, taking there at night all my belongings from the second class (for which I had a ticket), among them the cane which at some unknown point disappeared, causing me much sorrow. This circumstance was even more peculiar in that I had not taken the cane with me on the platform, so that no one could have stolen it, nor would anyone have attempted it. There's something extraordinary, supernatural, here. Unluckily I am somewhat superstitious and I can't help thinking that the loss of the cane means the loss of something good for myself, but I can see from here that you are laughing at me, so I conclude my discussion of this matter! I was quite well while traveling: my head didn't ache; I washed at the station and spent a lot of money on food; they pulled 50 kopeks out of me for a cold fish soup, with a rotten salmon which you, Romeo, would doubtless have loved. The only passenger I talked with was

---

[10] Vladimir Stasov was the only "member" of the Balakirev Circle who was not a musician: he was its ideologue, its spiritual and literary adviser, its propaganda minister. One peculiarity that he had in common with the rest of the Circle, with the single exception of Balakirev, was that his profession (criticism and history) was not his regular job, for he was librarian at the St. Petersburg Public Library. Over and above both profession and job was the all-embracing cause of panslavism, extending to his off-duty appearance (beard, boots, peasant blouses, boyar caps, etc.) and to an ancient Slavic vocabulary, intoned in a booming voice. Both for his extravagant manners and for his defense of Johann Sebastian Bach, the Circle members dubbed him Bach, and sometimes General Bach. In this letter Balakirev also calls him Romeo.

[11] Not only the ideas in this letter but the style as well was emulated by Musorgsky (see particularly Letter 10). In the Circle, Moscow was always referred to as "Jericho."

a doctor of the Imperial Guards Hussars Regiment, blond and very soft-spoken. For some reason he thought me a witty person and insisted that I was going to Jericho to write a humorous account of Jericho's provincial customs.

The ladies with me wept continuously and occasionally brought up my spleen in me. With us was Mme. [Julius] Gebhardt who, Piotr [12] says, showed . . . for 40 kopeks in the Passage. She attracted everyone's attention with her peculiar toilette: some metallic apparatus sat on her head—one Muscovite passenger observed that this was for preservation of the brain. You also, Romeo, were apparently attracted to her, while seeing me off. She is now showing Julia Pastrana [13] to the Jericho public.—On arriving in Jericho I left all my things with a friend, and went in search of Piotr, whom I found asleep. We went right off to the Troitzky tavern, and on the way passed Alexander Sèmen's print shop, whereupon Borozdin had a desire in the tavern to order Alex. Sèm.'s print shop covered with gravy. In general Piotr made me so gay that for a time I forgot about the cane. . . . In the evening we strolled through the Kremlin with great pleasure, sending me into a rapture, as ever. The evening was wonderful, the view over the Zamoskvorechy was beyond compare. In my soul were born many beautiful feelings which I can't describe to you. Here I felt with pride that I am a Russian.—In a few of my compositions I have expressed parts of the Kremlin, particularly the Kremlin towers: but now I will simply have to write a symphony in honor of the Kremlin.—Borozdin was more thrilled with Vasili the Blessed [cathedral] and grew quite indignant with me when I said that Vasili the Blessed is to other churches what Julia Pastrana is to other people. I named the Spassky Gate Bach or Romeo, the Nikolsky, as the most feminine architecturally—I named Dm[itri] Vas[ilyevich], but the Troitzky, which is highest of all—Nik[olai] Vas.[14]—From the Kremlin we wandered over to the Hôtel de Russie, where I am to spend the night, at Piotr's request: on the way Piotr made me laugh by stopping

[12] Nikolai Alexandrovich Borozdin (Piotr, Piotri, Petrusha) headed the Moscow branch of the Circle, providing the members with a gay host for their trips to that city. Borozdin's job was connected with the Moscow courts.

[13] Julia Pastrana was a bearded Mexican lady.

[14] Balakirev had nicknamed the Kremlin gates after the three Stasov brothers: "Bach" was, of course, Vladimir Vasilyevich; Dimitri Vasilyevich was the head of the St. Petersburg Bar Association and an energetic patron of music; Nikolai Vasilyevich was the banker and financial expert of the Stasovs. Alexander Vasilyevich, a fourth brother, apparently didn't rank a Kremlin gate.

8

the street walkers, without, however, erasing from my mind my wonderful impressions of the Kremlin.—Now, dear brethren, I await a letter from you to Nizhnii Novgorod . . .

6. *To MILI BALAKIREV, Nizhni Novgorod*

[Postmarked: 12 July, 1858
St. Petersburg]

DEAR MILI,

Yesterday at the Stasovs I had the pleasure of reading your letter to them from Moscow and I was mightily happy to learn that you are quite well. The story of the cane made me laugh a little (but when I recalled how fond you were of it—through habit, of course—I immediately stopped laughing); your observations on the trip were very amusing; the weeping ladies, the doctor from the Hussar regiment, the salmon (in the cold fish soup) that cost you 50 silver kopeks, that was terribly funny. Petrusha [Borozdin] on the Moscow streets attracted by the women, who very likely pushed him aside, all these scenes were extremely amusing.—Your description of the Kremlin, Mili, has plunged me deep in thought; however, thanks to you, these five minutes of reverie about it have given me unspeakable delight. And in general I must tell you that I read your letter with delight.— There's nothing to write about myself; the same absent-mindedness, the same occupations (music and literature), my departure to the country to attend a wedding, that is all I can tell you about myself. As for my musical activities, I will tell you that I'm beginning to write a sonata (in E-flat major), I'll manage it somehow; and I will try to make this come out well.[15] I plan to do a brief introduction in B (B-flat major) and lead up to the allegro by means of a pedal point; and in addition a scherzo is in work and in leisure moments I practice harmony; how terribly I want to compose decently! Kito bows to you and endeavors to embrace you from Krasnoye Selo, although I don't know how successfully he can do this. We played Schumann's symphonies (in B-flat major and C major), because he is very fond of them and reads music splendidly.—We are expecting him to come to town; he may add something to this letter, as he very much wanted

---

[15] This sonata, in E-flat major, was either left unfinished or was destroyed by Musorgsky, as it does not appear in the catalogue of his works which he prepared for Shestakova (No. 73) and the only fragments of it in existence are the themes noted in the following letter.

9

to do so. Cui is constantly at Bamberg's; [16] but it's not necessary to tell you this as you know it yourself.—Yesterday Stasov (Bach) suggested at the wedding that I should peep beneath the corset of the bride, but I was opposed to this for reasons that took two hours of argument about the mysterious parts of the human body, particularly women's; diseases were enumerated, the characteristics of the ace of spades (what an apt description!) were discussed, and all evening Bach pestered me: are you going to inspect the bride beneath her corset? . . . I was dreadfully bored by him. I played the introduction to Œdipus [17] (the overture) and some themes for other compositions, which Bach seemed to like, which was very gratifying.—What else can I write you, apparently nothing; yes—when I go to Tikhvin with Kito I'll write you my impressions from there, whether these will amuse you I cannot tell, but I'll write them anyway, for in the province of Novgorod there are some wonderful old things.—Now let me wish you a happy and pleasant time in the country, and most of all good health, which is also my mother's wish, she has just called through the door: Wish Mil. Al. from me the best of health, which is the most important thing! Write us oftener Mili, to be quite sincere, you give us very great joy.—Ach! it's horribly hot.—Till we meet, at least in a letter.

Yours forever,
MODESTE

P.S. In the first place excuse me for writing you so poorly, I've been

[16] Cesar Antonovich Cui, officer in the army engineers corps and professor in the Military Academies, was the son of a soldier in Napoleon's invading army who had been left behind, wounded, in the retreat of 1812. Having studied with the Polish composer Stanislaus Moniuszko, Cui felt that his musical education was slightly superior to that of the other "semiprofessionals" in the Balakirev Circle. His nicknames: Cesare and Kvey.

Cesar Cui was constantly at the home of Rafail Bamberg, pharmacist of Vilna, for an excellent reason: four months later he was to marry Rafail's daughter, Malvina Bamberg, whom he had met when she was studying with Dargomizhsky. It is not known who was being married at the wedding to which Musorgsky refers here.

[17] In 1852 the magazine Propilei (Propylaia) had published a new translation by Shestakov of Sophocles' Œdipus the King. It is generally assumed that it was this that gave Musorgsky the idea of doing incidental music for orchestra, chorus and soloists, but Gerald Abraham has suggested (Music and Letters, January 1945) that Musorgsky was working with an earlier and very free adaptation by Ozerov, entitled Œdipus in Athens. Judging by the text of a chorus (the only extant fragment of Musorgsky's incidental music), the dramatic situation resembles the climax of Œdipus at Colonus, but the words are not Sophocles'.

so absent-minded all week, and secondly—if you write any time from the eighth or ninth through the twenty-fifth, use this address: in Novgorod Prov., Tikhvin County, Nikolai Alexeyevich Burtzov, for delivery to us.

7. *To MILI BALAKIREV, Nizhni Novgorod*

[Postmarked: 13 August, 1858
St. Petersburg]

MOST PRECIOUS MILI,

Nothing can be more unbearable than absent-mindedness, and if to this is added confusion, then one is already done for.[18] I am in complete ignorance about you, and I have only myself to blame for this, for asking you to address your letters between the tenth and the twenty-fifth of July to Novgorod Province, and on the twenty-third of July I left there, so it is very possible that your letter is waiting there; at any rate I comfort myself with this possibility and I don't want to think that anything bad has happened to you.—Whether or not this is the case, I write you now, wishing to have in your absence at least this way of talking with you. Kito and I had a marvelous time in the country; there was a folk festival in honor of the wedding, and it was a splendid festival.—On this occasion I finally decided to write the sonata in E-flat major and dedicate it to the newlyweds; and by the way, here are the themes for you.

Introduction to the finale

Scherzo

You already know this,
First theme of the allegro finale.

---

[18] See Letter 15 for Musorgsky's actual mental state this summer.

I have also the other themes, but I have not yet quite decided to develop <all of> them.

I have brought them from the country; I am now writing a sonata in F-sharp minor, a very simple one, and I have written some songs.[19] Not long ago at Verigina's [20] we played the *Kholmsky entr'actes* [21] for eight hands; I have read Gluck's scores (*Alceste, Iphigenia in Aulis* and *Armide*) and then *Cinna* [22] and today I am finishing Mozart's Requiem, and playing Beethoven sonatas, ones I had not known previously, his *quasi fantasia* [23] I like very much.—*Œdipus* is always in my head and thus, as I want to dedicate it to you,[24] dearest one, I am thinking seriously about it, for if I don't, you will say that it's trash and one shouldn't compose rotten music.—Our dear Cesar was here for two days at Bamberg's, he flew here by train; coming away from B[amber]g we had a very pleasant chat together.—Write something Mili, I want terribly to hear about you. Ach! here's something: at the end of August, with God's help, I will go to Murom, near you,

---

[19] There is no record of this sonata in F-sharp minor but the songs of this summer were, according to Andrei Rimsky-Korsakov:

"Tell me why, dearest maiden" [dated July 13, 1858], dedicated to Zinaida Afanasyevna Burtzova.

"Meines Herzens Sehnsucht" [September 6, 1858], dedicated to Malvina Bamberg.

"Happy Hour" [dated April 28, 1859], text by Alexei Koltzov, dedicated to Vasili Vasilyevich Zakharin.

"Sadly Rustle the Leaves" [St. Petersburg, 1859], text by Alexei Pleshcheyev, dedicated to Mikhail Osipovich Mikeshin.

[20] Sofia Yakovlevna Verigina, a good friend of Stasov and of Anton Rubinstein, sponsored an intimate musical salon.

[21] From Glinka's incidental music for Kukolnik's tragedy, *Prince Kholmsky*.

[22] There are four possible *Cinna's*—by Asioli (1769–1832), Bianchi (1752–1810), Karl Heinrich Graun (1703–1759), and Paër (1771–1839). The last two are the most likely for Musorgsky to have known.

[23] *Sonata quasi una fantasia,* Op. 27, No. 2, the *Moonlight.*

[24] The piano score of a chorus (earliest version) from this incidental music is dated January 23, 1859, and is dedicated "To Dear Mili."

It may be of interest to record Musorgsky's stage directions for this earliest of his dramatic works extant: "Interior of the temple. The temple is divided into two parts; in the farther part can be seen an altar and three statues of gods. The people assemble in the temple, all are in anxious expectation. The priests perform the ceremony of taking the holy sword in preparation for a sacrifice . . . From the side-doors of the second part of the temple enter Œdipus, Antigone and Polyneices. At the sight of Œdipus, the people step back in horror. The high priest enters, sword in hand, followed by two priests . . . A distant thunder-clap. The people are struck dumb. The shield is struck a blow . . ."

if you will stay there till the middle of September; then we can go to Peter [25] together.—And I want to see Moscow, the Volga and to visit Vladimir.—We're having a splendid summer, and what about yours in Nizhnii? Now at leisure I am translating the letters of Lavater [26]— about the state of the soul after death, a very interesting subject, and besides the dreamworld has always attracted me; in his letters there are also especially interesting physiognomical observations, for he was, as you know, a physiognomist, and through physiognomy alone he could reveal the very character <of a man>. Here is his observation regarding a picture of Bacchus: "a sanguine enough temperament, but nevertheless a materialist rather than a divine element can be detected in him"; he is correct, this honors the artist.—Regarding the state of the soul he says: "the soul of the departed communicates its thoughts to a man who is capable of clairvoyance; these thoughts after they have been delivered to the friend left behind on earth give an idea about the soul's presence after death." Notice the correlation of souls; however, I think you will read this after I finish translating it; it is very interesting.

At this time I think think think, think of many sensible things, and many plans swirl through my head; if one could only bring these to fulfillment it would be splendid. When you come I'll explain these plans to you; it would take too much space to write now, anyhow I think my letters are not quite pleasant, as I am yet not accustomed to write seriously, and one soon gets tired of such drivel.

Mili, let me tell you an amusing scene with Kito in the country. We went off to swim, and just as he was getting into the water, he fell in, or more accurately, crashed in, making the waves rise fearfully and the whole watery kingdom moan, and at this time Kito could only say: "well done!" However, enough. Kito embraces you, Mili, and I kiss you from my soul and wish you good health. Please write quickly.

Your

MODESTE

2 o'clock in the morning, time to go to bed, it seems that this letter is incoherent.

---

[25] St. Petersburg was often referred to as "Peter," and by Slavophiles as "Petrograd," following Pushkin's example in *The Bronze Horseman*.

[26] This must be Johann Kaspar Lavater's *Aussichten in die Ewigkeit in Briefen an Herrn Joh. Georg Zimmermann* (first published in 1775). In the seventh letter (Book I) Lavater discusses Zimmermann's dream of his dead wife.

8. *To MILI BALAKIREV*

Wednesday

DEAR MILI,

We've taken a loge for the presentation of *Ruslan* [27]—in the *belle-étage*, No. 13 on the left, and *maman* [Musorgskaya] invites you to join us, sincerely requesting you not to ignore this summons, so be sure to come. I hope you will tell us how you found Serov's lecture [28] but I am sure in advance that you were bored, because the subject of the lecture is so intolerably boring.—I am angry with both you and Cesar for rejecting my polka; [29] however, it is so insignificant that there's no use thinking about it; polkas and waltzes and dancing pieces in general are in my opinion musical *"pigmies"* <among one's musical works>. In such things except a certain *something*—there is nothing. Till we meet, Mili, I and all of us hope to see you in loge No. 13 on Thursday.

Devoted to you from the soul,

MODESTE

P.S. Kitosha left for Slavyanka; he'll be back tomorrow, and asks to kiss you and to give greetings to Sofia Ivanovna [Ediet, Balakirev's housekeeper] and family.

7th of January, 1859

Performer

I wrote a libretto for *The Mandarin's Son,* and in a few months the opera was ready. We then arranged another performance,[30] also

---

[27] After a fifteen-year lapse from the Marinsky repertory, Glinka's *Ruslan and Ludmila* was revived on November 12, 1858, in a *bénéfice* for the basso, Osip Afanasyevich Petrov. Musorgsky had made a four-hand arrangement of the Persian chorus from *Ruslan*—manuscript dated May 23–27, 1858.

[28] The first (on December 30, 1858) of sixteen lectures given by Alexander Nikolayevich Serov "On Music from Its Technical, Historical and Esthetic Viewpoints." Serov's career as a composer may have been unexciting, but his career as critic, polemicist, and all-round fighter was tumultuous, to say the least. Nervous, ambitious, aggressive, overcandid, he seldom enjoyed a lasting friendship. His most worthy struggle was as Wagner's Russian champion.

[29] *Porte-Enseigne Polka,* whose publication, by Bernard in 1852, was paid for by Musorgsky's father. Musorgsky had waited a year and a half before daring to show his only published work to Balakirev and Cui.

[30] At the Cuis' wedding party, October 8, 1858, Victor Krylov's first one-act comedy was presented, *A Fair Copy,* in which Musorgsky played the role of Alexander Ivanovich Porogin, high-school teacher and writer.

in the apartment of the parents of Cui's wife. It was a very original apartment, consisting of two or three very small rooms and a huge *salle,* which made it inexpensive as well as convenient for arranging performances. The opera was studied a long time. Cui and I made the sets ourselves out of some wallpaper that looked Chinese; we obtained costumes and wigs, and in February [22], 1859, the performance took place. The female role was sung by Cui's wife; the mandarin by Musorgsky, he had a good voice; [31] the innkeeper by Gumbin, the talented baritone of the Russian opera; the tenor lover by Dr. Chernyavsky and the villain Zai-Sang by Colonel Velyaminov. Instead of an orchestra, the composer Cui played the piano, and he and Balakirev played the overture. There was a large audience, among whom were Dargomizhsky, Vladimir Stasov, and others.— VICTOR KRYLOV

9. *To MILI BALAKIREV, St. Petersburg*

[Glebovo] 12 May
[Postmarked: 18 June, 1859
St. Petersburg]

DEAR MILI,

The letter has started, so you only need time to read it.—You're familiar with this railway journey; I shall describe for you my trip from the station of Kriukovo, on my way to the Shilovskys.[32] At first the country was nothing special, but closer to the New Jerusalem [monastery] it is quite interesting. New Jerusalem occupies a splendid site, from five versts away its oriental, golden bulbs can be seen; it stands on a little hill, vis-à-vis is also a hill (however, a little to the side) where the old town of Voskresensk is; there's a river below, the cathedral is enclosed by a little wood, all around is a wall with little towers looking like those little machines in which you stick pastel crayons (I've forgotten what they're called) topped by weather vanes, the main cupola amazingly resembles *un gâteau Mathilde*—very amusing inside, they say it's lovely—I'll see.—What a man Patriarch

---

[31] "Of the five personages the chief role, of the mandarin Kau-Tzing, was played by Musorgsky with such life, gaiety, with such adroitness and comic quality of singing, diction, pause and gesture, that he made the whole company of friends and comrades roar."—Vladimir Stasov. Preceding this opera, Gogol's *Lawsuit* was given, in which Musorgsky played the role of the civil servant, Proletov.

[32] Maria Vasilyevna Shilovskaya had married into Shilovsky's money and luxury after a lurid career as salon singer, during which she dabbled in composing and exercised other less specialized talents which had earned her the distinction of "the most charming woman of her time." She had turned the Shilovsky estate into a rural musical center, inviting a stream of talented composers to rest and work on the estate. Musorgsky was talented, young, and handsome.

Nikon was—he chose a site that is not at all bad. It somewhat dominates the surrounding area and is very beautiful.—Now about the Shilovskys, their luxurious manor-house is on a hill; the English gardens (something like a park) are lovely—vis-à-vis is a dairy farm—all splendid (as it should be—what *canaille*-ishness, how rich Shilovsky is) a dear little church, like a tiny cathedral. The Shilovskys have a choir of singers, conducted by a M[onsieur] Dupuis (who is, incidentally, a Russian from the Sheremetyev choir [33]), the singers perform Bortnyansky [34] (except his concert pieces) and are rehearsing the introduction, the Polish chorus from the fourth act and the finale (the hymn) from *A Life for the Tzar* [35]—this is pleasant; I will work with them, they tell me that they sing not badly—they don't yell and they receive a decent domestic education.—At this time there's hardly anyone around besides Varfolomeyev [?] (a clever gentleman) but in a short while *tutta la compagnia* will arrive with Dargo and Liubonka [36]—*a due.*—The host and hostess are very nice and Shilovskaya takes good care of her guests. There's nothing more to write now; respects to Bach, to Piotr [Borozdin] and to the Cuis, if you see them. I will send notes to them, too.—Till we meet again, be well.

Your

MODESTE

P.S. Address your letters to Moscow Province, town of Voskresensk, to be delivered to the village of Glebovo, Mod. Petr. Musorsk.

---

[33] Count D. N. Sheremetyev's choir was an important institution in Russian music, reviving and solidifying the national inheritance of church and folk music.

[34] Dmitri Stepanovich Bortnyansky died in 1825, leaving a large number of compositions, mostly sacred choral works.

[35] Shilovskaya had employed Konstantin Lyadov to conduct this Glinka opera, in which she was to sing a role not available to her on the public opera stage.

[36] The forty-six-year-old Alexander Sergeyevich Dargomizhsky (Dargo, Dargun, Dargunchik, Dargopekh) was in Glebovo as Shilovskaya's singing teacher. He had, however, brought along his own heart interest, Lubov Miller. His music, especially his opera *Rusalka*, earned him the respect of the Balakirev Circle, a respect that was somewhat dimmed by the cluster of minor talents that now surrounded Dargomizhsky. This cluster was known in the Circle as "the invalids" and Dargo was "the president of the invalids."

10. *To MILI BALAKIREV, St. Petersburg*

June 23 [1859. Moscow]

MILI,

It has finally been vouchsafed me to see Jericho.[37]—I will give you my impressions. As I approached Jericho, I at once noticed its original character, a smell of antiquity came from the belfries and cupolas of the churches. The Red Gate is quaint and extremely pleasing. From here until you reach the Kremlin there's nothing of any particular note, but the Kremlin, the wonderful Kremlin—I approached it with an involuntary feeling of awe. Red Square, over which surged so many remarkable chaotic events, loses a little on its left side—from the Gostinni Arcade—but Vasili the Blessed [cathedral] and the Kremlin wall make one forget this defect—this is sacred antiquity. Vasili the Blessed gave me an extremely agreeable but strange sensation, it seemed that any moment a boyar in a long coat and high fur cap might pass by. Under the Spassky Gate I took off my hat, this is a folk custom that I like.—The New Palace is superb and among its chambers the best room is the former Gran[ovitaya] Reception Hall where, by the way, Nikon was tried.—Uspensky Cathedral, [the church of] the Savior-in-the-Forest, Archang[el] Cathedral, these are expressions of antiquity hand in hand with Vas. the Blessed. In the Arch. Cathedral I inspected with proper reverence the tombs before which I stood in awe, such as those of Ioann III, Dmitri Donskoy and even the Romanovs, before these last I recalled *A Life for the Tzar* and thus involuntarily stopped before them.—I climbed up the bell tower of Ivan the Great and from it beheld a wonderful view of Moscow; from the Kremlin, from the side of the palace, there is a good view of the Zamoskvorechye and there is even a better view from the Moscow River over the Kremlin in this direction.—At Samarin's, I ate an excellent cold fish soup and saw waiters in clean white shirts. Walking through Moscow I remembered Griboyedov ("a special mark lies on all Muscovites" [38]), at least among the simple class I was con-

---

[37] This letter should be compared with Balakirev's of July 5, 1858 (5a) for content, style, slang (Jericho), etc.

[38] Said by Famusov in Griboyedov's play *Woe from Wit.*

17

vinced of this truth. Such beggars and swindlers are here as the light has never shone upon. Such strange manners, such bustling struck me especially.—In general Moscow transported me to another world— an ancient world (a world that, although filthy, attracts me pleasantly for some reason) and it made a very pleasant impression upon me. You know, I have been a cosmopolite, but now I feel a certain regeneration; everything Russian seems suddenly near to me, and I would be annoyed if Russia should be treated without ceremony; at the present time I believe I am really beginning to love it. Ach, I forgot: in the Arsenal Hall stands the stagecoach of Tzar Al[exei] Mikh[ailovich], manufactured abroad—an enormous thing. Inside on a European seat was installed an armchair (a sort of *porte-chaise*). As I looked in I <remembered> imagined to myself the figure of Al. Mikh., issuing his orders to the voyevodes whom he is sending to Little Russia.[39]

Till we meet, Mili,

Your

MODESTE

11.   *To MILI BALAKIREV*

20 Sept., 1859, 10:30 P.M.

MILI,

The four-hand arrangement of your overture [40] is *baked*. I am contented with the transcription; all the *tutti* sections (in the orchestra) turned out very successfully, the interwoven imitative passages play easily, and in short *everything is in order!* Come early tomorrow, around six (while we can be alone) so that we can go through the overture together and can correct it where necessary. Come Mili, now I want to finish this quickly.

Your

MODESTE

P.S. The Cuis expect you tomorrow.

---

[39] Little Russia is the rather derogatory name which was used in the Russian Empire to designate the Ukraine. Musorgsky uses both terms.

[40] Overture to *King Lear*. One of the successes of this theater season was a German production of *King Lear* in which the title role was enacted in English by the famous Negro actor, Ira Aldridge. Attracted by this production, Balakirev's plan was to do a complete incidental score for this play. Vladimir Stasov encouraged this, hunting up and coyping old English tunes for him to use. It is also possible to identify the transcribed overture as Balakirev's *Overture on Three Russian Themes;* Musorgsky's manuscript transcription is undated.

12. *An Inscription on the Manuscript of* Impromptu Passionné

Dedicated to Nadezhda Petrovna Opochinina
To the memory of Beltov and Liuba [41]

1 October 1859

13. *To MILI BALAKIREV*

DEAREST ONE,

Neither Sofia Ivanovna nor you could have thought up anything better. We all await you with impatience. *Maman* asks me to tell you that "you are very nice and arrange everything beautifully." Yesterday we saw Alexander and Nikolai Stasov; they told us about the return [from abroad] of Dmitri, who has brought back a lot of interesting stuff.—If I am able to find out by tomorrow morning from Vladimir whether they will be home in the evening, that would be fine, and in any case we have promised to be at their place on Sunday. Bring *Schumann*, I am thirsty for work.

Till we meet, Mili, expecting you tomorrow.

Your

MODESTE

Thursday, 8 October [1859]

Enthusiast

In the autumn of 1859, I again encountered him at the house of S. A. Ivanovsky, an assistant professor at the Academy [of Medicine] and doctor at the Artillery School. Musorgsky had already left the service. He had grown much more manly and rather stouter in appearance; the flavor of a foppish army officer had disappeared. The elegance in dress, manner, etc., was the same as before but not the slightest trace of dandyism remained. We were introduced, but at once we recognized each other, and recalled our first meeting at Popov's. Musorgsky declared that he had left the service in order to "devote himself entirely to music, as it was impossible to combine

---

[41] The hero and heroine of Alexander Herzen's tendentious novel *Who Is to Blame?* "Beltov . . . is disappointed with life and with himself, until Liuba, by her avowal of love and the kiss she gives him, enlightens him as to the meaning of his existence, which, however, can never find its fulfillment, for Liuba belongs to another man, who is his best friend." Oskar von Riesemann, *Moussorgsky* (New York, Knopf, 1929) p. 45.
This is the earliest of the very few documents in evidence of Musorgsky's intimacy with Nadezhda Petrovna Opochinina.

military service with art—a complicated matter," etc. Our conversation then turned involuntarily to music. I was still an enthusiastic
Mendelssohnist at that time, and knew hardly anything of Schumann. Musorgsky was already acquainted with Balakirev, and had
already smelled out all sorts of new tendencies in music, of which I
had no conception. When the Ivanovskys saw that we had found a
common topic of conversation—music—they proposed that we
should play a four-hand arrangement of Mendelssohn's A minor
[*Scottish*] symphony. M.P. turned up his nose a little, and said that
he was very happy to do so, but only begged "to be excused from
the andante, which is not at all symphonic, but was just one of the
Lieder ohne Worte or some such thing arranged for orchestra." We
played the first movement and the scherzo. Then Musorgsky began
to speak rapturously about the symphonies of Schumann, of which
I was then quite ignorant. He began to play some fragments of the
E-flat [*Rhenish*] symphony; when he came to the middle movement,
he stopped, saying: "Now, this is where the musical mathematics
begin." This was all new to me and I liked it. Seeing how interested
I was, he played some other pieces, new to me. Incidentally, I discovered that he was composing music himself. As I expressed my
interest, he began to play some scherzo of his (I think it was the one
in B-flat); when he came to the trio, he hissed through his teeth:
"Well, this is oriental!" And I was terribly amazed at what were, for
me, strange new elements in the music. I cannot say that it pleased
me at first; I was rather puzzled by the novelty of it. After listening
for a while more attentively, I began to value it and enjoy it. I confess that I was incredulous when he told me he intended to devote
himself seriously to music. At first I took it for petty boasting and
was inwardly rather amused—but after becoming acquainted with
his scherzo I wondered: should I believe him or not . . . ? [42]—
ALEXANDER BORODIN

14. *To MILI BALAKIREV*

18 October, 1859. St. Petersburg

MILI,

Our argument today was of such great interest that on my way to bed
I determined to write you about this dispute.—If Moses himself told

---

[42] There is another reliable glimpse of Musorgsky at approximately this time,
as seen by P. Boborykin: "I met Musorgsky for the first time at Balakirev's. There
were two brothers: one [Philarète] still wore a Guards uniform; the other [Mo-
deste] had recently changed to civilian clothes . . . At that time he was still a society *jeune homme*, rather a dandy, with a pleasant appearance, very well-bred, and
without military manners. He maintained towards Balakirev an attitude of pupil
towards mentor; but with neither flattery nor servility. In my presence they often
played four-hand arrangements and discussed subjects which deeply concerned
the circle. Musorgsky had already tested himself as a composer . . . The ideas of
an innovator had already possessed him and Balakirev heartily sympathized with
him." ("For Half a Century," *Russkaya Starina*, February 1913.)

the people, "an eye for an eye, a tooth for a tooth," then I agree with you, because his is the fundamental law for the spirit and the policy of the people. It seems to me that this rule occurred to the people themselves independently of Moses, a consequence of harsh customs. —Your arguments—damnation and circumcision—are not enough: Christ replaced circumcision with baptism, which is somewhat gentler, but in essence is just as strange a rite. Damnation was decided upon for a crime, that is, for not carrying out one or another law; in place of damnation Christ introduced the idea of eternal torment—it's actually the same thing, except that He softened it a little through penitence. There is my explanation; give me your written answer, in case you know for certain that it ("an eye for an eye, a tooth for a tooth") was laid down by Moses himself.

Your

MODESTE

15. *To MILI BALAKIREV*

19 October [1859]
[St. Petersburg]

DEAR MILI,

You present me with two things, which you suspect in me. I will begin with the first—mysticism—or as you well expressed it—*a mystic trait*. As you know, two years ago or less I was in the grip of a terrible illness, which came on violently while I was in the country. This was mysticism—mixed with cynical thoughts about the Deity. This illness developed terribly after I returned to St. Petersburg; I succeeded in concealing it from you, but you must have noticed traces of it in my music. I suffered greatly, and became fearfully sensitive (even morbidly so).—Then, either as a result of distraction, or because I indulged in fantastic dreams which I fed upon for a long while, my mysticism little by little began to fade away; and when the development of my reason had taken a certain form, I began to take measures to destroy this mysticism altogether. Lately I have made efforts to conquer this idea, and fortunately I have succeeded. At present I am very far from mysticism, and I hope forever, since moral and mental development are not compatible with it.—As for my attitude toward you, I must clarify how I behaved toward you from the very beginning of our acquaintance.—In the first place I recognized your superiority; in arguments with you I saw the greater clarity of view-

21

point and firmness on your side. Mad as I sometimes was with myself and with you, I had to concede the truth. From this it is plain to see that my sense of self-esteem incited me to be stubborn both in our arguments and in my relations with you. Further:

You are aware of the former excessive softness of my character, which has harmed me in my relations with people who did not deserve it.—Once I felt my self-esteem wounded, all my pride arose. It goes without saying that I began to analyze people, and with this I made rapid progress and guarded myself against myself. But I have never overlooked the least fault of mine in the matter of the good and the true.—In relation to people, I am greatly indebted to you, Mili, you were splendid in knowing how to push me out of my stupor. —Later I understood you thoroughly and became attached to you with all my soul, finding in you, among other things, an echo of my own thoughts, and sometimes their beginning and their conception. Our latest relations have made your personality so completely akin to mine that I have begun to trust you absolutely.—The role of *pasha*, à la Darg[omizhsky] is too petty and worthless to be ascribed to you; it wouldn't fit you anyway.—The argument at Vasenka's [43] was not childishness, but just a deformity, which sometimes is encountered in me—this is an unhealthy loss of reason, even a result of physical factors.—I don't deny that the above-mentioned circumstances, rather than the mysticism, left their traces on me, but now this rarely happens, and thanks to your kind, nice letter I will prepare myself with renewed strength to banish this rubbish forever from my personality. —I finished *Oblomov* [44] today and have already argued with *maman* about love, with Kitushka supporting me. In the 4th chapter love is absolutely defined, love of an Oblomov sort, but love all the same. But you are wrong in one instance, Mili, that, with the exception of Agafya Matveyevna, no woman could love Oblomov.—*A propos;* I am reading geology, terribly interesting.—Imagine, Berlin stands on infusorial soil, several masses of which have not yet died.

Your

MODESTE

P.S. Thus my explanation, dearest one; write me how you like it, and when we may meet.—*Maman* very much wants to see you, and Kitosha kisses you.

---

[43] Vasili Vasilyevich Zakharin, a naval lieutenant and musical dilettante.
[44] Goncharov's novel, first published serially in *Otechestvenni Zapiski,* from January to April 1859.

An Article by ALEXANDER SEROV

THE FIFTH, SIXTH AND SEVENTH EVENINGS
OF THE RUSSIAN MUSICAL SOCIETY

in *Muzikalni Vestnik*, January 17, 1860

[Extract]

. . . It was even more pleasing to encounter the warm sympathy of the public to the Russian composer A. [*sic*] P. Musorgsky, making his debut with a fine but regretfully too brief orchestral piece.[45]

This scherzo has not the interest, in my opinion, that the scherzo of C. A. Cui has, performed in the fourth concert, but it shows decided talent in the young musician, beginning his career as composer.

It is noteworthy that the symphonic fragment of a composer as yet unknown, side by side with the music of a "famous" *maestro*,[46] not only lost nothing thereby, but gained a very great deal. . .

16. *To MILI BALAKIREV*

10 February, 1860

DEAR MILI,

Thank God, it looks as though I were beginning to recover from my severe, unendurably excruciating sufferings, mental and physical.— You remember, my dear, how two years ago we were walking down Sadovaya Street (you were on your way home); it was summertime. Just before our walk we had been reading *Manfred*,[47] and I became so electrified with the sufferings of this lofty human spirit that I immediately said to you, "How I would like to be Manfred" (I was a mere child at the time) and evidently fate decided to grant me my wish —I became literally "manfredized," my soul slew my flesh. Now I am obliged to take every kind of antidote. Dear Mili, I know you love me; for God's sake keep a tight rein on me when we are talking together, and don't let me go wild; for a time it is absolutely necessary to give up both musical activities and every kind of intense brain work so that I can fully recover; my prescription—everything must be done for the material cure as much as possible at the expense of the mental side. The reasons for the irritation of my nerves are clear

[45] On January 11, 1860, the Russian Musical Society, conducted by Anton Rubinstein, gave the first performance of an orchestral work by Musorgsky—his Scherzo in B-flat.

[46] The maestro was Meyerbeer, whose *Struensee* immediately preceded Musorgsky's scherzo on the program.

[47] Byron's *Manfred* was required reading among European romanticists, who may be considered the direct forebears of the Russian nationalists.

to me now: it is not only the result of masturbation (this is almost a secondary reason), but chiefly this: youth, an excess of enthusiasm, a terrible, irresistible desire for omniscience, exaggerated introspective criticism and an idealism that amounts to the embodiment of a dream in visions and actions—these are the chief reasons. At this moment I see, that as I am only twenty years old, the physical side of me is not sufficiently developed to keep pace with my strong mental growth <the consequence of which is that the latter (mental strength) has ascended and choked the former (material strength)> (the reason for my physical underdevelopment is masturbation); the consequence of this was that the moral strength choked the strength of material development. We must now come to the latter's assistance; distraction and as much calm as possible, gymnastics and baths ought to save me. —Today Kito and I were at the ballet (*Paquerette*), a very nice ballet, there were several pretty scenes, but the music, Mili, the music was of the worst sort; Pugni is positively a musical Scythian.[48]—The ballet made a strange impression on me; I felt ill in the theater, and when I got home and I lay down to sleep, the dreams were extremely tormenting, but were at the same time so bittersweet and blissful that to die in such a state would have been easy; that (fortunately) was the end of my sufferings; I now feel much better, and at any rate I am perfectly calm.—Although the reason for this epistle to you, Mili, was not really to tell all this, but once I took up the pen, I remembered you, and a pleasurable feeling overcame me, and thus what I've written you has poured out involuntarily. The immediate reason for the epistle is Vasenka [Zakharin]; we arranged to eat pancakes on Saturday at Vasenka's, and I want to ask you Mili, don't you fear there will be too many of us—if not, and if you find that we can eat pancakes, we'll all be very happy; Kito and I shall both be there, the latter together with *maman* kisses you. Auntie and old Markova and Lara bow to you. I kiss you, Mili, from my soul, it seems I have awakened from a heavy dream.

Your

MODESTE

---

[48] Cesare Pugni, an Italian composer working in St. Petersburg, does not deserve all of Musorgsky's severity for this score. The original score for *Paquerette*, a ballet by Théophile Gautier and Arthur Saint-Léon, was by François Benoist. For the Russian première at the St. Petersburg Bolshoi Theater on January 26, 1860, Pugni, occupying the official post of Composer of Ballet Music, was asked to write some additional numbers.

P. S. Tell Sofia Ivanovna that the ace of spades bows to her. I await an answer, Mili.

10 February
1860

17. *To MILI BALAKIREV, Nizhni Novgorod*

26 September [1860] St. Petersburg

I have barely collected my strength to write you, dear Mili. I've only just returned from the country, and learned your address from the Stasovs and hurried to talk with you—it's such a long time since I've seen you. I think you will be interested to hear how I passed my time in the Moscow countryside.[49]—My illness lasted almost till August so that I could devote myself to music only at brief intervals; most of the time from May to August my brain was weak and highly irritated. Nevertheless I collected some materials that will be needed later; *Œdipus* and the little sonata [50] have made some headway. The sonata is almost ready, something has to be cleaned up in its middle section, but the tailpiece is successful.—*Œdipus* has had two choruses added to it: an andante in B-flat minor and an allegro in E-flat major, which will be used in the introduction, and are being written now. —Besides this I have received extremely interesting work, which I must prepare for next summer. It is this: a whole act to take place on Bald Mountain (from Mengden's drama *The Witch* [51]) a witches' sabbat, separate episodes of sorcerers, a solemn march for all this nastiness, a finale—the glorification of the sabbat in which Mengden introduces the commander of the whole festival on Bald Mountain. The libretto is very good. I already have some material for it; it may turn out to be a very good thing. Of the smaller things I've written: "Lord of My Days," [52] which in my opinion turned out entirely satis-

---

[49] At Glebovo, with the Shilovskys.

[50] The manuscript of the Sonata in C Major is dated "8 December 1860," and this reference may be to that work. See list of piano works. Gerald Abraham (in Calvocoressi's *Mussorgsky*, E. P. Dutton & Co., 1946, p. 7) ingeniously supposes that this last work on *Œdipus* found its way into the opening chorus in Act III of *Salammbô*.

[51] Though many of Baron Mengden's plays exist in print or in manuscript, no copy of *The Witch* has been uncovered.

[52] "Lord of My Days" was possibly a song based on the prayer in Pushkin's poem, "Hermits and Pure Women, Too."

factorily, and a Kinderscherz,[53] which was heartily liked by Gussakovsky. These are my humble labors.—Mili, you would be delighted
at the change that has taken place in me and, without doubt, it is
powerfully reflected in my music. My brain has become stronger and
has turned toward realities, the fires of youth have cooled off, everything has evened off, and *of mysticism* at the present time *there isn't
even half-a-word*. My last mystic thing is this andante in B-flat minor
(a chorus) from the introduction to *Œdipus*. I have completely recovered, Mili, thank God.—However, enough about myself, we shall
see each other, God willing, and talk over everything. I've heard from
maman that you have collected quite a lot of Russian songs; [54] this is
pleasant news, Mili; Stasov said that some of them are very good.—I
hope to receive some word from you, Mili; I am now in Peter, you
know my address; Gussakovsky is producing very fine things, some
of them he played for me, and he is now orchestrating his symphonic
allegro.—By the way, Mili. The Zakharins have suggested that he
move in with them; he has asked me about this and has asked me to
decide. Not knowing exactly the manner of thinking and the attitude of Avd[otya] Petr[ovna Zakharina], I told him only one thing:
though I have nothing to suggest in this respect, I have inwardly
wished that he would adopt a more quiet way of living.—It seems he
wrote to you in reference to this; you know the Zakharins well and
you have probably satisfied Gussakovsky with a more definite answer.
Please write to me, Mili. My brother kisses you warmly. *Maman* sends
you her respects and wishes you much, much good.—Now I'm putting
all my little musical sins in order. For a new period of my musical life
has begun.—Till we meet, dear Mili, I kiss you warmly.

MODESTE

18. *To MILI BALAKIREV*

9 November [1860]

I inform you, dear Mili, of a completely pleasant situation for me
(and possibly for you, too). I was at D. Stasov's today—to get tickets
for the Shilovskys. With regard to my chorus [from *Œdipus*], the

---

[53] This is the second version, dated May 28, 1860, the manuscript of which is
now in the Library of Congress in Washington.
[54] On his trip down the Volga this summer, Balakirev recorded a number of
folk songs, for the purpose of issuing a collection (published in 1866).

committee, [55] he told me, decided: if I find at the rehearsal that it could safely be performed in public—they will play it.—An instinct of self-preservation made me tell Stasov that the chorus is agitato and short, and to make the agitato effective, it would have to be preceded by an andante, even a short one, and for this reason I requested them to give it back to me. Perhaps this imbecile outfit really supposes that it can teach me.—I have my chorus back, and am heartily glad that a collision with Rubinstein has been averted.—*Basta!* I've had quite enough of the Society.—My brother kisses you, my dear, and *maman* bows and asks me to tell you that she's making jam for you.—Give me an answer, Mili, I'm sure that you will approve of my conduct. I kiss you warmly.

MODESTE

P.S. The Selivachevs [56] are enchanted with you; I was at their place yesterday, and we had a nice talk with the students.

19. *To MILI BALAKIREV*

[Postmarked: 25 December, 1860
St. Petersburg]

Thanks, Mili, for letting me off the writing of another scherzo, all the more as just now I am in no scherzoish mood, but incline rather to a fine andante. I shall work at part writing, beginning with something in three voices [parts]. I intend to accomplish something really worth while, appropriate to the present occasion; it is a wholesome *stimulant* for me to think that my *harmony* looks like nonsense; this must not be, and enough for that. Don't be too vexed about your overture, don't forget it was my first attempt at transcription, as my ar-

---

[55] Dimitri Stasov was one of the organizers and moving spirits of the Imperial Russian Musical Society, whose concert committee was headed by Anton Rubinstein. This appears to be one of many skirmishes between "official" music, led by Anton Rubinstein and the Grand Duchess Yelena Pavlovna, and the "rebels," led by Balakirev and Vladimir Stasov. Rubinstein's firm fortifications—popular acceptance, his prolific composing talents, the conservatory, the Grand Duchess's financial support—worried the members of the Balakirev Circle into many desperate words and acts. They refer to him as "Dubinstein" (Dumbinstein) and "Tupinstein" (Dullinstein).

[56] Selivachev eventually took twenty lessons from Balakirev. Graduating from the course of study left him no less a dilettante than when he started. Elsewhere, Musorgsky describes him as an *"enfant gâté* with seven Fridays a week."

rangement of the Second Sp[anish] Overt[ure] [57] doesn't count.—
We'll see each other at the Stasovs.

MODESTE

20.　*To MILI BALAKIREV*

[end of December, 1860]

I should like very much to see you, dear Mili, but I can't, because
"it snows and blows outdoors" and a cough has so completely broken
me that *my nerves have turned to jelly,* and I shall stay home.

I am sending you your scores [58]—is the orchestration as it should be?
Do look it over; I have yet to note the instruments in the transcription. Bach is well; if you will be at the Stasovs on Sunday bring the
overture (the orchestration) and I'll give the entr'actes myself to Bach.
—Give a splendid answer for everything with *the formation which
results from Dargun's notification about Rusalka*—simply Yasha.[59]

Till Monday, January 2, at the Stasovs.

MODESTE

20a.　*MILI BALAKIREV to AVDOTYA ZAKHARINA* [Extract]

December 31, 1860

. . . Our entire company lives as before. Musorgsky now has a
happy and healthy appearance. He has written an allegro and thinks
that he has already accomplished a great deal for art in general and
Russian art in particular. Every Wednesday evening now I have an
assembly of all the Russian composers; new compositions (when they
compose any) are played for us and, in general, good, edifying things
by Beethoven, Glinka, Schumann or Schubert, etc. Even Cui has
waked up and comes every Wednesday; he jokes and amuses us
greatly, he's recently written a scherzo, a very good one, which he has
dedicated to us three: to me, Modeste and Apollonti [Gussakov-
sky] . . .

---

[57] This Glinka overture is also known as *Night in Madrid.* The score of Musorgsky's transcription for four hands is dated "Begun October 28, 1858, and
finished November 11."

[58] These transcriptions are possibly those done by Musorgsky for Balakirev's
overture and entr'actes for *King Lear.*

[59] "The meaning of this sentence is not clear. Yasha is possibly the lackey of
Dargomizhsky (Dargun)."—Andrei Rimsky-Korsakov. *Rusalka* (1856) is Dargomizhsky's most popular opera.

An Article by ANTON RUBINSTEIN [60]

In *Nash Vek (Our Century)*, January 4, 1861

"OF MUSIC IN RUSSIA"

[Extracts]

"He who has never moistened his bread with tears, who has never wept for entire nights, does not know you, O heavenly powers!"

These words of Goethe, of such profound truth for all who practice arts, including music, have little meaning in Russia, for here music is practiced only by amateurs, that is, those who, by virtue of their origin or social position, do not have to earn their daily bread with music, and practice it merely for their personal pleasure . . .

By a strange coincidence, Russia has almost no artist-musicians in the exact sense of this term. This is so because our government has not given the same privileges to the art of music which are enjoyed by the other arts, such as painting, sculpture, etc.—that is, he who practices music is not given the rank of an artist . . .

In order to prove the evil effects produced on Russian music by such an order of things, let us analyze the extent of our amateurs' abilities, starting with composers.

Who has ever been called witty for making one witty remark during his entire life?

Who has been called a philosopher for expressing a single lofty thought?

But this is not the case with amateurs in music. Once an amateur succeeds in composing a single song, more or less fortunate in content, he considers himself a composer. Woe to the person who tries to point out to him that his melody, though light and agreeable, does not fit the text of his song, or that there are harmonic errors in the accompaniment, or that one must study for a long time in order to compose even a small piece of music. The amateur looks scornfully upon the ill-disposed critic, publishes his song, forces some singer from the Italian opera to sing it, begins to pass judgments on art and artists, becomes a musical celebrity of the town, goes on composing songs without noticing that they are all repetitions of the same melody, does not care to penetrate into the rules of harmony and composition, begins to argue that melody is the only merit in music and all else is German pedantry, and will end by composing an opera . . .

21. *To MILI BALAKIREV, St. Petersburg*

13 January [1861] Moscow

I am obliged to disappoint you, dear Mili—I shall not be able to hear your and Gussakovsky's pieces—the frost is terrible, nearly 35 de-

---

[60] After the founding of the Imperial Russian Musical Society on May 1, 1859, Anton Rubinstein actively propagandized for the expansion of the society's school into the status of a conservatory.

grees [Réaumur], I caught cold and must not risk going out, the more so as I usually freeze at 10 degrees, and besides, we had to wait three hours because of an inability to get up steam in the locomotive. I am busy with serious and good work—writing an andante and scherzo for the D-major symphony,[61]—I've rented a piano from Lang and will make music.—The andante will be in F-sharp minor, the scherzo in B major is already being written. I was at Demidov's [62] but didn't find him in, but he may possibly come to me this evening. After you hear the entr'actes performed, if you find the transcription decent, give the first draft with the overture to Kito; he will send it to me here in Jericho.—Kiss Gussakevich and Mustafa [63] for me and write me how the entr'actes [for *Lear*] and Gussak's allegro went off. Write without fail and in detail, also that on Wednesday you will definitely play—please, Mili.

I found the Schumann fantasia here, the one dedicated to Liszt— *schwach*, and whatever is *fantastisch* in it is at the beginning.[64] However, it is his Op. 17, which means that it comes from his period of passion for Mendelssohn.—I am playing his Sonata in F-sharp minor (Schumann's); the introduction is not of his best, the best parts are both allegros, especially the first one. I picked up a silly transcription

---

[61] It is possible that this symphony was planned on some arrangement of the material for the "little sonata," dated December 8, 1860, since the andante for the sonata is in the key of D major and the manuscript of the sonata contains this note: "A symphonic exercise for orchestra."

[62] A. A. Demidov is another Preobrazhensky officer who has deserted to the cause of music.

[63] Alexander Petrovich Arsenyev, a composition and piano pupil of Balakirev's, known in the Circle as Mustafa and the Linguist.

[64] Schumann's Fantasia in C Major is noted at the opening, *Durchaus phantastisch.*

for two hands of the Schubert C-major symphony—by Reinecke—let's hope Demidov doesn't know it—I will play it for him. What a collection of portraits of the great maestros at Gresser's [shop]—imagine Yuri Golitzin [65] with a baton in his hand flourishing it at an orchestra as if he wanted to beat the musicians— O Jericho, that this should be in the foreground.

My respects to Bach. I have not yet been to Moscow's symphonic tribunal [66] but I'll probably go—they're admitting those with Petersb[urg] tickets. Ach, apropos, on the train I read a new magazine, *Vek*, with an article by A. Rubinstein. He says that in Russia there are not and never have been musician-artists, but there have been and are *musician-amateurs;* he bases his argument on this, that the genuine artist works for glory and money, and not for anything else, and then he clinches his argument saying that it is impossible to call anyone an artist and proclaim him a talent who has written less than three or four good things during his lifetime. What prerogatives does Rubinstein have for such narrowness—glory and *money and quantity rather than quality. O Ocean! O Puddle!* [67]

I am surrounded here by quite decent personalities, all former college students, but lively and efficient fellows. In our evenings we get all subjects going—history and administration and chemistry and the arts—everything, and it is pleasant to talk with them; but Jericho! these people form a sort of separate circle in Moscow—however, good people always stand aside and it is even better so, for, as one recalls, "blessed is the man that walketh not in the counsel of the ungodly."

Do write, Mili, about the performance of your pieces—and I shall go on working in Moscow, and return next week to Peter.

Till then, dear, I kiss you.

MODESTE

P.S. My address—near the Eye Hospital, in Degtyarni Lane, Shilovsky House.

---

[65] Prince Golitzin was the organizer of the Saltykov-Golitzin chorus, a conductor and composer—famous by virtue of his tour of Europe and America (1857–58) propagandizing Russian music.

[66] The Moscow branch of the Imperial Russian Musical Society, with Nikolai Rubinstein in charge.

[67] Anton Rubinstein's Second Symphony in C major (Op. 42), is known as the *Ocean Symphony.*

22. *To MILI BALAKIREV, St. Petersburg*

16 January [1861] [Moscow]

I've not received an answer from you, Mili; however, I hope to receive it tomorrow, because I wrote you on January 13.—On Friday
a lady froze to death in the train—her corpse arrived at Petersburg;
it's good I didn't go, having a cold, and no fur coat at that; the frost
in Moscow continues to be no less than 24 degrees every day.—The
scherzo is finished, only the second trio has not been done, and it is
being written: the scherzo is a big one, in a symphonic style, and is
dedicated (as is the whole symphony) to our Wednesday Fellowship—
our *jour fixe.* Demidov was at my place; he is a very nice fellow—terribly hot-blooded; I introduced him to Gussakovsky and Cui, and
played him your fifth entr'acte from *Lear,* and during the apotheosis
he ah-ed—he liked it so.—Played the C-major symphony of Schubert,
and tears almost came to his eyes.—He is still very young, but he definitely justifies your opinion of him; generally speaking I am very glad
to have made such an acquaintance. On Tuesday I am going to his
place (if well) with the Schub[ert] C major, which he begged me to
bring.—I have not been to the local Ger[man] Ministry of Mus[ic],
because the program for the Saturday concert did not attract me.[68]—
Nikolai Rubinstein is a worthy relation of Anton; he lets his homemade Moscow pianists play Chopin—*pièces de salon:* what a choice—
the height of absurdity.—I think Apollon [Gussakovsky] sprouted his
first feathers a little after the performance of his work; however, this
is understandable because it is the most necessary condition for further practice. Kiss him, Gussek, from me, the way I kiss him, finding
something nasty on his upper lip—I love him terribly.—Things seem
to be going all right now. If only God grants me strength—it will be
possible to write—I get quite tired, composing is not light work—
however, cold water helps.

I've become acquainted in Jericho with Pliushchikha, Arbat, Sofika

---

[68] The program for January 14, 1861, was as follows:

Symphony in D major	Haydn
Andante spianato et polonaise (Op. 22)	
(played by Volkov)	Chopin
King Stephen Overture	Beethoven
Cantata—Lauda Sion	Mendelssohn
Faust Overture	Wagner

—what distances—horror!—Lvov [69] is Haemorrhoid's [70] viceroy; he is not liked, but this will be the end of it, no one will like him but at the same time everybody will obey and be patient—this is Russian nature.

Please, Mili—write me, if you have time. Have you done anything new—what about your symphony in F-sharp minor? [71] I like it very much, judging from those little episodes that you played me; I often remember it—the freshness and a certain attractive coloring in it.— Has Cesar written anything—or does the Artillery [Academy] still drag everything out of him?—Write at least a few words, Mili, for I haven't heard a word from you.

Warmly kiss you my dear.

MODESTE

P.S. It seems I've already given you my address: near the Eye Hospital on Degtyarni Lane, Shilovsky House.

17 January

The scherzo is entirely ready and arranged for four hands neatly and cleanly, so that it is very convenient to play; I flatter myself with the hope of performing it for *our* judgment on one of our Wednesdays.—Still no news from you—maybe you are angry with me for having missed the Saturday universities [concerts] in Peter—but in any case you might have written anyway—well, curse, but give us some news of yourself nevertheless; one feels uneasy without any response.

I hope to leave on Friday—God grant that it will not be 35°—or I may freeze—the carriages are abominably equipped.—Till we meet, Mili.

MODESTE

P.S. No news from my own—also it is as if the whole conclave were against me.

---

[69] Leonid Fyodorovich Lvov, chief of the chancery of the Imperial Moscow Theaters, and brother of the composer of "God Save the Tzar."

[70] Alexei Verstovsky acquired this nickname after his opera *Gromoboi* (Thunder Fighter). His opera *The Tomb of Askold* (1835), however, entitles him to a more dignified niche in Russian musical history; its use of folk music and national subject furnished a steppingstone to Glinka's shore.

[71] This symphony must be numbered among the many unfinished Balakirev projects.

23. *To MILI BALAKIREV, St. Petersburg*

19 January [1861] [Moscow]

At last you've written, Mili.—I am happy about the fourth entr'acte and about Gussakovsky. Rubinstein had better not undertake "the dark soul" [72] with his limitations and his barren fantasy. "How amusing is your thought about the letter you wrote to Demidov"—I answer you: "I gave it to Demidov's servant for delivery to Al. Al. together with a letter of my own, which I prepared in case he would not be found at home."

About Demidov I wrote you a bit in my second letter [Letter 22]—now I add—he wishes to go to Peter and may arrive there alone on Monday, January 23, but this is just a plan as yet; in Moscow he has little opportunity to hear good music, good things fall to him but rarely in concerts; he is not yet fully formed, hardly touched musically, but with good instincts, he quickly grasps the development of a musical idea in a composition, he himself very often points out its phases and development—to speak simply, he has a feeling for musical logic. In his relation to esthetics he is a little youthful, but conscious esthetic feeling appears only in the perfect development of a musician.—Up to now he leans toward Mendelssohn, toward sour sentimentality, but this will fall away in time; we have all loved Mendelssohn; he already cannot stand Chopin. His teacher Wolf is *schwach;* I've seen him; he is the very image of a hairdresser. However, Demidov borrows only the mechanical part from him, without trusting him about the rest.—If I had known that I was to stay in Moscow for more than a week, I would have brought with me some things that Demidov is not acquainted with. In Moscow I have found only the Schumann sonata (F-sharp minor), the Schubert C-major symph., the F-major quartet of Beethoven (the Russian one)—which I have played for him.

As for my scherzo I will tell you that from what is written it is difficult to judge it, but after the thing is complete a decision can follow; I destroyed the 1st trio, I'll write another.—About your emphasis on *limited atmosphere* let us now speak.

The not very great difference between the names of Aslanovich and Ustimovich [73] provides a contrast in personalities. As to Aslano-

---

[72] Rubinstein was writing a song on Lermontov's translation of one of Byron's *Hebrew Melodies,* "My Soul is Dark."

[73] Konstantin Aslanovich graduated with Musorgsky from the Ensigns School; nothing is known of either Ustimovich or Shchukarov.

vich you are right, but as to Ustimovich—however, you spoke only of Aslanovich.—The parentheses within which you provoke me, as to my preference for *limited personalities*, that calls for only one answer: "tell me whom you love, and I will tell you who you are." And so logically—I, too, must be limited.—But Ustimovich is a strongly developed personality, besides being well educated and talented. Shchukarov, with whom I'm living, is intelligent and developed as well as being an original person; two or three former students—extremely nice fellows in the brain department—how I manage to breathe the atmosphere of these people and vice versa—they breathe my atmosphere—*I cannot grasp,* according to your opinion based on experience, [what you say] about my tendency toward limitation (experience because we've known each other for five years).—Undoubtedly my work will encounter prejudice from your side; this is natural because the active image of my personality sickens you.

As to my being swamped and having to be pulled out of the swamp, I say only this—if I have talent—I will not be swamped as long as my brain is stimulated—the more so, and if one has neither this nor that —is it worth while to pull a splinter from the mud? Speaking plainly, there was a time when I nearly went under, not musically, but morally —I crawled out; however, you will find out later what really happened—if our conversation should touch this matter—there was a female involved. In any case I know one thing, your letter was impelled by mistaken spite; it is time to stop looking at me as a child, who must be held up so he won't fall.

Here is the answer to your letter, Mili—heated and hasty as it was, but thanks for it; I was afraid that you would leave me without any answer.—I shall be in Peter soon.

Till then.

MODESTE

23a. *VLADIMIR STASOV to MILI BALAKIREV*

February 13, 1861

. . . Could you write a little letter to Musorgsky immediately, asking him to go at once to Maria [Shilovskaya], fall on his knees before her, cry, tear his hair . . . anything, to force her by hook or crook to summon [Konstantin] Lyadov, and compel him to give the third entr'acte of *Ruslan*. This seems the only means of settling this matter for good—it's about time for it to be brought into order . . .

35

24.   To MILI BALAKIREV

DEAR MILI,

Lyadov is positively taking your *Lear* for his concert, and asks for my *Œdipus* as well. We met at the Shilovskys, this is an urgent matter; therefore Lyadov and I, by his wish, want to catch you home tomorrow between twelve and one. Please be home, dear. Stephan de Schillon [Shilovsky] intends to honor you also, so we three, Lyadov, Shilovsky and I, will hasten to you.

All yours,
MODESTE

Friday
24 March [1861]

Lyadov's concert is to be very interesting.[74]

The Emancipation Proclamation [Extracts]

BY THE GRACE OF GOD
WE, ALEXANDER SECOND,
EMPEROR AND AUTOCRAT
OF ALL RUSSIA,
TZAR OF POLAND, GRAND DUKE OF FINLAND,

et cetera, et cetera, et cetera

Declare to all our loyal subjects . . .

All those people now bound to the soil will receive at the proper time the full rights of free rural residents.

The landowners, maintaining their possession of all lands now belonging to them, will place at the disposal of the peasants a certain quantity of field soil and other lands according to given regulations . . .

This new order, because of its inevitable complications, cannot be established at once, but will require no less than two years; to avoid confusion, therefore, and in the interests of social and private welfare, in the landowners' estates during this said period there must be maintained the present existing order until, the proper preparations having been made, the new order can begin.

To accomplish this in an orderly way, we judge it right to issue these commands:

(1) To open in each province a Provincial Office for peasant af-

---

[74] The concert on April 6, conducted by Lyadov, included, in addition to these compositions, excerpts from Dargomizhsky's *Festival of Bacchus* and from Cui's *Prisoner of the Caucasus*. However Musorgsky may have pleaded with Shilovskaya, Stasov's wish was not granted.

fairs, which will be entrusted with the supervision of the business of the peasant communities settled on the lands of the landowners.

(2) To appoint Mediators in the counties, and to form County Mediation Assemblies, for the examination of local disputes and misunderstandings arising from the execution of the new statutes . . .

Shield yourselves with the sign of the cross, orthodox people, and appeal with us for God's blessing on your free labor, a pledge of your domestic well-being and of the general welfare.

Given at St. Petersburg, on the seventeenth day of February, in the one thousand eight hundred and sixty-first year since the Birth of Christ, in the seventh year of our rule.

The lives of the landowning Musorgskys were to be immediately and deeply affected by this alteration in Russia's social structure.

25. *To MILI BALAKIREV*

Monday, 1st of May [1861]

I stand extremely guilty before you, dear Mili—I hasten to answer you because your letter frightened me. On Sunday I could not come, for from the morning on various people dropped in about our matter [75] and held me.—Tomorrow I want to find you in bed; why is it that you are always ill, dear? I want awfully to see you.

MODESTE

Maman and Kitinka kiss you.

26. *To MILI BALAKIREV*

Saturday, 14 Oct., [1861]

Yesterday I was just getting ready to drive to you, dear Mili, when a message arrived which forced me to fly to two businessmen (in regard to our matter). While my brother isn't here, I have to run around for him—very vexing, that such a necessity sometimes arises so urgently.

MODESTE

P.S. I'll try to drop in at Vasenka's today—but I can't be sure.

---

[75] "Our matter" must somehow be related to the Musorgsky estate, placed in the hands of the two brothers by their late father. This "matter," discussed in the next letter also, may have been brought to some new crisis by the manifesto of emancipation.

26a. *NIKOLAI RIMSKY-KORSAKOV* [76] *to* SOPHIA *RIMSKAYA-KORSAKOVA, Tikhvin [Extracts]*

November 26, 1861

DEAR MOTHER,

Last Sunday, Canille introduced me to M. A. Balakirev, a well-known musician and composer, and also to Cui, the composer of an opera, *The Prisoner of the Caucasus* . . . I am very pleased to make such an acquaintance and it may be useful for the music . . .

December, 1861

. . . Yesterday I was at Balakirev's as usual. I spend the time there so pleasantly that I simply don't know how to thank Canille for such a magnificent acquaintance. . . .

". . . How My Intermezzo Was Born . . ."

Among the instrumental compositions of [Musorgsky's] first period, undoubtedly the finest is the Intermezzo. It is full of power and beauty and is entitled by the composer himself *Intermezzo symphonique in modo classico,* which is indeed justified by the general manner; even the chief theme is somewhat in the manner of Bach. But it is wonderful that in spite of its external classicism and Europeanism, this composition bears in itself a national Russian content. At first Musorgsky did not tell this to anyone, but in the 70's, in the epoch of our most intimate friendly relations, he told me many times that his Intermezzo is "secretly" Russian, that it had been inspired by a certain rural scene which imprinted itself deeply on his imagination: in the winter of 1861 he was on his mother's country estate in the province of Pskov and once on a beautiful, sunny winter's day, a holiday, he saw a whole crowd of peasants crossing the fields and making their way with difficulty through the snowdrifts; many of them repeatedly falling into the snow and then scrambling onward. "This"—Musorgsky related—"was at once beautiful, picturesque, serious, and amusing. And suddenly"—said he—"in the distance there appeared a group of young peasant women, singing and laughing as they walked along an even path. This scene impressed itself on my mind in a musical form. And unexpectedly the first melody, rising and falling *à la* Bach, formed itself; I envisioned the happy laughter of the women as a melody from which I afterward made the middle section or trio. But all this was conceived *in modo*

---

[76] Nikolai Andreyevich Rimsky-Korsakov was an eager seventeen-year-old naval cadet who had just decided that music was the most important thing in life. He joined the Balakirev Circle with an almost childish enthusiasm and a wish to please. His nicknames in the Circle all derive from his name and naval career: Korsik, Korsinka, the Roman, the Admiral, the Corsican.

classico, in accordance with my musical studies at that time. And that's how my Intermezzo was born into the world . . ."—VLADIMIR STASOV

27. *To MILI BALAKIREV, St. Petersburg*

11 March [1862]
Village of Volok

I write the andante.[77]

I am splendidly situated, so far in good health and in comparatively good spirits.

I lead the life of a respectable person—go to bed at eleven, rise at eight and this schedule is proving very pleasant for me.—Snow, wind and frost. I wait with impatience for spring—to begin the cure—it's time to start my brain working, let's stop fooling around; I must work, I must do things, and one can do it only when the spirit's in a normal disposition, in a delirious condition one can only tremble, create fantasies and squander one's strength in vain—in its way it is a kind of masturbating—only spiritually.

How is your business in reference to the concerts and is Heirarch Dubinstein scheming or not? [78] Write me about it.—Has Korsik finished his scherzo [79] and is it good? (One must assume it is!) Write about this also—all these things are extremely interesting to know.

When one changes one's atmosphere and surroundings—one feels refreshed; the past becomes purified, standing in bold relief and then one can bravely analyze what one has lived through. Having realized this now that I've gone to the country—I see that, although I haven't run away from work, I have—with my Russian laziness—done little; I do not have any particular faith in my talent, although I don't have any doubt of it; therefore I want to work according to *my strength,* and I will, but I am searching for other activities where I could make myself useful. Moreover, I am discovering in myself something that is already obvious—a kind of looseness, a softness; you called it *doughiness,* I now recall, and I was a little hurt, because dough has the quality of retaining the impression of *dirty* fingers as well as *clean* ones.—However, I intend to get rid of this softness, it knocks me out;

[77] For the symphony, mentioned in Letter 21 and following letters.
[78] It is now difficult to say whether Rubinstein plotted against Balakirev or Balakirev imagined that he did.
[79] For Rimsky-Korsakov's first symphony.

39

I now feel this clearly, because I want to do things.—Do not consider this letter of mine as the Andante, judging by the emphasis at the beginning—as you might assume.—In the finale I'm still stuck in the second theme, the *rascal* simply won't come out, perhaps spring will force it out.—Kiss all of *ours* for me and don't forget the Linguist. I bow and press the hand of Malvinin Alcibiades [Cui]. Till the next letter, if it's not boring (if boring, tell me—I will take measures)—I wouldn't want you to think me a boring conversationalist in my letters.—I kiss you thrice, as always—write in detail about the affairs of the popular school.[80]

MODESTE

Respects to both Sofia Ivanovna and her husband; she is an ardent Catholic, and therefore believes that God has joined them together forever <inviolably> inseparably, so I won't have to separate them.

My address: In Pskov Province, Kholmsky County by way of the Tiapolovo Station, village of Volok, care of Natalia Yegorovna Kushelova, for delivery to me.—That will be more convenient, because I shall be here for a month.

28. *To MILI BALAKIREV, St. Petersburg*

31 March [1862]
Village of Volok

As soon as I got settled in this country place, I wrote you, Mili. But I've had no answer from you. I remain ignorant of the reason for your silence—I write a second epistle.

The andante is ready. The allegro for the finale is being worked on; I imagine the *birth pangs* will come in the spring, so I must get ready to *give birth*. In the meantime I'm shaping a little D major

---

[80] "It occurred to him [Balakirev] to submit to Gavril Lomakin, the conductor of Count Sheremetyev's choir, the idea of founding a school of music where instrumentalists and singers would be educated free of charge and would provide an orchestra and choir for performances of music old and new, Russian and foreign. A concert was given on March 11, 1862, in aid of the scheme; . . . and the foundation of the school was officially announced a week later. Work began soon afterward with Lomakin as the head of the school and Balakirev as his assistant. The first batches of pupils were government officials, university students, tradespeople, workmen, and women belonging to an equally great variety of classes. Eagerness to join was so great that Sheremetyev once remarked 'This is like people rushing to church on a Sunday.' "—M. D. Calvocoressi, "Mily Balakiref" in *Masters of Russian Music*.

sonata. Have already begun to write a scherzo in B minor.[81] From the
Beethoven quartet the allegro (first) and scherzo (first) are ready,
and I intend to finish the whole quartet in time for *our next season.*[82]
—There you have my musical activities. I am well and my head's all
right—it's convenient to work.

While my landlady's children forcefully bang their fingers on the
keyboard, creating all imaginable *accords possibles et impossibles* (this
is called taking music lessons)*—I am reading a very interesting
thing: concerning nature in general and human nature particularly.
The book bears this title: *De la philosophie de la nature* [83] and what
is pleasant is that it doesn't smell of that philosophic narrowness,
which lets into its circle only those acquainted with the terminology
and dogma of various philosophic gangs. This book is written by a
human being, one who expounds his thoughts freely, lucidly and with
a great knowledge of the matter.—Besides this, it has historical interest, of the gradual development of man's knowledge of nature.—
After the first revolution the book was sentenced in France (by the
stinking stupidity of Catholics and despots—dictators and presidents)
to the auto-da-fé.—O Frenchmen! O republicans! As usual the greater
part of the copies were saved, before the stupid sentence could be carried out.

In consequence of the approach of spring and the impossibility of
communication I am confined to my *petit réduit.*—My company consists of a *hot-blooded Prussian*—tutor of my landlady's children; a
clear and developed brain, a remarkably energetic and alert gentleman.[84] His Spartan character makes him quite useful to me; my Athe-
nian flabbiness seems to be losing itself, because he drags me through

* Musorgsky's note: Doing *this* they interfere with my music.

[81] This sonata and scherzo have not been preserved.
[82] This is Musorgsky's second transcription of a Beethoven quartet. His first
was a two-hand arrangement of the andante of the quartet in C major (Op. 59,
No. 3); the arrangement is dated April 9, 1859, dedicated to A. S. Gussakovsky,
and noted: "For the Opochinin Saturdays." This present work is an arrangement
for four hands of the five movements of the quartet in B-flat major (Op. 130). The
arrangements, by movement, are dated March 27, March 28, April 25, April 27,
and the finale allegro was left unfinished.
[83] *De la philosophie de la nature* (1769) by Claude Izouard Delisle de Sales.
This title has heretofore been mistaken in all Musorgsky biographies for d'Hol-
bach's *Système de la Nature,* a more familiar work.
[84] Research has not clarified either the identification or the activities of this
"Prussian." The best guess is that he is the Georg von Madeweiss mentioned in
Musorgsky's autobiographical note (p. 419).

snowdrifts up to my waist, finding that my half-stupor is due to sluggish circulation and that my organism requires regular jolts until *it
strengthens itself*. These *promenades monstres* really help me.

My Prussian plays the piano quite well and has some understanding
of musical matters.—He sometimes treats me to Bach's little fugues
(O Dargopekh!) and of these the one in E *together* with its prelude
pleases me especially—happily he plays it well.* I often sound out
my companion and on many subjects I find him, in his opinions, sympathetic.—I confess I've begun to doubt my opinions in regard to the
Germans in Russia and Germans in general (except for the scholars
and artists—who, understandably, have their own stature). As a German in Russia, he of course is an exception to the *beer-drinking
burgherdom* with Riga cigars, and this includes directors of depart-
ments as well as Dubinstein the Hierarch and crumpled Karl [85] in-
clusively.—But what about my German? On my birthday (March
16) [86] he showed himself at his most zealous. Before I had time to
awake, I received some verses with a rosebud pinned to them—*a
spring rose*. Poetry! Metaphors! This delicate attention was very pleasant for me, but—*a German! a thorough German!* The verses were not
without a certain strength—the author was too sensible to compare
me with a rose so they turned out not so badly.

Write me about everything interesting, concerning you and ours.
By the way: what about Korsik's lip—is it still drooping? I dare say
his scherzo is ready.—Isn't there news of Gussakevich? *Firmly*—thrice
—and in Russian style, I kiss you, and you are commissioned to kiss
all our brotherhood.

Kiss Linguist Mustafa where he has *something not so good*—he
knows the place—he'll show you.

What about the *famed match-maker?* [87] Is he still at Dubinstein's

* Musorgsky's note: The piano is a half-tone below pitch—the fugue comes
out in E flat major—I don't like E major.

---

[85] Karl Schubert, an outstanding cellist, at this time a director of the St. Petersburg Conservatory.

[86] Musorgsky always considered that his birthday was on March 16; it actually
was March 9.

[87] This may be Vasili Kologrivov who was, at this time, trying to patch up the
Rubinstein-Balakirev feud. In *Free Artist* (New York, Random House, 1939, pp.
180–181), Catherine Drinker Bowen tells of a musical joke, entitled *Fools' Scherzo*,
composed by Gussakovsky for the following combination:

| Violin I | Rubinstein I [Anton] |
| Violin II | Rubinstein II [Nikolai] |

mercy; does he dare or has he already put aside the thought of arranging a match for you?—Write about it.

I repeat my address: In Pskov Prov., town of Kholm, by way of the Tiapolovo station to the village of Volok, Natalia Yegorovna Kushelova, to be delivered to me.

Till our next chat.

MODESTE

29. *To MILI BALAKIREV, St. Petersburg*

28 April [1862] Village of Volok

Your letter delighted me greatly, Mili; I've derived a great deal of pleasure from it; to my interest in your letter was added the gratification of satisfied expectations; I waited and waited for an answer from you, and thus your letter gave me a twofold pleasure. I *exult* in your successful concerts and *I wish health* to the newborn school! I have already taken to my heart the two boys whom you picked out.[88] Their heads, naturally, are free of both the needed and unneeded things which fill the trained brains of medical students and internes.—It should not be assumed from this, that *learning* should be *obscurity*— but all the same, the natural, free development of natures, which are basically more fresh, and are considerably more pleasant than scholastic or academic (*cela revient au même*) training. These boys will receive impressions easily and clearly. One has only to imagine—what don't the professors cram into those young brains, and how those heads must break, before they become capable—of discarding unneeded things and keeping only essentials.—One is involuntarily re-

| Viola | Kologrivov |
| 'Cello | Karl Schubert |

with this program:
1. Kologrivov's joy at meeting Rubinstein.
2. Conspiracy against True Music.
3. Actions of the conspiracy.
4. Rubinstein gets ahead of everybody.
5. All bow before him.
6. Their deaths (of their musical careers).
7. Scherzo da capo (memories of the past).

[88] When Olya, Shestakova's daughter whose musical education had been placed in Balakirev's hands by Glinka, died in 1862, Balakirev, aside from his work in the new Free School, gave free private music lessons to two promising boys "in memory of Olya."

minded of the conversation between Mephistopheles and the mother's darling.[89]—With what satanic skill does this devil frighten the poor youthful novice, with all sorts of *antediluvian and new-fangled doctrines*—a real professor! Only this devil is more scrupulous than our professors: he frightens, and they lure.

I pursue all this for one purpose. From scientific schools I turn to music schools. In Peter, with only an insignificant distance between them, two [music] schools have been formed, absolute contrasts in character.—One is a *Professoria;* the other: a free association of those who seek to become kin to art.—In one Zaremba and Tupinstein, in their professorial, antimusical togas, stuff the heads of their students with various abominations and infect them in advance. The poor pupils see before them not human beings but two fixed pillars to which are nailed some silly scrawls said to contain the laws of music. But Tupinstein is a *tup* [a dullard]—consequently he scrupulously does his duty: *to be wickedly dull.*—But not Zaremba—a bold fellow. He cuts out measures for art. Being raised to the rank of a doctor of music—*a cobbler in an academic fool's cap,* he is not so childish as to base his opinions and advice on esthetics and musical logic—oh, no! He has learned the rules and uses this as a smallpox antitoxin to inoculate against free learning anyone who longs to study art.—*Into the dust before Mendel!* That is Zaremba's motto, for Mendel is Zaremba's god and Zaremba is his prophet.[90]

As for Auntie Helen—she can't live to Methuselah's age; she's only a passing affliction, and [. . .] has gray hairs, because she already [. . .] is very unsteady in her adorations and hatreds; [. . .] playfully and lovingly is famous for her inconstancy.[91]

---

[89] In Part I, Scene 4 of Goethe's *Faust.*

[90] Nikolai Ivanovich Zaremba, from a background as director of the choral society of the Lutheran SS. Peter and Paul Church in St. Petersburg, was brought into the newly opened Conservatory as professor of theory of composition. Zaremba's conservative theories and methods derived from those of his teacher, Adolph Bernard Marx. "Mendel" is, of course, Mendelssohn.

[91] This passage, on the Grand Duchess Yelena Pavlovna, has been cleansed of obvious indecencies by the Russian editor of Musorgsky's letters. The grand duchess was an important figure on many levels of Russian life. When this sixteen-year-old Württemberg princess crossed the Russian border in 1823 on her way to marriage with Nikolai I's younger brother, she said, "I feel that I am entering my native land," and all her many-sided activity in Russian interests prove her sincerity. She was instrumental in pushing Alexander II toward the "great emancipation"; she organized the first Russian Red Cross during the same Crimean War in which Florence Nightingale broke military tradition; opening hospitals

In the other school, there are you and Gashenka [Lomakin]. But what can be said here: you are a talent, and consequently all bold, free, strong things are yours by nature, and such *people* are needed by the *people;* and because of this—I wish success and prosperous life to your fine enterprise and once more I exult in the newly born!

Spring! Nature has shed its dead skin; how much more strongly one lives—and how kind she is, how many good things and healthy impressions she bestows.—My work goes on in its usual way. A trio is being written within the scherzo for the symphony in D major.— The 2nd scherzo and cavatina from the Beethoven quartet are ready, and I'm taking up the finale. I've put aside the D-flat major andante for the last.—I'm not sending my own andante. This is a tiny weakness —but let it pass.—Cui is arisen! [92] Bravo! *This is you again, Mili! Aller toujours, vous allez bien!* Poor Mustafa has put himself in chains and languishes there.[93] I congratulate Korsinka on his escape from the naval barracks.[94] Administer an especially big kiss to all of ours and *scribble* me something before you leave for the Caucasus.—I press your hand firmly! A good journey to you, Mili, and I hope you'll bring back some music.—Good luck!

MODESTE

P.S. Give me Mustafa's address once again; Kito has gone off to Peter, and Konstantin [?], while packing for the trip, threw in your letter; I'm left empty-handed, and I very much want to *write* Mustafa.—By the way, write about the boy,—whether he received my share yet or not—and give me Kalinin's [95] address.

Musical Recruiting

. . . After my return from abroad in the fall of 1862, I met Bala- kirev (in the home of S. P. Botkin) and my third encounter with Musorgsky was at Balakirev's, when he lived on Ofitzerskaya [Street] in the Khilkevich house. Musorgsky and I again recognized each other at once, recalling our two previous encounters. Musorgsky had

---

and clinics almost became her profession. But it was her leadership of the official Russian musical circle which made her the target of Musorgsky's private, and later public, attacks.

[92] Cui had gone back to work on his opera *William Ratcliff,* based on Heine's melodrama.

[93] Linguist Arsenyev had gone to Berlin to study Sanskrit.

[94] On April 8, Rimsky-Korsakov finished naval school, receiving the rank of midshipman.

[95] Possibly a voice student of Lomakin's.

already grown powerfully in music. Balakirev wished to introduce me to the music of his Circle and, above all, to the symphony of the "absentee" (this was Rimsky-Korsakov, then a naval officer, just departed [October 20] on a lengthy cruise to North America). Musorgsky sat down with Balakirev at the piano (Musorgsky at *primo*, Balakirev at *secundo*). The playing was not such as had been at our first two meetings. I was struck by the brilliance, the intelligence and energy of the performance as well as by the beauty of the piece. They played the finale of the symphony. It was here that Musorgsky found out that I also had some sort of inclination to compose music, and he began to ask me to show them something. I was terribly ashamed, and I categorically refused . . .[96]—ALEXANDER BORODIN

29a.   *CESAR CUI to MILI BALAKIREV* [Extract]

February 26, 1863

. . . Won't you be able to drop in on me for the evening (1) in order to release me from too heavy a dose of Modinka, who threatens us from dinnertime on and (2) in order to hear what I've sketched on Richard [97] . . . ?

29b.   *CESAR CUI to NIKOLAI RIMSKY-KORSAKOV, the Clipper* Almaz, I.R.N. [Extract]

April 22, 1863

. . . Modinka presented some sort of musical monstrosity to us—supposedly a trio to his scherzo, a huge, awkward monstrosity. Here are some church chants of endless length and the usual Modinkian pedaling and so forth—all this is unclear, strange, awkward and by no means a trio . . .

---

[96] In December 1862, Borodin was appointed assistant professor of organic chemistry at the Academy of Medicine.

[97] Richard Wagner had just come to St. Petersburg to conduct five concerts for the Petersburg Philharmonic Society. Musical and financial details of these concerts, largely made up of excerpts from Wagner's operas, may be found in Vol. III of Ernest Newman's *The Life of Richard Wagner* (New York, Knopf, 1933–37). The Circle's attitude to this "personal appearance" is given by an acquaintance: "At Balakirev's I never heard any conversations about the founder of 'music of the future.' And when Wagner himself came to St. Petersburg in the winter of 1862–63, to conduct several concerts with great success, our *narodniki*-realists, while granting that he was a splendid conductor, would not bow to him as a composer, did not try to meet him, nor did they invite him to visit them . . . The future "heap-ists" [see p. 85], of course, attended his concerts, but as I remember, neither Balakirev nor Vl. Stasov met him." (P. Boborykin, "For Half a Century," *Russkaya Starina*, February 1913.)

29c.   *VLADIMIR STASOV to MILI BALAKIREV, Pyatigorsk [Extract]*

St. Petersburg. Friday morning, May 17, 1863

. . . You can't imagine how unhappy it is for me now with you away. With whom else can I talk, whom can I tell tales to, with whom can I perform anatomy, profound and real, to the base, on all truths, incorruptible either by friend or by enemy, either by audience or by success, not by anything on earth? Where could I find such a man? I'm completely alone, there's no one to talk to. Even Cui has left for his *dacha;* God knows when he'll be back (incomprehensible apathy or flippancy). What is there for me in Musorgsky, even though he was [with me] yesterday at the theater? [98] Well, yes, his thoughts seem to agree with mine, yet I didn't hear from him a single idea or a single word expressed with real profundity of understanding, with the profundity of a raptured, moved soul. Everything about him is flabby and colorless. To me he seems a perfect *idiot.* Yesterday I could have flogged him. I believe if he were left without tutelage, if he were suddenly removed from the sphere where you have held him by force, and he were set free to follow his own wishes and his own tastes, he would soon be overrun with weeds like all the rest. There's nothing inside him . . .

29d.   *MILI BALAKIREV to VLADIMIR STASOV, St. Petersburg [Extract]*

Pyatigorsk. June 3, 1863

. . . Please write me, I have no one but you. I don't count Cui, he is a talent, but not a human being in a social sense; Musorgsky is practically an idiot. R.-Korsakov is as yet a charming child, of great promise, but by the time he blossoms into full light, I will already be old and will be useless to him. Besides you, I can find no one whom I need . . .

---

[98] The première of Alexander Serov's first opera, *Judith,* took place on May 16, 1863, at the Marinsky Theater, conducted by Konstantin Lyadov, with Valentina Bianchi in the role of Judith and Mikhail Sariotti as Holofernes. Musorgsky records this *première* and his criticisms, in detail, in Letter 30.

I I

Exploration
1863 — 1868

30. *To MILI BALAKIREV, Pyatigorsk*

Toropetz, 10 June [1863]

GREETINGS, MILI,

I share with you my impressions of Serov's opera.[1] All five acts are herewith properly laid out and justly appraised. It would seem that such a big thing would require more than two hearings; it is difficult to judge an opera's quality from first impressions; anyway this *Wagner's Kindchen* during its whole five-act life does not offer one place that deeply touches one, nor one scenic episode that makes one think deeply.

Besides, the libretto is extremely bad, the declamation is pitiful and un-Russian; only the orchestration is interesting in spots, although often too intricate. However, *Judith* is the first seriously worked-out opera on the Russian stage since *Rusalka.*—As all things must begin at the beginning, we have:

The Overture

Espèce de Vorspiel, without interest, chaotic, but with intentions which however are not realized—*suspected* intentions. A somber *largo* (the Jews), led astray by sudden wild blasts from the trombones (probably Holofernes); and after it, *agitato,* a harp (Judith); *husky Judith* was unthinkable for Serov without a harp, even though the personal-

---

[1] Alexander Serov, long in search of a suitable opera subject, had been struck by the effectiveness of a third-rate Italian melodrama, *Giuditta,* by Giacometti, in the visiting Italian theater's repertoire in St. Petersburg. Using this as a springboard, he wrote his own libretto with the help of the poet Apollon Maikov and his first opera, *Judith,* was under way. Musorgsky's "impressions" are not too violent for a twenty-four-year-old enthusiast who is dreaming of writing an opera himself.

ity and idea of Judith have far from a harplike nature; the *agitato* races on to some sort of *concluding theme*—a Jewish triumph.

1st Act.

which you know; I'll note here an important omission made by Serov. The phrase

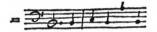

which describes the condition of the people lying about the stage in exhaustion is lost in the opening of the elder's recitative.—I would have continued it, I would have added some juice, and upon its development, on the movements of this phrase, I would have built the elder's declamation.—One needn't forget what is on the stage: the Jews suffering from thirst lie there silently and in confusion, and Serov forgets to think about them—he needs the people later for some sort of wonderfully trashy *fugato*. [Marginal note by Musorgsky: The thought of keeping the chorus quiet is correct, but Serov didn't control it.—This idea of the people gets lost in the orchestra, but if he had managed it otherwise—it would have turned out new and interesting.]—The very tail end of the first act is beautiful. The people curse, the people rage in the *fugato;* they lose their last hope, their last consciousness of their strength—powerless they surrender themselves to one feeling—some supernatural aid; a sharp transition to pianissimo (fifths in the bass during this make it sound especially mystic);—there is a kind of *solemn hush* which is left *unfinished,* and this is beautiful; the impression is a true and good one—this is the best spot in the opera.—I may be too partial to this tasty bit, but there is some indication that it is a good bit, if out of the whole opera it alone has aroused my enthusiasm.

2nd Act.

Judith alone. *Grand air et récitatif;* there is no creativeness, the declamation is laughable, but the mood is good, the instrumentation pretty and poetic; at the point where Judith says: "and to the enemy I will go, and diamonds and pearls I shall place on my head" the harp somehow pinches one especially pleasantly and beautifully. Avra enters and sings at Judith's request a war song of the Hebrews; thus:

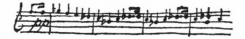

["The hills, thickets and valleys of Zabulon ring with triumph."]

As you can see: not so *very* good. During the last couplet Judith grows enraptured and joins Avra in the singing, repeating the words of the song after her. This develops into *un duettino*—which is natural and clever.—Enter the elders: wholly gloomy pizzicato in the bass of the orchestra. The elders bless Judith in her good intention to go to the enemy; without the authorities' permission Judith doesn't want to be a heroine.—In defiance of the authorities Avra begins to rage and to implore Judith not to go to Holofernes; *duo agité*—of a very bad quality; the curtain falls. For two acts, as you see, there has been no action.

3rd Act.

Entr'acte—Holofernes' march, ordinary, but not badly orchestrated

and so on, there isn't space for everything. Then only the tympani remain:

On this marches over the orchestra *pp,* alternating in the wood winds and strings, the following animal with its proper harmonies—*antique*. These are the basic phrases of the march.

I quote for you as much of the music as I can remember. In this *graphic way*, you will the sooner see what value the opera has; judgments of things you haven't experienced yourself are hard to make and to prove.—The act opens with a song of the odalisques:

recapitulated in 3/4, and then again in 6/4 in imitations with a canon; the orchestration is soft, with harps.—The chorus is interrupted by a dance of the odalisques:

and then the chorus again, and the dance again—in short, a *choeur dansé*.—Holofernes finally grows bored with the odalisques and throws them out (*le mal élevé!*), he jumps up and after getting rather fierce on the Jews' account, he goes out to *take the air* (under the pretext of inspecting the troops); evidently Holofernes treats the audience with *delicacy*.

In the meantime camels pass by, then troops; this entire Scribe-Halévy-Meyerbeerishness is lifted to its feet by the side-show efforts of Serov—*the march of Holofernes*—in two orchestras. While Holofernes is taking the air, soldiers in groups run in and shout at the eunuch *in coro scherzoso:*

["A Jewess of unheard-of beauty has come to us."]

51

Well-aired, Holofernes seats himself on the throne to receive Judith.—Everything that follows is so bad and talentless that it isn't worth expanding on.

4th Act.

Orgy.—The orchestra boils and bustles furiously, and the soldiers of Holofernes stand before him at attention and don't say anything, *they say only:* "Let the orchestra boil, what do we care!"—Holofernes feasts alone . . . vile, lifeless, empty! On such occasions one couldn't possibly do without a song and therefore: "Eunuch, go ahead with something Indian!" (How indelicate of Serov, to force a *castrato* to sing!) The eunuch sings (I've forgotten the theme of his song); the song is too complicated—too little simplicity, naturalness; it is clear that the eunuch knows counterpoint and imitation and *all sorts of things.* Holofernes becomes angry with his eunuch Bagoas for *knowing* music so well and, without any counterpoint whatsoever, he tears into some wild nonsensical song. Holofernes is as drunk as a devil, and begins to have hallucinations.—The 3rd and 4th acts show the complete lack of talent, the complete lack of passion in Serov—what a broad field for a musician—a carousing sensualist despot—how interesting it might have been to set the hallucination scene in the orchestra. There's nothing to this—only a banal French melodrama with howling Wagnerian violins.—The scene of the murder of Holofernes is also melodramatic, but very effective.

During this scene one can hear from the orchestra *reminiscences* of the aria of the second act: "and diamonds and pearls I shall place on my head," cleverly reminding Judith of her duty. Only at the very end an extremely funny thing happens—but it isn't really Serov's fault. Instead of the head in a sack, Avra drags in a twig, as if Judith and she were just coming from the steam baths. The twig ruins the impression of effective melodrama.

5th Act.

It is dark on the stage—and dark in the orchestra, too—before the appearance of Judith with the head, it is bad, very bad—

["Here is the head of Holofernes . . ."]

and after this there is a couplet of gratitude from the chorus, also of no enviable quality.

In general the opera reveals the lack of creative imagination in its author; besides this it has many musical blunders, which I call *musical anachronisms.*—For example: Jews go ahead and sing, without any ceremony, Catholic organ seconds (I have often heard these things),

in this way, while having no idea of the organ. It is known that for a long time in Christian music not only seconds but also thirds were considered proscribed dissonances; but putting aside these generally known musical questions—one shouldn't stuff these cloying seconds into Hebrew spirituality just because they look like choral, organ parts, in the way they are used by Serov.—It's about time to stop converting Jews to Christianity or to Catholicism. Mendelssohn in *Athalie* (Natalka) tossed off a Catholic chorale—because he is Mendelssohn, because he's a *routineur*—but Serov, worshiper of *Zukunftsmusik,* drove in the some direction—and *to what end?* No, if one dares *to take liberties,* one must renounce once and for all these *corruptions.* Must a high priest sing with a trombone accompaniment? Must the spiritual character of the Hebrews be expressed in the Gothic seconds of Catholic churches? Let's get rid of all this mildew!—Judith herself isn't true in the opera. From the logic of her behavior Judith is a *first-rate wench* who with one blow hacks off the head of Holofernes—so why have harps and a sweetly ideal orchestration? I won't say a word about the andantino of the second act aria, "and pearls and diamonds I shall place on my head, and I shall take from the sun its golden rays!" for here she plans to enchant Holofernes—the harps and idealization are appropriate. But what is this idealization doing in the overture and in several episodes of the opera; the idea of Judith is not tender femininity, but the idea of heroism, strength, energy! *Wagner's Kindchen* doesn't look like his daddy, *he couldn't grow up to him! the false beards hinder him!*

And the Petersburg-evaporated Jews, Leschetizky, Jacob Rubinstein and Co., are in raptures, along with the privileged German-invalid detachment.* *Das ist eine schöne Musik! eine sehr schöne*

---

* Musorgsky's note: The Russian-invalid detachment of *Dargo* seems not to be so enchanted.

Musik! Serov triumphator! Serov came, he saw, and he conquered! *veni, vidi, vici!* very well! another acquisition for the public.

Before going away I was at Cesar's *dacha*, where I had lobster soup and froze monstrously. Cesar was orchestrating Maria's aria [2] and very nice it is, too, *very tasty.*—I, great sinner that I am, as I run through the estates, come gradually to the conclusion that one cannot live on the income from *them*, and that one must definitely enter into a career of service, to feed and pamper my delicate body. This I'm going to do in Peter, i.e. I'll enter the service.—My affairs are bad, very bad! Before winter comes I shall orchestrate my *Intermezzo* [*in modo classico*] and leave it as a separate piece.

You, Mili, are luxuriating in the Caucasus; you must have many fine, fresh, healthy impressions.—Will you finish the Russian overture [3] before winter? I am very eager to hear it; I think I will love it more than all your works; judging from what I already know of it, it is very much to my liking, and besides, this is the first work which has no German influence.

There's nothing to write about myself, and one shouldn't chatter nonsense; I have no impressions to give you, for what impressions could there be in Pskov Prov., which in my own district I know by heart with all its blessed landowners. I can say one thing only: the peasants are far more capable than the landlords in the matter of self-government—in their meetings they bring their business straight to the point, and *in their own way* they ably discuss their interests; while the landlords in assemblies quarrel among themselves, acquire swelled heads—while the aim of the meeting and the business in hand are shoved to the side.[4] This is a comforting fact, this: *our cards are trump.* —There's nothing more; the same is all the same and *the very same.* Till we meet, dear Mili—perhaps into the next letter will fall something interesting for your tooth out of my Toropetz life or life in general, and till next time.—I warmly press your hand.

MODESTE

[2] For his opera *William Ratcliff.*

[3] *1000 Years,* or *Russia,* composed in 1862 for the celebration of the thousandth anniversary of the Russian nation. Musorgsky is speaking of the orchestration, then in progress.

[4] The manifesto of 1861 became law and reality in 1863. The serfs were now free laborers, offering themselves for hire, and the cries of the lesser Russian landowners were loud in the countryside. The scenes described by Musorgsky in this and the following letter must have been taking place all over agricultural Russia this summer.

P.S. Mother sends you friendly greetings and envies you your intimate neighborliness with the Djalmas.[5]

31. *To CESAR CUI, St. Petersburg (environs)*

Toropetz, 22 June [1863]

GREETINGS, DEAR CESAR,

. . . and boring, and sad, and vexing, and the devil knows what else![6] . . . and the overseer had to do some filth to the estate.—I had planned to get some decent things done, but here one has to make investigations, and inquiries, and run around from office to office, police and nonpolice. What a lot of impressions I get! And if mother weren't in Toropetz, I should go quite crazy in these ridiculous surroundings; it is only for this woman's sake that I am nailed here; she is terribly happy that I'm with her, and it gives me pleasure to give her this happiness.—And what landlords we have here! what planters! They are happy to have opened a club in town and rarely does a day pass that they don't gather there to *make some noise.* The business begins with *speeches, declarations to the Gentlemen of the Nobility,* and nearly always ends in such a fight that one feels like calling the police. One of the leading bawlers carries on a permanent dispute with the mediator, the mediator being his *bête de somme;* the bawler drives about town, collecting signatures in the name of Christ for the removal of the mediator. Another bawler, with a piteous brain, because of the lack of sufficient powers of conviction, emphasizes his arguments by raising his fists, which sooner or later *land where they're meant to land.* And all this occurs at assemblies of the nobility, and one meets these people every day, and every day they tearfully pester you about their *lost rights,* their *total ruin* . . . what howlings and moanings and scandals! The nobility are allowed to assemble—so they *do* assemble; they are allowed to fight about their business and the business of the *zemstvo*[7]—and they *do* fight, with fists and strong

---

[5] Djalma is the East Indian prince in Eugène Sue's *Le Juif errant;* this may be Musorgsky's or his mother's way of referring to the Caucasian tribes that Balakirev was seeing.

[6] "And boring, and sad, and no one to whom one can offer one's hand . . ."—Lermontov.

Andrei Rimsky-Korsakov characterizes this letter as a self-portrait by Musorgsky "in the role of a liberal Toropetz 'landlord,' an unwilling 'participant' in the 'social' disturbances of the manor nobility excited by their 'lost rights.' "

[7] Elected rural (county) government bodies.

words. *Force a fool to pray to God, and he'll smash his forehead!* And there they go, talking about their lost rights!—There are, it is true, some decent young fellows, but I rarely meet them; they are the ones who do the negotiating [with the freed peasants] and therefore they're always on the road.—And I, great sinner that I am, rotate in the *above-mentioned latrine atmosphere.* A latrine atmosphere rarely touches the finer instincts; you're concerned only with creating a big enough stink or preventing yourself from suffocating (how can one think about music here!) and thus you go as seldom as possible to the *latrine club;* when you do go, you can be sure it's necessary.—*Excusez de comparaison.* A few days ago I came across some verses by Goethe— short ones, I was happy . . . and set them to music; there is one place where the phrasing turned out pretty well:

I shan't be able to compose anything larger, my brain is stationed, thanks to the overseer, at the *police station,* but attempts at small things are possible.—The subject of Goethe's words is a *beggar,* from *Wilhelm Meister* [8] I believe—*and a beggar might certainly sing my music with no pangs of conscience*—I think so.—For the winter I shall prepare, in any case, the Intermezzo, and the instrumentation will be interesting.—You, dear Cesar, I expect, have already done something and are starting lots more—write: *how and what* you've been creat-ing, your work is of great concern to me and news of it will be very

---

[8] This is one of the Harper's songs in Vol. I, Book II, of Goethe's *Wilhelm Meister:* "*An die Türen will ich schleichen . . .*" Musorgsky's manuscript, dedi-cated to Alexander Petrovich Opochinin, is dated "13 Aug. 1863. Kanishchevo Village."

pleasing and will refresh me.—Write me directly to Toropetz, *c'est pas long!*

My respects to Malvina Rafailovna—yes, by the way, have you continued to be chilly at the *dacha,* or did it warm up after my departure?

Husky Judith evidently continues to hack (with harp accompaniment) at the head of Holofernes—for the glory of Serov. Have you heard her? Write me about it.—If you see Bach, bow to him for me and tell him that his article "After the Exposition" [9] positively thrilled me.—Please write me, Cesar, try to post a letter on Wednesday or Friday—those are the days the post comes to our district, and I for my part shall keep you informed about myself, and if anything interesting turns up, *I shan't hide it,* because I am *talkative.*—Till we meet, I warmly press your hand.

MODESTE

The "Commune"

. . . In the fall of 1863, returning from the country, he shared, with several young comrades, an apartment which they jokingly called a "commune," in adherence, perhaps, to a theory of shared living which was preached by the famous novel of that time, [Chernishevsky's] *What Is To Be Done?* Each comrade had his separate room where the others dared not enter without special permission each time, and there was also a large common room where they all met in the evening when they were released from their duties, to read, to listen to reading, to converse, argue, or just talk, or to listen to Musorgsky playing the piano or singing songs and excerpts from operas. . . . There were six of these comrades . . . three brothers Loginov (Vyacheslav, Leonid, and Piotr), Nikolai Lobkovsky, [Nikolai] Levashov, and Modeste Musorgsky. All were intelligent and educated; each practiced his preferred scientific or artistic interest, in spite of the fact that most of them worked at the Senate or in one of the ministries; none wished to be intellectually idle, and each of them looked with contempt on the sybaritic life . . . The three years of a new way of living with these young people were, according to stories, among the best of all their lives. And for Musorgsky—in particular. The exchange of ideas, of knowledge, of impressions from their reading, all accumulated for him material on which he lived for all his remaining years; in this period was strengthened forever that bright view on "equity" and "inequity," on "good" and "evil," which he never altered thereafter . . .

"At that time," says Philarète Petrovich Musorgsky, "my brother,

---

[9] Vladimir Stasov's article in *Sovremennik* (No. 4, 1863)—"After the [London] International Exposition of 1862"—contains Stasov's impressions of a Handel concert given in the Crystal Palace.

besides his music and compositions, was occupied with a translation of famous German and French criminal trials." [10]

Among the books read in the "commune" was Flaubert's novel *Salammbô* . . . All the "comrades" were enchanted by its picturesque quality, its poesy and plasticity; Musorgsky, more than the others, was impressed by its powerful Oriental color . . . —VLADIMIR STASOV

In October 1863, Musorgsky began work on the libretto for a grand opera based on Flaubert's Salammbô. *To his own verses he added passages from the works of Heine, Zhukovsky, Maikov, Polezhayev, and other poets. His plan, apparently, was for an opera in four acts, divided into seven scenes. Work started with the text of Act IV, Scene 1—Mâtho, chained, in a dungeon below the Acropolis (a scene omitted by Flaubert). During 1863 and 1864, Musorgsky found time for work on the text and music of the fragments listed below. In the process of work, the dramatic emphasis shifted from Salammbô to the figure of Mâtho, the Lybian soldier who rose to become commander of the barbarian army—and Musorgsky gave his opera project a new title:* The Lybian.

32. *Inscriptions and Stage Directions*

SALAMMBÔ

ACT I

Scene 1: At a feast in the gardens of Hamilcar

"Song of the Balearic Islander"—A young Balearic Islander is sitting on a cask; there are small metal cymbals in his hands, and he rocks to and fro as he sings.[11]

[Dated] Novaya Derevyna August, year 1864. Modeste Musorgsky.

War Song of the Lybians
[Dated] 10 April 1866. Peter. M. Musorgsky.[12]

ACT II

Scene 2: Within the temple of Tanit in Carthage. Salammbô alone, on the uppermost level of the catafalque. The moon rises . . . Salammbô descends from the catafalque (music from backstage). Genu-

---

[10] Oskar von Riesemann identifies this as Gayot de Pitaval's *Les causes célèbres.*

[11] Flaubert provides a description of the Balearic song much later in the text: ". . . in a shrill voice he intoned a Balearic song, a vague melody, full of prolonged modulations, broken off and replying to itself, like echoes answering echoes in the mountains . . ." *Salammbô,* Chap. 9.

[12] The orchestration of this War Song is dated: "Pavlovsk 17 June 1866. Modeste Musorgsky. See Appendix.

flects before the image of Tanit. Genuflects before the sacred lotus. Ascends the steps of the catafalque, scattering flowers . . . [Dated] 15 December 1863. St. Petersburg. Modeste Musorgsky.

ACT III

Scene 1: The altar of Moloch

Characters: Salammbô

> Aminakhar [not in Flaubert]—high priest of Moloch
> Priests of Moloch
> Carthaginian people and children

Costumes: Salammbô—in a gray tunic, over her shoulders is thrown a dark lavender cloak, the end forming a long train. Her braided hair falls onto her bosom; on her head is a yellow mourning veil.

> Aminakhar—in a garment of gold brocade, covered from neck to foot with precious stones; on his neck are several necklaces of sapphires; he is belted with a broad girdle studded with amber; on his head is a rich tiara; he wears gold sandals; over his shoulders is thrown a dark crimson mantle.

> Priests—in luxurious white robes, covered with precious stones; in red sandals with golden spangles; belted with girdles of braided gold thread, pearls and sapphires; tiaras on their heads.

> Children—in azure tunics, their heads wrapped in dark veils, clasped with wreaths.

> People—in tunics and various colored cloaks, women in yellow mourning veils.

Setting: On the left is the altar of Moloch—a lofty edifice of three tiered terraces. On the top semicircular terrace, ringed by a copper railing, stands the massive brazen statue of Moloch (a towering colossus). On the next terrace, also a semicircle, there is a small platform, from which deep steps lead to the lowest terrace; these steps are of black stone and must stand out sharply against the mother-of-pearl terrace below.

> To the right of the second terrace has been built an elevation for the children; it rests on six massive columns of black marble, forming a sort of rotunda; this elevation

is surrounded by a delicate gallery on which are flaming braziers.

In the center of this space there is a small elevation and a lectern of stone—on this lies the sacrificial shield.

Directly in front of the spectators, the bay can be seen at the left; at the right, a rock juts out of the sea on which can be seen the statues of the horses of Eschmoûn, and the sacred cypress grove of Eschmoûn. On the stage, slightly off center and nearer the footlights, is a stone idol; a brazier burns before him. (Behind Moloch, slightly to the left, the set represents a part of Carthage, whose buildings can be seen across the bay.)

Aminakhar stands before the lectern, surrounded by children; musicians (a military band) stand within the rotunda; there are priests on the second terrace, throwing dry twigs under the rail surrounding Moloch; people lie on the lowest terrace in various positions.

The evening is hot and sultry, forecasting a thunderstorm. The curtain is closed. (The chorus begins behind the closed curtain) . . .

[Dated] 10 November 1864. St. Petersburg. Modeste Musorgsky.

ACT IV

Scene 1: The dungeon of the Acropolis.

Characters: Mâtho

　　　　　　 Aminakhar

　　　　　　 Priests of Moloch and Pentarchs

Costumes: Mâtho—in worn woolen tunic, with neither corselet nor mail; over his shoulders there is a torn, bloodstained tiger skin; on his head is a golden band with a feather —the sole reminder of the former power of the leader. There are chains on his arms and legs.

　　　 Aminakhar and priests—in black mantles, lined with purple woolen stuff, wearing black tiaras; rich purple tunics are belted with sashes of precious furs.

　　　 Pentarchs—in luxurious long tunics of gold brocade, hemmed with large pearls; in golden cothurni; over their shoulders are thrown rich silk mantles of bright blue, embroidered in golden flowers (of a peculiar

eastern design); on their heads are black caps (Phry-
gian) with bands of precious fur.

Setting: The Acropolis dungeon, hewn from the rock. At the left a
deep excavation, looking like a cave; to the right and
nearer the center, a perspective of winding underground
passages. On the forestage, slightly to the audience's left,
is a great flat black stone, at the foot of which are scattered dry twigs, heather, leaves and handfuls of straw,
forming Mâtho's pallet. Semidarkness.

Mâtho in chains, despondent, exhausted by torture,
sits on the black stone, his head bowed; beside him is a
coarse, gray mantle . . .[13]

[Dated] 26 November year 1864. St. Petersburg. Modeste Musorgsky.[14]

Scene 2: Chorus of priestesses. The priestesses console Salammbô and
dress her in bridal robes . . .

[Dated] Peter. 8 February year 1866. M. Musorgsky.

*Musorgsky found his first civil service job in the Chief Engineering De-
partment of the Ministry of Communications, beginning work on December 1, 1863, with the rank of Collegiate Secretary.*

33. *To MILI BALAKIREV*

MILI,

A nervous irritation is beginning to work itself up in me rather persistently and forces me to give it my attention.—As I, to prevent any

---

[13] Subsequent stage directions in this original scene by Musorgsky: "Aminakhar,
four priests and four pentarchs enter. The priests hold torches in their hands.
They enter slowly, stepping cautiously, occasionally pausing and looking around.
Approaching Mâtho, they form a semicircle, holding the torches overhead; the
pentarchs, with staffs and red tablets, on which the judgment is inscribed, stand
forward . . . During the last words of the priests Mâtho springs up, but then
quickly falls back on the stone and, with bowed head, utters in a despairing voice:
'The end!' After the priests are out of sight, Mâtho looks in the direction of
their departure, shudders, approaches the dark ravine, then retreats from it with
horror . . ."

Flaubert is usually held responsible for the scenic details of Musorgsky's *Sa-
lmbô*, but in comparing these with the novel one is forced to suspect that
Musorgsky devised them on his own responsibility with some standard work of
operatic *décor* at his elbow.

[14] The libretto of this scene is dated: "Petersburg. October, year 1863."

harmful consequences, plan to sit at home and rest a little, I beg you not to count on me for *Undine*.[15]

I tell you about this in advance, so that those who should know will know about it, and also so that no *quid pro quo* will arise from it.

MODESTE MUSORGSKY

Thursday, 16 January [1864, St. Petersburg]

P.S. Could you obtain for me the 2nd song of Bayan; I should like to go over it during the coming week with the Cossack.[16]

Musorgsky was promoted to assistant head clerk of the Engineering Department's barracks division on January 20, 1864.

34. *To MILI BALAKIREV*

3 May. Sun. [1864]

MILI,

Yesterday I met Dargomizhsky, from whom I learned the following: Firstly, L[ubov] F. Miller has married Engelhardt, *le dit ami du compositeur;* the formal ceremony will be held at St. Simeon's.—Dargomizhsky is in a state of bliss.[17]

Secondly, and this is the primary aim of my letter, Dargomizhsky asked me to tell you that in Leipzig there is a man named Brendel [18] —a German who has some influence there in a certain <well-known> musical circle and who very much wants to have some Russian works. —Wouldn't you agree to send him one of your compositions?

Not knowing the day of your departure, I hasten to inform you of Dargomizhsky's proposition and I don't believe it would be bad for you yourself to stop in on that man who is now freed from earthly chains.—This is only in case you agree *to be shown* to the Germans; if you do not agree (which I foresee) just write me one word, *"no"*—

---

[15] Alexei Lvov's opera (1846), revived at the Marinsky on January 8, 1864.

[16] The song is from Glinka's *Ruslan and Ludmila,* but the "Cossack" singer remains a mystery.

[17] Apparently love had departed from the relationship between Lubov Miller and Dargomizhsky—departed from it so completely that Musorgsky describes Dargo's state of mind after Lubov's marriage to Engelhardt not only as "bliss," but also as "freed from earthly chains." Vasili Petrovich Engelhardt was a friend of both Glinka and Dargomizhsky—and an amateur astronomer.

[18] Karl Franz Brendel was the editor of the influential *Neue Zeitschrift für Musik.*

this shouldn't be too difficult for you and, on my part, I shall consider it my duty to turn over this "no" to Dargomizhsky.

Dargomizhsky *dreamed* that it would be possible for you to leave with me the score and parts of the piece that you choose to send to them, and as Khristianovich [19] is to be in Petersburg before going abroad, I could hand over your things to him.—But this dream is quite inconvenient for a matter like this. Khristianovich, if he leaves during the summer, will stop in at Dargomizhsky's and not at my place; I probably will have left to visit mother, and if I haven't left, then, living at the *dacha,* it would be extremely inconvenient *to shuttle back and forth* between the *dacha* and Dargomizhsky (*vu la distance*), so that, if you agree, you must see Dargomizhsky to give him your things personally.—Besides I am terrified of *unique* copies of a composition; a stranger's belongings must be guarded more closely than one's eyes, and I won't even guarantee that I can guard my own eyes.

Dargomizhsky goes abroad in August. Khristianovich will be here— I don't know when.—On the one hand it would not be at all bad to acquaint the Germans with your compositions, because I recall that you wanted to have *Lear* printed abroad.—The Germans are especially interested in folk motifs and, therefore, if you would send them your *Picture,*[20] it might be printed, which would be a very good and pleasant business.—However, that's up to you.

You afforded me enormous artistic delight at the evening in Shakespeare's honor.[21] Such a full, living sensation I had not received (up till then) from a single evening. Many thanks to you *for it;* you conducted *la reine Mab* superbly; the entr'acte * to the 3rd act of *Lear*

* Musorgsky's note: I had not previously heard it performed.

---

[19] Nikolai Filippovich Khristianovich successfully mixed his profession (law) with his pleasure (music). He was an able pianist, a pupil of Adolf von Henselt.

[20] *1000 Years* was first described as *A Musical Picture* (or *Tableau*).

[21] On April 23, 1864, the Society of the Literary Foundation celebrated the three hundredth anniversary of Shakespeare's birth by a concert conducted by Balakirev, consisting of the following program:

Overture, *Julius Caesar*	Schumann
Queen Mab, scherzo from the dramatic symphony, *Roméo et Juliette*	Berlioz
Overture and Entr'actes to *King Lear*	Balakirev
Wedding March, from incidental music to *A Midsummer Night's Dream*	Mendelssohn

produced so wonderful an effect on me that I gave it a place among the first class of symphonic dramas for its truth and full sensuous impression.—Well, I'm unable to express all I feel—I firmly press your hand.

MODESTE MUSORGSKY

34a.   CESAR CUI to MILI BALAKIREV [Extracts]

St. Petersburg. June 14, 1864

. . . Modinka—is resurrected. He's at my place weekly. He's composed two songs and Nekrasov's Kalistratushka, a *tableau de genre musicale.*[22] There's a new musical form for you. All this is not devoid of good turns, harmonies, thoughts, but as a whole—it's rather ridiculous . . .

August 15, 1864

. . . You are too hard on Modinka. To be indignant with him is impossible, but not to pity him is difficult. I sympathize with him in his avoidance of Zakharin; that's a terrific chatterer capable of making anyone shiver; but in his [Modinka's] work, of course, I don't believe . . .

35.   To MILI BALAKIREV

[St. Petersburg, end of February, 1865]

MILI,

The program of the Thursday concert on February 20 [actually given February 29] will be as follows:

(1) Symph. (C minor) by Spohr
(2) Excerpt from Lélio by Berlioz

---

[22] The manuscript of "Kalistrat" is dated May 22, 1864, dedicated to Alexander Petrovich Opochinin, and bears the inscription: "A first attempt at humorous music."

Two other songs dating from this spring, to which Cui may be referring, are: "Blow Winds, Wild Winds," with text by Alexei Koltzov (dated "28 March 1864. S.-Petersburg," and dedicated to Vyacheslav Alexeyevich Loginov), and "Night," a fantasy, with text by Pushkin (dated "10 April 1864. S.-Petersburg," and dedicated to Nadezhda Petrovna Opochinina).

(3) the Schumann concerto—Clara [23] will play

(4) Aria and chorus from *Life (for the Tzar)*

(5) Overture (Op. 124) by Beethoven [*Die Weihe des Hauses*]

I firmly press your hand.

MODESTE

The Death of Yulia Musorgskaya

In [the spring of] 1865, Musorgsky's mother died. This year he dedicated to her memory two new compositions which had an especially important meaning for him at this moment. One of these—two little pieces for piano, entitled: *From Memories of Childhood*—No. 1. "Nurse and I"; No. 2. "First Punishment (Nurse Shuts Me in a Dark Room)." 22 April 1865. At the top of the first page: "I dedicate this to the memory of my mother." The other composition: Lullaby—"Sleep, Sleep, Peasant's Son," to words by Ostrovsky from *Voyevoda*, 5 September, 1865. "To the memory of Yu. I. Musorgskaya."—VLADIMIR STASOV

The Song "Savishna"

. . . As he himself told me later, he conceived this piece in the country at his brother's (on the Minkino Farm) as early as the summer of 1865. He was standing at the window and was struck by a commotion that was taking place before his eyes. An unfortunate simpleton was declaring his love to a young peasant woman whom he liked, imploring her, all the while ashamed of his own ugliness and unfortunate situation; he himself understood that nothing on earth, especially the joys of love, could exist for him. Musorgsky was deeply moved; the figure and the scene fell powerfully on his soul; in an instant appeared the particular forms and sounds for the clear embodiment of the images that had stunned him, but he did not write down the song at once . . . —VLADIMIR STASOV

Breakdown

. . . In the autumn of '65, he fell seriously ill. A terrible disease (delirium tremens) was coming on, in consequence of which my wife induced Modeste to leave the "commune" and—at first this was against his will—to make his home with us . . . —PHILARÈTE MUSORGSKY

---

[23] Clara Schumann had first come to Russia in 1844 with Robert Schumann. This second trip was part of an extended European tour that perceptibly widened the popularity of Schumann's music.

36. *To MILI BALAKIREV*

DEAR MILI,   27 January [1866]

Sariotti [24] feels an irresistible craving for Ludmila's evening on Sunday; if he can be satisfied in this regard, then write me two words—I hardly know Ludmila's arrangements and I am too slightly acquainted with her,[25] to take on to myself the introduction of Sariotti. Till Sunday.

Yours,

MODESTE MUSORGSKY

37. *An Inscription on the Manuscript of "Desire"* [26]

Dedicated to Nadezhda Petrovna Opochinina
in memory of her judgment upon me
Peter. In the night of the 15th and
16th of April, 1866 (2 o'clock in the morning)

38. *To MILI BALAKIREV*

DEAR MILI,   Wednesday, 20 April [1866]

Tell me when I may find you at home; we haven't seen each other for so long, and I want very much to chat with you about several matters and to show you a new little piece (a War Song of the Libyans)

---

[24] Mikhail Ivanovich Sariotti, basso, began his operatic career in Italy but after 1863 he was permanently attached to the company of the Marinsky Theater, where his first new role was that of Holofernes in Serov's *Judith.*

[25] Ludmila Ivanovna Shestakova, though thirteen years younger than her brother, Mikhail Ivanovich Glinka, functioned as a superb moral support throughout his peculiar and disturbed career. It was due to her insistence that Glinka wrote his autobiography and collected his scattered songs. After Glinka's death she channeled her enormous energies into preservation of and propaganda for her brother's music and into mothering the circle of intellectuals and young musicians around Balakirev, to whom Glinka had willed his leading position in nationalist music. Musorgsky, though "too slightly acquainted with her" in January 1866, was to become, by January 1867, the favorite of this charming fifty-year-old manager of her late brother's affairs. See Bertensson, "Ludmila Ivanovna Shestakova," in *The Musical Quarterly,* July 1945.

[26] A song on a text by Heine: "Ich wollt', meine Schmerzen ergössen."

from my *Salammbô* [27]—a male chorus based on a theme that you know, with variations *à la Georgienne.*

I've begun to sketch the witches [28]—am stuck at the devils—the cortege of Satan doesn't satisfy me yet.

Impatiently waiting to be with you, I press your hand firmly.

MODESTE MUSORGSKY

39. *To MILI BALAKIREV, St. Petersburg*

Pavlovsk
14th of August 1866

DEAR MILI,

Tell me: will you be at home some morning this week, and on which morning exactly? By the first train I can arrive at your place by about ten o'clock in the morning.—I pledge myself to bring the score of my little Libyan chorus and I thirst to talk with you about the witches. If convenient for you, we could together burst in on Cesar to chew and while away the after-dinner time, which in Europe is known as the *avant-soirée.*

I haven't seen you for so long and a meeting would be extremely close to my heart.

I firmly press your hand.

MODESTE MUSORGSKY

Address: In Pavlovsk on the Soldatski Slobodka at Popov's *dacha.*

Salammbô Halted

. . . What compelled Musorgsky to give up such an outwardly interesting subject as *Salammbô?* . . . Once I applied to Modeste Petrovich with this question, why had he stopped the work that he had begun? He looked at me intently, then burst out laughing and, with a gesture, said: "It would have been fruitless, what a laughable Carthage would have come of it!" Then he stopped laughing and went on, seriously, "We've had enough of the Orient in *Judith.* Art isn't a pastime, time is precious." M.P. implied that one can't picture the Orient without having seen it or without knowing its melodies . . . —NIKOLAI KOMPANEISKY

[27] Musorgsky had returned to *Salammbô* for a short period of additional work on it, before leaving it forever unfinished.

[28] Gerald Abraham points out that at its first performance in Russia in March of this year, Liszt's *Todtentanz,* with Anton Rubinstein conducting, was played by Anton Herke, Musorgsky's old piano teacher—and that this event may have revived Musorgsky's "witches" of six years before.

"I Owe This to My Mother . . ."

. . . When I first saw Modeste Petrovich he was a young man of twenty-seven, a [former] splendid officer in the Preobrazhensky Guards. From our first meeting I was impressed with a particular delicacy in him and with the gentility of his manner; he was a man of extremely good education and control. I knew him for fifteen years, and during this entire time not once did I notice him allowing himself to lose his temper or, forgetting himself, to speak an unpleasant word to anyone. And more than once, when I remarked how well he was able to control himself, he answered: "I owe this to my mother, she was a saintly woman."

Musorgsky's attitude toward Balakirev was unchanging, with full respect for his great talent and his incomparable musical memory; they met regularly on completely friendly terms. . . .

Many often tried to talk Musorgsky into marrying; but his unwillingness to marry was almost laughable: more than once he assured me seriously that if I should ever read in the papers that he had shot or hanged himself, this would mean that on the day before he had got married . . . —LUDMILA SHESTAKOVA

40. *To LUDMILA SHESTAKOVA*

5 January, '67

Darling Savishna [29] begs most humbly of the honored Ludmila Ivanovna to advise her at her *dwelling-place* whether she, Savishna, may present herself to her on Sunday and at what hour, for Savishna, in addition to her desire to see Ludmila Ivanovna and to hang her guilty head before her, has also the purpose of bringing to her, "Kalistrat" and "The Dnieper" [30]—newly baked pieces.—Savishna has had the *grippe* all this time and she coughed a lot and her nose behaved most indecorously, wherefore she has not shown herself.

Devoted *Savishna* *

* Musorgsky's note: In the earthy orthography of Savishna.

---

[29] This is the first of Musorgsky's several fantastic letter-writing masks to which Lapshin refers (page xii). The Savishna "mask" is modeled, of course, on the peasant woman in Musorgsky's song.

[30] The first version of a song from Shevchenko's poem "The Haidamaks."

40a. *MILI BALAKIREV* [31] *to LUDMILA SHESTAKOVA, St. Petersburg*
[*A Sequence of Extracts*]

Prague, December 28, 1866

. . . By the last act I was ready for a fresh surprise. Here's how the solemn procession of Mikhail's coronation was managed: at first Venetians from the Council of Ten, followed by doges, then French troubadors and, finally, under a canopy carried by German pages, Tzar Mikhail passed by in the costume of the King of Sicily from *Robert* . . . Also I must tell you that evidently *A Life for the Tzar* doesn't please the local public. (There were very few there.) Nor will local musicians be pleased, for such heads as Shornik [32] and Smetana [33] can understand nothing sensible that steps out of the German frame. Interesting to wonder how they'll receive *A Life for the Tzar* (*V Praze*) as revised by me. Now the public attends only operas that are immediately understandable or that suit their vulgar German taste, like *Troubador* or *Wilhelm Tell,* and if *A Life for the Tzar* is given, it will be only because of the Russophile tendencies of certain local leaders, for example Rieger, who received me very kindly . . .

Prague. January 9, 1867

. . . This evening Kolař [34] and Pátera [35] came for tea along with Paleček, who sincerely loves Glinka's music and is a frank, dear

---

[31] In an appendix to Rimsky-Korsakov's *Chronicle,* Shestakova energetically writes: "M. A. Balakirev went to Prague for the first time in 1866, in the month of June, on my request to him to arrange a production of *Ruslan* there. But he returned toward the end of July without any success. In September of the same year, having obtained a letter of introduction from V. I. Lamansky to [Dr. František] Rieger, in Prague, I went there on the sixteenth, and, with the latter's assistance, the matter of producing *Ruslan* was settled in a few hours. On December 21 of that year, M. A. Balakirev went to Prague for the second time, taking with him all the sketches of scenery, costumes and accessories that Gornostayev had prepared at my request, and he there busied himself with the production of *Ruslan* and *A Life for the Tzar.*" Balakirev's first glimpse of opera in Prague was painful, a sloppy production of *A Life for the Tzar,* conducted by Smetana—whom he at once suspected of sabotage.

[32] Czech names were an added irritant to the worn Russophile nerves of Balakirev. He mistakenly refers to the composer Šebor (whose new opera, *The Templars,* was just opening) as Shornik, giving birth to a multitude of pointless puns, as *shornik,* in Russian, means saddlemaker and *smetana,* sour cream!

[33] The year 1866 was possibly the most important in Bedřich Smetana's entire career. Within this year his *Bartered Bride* was produced, and he was appointed conductor at the Provisional Theater.

[34] Josef Kolař, Slavophile scholar and writer.

[35] Adolf Pátera, scholar-philologist, and librarian of the Czech Royal Museum.

man.[36] The riddle has been solved: all the delays with *Ruslan* and *A Life for the Tzar* originate with Smetana, who appears to be the worst sort of intriguant, hates Glinka's music and calls it *Tartar!* He belongs to the pro-Polish party and he has dishonorably transferred his hatred of Russia to its art . . . But I'm no fool, either, and I will lead the attack myself . . .

Prague. January 11, 1867

. . . Much to my happiness Smetana doesn't train the chorus himself, but this is Mr. Tausig's work; he is a decent musician who is in sympathy with Glinka's music and therefore it is now easy for me to remove Smetana's influence from the Tartar operas, so let him ferment himself . . . The ringleaders of the local abominations are Poles, who live here in great numbers and have already succeeded in forming a whole coalition of Czechs—against the Russians . . .

41. *To MILI BALAKIREV, Prague [A Collective Letter]*

9/21 January, '67

[From Ludmila Ivanovna Shestakova]

As soon as we gathered together yesterday evening the conversation, of course, turned before all else to you; and just then your letter arrived, Mili Alexeyevich; so the idea occurred to me that each of us might write you a line; I know what pleasure this can give you in a foreign country; your departure has drawn me closer to Cui and to the others who truly love you. What does it matter if in *A Life for the Tzar* you will have to cast not quite suitable actors, but at least our *Ruslan* will be produced well (and Pátera has not yet informed me of the receipt of the scenery. *Nice fellow* he is! What more can be said!) I would be so happy if Kolař would send me all the newspapers that contain even a word about you and my brother's operas; ask him again about this for me. I also saw *The Bartered Bride* in Prague and Paleček astonished me, he is actually a younger version of our own Petrov; [37] he is wonderfully talented; I am happy that he pleases you

---

[36] Osep Paleček's performance of the basso role of Farlaf in Balakirev's Prague production of *Ruslan* eventually led to a contract and a lifetime at the Marinsky Opera in St. Petersburg.

[37] Osip Afanasyevich Petrov was already a veteran of Russian opera, against whom every dramatic basso was measured. Of gypsy and Ukrainian ancestry,

70

and I am convinced that you will give him a great push forward; I think that he, more than all the others, will be sensitive to your presence there.

And I haven't yet congratulated you on the New Year. Well, never mind, you can be sure that if my wishes for you are fulfilled, they will do you good. Tomorrow Anna Vasilyevna [Nikolskaya] is moving in for good with me. I've remained at home without going out once the whole holiday, for on the first day I caught cold and I'm still not well; but I am seldom alone; all my acquaintances visit me: a few days ago D. V. (Stasov) dropped in. Stellovsky [38] is playing all sorts of nasty tricks, but he won't be able to tie up Dmitri Vasilyevich—he's not the kind to be tied up and, very likely, he will apply pressure to him, and it's about time; however, to the honor of Stellovsky it must be said that he doesn't involve anyone, and only enjoys making fun of me; but there is a French saying: *rira celui qui rira le dernier*, this business doesn't alarm me in the least: Dmitri Vasilyevich took this on himself with love, and at the same time it is quite clear that he is interested in beating Theodor Stellow [Stellovsky] morally. You and your affairs concern me now; I am glad that you are well and I sense from your letter that you are calm—thank God—which makes me genuinely happy.

Your soul's
LUDMILA SHESTAKOVA

Petersburg, Gagarinskaya Street, house of Count Olsufev, in this drawing room we, the undersigned, have gathered around the table, this minute made happy by the receipt of your letter of January 3rd, Mili Alexeyevich.

LUDMILA SHESTAKOVA

[From Malvina Rafailovna Cui]

Now that the whole council has decided to write you, one and all,

---

he was at the age of sixty the pillar of Russian nationalism in opera, having created leading roles in both of Glinka's theatrical works. When Musorgsky knew him better, he called him "grandpa."

[38] Fyodor Stellovsky was the most serious obstacle to Ludmila Ivanovna's worthy and ambitious scheme to publish the full, original scores of her brother's two operas. Stellovsky owned the publication rights and was difficult about them as long as he lived. Even the legal mind of Dimitri Vasilyevich Stasov could not cope with Stellovsky's stubbornness and suspicion.

lo! I, slave of God, Malvina Cui, representing the second in senior-
ity, wish you all the best, particularly the best of health and success
in your undertaking and your early return to our circle.

M. Cui

[From Anna Vasilyevna Nikolskaya]

I take my turn, Mili Alexeyevich, to write to you, but, frankly, I
don't know what to write. I can only wish you, for the New Year, good
health and all possible success.

A. Nikolskaya

[From Cesar Antonovich Cui]

I have the most zealous manner.

"Straining the brain and wrinkling the brow," I tried to give birth
to some sort of pun, calculated to amuse you, but alas! at this moment
I am lower than Repetilov,[39] and my smartest remark at this moment is

Comme le chien de Jean de Nivelle
Qui s'enfuit quand on l'appelle.

Begging your pardon for this pitiful product of my pen, suitable
however to Shornik's music that you hear and to Smetana's conducting.

Your

C. Cui

[From Vladimir Vasilyevich Nikolsky]

To Your Ruslano-Ludmilish Majesty from a Titular Councilor
and magister of all sciences and various other dark arts, Vladimir, son
of Vasili, Nikolsky, alias Pakhomich [40]

---

[39] A gossiping character in Griboyedov's *Woe from Wit*.

[40] Vladimir Vasilyevich Nikolsky is known in the correspondence as Pakhomich
and as Dyainka (uncle). He was an inspector at the Imperial Alexandrovsky Lycée,
and a professor in Russian history and language at the Imperial College of Jurisprudence. Anna Vasilyevna Nikolskaya was his sister.
The "adventures of Pakhomich" figure in a song dated "22 Sept. '66. Nevsky
Prospekt. Bernadaki's House at Mili Balakirev's"—"Ach, you Drunken Woodcock!" The dedication is, naturally, to Nikolsky.

A Most Humble Petition
in which there are the following points:
The first point is also the second, and the last, as well:
Most humbly I appeal to you, Y[our] M[ajesty], not to forget that at
various points of the God-preserved city of St. Peter there is a Titular
Councilor, and so forth, as set down above, who remembers you and
wishes you all success.

[From Modeste Petrovich Musorgsky]

From darling Savishna to thee, my little dove, my darling falcon,
brightly wings the warmest greeting. Truly am I gladdened that thine
illness, O brother of mine, and the baleful malady have forsaken thee
and that thou art again radiant and shining like the fiery sun.—And
I feel bitterly offended that Shornik, the naughty one, has stuffed
himself with Smetana, and ruins our native music.—Receive, thou
sick one, my hearty kiss and nurse no grudge.

Savishna

[From Nikolai Andreyevich Rimsky-Korsakov]

I want to tell you something that will please you, this: I was very
nearly sent away to Kronstadt for permanent residence there, but I
managed to dodge it and now I am sure to be staying on in Peter for
good. Vladimir Vasilyevich [Nikolsky], by reason, supposedly, of my
emigration to Kronstadt, wrote a poem entitled "A Seven-teared
Elegy." Aside from this, I can inform you that I have thought out
the theme of the andante (D major) for the symphony,[41] and it doesn't
seem so bad; this may please you, too, and further, I wish you success.

N. Rimsky-Korsakov

41a. *MILI BALAKIREV to MODESTE MUSORGSKY, St. Petersburg*

Prague. 11 January, 1867
Dear Modeste!

How can you have completely forgotten Ludmila Ivanovna, she
writes that you've disappeared. If you want to know about me, go to

[41] Rimsky-Korsakov had returned from America with the squadron in the summer of 1865. His first symphony completed to Balakirev's satisfaction and successfully performed at one of Balakirev's Free School concerts, he was thinking
about a second symphony, in B minor—which he soon abandoned.

her; she has many letters from me. Besides, I've written to Cesar twice, and also to Korsinka.

I won't tell you everything because you can learn it all from my letters to Ludm. Iv., Cesar, and Korsinka, and this letter, so to say, is a continuation of the previous ones.

Here too I am vanquished by a conservatory: my landlady's nephew is being educated in this worthy institution and, in my absence, saw my collection [of Russian folk songs] on the pianoforte, grew interested in it, became acquainted with me, took the collection home, played it over with his comrades, all of whom shouted in *complete* rapture: "This is Slavonic music, while we have German." Their rapture was so great they even dared to show this collection or (more exactly) to play several songs for a professor. So that you'll understand how courageous their act was, I'll tell you that here, as throughout Germany, every conservatory professor is as much a blockhead as our Rubinstein, just as insolent to his awe-struck pupils. In Peter there are protests against the immaculacy of Rubinstein, but not here. So this is what happened: the professor became angry and told them that all this is *ganz falsch* . . . in a succession of chords he had found a hidden fifth, which is strictly forbidden here, and the melodies are in absolute nonconformance with the rules in their melody course. The conservatorists returned with downcast heads and sorrowfully declared that although all this is enchanting, it is *ganz falsch,* and they don't dare not believe the professor, and not one skeptical thought even occurs to them about the immutability of all these calves' laws of harmony and melody.

I questioned them, do they like such harmonies as . . . and so forth, and it seemed that they *truly* feel that Slavonic blood runs in their veins; they say other melodies cannot be, *but* according to the rules one must place C sharp. I finally persuaded them to throw the rules aside and reason with their own brains, as human beings should. At first they looked at me dully and then, when they realized what was the matter—*they were scared!* Next day my landlady's nephew reappeared and declared that such thoughts had kept him from sleeping all night, that he had lost peace (Gretchen [42]) and faith in harmony as it is taught in the Prague conservatory. If Petya Borozdin were

---

[42] From Part I, Scene 15, of *Faust*, "Meine Ruh' ist hin . . ."

with me, after such a *casus* he'd probably baptize all the conservatories in musical . . . As you can see, I am spilling about the poison of musical nihilism, as well as organizing a party for the support of *A Life for the Tzar,* which the Polish counts (there are plenty here), together with the conductor Smetana and several other gentlemen with musical authority, for example, Mr. Procházka,[48] want to chase off the stage, as a Tartar opera.

Today I visited classes of schools where the students assemble voluntarily to study Russian (a chair of Russian language is not allowed officially at the university). There are many of them and they're all going to hear *A Life for the Tzar,* which will probably be given on February 3, by the local calendar, conducted by me. The merchants will go, too. In a word I'm working with as much energy as [General] Kaufman in Vilna.

Today I was at the society called *Hlahol* [Tone], listening for two hours to a *Männer* chorus with extreme patience; to oblige me with Russian (!) singing, they sang some *Männerchor* by Rubinstein. Such anathema I've never heard.—Well, this is enough for you; write me more often, and get the address from Cesar, or Ludmila Iv., or Korsinka.

Your

M. BALAKIREV

The conservatorists call me nothing but *"Pane professore"*—which is flattering and pleasant.

41b. CESAR CUI to MILI BALAKIREV, Prague [Extract]

January 18, 1867

. . . Hasn't Modinka written you even once? This insane youngster is completely lost. When you get back, his "Gopak" [44] and "Savishna" will have to be printed . . .

---

[43] Dr. Ludevít Procházka—a Prague critic and intimate friend of Smetana's.

[44] The song, "Gopak," on a text from Shevchenko's *Haidamaks* (translated from the Ukrainian by Lyov Mey), has this subtitle: "Lute player. The old man sings and dances." It is dated "Pavlovsk. 31 Aug. year 1866," and is dedicated to Nikolai Andreyevich Rimsky-Korsakov. "Savishna" is dated September 2, 1866, and is dedicated to the author of this letter.

41c. *MILI BALAKIREV to CESAR CUI, St. Petersburg*

Prague. 23 Jan., 1867

DEAR CESAR!

I received your dear little letter and many thanks to you for having written. Korsinka has written only once, and then as if unwillingly, forcing himself, but the absurd author of the Libyans' and the Mixolydians' drama simply doesn't want to know me. Aside from his simpleton's postscript to the collective letter, sent from Ludm. Iv., I've had nothing from him. Tell him that this isn't correct even for the Carthaginian manner, and may great Moloch forgive him this!!! [45] In regard to Moniuszko,[46] I take back one-half of what I said. The rumors about his intrigues turned out to be untrue . . .

42. *To MILI BALAKIREV, Prague*

"Peter-Kashin Bridge"
23 January, '67

DEAR MILI—CZECH PANE PROFESSORE ALSO—

On the 16th of January you honored me with a pleasant awakening —I received your dear epistle [Letter 41a] and laughed over the conservatory capon-pupils in Czechia and over general-capon Tupinstein in regard to your suspicions about the *immaculacy* of that venerable capon. [. . .]

Three things have happened during your absence: (1) the Petersburg conservatory is dissolving—the general-of-music-corps Tupinstein has quarreled with the conservatory clique and plans to resign [47] —the poor professors are crestfallen and one may now see them on the streets in penitential rags, with penitential penny cigars (in place of candles) in their teeth (hands) and their heads scattered with ashes (from these cigars)—the very heart contracts when one encounters them. (2) The vision of the *in spe* sainted Druklin—of the flight of the Russians and the restoration of the Polish fatherland at exactly

---

[45] The references in this extract are to Musorgsky's *Salammbô* project.

[46] Stanislaw Moniuszko's *Halka* (1854), most famous of all Polish operas, was being prepared for a Prague production on February 28, 1868. Balakirev has cursed him roundly in his letters to Shestakova and to Cui, for turning up at this time.

[47] Anton Rubinstein did resign that June from both the conservatory and the Musical Society. Zaremba then became director of the conservatory and Balakirev was appointed conductor of the Society's concerts—apparently on Rubinstein's own recommendation.

that moment when in the former Polish kingdom thanksgiving services are being offered in the newly settled Russian provincial govern-
mental offices.—Pius IX took this deathbed hallucination of Druklin
as a revelation and ordered his elevation to sainthood.[48] [. . .] (3) I
have not kept my promise and have written nothing for orchestra for
the following reason. My sister-in-law has had a painful brain irritation, and the slightest sound strikes her in the head—which is understandable—so it's understandable also that I can't play; Botkin is
treating her and his lotion helps her considerably but not enough
for me to be able to play yet.

Turning to the usual pursuits, I tell you that I was at Ludmila
Ivanovna's, where I read your epistles, and from where we sent you
a conjoint letter which we wrote around her table.—All this week I
stuck fast at home because of terrible frosts, the instrumentation of
my chorus *à la magyar* [49] and a nervous fever with a villainous cough.
The frost reached 26 degrees [Réaumur] with a wind. The instrumentation of the chorus has been completed and I'm making a clean copy
of the score; the nerve fever passes, but the cough tortures me terribly.

It is because of these last two circumstances, do not be angry, Mili,
that I didn't immediately answer your letter; my brain was fooling
about in a most unpleasant manner, and in such a condition I avoid
writing.—And though the Polish *pani* hinder the production of
Russian operas in Czechia and desire the soft-sounding Czechs to continue to overeat on sour cream [*smetana*] and to make saddles [*shor-
niki*], this is as it should be, and still our operas—placing our hopes
in God—will be produced and under your supervision. From my
soul I wish for you to make whey of Smetana and send Shornik back
to shoemaking—*by the relationship of the materials* this is possible.
You, Mili, have energy enough, and I, spoiled child that I am, should
not advise you, but all the same you are higher and fatter than the
Czechs (*pas de calembour là dessus*) even though the Czechs from head
to foot are smeared with *smetana* and stink with saddle-makers' ma-

---

[48] A number of Polish priests (Druklin possibly among them) had recently
sought refuge at Rome, provoking arrogant statements from the Russian ambas-
sador to the Holy See. Pius IX had protested unceasingly against the oppression
of the Polish Catholics by Nikolai I's government, and a new break in diplomatic
relations between Rome and St. Petersburg was about to occur.

[49] The "Hungarian manner" is not exactly obvious in Musorgsky's chorus of
The Destruction of Sennacherib, based on Byron's poem as well as on the poem's
source, Isaiah XXXVII. The manuscript of this first version is dated "Petrograd,
29 January 1867," and is dedicated to Mili Alexeyevich Balakirev.

terials; as long as you have handled the Petersburg sweetheart—the public, so much the better will you handle the Czechs—I firmly trust and believe this.

I think that at this time you must be very busy, Mili, and you have no time to scribble me a line about your work, but if a convenient moment should turn up—dash off a line and in particular about your activity—it will make me happy.

Now avoiding the length so peculiar to my compositions, avoiding it because it already exists in this letter (another long drawn-out formulation), I close my scrawl and kiss you warmly.

Your

MODESTE MUSORGSKY

P.S. Tomorrow I'll be at Ludmila Ivanovna's, and the day after at Cesar Cui's—this is my release after my ailment. And what (it comes to my mind) if Shornik should smear his compositions with Smetana —he would spoil them, and if the *smetana* should spread itself over the saddle-makers' materials, it would stink of leather—it seems unquestionable and indeed it is so upside down that even if you have a dog's sense of smell, you can't tell where Smetana begins and Shornik leaves off—it is amazing to what incredible things music can lead humanity!

You ask me to write more often—I'll send you another letter the day after tomorrow.

43.   *To MILI BALAKIREV, Prague*

Peter. Kashin Bridge
26 Jan., '67

GREETINGS, DEAR MILI,

I begin this epistle with two delightful facts: (1) Dargunchik has failed in Moscow with the production of *The Festival of Bacchus* [50] and has failed brutally.—In *Sovremennaya Letopis* and in *Golos* mournful reviews appeared simultaneously about Dargun's *boring* festival. The former begs Dargun not to bore the public with his old worthless things and, further, they ask: did the ancient Greeks dance French galops and sing French polkas? The columnist of *Golos* collapses with laughter at the sight of eight muses playing clarinets on

---

[50] Dargomizhsky's *Festival of Bacchus*, an opera-ballet, was completed in 1848 but didn't reach the stage until this Moscow première in 1867, a dismal failure.

the stage, conducted by a 9th muse; what a Dargun! What an ugly Dargun! All nine muses reincarnated as clarinet players.

2nd fact . . . but allow me, dear Mili, to wipe away the gushing tears, and recover a little from a palpitation of the heart and gnashing of teeth . . . O *allemands!* O constantly vile *allemands!* I mourn your vileness and shed tears: "How much have you (scoundrels that you are) squandered, how many pittances have you plundered from the careless Russian people!" Now I have come to myself and I continue— In yesterday's *Golos* there is an article by Rostislav [51] on the conservatory—an amazing article. It begins as "a bear's good turn" [52] to the conservatory; its middle is a "great glorification" of *this* conservatory; it ends with a "begging solicitation" of society (not merely Russian musical society, but All-Russian—Rostislav's word) [. . .]— The thing is that Fifila Tolstoy, proving that the conservatory budget amounted this year to *only* 25 thousand, tearfully assures us that the *allemands* spent over 45 thousand, and they have spent this because no one supported them with substantial financial donations. What a fool! Fifila approaches an amazing degree of vileness (wanting to justify the pillage) in these lines: the *director* (Tupinstein) who is "wholly devoted" to the cause of music—(is paid) *only* 3500 rubles. "You must know, All-Russian society," quoth he, "that although in my opinion the director has been given much, he is *wholly devoted to the cause;* know further that all expenditures of the conservatory went the same way: each of the *allemands was paid just for that,* that he is *needed and wholly devoted to the cause;* each *needed* servant was paid *just for that—and the servant was also wholly devoted to the cause of music."* Regarding the servants I think Fifila was right; the servants were probably paid *just for that.* "*Tu l'as voulu, Georges Dandin —tu l'as!"* [53] The *allemands* wished to get rich out of the Russian pocket, dulling even the heads that are a wee bit capable—*they made their fortunes and they dulled them*—but for how long? Fifila howls in his jeremiad that the deficit is 20 thousand a year—a sword of Damocles that hangs over the conservatory; dear Fifila, it's too good to be true that this *sword should cease to hang,* in the literal meaning of the word . . . The best help for them would be to fight each other

---

[51] Feofil Matveyevich Tolstoy wrote under the name of Rostislav, and was known in the Circle as Fif. His article in *Golos* is entitled, "On the Graduation Examinations at the St. Petersburg Conservatory in December, 1866."

[52] A Krylov fable.

[53] From Molière's *Georges Dandin.*

(Wieniawski [54] has left, Rubinstein is leaving), and they would scatter, the devil take them, with their money, and the servants, who are wholly devoted, would merely have to brush away their footprints with a broom.—*Heraus, meine Herrn! und mit grossem Skandal, aber nicht ohne Geld.*

A speedy, just, and humane solution.

At present Cesar is preparing the *coup de grâce* for the conservatory. For this purpose I'm sending him Rostislav's article, which may be of use to him as reference.—From your letters to Ludmila Ivanovna, dear Mili, I can see that there is an intrigue against your activity in Czechia, and I have visualized myself in your position, but from your letters to Cesar I am convinced that if it is not especially good for you now, the devil knows how foul it must have been before. I admit that when you went to Czechia, I was sure that the affable invitations repeatedly sent to you came from a minority of select people —as was to be expected—so it occurred, but I was mistaken in the degree of influence that these individuals exerted over the whole Czech people. [. . .]—And as if it had been planned for your arrival in Prague, Pan Moniuszko arrives there at the same time with his Catholic operas.

This mating of the Polish clique with the *allemand*-conservatory stupidity represents for me a fruit similar to a vomiting nut. How happy I would be if after your conducting of *Life for the Tzar* and *Ruslan* these operas (at least, the former) would make such an impression on the public that all those Smetanas, Shorniks, Prokhvostkis [scoundrels] or Prokhaskis and Gnilushkis [rottennesses] would be choked with their own remedies—may the devil take them! Whatever good this all may be to say and even to write, it doesn't amount to much.—Archimedes invented a lever for his system, which could move the earth on its axis, and he was *killed by a Roman soldier,* but if Archimedes should propose to put the Czech brain onto the right track, he would certainly burst in vexation *without being killed by a Roman soldier.*—Must our music really be locked behind our borders: behind the western sea lanes of the Baltic Sea at Prussia, at Galicia, at the south on the Black Sea and at the east, at the north—in a word, geographically? Is it possible that even the countries of our

---

[54] Henri Wieniawski was the distinguished head of the conservatory's violin department. In June 1867, he resigned with Anton Rubinstein, in order to return to the European concert stage.

kinsmen cannot be inoculated with our native music? Note that in all Europe, with regard to music, two principles reign and fix the seasons: mode and slavery. Among the English, singers are imported and things are performed, and occasionally both are quite terrible—there, mode is in the foreground. Among the French—however the French have the cancan and *débarassez-nous de M. Berlioz!* Let's put the Spanish and Italians to the side along with the Turks and the Greeks.—Among the Germans there is the best and most convincing example of musical slavery: worship of conservatory and routine—beer and stinking cigars, music and beer, stinking cigars and music *ins Grün.* A German is capable of writing a whole tract on the fact that Beethoven has written a certain eighth-note with its tail below rather than above, where it should have been according to the rules; the German—a slave to *recognized (by himself) genius*—can't possibly imagine that Beethoven, in sketching hastily, could have made such a mistake, paying no attention to trifles.—This stupid and arrant side of beer bellies *mit Milch und süsse Suppe,* repulsive in true, genuine Germans, seems more filthy in the slaves of slaves, the Czechs, who don't even care to have a physiognomy of their own.—This long-drawn-out slander, my dear Mili, is caused by the fury that I got into when I realized your position among those cattle, a fury that induces me to block the road into Russia to the Germans, the Italians and the Jews (all equally), the road to cheating good-natured Russians.—It would be impossible to give a truer characterization of the Czechs than you have already done, although yours comes from a musical opinion of them. If you should force me to sing (not in jest) the lieder of Mendel[ssohn], I would be transformed from a gentle and polished person to a boor totally lacking in all social graces. Force a Russian peasant to love any of the *Volkslieder* of the rotten Germans—he will not love them. Suggest (don't force—a German-Czech can be forced to lick Austrian spittle—and lick it he will), suggest that a Czech delight his soul with German rot—he will delight in it and afterward say loudly that he is a *Slav.* Thus I understand the Czechs from your remarks, and this rot claims proudly that they want to hear Slavic things! They demand Slavic music! That is why your musical characterization of Czechlandia is true and relates to more than music alone. —A people or a society insensible to sounds that, like a memory of one's own mother or of one's closest friend, must vibrate all the living strings of a being, waking him from a deep sleep, making him aware of his peculiarity and of the oppression which lies on him and which gradually kills this peculiarity, such a society, such a people is a *dead body*, and the chosen of this people are doctors, who forcibly, by means of a revivifying electrogalvanic current, jerk the members of this dead body, as long as it hasn't undergone the complete chemical decay of a corpse.—The Jews leap with joy when they hear their own songs, which are handed on from generation to generation, their eyes lighting up with honest and not pecuniary fires—I myself have seen this more than once. [. . .] May one say that Slavic sounds have not reached the Slavic soul, because Smetana has sour-creamed that sound? This is not true! He could not possibly have mutilated the whole opera so much that there could not be found in it one *living place* to make a *living man* start upright. Dead ones sat in the theater, a dead one conducted an orchestra of dead ones, and you, my dear, fell into a Prague diversion *des revenants. A living man among the dead!* I sympathize with your gloomy situation, dear Mili, and I would be proud, my dear, if you revived them—those dead—for at least an hour. God help you, again and again God help you. Firmly, firmly I kiss you, dear—till the next epistle, soon on its way.

Your

MODESTE

The "Russian School"

. . . You can understand what interest arose in our school when we heard of the concert at the Hall of Nobility where our former cadet's *Destruction of Sennacherib* was to be performed [55] . . . By this time I had already spoiled a lot of music paper myself, and I rushed to the concert. I recall that I was very dissatisfied both by the *Destruction of Sennacherib* and by its composer. "Let's go over, I'll introduce you." Cavalry Captain M. of the cuirassiers suggested to me. "He's standing over there by the column on the top step." There I saw a young fop of medium height, not, I must say, of a very attractive appearance. Snub-nosed, popeyed, red-cheeked, with slightly curly hair, he was a real little rooster and quite cocky besides. I was almost ready to refuse the introduction, but it was too late, my friend was already speaking to him. Before me stood a very elegant, immaculately dressed aristocrat, lips tightly pressed, hands in lavender gloves, refined manners, his speech sprinkled with French words, spoken through his teeth—all this gave him the appearance of a high-society fop, but at the same time this little aristocrat had some-

---

[55] On March 6, 1867, conducted by Balakirev, immediately on his return from Prague.

thing very sympathetic about him, something unsuited to this vulgar
milieu. The swiftly changing expression of his face, now severe and
then suddenly laughing with complete frankness, the intonation and
rhythm of his speech full of contrasting changes, the broad range of
his voice, his abrupt movements, his provocative appearance which
at the same time showed shyness and timidity—all this indicated an
extremely nervous nature and a gentle character . . . —NIKOLAI
KOMPANEISKY

. . . in 1867, I met Turgenev once more, again at a concert, this
time in the Hall of Nobility. And here we became acquainted. This
was the 6th of March, a memorable date for me, and the concert
was one given by the Free Music School under the direction of Balakirev . . . [In our conversation] Turgenev turned to the subject of
the new Russian composers, whom he strongly disliked, and to whom
he referred with habitual contempt. "You saw in *Smoke* what I think
of them," he said, already considerably agitated. "But tell me, Ivan
Sergeyevich," I asked, "do you know many of them, or have you
had an opportunity to hear much of their work in Paris?" "When I'm
in Petersburg, I do my best to hear everything new that is being done
here . . . It's terrible . . . You needn't look far for an example—
it is sufficient to listen to what they're giving us tonight. In the first
part of [the program] they sang some sort of 'magic chorus' by Mr.
Dargomizhsky . . ." "From *Rogdana?*" "Oh, yes, from *Rogdana* or
some such place . . . A magic chorus! Ha, ha, ha! Wonderful magic!
And what horrible music! Emptiness itself, mediocrity itself. It
doesn't pay to come to Russia for such a 'Russian school'! You can
get this sort of thing everywhere—in Germany, in France, at any concert . . . and no one pays any attention to it . . . But here, now,
it's a great creation, an original Russian school! Russian, original!
And then there was this *King Lear* by Mr. Balakirev. Balakirev—and
Shakespeare—what do they have in common? A colossus of poetry
and a pigmy of music, not even a musician. And then . . . then there
was this 'chorus of Sennacherib' by Mr. Musorgsky . . . What self-
deceit, what blindness, what illiteracy, what an ignoring of Europe . . ."—VLADIMIR STASOV

44. *To LUDMILA SHESTAKOVA*

[Beginning of April, 1867]

OUR BENEFACTRESS THOU

LUDMILA IVANOVNA—BY MARRIAGE SHESTAKOVA

In these days of harsh frosts I feel greatly inflamed by a desire to coax
thee: allow me to present myself at thine home on Monday, God's
day, the day that follows Christ's bright resurrection.—Do not force
thyself, mine own, to spread an honorable feast, with a choice brew,
but permit me just to share with thee on that day some bread and
salt washed down with a goblet of the grape, and to indulge my aching

heart with thy kind speech.—How can I express my wish to see thee, my own, there will be no more than the four of us assembled: thou and I and the darling sister of Volodimer Vasilyevich, dear father Nikolsky, yes and he himself, her brother.

What a nice chitchat we shall have, heart to heart, and mind to mind—only behold, beloved—force not thyself to grant me this wish. But if thou wilt respond from the heart to Savishna's call—let me know at my dwelling place, perhaps through thine loyal Pakhomich —how great will be my joy. Aye, my own—we must see one another— only I don't feel like dropping in unexpectedly; it looks as though I have grown very fond of thee—and to tell the truth—thou art kind and wise—what more would one want! Aye, my grievous epistle is written on a scrap of paper, but don't hold this against me, my own; I borrowed it from a shopkeeper—a brother-in-law of mine—I had to borrow it because there's no chance to touch the state purse—or so people gossip, they should know—they can't help knowing. So and so, right or wrong, but I expect a response from thee, my dearest, my own.

Savishna

and I have been told that some fool has dubbed me Ivanovna, as they say in Pskov, and accordingly has scribbled some foolish music—here I stand—disgraced before the whole world and without my having known about it; so that's that!

Spit, my own, on this scribbler—all the same I am still

Savishna
in all her chastity

On April 26, Musorgsky was dismissed from the rolls of the Engineering Department.

An Article by VLADIMIR STASOV

"MR. BALAKIREV'S SLAVONIC CONCERT" [56]

in Peterburgski Vedemosti, May 12, 1867
[extract]

. . . As our readers already know from newspaper announcements and bill posters, Mr. Balakirev's concert consisted of pieces represent-

---

[56] A special concert at the city hall in honor of a delegation of Serbian, Croatian

ing one or another Slavonic nationality. Thus, the Great Russian element was represented by Glinka's Kamarinskaya, Little Russia by Dargomizhsky's Kasachok, the Czech element by Mr. Balakirev's Overture on Czech Themes, the Serbian by Mr. Rimsky-Korsakov's Overture on Serbian Themes, the Slovak by Liszt's Fantasia on Slovak (incorrectly called Hungarian) Themes, the Polish—by an aria from Mr. Moniuszko's opera [57] . . .

We conclude our note with a wish: God grant that our Slavonic guests never forget today's concert, and God grant that they may preserve forever the memory of how much poetry, feeling, talent and ability is possessed by the small but already powerful little heap of Russian musicians.[58]

45. To NIKOLAI RIMSKY-KORSAKOV, [St. Petersburg?]

Minkino Farm.[59] 5 July '67

MY DEAR AND KIND KORSINKA,

On the twenty-third of June, on the eve of St. John's Day [Midsummer Day] was finished, with God's help, St. John's Night on Bald Mountain—a musical picture with the following program: (1) assembly of the witches, their chatter and gossip; (2) cortege of Satan; (3) unholy glorification of Satan; and (4) witches' sabbat. The score was written directly on white without a draft—it was begun on the tenth day of June, and by the twenty-third there was joy and triumph. The composition is dedicated to Mili, according to his own orders and, needless to say, with my personal pleasure.—You must imagine, my dear, the situation—doing one clean score without sketches of any kind, and my trepidation at forwarding the score to the binder. In my picture your favorite bits passed over into the orchestra very successfully. Besides this in the general development of the composition many new things have been done; in the *unholy glorification,* for example, there is a bit for which Cesar will sentence me to the conservatory. Here it is:

and Bohemian artists and writers then visiting St. Petersburg. Balakirev completed his contribution to this program while still in Prague (composing swiftly for the only time in his life), and sent themes and instructions on to Rimsky-Korsakov, for his *Serbian Fantasy.*

[57] A gesture of contrition for unjust suspicions? There were two other vocal numbers on the program, Glinka's "Midnight Review," sung by Petrov, and Balakirev's "Gold Fish," sung by Yulia Platonova.

[58] This now famous term, *moguchaya kuchka,* was immediately seized from this article and used by both enemies and friends of "the little heap."

[59] Philarète's estate. The brothers had sold Karevo.

in B minor—these are the witches glorifying Satan—as you can see, stark naked, barbarous and filthy. In the sabbat there is a rather original call on a trill of the strings and a piccolo in B flat followed by this harmonic quarrel:

and directly on the trill in B flat this spot is repeated. Amusingly the G minor modulating into B-flat major alternates with G-flat major modulating into B-flat minor and all this is broken off with blasts of full chords in F-sharp minor; for this they would fire me out of the same conservatory in which Cesar had imprisoned me for the witches' glorification.—The plan and form of the composition is rather original. The introduction is in two series (the assembly of the witches); then a D minor theme with a slight development (the gossip) is linked with the cortège of Satan in B-flat major (I cunningly avoided the march clichés of [Liszt's] *Hungaria);* the cortège theme without development with a response in E-flat minor (this ribald character in E-flat minor is very amusing) is concluded with a *chemical gamma* [60] on a full movement *in moto contrario* in D major.—After this, B minor (the glorification) in Russian style with development, variations, and a semiecclesiastic quasi trio; a transition to the sabbat and finally the sabbat (first theme in D minor) also in Russian style with variations. —At the close of the sabbat the chemical [chromatic] gamma and the figures from the introduction in two series break in, which produces a pretty good impression.—You've hardly any idea of the sabbat—it has turned out very compact and, to my way of thinking, fiery.

---

[60] Borodin appears to have jokingly used the terms "chemical gamma" and "chromatic gamma" interchangeably. "Gamma" is used here as either a scale or a key.

The form of interspersed variations and calls is, I think, the most suitable for such a commotion.—The general character of the thing is hot; it doesn't drag, the transitions are full without any German approach, which is remarkably refreshing.—However, God grant that you will hear it for yourself.

In my opinion *St. John's Night* is something new and is bound to produce a satisfactory impression on a thoughtful musician. I regret *that distance divides us,* for I should like us to examine the newborn orchestration together.—Let us understand that I'm not going to start altering it; with whatever shortcomings it was born, it will have to live, if it does live. Nevertheless, by working together, we might clear up many things.—If this picture is played at a concert, Korsh's paper will surely carry a column of delicately paternal abuse from Cesar to Modinka.[61]

There is a book, *Witchcraft*, by Khotinsky,[62] containing a very graphic description of a witches' sabbat provided by the testimony of

---

[61] Cui was the music critic, under a signature of three asterisks, for Korsh's newspaper, *Peterbursky Vedomosti.*

[62] *Witchcraft and Mysterious Phenomena of Modern Times,* by Matvei Stepanovich Khotinsky, was published in St. Petersburg in 1866. Its "popular" retelling of more serious works in witchcraft provided Musorgsky with a ready-made scenario. Musorgsky's programs for Rimsky-Korsakov and Nikolsky should be compared with the following passage: "Sabbats or festivities of the evil spirit, where sorcerers and witches gathered, usually took place on the heights of isolated mountains, such as Brocken or Blocksberg in Germany, Blokula in Sweden, and Bald Mountain near Kiev. More women than men attended these gatherings, and witches were more honored by the devil . . . He who smeared himself with a special ointment fell into a deep sleep. He then saw the devil in the form of a black goat, seated on a stone or rotting treestump . . . The goat was worshiped in the most vile way, which we wouldn't dare to describe here in Russian, using the Latin original instead . . . Dances started in which people danced with other people, and also with the demons who made up the retinue of the devil. The majority of these had the appearance of wolves, goats, toads and all sorts of reptiles. They were at once transformed into handsome young men and became partners of the women who came to the Sabbat. They usually danced back to back. At this point unspeakably vile things started . . . Sabbats could occur any night and differed only in the character of the sins and vile things which took place there. However, they usually took place on Fridays, the eve before Saturday, and the main annual Sabbat was celebrated on St. John's Eve . . . [In Russia] at night the witches, hair falling over their shoulders, mount brooms, oven-forks, spades, besoms, or whisk-brooms, and fly up the chimneys to the Sabbat on Bald Mountain or the Devil's Lode where the sorcerers and demons and sometimes the *babayaga* [ogress] assemble. But in general the whole process of the departure to the Sabbat and what takes place there is very similar to that in Western Europe, described above."

a woman on trial, who was accused of being a witch, and had confessed love pranks with Satan himself to the court. The poor lunatic was burnt—this occurred in the sixteenth century.[63] From this description I stored up the construction of the sabbat.

Please do *Sadko*, dear Korsinka, it intrigues me so, and it would surely turn out so well in your hands. I wouldn't tease you to write on this subject if I weren't so sure that you could cook it well.[64] I press your hand firmly, dear one. Till we meet.

Write to me: via the Warsaw R. R. at the Preobrazhenskaya Station —to me.

Your

Modeste

46. *To VLADIMIR NIKOLSKY, St. Petersburg*

Minkino Farm, 12 July, '67

We thank you greatly for your message—in one way it was very diverting and pleasing, and in another way, very irritating and unpleasant.—Poor suffering soul; what on earth made Maximilian, as you call him, with Prince Salm-Salm,[65] bump into that copper, or possibly

---

[63] This "graphic description" can be found on page 40 of the Khotinsky book: "In 1578 Jeanne Hervilliers of Verberie near Compiègne, whose mother was burned for witchcraft, was held for investigation for the same crime. Without any torture this woman confessed that when yet an infant, she had been committed by her mother to the evil spirit, with whom she had had sexual relations since the age of 12. For 30 years the spirit had visited her, even on her nuptial bed, without arousing the suspicions of her husband. She confessed to committing several murders and to corrupting persons, and although such depositions had no proofs and were obviously invented, the judges of Ribemont sentenced her to be burned at the stake. It is remarkable that this unfortunate one should want to die so quickly that she did not consent to appeal her sentence, although there was hope that the sentence could be commuted."

[64] Vladimir Stasov had, for some time, been doing research work on Russian epic ballads (*bylini*)—his findings being published in 1868 as *The Origin of Russian Bylini*. Being particularly attracted by the colorful ballad of *Sadko the Rich Merchant of Novgorod*, Stasov proposed it to Balakirev, who in turn thrust it upon Musorgsky, who finally turned it over to the willing Rimsky-Korsakov.

[65] French rule in Mexico came to an end with the execution of Emperor Maximilian on June 19, 1867. Prince Felix zu Salm-Salm was an adventurer who had drifted down from the Civil War in the United States to attach himself to Maximilian in the last months of the "imperial tragedy." There are no further hints as to the St. Petersburg identities behind these names.

iron, lever—horrors! I am sure he must have seen stars.—It's obviously a bad accident if leeches had to be applied. This was unpleasant to read.—And disappointment seized me, when I beheld, with my roaming eyes, that my little dear didn't go abroad—for your health's sake it would have been better than to be in a Peter apartment with a porter, a samovar and a tasteless dinner—*all* covered with dust.—And how clever not to sign it—know ye, quoth he, that such nonsense, even of Homeric caliber, can be jabbered by no one but Volodimer Sire Vasilyevich [Stasov].—You know what worries me now and then: how is it that you, squared namesake of the *feuilleton* general, produce nonsense for the sake of jokes, and he—your namesake—perpetrates all sorts of rubbish seriously and, besides, not of an Homeric caliber. He should be told that his articles and particularly his discussions of important topics should all be done in an antique style, a majestic style, so to speak.—Imagine dear Bach orating political nonsense in hexameters and yelling this nonsense with a dignity appropriate to an ancient bard. This, my own, is worth a hotbed in Alyona's cattleyard.[66]

Well, my own, your most humble servant has deigned with God's help to cook up something: he has settled the witches for good, anent which you will hear from our hospitable Ludmila Ivanovna.—With you I shall discuss my witches from another viewpoint, for, aside from the fact that you do not sign your epistles, you further have my most sincere sympathy because of your Russophilism and your knowledge of Russian wisdom.

So this is what I'm going to tell you, and you may swear at me, or you may praise me for my arrangements.—The Witches—this is a popular title, or so to say. the nickname of my composition—in actuality it is *St. John's Night on Bald Mountain,* and is, as you will see, a hallowed little thing.—If memory has not played me false, the witches used to assemble on this mountain (of a baldness, do not blush, equal to that of your head) gossiping, playing lewd pranks, awaiting their superior—Satan. Upon his arrival, they, the witches, would form a circle around the throne, where he sat in the guise of a he-goat, and would carol glory to their superior. When Satan became frenzied enough at the witches' glorification, he would order the start of the sabbat, whereupon he would select the witches who had

---

[66] A teaching post in the Grand Duchess Yelena Pavlovna's conservatory?

caught his fancy to satisfy his needs.—So this is the way I did it. In the title of the composition I have indicated its plot: (1) assembly of the witches, their chatter and gossip, (2) the cortège of Satan, (3) the unholy glorification of Satan, and (4) the witches' sabbat.—I would wish that if my composition is performed the handbill should also indicate the plot, for the comprehension of society. In form and character my composition is *Russian and original*. Its tone is hot and chaotic.—Actually the witches' sabbat starts from the appearance of the little imps, because the unholy glorification, according to the legends, was included in the body of the sabbat, but I have given the episodes (in the plot) separate titles for greater ease in conveying this musical form—because it is new. I beg of you, my friendly Volodimer Vasilyevich, to write me whether I have understood the subject of my composition. You are aware of my musical convictions and you'll have no doubt as to the importance for me of this matter: the true representation of folk fantasy—wherever it appears—of course accessible only to musical creation.—Outside this artistic verity, I don't consider a composition worthy of note, or I won't give it a nickname but call it in the German manner: such and such in B-flat major or in A minor. —I wrote *St. John's Night* very quickly, directly in a fair copy in orchestral score, wrote it in about twelve days, and glory be to God, the second piece, Intermezzo for orchestra, was also dashed off directly in a fair copy in four days (most of it had already been written for piano alone back in '63).—For *St. John's Night* I didn't sleep at night and finished work, as it happened, exactly on the eve of St. John's Day; something so boiled up in me that I simply didn't know what was going on with me—that is, I knew, but it's not necessary to know this, for otherwise one may grow conceited.—In the witches' sabbat, I did the orchestration in scattered, separate parts that will be easily perceived by the auditor, because the coloring of the winds and strings produces sufficiently perceptible contrasts. I think that the character of the sabbat is this—scattered in continuous calls, until the final binding together of the whole witch rabble; thus, at least, the sabbat was carried in my imagination.—I think I chatter too much about my *Night*, but this I suppose comes from the fact that I see in my sinful pranks an original Russian production; not deriving from German profoundity and routine, but, like Savishna, springing from our native fields and nourished with Russian bread.

Till we meet, my little dove, write me at Minkino Farm, it will make me very happy.—Thanks for the hotbed and for the Pargolovo goddess—it gave me a good laugh.

Your

MODESTE MUSORGSKY

P.S. My warm greetings to Ludmila Ivanovna and Anna Vasilyevna [Nikolskaya]. And tell Ludmila Ivanovna that I have baked something more, and for orchestra.

46a. *NIKOLAI RIMSKY-KORSAKOV to MODESTE MUSORGSKY, Minkino*

Peter 10 July [1867]

In the first place, dearest Modeste, you have made me happy by writing to me, and secondly, by your completion of *St. John's Night on Bald Mountain*. How I yearn to examine your orchestration with my own eyes, for I am sure that I would find there much tastiness, as everything I have previously known from that source has been very much to my taste; but this will have to wait. The modulation of G minor and G-flat major interrupted by F-sharp minor on a trill must be quite beautiful. The glorification of Satan must certainly be very filthy, and therefore all sorts of harmonic and melodic filth is permissible and fitting, and there should be no reason to send you to the conservatory. The conservatory gentlemen would of course be horrified by you, but then they themselves aren't able to compose anything decent.

I recently returned from the country where I had been staying for three weeks, during which time I thought a great deal about composition, but wrote nothing, and now I have sketched some things in pencil; I have ordered music paper in twenty staves and the day after tomorrow I will begin to write the orchestral score. A large part of *Sadko* is composed thoroughly, to be exact—up to the trepak [a fast Russian dance], and this I now want to do in its final form. This is my plan: the beginning (in the nature of an introduction) is in D-flat major, in moderate tempo, which obliges one to picture a surging rather than a stormy sea, for Sadko was tossed into the water and had to float for a long time on a single plank. The very beginning goes this way: [musical quotation]

The next bar is again D-flat major and further in the bass [musical quotation] and harmonies from this figure [musical quotation] of the

91

violins and violas go into F-flat instead of F. After this, D-flat major, and through C-flat the bass goes over into B and the whole thing is repeated in B-flat major with the exception of the first two bars. The harmony is sustained by the clarinets and bassoons, afterward by the horns; bass drum and tympani *pp.* do a tremolo. There is a crescendo and forte D-flat major still on these figures; they go on in the basses, and in the brass the harmony little by little goes diminuendo; everything halts on the note D-flat, the tympani with drum doing a crescendo, and here I've done the appearance of the sea king, who lures Sadko into the deep; this begins with a two-note phrase, running through all the strings in turn and interrupted in turn by blasts of the trombones, horns and trumpets, and wood winds with a response from the chromatic gamma in violas on low notes with chords of the clarinets and horns also in the lowest register. Then *ff* this: [musical quotation]

This gamma ends in the basses with a chromatic gamma in brass chords diminuendo in this order: F-sharp minor is transformed into B-flat minor, D minor into F-sharp minor, B-flat minor into D minor; next the violins and violas with mutes *p* must portray the growing clarity before Sadko's eyes of the undersea kingdom: which [musical quotation] proceeds in D major, the melody the first time not being given in its entirety, but broken by phrases in the brass during trills of the violins in scherzando character, thus: [musical quotation]

Beginning without trills of the violins, and then with them.

Or thus: [musical quotation]

The gamma again becomes harmonized, as on a previous page, only with the fifth bar imagine for yourself the bass, modulating from A to G sharp.

Here the gamma also goes tremolo, but considerably lower and *pp.*

When the theme comes in in full, I give it an accompaniment, sustained by the clarinets and bassoons, leading the harmony, and harps, as in Mili's second Russian overture [67] (the B-flat major theme), and three flutes, [musical quotation] muted violas again in two parts *pp.* I think this will be a good effect. In general this part of the piece is given a scherzando character slightly passionate and at times strange, (such seems to me the character of the feast), the tone of D major, transformed to B and F-sharp major. I hope to orchestrate it entirely

---

[67] *1000 Years,* later renamed *Russia.*

transparently with harps and flageolets; the strings will not be muted all the time, but only once when they go to F. Alternating the bass from A to G-sharp in the gamma, as I've already told you, I change to D-flat major, and (at the very beginning with simple chords of harps in a low register) the trepak begins in D-flat major. I have everything composed till here, but it remains to be written, and all the details of this will become clear. The further plan is known to you: storm and at the very climax the church theme. How about this one which came to mind just recently? [musical quotation]

Pay no attention to the tonality.

I don't know, dearest, how much I could clarify to you what is being composed and what is being proposed; in any case I want to receive a reply from you. Of course, you can't judge these severely, as you know Sadko only in its previous fragments; I knew this when I wrote you, but nevertheless I wanted to share at least something with you. Now I am quite alone in Peter and I can tune myself to Sadko only by bathing in the Neva, which, by the way, I do, but of course not with this aim.

Till we meet, write.

N. RIMSKY-KORSAKOV

Thank you again for the letter and the good news of the completion of St. John's Night, which I terribly want to see with you. Rest a little and compose something else pretty.

47. *To NIKOLAI RIMSKY-KORSAKOV, St. Petersburg*

Minkino Farm 15 July [1867]

I anticipated your friendly wish, dear Korsinka. The orchestration is ready for the Intermezzo (in B minor, which was the little piano piece, without a middle) the middle is done in E major in the character of the trio from the scherzo of the 9th Symphony [Beethoven]; of course with the violins pizzicato in an easy, jovial sort of instrumentation.—I admit that the contrast with the B-minor part is rather sharp, but nevertheless it must refresh the impression, because the B-minor part is again repeated.—Throughout the B-minor part the rhythmic strokes

represent pizzicato of the strings in turn: the violins over the wood winds, and the double-basses and 'celli over the trombones playing *pp.* I think this effect will be pretty good.—The piece itself is nothing but a tribute to the Germans, and I have dedicated it to Borodin. In any case I am very glad that I did it, for what good would it be to lose the B minor piece entirely—which is quite decent.—Now I am laying out a poem about Poděbrad the Czech [68] . . . Several places, *stammpunkt,* already exist: the theme for the introduction is as follows: (slowly)

the introduction begins with two series, the second in C-sharp minor; then comes what appears to be a continuation of this little theme—in a Slavic *cantilena,* consisting of a tremolo in all strings over a *tutti* of the orchestra; crescendo gradually develops to *ff* (an explosion), then more and more soft.—The theme of *Poděbrad* (a prelude depicts the sorrowful situation of Czechia oppressed by the Germans) is the following: (rather fast)

There is an accompaniment to the theme. Very energetically and maliciously the papal wrath against Poděbrad comes out (in the piano sketch, only, so far). At the conclusion of the poem, after a scurrying of the strings alone in the gamma of A major *ff* and a little Slavic fanfare in the brasses, comes the theme known to you (I do it *à la guerre*—

---

[68] George of Poděbrad was the only possible king of Bohemia to inspire a Slavophile artist. He was the only native king of Bohemia and the only one not a Roman Catholic. On December 23, 1466, Pope Paul II excommunicated Poděbrad, pronouncing his deposition as king of Bohemia, at the same time that Emperor Frederick III and King Matthias of Hungary joined forces and invaded Bohemia.

These quotations are all that remain of Musorgsky's salute to Czech tradition. Two other tokens of Balakirev's trip to Prague did come to fruition, however: Balakirev's *Czech Overture* (later renamed *Bohemia*) and Rimsky-Korsakov's *Serbian Fantasy.*

Poděbrad—the King—Slavdom has won) and thus the poem, begun in
F-sharp minor, ends in D major.

Here you have, my dear, my intentions and my labors—let's get on
to yours.—If I were nearer to you, I would kiss you, just for the
introduction alone. The idea of a surging sea is much more menacing and impressive than a storm, that idea is fully artistic—the fulfillment of this is in accord with my soul. The appearance of the *sea
king* on the bare tone of D flat is splendid, the gamma of the descent
of Sadko to the undersea kingdom is very original in its harmonic
relationships, rather furious and bearing a strongly fantastic coloring
—this leaves a novel impression. The quiet and luminous turn of this
gamma to that of D major is very successful.—I like the planning of
Sadko and find nothing to object to in it.—And now for this—my
dear. Your first interruption of the D-major melody by the phrases
in the brasses is very much to my liking—it is exquisite and elegant,
but on the second example, noted in your letter, I will make this slight
comment:

(Serov in *Rogneda* [69]—I won't allow it)

Change this phrase, Korsinka—for God's sake get away from that
likeness to Serov's witch.—The transition of the bass from A to
G-sharp is audacious, and you know how I love audacity; this transition is assigned by you to the same gamma that you use for Sadko's
descent to the deep, only in the passing harmony at that time a tumult
will take place and the following cluster of sounds will occur:

---

[69] Serov planned *Rogneda* in 1842, but it was not until after the success of
Judith that he really wrote his second opera. *Rogneda* opened on November 8,
1865, with the contralto, Daria Leonova, in the title role, and Osip Petrov as
Vladimir the Great.

Schoking [shocking?] and furthermore, daring. This is comprehensible, but to be more accurate, it may sound false in the orchestra, or perhaps I lie.

The accompaniment to the undersea theme, needless to say, is poetic and, so to speak, lures one beneath the surface. But where you are really a clever fellow, Korsinka, is in your intention, holding the muted strings, not to carry them into the upper register. The strings under the mutes in the lower and middle registers have an enchanting character and positively draw us under into the undersea kingdom—master!—I don't agree with the church theme as you've written it out. It is quite nice, but it doesn't have that half-ascetic yet luminous imprint that one would like to feel in it. Coming at the very climax of the storm, it must instantly reshape the impression—find another one—*you have plenty to spare.*—Firm and unforgettable thanks to you for your warm participation in my first large work, *St. John's Night.* I have enjoyed this period, since the writing of the Intermezzo was not so pleasant—the German, not I, sits in it.—To you, dear, I say only this, that by those sketches which you sent in your letter, I can judge, if not fully, but I can guess that it was fitting, at least, for me to draw you toward writing the subject of Sadko; this is your first Russian thing, it belonged to you alone and to no one else—it was the first pancake—and it was far from spoiled. I am happy, soulfully happy, you know, that in the successful execution of *Sadko* I see something native; I am glad that you will work it out well, as much for the pleasure of having in Russia a good, original work, as well as, well—because it is extremely pleasant for me.—Write write write, my dear Korsinka. And at the end of August, if God so grants, I'll come to Peter on a visit, when we can get together and look through our scores.—Write me more often—anything you find necessary to tell me, put into your letter and send it to the proper address. I will be so glad to share with you anything that God sends to my brain. The letters arrive accurately and rather quickly.—My friends write me from Peter about the latest number, 6, of Serov's paper.[70] In this issue he jumped on Mili and knocked his education—well, in this case Serov is no authority; a fine sort of well-educated musician he is, inventing a high priest for Perun in a Russian epos

---

[70] Edited by Serov and published by his wife, the bimonthly *Music and Theater* had a heated but short career. It was begun in 1867 and lasted for seventeen issues.

and planting pilgrims in the Kiev thickets.[71] And in regard to musical and historical relationships he turned out to be lower than Verstovsky; [72] in Vladimir's feast he made use of a modern saloon song and dancing girls, as if Vladimir were Holofernes.—But in reference to Cui, Serov rode over him brutally: on account of a hint by Cui (an entirely tactless hint) that in the Slavonic concert [of May 11] they played nothing of Serov's, the author of two five-act operas writes: *A diplomatic regret, but a useless one* . . . How do you like the word *diplomatic?* Too bad about Cesar's tactlessness. And they say that we're all tagged in this number—so it must be, and I am sure of this, that Serov already hates us in the most wholehearted way.

Till we meet, my dear, I firmly press your hand and send you a friendly kiss—I'm so happy about Sadko.

Your

MODESTE

47a. *NIKOLAI RIMSKY-KORSAKOV to MODESTE MUSORGSKY, Minkino*
[*Extracts*]

Abo, 1 August, 1867

I write you, as you see, dear Modeste, from the chilly Finnish strand and you are probably quite surprised; but this is the reason, that I received an assignment to go for a cruise on the yacht *Wave* and was forced to leave Peter for one month and also to leave *Sadko,* to my great displeasure, now that I am wandering around in various Finnish places, but by the middle of August I will return for good to Peter and I hope to see you then and get down to the continuation of *Sadko,* which I've written in final form up to the first chords of the gusli player.[73] I received your letter at the very moment that I was setting down the Serovian phrase of which you don't approve—but somehow in a different way [musical quotation] and etc. exactly the same little thing in D major, only in the 1st and 2nd bars in place of ♩ I have ♫ . Do you understand all that I've told you? I hope that you will not now reproach me with *Serovisms* . . .

---

[71] These are the sneers of a nationalist who knows more about Kievan Russia, Vladimir the Great and Perun (god of thunder) than Serov does.
[72] Verstovsky's *Tomb of Askold* (1835) had drawn upon the same historical material that Serov later used in *Rogneda.*
[73] The gusli is an ancient Russian instrument, ancestor of the zither before it was supplied with a keyboard.

I'm very glad that you've gotten rid of your B minor Intermezzo, and started *Poděbrad*. Both of the suggested themes are good, and the one in B major is delightful, in my opinion; only you didn't write what it is to represent [in the program].

I await a letter from you in Peter, but it would be even better to receive you yourself.

Loving you,

N. RIMSKY-KORSAKOV

48. *To MILI BALAKIREV, St. Petersburg*

Minkino Farm, 24 September [1867]

DEAR MILI,

Your friendly appeal [74] is so strongly put that to refuse it would be, at least, a violation on my part of the sincere disposition toward me of my friends. This is the conclusion from your warm and sincere epistle which can be thanked only in deeds, not words, and so it is superfluous to write about it.—But this is how things are, my dear. If I were in such circumstances that I should have nothing to bite upon and could see *nothing in the waves* [75] of the future, the answer to your appeal would be explained by the desperate situation of a man.—Now though, in the present situation, I regard myself as *not justified* in alarming my friends and in deceiving them, for their disposition toward me is too valuable.—My means have shrunk—this is true, but not so far as to absolutely deprive me of any possibility of existing independently. Being accustomed to wealth and partly to luxury I am, in my present circumstances, not completely calm about the future and no wonder I made a wry face; at first sight of such a situation anyone would do the same in my place.—I can well understand the alarm that shows in your friendly letter and I am more than convinced of its authenticity.—But that is exactly why, for the sake of sincerity, I do not ask, I implore you to be calmed on my account and to pacify all those dear to me, for their fears for me weigh unbearably heavily upon me and my situation does not justify them.— Their fears weigh all the more heavily on me in that I am more afraid of deceit than of all else. Believe me, my dear Mili, that living in a

---

[74] It is not known what Balakirev offered to Musorgsky—another government job? financing?

[75] A phrase from the folk song, "Down the Mother Volga."

family and becoming bound to it for two years, rather spoilt in the family than ill at ease there, and entirely calm in regard to my living conditions, I had to consider well how to behave with diminished means.—After serious consideration of this matter and an arithmetical calculation of my finances I came to the conclusion that a deficit deprives me of the possibility of living in Peter at the beginning of October (as I wished) and commands me to skip this month with its Peter budget. From the beginning of November till April or May I can live quite easily in Peter. Consequently strained finances deprive me for one month from meetings and talks with my friends. —This is a great deal, but I am ready to consent to this deprivation for the sake of my own calm and that of my friends.—I am boldly able to say, thanks to the sincerity of your suggestion in the appeal, that all who sincerely love me will be still more happy to see me existing independently, rather than soaring as a meteor, and they will easily agree with me if one month of country solitude enables me to spend almost seven of the most lively, most interesting urban months and furthermore in a free and peaceful existence.—As for a job, to fuss for that I should wish for a permanent post (as the most secure) but such a post has to be kept in mind till after New Year's, for then in all ministries reductions and commotions occur in preparing for the new year.—From all this writing, my dear friend, extract an understanding of my situation and calm my friends and yourself—this you *must* do, for I adjure you by the fear of deceit, the most foul of all evils.

The change in circumstances did slightly oppress me, but only temporarily; with my nature, quite volatile, I landed on my feet and I should like to stay there. If I got into the dumps it was not because of a rural autumn or of financial matters but for another reason.— This was composer's dumps, although it is shameful to confess, but it is true that that was composer's *acidification* caused by your evasive response to my witches.—I rated, I rate and I will continue to rate this piece a decent one, particularly because in it, after several independent trifles, for the first time I independently approached a large work.— The dumps have passed, as much passes; I have accustomed myself to my composer's situation and at present am starting some new work, for the air of the pine woods stirs me to labor very well.—Whether or not you agree, my friend, to perform my witches, that is, whether or not I hear them, I will alter nothing in the general plan or in the

99

treatment, closely connected with the content of the picture, and executed sincerely, without pretense or imitation.—Each author keeps in mind the mood within which his composition grew and was carried out, and this feeling or the recollection of the past mood greatly sustains his personal criterion. I fulfilled my task as best I was able, within my powers. I shall only change a lot in the percussion parts, which I have abused.—But of the witches, later. But you, my friend, if an occasion can be found, write me at leisure about your positive opinion and then we'll have a talk.

Meantime, I firmly kiss you and thank you warmly for your sincere missive, which has greatly supported me, and, so to say, inspired me; it is pleasant, very pleasant to feel that one is the object of someone's regard and this is better than all sorts of financial excesses. I kiss you warmly, friend—give my friendly greetings to all who love me.

Your
MODESTE

I can just see how Solomonsha,[76] instead of Lermontov's *little fish*, will show you a Jew who is gulping Little-Russian dumplings and howling because they're so hot (remember the German portamento and the musical figure of the little fish). But anyway it's excellent that Solomonsha is dropping in.—*Hold on, Cossack, and thou wilt be an ataman.*

49. *To NIKOLAI RIMSKY-KORSAKOV, St. Petersburg*

[Minkino, end of September, 1867]

. . .[77] They want perfection! Glance at art from a historical point of view—and perfection doesn't exist. I do not speak of small tasks (which are, in actuality, not at all small). "Southern Night" is perfect, "Sing Not, Beauty, in My Presence" also "Forgive, Do Not Remember the Day of Degradation" also "Savishna" and among the Westerners *"Ich grolle nicht," "Doppelgänger,"* and how many our own Dargun

---

[76] Mme. Henriette Nissen-Saloman enjoyed extraordinary prestige in St. Petersburg as lieder singer and voice teacher. The bestowal of her favor on the Slavophiles had significance, and the inclusion in her repertoire of Balakirev's song, based on a Lermontov poem, "The Gold Fish," was a signal victory.

[77] The first half of this letter is missing, but something of its contents may be surmised from the opening of Rimsky-Korsakov's reply, October 8 (Letter 49a).

has, and "Midnight Review" [78]—with Russian perfection in this form, it is difficult for the Germans to compete.—But in large tasks—everywhere and in everything there are their own faults, but the matter is not in this, but in the general achievement of the aims of art.—We often abuse Wagner, but Wagner is powerful, powerful in that he lays hands on art and yanks it around . . . If he were more talented, he would do much more.—And Berlioz, and Liszt. Each of them and in each of their large-scale compositions they have their faults—and what faults! We are *excessively* strict with ourselves—every *excess* is dangerous.—After this, how can we not be frightened of *An Exercise for 10 Instruments!* [79] Up to this very moment I am afraid of Mili and this was said on his part after *Sadko* and in the discussions of my sinful witches.—And to want F-sharp major *à la Liszt's divina comedia* for the unholy glorification of Satan? *Corpo di bacco!* You, Korsinka, in the andante of your symphony showed your dear personality, in the Russian overture you said "God alone is without sin," in the Serbian fantasy you showed that one can write both quickly and pleasingly, and in *Sadko* you will declare yourself an artist. However, I kiss you firmly, till we meet and understand what I wanted to say in this letter and what I didn't say, for we would have much to talk about.

Yours firmly, very firmly,

MODESTE

Overlooking the faults which are hidden and occasionally stick out of the above-mentioned leaders in musical matters, apart from them, that is, from these faults, the works themselves will never die in the historical evolution of art and will always be bright points of intelligent artistic creation, and this is more important than passing, enthusiastic delights and praises.

---

[78] The composers of Musorgsky's favorite songs are:
  "Southern Night"—Rimsky-Korsakov
  "Sing Not, Beauty"—Balakirev
  "Forgive, Do Not Remember"—Cui (dedicated to Musorgsky)
  "Savishna"—Musorgsky
  "Ich grolle nicht"—Schumann
  "Doppelgänger"—Schubert
  "Midnight Review"—Glinka

[79] *An Exercise for 10 Instruments* was an idea of Balakirev's that he seems to have given up hastily.

P.S. If you will be at Ludmila Ivanovna's tell her that sitting in the country I have not forgotten her and am ever recalling her, and to her, the little dove, I have dedicated my new little piece ("Peasant Feast") by Koltzov.[80]

If you are intrigued, here it is:

Let it be granted for you to see that 6/4 and 5/4 constitute the whole *chic* of this little piece and came out as naturally as the 5/4 rhythm of "Savishna."—This, I consider for dear hospitable Ludmila Ivanovna, is Russian and, I dare to think, musical.

49a. *NIKOLAI RIMSKY-KORSAKOV to MODESTE MUSORGSKY, Minkino*
   [Extracts]

I received your letter, my dearest, the day before yesterday, and I thank you for it and also thanks for getting out of the dumps, which is best of all. At present I'm resting and doing absolutely nothing, for *Sadko* was finished on the 30th of September and has already gone to the binder's. I can tell you that I am quite satisfied with it, and that this is decidedly my best thing, even my very best; because the andante of the symphony, which the devil inspired me to compose so long ago, and successfully, and for which everyone reproached me, has given me absolutely no peace; but now *Sadko* has knocked it down, which makes me very happy. I do not regret the banishment of the sainted father Nikolai, for that business turned out perfectly without him, as Sadko himself could think to smash the gusli strings and the latter could not have withstood his playing. And Nikolai with the church theme would spoil the impression of the dance, and his appearance in the midst of the pagan world is a little ridiculous . . .

---

[80] The manuscript of "The Feast," on a text by Alexei Koltzov, is dated September 1867.

And thus *Sadko* is finished and to you, Modeste, great thanks for the idea, which you gave to me, remember, at Cui's, on the eve of Malvina's departure for Minsk. Thanks once again. Now I shall rest, for my noodle is a little weary after its intense strain; I'll rest, I'll laze around, I'll compose a few songs, and after that I'll take up—I myself don't know what, but the B minor allegro [of the abandoned second symphony] will hardly be resurrected from its ashes, but who knows what might happen!

Mili is definitely pleased with *Sadko* and found no corrections to be made. He wants to play it in the 6th concert along with the two episodes from Faust by Liszt. The 1st concert is scheduled for the 19th of October, giving the overture and full introduction to *Ruslan,* the *Dance of Death* [Liszt], the children's chorus from the *Prophet* [Meyerbeer], and the Fifth Symphony of Beethoven. If only you could come! Afterward the concerts will continue weekly; the Serbs will be in the 2nd; Borodin's [First] Symphony in the 3rd; and it appears that the 4th will include *Ocean* [Rubinstein], at the request of the conservatory, and the romance, recitative and chorus from the 5th act of *Ruslan;* I don't remember what is in the 5th, but I think it's a Schubert symphony. Come quickly.

I was so stupid that I haven't yet told you that Cesar finished the 3rd act [of *Ratcliff*] and *everything* from the love duet to the end is excellent. He has also written 3 songs, one exquisite, another nice, the third—more *schwach.* You will rejoice to hear that Mili has finally put aside the idea of an exercise for 10 instruments. He showed me your letter [of September 24] and I was not pleased with it (the letter). But I am glad you are composing; I can get nothing out of Poděbrad in its present form, for you didn't explain it in detail, and I will not judge the "Peasant Feast" until I can hear the whole song, for it is more difficult to judge a song from two bars than a symphony from four. But I like those quoted bars and I like their 11/4 rhythm.

Lodyzhensky [81] is here. He seems a very nice and talented gentleman. I haven't seen Ludmila Ivanovna for a long while; I dropped in to see her the day before yesterday but didn't find her home; I shall

---

[81] "Nikolai Nikolayevich Lodyzhensky joined our musical circle. Lodyzhensky, a ruined landowner in Tver Province, was a young man of education, strange, easily carried away, and endowed with a strong, purely lyric talent for composition. . ."—Nikolai Rimsky-Korsakov.

go there again in a few days and tell her all about you. Meanwhile, till we meet, or till the next letter. Even better if you could come sooner. I embrace you firmly.

N. RIMSKY-KORSAKOV

Peter, 8 October [1867]

50. *A Satire by MODESTE MUSORGSKY*

THE CLASSICIST
Dedicated to Nadezhda Petrovna Opochinina

In answer to remarks made by Famintzin in reference to the heresies of the Russian school of music.[82]

I am simple, I am serene,
I am modest, polite, and beautiful.
I am smooth, important,
And, within limits, passionate.
I am a pure classicist, and bashful,
I am a pure classicist, and courteous.
I am a raging enemy of the newest devices,
A mortal enemy of all innovations.
Their noise and hubbub, their terrible disorder
Worry and frighten me.
I see in them the coffin of art.
But I,
I am simple, I am serene,
I am modest, polite, and beautiful.
I am a pure classicist, and bashful,
I am a pure classicist, and courteous.

Petrograd, 30 December 1867

50a. *ALEXANDER DARGOMIZHSKY to MODESTE MUSORGSKY*

[1867]

(Epistle)

O you, excommunicated
By wardens and classical posers

---

[82] Rimsky-Korsakov tells that the direct provocation of this first of Musorgsky's "musical pamphlets" was Famintzin's review of the "heretic's" *Sadko*—thus the sea motif from *Sadko* is heard on the words, "of all innovations."

You who are heavenly mated
To all the Cui composers!
Make a date
With me, do not procras-
Tinate:
Otherwise—I pass.
I'll forget which cards have power
I'll be every bit as sour
As stale, old *kvas*.

A. S. DARGOMIZHSKY [83]

51. *An Inscription*

To the great teacher of musical truth [84]
Alexander Sergeyevich Dargomizhsky.—
Modeste Musorgsky
4 May, 1868
At Petrograd. [85]

---

[83] In the spring of 1866, at the age of fifty-three, and with a dangerously ailing heart, Dargomizhsky began the work that was to endear him to all members of the Balakirev Circle: *The Stone Guest*, not merely "based" on the poetic drama by Pushkin, but "without altering a single word" of Pushkin's text.

This doggerel "epistle" shows us some of the real affection existing between Dargomizhsky and the younger composers during his work on *The Stone Guest*.

[84] On December 9, 1857, Dargomizhsky had stated his basic principle in a letter to Lubov Karmalina: ". . . I will not go astray. My artistic position in Petersburg is not an enviable one. The majority of our musical amateurs and newspaper scribblers do not consider me inspired. Their routine viewpoint seeks flattery for the hearing of melody, towards which I do not drive. I have no intention of lowering music to the level of entertainment for them. I want the sound to express the word directly. I want truth . . ." A less sympathetic attitude to Dargomizhsky and his aims is provided in Tchaikovsky's diaries (entry for July 23, 1888): "Dargomizhsky wrote *The Stone Guest* near the end of his life, fully believing that he was demolishing old foundations and was building on their ruins something new, colossal. A pitiable delusion! I saw him in this last period of his life and in view of his sufferings (he had heart disease) it was not, of course, the time for arguing. But if anything is more dislikable and *false* than this unsuccessful attempt to introduce *truth* in a branch of art where everything is based on *pseudo* and where *truth*, in the usual sense of the word, is not required at all—I do not know it . . . During the period of his fatal illness he became much more good-natured, even displayed considerable *warmth* to his younger colleagues . . ." (translation by Wladimir Lakond, W. W. Norton, 1945).

[85] The two songs accompanying this dedication are: "Yeremushka's Lullaby," text by Nikolai Nekrasov, dated "16 March, 1868. Petrograd"; and the first number of the *Nursery* cycle, "With Nursie," dated "26 April, 1868, in Petrograd."

A Meeting at Dargo's

My acquaintance with Musorgsky began at Dargomizhsky's. This was when Dargomizhsky, in a blaze of creative inspiration, was composing with unprecedented speed one scene after the other of *The Stone Guest*, as if they had been prepared somewhere by him and were suddenly flourished before us like a magician's tricks from a bag. The second scene had just been written. My sister A. N. [Purgold] was studying the role of Laura, and I was accompanying.[86] Dargomizhsky set a day for the rehearsal and, in telling us this, said that the role of Don Carlos was to be sung by Musorgsky—a composer and singer. At that time we knew nothing of him and had never seen him. On the appointed day and hour we were at Dargomizhsky's, interested in making a new acquaintance and excited by the approaching performance, before a new authoritative person, of the difficult scene at Laura's. Musorgsky's personality was so unusual that, once having seen him, it was impossible to forget him. I shall begin with his appearance. He was of medium height and well built, with elegant hands, beautifully brushed wavy hair, and rather large and somewhat protuberant light gray eyes. But his features were very plain, particularly the nose, which was always reddish—owing, as Musorgsky used to explain, to its having been frostbitten once on parade. Musorgsky's eyes were by no means expressive; one might almost have called them tinny. On the whole, his face was not very mobile or expressive; it was as if it concealed some enigma. Musorgsky never raised his voice in conversation, but rather lowered it to a *mezza voce*. (I can still see him speaking, as if to himself, or mumbling some witty or piquant word, or chuckling, purposely abusing one of his friends when it was obvious that he was actually praising him.) His manners were elegant, aristocratic; he had the air of a well-bred man of society.

Musorgsky's personality produced an impression on both of us. And no wonder. There was so much in it that was interesting, peculiar, talented and enigmatic. His singing delighted us. He had a small but pleasant baritone and his power of expression, his subtle understanding of every shade of the soul's movement, and at the same time, the simplicity and sincerity of his interpretation, without the least exaggeration or affectation—all this had a fascinating effect. I was later convinced of the many-sideness of his talent as a performer; he was just as good in lyrical and dramatic as in comic and humorous things. In addition he was a splendid pianist; his playing was marked by brilliance, strength and elegance, combined with humor and vigor . . . —NADEZHDA PURGOLD (RIMSKAYA-KORSAKOVA)

[86] Alexandra Nikolayevna, the older of the two Purgold sisters, was a voice pupil of Mme. Nissen-Saloman. Nadezhda Nikolayevna had studied the piano under Musorgsky's old teacher, Herke, and composition at the St. Petersburg Conservatory under Zaremba. Their elderly uncle, Vladimir Fyodorovich Purgold, had taken their dead father's place, surrounding the two girls (and himself) with lively musical events. He occupied a high post in the Department of Appanages.

. . . I was very friendly with Musorgsky, but he never spoke with me about his youth; it was apparent that he himself was not satisfied with the way he had spent it; [however] he loved to tell me about his childhood, about how he grew up in the country on his father's estate, and this was one of his best memories; later he was in the army and, evidently, under the influence of bad comrades and spoiled his health for the remainder of his life. I became acquainted with him after he had retired [from military service] and was in very strained material circumstances. I know that he turned over [his share in?] his father's estate to his older brother, saying: My brother is married, he has children, and I will never marry and I can build my own road. . . . —ALEXANDRA PURGOLD (MOLAS)

52. *To CESAR CUI, St. Petersburg*

3 July, '68, village of Shilovo

My dear *Cesare,* greetings! Here I am, eating green fodder *en forme et matière.* I live in a hut, I drink milk and I remain all day in the fresh air, only at night do they drive me back to the stall.—Almost on the eve of my unpleasant departure, for I had not seen you, I finished the first scene of *Marriage:* [87] the first act consists of three scenes— with Stepan (the 1st) with the matchmaker (the 2nd) and with Koch-karov (the 3rd).—Being guided by the remarks by you and by Dargom I have been able to derive whatever is necessary from them, and have considerably simplified that which I showed you, and I have acquired for Podkolosin a very fortunate orchestral phrase, which can be used by me to the best advantage for the scene of the marriage proposal:

Dargom seems fully satisfied with it, and it makes its appearance for the first time in the conversation with Stepan at the words: "Well, and didn't he ask" and so on . . . about the marriage, in a word.— This, as you can see, is a *fragment* of the little theme which appears fully at the moment of the formal proposal in the third act, when

---

[87] Spurred by Dargomizhsky's example, Musorgsky is finding a musical form for a more difficult text, Gogol's comedy *Marriage.*

Podkolosin has already decided to get married.—On it can very well be constructed the stupid embarrassment of Podkolosin. In the first scene I have been able to do an ingenious little entry for Stepan . . . When he is called in for the 3rd time, he enters exasperated, but restraining himself (one understands) and at Podkolosin's words: "I just wanted to ask you, my good fellow" he answers *ff* "the old woman has come," perfectly disposing in this way of his boredom with his master.—At present the *second scene* (with the matchmaker) is roughed out in a draft. "Curs lie" and "the gray hair" have come out very well. I think that the little scene is interesting and not bad. —At the very end of it, the bear-like agitation of Podkolosin at the words "gray hair" has turned out very comically.—Now I am taking on *Kochkarov*. The first act will, after all, in my consideration, be able to serve as an experiment in *opéra dialogué*.—I should like to get the first act finished by winter; then we'll be able to judge and discuss it.—*Kochkarov sera fait spécialement pour vous, mon cher!* Tell your dear lady [Malvina] that the scene with Fyokla (the matchmaker) has come out well; she will be happy; my thanks to her for her sympathy in my extremely presumptuous work.—Now, contrary to my custom, I am composing the draft without a piano because there's no instrument here; I shall put everything in order in Peter. As long as I don't know if Korsinka is in the city or if he has sailed away to the "chilly Finnish rocks" [88] to freeze his flaming Antar,[89] I ask you dear to read to him my scribble if it should be interesting for him to read.—Well, and what about you, Cesar? *Comment cela va-t-il avec la versification?* Brave lad. Really what a blessed circle we are: if we lack a text—we scribble one ourselves! and somehow, it comes out all right.—Are you advancing in your instrumentation, how goes the prefinal composition [of *Ratcliff*]? What came of Dargo's audience with Alyona and how did it end? [90] There are the topics for your note,

---

[88] "From the chilly Finnish rocks to flaming Cholchis . . ."—Pushkin's *To the Slanderers of Russia.*

[89] Rimsky-Korsakov is completing a new programmatic symphony, based on the poem *Antar*, by Senkovsky (pseudonym: Baron Brambeus), suggested by Balakirev and Musorgsky. Originally planned as a second symphony (to replace the abandoned B minor project), the first and fourth movements had been completed earlier this year.

[90] As Honorary Vice-President of the Imperial Russian Musical Society, Dargomizhsky had interceded with the Grand Duchess Yelena Pavlovna on Balakirev's behalf. An unnamed German rival (Max von Erdmannsdörfer?) had appeared to fill the conducting post left vacant by Rubinstein's resignation, and Balakirev's chances were endangered.

if you, dear, take the trouble to cheer me up in my *réduit*.—In my *opéra dialogué* I am trying to underline as sharply as possible those changes of intonation, which occur in the characters during the dialogue, apparently for the most trivial of reasons and in the most insignificant words, in which is concealed, it seems to me, the power of Gogol's humor.—For example: in the scene with Stepan, the latter suddenly changes his lazy tone to one of exasperation after his master has worn him out on the subject of the boot-polish (I have eliminated the corns). In the scene with Fyokla such moments are frequent; from her bragging chatter to her rudeness or her shrewish behavior is for her only a step.—However, you will see all this better in actuality.—I firmly kiss you, dear, and to your dear lady my warmest greeting. I press the hand firmly and give a kiss to *Dottore doctissime*.[91]

YOUR

MODESTE MUSORGSKY

On the Moscow-Kursk Railway, at the Laptevo Station
10 July

This letter was delayed in being mailed, and it's just as well.—I have finished the *first act*. It rained for three days in a row, without a break, and I worked without a break, so that you might say that the weather and I pursued the same line.—For my part *Marriage* wouldn't leave me in peace, so I wrote it. Instead of three scenes four have turned up—as is necessary.—Now again the weather is wonderful, I am resting.—I kiss you firmly, dear. Give Dargomizhsky my salutations, and I have heard about Alyona from the Opochinins.[92]

YOUR

MODESTE

53. *To LUDMILA SHESTAKOVA, St. Petersburg*

[Shilovo] 30 July [1868]

I hasten to thank you with all my heart, dear Ludmila Ivanovna, for your two missives and for your warm and highly valued solicitude for this sinner;—(about the *apartment*) although I shall be settled

---

[91] Yuli Yulyevich Gubner (Julius Hubner), physician and friend of the Cuis.

[92] When Musorgsky returned to St. Petersburg that fall, he lived in the Opochinin apartment in Engineers' Castle, with Nadezhda Petrovna and her brother, Alexander Petrovich Opochinin, both of whom Musorgsky had known intimately for several years.

otherwise, that is, moved again, nearer to your neighborhood (in Engineers' Castle [with the Opochinins]), that's not the main point, but this above all, something nice responded in me to your lines about the *apartment* and I warmly kiss your little hand for this.—While you were growing angry with me for my scrawl, I was hurrying to share with you my success with *Marriage* and was rushing a letter to our station, because a two-weeks sojourn in a place which I was visiting for the first time, could not supply enough material for a letter—hence this little note was born;—it happened by itself, "and I am not guilty." [93]

O Kologrivov! [94] How long wilt thou remain in all sorts of obscurantism and mess! Look what he thought up! *il se panachait de l'impartialité*, this is certainly so;—O Kologrivov's impartiality! The action of Dargomizhsky shows good comradeship, and this is a great quality in a star of first magnitude, a rare quality. Only then will Russian musical affairs live, when our modest circle, staunchly, in a comradely way, without personal self-adoration (at least not in the application to affairs) will advance directly towards [its] aims through all the labyrinth of *Herrnhuter* [95] and renegade intrigues—staunchly and *cautiously, by degrees;* truth and honesty will be Ariadne's thread—truth in creation, honesty practically applied to both creation and musical activity.

Korsinka amazed me.—What a man! He traveled to the mythical kingdom! [96] Bravo! He wished to go to myths, but he *wished* it so hard that according to my way of thinking *he didn't wish it.*—Bravo! Kvey is charming, dearest Cesare is *une belle conduite!* I am happy both for him and for you, for the more one sees of fine people, the more pleasing it is, and the empty market, as will all empty things, has made a

---

[93] "May God bless you and witness that I'm not guilty," says the Mayor in Gogol's *Revizor.*

[94] Kologrivov, as one of the Musical Society's board of directors, was objecting to Balakirev's proposal to transfer a few classes from the Free School to the Conservatory.

[95] The Herrnhuter (Moravians) were a religious sect in Bohemia. Zaremba was a Polish adherent of this sect.

[96] The Borodins, vacationing on the Lodyzhensky estate in the Province of Tver, invited Rimsky-Korsakov to join them there. "Myth," in Russian, is the reversed spelling of "Fim," Lodyzhensky's nickname in the Circle. Borodin gave him the rank of "Ober-Fim."

lot of mischief; what a silly; fires are in fashion, so it had to have one too.[97]

Turning to my rustic life, I will say: (1) There was a fall of hail-stones, weighing about half a pound, five versts from us, from one windy corner three cartloads were collected, the hail killed a fine suckling-pig and the fields were given a really cruel beating. Those who saw the hail stated that the hailstones were as big as hen's eggs—one could have killed a bull. (2) We haven't had such a hay harvest for a long time, and I don't know how the wheat is, but in the fields it is pretty good.—In Yepifan county (in the province of Tula) and in Yeletz county (in the province of Oryol) the harvest of the trial yield is unheard of: 30 [? to the desyatin?].—50 versts from us, that is, from Serpukhov to Moscow, there is a complete drought, and the fields are literally dried up.—Hasn't the drought, dear Ludmila Ivanovna, at your place in Smolensk province, caused a deficit, that is, a reduction of the budget?—Such is our sorrow, that there is no possibility of maintaining a regular budget—this is all left to chance! After this, the "maybe" of the Russian peasant, who is mostly a tiller of the soil, is not surprising.—At present I am resting, as I have been raking hay, cooking jam and putting up pickles—*comment cela vous plaît?* The haying has turned out very well, the pickles and the jam are very tasty.—I'm now thinking over the second act of *Marriage,* I probably won't write any small things, I am not in the mood, but then, who knows! Maybe I will.—I am observing characteristic peasant women and typical peasant men—they all may come in handy. With how many fresh sides, untouched by art, the Russian nature swarms, oh, how many! and with what juicy ones, splendid ones.—A small part of that, which life has given to me, I have pictured in musical images for those dear to me, and I have voiced my impressions to those dear to me.—If God grant me life and strength I will speak on a grand scale; after *Marriage,* the Rubicon is crossed, but *Marriage* is a cage, in which I am imprisoned until I am tamed, but afterwards—to free-dom.—All this is desirable, and doesn't yet exist, but it must. Fright-ening! and frightening because what might be may not be, for it still is not present.—This is what I would like. For my characters to speak on the stage, as living people speak, but besides this, for the character

---

[97] The empty market across from Shestakova's apartment caught fire on the night of July 11, 1868.

and power of intonation of the characters, supported by the orchestra, which forms a musical pattern of their speech, to achieve their aim directly, that is, my music must be an artistic reproduction of human speech in all its finest shades, that is, *the sounds of human speech,* as the external manifestations of thought and feeling must, without exaggeration or violence, become true, accurate *music, but* * artistic, highly artistic. That is the ideal toward which I strive ("Savishna," "The Orphan," "Yeremushka," "The Child" [98]).

So now I work on Gogol's *Marriage.*—But the success of Gogol's speech depends on the actor, on his true intonation.—Well, I want to fix Gogol to his place and the actor to his place, that is, to say it musically in such a way that one couldn't say it in any other way and would say it as the characters of Gogol wish to speak.—That is why in *Marriage* I am crossing the Rubicon. This is living prose in music, this is not a scorning of musician-poets toward common human speech, stripped of all heroic robes—this is reverence toward the language of humanity, this is a reproduction of simple human speech. —Well, we went and went, and we came to a stop.—I should like to ask you, dear Ludmila Ivanovna, to read, or more truly: to give my little note to Dyainka to read, approximately from the words "turning to my rustic life," or all of it if it doesn't inconvenience you,— but particularly about my *chiefly predominant* idea; it so happens that everything I would have written him I have written you; what to do about it, that's the way it happened; I wanted to write both of you.—Till we meet, I kiss your little hand warmly.

MODESTE

* Musorgsky's note: Read: which means.

54. *To NIKOLAI RIMSKY-KORSAKOV, St. Petersburg*

DEAR FRIEND KORSINKA.

[Shilovo] 30 July [1868]

I hear from Ludmila Ivanovna that you are in Peter and so I write you.—If you have seen Cesare you will have learned that the first act of *Marriage* is ready, and knowing this, you cannot doubt that I have been working.—Cesare has offended me by not answering my letter. When I receive no reply I, in my peculiarly suspicious way, suspect

[98] "The Little Orphan Girl" uses Musorgsky's own text. It is dated "13 January 1868. Petrograd," and is dedicated to Yekaterina Sergeyevna Borodina. "The Child" is better known as "With Nursie," No. 1 of the *Nursery* cycle.

that I have committed some sin, and when I suspect this, I worry, and when I worry—I get angry. The unpleasantness of such a situation is understandable.—From Ludmila Ivanovna I learn also that you have been in the financial kingdom with the chemical gentleman [Borodin]. What came of this? Write me about Antar and write me about the *Pskovityanka* [99] scene.—And placing the letter in a suitable envelope, address it to: on the Moscow-Kursk Railway, at the Laptevo Station— to me. I left Peter without saying goodbye to you or to Cesare. I ran in twice to the latter but didn't catch him, and I had to leave very fast, for my brother, with whom I'm staying, had to leave the estate urgently for Peter, and because it is the first time I am in Tula Province, in general I had to make thorough inquiries in order to select a proper house, because we live quite rustically, that is, with as much comfort as possible, on rather slender means.—The estate begins to be straightened out because the railroad is so near it; some sort of superintendent lived in it formerly. *Où donc voulez-vous trouver le confortable!* I don't inquire about the Fims, for Fims are Fims, as the wind is wind.—I have looked over my work—in my opinion it is quite interestingly carried out—however, who knows! I worked as well as I was able, and now it's up to all of you to judge its success—I am on trial. I say one thing only: if one completely renounces opera traditions and visualizes musical dialogue on the stage as just ordinary conversation, then *Marriage* is an opera.

I want to say that if the expression in sound of human thought and feeling *in simple speech* is truly produced by me in *music,* and this reproduction is musical and artistic, then the thing is in the bag. This is what you must discuss, and I will stand aside.—I did it as well as I could and I surrender myself wholeheartedly to all sorts of torments. I have calmed down, as much as I could, and I await judgment quietly, although the labor was not easy. I have worked briskly—as it happened, but brisk work tells on one: whatever speech I hear, no matter who is speaking (nor what he says) my mind is already working to find the musical statement for such speech. Now I have rested—this is over, it was really hard on me before, because I had no calm.—By the end of August I hope to come to Peter, then we shall see each

---

[99] Mey's play, *The Maid of Pskov,* had attracted the Circle as an opera subject for some time. Balakirev had first suggested it to Borodin, who gave it up when Stasov proposed the subject of *Prince Igor.* Balakirev and Musorgsky had then pushed Rimsky-Korsakov toward this work. *Pskovityanka* is usually performed outside Russia as *Ivan the Terrible.*

other, and I very much want to see all of you,—this is understandable, isn't it true?

[Unsigned]

54a.   *CESAR CUI to MODESTE MUSORGSKY, Shilovo*

DEAREST MODESTE!

I've long wanted to answer you, but all my laziness found proper pretext for its justification.

First, I wanted to write you something quite *positive* about *Ratcliff*, but at this moment I simply can't do this fully. Two days ago I took the score of two acts to Fyodorov: [100] the second act—230 pages, the third—140, altogether 370 pages—92½ leaves; the paper came to 1 ruble 53½ kopeks silver. Fyodorov has given them to the copyists, but he couldn't give me a tentative date for the staging of the opera. All dates till January, he says, have been assigned, which means that the opera can go on only after New Year's. Besides, Serov has sent two acts of his new four-act opera [*The Power of Evil*], and these two acts are already being copied. However *everything depends* on the Director.[101] As long as I haven't given in the whole opera, I can't consider I have a right to press an exact date for the production. Very likely the swifter in sending his completed work will go on first, which is quite just. However, I will see the Director himself in a few days.

Thus the vagueness of *Ratcliff's* fate was the first, or so to say, legal reason for the tardiness of this reply, when all of a sudden, to make things worse, I came across Samarin's book on the Jesuits,[102] I am reading it, I look into their doctrines, and I find an inestimable treasure: a justification for all kinds of mischief, within the theory of "plausibility." If you have before you several paths, you may choose the one of least "plausibility" (least honest, least in harmony with your conscience, with your *inner* convictions) if only it coincides with your benefit, with your inclination. I may answer you or not. Not to answer would be less "plausible," but would coincide with my laziness.

---

[100] Pavel Stepanovich Fyodorov was head of the repertoire department of the Imperial Theaters of St. Petersburg.

[101] Stepan Alexandrovich Gedeonov had, the year before, begun his valuable eight years of work as Director of the Imperial Theaters. He was also director of the Hermitage Museum.

[102] *The Jesuits and Their Relation to Russia.*

However, you see that my virtue triumphed. For the application of this wonderful theory I await more capital mischief.

I am glad about the completion of the first act of *Marriage* and look forward with enormous interest to becoming acquainted with it. With words of my own (the scene of Lesley with chorus before his song) I wrote music that I deem in the manner of its execution—*irreproachable.** I am writing lyrics (rather odious) for the finale of the 1st act. I am orchestrating Douglas's story.

"Well, that's that." I'll tell you more when we meet. Dargun, Wife, Doctor, *Nikolas* all greet you.

Adieu dearest.

Your

C. Cui

27 July, 1868
S.P. Burg

* Cui's note: This would be a more accurate term than "model." And regarding one's self it is more becoming to maintain *accuracy of expression.*

54b. *NIKOLAI RIMSKY-KORSAKOV to MODESTE MUSORGSKY, Shilovo*

I received your epistle yesterday, dearest friend Modeste, and I hasten to reply, for I do not want you to leave off writing to me, nor to begin to be cross with me. To start with I'll tell you that Cesar has written you and that you probably haven't received his letter and therefore your apprehensions are quite in vain. In case his epistle has gone astray, I will tell you something of it in this letter. Now I will tell you that I await you impatiently, for I never have enough of you, and I am eager to have an idea of your *Marriage,* for the *Marriage* of such a talented composer as yourself, presents a fact that is quite interesting. See how witty I am and bad, too! Truly, you are acting splendidly in this matter. A whole act written, no joking? But to me this is incredible, the event interests me frightfully, not that it is so incredible as that it is unprecedented in music; and for the existence of the unprecedented—the more honor and glory to you. Really, your work is terribly interesting, and besides, there are surely perfect things in it, and too, it must clarify a good deal. Come, and bring it. Looking at you I am always wondering when the time will come, when I will prepare one number after another for *Pskovityanka* and will show them to you, but meantime one must be content that something begins to turn up for the first act, and especially for the scene of Olga and Tucha and for the fairy tale. Thus in September, when *Antar* will be finished and I will have rested a little, after that I will approach these things seriously. As soon as I write it, I'll show it and it's up to you to judge it.

"Vengeance" has long been orchestrated, and at present I am orchestrating "Power." [103] I've already told you that I am drawing the atmosphere of an Oriental potentate rather than an abstract feeling; I hope that it will not be too bad from this aspect, it will be awfully elegant, there will also be rather strong things. The beginning which you know is produced alone by the wood-winds and brasses with cymbals. The second theme in A major (the harem), with a sufficiently original accompaniment of tambourines and cymbals, has a certain oriental *chic*, and then—Power (Antar's theme in F major with fanfares); after a short middle section there is a return to the first theme and Antar's theme in D. Then a not very big tailpiece. I plan to do the shortest prelude for the fourth part, based on [musical quotation] and so on.

This will again recall the ruins (from the first part) and the kingdom of the Peri, and besides it will serve pleasantly as a link between the D major (the third part) and the D flat major (the fourth). Now I hope that *Antar* will be entirely finished in a few days. Mili will hate "Vengeance" and won't be pleased with "Power," for I didn't do it as a grand *allegro* with a broad symphonic development of the theme; but I won't redo anything,[104] for the idea is conveyed and that's good, except that the symphonic development is not always good or suitable. Yes, the shore is in sight.

I stayed among the Fims for three weeks, spent a pretty good time, Borodin and the rest of us rode horseback, ate a frightening quantity of berries and cream, and walked. At a choral round dance I heard a rather good little theme, which I remember. No matter how much

---

[103] The last three movements of the Antar symphony (or suite) are: Second ("Joy of Revenge"), Third ("Joy of Power"), Fourth ("Joy of Love").

[104] ". . . in the spring of 1868, during the composition of *Antar* certain indications of coolness began to be felt between Balakirev and me for the first time. The independence which had gradually begun to awake in me (I was twenty-four) had, by that time, begun to assert itself, and Balakirev's acute, paternal despotism began to weigh heavily. It is difficult to determine what these first indications of coolness were, but soon my complete frankness toward Mili Alexeyevich began to decrease, and the necessity for frequent meetings also began to decrease. It was pleasant to spend an evening with him, but it was still more pleasant to spend it without him."—Rimsky-Korsakov, *Chronicle*.

the Fims are Fims they are nevertheless an extremely cordial people, and the chief Fim [Lodyzhensky] is positively a kind and good man, and the fact that he has a disorderly mind doesn't concern me; sad though this may be, he harms only himself. After the trip to the Fims I went on into Finland to visit my family, lounging around for a week; in general this summer has passed pretty well for me. We are still having summer, excessively hot and the air is so filled with smoke that if you try to look at the sun, the smoke makes your eyes smart. As we are having good weather Dargun is always idling, and does no work at all; he again complains about his health, but he is cheerful and gay. The business has been settled with the German [?], we made Alyona [the Grand Duchess] angry, but the German is thrown out.[105] Not a sound or a smell of Mili, he writes no one.

Now I'll tell you about Cesar. He is really doing fine. The third and second acts have been given to the Directorate, and the first is half ready, all that remains is to orchestrate the tale of the MacGregors and write out the finale. He has gone ahead powerfully in orchestration, and I hope that much of the work will go into the orchestra excellently. Dargun still cannot digest all of his [Cui's] orchestration, but this is because he, aside from Weber's, Glinka's and his own, hasn't seen other scores. Let's hope that we shall finally hear *Ratcliff* this winter.

However, it's time for bed, and consequently, time to end this meeting with you; and so, farewell, dear, come quickly, bring your work, and if you won't be lazy, write further to me.

If you have rested, go ahead and work on. Come.

N. Rimsky-Korsakov

7 August, Peter.

I'm dining tomorrow at Ludmila's with Dyainka.

55. *To CESAR CUI, St. Petersburg*

[Shilovo, 15 August, 1868]

Thanks, dear Cesare, for your missive.—And I was hurt on your account. What's to be done?—it is my fate to be eternally suspicious where there is no reason to be and not to be suspicious where there is a reason.—*Cela doit vous prouver un peu ma stupidité.—Qu'en faire?* I have brought my composition [*Marriage*] into order and I

---

[105] See footnote 90 on page 108.

am hammering it into my memory in order to show it to you. Without a piano it is more difficult to memorize it than to write it.

From Korsinka's letter I have been once more convinced that you have rescinded your *renunciation of instrumentation.* Honor to you and glory! From your dear epistle I extract hope of hearing *Ratcliff;* though we wait, we shall hear.—Well, good things always oblige one to search and to wait, and *Ratcliff* is more than a good thing,—of which I speak. *Ratcliff* is not only yours, but ours. It crept out of your artistic belly before our eyes, it grew, became strong and now goes out into the world before our eyes and not once has it disappointed us. How is it not possible to love such a dear good creature, one can't help saying that it is more than good!—Concerning what you've done recently, I am firmly convinced that in the mood in which I left you, you've done superb work. Mood for an artist is a great thing!—And that you would give me *joy* when you arrive—of this I am also convinced.—Around the twentieth (or a few days later) of this month we shall see each other. I am still resting from the 1st act, that is, thinking over and shaping the 2nd act, but I have not come to the writing of it. I feel that I must take my time—so that the merchant character (at the beginning of the act) as well as Zhevakin and Yaichnitza will come out as properly colored as were Fyokla and Kochkarov.—And much is being shaped up. This is truly "the deeper you go into the woods, the more firewood there is"! And how capricious and subtle Gogol is.—I have been observing peasant men and women—and have caught some appetizing specimens. One peasant is a very copy of Antony in Shakespeare's Caesar—when Antony delivers his speech at the Forum over Caesar's body. A very clever and malicious (in an original way) peasant.—All this will find some use, and the types of peasant women are simply a treasure.—It's always thus with me: my eye catches certain kinds of people, and then on the proper occasions I set them down [on paper]. And what fun for us! That's what I'm doing at present, my dear Cesare.—And as, in ten days at the latest, I hope to see you, therefore I leave off this chattering.—Leaving it I kiss you firmly, dear, and to your lady and to the *dottore doctissime* also I send my warm greeting.

MODESTE

Mili, so they say (or rather, as they write) doesn't write to anyone although there is some news of him. This is what's strange: Heine's *Ratcliff* is stilted—your *Ratcliff* is a figure of wild passions and so

living that the stilts cannot be seen in your music—it is blinding.[106]
That's another reason why *Ratcliff* is more than a good thing, because
it is the first such figure in music—*fully* realized. *A vous l'honneur—
le charme à nous!*

56. *To NIKOLAI RIMSKY-KORSAKOV, St. Petersburg*

[Shilovo] 15 August [1868]

Dear friend Korsinka, again greetings! There is in the eleventh
line of your dear epistle (I counted it) the speech: "I await you impatiently, for I miss you" and I thank you friend for your warm speech,
and doubly for your support.—Yes, this is the comradely way: *to support,* when necessary; and your warm words poured warmth over me,
even though the air is hot. Thanks! These days I have been bringing
order to my country composition, the second, third and fourth scenes
of the first act of *Marriage,* that is, the whole first act.—I did not expect to do this. For the first time in my life I *wrote* without the aid of
an instrument, that is, without verification of the composed work *
and I thought, that in such a thing, as musical prose (where the harmonic conditions are terribly capricious), I would not be able to dis-
pense with the instrument.—But having received your and Cesar's
epistles, I was inflamed with a fever for order and I cleaned and
brought order to what was composed, and it was *opportune* to do so—
there are no mistakes, and I did it so that as soon as *Marriage* is bound,
I could show it to you, my dears. Now I am memorizing it. It's coming out quite amusingly.—The second act exists only in thought and
plan—it cannot be composed yet—too early! Patience, otherwise one
would fall into a monotony of intonation—the most horrible of sins
in this capricious *Marriage.*—However, the fortune-telling with cards
of the fiancée and the character of Zhevakin are already visualized
. . . —I'm glad that *Pskovityanka* is harassing you and I was positive
that you would begin with the love scene and the fairy tale, and thereafter: the deeper you go into the woods, the more firewood there is,
as I've already written you.—I am again happy about *Antar*—finish it!

* Musorgsky's note: Always turn back, but I didn't observe this in the past.

---

106 Heine wrote *William Ratcliff* within three days in January 1821, and was
never very proud of the results. Louis Untermeyer describes it as "a combination
of thick melodrama and thin mysticism," and Cui does not appear to have improved the mixture perceptibly. The opera had its première on February 14, 1869,
enjoyed eight performances, and has since been heard only once.

Concerning your intentions about "Power" I won't argue and I think that oriental power, considered externally, is not contradictory to artistic requirements, for this power loved and loves to express itself *chiefly in pomp.*—But regarding the last scene "Love" I argue against the prelude, for I think it should be, as you had it, without preludes. It would be more artistic, more simple and more sincere.—Is it possible that for esthetic taste, after the D major pompous character, for D-flat major's melancholy-pathetic character, that A on the horns is needed? And it is you who are saying this—a Glinka of esthetics!—Do not be embarrassed!—What could be more poetic, after the *forte* D major, *pomposo* (as I remember you finish the scene of "Power") than the melancholy D-flat major, directly, without any sort of preliminaries?—If you like the allusion to the ruins and the Peri, then if you please, be faithful to the Senkovsky original and before each scene do a prelude from the ruins with the Peri (this is logical).— What nonsense would come out! Such is my opinion, that the more simple and sincere it is, the better.—Vengeance—without any preliminaries, Power—also, but why do you want to borrow Love from the Germans?—So I argue—thus it seems to me, that I have the right to argue. Remember Sadko and its conclusion.—You know that after Antar's C-sharp minor and D major, D-flat major *directly* carries Antar above the clouds, into that world of houris, peris and nice people in general, which purifies, and temporarily soothes (pacifies) Antar and poetically exalts him.—O preliminaries! How many good things have they ruined!

And further, regarding *symphonic development.*—You seem appalled that you are writing in a Korsakov manner rather than in a Schumann manner. And I tell you (scorn fear—*vous êtes brave*) that cold *borsch* is a calamity to a German, but we eat it with pleasure *point de comparaison s'il vous plaît, comparaison n'est pas raison.* The German *Milchsuppe* or *Kirschensuppe* is a calamity for us, but it sends a German into ecstasy.—*Bref, symphonic development, technically understood,* is developed by the German, just as his philosophy is—at present destroyed by the English psychologists and our Troitzky.[107] The German, when he thinks, first *theorizes* at length, and then *proves,* our Russian brother proves first, and then amuses himself

---

[107] Troitzky's *German Psychology of the Present Century; A Historico-Critical Study with an Introductory Essay on the Advances of Psychology in England at the Time of Bacon and Locke,* published in 1867.

with theory: (at Borodin's you didn't have a prelude for "Love," but now you do): [108] I'll say no more to you on the score of symphonic development.—Now, my dear Korsinka, listen to one thing: creation itself bears within itself its own laws of refinement. Their verification is inner criticism; their application is the artist's instinct. If there is neither one nor the other—there is no creative artist; if there is a creative artist—there must be one as well as the other and the artist is a law unto himself. When the artist revises, he is not content (as in Vengeance—which makes me glad). When he, contented, revises or, what is worse, adds to it, *he germanizes, relives* what has already been said. We are not ruminants, but omnivorous animals. This would be a contradiction!—and of nature.

"So when you are alone, like this, and you think things over, at leisure, you do come to feel that, after all, one has to . . ." [109] become *one's self.* This is hardest of all, that is, it is the rarest of things to achieve, but it's possible.—And as it's possible, there's no use theorizing, but I kiss Korsinka firmly and even wish him very pleasant dreams, as it is two o'clock at night.

MODESTE

I'll be with you at the end of August.

57. *To VLADIMIR NIKOLSKY, St. Petersburg*

[Shilovo] 15 August [1868]

Rumors have reached me that my priceless treasure in the dear figure of *dyainka,* with his characteristic craftiness, has sneaked into my dwelling in my absence.—This treasure of mine had read in the church calendar that June 15 is the day of St. Modestus,[110] hence the sneaking in, the treasure wanted to drag me along to a favorably disposed man to enjoy dainties and a heart-to-heart talk.—Thanks to him for this—forsooth! Exceeding thanks, for when a little man feels good he is pleased, and when he gets pleasure from another person then—happy as he is, he says thanks!

---

[108] Despite Musorgsky's caustic remarks, Rimsky-Korsakov held on to this brief introduction to *Antar's* fourth movement.

[109] "So, when you are alone, like this, and you think things over, at leisure, you do come to feel that, after all, one ought to get married . . ."—the opening lines of Gogol's *Marriage.*

[110] Musorgsky's patron saint, St. Modestus, was the tutor of St. Vitus and achieved martyrdom with him.

I am forever intending to write to my treasure, and only now do I get to it.—At first I didn't write for lack of material, then I wanted to write, and wanted to badly, but it came to pass that the subject, which was supposed to be written to you, haply rolled over towards our little dove Ludmila Ivanovna.—So it is only now that I actually get down to writing you.—But what to write? Why, words, speeches, sentences, of course.—But what to write about? About the following.

The Greeks worshiped nature, meaning man as well. Great poetry and the greatest arts originated in this.—I continue: In the scale of nature's creation man constitutes the highest organism (at least on earth) and this highest organism possesses the gift of speech and voice without equal among earthly organisms generally.—If one can assume a reproduction, through an artistic medium, of human *speech*, in all its most delicate and capricious shades, a natural reproduction, as natural as is required by the life and character of a man—would this be a deification of the human gift of speech? And if it is possible to tug at the heartstrings by the simplest of methods, merely by obeying an artistic instinct to catch the intonations of the human voice—why not look into this matter?—And if, at the same time, one could capture the thinking faculty as well, then wouldn't it be suitable to devote oneself to such an occupation?—Without preparation you can't cook a soup. Meaning: preparing oneself for work, even though this may be Gogol's *Marriage,* a most capricious thing for music, wouldn't that be the achievement of a good deed, that is, wouldn't that mean a closer approach to the most cherished aim of life? One can say to that: Why is one always preparing oneself—it's about time to do something! The trifling little pieces were preparations, *Marriage* is a preparation—when will something finally be ready? To this there is only one answer: *the power of necessity;*—some day it may be ready.

My activity, the activity that I hold under my arm, which I'm not ashamed to show others, if they should question me, started with those trifling little pieces.—It's silly to be bashful and put on modest airs when one realizes that those trifling pieces have given me a name, as well, though only among a limited circle, but at least a circle of people who are not narrow-minded.—These trifles have provoked a desire in persons who are rather imposing in music to set me an untouched (in the historical course of music) problem—musically to set forth everyday prose in the form of musical prose. For proof that the solution of such a problem is not easy I offer my humble self.—I have composed a whole act of musical prose, I have painted it with four characters—from my point of view the act turned out well, but I don't know what will happen to the other three acts. I know that they *must* be good, but I don't know whether they *can* be good. However, one must finish the work that one has begun, and then bring in the verdict. —But through the darkness of uncertainty, however, I see a bright spark and this spark is the complete renunciation by the public of the opera-traditions of the past (which, moreover, still exist).—*Impossible!* But why is that spark bright? Because when one opens a new road one feels *doubly* strong, and when one's strength is doubled (four is exactly twice two) one can work, and work joyfully. This situation can end only with the thieves' formula: *la bourse ou la vie—la vie ou le drame musical.* It is needless to say that both life and musical drama are necessary because one without the other is unthinkable. —With this I end my rot.

The other day I received a most charming epistle from Ludmila Ivanovna, but I must express a reservation about it.—Speaking of my talent our little dove added a word which would lead my humble self to Olympus.—It's no use to climb the hill—I'm lazy and I fear fatigue. I don't understand the word *genius.*—To my way of thinking a clever and capable interlocutor is a very good thing. I have no reason not to like the little man and I wish him well and as best I can I talk with him and if my talk finds a response in his soul and his brain—I have done my work and what happens later is *in the hands of the authorities,* as dear Piotr Mironovich Perevlessky [111] used to say.—Once, before my departure, the little dove threw this word in my face (I shuddered) and now she has written it (and I broke out in a sweat—it was 23°), why, first fever, and then sweat? I am not a malicious sort, and there is no reason to punish me.—I am firmly convinced that only modesty in work and a sincere wish to have a hearty talk with nice little men can guarantee independent creative activity.—Why force a man to depend on the garnishes of a creative full-dress uniform? I am a man and I am prone to every human nastiness as well as to some good sides of humanity,—but let the passions loose, as they say. I haven't let them loose and I will not let them loose until I have the strength for it. A calm conscience is the most enviable thing.—However, I firmly kiss my dear *dyainka* and beg him to tell

---

[111] Perevlessky was the previous occupant of Nikolsky's chair of Russian Letters at the Alexandrovsky Lycée. He died in 1866.

Ludmila Ivanovna that I have given a bit of thinking to her little letter and when we meet (about the 20th of August) I'll have a talk with
her. I don't write her because there's nothing to write about, and it's
better to talk about this looking into each other's eyes rather than at
a distance of 700 versts.—My hearty greetings to Anna Vasilyevna,
don't forget your lady, too, for I haven't forgotten her.

MODESTE

57a. *ALEXANDER BORODIN to YEKATERINA BORODINA, Moscow*

S. Petersburg 25 September [1868]

. . . Afterwards Musorgsky played the first act of *Marriage* by
Gogol, written directly from the text of that writer, without any alteration. It is an extraordinarily curious and paradoxical thing, full
of innovations and places of great humor, but as a whole—*une chose
manquée*—impossible in performance. Besides, it bears marks of too
hasty labor . . .

Marriage, *Act I*

. . . When Musorgsky's *Marriage* was played at our home, A. S.
[Dargomizhsky] sang the role of Kochkarov, roaring with laughter
till the tears came to his eyes, and enchanted by the wit and expres-
siveness of this music. In the place where Kochkarov says "these
darling little mail-clerks, these sweet little rascals"—A. S. was always
obliged to stop, he was so overcome with laughter, and he said to me,
"You're playing some sort of symphony there, you're hindering my
singing." (in the accompaniment at this point Musorgsky had some
amusing curlicues) . . . —NADEZHDA PURGOLD (RIMSKAYA-KORSA-
KOVA)

. . . Early in the season [1868–69] Dargomizhsky's soirées recom-
menced. *The Stone Guest* was sung in its entirety. *Marriage* also
roused considerable interest. We were all amazed at Musorgsky's task,
enthusiastic about his characterizations and many recitative phrases,
but perplexed by some of his chords and harmonic progressions. At
this performance Musorgsky himself sang Podkolosin with his inimitable talent; Alex[andra] Nik[olayevna] sang Fyokla; [General] Velyaminov sang Stepan; Nad[ezhda] Nik[olayevna] accompanied, while
Dargomizhsky, extremely interested, copied Kochkarov's part in his
own hand and sang it with enthusiasm. Everybody particularly enjoyed Fyokla and Kochkarov—the latter expanding on "the darling

little mail-clerks, the sweet little rascals," with a most amusing characterization in the accompaniment. V. V. Stasov was in ecstasy. Dargomizhsky occasionally said that the composer had gone a bit too far. Balakirev and Cui saw in *Marriage* nothing more than a mere curiosity with interesting declamatory moments.

However, having composed Act I, Musorgsky could not make up his mind to go on with *Marriage*. His thoughts turned to Pushkin's *Boris* . . . —NIKOLAI RIMSKY-KORSAKOV

III

Boris Godunov
1868 — 1872

"... *the friendly companionship in the home of Shestakova with Professor V. Nikolsky caused the creation of the grand opera* Boris Godunov, *based on a subject by the great Pushkin." Thus Musorgsky records (in No. 219) the inception of his best-known work.*

No sooner had Musorgsky conceived the idea of an opera on this subject than he received from his hostess the volume of Pushkin's works containing the historical drama of Boris Godunov, *with interleaved blank pages on which Musorgsky could sketch his libretto.*[1]

This work copy, now in the Russian Public Library, Leningrad, contains Musorgsky's text of the first version of his libretto (to the end of Act II) as well as the following notations, the only factual record, aside from the dating on the autograph scores, of Musorgsky's activity during this most satisfying period of his life.

At the close of the first period of this work on Boris Godunov *Musorgsky returned this working text to its donor with one more inscription on its first page:*

> *Here you have, dear Ludmila Ivanovna, the completion of the labors of which you have been witness.*
>
> > *27th January, 1871.*
> > MODESTE MUSORGSKY.

Underneath this inscription there is another, to the other firmest ally of Boris Godunov:

> *1874, 31 March, I transfer all rights in this book to Bach, i.e., Vladimir Vasilyevich Stasov.*
>
> > LUDMILA SHESTAKOVA.

---

[1] Gerald Abraham has demonstrated both the physical and artistic relationships between Pushkin's drama and Musorgsky's opera. This useful analysis was published in *Music and Letters*, January 1945.

58. *Title Page and Scenario of* Boris Godunov

BORIS GODUNOV

A MUSICAL PRESENTATION [Effaced]

AN OPERA

IN FOUR PARTS

By M. MUSORGSKY

Subject taken from the dramatic chronicle of the same name by Pushkin with the preservation of the greater part of his verses.

Composition of the opera and its instrumentation completed in July 1872 in Petrograd
M. Musorgsky.

N.B. Opera planned during the autumn of 1868, work begun in October 1868.—For this very work this little book was prepared by Ludmila Shestakova.

[Inscriptions and Stage Directions]

Prologue

[The scenario for the Prologue, first tableau, in the complete libretto, reads as follows:]
Courtyard of the Novodevichy Monastery, near Moscow, surrounded by a wall with turrets. On the right, near the middle of the stage, a projection, the great monastery gates under a wooden canopy. When the curtain rises, a little handful of people are assembled in the courtyard in front of the wall; their movements are languid, they walk lazily. The boyars cross the stage (headed by Prince Vasili Ivanovich Shuisky) and, exchanging bows with the people, make their way into the monastery. When they have disappeared, the people begin to stroll about the stage. Some, chiefly women, peer through the gates; others whisper, scratching their heads. The Bailiff enters; on seeing him in the gateway the people crowd closely together and stand motionless, the women—with their cheeks on the palms of their right hands, the men—with their hats in their hands, which are crossed on their bellies,

127

and with hanging heads. Curtain. The people crowd into the court-
yard. The Bailiff appears at the gates . . .[2]
[At the end of the tableau:] Music and text of the tableau finished
November 4, 1868, at Petrograd. M. Musorgsky.

[Complete scenario for the Prologue, second tableau:]
Square in the Moscow Kremlin. Directly opposite the audience, in the
background, the grand staircase of the Tzar's palace. Right, nearer the
proscenium, the people, kneeling, occupy the space between the
Uspensky Cathedral on the right and the Archangel Cathedral on
the left; the porches of the cathedrals are visible. The bells ring a
solemn peal. Curtain. Great chiming of bells on the stage. From the
grand staircase a solemn procession of boyars sets out for the Uspensky
Cathedral: headed by the bodyguards, streltzi, the boyars' children;
Prince Shuisky follows, with Monomakh's crown on a cushion; behind
him come boyars, Shchelkalov with the Tzar's staff, more streltzi. Behind these, the leading boyars, scribes, etc. The procession, passing
through the crowd, enters the Uspensky Cathedral. The streltzi line
the porch and the steps. The pealing of the bells continues. . . .
[at end of tableau:] The music and text of the first part finished 14
November 1868, at Petrograd. M. Musorgsky.[3]

ACT I

Scene 1: Night. Cell in the Chudov Monastery. Pimen is writing by
the light of a wick. Grigori sleeps . . .
[At end of scene:] The music and text of the tableau were finished
on 5 December, 1868, at Petrograd. M. Musorgsky.[4]
Scene 2: Inn on the Lithuanian frontier. At the spectators' right is a
door to a storeroom. Directly ahead is the entrance; a little to the left
a window. Curtain. The Hostess is darning an old house-jacket . . .
[There is no date on this scene, either in the piano score or in the
full orchestration.]

ACT II

The Tzar's chambers in the Moscow Kremlin. The sumptuous fur-
nishings of the Moscow Tzars. In the background at the audience's

---

[2] In the vocal score of 1874 these indications are reduced to: "Courtyard of
the Novodevichy Monastery, near Moscow. In the foreground the exit gates in
the Monastery wall, with a turret. People are loitering listlessly."
[3] Date on the full score: "Petrograd, 30 September, 1869. M. Musorgsky."
[4] Date on the full score: "Petrograd, 13 September, 1871. M. Musorgsky."

left, there is a globe and a small table, at which Fyodor is occupied with a volume of *The Book of the Great Map*. Right front, an armchair. Right, nearer the front, the nurse is engaged in some handiwork. Xenia sits at a little carved table. Curtain. Xenia, at the little table, looks at a portrait of the King of Denmark's son, kisses the portrait, weeps and laments . . .
[At end of act:] Finished 21 April, 1869, at Petrograd. M. Musorgsky.[5]

ACT III

Scene 1: The dressing-room of Maryna Mniszech in the Sandomierz castle. Maryna is at her toilet-table. Ruzia is dressing her hair. Maidens entertain Maryna with songs . . .
[At end of scene, in full score:] 10 February, 1872, at Petrograd. M. Musorgsky.
Scene 2: The castle of Mniszech at Sandomierz. Garden. Fountain. Moonlit night. Dmitri comes from the castle, thoughtfully . . .
[At end of scene, in full score:] 29 March, 1872, at Petrograd. M. Musorgsky.

ACT IV

The square in front of the Cathedral of Vasili the Blessed in Moscow. A crowd of impoverished people wanders about the stage. The women sit on the ground apart, a short distance away, in the direction of the side entrance to the Cathedral. Bailiffs frequently circulate through the crowd. Curtain. Enter a handful of men from the Cathedral; Mityukha is ahead . . .
[At end of scene:] On the night of 21–22 May, '69, at Petrograd. M. Musorgsky.[6]
Scene 1: The Granovitaya Reception Hall in the Moscow Kremlin. At the side, benches. At the right, the exit to the grand staircase, left, the entrance to the [Tzar's] chambers. Right, nearer the footlights, a table covered with purple velvet, on it writing materials. To the left, the Tzar's chair. Extraordinary meeting of the Council of Boyars. Curtain. On the left Shchelkalov enters from the chambers with a decree in his hand and bows to the boyars, who bow in return . . .
[Dated on the full score:] 15 December, 1869. M. Musorgsky.

---

[5] Date on full score of first version of this scene: "Petrograd, 18 October 1869. M. Musorgsky." Date on full score of second version of this scene: "11 January, 1872, at Petrograd. M. Musorgsky."
[6] This scene was never orchestrated by Musorgsky.

Scene 2: A forest glade near Kromy. At the right a rolling slope and behind this, in the distance, the walls of the town. From the slope, crossing the stage, is a road. Directly before the audience, a forest thicket. Near the slope a great tree stump. Night. Curtain. Cries of the crowd offstage. Onto the stage bursts, from the right of the slope, a crowd of tramps. In the crowd is the boyar Khrushchov, bound, in a torn cloak, without a hat. They seat Khrushchov on the stump . . . [Dated on the full score:] 23 June, 1872, at Petrograd. M. Musorgsky. [At end of volume:] Composition and scoring of the opera finished in July 1872, at Petrograd. M. Musorgsky.

58a. *VLADIMIR STASOV to HECTOR BERLIOZ,*[7] *Paris [Extract]*

October 4, 1868

. . . Tonight "Lohengrin" will be played for the first time at the Petersburg Opera. Possibly part of the audience will like this brutal, heavy-handed music. But *we all* do not believe that Wagner is a prophet: we hold that he marks a retrogression from the music of Weber. We find in him a lack of taste and measure, vulgarity, noisy scoring, no gift for the recitative, horrible modulations [8] . . .

On December 21, 1868, Musorgsky was appointed assistant head clerk in the Forestry Department of the Ministry of Agriculture.

Boris Tested

. . . From this winter of 1868 . . . fragments of the opera [*Boris Godunov*], followed by the whole work, were performed dozens of

[7] Balakirev's first action as permanent conductor of the Musical Society's concerts had been to invite Berlioz as guest conductor for the first half of the 1867–68 season. During this second visit to St. Petersburg Berlioz renewed the acquaintance he had made in 1847 with Vladimir Stasov, and after his return to Paris maintained an affectionate correspondence with him, writing him, for example, on August 21, 1868: "Je sens que je vais mourir, je ne crois plus à rien, je voudrais vous voir, vous me remonteriez·peut-être . . ." Stasov was well aware that an anti-Wagner attitude would not displease Berlioz, as the latter had rejoiced in Wagner's Paris debacle in 1860, greatly disliking both music and orchestration. The extract from Stasov's letter is quoted by Calvocoressi in his essay on Balakirev in *Masters of Russian Music.*

[8] Rimsky-Korsakov reports this event: "K. N. Lyadov conducted. Balakirev, Cui, Musorgsky and I occupied a loge with Dargomizhsky. *Lohengrin* called forth complete scorn from us, and an inexhaustible torrent of humor, ridicule and venomous caviling from Dargomizhsky."

times in the little circle of his comrade-composers. The delight, enthusiasm, and admiration were general; each of these talented men, while finding various defects in the opera, felt nevertheless that something big and new was being created before his eyes. In the last months of his life Dargomizhsky also heard some of the most striking bits: the first scene and the scene at the inn, and notwithstanding that at the moment he was engaged in the completion of his great work of genius, *The Stone Guest,* crown of his artistic career, with generous enthusiasm he freely repeated in the presence of all that Musorgsky "goes even further than I." At these musical gatherings Musorgsky usually did everything himself—the choruses, recitatives, ensembles, and the solo roles. For the female roles he had a wonderful helper in Al. Nik. Purgold; she performed the parts of Xenia, the Tzarevich, the Nurse, Maryna, the urchins who tease the Simpleton, and performed them with artistry, fire, passion, grace, fury, playfulness, and, above all, with simplicity and naturalness, closely resembling the incomparable renderings of Musorgsky himself. These trials of *Boris* took place in gatherings at the home of L. I. Shestakova, V. F. Purgold, and Al[exandra] Al. Khvostova . . . —VLADIMIR STASOV

58b. *VLADIMIR STASOV to DIMITRI STASOV [Extract]*

July 18, 1869

. . . Musorgsky has definitely finished *Boris Godunov* and nearly at the end he has Pimen's story about the appearance to him of the Tzarevich Dmitri—the story is so magnificent that it equals Finn's Ballad [in *Ruslan*], and the best places in the first and second acts of *Boris,* i.e., the people's scenes with the forced weeping and howling of the women [Prologue, Scene 1] and the scene at the inn with the police-officers . . .

59. *To MILI BALAKIREV*

[27 September, 1869]

DEAR MILI,

I regret very much that I can't be of any help to you: In the first place, I've had a severe cold since Wednesday, but that would be nothing—today I forced myself to go to the office, and consequently moreover would be able to go tomorrow to help you in our common cause. But the second reason is considerably more severe than a severe cold. I do not consider it necessary to lie, and so I speak out directly: Among a large company of people not at all known to me, I do not consider myself at all skilled enough to perform at the piano, and due to my being *out of practice,* particularly in playing Schumann's *Faust* [9]—I would be more of an embarrassment than a help to you. And that thought—of accompanying your chorus—is so repellent to me and it so alarms my brain, that if in your soul you should accuse me of a ridiculous caprice, even in such a case *I would not come*—although it would be heavy for me to bear the accusation of a ridiculous caprice. —Nadezhda Petrovna [Opochinina] said she wasn't home because she wasn't dressed, this is the arrangement she has established: Till two o'clock she is not at home to visitors—and today she planned to go out at three o'clock on various tiresome errands.

Firmly kiss you, dear, and I beg you not to impose on me any accusation for my refusal.

Your

MODESTE

I received an envelope with tickets for the quartet and symphony concerts of the *musical slum.*[10] I decided—at once to send back these tickets to the musical slum.—Demidov has gone out of his mind and is staying at *Stein's.*[11] He bit Rubinstein and at once landed at *Stein's.* —How sad.

60. *To KARL ALBRECHT, Moscow*

[December, 1869]

DEAR SIR,

KARL KARLOVICH:

Our indirect acquaintance must begin on my part by my begging your pardon for my tardy reply. The fact is, that with full sympathy

---

[9] The church scene from Schumann's secular oratorio *Faust* was performed by soloists, chorus and orchestra at a concert of the Free Music School on October 26, 1869. Platonova sang the part of Gretchen, Kondratyev the part of the Evil Spirit. Balakirev had asked Musorgsky to accompany choral rehearsals of this work.

[10] After the break between Balakirev and the Imperial Russian Musical Society, the Society attempted a friendly gesture toward the members of the "nationalist" group by sending them all free season tickets for their symphonic and chamber music concerts. For contrast to Musorgsky's reaction to this gesture, we have Borodin's happy gratitude for the tickets, expressed in a letter to his wife.

[11] Grigori Alexandrovich Demidov was inspector of music classes at the St. Petersburg Conservatory. Mme. Stein operated a nursing home for mental cases on Vasilyevsky Island.

for your undertaking,[12] I wished to answer you properly, that is, with the sending of the choral works, but misfortune intervened.—And the misfortune is that I can't control my time according to my wishes —and I have no prepared choral works.

In any case, I beg you to be assured, dear sir, that at the first opportunity I shall hasten to fulfill your proposal, and your belief need not be shaken because the fulfillment of my promise is guaranteed by the purpose, which lies at the base of your undertaking and which cannot but be close to Russian musicians.

With my sincere respects,

Yours,

M. MUSORGSKY

60a. NIKOLAI RIMSKY-KORSAKOV to MODESTE MUSORGSKY

Saturday

If I'm not mistaken, it's the 13th of February [1870]

FRIEND MODESTE.

I miss you, because it's so long since I've seen you; you didn't come to the Purgolds on Tuesday for some reason, and I thought that perhaps on Wednesday you would come to the Borodins, but again you weren't there. The former, the Purgolds, having grown used to seeing you at their home every Tuesday, are disturbed that you may be ill, and the latter, the Borodins, have also not seen you for a long while. This evening I may go around to the Borodins, couldn't you come too, and if we don't see each other there, do write me whether you are planning to be at Cui's tomorrow, for I too would go there for dinner and would bring *The Stone Guest*. Address me at the Naval Academy at the apartment of the Chief of the Academy.

Your

N. RIMSKY-KORSAKOV

"Musolyanin"

. . . My recollection of Musorgsky dates from when I was seven years old—or, rather, I was seven years old when I began to notice

---

[12] On October 28 Tchaikovsky had written Balakirev, asking for the full names of the members of his circle for the following purpose: "Your fervent admirer Albrecht plans to publish a collection of choral pieces, written in the numeral system. For this purpose he has composed a circular letter to be sent to all Russian composers."

his appearance at our house; he had probably been a frequent visitor before then, though I was unaware of it. But all at once he came into the circle of our child life as "Musoryanin," as our elders called him, and as we children [18] began to call him, deciding that this must be his real name. He came very often to see us, both in the city and also at our *dacha* in Zamanilovka, near Pargolovo, and as he wasn't hypocritical with us and never talked to us in that false way that grown-up people who are friends of the family usually talk to children—we soon not only grew attached to him, but even eventually counted him as one of ourselves. My sister Zinochka and I were particularly impressed by the fact that he, in greeting us, always kissed our hand as if we were grown-up ladies, saying "Good day, *young lady*" or "Your hand, *young lady*"—strange and astonishing it seemed to us, and amusing, so we came to talk with him quite freely, as with an equal. My brothers, too, were quite at ease with him and used to tell him all the events of their lives, though the youngest was not yet able to pronounce his name properly, but said "Musolyanin," and when Musorgsky came to visit us, he would call out to us, from some way off: "Musolyanin has come." The musical scenes "Naughty Puss," "By Hobby-Horse to Yukki," and "The Dream" (this was one of Zinochka's tales—apparently not published, and I am not sure whether it exists in manuscript, though Musorgsky often played it on the piano), and a fourth scene from child life ["A Children's Quarrel"] were all based on our child stories.

As I was the eldest, Musorgsky would often talk to me on "serious subjects." Thus he was the first to explain to me how the stars in the sky were arranged in constellations, and how they all had their own names; he taught me where to find the Great Bear, Cassiopeia, Orion, Canis Major, and Sirius. I remember, too, a talk we had one New Year's Eve, when he explained to me—up till then I had never thought about it—why the New Year began on the next day and why this is celebrated in the middle of winter and not in autumn (for, as the child sees it, the new year begins in the autumn, when they return to town from the *dacha*, and ends in the spring; as for the summer—that is a thing apart, outside the year).

Musorgsky often visited us at our *dacha* in Zamanilovka, where it was quite customary for him to take part in all the incidents of our life; he was present when my little two-year-old brother, who was being bathed in the sun, in the courtyard, gave a scream and ran off stark naked across the sands, to be enticed back only by a promise of strawberries; and Musorgsky would later reproduce this comic scene and would mimic our brother, demanding the promised "berries-berries! . . ."—Varvara Stasova-Komarova

---

[18] The children of Dimitri and Polyxena Stasov (at this time) were: Varvara, Zinaida (Zinochka, Zizi), Andrei (Andrushka), Boris.

61. *To VLADIMIR NIKOLSKY*

Tuesday 19 May [1870?] [14]

Dear little friend *dyainka*, I am enclosing herewith the tomes with many *rémerciements*, especially for Vygovsky and for Troitzky.[15]— The Forestry Dept. continues to interpolate corrections of the Russian language and to write introductions, and plenty of them, etc., but I keep *Me* invulnerable and continue to write as it sounds best to me. Perchance *dyainka* dear, weary and harassed as he is, has lain down to snore a little, therefore I send him a short scrawl and taking advantage of a casual chance, I heartily request the following of him:

(1) Don't pay any attention to my request, because it really isn't fair:

(2) Do pay attention to it, because it is fair, and the substance of the request is the following: V[otre] S[ervice?] tomorrow the brains of the small Opochinin [16] will have to stand trembling before *dyainka*, and as I have become quite fond of this small thing, i.e., the above-mentioned youngster, I beg you, during the test of his brains, to give him *a little piece of your warmth* *—*if he's worth it;*—I hope, however, that he will be worth it: the youngster is not devoid of a sense of humor—and he has originality, and this is a good thing.

I scare myself with what I have written! Do I understand *dyainka* properly?—In any case, I deign to kiss him, my *dyainka*, most firmly —and this I'm *not at all scared* to do.

MODESTE

* Musorgsky's note: I mean—don't scare him too much.

---

[14] Musorgsky played with this date, rearranging the letters to create nonsense words whose flavor does not survive translation.

[15] The first of these books is *The History of the Vygovsky Hermitage,* as recorded by Ivan Filippov. If Musorgsky was in the habit of keeping borrowed books for two years, the Troitzky book may be Matvei Troitzky's work on German psychology (see p. 120). It is more likely that this refers to a work by Ivan Troitzky, *The History of the Schism.* In this case, the mention of "Vygovsky and Troitzky," being both concerned with the period of the dissenters, would then be a remarkable forecast of Musorgsky's next major work, announced two years later: *Khovanshchina.*

[16] One of the child relatives of his hosts, the Opochinins, was apparently to be given an examination by Nikolsky at the Alexandrovsky Lycée.

61a. *LUDMILA SHESTAKOVA to VLADIMIR NIKOLSKY* [Extract]

June 1, 1870

. . . On Sunday evening I was at the Purgolds, where it was not at all boring, and I was taken home from there at one o'clock in the morning, not only by our company but also by the hosts and their guests; there were almost twenty of us and, truly, hearing the talk and laughter, the residents along those streets must have thought us a crowd of drunks. Yesterday I had the two Purgolds, Korsinka, Mili, Bach, your *dyainka* [Musorgsky], Paleček and Petrov. There was lots of music and singing and I felt fine. But it was too bad that you didn't hear . . . what your *dyainka* was doing with the Purgolds, what he said, was simply awful; and later in *mezza voce* in their presence he whispers to me quietly (in Bach's manner): "You can do anything you want with these people. They won't understand"; he was awfully prankish, he simply astonished me; I had never seen him like this before . . .

62. *To ALEXANDRA and NADEZHDA PURGOLD, Pillnitz near Dresden*

18 June
1870 Petrograd
On the very *Thursday*

To Doña Anna-Laura and to the charming Orchestra, greetings.

He is grateful, he writes, he sends [17]—he long since risked his neck, because risk is necessary.—Thus the Seminarist is abandoned to the printer's sacrificial altar.—So be it!

He is very grateful—he asks the dear Orchestra to keep the proof-reading in mind; he asks this especially because he is assured of the Orchestra's good and even excellent memory—of her musical memory.

He is extremely grateful and asks to take care of the sending of the sacrificed "Seminarist" to his address, notwithstanding the censor, because in the above-mentioned "Seminarist" there is nothing forbid-

---

[17] Note on the envelope: *Einliegend fünfzehn Thaler.* This was to pay for the printing abroad of Musorgsky's song "The Seminarist," which the Purgold sisters were to watch over during their trip abroad that summer. The printer was to be W. Beinicke, in Leipzig. The manuscript of "The Seminarist" is dated "27 Sept. 1866," and the dedication is to Ludmila Ivanovna Shestakova. On one of the rare copies of the censored first edition, a presentation inscription to Arseni Golenishchev-Kutuzov contains this remark: "I did this one morning as I woke, in '66, beginning only with the rhythm."

den, and furthermore as—I am sure that they will know how to take care of it.

I have composed *Penny Paradise;* [18] a little thing that provokes hearty laughter; when you arrive you will see it and you can hear it. —Doña Anna-Laura who is so kind to the *small animals* (the Berlin Aquarium), will, I hope, be even more kind to the *large* animals.[19]— Regarding the dear Orchestra, as she is already slightly habituated to my musical monstrosities, she will charmingly depict, in assisting me, the *large animals* which, it is acknowledged, I have depicted with all possible love and warmth, which is so characteristic of my musical monstrosities (sic) . . .

Korsinka has sailed away to the Finnish shore. Before his departure from Petrograd, I was at his place and sensed something wonderful. This was none other than that there is a little feature in Korsinka's talent, that he has perceived the dramatic essence of musical drama. —He has cooked up history splendidly with a chorus of the *Veche* [in *Pskovityanka*] just as it ought to be done: I even laughed in my delight.—Mili goes off to Muscovy in a few days, and I will deliver your bow to the remaining gang of bandits. By the way, the word *bow* reminds me that the charming Orchestra sent a bow to the musical mischief-maker; I am very grateful

[Our dear Orchestra]

and I deign to bow low back to her.

As you have urged me to answer, Doña Anna-Laura, I have hurried my reply, and so I will execute in writing, your dear commissions (the number of Ludmila Ivanovna's house and what German things you should sing) following hard upon this epistle. But why am I a mocker

[18] The full text of this large-scale musical satire is given in Letter 64. In answering Stasov's letter describing Musorgsky's performance of *Penny Paradise,* Nadezhda writes from Pillnitz, July 11: "I'm already familiar with part of the new thing by Musorgsky that you speak about. Before our departure he played us all of it that had been done. And almost everything but Serov was done . . ."

[19] The distinguished personages of St. Petersburg's musical world who are portrayed in *Penny Paradise.*

[20] This is Don Juan's phrase in Dargomizhsky's *Stone Guest:* "Dear Leporello!"

—I don't understand—I am modest, simple and courteous,[21] only not bashful—this would be going too far.

I thank you firmly once again and firmly press your hand. I beg you to give my sincere greetings to your people.

MODESTE MUSORGSKY

P.S. If Vladimir Fyodorovich [Purgold] is in Teplitz[-Schönau], do me the favor of telling me; I'd like to let him know about the cooking of the *penny-paradise* and would like to do this because there is in me something that very warmly responds to his interest in my musical pranks.

63. *To ALEXANDRA and NADEZHDA PURGOLD, Pillnitz near Dresden*

20 June, 1870. Petrograd

To Doña Anna-Laura and to the dear Orchestra, once again greetings.

I execute the commissions: The number of the house in which Ludmila Ivanovna lives is 30, the house belongs, or rather, belonged to Count Olsufev. Of the German things sing the ones you like, because it's better for you to make the choice *accidentally,* than for me—at a distance: *accidentally,* for I am very doubtful about German vocal music in general and modern German music in particular.—German men and women sing like roosters, imagining that the more their mouths gape and the longer they hold their notes—*portamento,* the more feeling they show.—To speak harshly, *Kartoffel, Kirschensuppe, Milch* and *Tchernickensuppe* do not have an especially good influence on the power of feeling and particularly on artistic feeling, and for my taste the Germans, moving from their leather fried in pork-fat to the seven-hour operas of Wagner, offer nothing attractive *for me.* On the other hand, the Germans who left the *Vaterland's* leather and its rooster-stretching, far behind—they have always interested me, but such Germans don't write romances and lieder.—However, as a curiosity, take Robert Franz—he alone could quiet one's desire to eat that German cloying-*Vaterlandish* musical cookery. I say all this in envy and for the sake of mockery, but I do not envy the Germans and I do not laugh at them, because one can't laugh at that which is boring, but may only avert one's face. You yourself know: the greatest

---

[21] From *The Classicist.* See page 104.

German geniuses, Beethoven, Weber and Schumann (each in his own way) were poor vocal composers, including the characteristic and yet, in many ways, fresh Weber. The Germans sing as they speak, but they speak *à faire tonner le gosier,* but when they compose for singing, then they do not think of the *gosier,* forcibly cramming human thought into the frame of a preconceived musical phrase.—These are a people, theoretical in music, too, who with nearly each step fall into abstraction. You, educated on the Russian soil of realism, will not (I hope) like the German roosters' *Sehnsuchten.*

I considered it necessary to speak this whole diatribe to you, because I was astonished, or rather, perplexed, by your question, what German things to sing: sing all or nothing—the result will be the same;—didn't you really know this yourself, and if you knew, then why, for the sake of fun, did you ask me, Doña Anna-Laura? Our dear Orchestra will be displeased when you read her this epistle. The Orchestra is by preference theoretical, and doesn't wish and never wished to see nonsense that is beyond musical beauty. I hope to receive a few lines from you and from the dear Orchestra. It's so easy to do this: take the pen and write, of course previously dipping the pen into ink or some such outstanding liquid—for example, coffee, of which so much is drunk in chicory Germany.

And meanwhile I firmly press your hands, Doña Anna-Laura and dear Orchestra, and ask you to write, and to those of your folks who know me, I bow.

MODESTE MUSORGSKY

64. *To VLADIMIR NIKOLSKY*

28 June. Petrograd [1870]

Because we thirst for you—greetings, little friend *dyainka,* and with a firm kiss—more greetings. And in your absence we have committed the sin of composing *Penny Paradise,* and it so happens that this *Penny Paradise,* as in a mirror, reflects the infamy of extremely important musical persons: and they, the darlings, are diversely named. And how they are called and why they are called, so and not otherwise—we beg you to listen. First of all among them, appears myself, a slave of the Lord, your own, *dyainka,* to lift the veil of *paradisiac* charms, causing said persons to pass in review, each with an appropriate accompaniment of musical harmonies—but never mind: it turns out thus, and I dare say it *turns out all right*.—Because of the great benefit to me of my friend *dyainka's* impartial judgment and calmed by the goodhearted thought that said *dyainka* is accustomed to read *all sorts of hodge-podge* (because he has a vocation for it and can read with sufficient patience), I take the impertinent liberty of presenting my *paradisiac* invention graphically:

PENNY PARADISE [22]

Prelude (I myself)
    Hey, honorable folks,
    Open your eyes,
    Come here—take a look,
    Enjoy the show—marvel
    At these greatest of men
    At the musical leaders,
          They're all here!
    A rivulet ran high
    And parted into three streams:
    One stream ran by the woods,
    Another turned onto the sands,
    And the third—under the mill,
    Under the elm wheel,
    Under the grindstone itself.
    Turn on, my wheel,
    Grind on, millstone.
    Grind out the truth
    About these dashing fellows,
    These musical swaggerers.
          They are displayed!

    No. 1. (Zaremba)

Just down from the clouds,
A denizen of fogs eternal,
To us poor mortals he reveals
The meaning of mysterious things,
Of the most commonplace things.

---

[22] At the end of another copy of this text, presented to Stasov, there is this note: "All phrases, enclosed in pot-hooks [quotation marks] and underlined [here italicized], are the authentic words of each of the leaders.—Musorgsky."

"With God's help."
He teaches that *"the minor key—*
Is our original sin,"
And that *"the major key—*
Is our sins' redemption."
Thus, floating in the clouds
With the celestial birds,
He showers us mortals
With incomprehensible verbs
(*"With God's help"*).—

Music from Handel's
oratorio "Maccabaeus" [23]

No. 2. (Rostislav—F. M. Tolstoy)

Behind him comes a-hopping
Fif, youth eternal,
Fif, the restless,
Fif, the mediator,
Fif, the all-sided.—
All his life he's whirled,
Whirled until he's dizzy:
Hearkens to no one,
And cannot help it,
Listens but to Patti,
Patti he adores,
Patti he hymnifies:
"O Patti, Patti,
O Pa-pa-Patti,
Wonderful Patti,
Marvelous Patti,
O Patti, Patti,
O Ti-ti Patti.
Wonderful Patti,
Glorious Patti!
But why, O Patti!
A flaxen wig—
Flaxen?
O Patti, Patti,

A salon valse [24]

[23] A paraphrase of two choruses from *Judas Maccabaeus: Sing unto God* and *See, the Conqu'ring Hero Comes!*
[24] Based partly on the traditional gipsy tune, *Dark Eyes.*

O Pa-pa Patti,
Wonderful, marvelous,
Dearest and glorious,
Pa-pa, Ti-ti,
Ti-ti, Papa,
O Pa-pa, Titi,
O Titi, Pa-pa!"

No. 3. (Famintzin A.)

Here comes trudging step by step
A grievously wounded Infant,
(Pale and sombre and exhausted).
"*Wash away the stain,*" he begs,
—A quite indecent stain.
Once upon a time, he (too) was innocent ⎤
And charmed his elders. By obedience,   ⎪
Dear, bashfully childish prattle   ⎬ One of his "pieces" [25]
Many a heart then he won.   ⎦
But that time has passed. All of a sudden
Feeling a great will power, he saw the foe,
—He crossed swords with him and fell! . . .
"*A moral blow*" the poor wretch suffered
—A great blow to his will-power! . . .

No. 4. (A. N. Serov)

Here he is—Titan!   ⎤
Ti-tan, Ti-tan!   ⎪
See him race and chase and stir,   ⎪
Rage and fume and blow and threaten, ⎪
Shaggy, frightening . . .   ⎬ From the glorious
On Bucephalus Teutonic,   opera *Rogneda*
Run down by the Zukunftists   [themes from Acts I
With a bundle of thunderbolts,   ⎬ and III]
In a printer's shop prepared: ⎪
Quick, an armchair for the genius!— ⎪
The genius has no place to sit,   ⎦

[25] The Famintzin "piece" has not been identified. The "stain" is an article by Stasov, "Musical Liars," attacking Serov, Rostislav, Famintzin, and "Mr. P."

Do invite him to your dinner!— [26]
The genius dearly loves a *speech*,
Down with the whole Directorate!—
He alone will replace them all.
(Adorned with a wreath
Put on dashingly awry,
Made of dry laurel leaves
Rented from the shop,
Here's the creator of the great era,
The Musico-All-Russian one!
He alone leads art,
Aside from him there's no perfection,
He alone fills all places,
Encompassing, creating, preserving.) [27]
There he goes in his simplicity
In his loftiest simplicity,
His curls tossing, blowing.
There he bubbles!—There he goes,
And goes and goes and goes,
Straight to them, straight
To the leaders bold;
This Titan, this Titan
In his Titanic pride,
O scandal, O scandal,
Into their company he fell,
And thereupon grew wrathful,
With rage assailed them all,
And beat them all full sore.
Oh how he beat them, how he beat them . . .
And he beat and beat them
But a thunder clap was heard . . .
And darkness fell,

[26] During the last visit of Berlioz to St. Petersburg, his birthday on December 11 (N.S.), 1867, had been celebrated with a supper at which Berlioz was made an honorary member of the Imperial Russian Musical Society. The supper was arranged by Berlioz' admirers, among whom the foremost were the young composers and the staff of the Free Music School. As Serov had not disguised his dislike for Berlioz, he was not invited—an action that Serov interpreted as a public insult.

[27] The parenthesized lines are omitted from the final text.

"A nocturnal mist did tremble."
And they knelt in sacred awe,
The denizen of clouds, and Fif, and Infant,
And this proud Tita-tan.

    And in a wreath of rose and lily
    And camellia white as snow
    Appeared the Muse.
    And an aroma was wafted . . .
    The leaders calmed down,
    And chanted their hymnal prayer:

    Hymn: in place of No. 5

O, Most Glorious Euterpe
O, great Goddess,
Send us, do, some inspiration,
Lend life to our infirmities!
And with the golden rain of Olympus
Irrigate our arid meadows.
O, blonde-tressed Goddess,
Heaven-dwelling Muse!
We will praise thee for eternity
We'll sing of thee on sounding zithers!

Music "From under the Oak and the Elm" *grandioso* [from *Rogneda*]

The dedication is to the very great general Bach with this inscription "Of thine own have we given thee." [28] He is so pleased that he kissed me repeatedly, which is a rare thing with him, but to me, slave of the Lord, it was pleasing. Well now, little friend *dyainka*, pass judgment on me, *cautious buffoon* that I am, and we shall put this picture on the press—let the leaders rejoice.—Now I beg you to proceed to the next page: I have read your notes on the *History of the Russian language* [29] with great interest as well as with great benefit. The exposition is clear, compact, and if the boys will cram into their brains what appears through these notes, they will be blessed and the Russian people will thank you for such a preparation of Russian brains—(in a mental and not a kitchen sense, dear *dyainka*). I for one,

---

[28] I Chronicles 29:14, "All things come of thee, O Lord, and of thine own have we given thee."

[29] This appears to be a syllabus for Nikolsky's students, rather than a published work.

having read the notes, have sensed the sound of a native string—the appeal of the vivid folk-speech of Russia, of that mighty word which appears to be just a hint—but actually says everything.—And there undoubtedly is a need to awaken the natural resources of the crippled Russian speech; undoubtedly, too, with the proper use of Russian speech, Russian thought will also recover. Modern Russian speech is like a person wearing high heels and tight shoes, making his toenails grow all crooked, forming excrescences of proud flesh. These excrescences must be removed and the patient must be given bark sandals (even temporarily); otherwise instead of a human gait there will be a hobble.—Recently I chanced to read something about Russian warriors—particularly those of Novgorod and Pskov—naturally I mean to say ancient warriors. What a colorful imagery of terms (terms still used in our army) and what an angry, tasty, original *terminology*.

What a longing I've always had for those native fields that I know and *dyainka* knows—no wonder that in childhood I loved to listen to the peasants and to test myself with their songs.

A. P. Op[ochinin] is reading your notes, following his wise rule that one must never stop studying; he devotes much attention to the notes.—I won't go into details about your work, dear *dyainka;* one must understand more than I do for that, but whatever I learned from them and whatever conclusions I drew appeared very tasty to me, and a tasty dish is always followed by a kiss, therefore . . .

Yours,

Dyainka

Write to me, my own, to the [Engineers'] Castle, to me—apt. of the Opochinins.

64a. *VLADIMIR STASOV to NADEZHDA PURGOLD, Pillnitz near Dresden [Extract]*

Spb. July 9, 1870

. . . After your departure we continue to assemble at Ludmila's and you know what is played there more than anything else? No, you don't know—it's an entirely new thing by Musoryanin, straight from the oven, but so wonderful that it's impossible to tell you! When I set him this theme I never imagined that it would turn out to this extent. This is *Penny Paradise* . . . a magnificent caricature and it's true that there has never been anything like it in music heretofore. However, you know that in originality and inventiveness Musoryanin outstrips everyone and is simply a genius. Even your *idealist* Balakirev, against whose grain Musoryanin's *realistic* music goes, agrees with this . . .

65. *To ALEXANDRA and NADEZHDA PURGOLD, Pillnitz near Dresden*

Petrograd
13 July
1870

To hostile Doña Anna-Laura and to the dear Orchestra who makes *lunga pausa*, greeting, notwithstanding Doña Anna-Laura's and the dear Orchestra's imperturbable silence. Ludmila Ivanovna delivered to me in detail your fit of fury, Doña Anna-Laura, and here is my reply to it:

"I am an enemy of advice and a friend of conference."

I ask you to arrange the title-page of "The Seminarist" according to your own kind judgment, but preferably with simplicity—I love that as much as I love conference.

At present, when Prussia and others, and at this immediate present, when France without any others, intend to grapple with each other,[30] the position of the "musical priestesses" intrigues me.

I imagine that the very dear, although capricious, "priestesses" are contemplating the unknown quantity—who will beat whom? And having such a thought, I do not doubt that the outcome of this question is slightly disturbing to the "priestesses" and disturbs because the "priestesses" are unable to determine the outcome, because, strictly speaking, no one, aside from those contenders, can decide it: I think I have deliberated truly.—You must be surrounded by the tragic scene of war preparations, a scene of "sacrificial victims" always as innocent as sheep, if these latter are really innocent.—Danger threatens the *Vaterland*, which means that the limbs of the *Vaterland* must be inflamed with the zeal to kill men—and the limbs are inflamed till amputation.—From the other side the *grrrande nation* [France], stung by the wise Schönhausen serpent [Bismarck] and the

---

[30] If M. dated his letter by the Russian calendar, these stages of the Franco-Prussian crisis had already been reached: German mobilization on July 15, and French declaration of war on July 19. Russia's benevolent neutrality was guaranteed by Gorchakov.

action of the serpent's poison, appears to have the same zeal for killing men—there also is an inflammation of the limbs and a straining toward amputation—the result will be that clinical experts will be called, and the newspapers will write "war."

I've been to the Director: he said that this year they can't produce anything new, however they might send for me in the middle of August or at the beginning of September to frighten them with *Boris*.[31]

That's all: I am "an enemy of advice" really because in my humble opinion each man is an individual, and as such, has much that is distinctive to him alone. Consequently, again in my humble opinion, conference, that is, the exchange of ideas and viewpoints, is the best soil for free acquisition of that which is called advice. In my letter I said what I thought, and I *conferred* with an independent nature independently.

However, I firmly press the hand, throbbing with rage, of Doña Anna-Laura and the immobile extended hand in *lunga pausa* of the dear Orchestra.

MODESTE MUSORGSKY

66. *To NIKOLAI RIMSKY-KORSAKOV*

23 July, '70
Petrograd

Little friend Korsinka, greetings . . .

Cesare tells me that *The Stone Guest* is to be staged this season without fail [32]—such is Gedeonov's wish. The financial end of the business, evidently, has already been clarified and the agreement has been drawn up; however, you will hear about this from Cesare himself, but I am afraid that I will misinterpret something and represent myself as an *old-woman–newspaper*.—So we shall soon hear "The Guest" in your charming instrumentation and we shall see *The Stone Guest* in the *stony* performances of our artists.—Besides Petrov,[33] a superior *ace*, I have no hopes, as you know, for any of the others.—In spite of

---

[31] This half-promise by Stepan Gedeonov was not kept until February 1871, when *Boris Godunov* was officially submitted to the Theater Committee.

[32] According to the wish of Dargomizhsky, who died on January 5, 1869, before completing his *Stone Guest*, Cui completed the two unfinished scenes, and Rimsky-Korsakov scored the entire opera.

[33] Who was to sing the role of Leporello. Kommissarzhevsky was Don Juan; Platonova, Doña Anna; Abarinova, Doña Laura; Melnikov, Don Carlos.

my expectation of a sad production (in the main) of Dargomizhsky's *swan-song*, I am sure that an extraordinary stir will be produced by the production of *The Stone Guest*. What a *Babel and a confusion of tongues* there will be! And maybe it's good that this confusion is taking place while Dargomizhsky is among his ancestors, because although he expressed a wonderful energy and perseverance in his musical activity, pursuing his desired artistic aims, as a man, Dargomizhsky belonged to the people of the 40's; consequently, the perplexity of the *public souls* regarding his "Guest" would find in him a painful reflection, and maybe even our company would not be able to save him from a new moral downfall,*—who knows? Dargomizhsky grew embittered extraordinarily fast and an acid was distilled from his bitterness, yielding slowly to treatment. Taken to his ancestors (although, in my opinion, far prematurely), Dargomizhsky stands at the peak as an artist-genius, and in his impregnable position no dirty gossip can cling to him there, and for an influence on the course of musical matters, this item is very important. Confidence, bravery and perseverance—that must be our motto and this *should have been* Dargomizhsky's motto, because he has contributed something to art which no one before him suspected, and which in his time and even since is not fully recognized for its future possibilities. Thus must one *smash* through, because this something *is;* meaning: confidence, bravery, and perseverance, and the lack of these was his sickness.

I've been at Pargolovo twice and yesterday I played my *pranks* before a large audience. As regards the peasants [34] in *Boris*, some found it to be *bouffe* (!), others perceived *tragedy*.—*Penny Paradise* produced roars of laughter, but many were perplexed by the inn scene in *Boris*.—By the way, I also went to Gedeonov: he was firm but just, and I was firm but just; the result—I am to be summoned some time after August 15 (?), but *They* cannot stage anything new this year.— How is the work going on *Pskovityanka?* I ask because [I know] the instrumentation of *The Stone Guest* is already shaped and is therefore only in the process of being set down on paper, which won't hinder the brains with their strolls through the land of Pskov and

* Musorgsky's note: A great brake on the propaganda of art during the lifetime of an artistic worker.

[34] Apparently the opening scene, before Novodevichy Monastery. The Kromy scene did not yet exist at this time and it would be difficult to interpret the scene before the Cathedral of Vasili the Blessed as "bouffe."

bumping into Vanka the Terrible.—Please write, little friend Korsinka, I thirst greatly for your missives.—Ludmila Ivanovna is ailing
and feels sad—*mauvais!* I have been dropping in to see her, but it
doesn't help: I think it's difficult now for her to write you. Mili had
a consultation about his ear in Jericho, but now I think he is all right.
I *don't correspond* with the chemical brigadier [Borodin] and I don't
know where he now drinks his tea. I have news from the Purgolds—
the proofs of "The Seminarist" are already read; I have prepared the
rest of the songs [35] and the penny-paradise for the press.—Firmly kiss
you, little friend. Write me.

MODESTE

66a. *VLADIMIR STASOV to MODESTE MUSORGSKY*

Tuesday, 26 July, '70

I send you a sketch of the libretto for *Bobyl*.[36] I will be very glad if
this thing proves useful to you. And it seems to me, that here are
types, humor, and poetry, and even tragedy—enough of everything,
and the tasks are exactly fitted to your nature. I'm going to Pargolovo
on Friday evening or Saturday morning. This means that, if you find
it necessary, you can let me know before then, personally or by letter,
of any remarks or questions you may have. It seems to me that it would
be best of all for you to stop in on *Thursday evening:* I shall be home
with Meyer, your new and unexpected *admirateur.*[37] But however, as
you see fit. Till we meet.

Your V. S.

[The sketched scenario follows.]

---

[35] In 1871, along with *Penny Paradise,* there were printed several of Musorgsky's
songs which he had long since composed: "Cradle Song" (1865), "The Goat"
(1867), "The Little Orphan Girl" (1868), "Children's Song" (1868), and "Yeremushka's Cradle Song" (1868).

[36] A *bobyl* is a recluse—but not necessarily a hermit. In Stasov's libretto, his
bobyl is accused of poaching on some private forest preserves. Did Stasov hope
to catch the interest of a composer part of whose government job was the prose-
cution of poachers on state lands? The origin of this opera project is described
by Stasov in the following extract.

[37] Alexander Vasilyevich Meyer was a lively character in this era's intellectual
life in spite of the fact that his only concrete claim to fame was as the brother
of the doctor who was the original of the Dr. Werner in Lermontov's *Hero of
Our Times,* and in spite of being blind for his last thirty years of life. He was a
friend of the whole Stasov family and he and Musorgsky became great friends.
Musorgsky once referred to him as "Alexander-Gottfried-Heinrich-Karl-Max-

66b. *VLADIMIR STASOV to DIMITRI STASOV and POLYXENA STASOVA* [Extracts]

July 29, 1870

. . . Yes, by the way, Lady Paulina, we spent the day of your *bénéfice* [Polyxena's birthday—on July 22] in a splendid manner: the Hartmanns [88] came to the *dacha* in the morning . . . Musorgsky arrived for dinner and in the evening he sang *so*, that all the ladies and girls applauded him and he had a sort of triumph. I recalled the days of Glinka, he himself sitting down at the piano. Since then I haven't seen anyone give such a *unanimous* impression to everyone without exception. It was so hot that Musorgsky sang the whole time in a white Russian blouse of mine.[39] But there was something that amazed me more than everyone's enthusiasm: the other day Musorgsky was at my place on the Mokhovaya on a matter relating to his opera [*Boris*]. Meyer was there and I made Musorgsky sing all his best things: well, what do you know, Mr. Meyer, the driest and most wooden of persons, as anti-poetic as a shriveled mummy, suddenly went into raptures and declared that this is the best of all music in the world (with the exception, of course, of the Italians). So more than ever I say that Zukunftsmusik is not Wagner, but Dargomizhsky and Musorgsky.

. . . One more last piece of news—musical news. Musoryanin definitely wished to get to work on an opera, but hadn't been able to find a subject; he even tried, on Cui's suggestion, to decide on [Ostrovsky's] "Sin and Misery [Visit All]," but somehow nothing came of it. Then we both happened to speak about this matter and I offered to concoct a libretto. Suddenly there came to my mind, I don't know why—the plot of a piece that Paulina gave me to read this spring. I immediately began to tell this to Musoryanin, extempore, right off, with the changes and inserts which I began to visualize, and Musorgsky was very pleased. Next day, at Cherkesov's [Library] I obtained the book, and reread it very attentively, finishing it by night, and immediately, as I was falling asleep, laid out the whole plan in my mind,

---

Franz-Otto-Hans-Friedrich von Meyer." His "new and unexpected" admiration for Musorgsky's music is described in the following extract. It was Meyer who gave Stasov the rank of *"généralissime."*

[88] Victor Hartmann was an original and congenial architect and designer. His concern for "national" sources for his art made him a firm ally of Stasov and the Balakirev Circle.

[39] Musorgsky's description of this evening is on p. 148.

and next morning wrote out the entire libretto (six whole pages), us for a plot which I trust will play a rather important role in Rus- and Musorgsky is to give me, today or tomorrow, his definite answer, whether or not he accepts this thing, and if it's *yes*, then in what shape it's to be. So, dear Lady Paulina, the Russian stage will be obliged to sian music. You've probably long since guessed what the piece was: *Hans and Grete* by Spielhagen. We're calling the opera *Bobyl*. But I've made *tremendous* changes and inserts, so actually only one of the original motifs, with the gun in the forest, has been kept; it is self-understood that the Landgraf and Landgrafina (at the end) have been transformed into [Russian] landowners in some distant prov- ince . . .

August 20, 1870

. . . I've lots of news . . . Musorgsky has already begun the *divi- nation scene* of his new opera: it's simply a miracle . . .[40]

67. *To VLADIMIR STASOV*

18 August, 1870

Being extremely fearful (as you know) of the little musical sins of my cookery, it may be that I should never have decided *to print*, within my lifetime, the damned "Seminarist" and I acknowledge you, my dear, together with Ludmila Ivanovna, as the cause of its appear- ance in public, as you (and one other good man A. P. Op[ochinin]) were able to electrify me with warm words.

I deem it useful to describe for you the procession of the above- mentioned "Seminarist" through the fires of Gehenna. This prodigal

---

[40] Later, in writing of *Khovanshchina*, Stasov said: "Much more complex and profound is the figure of the old-time landowner, portrayed by Musorgsky in his Prince Ivan Khovansky . . . This old man, sometimes kind and placid, sometimes fierce and evil and merciless; proud of his ancestry and of his unlimited power, raising storms over trifles in his own harem, irascible to the point of rage, with limited brains, looking on everything around him as born into slavish servitude. It was this very figure of a landowner that Musorgsky planned to use in his opera *Bobyl*—the scenario of which [by Stasov] has been preserved in his papers and about which we both had many discussions soon after *Boris Godunov*. A few things were already composed for this. The scene of Marfa's divination for Prince Golitzin in Khovanshchina was taken directly from the divination scene for the old landowner in *Bobyl*. There was also to be in this opera a trial by the land- owner in his house, acting as justice of the peace, of the poacher-*bobyl*."

son, detained for a while in the *external censorship*, has completely
stuck in the *internal*: he's not allowed to be sold, *on account of the
Seminarist's concluding statement, that he "was tempted by the devil
in the very temple of God."* Judge for yourself, what is there objec-
tionable in this? Nearly every day before the altar of the Most High
do the priests beat up the deacons (and vice versa) with crosses and
the holy chalice, and, filled with the Holy Spirit, run unashamedly
into each other's "manes": isn't that a "temptation of the devil?" Why,
the *material* conflicts of the *non-material* in St. Isaac's Cathedral have
been officially announced to the reading public.[41]—The history of my
"prodigal son's" return from the German *manège* to his native land
through the external Gehenna is a very simple one. A customs official-
zealot observed the Latin language in "The Seminarist," and therefore, in his opinion, this meant *religion* (!)—and must be a *censorship matter*. The trembling speech of this zealot, when he pulled this
opinion out of himself, filled me with pity, and I was transformed
from a "sacrificial victim" to a "preceptor," endeavoring to appease
the aroused flame in the heart of the customs official by assurances
that this *Latin* signifies exceptions in declensions and is taken from
the Latin grammar, examined, re-examined, consumed and digested
by the constituted authorities and subsequently approved by them.—
But it didn't work: "zeal knows not the persuasion of reason!" Today
I was at the censor's: he recommended my filing a petition (copy enclosed); What will be—I know not.—I am sending you, my dear,
one of the hundred Seminarists, receive the "prodigal son" with paternal love; I could not refrain—and I part with the only remaining
copy of the three presented to me by the benevolent hand of the
divine censor.—This epistle will serve as a guarantee (between us)
of the first *baptism by fire* [42] and the relationship between the government and a musician. Heretofore the censor let musicians be; the ban
(on "The Seminarist") shows that from being "nightingales, leafy
forests, lovers sighing in the moonlight" musicians have become members of human societies, and if they should ban *all of me*, I would not
cease to peck at the stone, as long as I had strength; for "brains cannot

---

[41] This may refer to the newspaper accounts of the fights that took place between the priests and deacons "before the altar of the Most High" in St. Isaac's
Cathedral.

[42] Recently said of the young Wilhelm I at the opening skirmish of the Franco-
Prussian War.

be tempted and prohibition creates in me a terrific eagerness."—*Vade retro satanas!*

Your soul's
(MUSORYANIN)

[Enclosed:]
(Copy)
(To the Committee of Foreign Censorship)
From Collegiate Assessor
Modeste Petrovich Musorgsky
A Petition.

In consequence of the recognition by the Committee of Internal Censorship, that my musical composition "The Seminarist," published in Dresden [Leipzig] is not allowed for circulation in sale, I have the honor to humbly beg the Committee of Foreign Censorship to allow the release to me of *ten* copies of the named composition, for distribution to the following acquaintances of mine:

1. To the Widow of a Lieutenant-Captain, Ludmila Ivanovna Shestakova (born Glinka) .... 1 copy
2. To the Daughters of the Actual State Councilor, Nadezhda Nikolayevna and Alexandra Nikolayevna Purgold 2 copies
3. To Lieutenant Nikolai Andreyevich Rimsky-Korsakov 1 copy
4. To the Director of the Free School of Music, under the patronage of the Tzarevich, Heir to the Throne, Mili Alexeyevich Balakirev............................. 1 "
5. To the Professor of the Imperial College of Jurisprudence and Lycée, Vladimir Vasilyevich Nikolsky........ 1 "
6. To the Professor of the Nikolayevsky Engineers' and the Mikhailovsky Artillery Academies—Captain of the Engineer Corps, Cesar Antonovich Cui................... 1 "
7. To the attaché to the second department of His Imperial Majesty's Chancery, Actual State Councilor Vladimir Vasilyevich Stasov.................................. 1 "
8. To Privy Councilor Vladimir Fyodorovich Purgold.. 1 "
9. To the Professor of the Imperial Medical-Surgical Academy, State Councilor Alexander Porfiryevich Borodin 1 "

A total of 10 copies

19 August 1870, St. Petersburg.
Collegiate Assessor Modeste Petrovich Musorgsky

68. *To VLADIMIR STASOV*

I'm sending you, dear *general*, the *Kinderbalsam.*[43] If you wish to play it—pay no attention to the pencilings. Tomorrow, if it's fair, I shall be in the Pargolovo country. Great thanks for the "A saying, *boyar*," [44] I'll put to use what you say concerning *Boris*. I firmly kiss you. The Shashas [Purgolds] have come back, I was there today—they were splendid, to pull "The Seminarist" through.

Your
MUSORYANIN

22 August 1870.

Extracts from the Diary of Nadezhda Purgold

29 August, 1870.

. . . it's time for her [Alexandra Nikolayevna] *to have a husband*. However, she sees only coldness in the man [Musorgsky [45]] who might inspire passion in her if only he would show a little more interest in her. Not seeing what she would like to see in him, she exaggerates, and refers to his attitude as almost hatred, and says that he doesn't even like her singing, and that his visits are not for her sake. Out of this come endless conversations with me, about how I am much more attractive to him, and that he visits us only for my sake, and perhaps for the sake of Uncle O [Vladimir Fyodorovich], and that he doesn't value her opinion and so on and so on . . .

I find that he pays equal attention to us both, although he treats us slightly differently. For example, he often speaks seriously with me, but he can hardly speak to Sasha without joking . . .

He has a certain manner which probably comes from his extreme egotism. He won't start a conversation with anyone, but waits for the other person to start it; he won't force anyone to talk, as though he were afraid to show the other person that it pleases him to be talked to. He cares to talk only with persons who consider it a special pleasure to talk with him. It's the same with the rest of his behavior: this extreme egotism prevents him from offering to bring his songs with him. Although he knows the enjoyment they afford, he waits to be asked. For the same reason, he never asks Sasha to sing, although I am convinced and I know positively how highly he esteems her singing. This happens particularly when he is the only guest here (it has also happened when everyone was here, although Sasha insists this isn't so . . .) . . .

Well, as long as I've started on his characteristics, I may as well

---

[43] Meyer's name for *Ein Kinderscherz.*

[44] It is not clear why Musorgsky should thank Stasov for a phrase used by Rimsky-Korsakov in his *Pskovityanka.*

[45] Musorgsky is awarded two nicknames in Nadezhda's diary and correspondence: Humor, and Tiger.

go on. Some people think he isn't very intelligent, but I don't agree. He has his own kind of brain, original and very witty. But he sometimes misuses this wit. This may be either a pose, to show that he is not like other people, or this may be just the way he is. The former is more believable. He has too much pepper, if one may say so. When Sasha and I gave everybody a nickname, the one we gave him—Humor—I find proper, because the main feature of his brain is a sense of humor. But he lacks warmth, softness—just the opposite of dear Sincerity [Rimsky-Korsakov], who has so much of this. Perhaps he isn't able to become strongly enthusiastic and to love. I'm not yet sure about this . . .

31 August (late evening)

. . . Humor was very sweet today, he spoke so nicely and cleverly, at times especially so; today he was at his best. And he sang so nicely! I still can't quite understand his relation to Sasha. Anyway it seems to me that she interests him, and that he sees her as a puzzling, original, capricious but powerful nature. But whether he is able to be attracted by her, to fall in love with her, I don't know. He is an egotist, a terrific egotist!

New Finale

. . . During the winter of 1870–71 Musorgsky made another decisive change in his opera. He decided not to end with the death of Boris, but with the scene of the rebellious people [at Kromy], the triumph of the Pretender and the cry of the Simpleton about poor Russia. How much the opera gained by this conclusion, in stunning and tragic force, and in menacing significance! This important change was suggested to the composer by his friend, V. V. Nikolsky. Musorgsky was in raptures, and in a few days he reconstructed and fitted this final scene. I admit that I felt despair and a profound feeling of envy that it was Nikolsky and not I who suggested such a splendid idea to Musorgsky . . . —VLADIMIR STASOV

68a. *NIKOLAI RIMSKY-KORSAKOV to MODESTE MUSORGSKY*

[Thursday, 7 January, 1871]

FRIEND MODESTE.

I've already written to Ludmila Ivanovna that today I again cannot be at her place, because I am again on guard (on the occasion of the Twelfth-Night parade [46] a large number of the officers are occupied, and it is necessary to maintain the watch, as you see, frequently), but I am afraid that my letter to Ludmila Ivanovna will not be received until tomorrow and you will not know anything about it, therefore I am sending you this missive. Write me at once, so I will

---

[46] See postscript to Letter 3.

know by evening tomorrow, when you plan to go to the Purgolds, for it *would be* good to do this together and for this it *would* be necessary for me to *have* known this beforehand. I notice that today I am writing quite illiterately, but however I've always written illiterately. Don't be surprised by this nonsense, why should such nonsensical wishes come to mind. By nonsense I mean foolishly underlining mistakes and making new ones at the same time. The devil knows what nonsense. Till we meet.

Your

N. RIMSKY-KORSAKOV

69. *To NIKOLAI RIMSKY-KORSAKOV*

8 January [1871]
11:30

Just now I have received your epistle, little friend Korsinka, and I answer at once, as you have demanded. I am vexed about the guard-duty—but what's to be done! Yesterday, after having left Ludmila Ivanovna at the moment when she had to be placed in a soda bath, I ran off to the Purgolds, at the suggestion of our little dove, and stayed there kidding from 9:30 to 10:30.—And as you will probably receive, if you haven't already received, an invitation from Ludmila Ivanovna to eat with her on Monday, together with the musical young ladies, therefore I don't imagine that (before Monday) we'll have a chance, little friend, to journey off to the high-spoken damsels.

"Therefore all is in order,
Some honor has been rendered."

I picture you in a good kind disposition—that makes *me* happy; I am writing a little piano piece [47]—this makes *you* happy; we'll see each other Monday—that makes *us* happy (I also underline it). And what would it be, if I were not I * but of that, I reckon, we haven't the slightest idea (!!!) there's some nonsense!

I firmly embrace you, till we meet, friend.

MODESTE

P.S. Ludmila Ivanovna is giving a spread on Monday, because she wishes gradually to shove the damsels back on their previous tracks;

* Musorgsky's note: Underlined in your epistle.

---

[47] Possibly his Scherzino (*The Seamstress*).

and she considers it more convenient to start with us and towards evening to proceed to *the unbridled barbarians.*

A Soprano Sponsor

. . . I don't know if you are aware of all that took place up to my acquaintance with Musorgsky and before the fate of *Boris,* but I don't consider it superfluous to acquaint you with a few episodes—quite edifying—of that time.

Musorgsky, with whom I became acquainted at my house,[48] but had seen previously at Ludmila Ivanovna's, with Lukashevich,[49] Kondratyev,[50] Kommissarzhevsky,[51] Leonova,[52] Petrov, captivated all with *his extraordinary sympathy;* to become acquainted with him meant to love him—even hardened enemies of the new Russian school, of which Musorgsky was a representative, were involuntarily conquered by his charm, saying: "What a sympathetic man, it's a pity that he has gone astray musically." These were the words of N[apravnik] [53] and several other artists not in sympathy with his inclination.

On Saturdays I had gatherings of admirers of *new* music; the only one of my comrade-artists who came regularly was Kommissarzhev-

---

[48] Yulia Fyodorovna Platonova was born in a Russianized German family of Kurlandia only a year before Musorgsky's birth. Her début as a soprano was made in 1863 on the Marinsky stage, and her combined lyrical and dramatic talents soon made her a power in that theatre.

[49] Nikolai Alexeyevich Lukashevich had been a pupil of the painter Bruellow, and a curator of the Hermitage Museum. At this time he occupied the responsible post of Head of the Art Department at the Marinsky Opera.

[50] Gennadi Petrovich Kondratyev was about to change his function in the Marinsky Opera from singer to régisseur.

[51] Fyodor Petrovich Kommissarzhevsky—one of the leading tenors at the Marinsky.

[52] Daria Mikhailovna Leonova—the foremost contralto at the Marinsky. Her enormously successful debut was made in 1852 in the role of Vanya in *A Life for the Tzar* (in which she was coached by Glinka), and to her friendship with Glinka she added more composer-trophies in the persons of Meyerbeer and Auber on a tour abroad in 1858.

[53] Eduard Franzovich Napravnik's arrival at the powerful post of conductor at the Marinsky Opera had been swift and romantic. Born in a Bohemian town, educated in Prague, he had accumulated fourteen opus numbers by the age of twenty, and had left Prague at twenty-two to become the conductor of Prince Yusupov's private orchestra in St. Petersburg. Happening to be at the Marinsky Theater for *Ruslan and Ludmila* when the orchestra's pianist fell ill, Napravnik impressed the conductor Lyadov by his unrehearsed performance of the piano part, and Napravnik's long career at the Marinsky was under way. When his contract with Prince Yusupov expired, the directorate of the Imperial Theaters engaged Napravnik as organist and vocal coach. He was soon advanced to an associate conductorship and finally to general musical director, replacing Lyadov. His good will was of critical importance to a young Russian opera composer.

sky, who took very warmly to his opera *Boris*—but there were many strangers, and Musorgsky was the life of the party: he played and sang till late at night from his *Boris,* his *Khovanshchina* and all his smaller pieces—his declamation surprised even people who were not connoisseurs of music.

My late husband and I enlisted more and more admirers of Musorgsky's talent, inviting them from all quarters to *listen to Musorgsky,* and in such a way that already there was formed at my house a circle of warm admirers of his talent. Lukashevich was at that time a warm admirer of mine, and both my husband and I made use of all of our influence on him in order to enlist him in our circle, in which we succeeded, just as the charm of Musorgsky's talent began to work on him . . . —YULIA PLATONOVA

69a.   *GIOVANNI FERRERO to STEPAN GEDEONOV (A Report)*

By order of Your Excellency the score of the Russian opera proposed for production, *Boris Godunov,* the composition of Musorgsky, was examined in the presence of MM. Louis Maurer, Napravnik, Voyaček, Klammrodt, Popkov, Betz and myself,[54] who unanimously decided to have a balloting in the presence of the aforesaid seven persons, in consequence of which there appeared six black balls and one white, so that I have the honor to return the aforesaid score to Your Excellency.

IVAN FERRERO

10 February, 1871

New Version

. . . At the beginning of 1870 [1871] Musorgsky presented his opera *Boris Godunov* to the Directorate; it then had only three acts and was written with male roles only.

Soon after this Yu. F. Platonova had a luncheon at her home on the occasion of her *bénéfice.*[55] She came to invite me and added that on that very morning the fate of Musorgsky's opera was being decided, and that Napravnik and Kondratyev were coming to her

[54] This Musical-Theater Committee was made up of the conductors from each of the St. Petersburg imperial theaters. Only one member was Russian (A. D. Popkov, the ballet conductor), and there was apparently no age limit, Louis Maurer (Inspector of Music) being eighty-two at the time. It is comforting to imagine that the one white ball was cast by Napravnik, the most intelligent member of this group—and its youngest; he was thirty-two, Musorgsky's age.

[55] The *bénéfice* is a theatrical custom originating in France, whereby some actor, singer or other member of a theatrical company is awarded a percentage of that performance's gross. Such occasions were provided for in the actor's or singer's contract; no charity is implied.

[luncheon]. I went to her home and with great impatience awaited the arrival of those persons. Naturally I greeted them with the words: "Is *Boris* accepted?"—"No," they answered me, "it's impossible for an opera to have no feminine element! Musorgsky undoubtedly has a great talent, let him insert one more scene, then *Boris* will be presented!" I knew this news would be unpleasant for Musorgsky and I hesitated to tell it to him at once; but I immediately wrote to him and to V. V. Stasov, asking them to come to me at six. By the time I returned home, I found them already there and I told them what I had heard. With warm concern Stasov began to discuss with Musorgsky the new insertions to be made in the opera and Modeste Petrovich himself began to play various themes, and the evening passed in great animation. Musorgsky started this further work without delay . . . —LUDMILA SHESTAKOVA

69b. *PAVEL FYODOROV to MODESTE MUSORGSKY*

DEAR SIR,

By order of the Director of the Imperial Theaters, I have the honor to advise you that upon examination by the Musical-Theatre Committee of the score of the opera of your composition, *Boris Godunov*, this opera was not approved for production on the Russian stage of the Imperial Theaters. Returning the aforesaid score and the libretto of the opera, I sincerely ask you to accept this expression of my respects.

P. FYODOROV

17 February, 1871

70. *To NIKOLAI RIMSKY-KORSAKOV*

27 March, 1871 [Saturday]

Friend Korsinka, here you have a text for the girls who are honoring Vanka; [56] according to my understanding it's better if they would honor the Tzar at the very end—because not without reason is he *the terrible.*

> Under the hillock—
> Under the green mound
> Springs a swift brooklet
> Rippling and running.

---

[56] For the arrival at Pskov of Ivan the Terrible (he of the "bright eye" and "black brow")—Act II, Scene 2 of *Pskovityanka*. Rimsky-Korsakov used this text, omitting only the seventh and ninth stanzas.

Over the brooklet,
Over the ripples
A small wooden span
Was builded across.

Now across the bridge
Marching and riding
Steps like the thunder—
A boyar's army.

And this army marches,
This armed boyar,
Not toward bloody fray—
But friendly visit.

Out to meet it rides
A brave young fellow
On a steed of mettle
All bedecked with gold.

All bedecked with gold
He glistens and gleams
Like the very sun
On a morn in spring.

And what did it do,
The boyar's army,
Did it bow full low
To this brave fellow?

Ah, he draws nearer
Like a stormy cloud—
Knitting his black brow:
What a noble lad!

And from his bright eye
There began to flash
Such a burning fire
On the boyar's ranks,

That like the tall grass
Under the strong man's scythe
The army was felled,
The proud boyar's ranks.

And so to him we sing,
This brave young fellow,
Honor and glory
In Russia holy.

Glory in Heaven
Glorious sun above
Glorify father—
Ivan the Terrible.

I firmly kiss you, friend, till Wednesday.

Your

MODESTE

70a. *NIKOLAI RIMSKY-KORSAKOV to MODESTE MUSORGSKY*

I send you, friend Modeste, the little song of the girls in the forest,
from Krestovsky's libretto [for *Pskovityanka*]. Here it is:

Ah, my forest, my sweet father,
How dark you've grown, how noisy!
How he roars and sways,
Thinking his dark dread thoughts,
Swaying with his dark thoughts,
Like my own sweet father,
Like my own sweet father
Rustling, roaring, growing angry!
Under the thunder-clouds and rain
He will shelter his dear daughter
From the flitting, flying evil,
He will shelter the wanderer with love.

The meter of the verses fits my little theme and the lines are also
just right. I think the verses pretty good and I send them to you. In
case you find them suitable, because in these matters you have eaten
dog * [because this is your strong point] you will not have to trouble
inventing new verses. If you consider it necessary, make corrections
in the verses.

Till we meet, dear friend,

Your

N. RIMSKY-KORSAKOV

Sunday, 9th May [1871]

* Rimsky-Korsakov's note: An Expression of Auntie Malanya.

161

[On the back of this letter there is Musorgsky's penciled version for this song:]

IN PSKOVITYANKA

(The girls sing in the forest, Act I, Scene 4)
(borrowed from a Pskov song)

Ah, you grove, you little grove,
Mother mine, little green grove,
Why such noise—you'll hurt yourself,
You must see dark clouds up there.
The darkness covers us, dear grove,
The noise drowns the crying birds.
Cuckoo cries there cuckoo,
Grief to us and sorrow.
Ah, this little cuckoo,
A sly and restless bird,
Like an unmarried wife, bold, young.
She has no snug and warm nest.
She has none and needs none,
Like the unmarried wife, she's free.
The little grove offers plenty
Of other birds' snug warm nests
There, in the stormy weather,
To shelter the free little bird.

---

71. *To VLADIMIR STASOV*

Your epistle, dear *généralissime*, was received in my absence; I thought I would catch you at Hartmann's but this didn't happen— that's the reason for my tardy reply.—At "The Power of Serov" [57] I will be with my people, because this arrangement was made long ago; Korsinka surprised me at Ludmila Ivanovna's when he announced that the "company" would be united in a loge—I knew nothing about this. Well, what of it? We'll run into each other in the entr'actes and

---

[57] On the following evening, April 19, 1871, was to be given the première of Alexander Serov's posthumously produced opera, *The Power of Evil*, based on Ostrovsky's play, *Don't Live as You'd Like To* (1855). Serov died in January of this year. The playwright had adapted most of the libretto himself, only quitting when his wish for fantasy collided with Serov's urge toward naturalism. Victor Hartmann had designed the sets for this production at the Marinsky Opera.

somehow manage to sit through the power of Serov.—Judging by the libretto, I expect excellent scenic situations (drunken Vasya with the little song and the questioning Dasha—Dasha's appearance in the inn and Grunya's recognition of Piotr's tricks, Yeryomka—this Russian Bertram [58]—in the larger part of his pranks; but because Serov's ingenuity is in general to twist and turn, and *suspecting* the sincerity of his opera's nationalism in a musical sense, I expect a caricature in the trivial meaning of this word. However, we'll see and hear.—Your lines about Mili, my dear, were a blow to me, although I wasn't an eyewitness to the freezing.[59] Thanks to my impressionability, something horrifying appeared before me: Your lines seemed to me like the burial service for Mili's artistic ardor—terrible, if this is the truth and if, on his part, this was not a mask! It's too soon; *it's too horribly soon!* Or is it disillusionment? well—it may be this too; but where then is his courage, and maybe his consciousness of matters and of artistic aims, which are never achieved without a struggle. Or was art only a means, and not an aim? *Diavolo, diavolo!* . . .[60]

I am finishing the scene—the Jesuit [61] has given me no rest for two nights in a row—that's fine—I love it, I mean, I love it when I compose this way.

Your
MUSORYANIN

18 April, '71.

---

[58] In Meyerbeer's *Robert le Diable.*

[59] Stasov's lost report to Musorgsky on Balakirev may have been similar to his letter of April 17 to Rimsky-Korsakov: "In general I can say that Balakirev made a most sad impression on me yesterday. In his appearance it was as if everything were the same and nothing had changed: voice the same, figure, face, words—all the same, yes,—but actually everything had changed, and of the past not one stone stands on another . . . Can you imagine, from time to time silence would suddenly set in and continue for several minutes . . . I tried, in this way and that, to begin [the conversation] anew, starting first from one end and then from the other, carefully skirting anything that might be unpleasant, such as the [benefit] concert for *The Stone Guest*—nothing helped me; he would answer in a few words, and again silence. When has anything like this ever happened, why it's fifteen years that I've known him. No, this is an entirely different man; it was some sort of *coffin* before me yesterday, not the former lively, energetic, restless M.A. . . ."

[60] An exclamation in *Fra Diavolo.*

[61] The first scene of the new "Polish" Act III of *Boris:* Maryna, with the disguised Jesuit, Rangoni. Musorgsky's anti-Polish-Catholic attitudes have been previously indicated in Letter 42.

163

Extract from the Diary of Nadezhda Purgold

. . . I'm sure that some of Musorgsky's works would not have been written if it weren't for Sasha. Without himself realizing it, he wrote his children [*The Nursery*] because of her, and for her, because he very well knew that no one else could do them as they should be done. She inspires others by her performance . . .

72. *To MALVINA CUI*

Thursday 1 July [1871, Petersburg]

Dearest lady, because of my brother's arrival in Peter for two or three days, on business, I can't take advantage of your joyous summons for Friday, as Brother is staying with me and part of the business that brings him concerns both of us. Your errand at Bessel's is carried out: he is planning a good thing,[62] about which we will talk fully when we meet, which let us hope, will be soon, *with your kind permission*, because you well know: I feel comfortable at your home and with you.

Your soul's

MODESTE

I could smack dear Alexander [63] on that place which doesn't hurt now.—I greet the *dottore* [Hubner].

73. *A Catalogue* [64]

[July-August, 1871]

MUSORGSKY

The first composition, published, to the author's regret, by Bernard in 1852, was *"Porte-enseigne Polka,"* dedicated to his comrades of the Cadet School (the author was 13 years old).

1856 An attempt to write an opera on the subject of V. Hugo's *"Han d'Islande"*—nothing came of this, because nothing could come of it—(the author was 17 years old).

---

[62] Bessel's project to publish a magazine, *Muzikalni Listok*, was realized in September 1872.

[63] It is to Alexander Cui—now one year old—that "Going to Sleep," No. 5 of *The Nursery*, is dedicated.

[64] Ludmila Shestakova asked all members of the Balakirev Circle—Balakirev, Cui, Borodin, Musorgsky, and Rimsky-Korsakov—for catalogues of their works. Musorgsky provided not only his own, but Cui's as well (omitted in this volume), and Rimsky-Korsakov prepared dilatory Borodin's as well as his own.

1858 *Scherzi:* (1) in B-flat major—performed in 1860, conducted by A. Rubinstein in a concert of the Russian Musical Society.
(2) in C-sharp minor (for piano—unpublished). Songs—of these "Tell me why, dearest maiden" is published. Music undertaken for Sophocles' tragedy "Oedipus."—Chorus at the temple of the Eumenides, before the appearance of Oedipus, was performed in '61 in a concert of K. Lyadov.

1859 Nervous disease.[65] Bathed in the springs of Tikhvin county, province of Novgorod, and composed *"Kinder-Scherz"* (being printed).

1860 Exercised my brains.

1861 *Intermezzo [in modo classico]* (being printed).
Preludio in modo classico.[66]
Menuetto.[67]

1862 Put my brains in order and nourished them with valuable knowledge.

1863 A few songs [68]—of these "King Saul" is being published.

1864 Opera undertaken on the subject of Flaubert's "Salammbô" (from the Punic Wars).—Toward the end of the year 2 scenes were ready in piano sketches.
"Night" (a song-fantasia) is being published.
First attempt at humor: "Kalistrat" by Nekrasov.

1865 About 10 unpublished songs.[69]

[65] Musorgsky is a year wrong in his memory of his "nervous disease." It was in the summer of 1858 that he went to Tikhvin county (see Letters 6 and 7). In the summer of 1859 he visited the Shilovsky estate and Moscow.

[66] This may be another slip, as there is no other evidence of a *Preludio in modo classico* among Musorgsky's manuscripts.

[67] Neither a *Menuetto* nor a *Menuet monstre* (mentioned in Musorgsky's later autobiographical note) has been discovered.

[68] The "few songs" of 1863 may include: "Old Man's Song" (see page 56); "If I Could But Meet You" (text by Vasili Kurochkin, dated "15 August, year 1863. Village of Volok," dedicated to Nadezhda Petrovna Opochinina); "Many Chambers and Gardens Have I" (text by Alexei Koltzov, dated "Peterburg. Year 1863," dedicated to Platon Timofeyevich Borispoletz). "King Saul" uses the text of one of Byron's Hebrew Melodies, "Song of Saul before His Last Battle," as translated by Pavel Kozlov. The manuscript is dated "year 1863. Village of Volok," and is dedicated to Alexander Petrovich Opochinin.

[69] It is difficult to establish even "about ten" songs for 1865; "Prayer" (text by Lermontov, dated "2 February, year 1865"), "The Outcast" (text by Ivan Goltz-Miller, dated "5 June 1865. S-Pbg," and inscribed "An Experiment in Recitative"). In addition to those he lists for 1864, there are: "Blow Winds,

Scene for the opera "Salammbô."
"Lullaby" from Ostrovsky's "Voyevod" (being printed).

1866 *Chorus* on a Hebrew melody by Byron, "The Destruction of
Sennacherib" (performed in 1867 under the direction of
M. Balakirev and G. Lomakin in a concert of the Free
Music School) published in 1871.
"Savishna" (published).
"Gopak" (from Shevchenko's "Haidamaks"—published).
"The Seminarist" (published and forbidden by the censor).
"Yaryoma's Song" (from Shevchenko's "Haidamaks").
Symphonic picture undertaken, "Night on Bald Mountain."

1867 Completion of the scoring of "Night on Bald Mountain."
"Gathering Mushrooms."
"Jewish Song."
"The Feast."
"The Goat."

(published)
"The Magpie."
"The Naughty Boy."
"The Classicist" (the beginning of the musical pamphlets—
published).

1868 "The Little Orphan Girl."
"Child's Song."
The first act of Gogol's "Marriage" (written with some slight
abridgment of Gogol's text).
Planning of the opera "Boris Godunov" (after Pushkin).
"Child with Nurse" (being printed).
"Yeremushka's Lullaby" (being printed).
First act of the opera "Boris Godunov."

1869 Completion of the opera "Boris Godunov."

1870 "Penny Paradise" (a pamphlet—published).
"In the Corner."
"With the Doll."
"Going to Sleep."

Being published:
"The Beetle."
Scherzino (the seamstress).

Wild Winds" (text by Alexei Koltzov, dated "28 March, year 1864. S.-Petersburg,"
dedicated to Vyacheslav Alexeyevich Loginov, one of the "commune"); and,
stretching a point or two, one might include the "Song of the Balearic Islander"
from *Salammbô*, and Musorgsky's arrangement for duet of Gordigiani's "Ogni
sabato avrete il Lume Accesso" (dated "Anno 1864. San-Pietroburgo," dedicated
to "signor Vold. Grodskii").

"Boris Godunov" is submitted to the Directorate of the theatres—rejected.

1871 New version of "Boris Godunov."
Planning of a comic opera on a subject by Gogol. Planning
of work on the beginning of a historical musical drama
concerning the Volga Cossacks.[70]

74. *To VLADIMIR STASOV*

10 August, '71

Centuries have passed, my dear, since I last saw you and talked
things over with you; no one is to blame for this but the vicissitudes
of fate. And I have a lot to tell you on our account, and for that "my
own eyes" are burning to behold you and to torture your hearing
"with my obscenely hoarse voice."—The criminal Tzar Boris perpetrates a certain *arioso;* in the opinion of musical sages, and above all,
originating from Lodyzhky known as Fim, as well as from the knight
of the marine tempests [Rimsky-Korsakov] so laudably transformed
by you into the admiralty, this criminal *arioso* is very lovely and tickles
the ear rather amusingly, and the words of this *arioso* have been
cooked up by me.[71]

Since it is disgusting and boring to watch and listen to the grinding
of the criminal's teeth, the little mob of nurses breaks through after
this, bawling and clamoring unintelligibly, whereupon the Tzar
drives them away and sends his son to find out "why these women are
howling there." . . . Whilst the son attends to this, a boyar in attendance presents himself and informs against Shuisky, and when this
spy slips away the Tzarevich returns and in answer to Boris's question: "Well, what's going on there?" explains as follows:

Tzarevich

Sire, permit me to begin a true story.

Boris.

I am listening, my son.

---

[70] Andrei Rimsky-Korsakov can identify neither of these projects. The Gogol
project may be related to that mentioned in Letter 78, and the Cossack project
to the interests of Kenevich (see pp. 292–293).

[71] The music for this *arioso* is taken from the unfinished *Salammbô* score—
chorus of the people, Act IV, Scene 1.

Tzarevich

Our little *parrot* * perched in the nurses' chamber,
He chattered unceasingly, and was gay and affable.
He went up to the nurses, and begged them to scratch his poll:
He visited each one in turn, observing the proper order.
Nurse Nastasya did not want to scratch him;
The parrot stepped aside—he called the nurse a fool.
Nurse, much offended, seizes him by the neck.
The parrot begins to scream, and flap his wings.
Well, they coax him, they pet him, they fondle him.
Imploring him by all the clergy, they caress him, soothe him.
But no—he will have none of it:
He sits and scowls, his beak buried in his feathers,
He won't look at the nurses, he keeps on muttering something.
Suddenly he springs at a nurse.
(The one who wouldn't scratch him):
Begins to peck her—the nurse flops on the floor.
Then the nurses seemed to go mad with terror,
They began waving their arms, screaming, wanting to drive the
    parrot away,
But he was not at a loss: he marked each of them adroitly.
That, my royal father, was why they all rushed in here,
Interfering with the deliberations of thy royal thought.
Well, it seems that's all—all that took place.

With the music this fibbing turns out to be so pleasing that the above-mentioned musical sages kept their ears wide open so that by cramming them with this pleasing stuff they might please themselves sufficiently. It would be pleasant to grab you in your residence on Thursday, and if you're not terribly against it, write me, my dear, at the House of Zaremba (near St. Panteleimon's) apt. No. 4.

Your

MUSORYANIN

Mayhap you have *anathematized* me, but the nurses prove how firmly you are seated in my brain and soul.

N.B. I seem to remember that *somebody* presented Boris with a parrot as a novelty in the Russian Kingdom—*is that so?* [73]

* Musorgsky's note: *Already the seventh creature* about whom I have amiably sung: in the historical order of their appearance have jumped out (1) a *magpie*, (2) a *goat*, (3) a *beetle*, (4) a *drake*, (5) a *mosquito* with a *bedbug*, (6) a *screech-owl* with a *sparrow*, (7) this *parrot*.[72]

[72] Musorgsky's allusion is to: (1) *The Magpie* (text by Alexander Pushkin, dated "26 Aug. '67. Peter," dedicated to Alexander Petrovich Opochinin), (2) *The Goat* (text by Musorgsky, dated "Petrograd, 23 December 1867," dedicated to Alexander Porfiryevich Borodin), (3) *The Beetle* (No. 3 of *The Nursery* cycle), (4) the hostess's song that opens the inn scene of *Boris*, (5) and (6) the children's songs brought into this new version of Act II, and (7) the above.

[73] Remembered from Karamzin's *History of the Russian State,* where a list is

75. *To NIKOLAI RIMSKY-KORSAKOV*

Dear friend Korsinka, they have not yet paid me the money at the postoffice, again some formalities have not been observed, therefore I again have to wait a fortnight; the shameful postoffice has finally worn me out. Because the administration exists to give people an anticipation of the devil's grills in hell, it undoubtedly therefore consists of the most loathsome rogues who get a chance at promotion—that's logical. However, get as furious as you wish, but in Russia one has to learn to have patience, "which many cattle have." I let you know about this new adventure for your deliberation as well as for a warning in case such incidents occur [to you], and at our meeting, tomorrow, we'll have an explanation between ourselves.—I've received a summons from Ludmila Ivanovna for both of us *on Thursday the 19th with dyainka.*

"in the evening . . . aaaa!" [74]

Didn't you promise the Purgolds—if you did, *do something about it.* I firmly kiss you, dear friend. O abominable All-Russian desolation!

Your

MODESTE

17 August, '71.

A Furnished Room for Two Composers

In the fall of 1871 . . . Musorgsky and I agreed to live together, and we rented an apartment or rather a furnished room in Zaremba's house on Panteleimonovskaya Street. This stay with Musorgsky, I imagine, was a unique example of two composers living together. How could we avoid disturbing each other? Like this. Mornings till about noon, Musorgsky used the piano, and I copied or orchestrated something I had fully thought out. At about noon he left for his duties at the Ministry, and I used the piano. The evenings were arranged by mutual agreement. Moreover, twice a week, I went to the Conservatory at 9 in the morning, while Musorgsky frequently dined at the Opochinins; so that things adjusted themselves as well as possible. That autumn and winter the two of us achieved a great deal, constantly exchanging ideas and plans. Musorgsky was composing and orchestrating the Polish act of *Boris Godunov* and the people's

cited of the gifts brought by the minister plenipotentiary from Austria to the Russian court on May 22, 1597, including not only "a clock with chimes" for Boris Godunov, but also "6 parrots and 2 monkeys" for Fyodor, son of Boris (5th edition, Vol. X, p. 108 and footnotes).

[74] The "aaaa" comes from the opening scene of *Boris.*

scene "near Kromy." I was orchestrating and finishing *Pskovityanka*
. . . —NIKOLAI RIMSKY-KORSAKOV

. . . I shall never forget that time when they, both still young,
lived together in one room, I used to visit them early in the morning,
find them still asleep, wake them, haul them out of bed, help them
wash and hand them their stockings, trousers, dressing gowns or
jackets, and slippers. Nor how we used to drink tea together, eating
slices of bread and butter with Swiss cheese, of which they were so
fond . . . And directly after this breakfast, we would turn to our
chief and favorite occupation—music, beginning with singing and
piano playing, and they would show me with delight and great excitement what they had written during the last day or two. How good
it all was . . . !—VLADIMIR STASOV

76. *To VLADIMIR STASOV*

(Zarzhemba's House, Panteleimonovskaya,
apt. No. 9 from the stairs along the cor-
ridor to the right, 1st door on the left)
Saturday 11 Sept., '71

Very most superlative, most inimitable, most thorough picker of
my brains and helper of their perfection—hear ye! In case we don't
see each other today at the house of Hartmann, master of the architectural craft, I write you this epistle, consisting of the following
points, immediately below:

(1) Yesterday I saw dear Rubin[stein]—he, as much as we, thirsts
passionately for a meeting;

(2) He has fixed Wednesday for that purpose;

(3) He'll come on Wednesday with his new opera [*Demon*], to show
it to us, meaning: General Bach, Dmitri Sire Vasilich, the Admiralty,
Kvey, and me, great sinner that I am;

(4) He mentioned Balakirev and Borodin among those to be present, but this is not likely.

(5) He will sing his own opera, and for that reason begs us not to
let anyone but ourselves be present.

It would be useful to know where Rubin is to bring his opera—to
you or to Dmitri Vasilyevich—decide this and let Rubin know—
(preferably personally); they say he is staying at the *Hôtel-de-France*,
and probably is at home in the morning until 11 or noon. Rubin was
delightfully warm—a living and genuine artist.[75]

---

[75] On September 17, 1871, Musorgsky, Stasov, Rimsky-Korsakov, Cui, Laroche,
and Azanchevsky gathered at Dimitri Stasov's to listen to Anton Rubinstein's recently completed opera, *The Demon,* played for them by both Anton and Nikolai

I have the honor to inform Your Grace that Pimen and I have accomplished the abbreviation,[76] have improved Grishka in it (i.e., be it understood, we have composed Grishka anew) and the Corsican admiral says that it is now *great* and is "our trump card." The *vagrants'* scene [Kromy] is being thought out: (*novelty and novelty,* out of novelties, novelty)—terribly pleasant.

I firmly embrace you, my dear.

I almost forgot, Shustov said that at the Conservatory, too, a collection was taken for *The Stone Guest* and wanted to see you about this—only is this true and who did it?

Your

MUSORYANIN

76a. *ALEXANDER BORODIN to YEKATERINA BORODINA, Moscow*
    (*A Sequence of Extracts*)

Monday [September 20, 1871]

. . . Korsinka has completely finished *Pskovityanka*. Modinka has revised and added a great deal to *Boris*. For example, he has added a whole act with Maryna—a Polish act. Besides this, a large scene where the Pretender appears in the province of Orel, already as a conqueror. To the scene of the children with Boris have been added a little song by the tzarevich about a parrot, "clocks with chimes" and a story about them. He has radically revised a number of earlier scenes. For Boris himself he has done an "arioso." And this is all delightful. Cui has written a whole scene [of *Angelo*] and three of the most charming little choruses, one of which is simply a *Meisterstück* in the choral field. Today Modya and Korsya are coming here to perform all this . . .

Tuesday [September 21, 1871]

. . . Modinka and Korsinka played over for me all that they've

---

Rubinstein. Vasili Bessel may also have been there, as he has left the following memoir of the occasion: "Notwithstanding the composer's marvelous playing, the new opera made no very favorable impression on its audience. The dances, the march, and the procession of the caravan (introduction to Act II, scene 2) pleased them best. Only after supper, when the great artist sat down to the piano [as a pianist, not composer], their mood changed and they became enthusiastic; when he left, they all escorted him to the door, expressing their admiration."

[76] The new music composed for Grigory's speech in the cell scene (Act I, Scene 1).

written. How fine *Boris* is now. Simply magnificent. I am sure that it will have success if it is produced. It is remarkable that among musicians *Boris* positively affects one as stronger than *Pskovityanka,* which at the beginning I did not expect [. . .] Azanchevsky is energetically bustling about to stand the Musical Society on sturdy feet. They're going to play the whole *Elisabeth* [Liszt's oratorio], *Der Rose. Pilgerfahrt* by Schumann, the latter's E-flat major [*Rhenish*] symphony, a chorus and scene from Modinka's *Boris* and a great many other good things . . .

Monday, 4 Oct. [1871]

. . . . At the Makovskys' I saw the famous concocted caricature of our circle: in the center is pictured Bach—a Russian peasant, leading a bear for show. Bach holds in his hand the trumpet of fame, which he is blowing. Sitting astride the trumpet is Hartmann, as a monkey; on [Stasov's] right shoulder is Antokolsky [77] as Mephistopheles. The bear is, it is understood, Mili; holding a conductor's baton in his right paw. Cui is pictured as a fox, wagging his tail, holding in his forepaws laurel wreaths, intended for his chosen ones, his paws are adorned with healthy and menacing claws, bared significantly; in a word: "Don't come near me! unless you want to be hurt!" Modinka—a rooster, with a stately step. Korsinka is pictured as a long lobster, one claw holding Bach's hand, the other embracing Nadezhda Purgold. Both Purgolds are pictured as little dogs, dressed in children's clothes and dancing for the entertainment of the others. I am depicted in a dress-uniform, and spectacles, clapping my hands to my ears, and fleeing from all this confusion. Further improvements are proposed: Mili will wear red gloves, Cui will be seated in a fortress, and they're going to picture me stuck inside a retort, for which Kostya [Makovsky] asked me to obtain a retort for him. The whole allegory may be understood thus: the Makovskys have a grudge against the entire circle [78] except

[77] Mark Matveyevich Antokolsky is one of Stasov's "troika," the other two being Repin and Musorgsky. Born in 1842 in a poor Jewish family of Vilna, Antokolsky became Russia's leading sculptor. The caricature portrays him in the pose of his own "Mephistopheles."

[78] Shestakova's memoirs contain an explanation of this grudge: "In May 1870, I. S. Turgenev was in St. Petersburg and promised the Makovskys that he would spend an evening with them. The Makovskys decided to invite our musical circle to this party, but everyone refused the invitation categorically, due to Turgenev's antagonism to modern Russian music [see p. 83]. Yelena Timofeyevna [Makovskaya] got really angry and, of course with the help of Konstantin Yegorovich, she drew a caricature in pastels of all the members of the circle . . ."

me, and therefore they want to justify me as though apart from the others . . . Modya, Korsya and N. Lodyzhensky were here, and they all went wild over the finale of my [second] symphony; only the very end isn't ready. But the middle section turned out—unsurpassable. I myself am very satisfied with it; it is strong, mighty, dashing and effective. I'm on my way to Ludma [Shestakova], who is having her Mondays as she used to . . .

Sunday & Monday [October 24–25, 1871]

. . . [Pskovityanka] was performed on two pianos. One was played by Nadezhda Purgold, the other by Korsinka supporting everything that she couldn't play alone. Modinka [as Ivan the Terrible, Tokmakov, and other roles], [Vasili] Vasiliev and Alexandra Purgold sang the parts. I don't understand why Balakirev turns away so stubbornly from our circle and obviously avoids any encounters. I fear that his mind is not quite in order, but perhaps it's only his conceit gnawing at him. He is so despotic by nature that he demands complete subordination to his wishes, even in the most trifling matters. It doesn't seem possible for him to understand and acknowledge freedom and equality. He cannot endure the slightest opposition to his tastes or even to his whims. He wants to impose his yoke upon everyone and everything. And yet he is quite aware that we all have already grown up, that we stand firmly on our feet, and no longer require braces. This evidently irks him. More than once he has said to Ludma: "Why should I hear their things, they are all so mature now that I've become unnecessary to them, they can do without me," etc. His nature is such that it positively requires minors around whom he can fuss like a nurse around a child. So he pulls to himself Miloradovich,[79] Pomazansky,[80] and even, so they say, the "flagon of perfume," i.e., Shcherbachov,[81] although he must realize clearly that there's nothing that can come from this last one. He's run Pomazansky quite breathless, forcing him to write a Russian overture in which nine-tenths has

[79] M. A. Miloradovich was little more than a Balakirev satellite.

[80] Ivan Pomazansky had entered the court choir at the age of nine and had remained until 1863. After a brief service in the Forestry Department (before Musorgsky obtained his post there), he entered the conservatory to study the harp, and in 1870 was appointed junior coach for the chorus of the Marinsky Opera. He appears to have had short-lived ambitions as a composer.

[81] Nikolai Vladimirovich Shcherbachov was a late-comer to the Balakirev Circle, being eighteen years old at this time. Borodin's negative opinion of him was not shared by the others; Stasov expected great things of him (see Letter 100a).

been composed by Mili himself, for he doesn't give Pomazansky the slightest freedom to act according to his own wishes. However, the overture is very good, interesting in its themes and development and is beautifully orchestrated, and so on. But all this is Mili, Mili, and Mili, while Pomazansky as a personality doesn't exist here. Meanwhile the alienation of Mili, his obvious turning away from the circle, his sharp remarks about many, especially about Modeste, have considerably cooled sympathies towards Mili. If he goes on like this, he may easily isolate himself and this, in his situation, would amount to spiritual death. I, and not I alone, but the others too, feel very sorry for Mili, but what's to be done? Even Ludma, who used to be able to pacify him, has lost all influence over him. There may also be a reason for his estrangement in his strange and unexpected switch to pietism of the most fanatic and most naïve sort. For instance, Mili doesn't miss a single morning mass or a single night mass, breaks a piece from his holy wafer, fervently crosses himself before each church, etc. It's quite possible that in these circumstances it's unpleasant for him to meet people who are unsympathetic to all this; he may even be afraid of the tactless and coarse mitrailleuse of reproaches from Vladimir Stasov who, whenever he meets him, starts forthwith "demonstrating" to him that all this is nonsense, that he "cannot understand" how an intelligent man like Mili, and so on and so on. Moreover, most of the reproaches fall upon his apathy to musical matters, especially during the past year. For example, Stasov cannot forgive Mili for his attitude toward the concert for the benefit of Dargomizhsky's *Stone Guest,* for which all was arranged, but which didn't come off solely because Mili, without any excuse, postponed the concert and dragged out the affair mercilessly. Ludma cannot forgive his inexplicable indifference toward *Ruslan,* when Mili, having talked Ludma into reserving a loge especially for him, suddenly spent the entire evening at Zhemchuzhnikov's,[82] without any cause, and appeared at none of the other performances. Modinka is offended by Mili's unjust and high-handed remarks about *Boris,* expressed tactlessly and sharply in the presence of people who on no account ought to have heard them. Korsinka resents his indifference to *Pskovityanka* and is pained by Mili's behavior.

---

[82] Vladimir Mikhailovich Zhemchuzhnikov, together with his brother Alexander and Alexei Tolstoy, published satirical works under the collective *nom de plume* of "Kuzma Prutkov."

Cui also is indignant about Mili's apathy and his lack of interest in what happens in our musical circle. Before, Mili was concerned with the slightest novelty, even in embryo. There is no denying that the abyss between him and us grows wider and wider. This is terribly painful and pitiful. Painful chiefly because the victim of all this will be Mili himself. The other members of the circle now live more peacefully than ever before. Modinka and Korsinka particularly, since they began to share a room, have both greatly developed. They are diametrically opposed in musical qualities and methods; one seems to complement the other. Their influence on each other has been extremely helpful. Modeste has improved the recitative and declamatory sides of Korsinka who has, in his turn, wiped out Modeste's tendency towards awkward originality, and has smoothed all his rough harmonic edges, his pretentiousness in orchestration, his lack of logic in the construction of musical form—in a word, he has made Modeste's things incomparably more musical. And in all the relations within our circle there's not a shadow of envy, conceit or selfishness;—each is made sincerely happy by the smallest success of another. There are the warmest of relations, not even excepting Cui who, for example, ran over to me only for the purpose of hearing the end for my finale. Mili alone shuns this *family* equality! Well, what of it! . . .

Sunday, 14 November, 1871

. . . Yesterday, I'm sorry—the day before yesterday, on Friday, at the Purgolds they performed *Boris* in its entirety, except for the last act. A delight! Such variety! Such contrasts! How rounded off and motivated it all is now! I liked it very much. As an opera, Boris—in my opinion—is stronger than *Pskovityanka,* though the latter is richer in purely musical beauties . . .

76b. *NADEZHDA PURGOLD to NIKOLAI RIMSKY-KORSAKOV*

[December 14, 1871]

. . . Yesterday Sasha talked with the Tiger [Musorgsky] about Dobryna.[83] He also finds that many things must be changed in it, and wants to rearrange these himself, after, of course, discussing them with

---

[83] Dobryna Nikitich, an ancient hero, about whom Rimsky-Korsakov was writing.

you. But my opinion is that nothing good can come out of wreckage
and rearrangement . . .

77. *To VLADIMIR STASOV*

[December 14, 1871]

My dear, I fully share your thought not *to mignonize*,[84] and so I am
writing the last chord of the fountain scene: Till Friday. I firmly kiss
you.

MUSORYANIN

A Composite Painting

. . . In the winter of 1871–72, on the commission of A. A. Porokhovshchikov, constructor of the "Slavonic Bazaar," I painted a picture of the group of Slavonic composers: Russian, Polish, Czech.
Stasov took part in the development of this theme. He insisted on the
necessity of including among the number there the figures of Musorgsky and Borodin. An inquiry, addressed to Porokhovshchikov,
resulted in this reply: "There you are, you're going to sweep all sorts
of trash [*musor*] into that painting! My list of names was provided
by Nikolai Rubinstein himself, and I don't dare to add to it or take
anyone off that list that was given to you . . . I am sorry about one
thing, that he didn't write in Tchaikovsky . . ."—ILYA REPIN

78. *To ALEXANDRA PURGOLD*

3 January, 1872
[Monday]

Many thanks, Alexandra Nikolayevna, for the information concerning Saturday and I heartily beseech you to arrange for *Boris* on *Saturday,* as long as there are no hindrances of any kind for Vladimir Fyodorovich [Purgold] and those acquaintances of his who wished to
hear my little sins. I'm quite familiar with the Gogol subject [*Fair at
Sorochintzi?*], I thought about it two years ago, but the matter does
not fit into the path chosen by me—it doesn't embrace Mother Russia
in all her simple-souled girth. I'll inform Kvey, but I haven't yet informed him: I'm coming earlier tomorrow, for around 10 I have to

---

[84] This remark has borne some weighty interpretations, but the fact is that
Stasov and Musorgsky were merely unable to attend a performance of *Mignon*
that night.

be at Lukashevich's—very necessary.[85]—My reply is laconic, but the orchestration is right under my nose, and so, etc.—excuse me.

I firmly press your hand.

MODESTE MUSORGSKY

I am inventing *Grabbe Spunskij.*[86]

Why is there no word from you about the health and powers of the *dear Orchestra* [Nadezhda Purgold]?

79. *To VLADIMIR STASOV*

Friday Jan. 7, '72

MOST DELIGHTFUL *généralissime,*

Tomorrow, Saturday, at the Purgolds', beginning at 8:30 P.M. we are going to pull *Boris* by the hair. Naturally we shall meet, naturally we shall have a talk, naturally it will be pleasant for me to see the dear *généralissime,* naturally it's always pleasant for me to see him, naturally I've chattered too much, and I may be too late with the news —naturally I finish the letter.

MUSORYANIN

80. *To VLADIMIR NIKOLSKY*

[February, 1872]

Dyainka,

Such is the pastille extracted yesterday by Korsinka from the belly of the Directorate for our use:

```
┌─────────────────────────────────────┐
│                                      │
│        Marinsky Theater              │
│                                      │
│      Lower Loges    16 Febr.         │
│                       1872           │
│                                      │
│      No. 2 on the right              │
│                                      │
└─────────────────────────────────────┘
```

and this pastille was extracted on the occasion of *The Stone Guest* [87]

---

[85] Possibly in regard to the *Boris* conspiracy.

[86] This may be a figure (since discarded) in the "Polish" Act, on which Musorgsky was working at this time.

[87] *The Stone Guest* finally achieved its première on February 16, 1872.

and for the joy of beholding and hearing it. And *dyainka* should scribble on a scrap of paper whether he accepts the proffered cabbage and whether he'll be in the loge, which is designed to hold: *Vasili Vasili Vasili* * with his spouse, *dyainka*, Lodyzhensky, Korsinka and me.

But one can kiss, so I do.

Dyainka

* Musorgsky's note: Read: Vasili Vasilyevich Vasiliev; he has begged to be there with his spouse.—In view of—but then there's nothing to view.

81. *To ALEXANDRA and NADEZHDA PURGOLD (A Satirical Ode)*

Hey, you girls so lovely,
Girls who play and sing,
Listen to my story—
In a mighty kingdom,
In the broadest country,
There lived two boys of talent,
Two musicians of great talent,
Just like you, you lovely girls,
Both are young and handsome,
Singing praises to Apollo,
Charming all around them.
The majestic air of one　　　　　[Rimsky-Korsakov]
Recalls the Colossus of Rhodes,
Like an eagle he soars above,
Thus he flourishes on earth
With all four of his eyes.
He sees all and watches all,
Even little ribbons in the hair,　[of Alexandra Purgold]
Even that he sees and watches.
Although his thought sublime
Often sojourns in heaven,
Nevertheless his tongue
Often wags unnecessarily.
Once, in an hour of solitude,
Forgetting worldly vanity,
Absorbed in sweet oblivion,
He had plunged into reverie.
And in this blessed moment

He saw a lovely vision,
Inspiration descended from Heaven
And he created *Pskovityanka*.
This great work of art
Will go down to posterity,
And the Ancient, full of emotion,   [V. F. Purgold]
Will shed at its name—a tear.
The other hero of my story   [Musorgsky]
Does not lag behind his friend,
In skill and wit a Mephistophel he,
But in talent—an Apollo.
When he sings or plays,
Gracioso lifts his little hand,
And at each lofty note
He uses a lorgnette.
His eye with flame flashes,
His lips drip bitter humor,
His look inflames the heart,
But in his word is poison heard.
A fancy to become a saint,
To take on a higher order,
The Cardinal's mitre to don,   [Rangoni, in *Boris*]
To save the lovely sex's soul.
Such a thought is quite lovely,
Basically and charmingly,
But these blessings of his
Don't guarantee you paradise,
Because your dear salvation
Will require a little more—*Mesdames.*
But he has raised himself a monument,[88]
He has glorified the proud Boris,
And his work, henceforth imperishable,
Has brought to Russian music glory.
To you, great talents for these deeds,
Let there be resplendent rewards,
Let your brethren musicians
Clap on you the laurel wreath.
Over the flower-carpeted path,

[88] "I have raised myself a monument . . ."—Pushkin.

> Let the god of arts lead you,
> With speeches ringing with your fame,
> Let word of you pass from year to year.

M.M.

FEBRUARY 1872

82. *To MILI BALAKIREV*

22 March
1872

MY DEAR MILI,

Your note came to me simultaneously with a card from Gayevsky, on which it is indicated that the concert of the literary foundation will be conducted by Leschetizky—well, let him conduct.[89]—If, my dear, you find the polonaise worthy of inclusion in the program of your concert,[90] I am delighted and I don't see any harm in the fact that it goes on at the end: those who remain in the *salle* will be those who are *really* interested in this work. And for that which can be read between the lines of your note, I firmly and warmly thank you.

MODESTE MUSORGSKY

You will do me a great service by performing the polonaise; it is indispensable for me to hear myself on the orchestra, without the participation of the chorus, which hasn't occurred since I began to compose [*Boris?*].[91]

A Group Commission

. . . the following work fell to the lot of the members of our circle. Gedeonov, Director of the Imperial Theatres at the time, had considered the idea of producing a work which should combine ballet, opera, and féerie. For this purpose he had written a program for a

---

[89] Balakirev's ties to music and musicians were being cut—one by one. The Literary Foundation, where Balakirev had conducted his successful Shakespeare program, had now put its concerts in the hands of Theodor Leschetizky.

[90] The last concert for the Free Music School which Balakirev conducted. During the preceding month Napravnik had programed the Coronation Scene at a concert of the Imperial Russian Musical Society.

[91] Balakirev later wrote Stasov in regard to this polonaise: ". . . I made several suggestions to him which he made use of, as I can see from the published *Klavierauszug*. I don't know if his orchestration was corrected. I never heard it on the stage. The remaining numbers of *Boris* were instrumented and composed without any participation of mine . . ."

theatrical production in 4 acts on a subject taken from the Elb Slavs and had commissioned V. A. Krylov to develop the text. *Mlada*, with its fantastic and genre scenes, appeared a most grateful subject for a musical portrayal. Gedeonov offered the composition of this music to Cui, Borodin, Musorgsky and myself; moreover the purely ballet numbers were to be composed by Minkus, the official ballet composer of the Imperial Theatres. From where this order originated, I do not know. I presume here the influence of Lukashevich . . . I also assume that this affair would not have happened without V. V. Stasov's participation. The four of us were invited to Gedeonov's for a joint discussion on the work. Act I, as the most dramatic, was entrusted to the most dramatic composer—Cui; Act IV, a mixture of the dramatic and the elemental, was entrusted to Borodin; Acts II and III were distributed between Musorgsky and me. Some portions of Act II (folk choruses) were assigned to me; and in Act III, I was given the first half: the flight of the ghosts and the appearance of Mlada; while Musorgsky undertook the second half—the appearance of the Black God, into which he wanted to fit his Night on Bald Mountain, which had been left inactive . . . —NIKOLAI RIMSKY-KORSAKOV

83. *To VLADIMIR STASOV*

MY DEAR,

You don't complain that I did not answer your letter, and this troubles me; this event occurred because our writing table looks like the Augean stables and only now was I able to find a scrap of paper. How delightful you are—this you know. And that I don't stop kissing you, that you also know. I am sending the requisition to Repin this very day,[92] but *Mlada!*

> *And beyond the damp sepulchre*
> *There is no peace for me* *
> *From her, the dear departed* (read "still-born").

It's a shame to take my pen to picture "Saganu, hush!" and such rot, written by somebody, sometime, perhaps, with a drunken eye and brain [93]—and I am expected to be inspired by these fumes of *delirium*

* Musorgsky's note: Who is "beyond the damp sepulchre"—the author of the text [Victor Krylov] or Mlada or both? Decide yourself.

[92] Bessel wanted an impressive cover on the *Nursery* album and Musorgsky was asking Repin to design one.
[93] This "drunken" text, or an expansion of it, was brought, along with the "Bald Mountain" music, into the later *Fair at Sorochintzi*, and there dignified with this note in the score: "The text for this part of the scene was borrowed from Sakharov's collection. M. Musorgsky." This source, *Narratives of the Russian*

tremens. Disgusting! By my nature I have long struggled against a
nasty feeling that certain little people attribute to me, but when the
cause, giving birth to this nasty feeling, is not wiped out or it is not in
my power to wipe it out, then the struggle is transformed from acute
to chronic (this parallel is a true one: a nasty feeling, long sickening
a man, is a disease, a chronic disease—permanent, *récidive*). The hire-
ling attitude of the collaborators of *Mlada,* their appraisal of work—
blockheaded to an indecent degree, the lack of all *ethics* in our worthy
contractor [Gedeonov], and consequently the moral *fiasco* (not so far
beyond the hills) of our circle—that's what sickens me. My kind and
dear friend, you know that I can't carry rubbish in me and nurse it;
therefore I must change to an active position—it is simpler, more direct and better. I declared (as inoffensively and as delicately as I could)
to Korsinka and Borodin, that in order to save the maiden innocence
of our circle, to prevent its becoming a street walker, I will, *in the matter of our hiredom,* do the prescribing, not the listening, the questioning and not the submitting to questioning, and this, of course, only
with Korsinka's and Borodin's permission to speak for them and for
myself, and as for the contractor—let him do what he wants.

I am writing the Black God, which is turning out quite well, very
good in the voices.

And in the meantime, here is a joy for you. Korsinka implores me
to manufacture another *penny paradise* with a description of us sinners, and instead of Euterpe—Ged[eonov]. The idea is a capital one
because he, Korsinka, asks me to give us all a *hiding* with love (of
course myself too—*chic*), so that if this little thing is a success, our

---

People, collected by N. Sakharov (St. Petersburg, 1841) includes the following
items of interest:

13. *Song of the Witches on Bald Mountain.* Among the narratives forbidden
by the villagers there is a legend that a Cossack who climbed Bald Mountain over-
heard the witches' song, and that the Sabbat assembly, discovering this, drowned
the Cossack in the river. Ever since, the song wanders over the world . . . There
is little possibility of comprehending the meaning of its words, for they are a mixture of sounds from a language unknown to anyone—perhaps one that never
existed . . .

14. *Sabbat Song of the Witches.* This Sabbat song of the witches, say the villagers, was revealed by a young girl who, from being a witch, was brought back to
her former [natural] condition.

    Gutz!
    Alegremos!
    Astaroth, Behemoth! [etc.]

circle is saved: [because] no Philistines of any kind punish themselves
for their own blunders.—Wonderful! Wonderful.

I firmly kiss you, my dear,

MUSORYANIN

Till tomorrow

Boris and the Historians

. . . I don't remember the exact date, but I think it was probably
March or April, 1872, when I invited Kostomarov [94] to my home to
hear excerpts from *Boris Godunov*, which Musorgsky was to play.
Both Musorgsky and I were very eager to hear what our highly
esteemed Kostomarov would think of the plot and libretto of the new
opera, and perhaps of the music as well. Kostomarov brought Gay [95]
along with him, which delighted Musorgsky and me. Kostomarov was
extremely pleased with *Boris*, even with the new and unusual music,
and kept exclaiming delightedly—about the libretto, the personality
of the characters, the scenes—"Yes, this is real Russian history."
. . . Gay was also very pleased, although it was Italian music that
he loved and knew well. In one of the intermissions, when Gay perhaps felt especially moved by the historical creative power of Musorgsky, he began to tell us the plan for a new painting he was thinking of doing. It was a scene in Uspensky Cathedral—the youthful
Tzar Alexei Mikhailovich, placing his hand on the tomb of the
sainted Metropolitan Philip, in order to retain Nikon as Patriarch,
swears never to interfere in the clerical affairs of Russia. Although
the subject seemed to me very interesting and picturesque, I rose up
at once against it, and warmly began to prove to Gay that in my
opinion he should not have taken such a subject—a triumph of clericalism, of a despotic and arrogant clericalism, over the frightened,
youthful Tzar. Gay naturally defended his idea, but Kostomarov and
Musorgsky were on my side, and finally Gay capitulated and the picture was not mentioned again. He never even started to paint it.—
VLADIMIR STASOV

84. To VLADIMIR NIKOLSKY

LITTLE FRIEND *dyainka*,

Tomorrow, Saturday, at Vladimir Fyodorovich Purgold's, *Boris*

---

[94] Nikolai Ivanovich Kostomarov—possibly the most distinguished Russian historian of his day—a valuable academic bulwark for the nationalist group.
[95] Nikolai Nikolayevich Gay—a painter of historical and genre subjects. In a
letter written some time after this occasion, Stasov mentions that Daniil Mordov-
tzev, the historical novelist, was also present this evening.

will be in all his inviolability, and so do come, and *we bow to thee and await thee.*

Very much *dyainka* Musorgsky.

Friday, 7 April

Many thanks for the dress-suit, and regarding the tramps,[96] that is *turning out well.*

85. *To MILI BALAKIREV*

DEAR MILI,

I must have the score of my polonaise for correction and submission to the Theater Committee. Be so kind as to tell me: *When may I send to you for it?* In order to avoid disturbing you, dear Mili, I ask you earnestly to leave the polonaise with your servant, so she can hand it over to my messenger on the day that you set. I firmly press your hand and implore you not to delay me.

Your

MODESTE MUSORGSKY

Monday
24 April, 1872

86. *To VLADIMIR STASOV*

DEAR *généralissime,*

I implore you to be at Cui's this evening, that business with the kids [97] is not lost, *there may still be time;* I saw Bessel, he will be at Cui's, too: it would be good to talk over how to prevent that misfortune. Bessel is very eager for the children to have a drawing. I implore you to help Musoryanin.

Your

MUSORGSKY

1 May, 1872

We'll go through the whole *Mlada* at Cui's and we'll all be there.

---

[96] The new final scene—near Kromy ["A forest glade near Sokolniki on the Dniepr"].

[97] This is still in regard to Repin's drawing for *The Nursery.*

I V

Khovanshchina: Sketched
1872 — 1873

Sometimes one must express something, "although a stake be sharpened on the head." I am pregnant with this something and I am giving birth—and to what I am giving birth you will see, my dear *généralissime.* What can it mean, that occasionally I feel your absence very keenly? that feeling your absence, I grow disquieted? (I am no woman.) What must this mean, that when I am disquieted—not firm —I miss you? Do not think that this means "O thou, whom I fear to love" and so forth. All this and other such obscenities to the side.

Ex abrupto:
How dared you think that I do not acknowledge the fact that you acknowledge me? *Slav, see how great are your trespasses!* And what if Musoryanin were to thunder over Mother Russia! More than once have I plowed the black earth, and I want to plow the unfertilized, virgin earth; not merely to become acquainted with the people, but I thirst to be their brother: frightening, but good! What then? and why did I accuse this *Russian* of heresy? Am I not aware to what I should echo? do I not sense where power is hidden, where truth clouds the eye, and perhaps the nostrils too: I could sneeze for spite!

The black earth's power will manifest itself, when you plow it to the very bottom. It is possible to plow the black earth with tools wrought of alien materials. And at the end of the seventeenth century they did plow Mother Russia with *such* tools, that she could not immediately discern with what they plowed, and how the black earth *opened up* and began to *breathe.* And there the beloved Mother gave herself to sundry actual and privy state councilors and they gave her, the long-suffering, no time to collect herself and to think: *"where are you pushing me?"* The ignorant and confused were executed: *force!* and officialdom goes on and the search is ever as of oft: only the times have changed: the actual and privy state councilors disturb the *breathing* of the black earth. The past within the present—that is my task.

"We've gone ahead!"—you lie, *"we're still here!"* Paper, books, they've gone ahead—we're *still here*. So long as the people itself cannot verify with *its own eyes* what is being cooked out of it, so long as it does not *itself* will what is to be cooked out of it—we're *still here!* Divers public benefactors are quite apt to glorify themselves, and to fix their glory in documents, but the people groans, and drinks to stifle its groans, and groans all the louder: *still here!*

You are dear to me, not because you are necessary to me, but because you demand much, but I demand still more, it is so tempting, so fascinating. And you are beloved to me because you are cunning at pushing the All-Russian woodchucks who sleep and stay awake, both at the wrong times. Once I had a thought: what if *he* shouldn't exist? And now, at this very minute, I am awe-struck and bitter and I was just as awe-struck and just as bitter then. Without you I should fail in $3/4$ of my attempts. No one sees better than you in which direction I wander, what excavations I dig, and no one looks more directly and further than you upon my distant path (and the path is remote—I have barely skirted the open fields); and therefore no one besides myself is aware of your might, and therefore I am aware of it *with all my guts* (a metaphor you love).

If, some day, the thought should unexpectedly knock at your brain that you are not understood in music, in the same sense that you are understood in the arts of sculpture, painting, architecture,—tell that thought that she is lying and immature, and that she should run to me; I will give her evidence on that account to be delivered properly. And if the lady-thought, being of the female gender, falsifies or leaves the message incomplete, I myself will be able to knock at your brain (maybe I've already knocked) in order to avoid this feminine and therefore (they say) *gentle half-spoken thought.*

E basta! I wished—I did.

MUSORYANIN

16 & 22 June, 1872

I ask you to count this epistle in a numerical order as No. 1, for other epistles, too, will occur consecutively, of various tastes and leavens, but on the subject of the *streltzi*.[1] May this be in memory of our new work, our bold work.

HE, MUSORYANIN

Stasov Proposes a New Opera

   . . . It seemed to me that the fight between old and new Russia, the exit of the former and the entrance of the latter, would provide rich soil for drama and opera, and Musorgsky agreed with me. In the center of the plot I wanted to place the majestic figure of Dosifei, the leader of the dissenters [or Old Believers], a strong, energetic man of keen intellect and vast experience, who, as a controlling force, guided the acts of the two Princes—Khovansky, the representative of the ancient, gloomy, fanatical, dense Russia, and Golitzin, the representative of Europe, which was beginning to find favor even among the courtiers of the Tzarevna Sofia. Various characters and events in the German and *streltzi* quarters, the German pastor and his old sister, their young niece, two members of the sect of the Old Believers, one, Marfa, aflame with youth and passion (a Potiphar's wife), the other, the withered, yellowed, malicious, fanatical Susanna, both ever at strife, the ten-year-old Peter, with his personal guards, clever, energetic Sofia, with her savage *streltzi*, the monastic retreat of the dissenters, the sectarians burning themselves at the close of the opera, when Dosifei realizes that "old Russia" is passing away and a new age beginning—all that seemed to us a grateful task.—VLADIMIR STASOV

88. *To LUDMILA SHESTAKOVA*

LITTLE DOVE OF OURS, LUDMILA IVANOVNA,

Five years ago you realized your blessed wish to gather together a Russian musical circle in your home. You have been a witness of heated doings, occasional struggles, aspirations, and again struggles, of the circle's members and your heart always responded in a lively way to these struggles, aspirations and heated doings. Much good has

---

   [1] The *streltzi* were a regiment of musketeers, almost independent of the rest of the Russian army, and used as a powerful political weapon by the struggling factions around the Russian throne in the seventeenth century. When Peter I threatened to assume full power, the *streltzi* were incited to rise against him. Peter put down the uprising and eliminated this political weapon forever. This is the period and pivotal event of Musorgsky's projected opera *Khovanshchina*, of which this is the first note in his letters. This title is the single word used contemptuously by Peter on receiving the news that the Princes Khovansky had organized the rebellion of the *streltzi* in order to seize the throne for themselves.

been accomplished and for this good you deserve a tribute, yours by right.—The circle's past is bright—its present is overcast: gloomy days have begun. I do not accuse any one of the members, "because my heart holds no malice," but owing to my inborn good-natured laughter I can't help honoring the circle with a quotation from Griboyedov: "Some have been expelled, others, see, are killed;" [2] but what has benefited Skalozub is very sad for the circle, and try as I may to drive away a tiresome fly that buzzes the evil phrase "fallen to pieces," the fly stays there buzzing—it is as if one could hear laughter, wicked laughter, in its buzzing. You will have to rally, little dove, the remnants of the shattered holy army, and even if it is impossible to face all sorts of Chaldeans in battle, we must go on fighting to the last drop of blood, literally. Fighters will be found from whose hands one cannot tear the banner, and these fighters will rally, although clothed in rags, but their own rags, not borrowed, and not the women's robes and skirts worn by the holy army of the grand executor.[3] The artist believes in the future because he lives in it. This faith has prompted me, while laying my tribute at your feet, to confess to you. Accept my *Boris* under your wing and may he be blessed and start out from you on his public ordeal.

MUSORGSKY

Petrograd
11 July, '72
Olya's day [4]

89. *To VLADIMIR STASOV*

"Soon the foe will come and darkness will set in."
"Black impenetrable darkness"—thus whines the simpleton in my

---

[2] Skalozub speaking in Griboyedov's *Woe from Wit*. The members of the Balakirev Circle were functioning less as a group, and were now pursuing more individual careers.

[3] Napoleon's *Grande Armée* in its winter retreat of 1812.

[4] The name-day of Shestakova's dead daughter, Olga.

Boris [5] and, I'm afraid, not in vain. The city of Himself-Peterbuch and its environs depict, in the two-legged department, a continuous children's camp; factory-hands wander in the streets, whistling or hoarsely singing military marches, even the women berry-vendors call and whine in a military manner, for instance:

[Berries, juicy raspberries!]

and non-Russian sevenths and raspberry fanfaronade.

Innocent angels—the children, exercise with the help of carefully tooled muskets in the application of the Malthus theory [6] and patiently wait for the commander, a more mature innocent angel who, in his turn, awaits the arch-commander, this time a young telegraph boy "carrying messages" with Zeus' thunderbolts on his shoulder straps and in his cap band, and with the face of a peasant-girl. In *Pärgala* I heard the savage war cries of those human minnows, I saw from afar the banners, badges, sabers, muskets . . . these minnows are being drilled, they say, by some hussar officer. Froggies with hanging bellies, bowed legs and also with homemade muskets can be seen marching on the *Platzparade* . . . What will come of this? Even the roosters crow marches! What is to come?

By the time you return, dear *généralissime,* all the materials for our future opera will probably be collected. I have put together a notebook and entitled it *"Khovanshchina, a people's musical drama—materials";* [7] on the title page I listed my sources—9—not at all bad, that: I am swamped with information, my head is like a caldron, just keep throwing stuff into it. Zhelyabuzhsky, Krekshin, Count Matveyev, Medvedev, Shchebalsky and Semevsky are already sucked dry; now I am sucking at Tikhonravov, and then comes Avvakum—for dessert. Some days ago I plunged into the very depth and found the following pearl (the dissenters' retreat in Myshetzky's narrative): "To the Germans has been sent an entire horde of demons, to cause them to be insubordinate, without unity or obedience; and to them went

[5] These are the final words heard in *Boris Godunov*—in the Kromy scene.

[6] In his *Essay on the Principle of Population* (1789) Thomas Robert Malthus sees one advantage in war: it helps to keep population figures at a reasonable level.

[7] See inscription at end of Letter 90.

Teut with a regiment of demons and taught them to spread corrup-
tion; those who accepted this teaching were named Teutons and pride
themselves in being sage in the accursed learning. So also to us has
Lucifer dispatched his cohorts—to snare and draw us to great lust,
and in particular to pride, drunkenness, *to idleness and dancing*. He
also dispatched accursed women—all-knowing witches, fortune-tellers
and *seers:* Thus have Bacchus and Gordad with their comrades over-
whelmed the entire land of the north!" (With this there is a close connection between heavenly and aerial phenomena: a thunderstorm in
January and the *destruction of the sun*). "And when they had set up
their kingdom, Lucifer sent a certain man (no one knows his name):
and he said to the woman in childbirth: 'I wish to kiss the great one
in your womb,' and when he had kissed, he said: 'Great One! 53
sazhens in height! Thou wilt wield the great cudgel.' And then a
thunderstorm broke over Moscow, it was the 6th day of January, and
the sun perished. In such wise, brethren, the evil spirit led . . . from
the womb, and that was the Antichrist!" [8]

On such a framework one may do much: it is pictorial, mystical and
a delightful caricature of history. There's much substance in the materials.

This epistle will not go to Moscow, but *nearer,* to [Stasov's] Melikhov house erected in Petrobourse; this occurred because of the sitting
together of many people in the *izvoshchik* (namely, the drivers) and
an observation of all sorts of sinful stuff among the ever criminal and
lecherous Germans close to the *Stenbokovsky Passage*—they love
money greatly and plunder a lot, therefore this is written: [9]

Even if the authorities do permit our opera, I shall still get a beating for my many great sins from the various Laroches, Fifs, Tomsons [10]
etc., etc., perhaps, however, by the time everything is ready, the par-

---

[8] This "pearl" is from the dissenters' story "Teuton and Gordad" (actually a
translation of a Polish work, "The Devil's Attack on the Race of Man") which
Musorgsky found in Tikhonravov's *Chronicles of Russian Literature and Antiquity*. It is Peter whose legendary birth concludes the narrative, his name being
cautiously omitted in Musorgsky's quotation. Peter returned from abroad in 1699
(the year of the *streltzi* uprising), fulfilling the dissenter prophecy of the coming
of the Antichrist.

[9] This mysterious paragraph is open to a number of interpretations. The *Passage* (built by Count Steinbock-Fermor) was also used as a promenade by St. Petersburg's prostitutes.

[10] "Tomson" is a labored English rendering of the Russian Famintzin. "Fif,"
of course, is Feofil Tolstoi.

ticle *in* may be discarded from the word *Ingermanland,*[11] and Laroche will enter the chancery of the German musical guild as a watchman (in the literal sense), Fif will become the apprentice of Bismarck's cook, and Tomson, because of his extreme and respected, although sterile, industry—will be driving away the flies from Bismarck's bald spot—and flies there will be for sure, Russian flies, no more easily driven away than the cockroaches, and in Germany there are such a lot of bedbugs that it's no wonder Shcherbina once ordered a waiter in Koenigsberg to bring a *Klopstock um Klopy zu schlagen.*[12] But however let's see who wins—we shall get a beating, and a hard one, and I am being beaten already but still who knows who will win.—(A rotten pen, but the heat is so fierce, that I'm too lazy to take another) (—meaning irresponsibility or extenuating circumstances). Why, *tell me,* when I listen to the conversation of young artists—painters or sculptors, not even excepting the monumental Misha,[13] I can follow their turns of thought, their ideas, aims, and seldom do I hear anything said about technique—unless it's necessary. Why do I, *do not tell me,* when I listen to our musical brethren, seldom hear a vital idea, but mostly stuff from a school-room bench —technique and musical ABC's?

Is musical art young only because its practitioners are half-educated adolescents? How many times, unintentionally, *through absurd habit* (in a roundabout way) I would start a conversation with the brethren—and this is what happened—either I was repulsed or not given a clear answer, or, more often, was just not understood. Well, let us assume that I am unable *to present my thoughts clearly*—that is to say: to present on a tray brains with thoughts printed on them (as on a telegram). But what about themselves? Why don't they start?—evidently they don't want to? *And evidently, you, généralissime, understand me, and furthermore, you touch that very place where you should touch—with a brave, firm hand.*

---

[11] Ingermanland is the name sometimes used for the Baltic area including St. Petersburg, Novgorod and Pskov. It was Balakirev who often said that the first act of invading Germans would be to rename this area *Germanland.*

[12] Nikolai Shcherbina was a punning poet, a friend of Balakirev. This pun hangs on the Russian word for bedbug—*klop.*

[13] Mikhail Mikeshin, a friend of Musorgsky and a colleague of Victor Hartmann, is best remembered for his monuments: the bell-shaped structure to Catherine the Great in the park before the Alexandrinsky Theater, and the Russian Milleniary monument, on which he collaborated with Hartmann, in Nizhni Novgorod.

Maybe I'm afraid of technique, because I'm poor at it? However, there are some who will stand up for me in art and in this respect also. I, for example, cannot bear it, when the hostess, in serving a good pie which she has prepared and we are eating, says: "A million *puds* of butter, five hundred eggs, a whole bed of cabbages, 150¼ fish . . ." You eat the pie and it tastes good, then you hear about the kitchen, and you at once can imagine the cook, always dirty, a chopped-off chicken head on a bench, gutted fish on another, and sometimes side by side, and somebody's intestines peeping out of a sieve (as though the Prussians had honored us with their presence), and more often one can visualize a greasy apron, the same apron that is used as a nose-rag, and which later will be used to wipe the edges of the pie dishes, in order to clean them . . . well, the pie grows less tasty. There is in ripe artistic productions that side of chaste purity, that when touched by dirty paws, grows loathsome.

In truth—until the artist musician rids himself of his diapers, his braces, straps, so long will the *symphonic* priests rule, setting up their Talmud "of the 1st and the 2nd editions," as the alpha and omega in the life of art. The little brains sense that their Talmud cannot be used in living art: where there are people, life—there is no place for prejudiced paragraphs and articles. And so they cry: "Drama, the stage, they cramp us—give us space!" And here they go giving free rein to their brains: "The world of sounds is unlimited!"; yes but their brains are limited; so what use is this sound of worlds, or rather world of sounds! One gets as much space when lying on "the lawn and following the flight of the heavenly clouds": there's a fleecy lamb, there's an old granddad, there's simply nothing at all, then suddenly, a Prussian soldier. I can't blame Polonius for agreeing with Hamlet about the clouds. The esteemed cloud is very changeable and in the wave of the hand may turn from a camel, to, perhaps, a Laroche.[14]—It isn't symphonies I object to, but symphonists—incorrigible conservatives. So do not tell me, dear *généralissime,* why our musicians chatter more often about technique, than about aims and historical tasks—because, this derives *from that.*

But all the same a thought puzzles me: why do the "Ivans" (IV and

[14] Musorgsky may not have known Shakespeare in English, but he certainly knew him in German, for the dig at Laroche has point:
Hamlet: Do you see yonder cloud, that's almost in shape of a camel?
Polonius: By the mass, and 'tis like a camel indeed.
Hamlet: Methinks, it is like a weasel. (Act III, Scene 2)

III) and especially the "Yaroslav" of Antokolsky, live, why do Repin's "Volga boatmen" and even the scrofulous boy in Perov's "Bird-catcher" and the "first couple" in his "Huntsmen," and likewise the unexhibited, but seen by me "Village Religious Procession" [by Repin] live, and they so live, that when one gets to know them, one has a feeling that "you are the ones I wanted to see." And why does all that is done in the latest music, in spite of its excellent quality, not live thus, and when you hear it, it seems: "Ach, yes, I thought, that you . . ." and so on.—Explain this to me, only leave aside the boundaries of art— I believe in them only very relatively, because *boundaries of art* in the religion of the artist, means *standing still*. What if someone's wonderful brains did not think and come to any conclusion; but other brains did think and did come to conclusions—where then, are the boundaries? But relatively—oh, yes! sounds cannot be chisels, brushes—well, of course, as *in each best thing there is a weakness and vice versa*—even children know this.

There's a diatribe for you to read. I saw a curious thing in *Kladderadatsch* today: the Germans ridiculed Bismarck for his desire *to be left undisturbed in Varzin*. (This was declared by him in the newspapers, as is already known). There those most respectful ones have pictured him in dressing-gown and slippers, with a dozing dog at his knee, feeding ducks and geese. As long as you are, it says, a statesman, don't dare relax.[15] I should have said: "Feed the ducks, my dear, feed them! Only don't put the Malthus theory into practice—and even without you it will be done: people are dying off like flies." Maybe there is a hidden meaning: maybe, think the Germans, "As soon as Bismarck retires on his laurels, he will invent the destruction of men." Well, then I am in agreement with them: "Let the criminal think, but only guard us, God, lest he come to a conclusion." . . .

The epistle was intended for the ruling city of Moscow and was to have been filled with a warm thirst for a close embrace. In the hope of doing this in person (the epistle should have been received by you on May 15) I control myself and because I control myself I will have to let myself go (like a spring) and I warmly kiss you, my dear. I've taken

---

[15] The caption under Wilhelm Scholz's cartoon, in the German humorous magazine *Kladderadatsch,* reads: "Prince Bismarck urgently requests, during his vacation in Varzin, to be spared from letters." Musorgsky is expressing a common fear of that period, that after the German victory in 1870, the newly strengthened German Empire would turn toward the east.

up the cross and with lifted head, bravely and happily, I shall go forth, against *all sorts of things,* towards bright, strong and righteous aims, towards a genuine art that loves man, lives with his joys, his grief and his sufferings. I do not ask for your hand: you long ago extended it and I've long held it firmly, my best, my dear support.

Your
MUSORYANIN

13 July, 1872, in Petrograd

90. *To VLADIMIR STASOV*

To Vladimir Vasilyevich Stasov, in dedicating *Khovanshchina.*

To me it doesn't matter and needn't matter that there is no precedent for dedicating such works as do not yet exist. No fear in my heart holds me from this dedication or makes me look back. I want to look forward, not backward. I dedicate to you all that period of my life occupied by the creation of *Khovanshchina;* there would be nothing funny in my saying: "I dedicate to you both myself and my life for that period," for I still vividly remember: I *lived* Boris in *Boris,* and the time I lived in *Boris* has left precious and indelible marks on my mind. Now the new work, your work, will boil, I already begin to live in it—how many rich impressions, how many new lands to discover, glorious!—So I beg you to accept "all my disorderly being" in the dedication of "Khovanshchina," *whose beginning came from you.*

MUSORYANIN

15 July, 1872, in Petrograd

[Inscribed on the cover of the enclosed notebook:]
I dedicate to Vladimir Vasilyevich Stasov my work, done to the best of my ability, inspired by his love.

15 July, 1872

MUSORYANIN

KHOVANSHCHINA

A people's musical drama

in five parts

by M. MUSORGSKY

194

Materials
1. *Annals of Russian Literature and Antiquity* by N. Tikhonravov (Moscow '61)
2. Journals of I. A. Zhelyabuzhsky and Silvester Medvedev
3. *History of the Vygovsky Hermitage* [16]
4. *Deeds of Peter the Great* by Golikov
5. *Regency of Tzarevna Sofia* by Shchebalsky (Moscow '56)
6. Extracted from *Russkoye Slovo*, 1869. No. 12: "Contemporary portraits of Sofia Alex[eyevna] and V. V. Golitzin" by M. Semevsky
7. Journals of Count Matveyev (St. P. 1841)
8. and of Archpriest Avvakum

M. MUSORGSKY   7 July, 1872 at Petrograd

I've been told that Tikhonravov is publishing a collection of folk miracle plays around September, 1872. One must wait for this, and when it comes out, it will also be included.

Collected between 14 & 15 July, 1872

M. MUSORGSKY

91. *To VLADIMIR STASOV*

You are right, my dear; if you had impudently received yesterday's guest—*it would have been fierce for us.* Paskhalov [17] is talented—obviously. Paskhalov is beaten down by fate—that's even more obvi-

---

[16] This source provided a prototype for the leading character of *Khovanshchina*, the towering figure of Dosifei, who had left behind him his life as Prince Myshetzky to become the leader of the dissenters. Musorgsky's Dosifei is also partly drawn from the character of Avvakum. Although Musorgsky refers to this volume as "Myshetzky's narrative" (page 189), it may be the Filippov record mentioned in Letter 61, or one of the 119 works left by Andrei Dionisevich Denisov, a prior of the Vygovsky hermitage, and the chief leader of the dissenters during the first half of the eighteenth century.

[17] Victor Nikandrovich Paskhalov was only two years younger than Musorgsky. His brief, frustrated musical career appears to have begun officially on "words" with Nikolai Rubinstein, abruptly concluding Paskhalov's term at the Moscow Conservatory.

On September 25 Stasov wrote Paskhalov of Musorgsky's enthusiasm, "and our whole circle was unanimously ecstatic."

ous. Paskhalov will have to be fished out of the mire, but so *that the fishing-rod will not be broken*—that's the problem. The vocal compositions of Paskhalov vouch for a finely shaped head: there's nothing affected or forced in them, although most of his chosen texts are so forced that they are capable of producing corns. But on the other hand these things bubble with Moscow malt and they're already bubbling over. I think that it's necessary, for a while, to forget about Paskhalov as a composer for the human voice. The time will come when Paskhalov will taste of "the tree of knowledge of good and evil" and will be ashamed of his nakedness, as was our venerable ancestor. The serpent's means will have to be replaced by an irritation of Paskhalov's oppressed conscience, and this matter I take on with the greater desire for I've never played the role of serpent-tempter.

And I was very pleased with the "wedding procession"; like a lively little stream on a day so hot that the forest is almost suffocating to death—that is how the procession affected me: its luster, strength, rhythmic riches, simplicity and ease of exposition roused me from the drowsiness induced by the bitter-sweet fizz of Moscow malt against a background of social sorrow—

> Band, and gusset, and seam,
> Seam, and gusset, and band,—
> Stitch—stitch—stitch! . . .[18]

Pfui! devil take these social rimesters, these pharisaical weepers!

I believe in Paskhalov and, as "faith without works is dead," I intend to act. In a few days I will open a campaign and strike directly at Paskhalov's weakness—his cordiality. However, of course, this letter will inform you, my dear, we shall talk it over, because the cause which we begin—is a holy cause.

MUSORYANIN

The night of 12-13 September '72.

The theme of Paskhalov's "wedding procession"—for a memo, until the whole piece can be sent you from Moscow.

---

[18] Paskhalov had set to music Thomas Hood's "Song of the Shirt."

92. *To VLADIMIR STASOV*

Généralissime,

Nothing is happening at the Purgolds tomorrow in regard to music, because it is impossible for Nadezhda N. Rimskaya.[19] You need not doubt that your little letter of yesterday had an effect, any more than you may doubt that I am rereading the travels in the Holy Land of the priest Lukyanov. The perusal of this will be the subject of an epistle to you in the swiftly flowing stream of time. I report to you, that this observant old-believer fellow of a priest is quite appetizing; one can find something about the Little-Russians, about the Turks and many other good things here. A scroll is being prepared for notes on important points, in order to embellish our *Khovanshchina*. Lukyanov's travels are almost exactly contemporary with the operatic life of *Khovanshchina* and in any case are stuffed with the most characteristic material. Altogether—you always hit the mark truly—remember your running comment yesterday to an accompaniment of Petya's [20] interjections. Well, *Boris* is beyond him. Yes, and "The Nursery" was requested by him only because Balakirev had praised it.

MUSORYANIN

When a gathering can be arranged at the Purgolds—we'll let each other know.

Entertainment at the Repins'

[At my request] V. V. Stasov agreed to stand as godfather to my daughter Vera [born October 6, 1872] and V. V. came along with M. P. Musorgsky. Both great musician and great historian stayed with us little people till late evening. M. P. entertained us, playing great Mozart on a poor piano. He improvised a lot [and played] "The Seminarist" and other things. He remembered many beggars' chor-

---

[19] On June 30 Nadezhda Purgold had married Nikolai Rimsky-Korsakov in the church of Shuvalovo—with Musorgsky as best man. Her sister Alexandra, whom Nadezhda had thought of marrying to Musorgsky, did not hesitate long after her sister's wedding—marrying in November of the same year a government official and amateur landscape painter by the name of Nikolai Molas. Musorgsky was best man at this wedding too.

[20] "Petya" is Piotr Ilyich Tchaikovsky, whose immediate reason for a trip to St. Petersburg was the submission of his new opera *Oprichnik* to the Imperial Theater Directorate. Could "Petya's" negative response to *Boris* be partially explained by his having composed a scene from Pushkin's *Boris* (in 1864–65?)—the fountain scene between Maryna and Dmitri?

uses. I guess he had learned them at the fairs. We laughed a great deal. He sang all this himself . . . —ILYA REPIN

93. *To VLADIMIR STASOV*

To Volodimir Vasilyevich Stasov the Wise,
an epistle from Musoryanin:

Verbal discourse with wise men cultivates the brain and trains the tongue, and the reading of wise men saves the soul. All this I have uttered with respect—with respect to the 1st and with respect to the 2nd. In respect to the 1st: it's clear to me that if I didn't push without permission into all sorts of arguments of any interest or sensible discussions I would *not* be myself; in respect to the 2nd: it's even clearer to me that if something or someone had not incited me to read *between the lines of wise men,* then—I should long ago have been confused in spirit and should resemble a holy pilgrim, viz.: one step forward and two steps backward.

Well, my dear soothsayer, I enjoy bliss in spite of the blue-gray gendarmes' trousers that block out Heaven; the source of this bliss is to be found in the books lent me by my Opochinin: such a *worthy* man—before he himself finished Darwin "On Man," [21] he has already lent me the first volume—he couldn't help it, and thanks to him. I am reading Darwin and I am in bliss; it is neither the power of Darwin's brain nor its clarity that enthralls me—I am already familiar with these attributes of the Darwin colossus through his earlier works; it is this that enthralls me: while instructing Man as to his origin Darwin knows exactly the kind of animal he has to deal with (how could he help but know!). Accordingly, without Man being aware of it, he is *gripped in a vise,* and such is the mighty genius of this colossus that not only is Man's pride not torn from him by this violence, but sitting within Darwin's vise is even pleasant, to the point of bliss. When a strong, burning and loving woman clasps her beloved to her, he is conscious of violence, yet he has no wish to free himself from her embrace, because this violence sends him "beyond the borders of bliss," because from this violence, "youthful blood roars with flames." I am not ashamed of this comparison: however we may twist and

[21] Darwin's *Descent of Man* had appeared in England a year before—in 1871. In Musorgsky's several comments on it in this and subsequent letters, he appears to have been more stirred by its implications than by its ideas.

coquet with the truth, he who has experienced love in all its freedom and power has *lived* and will remember how *wonderfully he has lived,* and will permit no shadow to fall on the bliss he has known.

You, my soothsayer, read Darwin in English, a year ago, therefore I bite my tongue *e basta!* But what I want to discuss is "between the lines" of Darwin. This colossus from the island shores is so colossal that all oceans, rivers and lakes show his reflection, and very probably the moon does, too; so it is not astonishing that the force of his ideas has penetrated to a Lilliputian, strengthening him forever in what might not be, after all, such Lilliputian endeavors: it was little David who slew great Goliath!

In spite of naïve tendencies towards the elegant delicacy of contour in naked Venuses, in Cupids and Fauns, with flutes or without flutes, with fig-leaves or "as their mother bore them," I maintain that the antipathetic (I meant to say *antique*) art of the Greeks is coarse. The Lilliputians are compelled to believe that the classical school of Italian painting is the absolute, while in my opinion—it is deadly and as repulsive as death itself. In poetry there are two giants: coarse Homer and refined Shakespeare. In music there are two giants: the thinker Beethoven, and the super-thinker Berlioz. When around these four giants we gather all their generals and *aides-de-camp,* we have a pleasant company; but what has this company of subalterns achieved? Skipping and dancing along in the paths marked out by the giants—but to dare to "go very far ahead," this is terrifying!

"And our own?" Glinka and Dargomizhsky, Pushkin and Lermontov, Gogol and Gogol and again Gogol (there is no one to approach him)—all great generals who led their armies of art to the conquest of good lands. Since then their artistic descendants have spent their time in manuring the soil of the lands, conquered, but not by them, although it is so naturally fertile that no fertilizer is required (the black-earth Little-Russians are wiser). Darwin has finally confirmed my most ardent dream which I have never ventured to approach without a certain thick-headed shyness. The artistic depiction of beauty alone, that is, in its material sense, is sheer childishness—art in its infancy. *The finest traits in man's nature* and in *the mass of humanity,* tirelessly digging through these little-known regions and conquering them—that is the true mission of the artist. "Towards new shores!"—fearlessly through storms, and shallows and treacherous rocks, "towards new shores!" Man is a social animal and cannot be otherwise; among masses of men, just as in each man, the finest traits always escape our grasp, those traits untouched by any one: to observe and study these, by reading, by observation, and by conjecture, to study them with *all one's inner being,* and feed humanity with them—such a healthy dish as they have never before tasted—there's a task! rapture and everlasting rapture!

Isn't this what we must try for in our *Khovanshchina,* my dear soothsayer?

MUSORYANIN

18 October '72 in Petersburg.

Although I am no woman, here is a P.S.:

Repin—"Volga Boatmen"   ⎫ pioneers in new lands
Antokolsky—"The Inquisition" ⎭ "towards new shores."

Another P.S.: Sculpture limited to *light and dark tones* is unsatisfactory.

Painting, regardless of the wealth of colors, is not satisfactory enough. Sculpture in colors must be developed, and for this, materials must be invented, the process to reveal the most delicate touches. What might Antokolsky have done with this in his "Inquisition," especially with the use of light that he already has!

94. *To VLADIMIR STASOV*

26 December, '72 [Tuesday]

MY DEAR *généralissime,*

I've had to spend all these days in the company of worshipers of absolute musical beauty [22] and have experienced a strange *feeling of emptiness* in conversation with them; this strange feeling of emptiness was replaced by an even stranger one, but an inescapable feeling—I cannot name it: it is such a feeling as hurts one in losing a very near and dear person, with whom, as they say, "the days were spent and the nights beguiled." Life boils and springs with such a person and one wants so passionately to live; this dear person passes away—and it is as if one were in a dense forest, at night, hearing only some sort of

---

[22] One of these was Tchaikovsky; among the others were certainly the recently wed Nikolai and Nadezhda Rimsky-Korsakov. On December 30, apparently immediately after the receipt of this letter and after Tchaikovsky's return to Moscow, Stasov sent him the well-known detailed program for the *Tempest* Overture. One cannot help wondering if Musorgsky was aware of this before planning his touching birthday present for Stasov, described in Letter 95.

Nikolai Rimsky-Korsakov
A photograph of the early '70's

Modeste Musorgsky
A photograph by Alfred Lorens in 1870

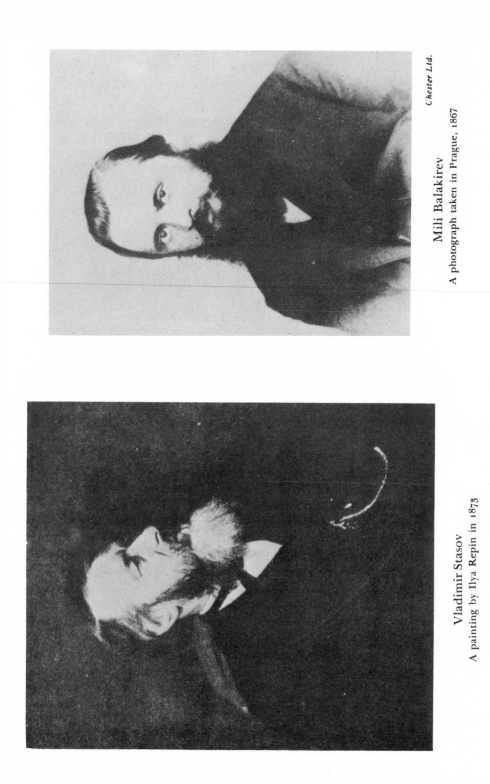

Chester Ltd.

Mili Balakirev

A photograph taken in Prague, 1867

Vladimir Stasov

A painting by Ilya Repin in 1873

incomprehensible sounds, and one is somehow frightened amidst the inhuman and lifeless sounds.—It was such an experience that began for me on Sunday. That day I had not dropped in to see you, because I was afraid of an attack of sore throat after Saturday's exercises. At Cesare's I felt an anticipation of this attack and, when I heard that it was pouring rain, I didn't dare come to you—there was no attack, after all. *The Oprichniki* was not shown on Sunday—the author [Tchaikovsky] had brought neither the score nor the piano arrangement with him; so other things were shown him in the following order:

Tisbé [23]—fiasco.

Mlada—was liked, except for "Morena" [in Cui's Act I]—fiasco (!), the trio—furore.

Nursery—he didn't agree with the type and aim of the composition; declared that the composer's rendition sells one the composition, but in itself, it is trash.

"Tramps" [24]—fiasco.

"Story of the Parrot"—furore.

Sadyk-pasha [25] was half dozing, dreaming of Turkish sweetmeats, or perhaps about Moscow leaven, into which he transformed himself all through the playing of the excerpts from *Boris*.—I always watch (instructively) the auditors, and noticing in Sadyk-pasha an unmistakable (serious) tendency to become leaven, I awaited fermentation. —Well, the leaven fermented after the "parrot," fermented and bubbles began to burst with a dull, lazy and unpleasant sound. From the sum of sounds (there weren't many) of bursting bubbles, I gathered: "a powerful one . . . (you know who), but dispersed powers . . . useful to work on . . . a symphony . . . (naturally *en forme*)." The powerful one thanked Sadyk-pasha and no more. Yesterday I happened to see Sadyk-pasha at Bessel's. The same Savka and the same hobby-horse: "Give musical beauty—only musical beauty!" Balak-

---

[23] Cui had found the subject of his next opera in Victor Hugo's play, *Angelo, Tyran de Padoue* (1835), which Ponchielli also used—for *La Gioconda* (in 1876).

[24] The Inn scene of *Boris*.

[25] Michael Czajkowski (the Polish spelling of Tchaikovsky) was a Polish writer and a thorn in Russia's side. Along with Mickiewicz he had formed legions in Turkey to fight by the side of France and England against Russia in 1855. Recently Czajkowski had adopted the religion of Islam and the name "Sadyk Pasha." Musorgsky could not resist attaching this title to his antagonist of the same name, Piotr Ilyich Tchaikovsky.

irev came in—with him I played Dargo's Finnish [Fantasy]. Sadyk-pasha did not approve—Pomazansky discovered a close relationship to Korsakov and was betrayed, head and all, by me to Balakirev. The encounter with Balakirev was quite warm, but while I was there he stayed only about half an hour (it was 10 in the evening); he said that as long as he had not recovered sufficiently to abandon music as a profession—until then he would not have the strength to practice music as an art (which is what he said to Shestakova too); he was in an excited state, played well, but too nervously and sharply. The object of Balakirev's visit was, apparently, Tchaikovsky's [second] quartet, played before my arrival; while I was there Balakirev corrected the transcription of the Finnish [Fantasy], made by Dargo himself, and corrected it well. After Balakirev left, they asked for *Boris*. Sadyk-pasha asked for "the parrot" and fermented himself into a frenzy, into a loss of the ability to listen; he didn't accept the polonaise.

On that I'll close.

MUSORYANIN

Orlov intends to spite the Russian Opera and God knows when *Pskovityanka* will go on, they are babbling about all sorts of intrigues —I don't understand a thing.[26] *The Oprichniki* is written with the aim of becoming a favorite with the public and to gain a name; the author has ingratiated himself with the public taste (O pasha!) and at the same time did his work very warmly and sincerely (O Sadyk!). In the first place, tastes are changeable, in the second place the public demands Russian things of Russian artists, in the third place—it is disgraceful to play with art for personal ends. It turns out that Sadyk, like a real pasha, is not devoid of cynicism, and openly embraces a religion of absolute beauty: *où qu'elle va se nicher alorsse la maman raison, comme vous venez de dire tantôt* (from the *Journal amusant*—speaking *"en patois,"* by such a *"novice"* to his *"brigadier"* or *"Sargent,"* which I read long ago)!

MUSORGSKY

---

[26] Whatever spite the tenor Orlov had in mind does not appear to have materialized in time to hinder the production of *Pskovityanka*, in which he sang a leading role.

95. *To VLADIMIR STASOV*

2 January, year 1873

To Volodimer Vasilyevich
from Musoryanin
Good health and glory to him!

No one more zealously than you has *kindled* me in all respects; no one has more simply and, consequently, more profoundly than you peered into my inner being; no one has more clearly pointed out my pathway. You are beloved by me—you know this; and I by you—I sense this. If our mutual attempts to produce a living man in living music are to be understood by living people; if *vegetating* people fling fine lumps of earth at us; if the musical Pharisees crucify us—then our cause will begin to progress, the fatter the lumps of dirt, the more furious they become, yelling hoarsely for our crucifixion, the more swiftly will our cause progress. *Yes, judgment is at hand!* It is so joyful to dream of our standing on the place of execution, thinking and living *Khovanshchina*, while they judge us for *Boris;* with a courage amounting to recklessness we gaze into the remote musical distance that beckons us onward and judgment cannot frighten us. They will tell us: "You have trampled all laws, divine and human, under foot!" We shall answer: "Yes!" and think to ourselves: "There's more to come!" They will croak: "You will be forgotten soon and forever!" We shall answer: *"Non, non et non, Madame!"* We have enough audacity to portion out to all judges.

On this *birthday of yours,* so dear to me, you do not leave my thoughts, *généralissime*—this comes "of itself" and it is understandable that if this is so, then the thought comes—how can you please a man dear to you? The answer comes without the slightest hesitation, as in all the boldest hotheads: give him yourself. And so I do. Take my youthful work on Gogol's *Marriage,* examine this attempt at musical speech, compare it with *Boris,* bring 1868 and 1871 *face to face* and you will see that I give you myself, irrevocably. I have included Kochkarov's part as copied out by Dargomizhsky himself, as a precious memory of what Dargomizhsky was to us in his last days; the part was copied by him in spite of a serious illness and his work on *The Stone Guest.*

I can't stand darkness and I think that for a connoisseur, *Marriage* will illumine much in regard to my musical audacities. You know

203

how *greatly* I value it—this *Marriage,* and for the sake of truth, you must know that it was suggested to me by Dargomizhsky (as a joke) and by Cui (not as a joke). The length and the date of the work are indicated, the place is also indicated, in other words—everything is in order and nothing is hidden away. So take me, my dear, and do with me what you will.

MUSORYANIN

(A note with reference to *"Non, non et non, Madame!"*).

During graduation at Smolny Monastery, the Empress Maria Fyodorovna was speaking to the girl with the highest marks, the Princess Volkonskaya, and happened to make a mistake in some historical reference. Volkonskaya remarked to the Empress: *"Non, Madame,"* and when the Empress rebuked her: *"On ne me dit pas non, ma chère,"* she replied: *"Non, non et non, Madame!"*

[Accompanying this letter is the manuscript of *Marriage* with this inscription on the title-page:]

An Experiment in Dramatic Music in Prose

MARRIAGE

(a completely incredible occurrence in three acts)

Words by N. V. GOGOL

Music by M. MUSORGSKY

I present my student work in eternal hereditary possession of dear Vladimir Vasilyevich Stasov on his birthday,
2 January, 1873.
Modeste Musoryanin,
that is, Musorgsky.
Written with a goose-quill in the Stasov apartment:
Mokhovaya, house of Melikhov, in an enormous press of people.
He, also Musorgsky

First Act
(in four scenes)
Characters: Podkolosin
—an aulic
councilor
Kochkarov
—his friend
Fyokla Ivanovna
—a matchmaker
Stepan
—Podkolosin's
servant

96. *To VLADIMIR STASOV*

30 January, '73

MY DEAR *généralissime,*

Zhemchuzhnikov's seat is reserved in *his* name in the 4th row on the left, Ivanov's [27] in *your* name in the 9th row on the left, and I'll make a note about Clark [28] right away; but the 3-ruble seats begin at the 13th row—what about this, does he want it? O Sadyk Pasha! we'll chatter about the rest when we meet.—I'm rushing off to an orchestra rehearsal: [29] "To be or not to be, that is the question."

Your

MUSORYANIN

Public Trial of Boris

. . . Toward the end of the theatre season, for someone's *bénéfice,* two [actually three] scenes of *Boris Godunov* were staged: the inn scene, [Maryna's dressing-room,] and the scene at the fountain. Petrov (Varlaam) was splendid, and Platonova (Maryna) and Kommissarzhevsky (Dmitri) were also good.[30] The scenes had a tremendous success. Musorgsky and all of us were in raptures, and plans were made for the production of *Boris* in its entirety the following year. After this performance Musorgsky, Stasov, Alexandra Nikolayevna (my wife's sister, who had married N. P. Molas in the fall of 1872), and other people who stood close to musical matters assembled at our home; at supper, champagne was drunk, with wishes for the speedy performance and success of the whole *Boris.*[31]—NIKOLAI RIMSKY-KORSAKOV

[27] Mikhail Mikhailovich Ivanov, critic and composer, was, as yet, still friendly to the Circle.

[28] Either William or Alfred Clark, brothers of Nikolai Stasov's wife, Marguerite.

[29] Of three scenes of *Boris Godunov,* to be given at the Marinsky Opera for Gennadi Kondratyev's *bénéfice* on February 5. The rest of Kondratyev's program consisted of Act II of *Lohengrin* and Act I of *Der Freischütz.* The conductor was Eduard Napravnik.

[30] Other roles in these scenes were sung by Dyuzhikov (Misail), Abarinova (the hostess), and Kondratyev (Rangoni).

[31] Musorgsky came home from this celebration and in the dark touched something prickly and strange on his table. His fright was transformed into a more pleasurable emotion when he lit the lamp, and found that a wreath from Polyxena Stasova had been laid on his table in his absence. He thanked her on April 22 by sending her a photograph with this inscription: "To the dear and nicest lady, for frightening me on 5 February 1873."

97. To EDUARD NAPRAVNIK

6 February, '73

Eduard Frantzovich, you do not accept eulogies—which makes you all the stronger and loftier; but won't you receive the confession of a musician?

On Monday, February 5, you did an unheard-of thing; only your artistic strength could have, with 2 rehearsals, interpreted the scenes of *Boris* with such fire and artistry. Considering all my painful excitability, your first assault, and the following ones, on *Boris*, made me begin to love you warmly, as a champion-artist (you can't forbid me this). You probed not only into the details of orchestral performance, but into all the finest shades of staging and declamation; in all your remarks I perceived a sincere desire for the success of the work; I considered and I consider your remarks an honor and reward to my student labor: such fine, such artistically true understanding of a composer's intentions could only come from an artist of great talent.— Neither in thought nor in dream, in spite of the ovations, not once did I attach any importance to myself (this was my only merit on the evening of February 5): all the honor and glory of the performance of the scenes of *Boris* I ascribe to you, Eduard Frantzovich, and to our dear comrade-artists and to the glorious orchestra. I tell you frankly that I bless your name for enabling me to continue my studies.

MUSORGSKY

P.S. They say that *gingerbread* [Gedeonov] felt abominably and conducted himself likewise on the evening of February 5, they say that his lip reached out towards your conductor's baton wishing to catch it and swallow it, but was limited to his customary chewing, because of his total weakness from senility.

Announcement by *VASILI BESSEL Printed in* Muzikalny Listok, *March 25, 1873*

Having obtained the copyright in all countries for the composition *Boris Godunov* (opera in 4 acts with prologue, the subject taken from Pushkin and Karamzin), music by M. Musorgsky, we have the honor to announce the opening of a subscription for an edition of the complete piano and vocal score of this opera. The subscription price is 10 silver rubles. The sales price will be 15 silver rubles. In this published transcription there will be included scenes which, in order to avoid length in the spectacle, will not be performed in the opera's theatrical production, and the size, therefore, will be quite imposing. The transcription is by the author. In view of the approaching summer season, the subscription will shortly be closed. The *Klavierauszug* will appear next fall.

98. *To VLADIMIR STASOV*

[May 3, 1873]

DEAR, SPLENDID, MOST SPLENDID *généralissime*—

How important! "Fomka, Yepikhan! behind the boyar!" "How important!" [32] *I am utterly happy.* Thank you, my dear, I am ready to talk, write and do all sorts of foolishness. *Our common cause, dear to us, is safe.*

MUSORYANIN

Mission to Liszt

. . . My acquaintance with Fr. Liszt grew out of the policy of our publishing house. I went to Weimar for the first time on the advice of Musorgsky and C. A. Cui to show him the piano scores of the operas, Dargomizhsky's *Stone Guest* and Cui's *William Ratcliff*, which had just come off the press. In order to make the text of *The Stone Guest* intelligible to him, a German or French translation had to be added (*Ratcliff* was published with both Russian and German texts). Then M. P. Musorgsky, who had mastered the German language, undertook to interline Bodenstedt's translation of *The Stone Guest*, which seemed quite close to the original, and gave me this copy for Liszt . . .[33]—VASILI BESSEL

98a. *ADELHEID VON SCHORN*[34] *to VASILI BESSEL, St. Petersburg* [Extracts]

Weimar, 19 May [O.S. May 7], 1873

HIGHLY ESTEEMED M. BESSEL!

It is indeed a pity that you left our Weimar so soon; reading my letter, you will undoubtedly agree with me that it could not have been more unfortunate for you, for Russian musicians and for all that is represented by your interests, for you to have left on the eve of that

---

[32] From the Kromy scene of *Boris*—the peasants are ridiculing the captured boyar.

[33] Bessel must have kept this copy for himself, preparing Liszt's copy otherwise, for Musorgsky's labor of love, dated June 1872, is still in Leningrad.

[34] The Canoness Adelheid von Schorn was one of several noble female aides to the aged Liszt.

very day which would certainly have shown you how warm are the feelings held by our dear, great Liszt for your friends and for their compositions, so original.

. . . You cannot have known that after your visit, during which you brought to M. Liszt the latest compositions of your compatriots, MM. Balakirev, Borodin, Cui, Rimsky-Korsakov and others—he had the idea of giving to an orchestra for performance those of these compositions in which he was most interested and which the broad inquisitiveness of his great wisdom found required the most attention . . . This performance was finally given yesterday, but your men sustained a victory without you, and I must say that this first victory, however brilliant it was, considering those extremely distinguished and select auditors who acknowledged it—all this was as nothing to the victory which stole that evening; its unexpected hero appears to be M. Musorgsky, whom you particularly praised during your stay and who would be pleased to hear of it, and if he is able to understand its significance, he can be proud of it as well.

The memory of this performance will, I think and hope, long be treasured by those who had the honor and pleasure of attending it: it took place on the day after your entirely unexpected departure. You know that M. Liszt occasionally gives himself the rare pleasure of performing with the orchestra, which the Grand Duke has placed at his disposal—for himself, for his pupils and friends—those compositions known and unknown which he may wish to hear. This usually takes place in the morning at the theater, by the light of a few lamps and with no ceremony of any sort . . . In the half-dim salle, yesterday morning, there were not more than 30 of us but, with the exception of your humble servant who is quite inexperienced in musical matters, the auditors were highly qualified: His Highness the Grand Duke arrived in good time for the beginning, and shortly after, Her Highness the Duchess [35] and a few members of the princely family arrived; there were several close friends of the Maestro (R. Wagner), then visiting in Weimar, among them Otto Lessman, editor of the *Allgemeine Musik-Zeitung*, the only music critic in whom M. Liszt has faith; a few of his pupils, M. Urspruch, the young girls [Cecilia] Gaul and Amy Fay—talented young American girls, not to mention the very

[35] Maria Pavlovna, sister of Tzar Alexander II. This Russian occasion may have been partially in her honor.

young French composer and organist, M. d'Indy, of whom M. Liszt speaks with the highest praise.[86]

One of the compositions, arranged on the music racks, was M. Rimsky-Korsakov's ballad *Sadko*, printed copies of which you so kindly brought us; the most living curiosity, filled with the most sincere interest, lighted up the great ardent face of our conductor, and when he lifted the baton, the virtuosi, bent over their parts, with obvious passion, started the performance of the strange, most brilliant and yet perplexing composition of your symphonist. The enthusiasm in communicating the unfamiliar composition, about which the most incredible, the most legendary tales have been circulated, the intense attention with which the auditors followed the composer's ideas, embodied by a great interpreter, whose cassock emphasized each gesture of his—all this presented the most fantastic vision. You, dear sir, better than anyone else, would have sensed the profundity of its meaning, and your Petersburg friend, the author of this ballad, at the conclusion of which the Abbé Liszt could not find sufficient praise—indeed he would have felt it more than you.

After the performance . . . M. Liszt was in a gay mood at the table, several times speaking of his affection for Russian music, which you revealed to him. Your name called forth gratitude several times, especially in connection with the compositions of M. Rimsky-Korsakov, and also in regard to the *Klavierauszug* of *William Ratcliff* by M. Cui, the edition of which you presented to him and which seemed to him to be full of interest and novelty. And M. Liszt explained to the reverent listeners what it was that he particularly liked in the works of your musicians, which are worthy of serious consideration by modern musical Europe: having developed independently far from and apart from any foreign influence, they have brought something new into music which delights him in its rhythm and fresh taste. On his part he would be very sorry if your musicians, who discovered themselves while locked inside a fortress, indeed an extremely Russian fortress, would one fine day stop this energetic defense against foreigners. In his opinion nothing worse could happen to them than that, after such a zealous struggle in their youth against Mendelssohn and the Leipzig

[86] No record of this significant occasion has been left by any of these auditors, including Miss Gaul, of Baltimore, and Miss Fay, whose letters home were published as *Music Study in Germany*.

influence, they should suddenly fall under some other influence, even that of M. Wagner himself, despite his genius.

In regard to this there began a certain dispute between the Abbé and his friend and neighbor at the table, M. Lessman, who, without denying the originality of these composers, reproached them for the strange forms of their works and, from a current viewpoint, the barbaric aspects of their technique; this dispute dragged on because neither opponent would give in; both grew even more stubborn because of their love for each other and they spoke with complete frankness— and thus the dispute continued throughout the return, past the court greenhouses, to Liszt's drawing room . . .

. . . The large, bright crimson room awaited its master with windows opened onto the park's spring fragrance from the lindens; the great piano was also open, awaiting the inspiration of its master. While M. Liszt lit a fresh cigar at a candle kept burning on his writing-table, his glance fell upon one of the albums which you had given him and which, until now, he had not had time to examine: this was M. Musorgsky's "Nursery"; the album caught his attention; perhaps he hoped that here would be found fresh confirmation for the thoughts then filling his mind regarding your friends.

"There," said he to M. Lessman, "there is another of those compositions without familiar form; I had forgotten it . . . but I should be astonished if it doesn't contain a surprise for us . . ."

So speaking, he carried the album to the piano and, without removing the cigar from his mouth, began to play; the critic followed him and with a trace of a mocking smile as he glanced at the time indications on the first page, prepared to celebrate his triumph; on that page the time indication changed in each bar, beginning, as I, along with the others, was able to confirm, with 7/4, continuing in 6/4 and 5/4 and reaching 3/2, 3/4 and 4/4—seventeen times within 24 bars.[37] But Lessman had not taken into consideration the spiritual height and power of expression of M. Liszt . . . Hardly had the latter played, with great simplicity, several bars of this little song which clearly overcame him, than we were swept up in his emotion and M. Lessman's irony faded away.

. . . You should have heard Liszt crying out at each new page: "How interesting! . . . and how new! . . . What discoveries! . . .

---

[37] No. 1 of the *Nursery* cycle is "With Nursie."

No one else would have said it this way . . ." And thousands of other exclamations of satisfaction and pleasure which we all shared and which finally led to an action which is rare in him in regard to the innumerable worthy composers who daily bring him their works.

You know how little he likes to write letters and how difficult it is for him to express his thoughts on paper, so that, according to his wish, I must often be the more or less responsible interpreter of his thoughts. But this night the flame of his enthusiasm made him forget the presence of his "Mlle. Providence," as he calls me. Without a moment's hesitation and with the impulse of a lion, he dashed to his desk and at one sitting wrote to M. Musorgsky his impressions as he felt them; I myself sent off this letter, and it is with delight that I inform you of its sending . . ."[38]
[The original text of this letter is in French.]

99. *To VASILI BESSEL*

DEAR SIR.

VASILI VASILYEVICH,

The only answer to your letter of the 2nd of this May would be the fulfillment—and of course the prompt fulfillment—on my part, of your desire to have the manuscript of *Boris*. Here it is—I've been as fast as I was able. As to the terms of publication, I think we can discuss these in a few days, if not this very day; anyhow, what has been verbally agreed between us will remain unaltered when embodied in a document.[39]

Ever warmly greeting your activity,

MUSORGSKY

14 May, '73

[38] This letter, which might have determined Musorgsky's plans for this year (see page 227) and consequently his subsequent career and life, was never received by him. "Mlle. Providence" must have stumbled.

[39] This document was not drawn up till January 31, 1874—four days after the première of *Boris Godunov*. Musorgsky was to be paid 600 rubles by Bessel for all publication rights, 300 in the course of the opera's first season, the remainder in the course of the second. (See p. 317.) Bessel also claimed a portion of any royalties, etc., that Musorgsky might receive from abroad for foreign performances of *Boris*.

100. *To VLADIMIR STASOV*

MY WONDERFUL *généralissime,*

Do not expect me for dinner: I've been summoned to Bessel to set up and number *Boris* for printing; the matter is urgent, so I don't excuse myself, because it would be nonsense to do so. Cesare will be at your place this evening with *Tisbé,* I'll be there at about 9, of which Cesare has been informed.

Yours very firmly,
MUSORYANIN

16 May, '73, here in Peter

100a. *VLADIMIR STASOV to ZINAIDA STASOVA, Bad Reichenhall [Extract]*

May 21, 1873

. . . Yesterday evening we again had a little musical gathering. . . . Later we heard the *finally* finished and considerably revised Valse by Shcherbachov (dedicated to me, because I forced him to complete, to revise and to compose it): this was so incomparable, along with several other new things, that Cui spoke right out that he simply *envies* his creativeness, that what was done in the finale of the symphony would be enough to place him among the *first-class* composers; Borodin was as pleased and delighted as only that good and pure soul of his can be; I need say nothing about Musoryanin because it's we two who most of all have pushed Shcherbachov. For myself, secretly, I place this Shcherbachov (if only he doesn't stand still)—third, counting the first two as Musoryanin and that giant Borodin . . .

101. *To VLADIMIR STASOV*

Night of 1 June, '73

MY DEAR *généralissime,*

Here's the thing: if, 'gainst expectations, you run into Cesare, don't mention *that certain* mysterious document, which was dropped, not into the lion's mouth, as among the Venetians (*du temps*), but into the pigs' trough.[40] Cesare, after the letter from "Franciscus," [41] is in a

---

[40] Possibly one of the many anonymous letters sent to members of the Circle about Cui's music and criticisms.

[41] Musorgsky did not receive his epistolary benediction from the Abbé Liszt, but Cui received his. The formally friendly text of the latter letter can be found in *The Letters of Franz Liszt* (New York, Scribners, 1894). In May, Liszt also wrote

KHOVANSHCHINA: SKETCHED (1873

better mood and is getting down to good work, and if one should knock him with *this* message, then surely he would "turn sour."—Protect the man—serve the art. The devil take all this "dirt" [42]—but who cares.

My dear, *up to a certain time,* you must keep silent about "that certain thing"—I trust you.

Of course as ever Musoryanin, and not otherwise.

P.S. (Ladylike) There's so little time, that I delivered this letter on the next day. This resembles a man who, during an animated conversation, thinks of a *particularly witty remark* and only on the following day, tells it to his companions so it wouldn't be lost. *Fouchtra.— (bretone).*

101a. *DIMITRI STASOV to POLYXENA STASOVA, Salzburg [Extracts]*

Petersburg, June 6, 1873

. . . Musorgsky himself told Volodya [Vladimir Stasov] a few days ago that on Trinity Sunday, he felt fits of dementia such as he had had some years ago, and in saying this he himself emphasized that he is drinking very little, even though he loves to drink. It would be unfortunate if this should happen . . .

June 7, 1873

. . . Yesterday I dined with our family, stayed the whole evening; Musorgsky, whom I found considerably altered, also came to dinner; he is somewhat sunken, grown thinner, and considerably more silent, but he composes as before—well . . .

102. *To ILYA REPIN, Paris*

13 June [1873], Petrograd
at Vladimir Stasov's on Mokhovaya

So that's it, glorious *shaft-horse!* The *troika,*[43] though scattered, still

---

Bessel, thanking him for Dargomizhsky's *Stone Guest, Finnish Fantasy,* and *Baba-Yaga,* Rimsky-Korsakov's *Sadko,* Musorgsky's *Nursery,* and a Tchaikovsky score, and asked for orchestral parts for these, for which he was willing to pay.

[42] "Dirt" is written in Napravnik's Czech accent.

[43] Stasov's "troika" was composed of the painter Ilya Repin, the sculptor Mark Antokolsky, and the composer Musorgsky. When Andrei Rimsky-Korsakov asked Repin in 1927, then living in Kuokkala, Finland, to comment on this letter, Repin replied, denying his leading role in the "troika": "Well, what sort of a

pulls what has to be pulled. It doesn't let up its ceaseless pulling: it looks and sees, *but doesn't merely look*. Takes up one work—and is already thinking about another, that is to be pulled further. So that's that, *shaft-horse*. "Well are we bounden to thee." What a Sire Volodimer you have portrayed! [44] he already seems to crawl from the canvas into the middle of the room; what will happen when the canvas is varnished? Life, power—pull on, *shaft-horse,* don't get tired! And *I,* in the capacity of *side-horse,* pull once in a while just to avoid disgrace —I'm afraid of the knout. But tell me, *shaft-horse Ilya Yefimovich,* is it true that Europe is really better than Tartary, called in books Russ, Russia and Rossia? Personally, I feel quite nauseated with the Russian order, but this is because, as *side-horse,* I'm afraid of the knout. And would life be easy—if? Well, to hell with them!

Let us turn to the next page:

I'm terribly happy that you've gone to Europe, but I'll be even more happy when, after looking around and gazing to your heart's content, you settle down in some secluded spot, devoting yourself to work. Pull on, *shaft-horse*—the load is heavy, and there are plenty of broken-down jades. I should think that in surroundings quite different from the All-Russian bog, your coloring would stand out in more relief and with more dash, *Mr. Shaft-Horse.* However, who can figure out an artist: no one but oneself can understand oneself and lay down one's own laws. Shut up, *side-horse!* What a strong desire to do things, but Mother Russia keeps giving me only investigation work—of a bureaucratic nature—how vile! It's a good thing that's boiling, only I'm afraid that instead of good thick peasant cabbage soup it will turn out to be some thin broth. Anything can happen in the All-Russian kitchen! More than once have Russian artists, and great ones at that, shot at a crow and hit a cow; verily, there is one consolation: even aces can lose tricks, but this is small consolation, for there always were and always will be impotents. It's true, that "I feel no fear"—*push on and push on,* and some day we'll talk over what comes of all this.

I feel the direction in which one must pull, I tug at my lead-rope

---

shaft-horse was I! His genius astonished my spontaneous nature, but I could only sense it—I was unable to judge or recognize it." The Repin family left St. Petersburg at the beginning of May on their way to Italy, stopping on the way to see the International Exposition in Vienna. They did not reach Paris till October 10.

[44] Repin painted approximately eight portraits of Stasov. This one now hangs in the Tretyakov Gallery, Moscow.

and I need no driver, but suppose there's a barrier: or the lead-rope breaks, eh? or I strain and hurt myself. This is the thing: it is the people I want to depict: when I sleep I see them, when I eat I think of them, when I drink—I can visualize them, integral, big, unpainted, and without any tinsel. And what an *awful* (in the true sense of the word) richness there is in the people's speech for a musical figure, as long as all Russia hasn't been pecked open by the iron horse! What an inexhaustible (that too, as long as—) ore there is in grabbing everything that is *real* in the life of the Russian people! Just choose—one could dance for joy—if one is a genuine artist. Take your Volga boatmen, for example (I can see them, alive, before me)—there's an ox and a goat and a sheep and a broken-down jade and the devil knows how many other domestic animals, and musicians get away with a variety of harmonies, and deal with technical peculiarities, and imagine that they are "creating figures." It's sad. Long ago the artist-painter learned how to mix his colors and work freely, if only God gave him a mind; but we musicians—first we think, then we measure off, then after measuring off, we think again—what *childishness*, real childishness—*kids!*

Well, if I can succeed—thanks; if not—I shall remain in mourning, but the people will not get out of my mind—no, sir!

I kiss you firmly and warmly, dear Shaft-Horse Ilya Yefimovich, and to the lady and the young miss, greetings and best wishes.

MUSORYANIN

If you can send me a couple of lines about yourself, or about what you will (an artist must be free), I'll be grateful, even if these lines should be in a letter to Sire Volodimer, who is climbing out of his canvas.

I'm living on Shpalernaya Street in the house of Sinebryukhova, No. 6, apt. 15, in Peter-town.

Enter Poet

. . . I remember, as if I were hearing it now, my impression when I first heard the famous *Penny Paradise*,—I understood absolutely nothing; the others present laughed themselves sick; from all sides came exclamations: "Splendid!" "An ace!" etc. I was at a loss and looked around questioningly. Finally the meaning of the satire was

explained to me, and they told me the names of those against whom
the satire was directed—and I finally managed to convince myself
that *Penny Paradise* was really a wonderful work. In spite of this,
when Musorgsky and I were on our way home late that night, I decided to ask him, but not without considerable timidity: did he himself consider his *Penny Paradise* a work of art?

"You seem displeased, Mr. Poet?" said Musorgsky with a good-
humored chuckle.

"Oh, no, no," I said hastily, "not at all! It only seems to me that
Penny Paradise is—a joke; witty, wicked, talented, but all the same
only a joke, a prank . . ."

"And how could you be so irritated with me for this joke?" interrupted Musorgsky. "At the concert you met me, pressed me against
the wall as a kind of politeness, shouting that you recognize yourself
in me." He laughs, but at the same time he is convulsed with anger.

We neared our house.

"I don't want to sleep," Musorgsky says, "let's go to your place, and
I'll show you some other things."

We went in, lit the candles, and he sat down at the piano.

"I know what you need," he told me and played the "Lullaby"
from Ostrovsky's "Voyevode"—a work that is beautiful, musical, and
full of feeling and sincerity, and which sent me into a perfect rapture.

"There, that's no *Penny Paradise!*" I exclaimed, without restraint.
Musorgsky grinned again.

"This is dedicated to the memory of my late mother," he said.

"And to whom is *Penny Paradise* dedicated?" I asked.

We both burst out laughing.

Musorgsky stayed until early morning. Throughout the night he
played and sang without tiring, selecting all that he thought would
especially please me. I remember that, among other things, he played
"Saul," "Night" with words by Pushkin, the end of the fountain
scene from *Boris,* the scene of Maryna and the Jesuit, and the death
of Boris. It was only when the light of dawn came in the window that
we were reminded that it was time to part. We clasped hands firmly
and parted, but parted with the feeling that we had much more in
common than we had thought a few hours before, and that we must
see each other more often.

And we did see each other often . . . —ARSENI GOLENISHCHEV-
KUTUZOV [45]

[45] In the summer of 1873 Count Arseni Arkadyevich Golenishchev-Kutuzov
was 25, a young poet of promise. It was inevitable that he should meet Musorgsky:
both artists, leading a vaguely Bohemian existence, both also came of ancient and
illustrious, but now impoverished, noble families; they were even distantly related. And, at this time, they were both looking for a new friend: since Rimsky-
Korsakov had drifted away from intimacy with Musorgsky, the composer needed
a friend slightly less godlike than Stasov; and the poet, recently launched into
the literary arena, was in urgent need of genuine friendship.

103. *To VLADIMIR STASOV*

Petrograd. Tuesday 19 June, '73

MY DEAR *généralissime,*

I was in to see *Msr. le président*,[46] about whom the *"admiralty"* [Rimsky-Korsakov] had told me *frightening things,* and this is what appears: A newly born poet Count Arseni Arkadyevich Golenishchev-Kutuzov, of whom I've already spoken to you, consoles me both with his artistic nature and sympathetic mind, to such an extent that I took the liberty of making it possible for him to see you, my dear one. Because this highly audacious *thought* does not leave me, and I have been filled with grace that your contact with *Arsenti Arkadyevich* will be beneficial to his muse, as much as "he thirsts with trembling to behold you," I begin, and this is how you should interpret my beginning:

Since Pushkin and Lermontov, I have not encountered what I find in Kutuzov: this is no manufactured poet, like Nekrasov, and without the birth pangs of Mey (I place Mey above Nekrasov). In Kutuzov, almost everywhere, sincerity springs up, almost everywhere one can sniff the freshness of a good, warm morning, all with a superb technique, inborn in him. It is remarkable that while he was at the University at a time when etc. . . .[47] our young poet (and *he is very young*) was not inspired by social motives, that is, he didn't follow the fashion and ape, like a marmoset, the grimaces of Mr. Nekrasov, but hammered into verse those thoughts which occupied *him,* and those longings, which belonged to *his* artistic nature. This *lordship of the mind* particularly delighted me, when I looked into Kutuzov's notebooks (sometimes in pencil, sometimes in ink, and sometimes with blank pages between—a photograph of the brain activity of an artist), and delighted me immensely. Kutuzov is a *good judge of himself* (Balakirev used to say "an inner critic") as a genuine artist must be, and I guarantee that Kutuzov (judging by his rough drafts) shapes himself in a "forge" (and in my opinion simply in an oven, because he works himself into a sweat, as I do, poor sinner); and how attracted he is by the people, by history! One further observation: a poet can be fully

---

[46] Alexander Vasilyevich Stasov, being in charge of the financial and business affairs of the Stasov brothers, became known as the "president" of the Stasov clan.

[47] At a time when students were assuming political roles and a wave of social consciousness stormed against the walls of higher education.

sincere only with those things which he has known *closely:* thus Kutuzov hasn't done one social motif, not one Nekrasov grief.

I think that you will allow me, my dear, to come to you tomorrow with Kutuzov and if you approve of him you will accept him as closely as you have accepted me: I know what a blessing your close acceptance is. *I dream of a four-in-hand.*[48]

MUSORYANIN

104. *To ARSENI GOLENISHCHEV-KUTUZOV, Tver*

The eve of SS. Peter and Paul, 29 June, '73

Let this be my first epistle. These three days [that you will be] away from the city, these three days my mind mourns—so I write to you.

Man is a social animal; a social animal seeks the society of its fellows, 2 lions and 3 ostriches could not set up a society and would remain two lions and three ostriches, violating even the mathematical law of common multiples, i.e., they could not even add up to five. 2 barrels + 3 diamonds = 5, but 5 what? what are the ingredients?

Thus I travel to you, Arseni Arkadyevich, and I travel—without mercy, even if it brings sin on my soul.

Life is struggle; struggle is power, and power is unity, i.e., a community of vital interests, enthusiasms, sufferings and curses to primitive evil. External nature makes peace with one; nature calls the "wrestler with nature" to arms. Heine has successfully prompted the plot of *Belle Hélène;* [49] all is there (in the heroic epos of the Greeks) —beauty, grace, incarnate art and even virtue, but wisdom, where is wisdom? Renowned, hallowed Troy did not deign a glance at what kind of horsie had arrived, and didn't even take the trouble to be curious to look inside this horsie.

He who senses man in the whisperings of nature, or in its fearsome uprisings; he who senses man in the drowsy surges of the sea, or in the evil mutterings of the deep; he who sees and imagines, in the warm sunset seen through cloudy mist, that last little cloud in capricious flight, clothed in a rosy garment; here is flying youth, that moment

---

[48] To add a poet to Stasov's "troika."

[49] In Heine's *Mädchen und Frauen des Shakespeare* there is a sketch of Helen (in *Troilus and Cressida*), so ironical that it may well have caught the sympathetic eye of Offenbach or Halévy.

of fleeting happiness, and there the reckless, impenetrable night, and sorrow and dismay—such do not have to go to the Caucasus.[50]

That, for now, is the first journey to you, Arseni Arkadyevich.

Your

MUSORGSKY

Till Monday morning. In Petrograd.

105. *To ARSENI GOLENISHCHEV-KUTUZOV, Tver*

Petrograd, 22 July, '73
Midday.

DEAREST COUNT ARSENI ARKADYEVICH,

Your delightful epistle, entitled a Tveriad, afforded me a cluster of delights and I thank you. Sepulchral Tver, standing in the very center of the "field of death of Russians," the provincial heat-lightning lady and heavy-jowled governor-moon himself, these sprinkle my memory with such fresh and lively recollections of that which has just happened, but is already past—drawn aside to the historical path and risen again in those welcome shining images which so brightly lured me to the house of Zaremba, the Empire of China or the Province of Kaluga. I thank you once again. Just as my sinful dissentress, Sister Marfa, found greeting and sincere response in your artistic mind, this martyr of yours, refreshing her pricked bare feet with the tears of the first beatitude, trembling at the thought that a stranger, that an impertinent eye could slyly watch and soil her complete sincere surrender to her beloved, will not leave my mind: thus truly and full of love the picture sketched by you is completed by the shuddering of the martyred criminal on trial before human justice, rotted through to the last fibre, and, very likely, in the presence of an extremely pure public, able only to buy and sell.

Write your martyr, dear, and if, accidentally, in Russia's "field of death" at Tver, should arise a depressing ghost that would, for a moment, stop your hand—drive it away: *"Vade retro Satanas"* and remember: the inspired artist *always* is an impartial judge, and further remember: "Burn away the hearts of men with the Word of *prophetic truth"* [51] (the Gospels and the Bible).

And I begin the writing of my *Khovanshchina.* I received your

---

[50] At the beginning of 1873 Golenishchev-Kutuzov had ignored a decree ordering him to serve in the High Office of the Governor of the Caucasus at Tiflis.

[51] The altered last lines of Pushkin's poem *The Prophet*—inspired by Isaiah 6.

219

epistle and, instead of a reply, sketched my dissentress in a shroud with a green candle, whispering to her lover Andrei Khovansky, before the self-immolation [in the final scene], and on this motif that you know, there is the following:

> Your mortal hour has come, my dear,
> Clasp me to you for the last time,
> Beloved by me unto the very grave
> Dying together—as if we sweetly sleep.

Alleluia! (with the burial service for Andrei Khovansky).

This first scrap is your property, and the second is prepared, in which there will be the incantation of the dissentress and this too will be for you. Take this first piece of that which is being created in your home,[52] in your presence, and inspired by you—this is true, because, besides us, only Zaremba's walls have heard and witnessed [this], and in a certain kingdom, in a certain country, walls are able to hear. Suspending my confession for the time being, in order to go to my appointment with A. Zhemchuzhnikov, P. Naumov [53] and I. F. Gorbunov (I recorded some more of his song [54] yesterday), I dare to assure *Your Highness*, that your epistle *from Tver* will eventually crawl into a public library among the manuscripts of good men, so *I beg you to be still, Your Highness: it's all my grandmother's* [55] and my fault that I use such a bureaucratic-peasant form of speech, for what good can

---

[52] After living alone for a year (following Rimsky-Korsakov's marriage), Musorgsky shared his apartment in Zaremba's house with his new friend. But sometime during the approaching winter Golenishchev-Kutuzov wrote to his mother: "I want to find an apartment for myself. It's crowded and cold at Musorgsky's. I hope I can drag him along with me."

[53] After the departure of Pavel Alexandrovich Naumov from naval service, his sole concern was to enjoy "the good things of life"—the mechanics of which he managed by marrying a well-to-do lady. As he numbered theater, music, literature among these "good things," his circle of acquaintances included the Zhemchuzhnikovs, Kommissarzhevsky, and at least three former officers of the Preobrazhensky regiment who were now dabbling in the arts. Naumov did not even dabble—he frankly characterized himself as a "good-for-nothing."

[54] Ivan Fyodorovich Gorbunov was famous as an actor (particularly in the plays of Ostrovsky, a friend of his), and even more famous as a *raconteur*. The song, "There passed a maiden," as recorded by Musorgsky, appears in Rimsky-Korsakov's collection of Russian folk-songs. Musorgsky used it as the basis for Marfa's "divination" aria, in Act II of *Khovanshchina*.

[55] Musorgsky blames (jokingly?) his grandmother, Irina Georgievna Yegorova, for having been an attractive serf-girl (see page 1), but this need not have interfered with Musorgsky's aristocratic standing.

one expect from a civil servant born from a union of a serf with an aristocrat-landowner? the latter will always be drawn toward the civil servant in officialdom, especially since that genius Count Speransky,[56] "for whom at present is being raised a proper monument"—only, mind you, such a civil servant will never have aristocratic standing— *that serf interfered and the welfare of Russians has been protected.*

From the 22nd to the 23rd of July,
long after midnight, of course.

I've seen Alexander Zhemchuzhnikov. Such charm, such lack of artificiality! And what a rare and original turn of speech along with an illumined and educated mind! I'm glad to have made such an acquaintance. We spent the whole day together, you, of course, were read and, of course, with success: the characteristics of the pretender (the youthful hero) without setting a finger on the word "Pretender" (a delicately artistic touch in your epistle) evoked enthusiasm.[57] *And we bow before thee.* Write and *"vade retro Satanas!"* A sincere, extremely sincere denial *of the enthusiasm for pictures of nature, i.e. landscapes,* shown in depictions of heat-lightning and the moon and an approach toward human sorrows and passions, *came out right well.* "Burn away the hearts of men with the Word of prophetic eternal truth!"—Write, create and write again, my dearest. I'm glad that your *maman* is in good health, and I trust we shall soon meet.

Your soul's
M. MUSORGSKY

P.S. Where is Count Piotr Arkadyevich? Verderevsky is waiting for the balance of the money on the estate; it would be fine if Piotr Arkadyevich would correspond with him, otherwise it wouldn't be so fine: the term, it seems, has expired.[58]

---

[56] The reference to Count Speransky has two possible motives: he broke tradition by changing his social status (that of a priest's son) to that of nobleman; and he was the author of a project for freeing the serfs during the reign of Alexander I.

[57] Golenishchev-Kutuzov had begun to sketch a poetic drama, *Shuisky,* begun under the influence of Musorgsky's *Boris,* and continued through Musorgsky's constant encouragement. Fragments of a long poem, entitled "The Death of Godunov," have also been found among the poet's papers. The other work evidently mentioned in Golenishchev-Kutuzov's letter to Musorgsky, *The Martyr,* has not been preserved.

[58] Piotr Arkadyevich is Arseni's brother; Verderevsky may be a relative of Shilovskaya (*née* Verderevskaya).

105a. *POLYXENA STASOVA to MODESTE MUSORGSKY, St. Petersburg*
    [*A Draft*]

[Salzburg]

Nice, dear Musoryanin (what is this I hear) my husband writes me that he has found you looking considerably thinner, changed, (not the one we knew in Pargolovo), in general not Musoryanin-like.[59] What does this mean? I implore you, not in the name of a woman who is dear to you (there are interests higher than those of the heart), but in the name of Russian art so dear to you and art in general, which you serve—take care of yourself. What depresses you? If it is office work that has exhausted you—let them pass over you with their promotions, ranks, rewards, the gracious looks of His Highness or Any Other Ness—don't waste yourself, don't be too zealous; sit in the same spot for 10 years, you'll lose nothing by it, and Russian music will only gain, because you will have conserved your strength and health for it. Do the failures of life worry you—but who among the great have ever had an easy life? . . . Financial conditions bad?—but what are your friends for? Is it possible that we all exist only to hear and to enjoy or disapprove your musical creations? Won't all of us really be happy to welcome you to all we have? What then is the value of friendship if it consists only of pleasant conversations and music? However, why should I dwell on my feelings toward you, which, I trust, are slightly familiar to you? But perhaps all this is nonsense and there is simply some physiological cause that disturbs you. Then brush it aside. What are doctors for? . . . Let's speak frankly and directly, the way people should long ago have spoken: your head often aches—perhaps this is caused by the very remedies you are using for your throat ailment? Instead of these, as I long ago said, one could call upon Dr. Rauchfus [60] or some other ace of his specialty—they will cure you. My little dove, dear Musoryanin, just think, he who began with *Boris* has much ahead of him, oh, so much! Is it possible that you would ruin yourself prematurely, just as Glinka ruined himself, but not in the same way.[61] No, I don't even want to think of it. Listen, when I come back to Petersburg in September and when all my ailments have vanished, I want again to luxuriate in your music, as we used to last year in Pargolovo

[59] See Letter 101a.

[60] Dr. Karl Rauchfus was a famous specialist in children's diseases. Why does Polyxena Stasova recommend him to Musorgsky?

[61] It was not one of Glinka's eternal petty complaints that killed him, but syphilis.

on Saturdays and Sundays, only I want to hear something new, a lot of new things, and not I alone, of course—you must be a good boy and not be sick and not hurt yourself.

Goodbye, my dear, don't be angry with me for this letter—it was Georges Sand who long ago said in some novel: "*Il n'y a pas de despotisme plus grand, que celui de l'amitié*"—I only confirm this truth; but this despotism may justify itself by the good, heartfelt feeling that motivates it. I press both your hands firmly, firmly. The Tyapas and Mishinkas [62] all greet their dear Musoryanin.

P. S.

106. *To POLYXENA STASOVA, Vienna*

Petrograd, 23 July, 1873. Shpalernaya No. 6.

NICEST AND DEAR LADY,

It is with horror that I think of your perplexity concerning my prolonged silence. But whatever I may have to pay for this silence (see the civil servant in me), my soul hasn't yet become so black that I can't make a full confession. Stingy housewives usually put the cat in pantries where no mice could possibly be, because all the edibles have rotted there and mice can't be expected to eat rotten food; so it's good for the cat to seize the proper moment and sneak away from his guardhouse—otherwise he'd die of hunger. After reading your nicest epistle, I feel like the cat who has sneaked away from his guard-house and has fallen upon fresh food. There is only one unfair item in this epistle: fear for the man-musician. You are too intelligent a woman to make such a mistake! If there is the slightest doubt as to the independent state of a certain man's (named so-and-so) creative powers, then there should be no doubt about what often pushes him on, i.e., this gentleman, towards creation; but if the fruits of this pushing aren't on paper "because there's no time," then truly this is the fault of a country which produces grains about whose existence it doesn't know itself, because it doesn't need them. In Russia one does encounter art, but art—that's an object of luxury: I do not speak of music alone, I love (and I think that I have a feeling for) all arts. So far a lucky star has guided me and will guide me further—I believe this, because I love and I live with such love, and I love man in art.

The Introduction to *Khovanshchina* (dawn over the Moscow River,

---

[62] Characters in the *Nursery* cycle, drawn from the lives of the Stasov children (see p. 134).

matins at cockcrow, the patrol and the taking down of the chains) and the opening moments of the action are ready, but not written down,[63] because I have been working on a file of 2000 sheets, and now I have the same thing to do, not exactly the same, but 4000 sheets this time: [64] I make a face, grow angry and work on the opera. I have another good device, bearing some resemblance to the truth (this is inherent in the fashionable manner of a Preobrazhensky guard); the dissentress, madly in love with the young Andrei Khovansky, exorcizes him in the retreat with the spell of the "wild wind," and right at the climax of her intoxication of passion, she is interrupted by the song of the dissenters, known to you, about the "Alleluia wife." Sensing that the time has come to prepare herself for death, the dissentress pierces the stage action and the orchestra with a desperate cry: "Death approaches." The dissenters, dressed in shrouds, come out of the forest, green candles in their hands, ready for the self-immolation, and they lock themselves in their cells to pray, ready for the summons of Dosifei (Prince Myshetzky) to stand by their coffins: the dissentress rises, follows them, "to clothe herself in chaste, white vestments," but she goes not to pray. When Andrei Khovansky comes from the cell, dreaming of his German girl, the dissentress in shroud and with candle in hand watches him. And this little fool sings a love song under the window of the cell where Dosifei has hidden the German girl, kidnapped by Khovansky from the German settlement. When the little fool has sung his fill the dissentress approaches him and, on the motif of the incantation, sings Andrei Khovansky's burial-service. This is all almost ready, but as with *Boris,* will be written only when the fruit has ripened. Here, my dear and nicest lady, is the answer to your more than friendly missive sent from Salzburg. Firm thanks to you, and now I am living *Khovanshchina* as I lived *Boris,* and I am the same Musoryanin, only I have become more strict with myself after the success which you crowned, and after my aspiration to approach the people (But Peter and Sofia are kept off stage [65]—this is decided; better without them), and I am eager to do a people's drama—*I am so eager.*

---

[63] The manuscript of the piano score for this introduction is dated September 2, 1874.

[64] Most of Musorgsky's office work consisted of copying or filling in foresters' certificates—thus the 2000 sheets, the 4000 sheets, and (in letter 108) the 6000 sheets!

[65] But not only for dramatic reasons; Tzar Peter I and Tzarevna Sofia, being of the Romanov dynasty, could not be represented on the stage.

Dearest Dimitri Vasilyevich may like my first efforts for *Khovan-shchina*—well, he is welcome to all I have, and I firmly press his hand. I kiss the boyar's little daughters and sons, without shame, in their absence. They say that Liszt became so enthusiastic over *The Nursery* that he wants to dedicate to me a little piece of his; the text and story were interpreted for him by Baroness Meyendorff,[66] who is constantly at his side at Weimar. Your hand, my dear and nicest lady, and till we meet.

MODESTE MUSORGSKY

107. *To VLADIMIR STASOV, Vienna*

Petrograd, 23 July, '73. Shpalernaya No. 6.

MY SPLENDID *généralissime*,

Greetings and please give the attached letter to Paulina Stepanovna —you know where to catch her, yes, and by the way, you read it too— *I want you to.* Our work boils at all points, my mood is good—I have a desire for solitude and thinking; it's too early to put this into writing—let it ripen; one can't play jokes with a people's drama. The dissentress, our beloved, has been *so planned, ai, ai!* From the letter to Paulina Stepanovna you will see only a slight hint of what really exists; when we meet we'll talk it over and listen to it. Meanwhile I can only tell you that no matter to whom I showed the *love burial-service,* his eyes popped, this is such an unprecedented thing; what Jesuits are here; it is the death-sentence of a loving and deserted woman, and how the stupidity of Andrei Khovansky explains *itself* here, that he preferred a German girl as stupid as he to this vigorous and passionate woman: the dissentress taunts Andrei with the German girl's dislike and pities him and her, lamenting "alleluia," circling him holding a green candle in each hand and wearing a shroud, on the motif of the magic spell or the incantation of the "wild wind," only in a different key and in a different harmony, until Dosifei enters, in the same sort of shroud and with a candle, and declares, that "the time has come to be cleansed in a baptism of fire and to ascend to the heights in the bright mansions—of God, where Antichrist is powerless, and so save our souls." Besides, there's this matter: I've talked with a sensible priest in regard to the character of the dissenters' tunes. He declared:

---

[66] Madame la Baronne Olga de Meyendorff (*née* Princess Gorchakova) was another close companion of Liszt at this time.

if, living in a village, you found and heard old sextons—then you should clothe your dissenters in traditional tunes. I found and heard the sextons, but I forgot the sensible priest's advice until I needed a motif for the chant of Dosifei and for the baptismal chant during the self-immolation. I told Korsinka—he was in perfect delight about the project of a coloratura church hymn of the whole chorus in unison. The sensible priest testified that Razumovsky [67] had the same opinion. This project is original, well, that means our suit is trump, the more so as the dissenters' howl will be in perfect contrast to the Petrovsky theme.[68] That's what Musoryanin is doing, my dear, and from Gorbunov I have two extremely valuable ancient Russian songs; he's promised more, but his wife is ailing—I'll have to wait.—With such methods I am gathering such folk-honey from all quarters, to make the honeycomb tastier and *sweeter*, because, after all, this is a people's drama. The brother of Bessel, who had seen Liszt more than once in Weimar, stopped his *izvozchik* and ran after me to tell me that Liszt was enthusiastic about the latest Russian music and, by the way, that he had informed V. Bessel that *The Nursery* stirred him so that he had grown fond of its author and wanted to dedicate *une "bleuette"* to him. If this is true and not an overestimation of his own enthusiasm, then Liszt amazes me with this inspiration of his talent, *this is incredible!* Fool or not in music I may be, but in *The Nursery* it seems I am no fool, because an understanding for children and a view of them as people in their own little world, and not as amusing dolls, prevents the composer from having a foolish attitude. All this may be so; but I never thought that Liszt who, with but few exceptions, pictures colossal subjects, could *seriously* understand and evaluate *The Nursery*, and especially, be moved by it; why, all these children in it are Russians, with a powerful local smell. What will Liszt say or what will he think, when he sees *Boris*, if only in piano score. In a word, if this *event* is to be believed, how happy Russian music should be, to find such recognition from an ace like Liszt. I am thinking not only of myself, but of the fact (delivered to me by this brother of Bessel) that Liszt never wearies of talking about Russian musical workers and

---

[67] Dmitri Razumovsky—a learned divine, a great authority on old Russian church music. He is the author of an important study, *Church Song in Russia* (1867–69).

[68] The theme for the soldiers of Peter, sent to arrest the dissenters in the last act of *Khovanshchina*, is based on the official march of Musorgsky's old regiment, the Preobrazhensky.

reads over their works from time to time. God send him long life and perhaps when it will be possible, I will skate off to him in Europe and entertain him with novelties, but only in your company, *généralis-sime*, and not otherwise. But now I am destined to wither and grow sour among the Chaldeans, with wasted labor and time spent on business that would be done better without me. I am destined to be aware of the whole fruitlessness and needlessness of my labors *in the Forestry Department* and, in spite of this awareness, to go on toiling *in the Forestry Department*. It is horrible! How many new worlds, perhaps, might have been discovered in talks with Liszt, how many unknown corners we might have explored together; and Liszt, by his nature, is daring and has no lack of courage, and with the recommendation, which took place "of itself," it evidently would not be difficult for him to take such an excursion with us into new lands.

Will you see Liszt, *généralissime?* If in Petrograd, on the soil of putrefied human corpses, here and there gleams a sensible idea, something boils away inside somewhere and the half-sleeping All-Russian creative spirit will wake, what must be there, in Europe? The All-Russian creative spirit is like some scared sparrow, afraid to speak out; if he flies "high under the clouds," he sits and dozes off, or if he "turns downwards," he is reduced to a petty money-changer and mixes himself in all sorts of interests of interest to no one; it is not possible for this half-sleeping creative spirit to rid itself of its banner: "as the gentleman commands." The mystical picture of the Dance of Death based on the liturgical theme of Dies Irae in the form of variations, could only have been born from the head of the courageous European Liszt (Serov didn't understand this) and this courageous European proved the artistic relation between piano and orchestra particularly in the Dance of Death. By the simplicity of the yeast, i.e., the variations and (apparently) nothing more, I compare it with Repin's "Volga Boatmen": a group of portraits and also, apparently, nothing more. The colossal Te Deum, standing in relation to the tremendous 2nd Mass of Beethoven, as the Roman St. Peter's does to our St. Isaac's, could only have been reared in the head of the brave European Berlioz. With this colossus I can compare in grandeur only the introduction to *Ruslan*—a composition of the Europeanized (pfui, what a word) Glinka. *Et nous autres?!* We need Europe, but not just to ride around on it: it's necessary to examine it; not to admire the lifeless waterfalls of Switzerland or the view from the Brühl Terrace [in Dresden], not

227

to determine where they set the best table, in Paris or in Vienna—no, this is not what is needed. This can be done by those landowners who are not yet ruined or by fat-pursed financiers. But, unfortunately, from our musician-*voyageurs* I hear little more than this about Europe.—This half-asleep Empire of All the Russias! In the world of learning, where brains must perforce act faster, scientific workers keep in touch with each other, with workers in almost all countries. I don't know how it is with other branches of the arts, but in our musical part such problems have not yet been conceived in the brains of our musician-*voyageurs* through Europe. "*She sleeps, sleeps* . . . and no one knows the hour of her awakening" (I purposely wrote "sleeps" twice, as it is in Borodin's song,[69] because it's sillier that way; and what a sleepy goblin he is; as if one must say that "she sleeps, sleeps" . . . how often I've asked him to cut it). If our present relations in the European vestibule have proven so useful to all of us, then, naturally, relations with Europe itself might push us even further.

Yes, and now: suppose Shaklovity dictates the denunciation to the scribe; he should be a characteristic personality—an arch-swindler with an additional affected importance, a certain grandeur even in his bloodthirsty nature. It is possible furthermore, that the 3rd conspirator remains unidentified, but Shaklovity, though literate, did not wish to be known by the Khovanskys, against whom he was intriguing. I would like it thus, because the scene with the scribe [Scene I] is not badly thought out, and *in our way*.

Yes, *généralissime*, I feel that, glory to God, I am still alive: ah, if only there were time and health.

Count Arseni Kutuzov is writing a poem,[70] that came to him after the meeting with you, that very night. Judging by the fragments, it will be important; although he doesn't know Coppée's "Blacksmith," he is doing something suitable in idea and in problem; only not a martyr blacksmith, but an involuntary martyr woman; there will be a court session in it, which, in my opinion, has been masterfully conceived.

I firmly embrace you, my dear, till the next time; *take care of yourself for us and for me, for the sake of Christ himself.*

MUSORYANIN

[69] "The Sleeping Princess" (1867).
[70] The lost "Martyr."

228

108. *To POLYXENA STASOVA, Bad Reichenhall*

Petrograd, 26 July, '73. Shpalernaya No. 6

My dear and nicest lady, yesterday's visit to the Melikhov house created a certain perturbation in my musical, perhaps, but certainly disorderly brains; my epistle to you will get stuck in Vienna and won't catch up with you, despite all the steam I raised in regard to *Khovanshchina,* whose construction boils; *and how it boils;* this sorrow turned to joy when I learned that the *généralissime* is not going to Vienna, that this excursion was forbidden to him by those who love him (I implored him not to go to Vienna); but as for my dear lady, I think I shall write to her—after all I'll find the lady somewhere in Europe. So I do this: this joy changed and *turned topsy-turvy* when I learned that our dear Vityushka Hartmann had died in Moscow of an aneurysm.[71] Grief, grief! O greatly suffering Russian art! During Victor Hartmann's last visit to Petrograd, the two of us took a walk, after some music, along Furshtadtskaya Street; at one of the by-streets he stopped, paled, leaned against the wall of some house, and couldn't catch his breath. At that time I didn't attach much importance to the incident and only asked him: did this sort of thing happen to him often (yes, often), fooled with him with some sort of nonsense, I distracted his mind for a time from that which the mind didn't realize, and we went on, at first at a slow pace, and then in a normal manner. Having myself experienced shortness of breath and heart palpitations (the absurd *"palpitatio cordis"*), I thought that this is the fate of nervous natures mostly, but, as it appeared, I was bitterly mistaken, as it turned out, even in better days, when Hartmann's talent so gushed out that it was impossible to approach him. I remember (how can I ever forget!) my last talk with him: he was cheering me with a project for a building in Russian style, although adapted to the demands of the times, still a Russian style, as he loved to say—"well-bred." He was already bringing his project to life, his brains were busy with plans for the building of a house in Russian style for Mamontov, in Moscow. Whether Hartmann finished this work—I don't know; this talentless fool of a death mows on, without considering whether there is any necessity for his accursed visit. Little did I expect that I should have to send a brief

---

[71] On July 23, 1873, at Mamontov's country estate near Kireyevo—at the age of forty-one.

obituary to the *"Peterburgsky Vedomosti."* [72] I would understand that if talents sprouted like mushrooms, but then out of the recognized talents the majority are so many green jackasses, thoughtful fools, who propagate only many-volumed and very monotonous corpses: as it's said—neither flesh nor snout, and even less reason.—As your brain recalls impressions (precious ones) of the houses *à la* Makarov, the chapel in the Summer [Garden], the staircase [of the Russian pavilion] in the Vienna Exposition which greeted, "bowing low," and has probably "bowed low" before the entire world (All-Russia, the slave, in this case, too—could not hold out), yes, and then contrasts these with the architectural skeleton of the People's Theatre in Moscow (I don't speak of its elegance and originality), but simply its skeleton, how frightful it's becoming: what might Hartmann not have done! Hartmann who, quietly and unobtrusively, saved the lives of thousands with a hint to the *authorities* about the imminence of the ceiling falling in the Marinsky barn. The authorities pretended not to believe, but "they didn't have the heart" and reinforced the ceiling. But Hartmann had only glanced:—chance, naturally. This has nothing to do with the creative power of the artist, but at the same time it forms its base; beautiful sounds are always beautiful, and during a dumpling session they so fascinate a Little-Russian that, as he gobbles up his dumplings, he is drenched with melted butter and tears, and gulps both dumplings and beautiful sounds. But something more concrete is needed. Art must embody more than beauty alone; a building is only good when, in addition to a beautiful façade, it is well planned and solid, when one can sense the aim of the construction and can see the artist's spirit. This was in the perished Hartmann. Poor, orphaned Russian art! Antokolsky busies himself with Gena's son, and Repin with his two Verushkas (one smaller than the other). However, why should I . . . ? what evil genius made me say this? Well, *basta!* In the letter that lies in Vienna, which I compared with the sleeping Prince Marko [73] (I think that, in his turn, Prince Marko is doomed forever to be compared with my Vienna letter), as in that letter I explained to you, my nicest lady, what a nice little epistle you have graciously sent to me and how you, lady-wise woman, how you were troubled, you

---

[72] The brief obituary, as published, shows no sign of having been written by Musorgsky.

[73] A Serbian hero of the *bylini*. The song tells that Marko Korolevich killed his horse, broke his sword, and fell asleep under a tall tree.

little dove, about Musoryanin. There are days when cats scratch at the heart, but those days pass on, as all passes on. But know that the work boils, and your Musoryanin is still the same Musoryanin, only he has become more severe with himself since he undertook a people's drama: and more fastidious in regard to his brains, and 6 thousand sheets of the department's work idle there, while the forester waits for his license,—what's to be done! So that's how we live in Russia! There was further written about how Liszt fell in love with *The Nursery* and its composer, and intends to dedicate a little piece to its author. Further there was written about the dissentress abandoned by Andrei Khovansky, though she honestly and passionately loved him, and on a love motif she *sings a burial service* to Andrei Khovansky, preparing him for the self-immolation, and further, various other things were written. Well, when we meet you will hear and weigh the quality.

To Dmitri Vasilyevich, naturally the dearest one, I extend my arms as far as I can to embrace him and with all my might I thank him for forbidding the *généralissime* to go to Vienna: I've written him, to take care of himself; for the sake of Christ, for us and for me. I kiss the little ladies and the little gents in their absence.

Your little hand, my dear and nicest lady, and till we meet, but if I know where you will be, I shall write further.

MUSORYANIN

109. *To VLADIMIR STASOV, Wiesbaden*

Petrograd, 2 August, '73. Shpalernaya No. 6

My dear, my splendid one, such horror, such sorrow! "And why should curs and cats live," and the Hartmanns perish.[74] I remember on his last visit to Petrograd, Vittyushka and I (after waiting for Your Grace at Molas's) were walking from Molas and at the corner of a by-street and Furshtatskaya, just opposite the *Annen-Kirche,* dear Vittyushka leaned against the wall and turned pale. Knowing our brethren from my own experience, I asked him (*calmly*): "What's happened?"—"I can't breathe," answered Vittyushka. Again, for all that, knowing from my own experience the nervousness, heart-sensitivity (by reason of palpitations—*palpitatio cordis*) of artists, I (*still calmly*)

---

[74] Over Cordelia's body, King Lear cries: "Why should a dog, a horse, a rat, have life, and thou no breath at all?"

told Vittyushka: "Rest a bit, little soul, and then we'll go on." That was all that was said about something that has hidden forever beneath the earth one dear to us. What a fool man is, in general! And when I now recall this conversation I feel wretched that I behaved like a coward before my fear of sickness.* *Généralissime,* believe me: it was as an actual fool I looked then upon our Hartmann. Powerless, "who hasn't the strength to help," a pawn—that's what. But a man, and such a man, feels bad; and you push it aside with ridiculous "little souls," with insipid cold-bloodedness: base social slime! And here in the foreground is petty self-love—a coin, a counterfeit coin, not needed by anyone. I remember, I well remember this incident, and I hope I shall remember it—I may grow wiser.

That's it, that we sense danger for another man only when he's drowning or when "ready to die." Fool! and if we had foreheads seven feet high, we'd be fools all the same, hopeless fools! and all these little men are such fools, not excluding the doctors who, with the importance of Indian peacocks, beneath the gentle rustle of their tail-feathers, settle questions of life and death.

Thus the wise console us fools in such cases: "he" no longer exists, but what he had time to do exists and will exist, but then, are there many people who have such a happy lot—not to be forgotten. Again that beef-cutlet (with horseradish for tears) of petty human self-love. Devil take your wisdom! If "he" has not lived in vain, but *created,* what a scoundrel one would have to be to reconcile oneself with the delightful "consolation" that "he" *"no longer creates."* There is not and there cannot be repose, there is not and cannot be consolation— this would be weak-kneed. If nature is only coquetting with man—I have the honor to make her acquaintance as with a coquette, that is to trust her as little as possible and watch over her sharply, if, by chance, she so fascinates me that heaven seems a sheepskin; or, like a hussar, to throw oneself into the slough—choking oneself to death, but enjoying oneself: with what? with the spongy, clammy earth that no longer coquettishly, but frankly takes into her vile embrace every "king of nature," no matter who he is, like some old stale girl, for whom all are good, because there's no choice.

There's the fool again, what good is anger, when it's powerless. Well, *basta!* let's shut up.

* Musorgsky's note: This fear existed because I was afraid of frightening Hartmann, so I behaved like a silly schoolboy!

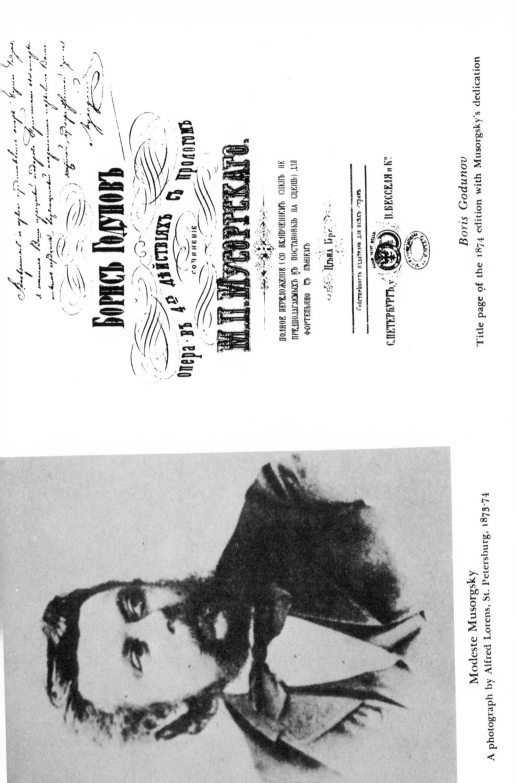

Modeste Musorgsky
A photograph by Alfred Lorens, St. Petersburg, 1873-74

Boris Godunov
Title page of the 1874 edition with Musorgsky's dedication

Prologue, first tableau: Novodevichy Monastery

Act IV, Scene 1: Granovitaya Reception Hall

Designs by Matvei Shishkov for the first production of *Boris Godunov* in 1874

That's what has happened during this time, my dear *généralissime*. Yes, then, I remembered:

> Sleep, dead, sleep peacefully in the grave.
> Enjoy life, you who yet live.[75]

That's bad, but sincere.

In regard to music something has happened: a new, unmistakable, original and *Russian* young talent has appeared, the son [76] of Konst[antin] Lyadov, and a pupil at the Conservatory, who not once in an encounter has given a hint about six-four-chords (by the length of this word—may you judge the length of its stretched stupidity). A genuine talent! Easy, natural, daring, fresh and with *power:* O, yes! Kvey and Drigabier! (who, the other day buried his decrepit old woman of a mother whom in his inborn simplicity he always called "auntie" in front of us—he-he!) [77] thus Kvey, Drigabier and my debauched self are highly *delighted with him.* A description of his exterior: fair-haired, thick-lipped, with little wrinkles, designed by nature as channels for tears direct to the mouth, namely, between the outer surface of the nostrils and the rotundity of the wise jowls are irregular fissures —full of character; the forehead is not lofty, but is especially imposing in conjunction with a prominent temple, well filled out, nervous to a terrible degree, taciturn to a more terrible degree, he listens—he doesn't praise, only the wrinkles around his nostrils begin to work—good!—You'll hear what this youngster scribbles, but Korsinka long ago read a sermon on him. Kvey did a very good scene of Rodolfo with Anafesto and a wonderful narrative of Tisbé before Angelo about her mother, on our favorite theme:

---

[75] Zhukovsky's very free translation of the last lines of Schiller's "Das Siegesfest":
Morgen sonnen wir's nicht mehr,
Darum lasst uns heute leben!

[76] Anatoli Konstantinovich Lyadov—just beginning his composing career.

[77] Borodin's illegitimate birth (his father was the Caucasian Prince Gedeanov) had been officially covered by registering him as the son of one of the family serfs (Borodin) for adoption. His mother, Avdotya Konstantinovna Kleinecke, [*née* Antonova] died on July 23, 1873.

1873)

THE MUSORGSKY READER

O, what Kvey has put in there—how great!

In the 3rd act he has done a Notturno that is very nice, very Italian —it could be instrumented enchantingly. And there is, hmm! a tarantella—on *pifferari*—and I insisted that he keep <withhold> it: * I was importunate to an impossible degree, I had heard it in *Pargolovo and in Novaya Derevnya from Italians of the Neapolitan district* (ha, ha, ha!) I insist, I sense that this—this is that very thing! Korsinka is behaving excellently in regard to the *sea* sirens,[78] he drops in and pleases me a great deal in regard to himself and even in regard to myself: regarding himself—he is orchestrating the [third] symphony, but regarding myself—hmm! *Too early, it's not yet time.*

It was with delight that I, along with Meyer, read your letters, my dear, to Nikolai Vasilyevich [Stasov] at his place. I share that hate for the sea.[79] A nice sort of world, where cold-blooded creatures live:— nothing is left but *"rendre contre elles ce qu'on vient de mâcher."* I marvel at Aivazovsky [80] and I recall Grigorovich,[81] charmed by the suggestion of a trip to the southern shore. I leapt with joy at the telegram about the canceled flight to Vienna (what a wise man!). Yes, then, as was agreed . . . however—that's for our meeting, and that's not the point. And now I write to you in Wiesbaden, and if the letter will not be found there, I ask the little dove Nadezhda Vasilyevna [Stasova] to forward it to a point where it might catch up with you. I've written Polyxena Stepanovna twice: to Vienna with your letter, to be forwarded, and to Reichenhall on the 26th of July, because Nikolai Vasilyevich told me, figuring out the time, that one may write there till the 31st of July. I will be disappointed if she hasn't received the letter. Work on our opera boils, but it's been upset. You remember, of course, that I made an attempt at the first act, but "I've been halted" by the post with inscriptions, upon the reading of which I want to construct an interesting folk scene.[82] Must talk this over with

* Musorgsky's note: *I insist—it was dirty to withhold it!*

[78] Rimsky-Korsakov has been placed in charge of all navy bands.

[79] That summer Stasov was sent by the Archeological Society to Kerch, to supervise research and copying of frescoes in the catacombs there. In his letter to his brother Nikolai he wrote, ". . . I hate and curse the sea and every sort of water except water for bathing."

[80] A marine painter.

[81] The writer Dmitri Grigorovich often entertained at the Stasovs' with stories of amateur seagoing and its consequences—mainly seasickness.

[82] Early in Act I, between Shaklovity's dictation of the anonymous denunciation to the Scribe, and the mobbing of the Scribe, Musorgsky's original version

234

the censor, and must talk things over in general with the censor. Meanwhile, 3 bits of news: 1st, the incantation "to the wind" overlaps the song of the dissenters about the "Alleluia wife," as they come from the forest in shrouds and with green candles; on one of the paraphrases of the chorus the dissentress pierces the scene with a cry, "Death approaches," and follows the brothers "to clothe themselves in white vestments and to take the candle of righteousness." Meanwhile Andrei Khovansky appears beneath the little window of the cell where the German girl is hidden and sings his "nightingale's song." Hearing this, the dissentress in shroud and with candle comes from the retreat, steals towards Khovansky and the latter, as if hit over the head with a club—like a fool doesn't notice what is being prepared in the retreat.—On the love theme of the incantation the dissentress whispers to him: "Your mortal hour has come, my dear; clasp me to you for the last time; beloved by me unto the very grave; dying together— as if we sweetly sleep. Alleluia!" (she circles and bows low before him). *Everybody, without exception likes* this love burial-service and even I like it myself.*

A note: I recalled my talks about the dissenters with a wise priest (at this moment I can't remember his name), but he is a member of our committee on applied science in Solyani Gorodok; what I tell you is shared in full with Razumovsky. The chorus of the dissenters, on their way to their coffins, preparing for the self-immolation (they come out, not all at once, but in groups, naturally), is based on a coloratura theme *unissono* of an ancient liturgical tune—and is led by Dosifei himself. Korsinka likes such an undertaking very much and he admits that it is incredibly original. *A coloratura chorus.* This novelty is as old as original sin, but that's what I like about it. (2) As prelude to the scene in the retreat there is a rustle of the forest in the moonlit night, growing stronger, then dying away, like the wash of waves; on this background, Dosifei will begin his confession (will *begin, bien entendu*), because the confession will be extremely varied, and in *invention* too—one has to imagine something out of the ordinary: this matter is now fermenting in my brain. (3) You know whom

* Musorgsky's note: This duet: the powerless struggle of Andrei, his horror, the scathing words of the dissentress about both the German girl and the self-immolation—this pleases me no end.

shows strangers to Moscow examining and spelling out the various inscriptions on a post in the street, including a proclamation on the punishment of traitors and conspirators.

I should like to dictate the denunciation to the scribe: Shaklovity—
he, stronger than the others, intrigued against Khovansky, but then
the third of the *hiding* informers was never discovered: neither in
Zhelyabuzhsky, nor in Matveyev is there any evidence on the *third*.
But I already have a theme for him—a good theme, and a bit of its text
is stirring.

At first I didn't want to write you anything, dear, because of our
deep mourning. But I couldn't hold out—I wanted to blurt it out,
and the minute I took up the pen "there was no end to it." [88] And besides something crawled into my head from somewhere: when a
mother loses one of her beloved children, she finds a slight consolation for her sorrow in the others who have so far survived; hoping
that, perhaps, my epistle—in which, *regardless of anything,* I have not
changed my habitually inconsistent style one iota—will relieve you,
if even mechanically, from the oppression of a bad feeling, I decided
to send this epistle.

Liszt liked *The Nursery* so much that he wants to do *une bleuette*
on little themes from it. They haven't yet sent the proofs of *Boris.*

The introduction to *Khovanshchina* is almost ready, the growing
light of the rising sun is beautiful, has been brought to that point
where the denunciation is dictated, that is, with a tiny scene of Shaklovity and the Scribe preceding the dictation, the text of which is, naturally, ready. The working out goes on laboriously, six times you
measure off and once you slice off: you can't do it otherwise, something sitting inside me pushes me toward severity. Sometimes you
dash ahead, but no, stop! The inner cook says that the soup is boiling,
but it's too early to put it on the table—it's too thin, perhaps it needs
a bit more root or salt thrown in; well, the cook knows his business
better than I do: so I wait.—Then as soon as the soup reaches the table
—*I'll gulp it down.*

That's what I wanted to tell you, my dear; but that which crawls
in the brain—let it crawl a while. Ekh, how I would like to see you
with us sooner. Take care of yourself—for all of us, for the sake of
Christ, or Musoryanin will fade away—this is true.

HE, THE SAME MUSORYANIN

---

[88] From Gogol's *Dead Souls.*

110. *To NADEZHDA STASOVA,*[84] *Wiesbaden*

Petrograd, 2 August, '73

My dear little dove, Nadezhda Vasilyevna, do spoil Musoryanin as you used to by forwarding, I beg you, the *enclosed* to Vladimir Vasilyevich to whatever country he's now in, in case this epistle does not find him amongst you:—I am glad he has been talked out of his trip to Vienna, although I wrote him there; I also wrote Polyxena Stepanovna there for forwarding, but as soon as I learned that she was to be in Reichenhall at the end of July, I hastily wrote her to that same Reichenhall. I don't know if my epistle has been received.—How are you getting on, my little dove? And I, disorderly man that I am, see nothing but paper, so much do I labor in the defense of government interests. However, our new opera *Khovanshchina* is in work and the work boils, although it is too soon to transfer it to paper. I've become so severe with myself that it's laughable, and the more severe I become, the more disorderly I behave. How people get anything done in an orderly way—I don't know; but I can't and because of this, very likely, I attempt to overcome Sisyphus himself. I'm in no mood for small things; however, the composition of small pieces may be relaxing during the contemplation of larger works. But my relaxation is in the contemplation of the large works, when I manage to get away from government cookery, and land in my own sphere: thus all that goes topsy-turvy with me—downright disorderliness.

I bow very low to Marguerite Matveyevna,[85] because I remember her very well; I greet the young lady: [86] probably she has grown so tall, if one could only realize that people always grow up. And I stand guilty before Fräulein Ernestine [Kiel, governess]—I didn't do what I was supposed to and what I wished to do. But I haven't given it up, not at all do I give it up and I will do it.

Now your little hand, my dear little dove; all right, do spoil Musoryanin.

Severe to myself and still disorderly,

MUSORYANIN

---

[84] In a family of energetic, intellectual and social-minded brothers, it is not surprising that around Nadezhda Vasilyevna whirled a legion of societies for cheap housing, Sunday schools, women's higher education, translators' co-operatives, women's publishers, women's aid, children's aid, etc.

[85] Marguerite Matveyevna Stasova—Nikolai Stasov's wife—daughter of an English merchant, Matthew Clark.

[86] Olga Nikolayevna Stasova, Nikolai Stasov's daughter.

At the beginning of August the généralissime *granted Musoryanin's fondest wish by telegraphing him an invitation to visit Liszt together. Musorgsky's telegraphed reply was in a single word: "Impossible."*

111.   *To VLADIMIR STASOV, Vienna*

Shpalernaya, No. 6, Petrograd. 6 August '73
Transfiguration Day [87]

This is what a Russian musician must answer, my dear *généralissime.* To refuse the most wished-for, the most living life, to go on plodding through rubbish. Frightful! because it is true. Your warm summons to me almost pushed me to say farewell to the official uniform, but this is the thing, that I didn't have the heart to injure my friend and chief, with his eye trouble—this would be inhuman and bad. As long as he helped me, I must help him, too—anything else would be weak-kneed.

And *what* might have been said in a meeting with Liszt, how many good things might have been done! No, one must seek other means, according to one's strength and ingenuity, *to provide the daily bread;* one must save both sheep and wolves, if possible. You will see Liszt, I would be ready to ask you, my dear, to hand him from me a little note, but again it turns out badly; in the first place, do I have the right to act like this—in the second and last place, what would this note mean to him. Silence and silence: exactly like a Trappist. However, I trust in my star; it is surely not possible that some time or other I will not see the men of Europe face to face. If this doesn't turn out—we will endure it, and will endure it as we now do. To you, my dear, it is not possible to tell everything, well, I'll tell you anyway—as long as "the far distance" saves me. Your proposal, as valuable as you are yourself, to go to you for a trip to Liszt, your guarantee of the financial side arranged by you for this aim—all has crashed and there's no way out. Only one rich, living impression remains from your plan, living as if I could see Liszt, hear him, and talk with him and with you. This is not a dream, not an irresponsible phrase. There is still enough living strength to raise in myself the mighty image of the European artist, to move my brains on all that is done by this artist and in a single blink of the eye to stand before him, to look at and listen to him. Without you, perhaps, I should never have so much turned my attention to

---

[87] The special holiday of the Preobrazhensky (Transfiguration) Regiment.

Liszt, would never have gazed at him *so fixedly*. And such gazing is
terribly important; *I know how important it is,* particularly after that,
as Bessel-*frère* informed me, that he still has recognized me, although
he hasn't recognized me fully. That's what I wanted to tell you, my
dear. Call it a Platonic affair, but the substance is in this, that the
brains have been roused, and for a Russian this is always useful, because a Russian (whoever he be) can be compared with a Petersburg
izvoshchik who with particular gusto dozes off at that very moment
that he carries a customer. Well, so thank you, naturally. But when
you return *I do not ask* you *not to remind* me that I didn't get to Liszt;
on the contrary, I ask you to remind me more and more often: once in
a while a disgusting feeling brings good results and a feeling of aver-
sion in this instance is salutary: let me be shocked that I wear my official uniform.[88] I bathe in the waters of *Khovanshchina,* dawn approaches, objects begin to appear, sometimes outlines as well—this is
good. I don't know how to become bitter over failures. Vile and pitiful, but I crawl further and further, always forward—this is my sluggish nature—always asking for novelties. Ekh, if! What new characters, as yet untouched in art, rise before one. For example (you have
minutes when satiation demands some novelty, even though it be
caviar from a shop); well, thus, for example: let us take our dissentress
(the boyarina Princess Sitzkaya, who ran away from "the upper level,"
in other words, from the women's quarters, from the stuffiness of in-
cense and of feather beds) and let's take her, the good heart, the quasi-
streletz-dissenter—Marfa in nunhood, to Prince Golitzin to tell him
his fortune. Golitzin, who little knew the "high court" and had not
been admitted to the Tzaritza Natalia, could not have seen Sitzkaya
as a young woman. As they "at the top" had gossiped about important
matters in Moscow, over sweetmeats and 100-verst-long pies!, the dissentress Sitzkaya-Marfa was quite familiar with Golitzin's affairs,
while Golitzin knew little, if anything, of *her.* So she told his fortune
and as soon as she made it clear to him that she could *see through*
everything, he at once rang his little European hand-bell and gave

---

[88] Stasov later provided this opinion of Musorgsky's refusal: "Musorgsky
couldn't quite trust Liszt's sympathy and was surprised by it. Not he alone, but
we also, many of his comrades and friends—why were we all surprised? Because
we were still unfamiliar with that great sun-like beneficence and profound mother-
like loving nature of Liszt . . . none of us comprehended what life-giving and
loving strength resided in that man, how he understood and valued many of those
to whom the rest of Europe was deaf and blind."

orders for her to be drowned "in the marsh, so that there would be no denunciation." But nothing of the sort: she slipped away—she was no fool, and then she suddenly appears at the start of the meeting of the "trio," and her mere appearance makes Golitzin's "tongue stick in his throat" and makes him realize how undependable his spies are, so it turns out to be a "quartet."—The dissentress tells him some story like this: "Execute me or not, Prince, as you wish, but I come to you with a confession. Coming from you and ere reaching the marsh, your serf, whose name I don't know, and who was probably spying around the yard, threw himself at me, and the sly one began by assuring me that he's in love with me and wouldn't let me go. I took him for a thief and called him thief and filthy serf. And he took offense, drawing himself up with pride: the Prince and I, says he, have seen Europe and were received there with honors; then he started to paw me. Well, it's time, I think, and I showed him this toy (a big knife). Your fool got scared and raised such a Sodom-Gomorrah [an uproar] that passers-by began to collect: they laughed and yelled and I went on mocking him. It was here that a calamity occurred: do not get angry, but your dunce confessed, and in the presence of all, that you had supposedly ordered him to take me to the marsh to drown me, slave of God, as a witch. Peter's men grabbed him and till now keep him under lock and key; they didn't believe the fool nor do I, Prince, so you can punish him so that there will be no denunciation" (she laughs aloud). Golitzin might have become excited and given the order "to drown her so that there would be no denunciation" too soon. Marfa, before leaving, had heard and understood this, and had prepared herself with a weapon that she could wear under her cassock, transformed from boyarina to quasi-*streletz* and knowing the *streltzi* well. For Golitzin this is a European business (of the time): the serfs being instructed in this way, *not to destroy in a body* those witnesses of his *old Muscovite practices* to which he reverts occasionally due to his flabbiness, but with ruse and lure to drag them singly into remote corners and there do away with them. And this was revealed because contemporaries knew Golitzin's tricks and described them. Besides for an opera it seems to me that such a twist of the action is important to expose this actually vile conference at Golitzin's in its true light, where they're all grabbing at the throne and scepter, and probably Dosifei is the only one with a firmly fixed conviction. It is in this way that the "trio" of Golitzin, Khovansky and Dosifei are interrupted by the *Moscow disorder,* and the Fool-Babbler Khovansky takes this opportunity to make fun of Golitzin, who doesn't know where to turn. Marfa plagues him: "But, Prince—give orders so there won't be any denunciation," but Dosifei, standing aside, evaluates the merits of the whole business: "Overtaken by pride, obedient to Mammon and the Asp, you are given boundaries by the centuries—over which you cannot step; you will perish in shame and dishonor. And the meek whom you persecute will be comforted in the mansions of the Lord, the hungry, the orphaned,—there is a refuge for them by the side of the Lord." This confusion is resolved by the entrance of Shaklovity (the informer), telling of the receipt of the denunciation and of the wrath of Sofia and Peter. Tableau on a single menacing chord *pp.* as the curtain falls.[89]

This is just a little sketch, *généralissime,* but it can be worked out. I've written you, my dear, at Wiesbaden; consequently that letter won't be lost. Once more I ask you to take care of yourself, for the sake of Christ, for all of us and for Musoryanin, because he loves you.

HE, MUSORYANIN

111a. *VLADIMIR STASOV to MODESTE MUSORGSKY, St. Petersburg*
[*Extract*]

Vienna, 15/27 Aug., 1873. Wednesday morning, 9:00

. . . When your telegram arrived, saying—*Impossible,* this hit me quite hard, but I didn't lose courage. When I noticed that your promised letter was a long time coming—it couldn't be that it was lying somewhere [on my itinerary] or that you wouldn't have answered me *immediately* on a matter so important to me, I couldn't for a moment think you would hesitate, or postpone without some serious necessity, —so I said to myself: "He's probably thought it over, and come over to my way of thinking; on Sunday and Monday (after Saturday's telegram) he met so-and-so, talked it over with him, figured and measured things out, and is now bustling around for a leave and a passport." But the letter, dated *Transfiguration* Day [August 6] suddenly crashed all my last hopes. You write me quite definitely (it is a whole week later, so this means it's conclusive), that you *can't possibly* come. This was a real blow to me. But do you know? I nevertheless still stand in the breach, not allowing the foe to pass, and I will go on fighting, to the

---

[89] This plan closely approximates the action in the final version of the last half of Act II of *Khovanshchina.*

last possibility. At first I wanted to send you a long, enormous telegram, a double one, about 40 words; but then I considered that *now* it's too late anyway; I shall probably stay in Vienna a week longer, or at the most a week and a half, till next Wednesday, Thursday or Saturday (i.e., 22, 23 or 25 our August); I have to catch Korf [90] in Wiesbaden and he is leaving there at the end of *our* August. So when would you and I have time to attend to our matter? Therefore I don't consider our matter completely ruined, but only *postponed*. Whether or not I go to Paris and London—I don't yet know myself; this will be decided for me in Wiesbaden. And thus, from either Wiesbaden or Paris or London, I still hope to carry you off to Liszt, and in this regard Mitya [Dimitri Vasilyevich], who left here with his family the night before last (Mon., Aug. 13/25) according to our arrangement, will urge and persuade you; yesterday they were supposed to be in Prague, tonight they must be in Berlin where they will stay for 2 or 3 days (Hohenstein Hotel, I note this in case some one of ours needs it and please let them all know about it as quickly as possible), then they'll stop over for half a day in Königsberg, Eydtkuhnen or Vilna, and will reach Petersburg next Tuesday or Wednesday, the 21st or the 22nd of August. (I hope that no illness of Paulina's alters their plan). And will you be so kind as to drop in on Mitya on Tuesday or Wednesday morning (Wednesday is *surer*), on your way to the office—he's only a couple of steps away from your Ministry: you can agree together when to return Mitya's piano, which of course will be needed immediately for the children's lessons, and then you two can have a talk about your trip to me and Liszt. I think you know Mitya's new address: Malaya Morskaya, house of Tatishchev, where *Berrin's* confectionery is. Mitya will tell you everything possible to persuade you. He and I had several chats and discussions on this matter, and it's always more convincing verbally, but nevertheless I shall present my reasons to you on paper. Your colleague and chief may be sick—but he won't be sick forever, and after a rest of some sort he will have to put on the department harness again. I can't imagine that his illness will continue throughout the autumn: this won't be tolerated by the general rules of the office, particularly those pedantic and petty rules established by your lovely Khaluyev. [91] And if this is so then there's

---

[90] Baron Korf, Stasov's superior at the Public Library.

[91] This may be a rude reference to the Minister of Appanages, Piotr Valuyev, who was campaigning for greater efficiency in government offices.

nothing more legal or simple than your obtaining a *2-week leave,* if not because you have a right to it, then at least as a reward for doing another man's duties throughout an entire spring and summer. Finally, I'll tell you straight, from the start I've always counted, in the *last* resort, on your quitting the Forestry Department: in any case you won't be staying there, for in the fall you'll move to [the Department of] Appanages.[92] This means that no one could possibly prevent you from taking a *temporary* leave *before* the move to another ministry. And any [financial] difference in this *entr'acte* I would naturally furnish you, and with the greatest of pleasure. You could return it later when you receive something from the estate, or from *Boris,* or from somewhere—it makes no difference, I would of course include your fare, as well. You have only to say a word to my brother Nikolai— my previous instructions to him of course remain valid. After discussing all this with Mitya and arranging everything finally (as I hope), write me quickly, by the end of the week—at Wiesbaden, where I shall stay, as I said, for 4 or perhaps 5 days, depending on the circumstances. For us to lose Liszt—this would be an unpardonable sin: naturally I won't go to him alone, but together—God knows when we would have another such opportunity. Only you must see Bessel before: it's *today,* I think, that he leaves Vienna, meaning that he may be in Petersburg along with this letter. You'll hear from him *when, where* and how Liszt will be—this is essential for us. And so I continue to hope.—Hartmann's death simply bowled me over and last Wednesday, a week ago today, I got simply sick when I received two lines from Adele Hartmann. I scribbled something hastily for the newspaper (a long article is to follow), sent it off, and fell right into bed, where I lay sick the whole day till evening. This death so bowled me over that I don't have the heart to talk about it again: if you wish, you may read my letters home, written at that time. You'll probably see in them how I felt then!!—Here I've reached the 5th page and I've not yet said anything in particular about *your* affairs, about the opera and your new plans. I'll tell you in two words that to me they seem— *splendid,* and I detect here the artistic paw of a powerful talent. But why should I praise you—you've heard enough of this from me, but you may as well listen to my remarks—you know that I can't be silent about things I consider important. And so this is what I find: (1) All

[92] Where Musorgsky would have a great deal more freedom, his friends Purgold and Molas being firmly entrenched there.

that you've planned for the dissentress, half a *Potiphar's wife* (in at least one scene)—is *excellent*, but what devil pushes you to make her —a Princess?!! The entire opera will finally consist so exclusively of princes and princesses that it will be a chronicle of princely *spawn!!* Golitzin—a Prince, Khovansky senior—a Prince, Khov. junior—a Prince, you plan Dosifei as the former Prince Myshetzky, the dissentress as the Princess Sitzkaya. What is this finally to be, *an opera of princes*, while I thought you were planning an opera of the *people*. After all, who among your characters will not be a *prince* or an *aristocrat*, who will come directly *from the people?* No, no, I energetically protest with all my might and I simply implore you to prevent both the dissentress and the dissenter from being *aristocrats who have laid aside their rank.* No, I implore you to have both of them abhor all sorts of aristocracy, letting them recall it only with proper hostility. Let them both be *of the real people from the soil*, from hut, from village and field, from plow and distaff, from tough, oppressive labor and with calloused hands. This will be more interesting and better! But you have a splendid motif—this: the attitude of the dissentress toward "those above," from whom she has run away and whom she knows and remembers well. This is good, and should be used to the limit. It would pay you only to arrange it so that this dissentress would have been taken "above" from a hut or village, either for love or as a serf, and should live there for long enough to see all, suffer all—and then abandon all and run away. Thus you gain the *tremendous* advantage that her stories and memories would be a rich blend of a peasant's village life—and an aristocrat's life. Would this be bad?!! There are some entirely new motifs for your talent. And at the same time these memories and stories, picturing ancient Russia and the ancient Russian woman on various levels of society, will be of an entirely different shading and coloring than the stories and memories (told by himself) of Dosifei—this mighty Russian Mohammed, this fanatic, this accuser, this Savonarola, this John the Baptist, crying: "Repent ye, the time is fulfilled!," while at the same time he forges weapons in the darkness for the doom of the incomprehensible *new* and for the rescue of the passionately beloved and ideally comprehended *old*. (2) You seem to have completely forgotten the second dissentress, a dry, pedantic and cruel fanatic, cruel and pitiless to the point of brutality, as withered and yellow as parchment. It would be splendid for her (in the last act) to attack and expose the first dissentress, the good *Poti-*

phar's wife—this would be an attempt to show the dissenters' inner court, consisting of people selected by—Dosifei. Dosifei, though loving and respecting Marfa, *must* unwillingly sit in judgment on her, but Marfa no longer hears or understands anything—she stands like a pillar, like one who has perished: since her understanding, her final understanding with Andrei Khovansky, she has long borne a sense of death in her breast. I think that if this project suits you, the drama would turn out more broadly and its women characters, who are too little on the stage, would stand out in their great richness and fullness. Besides, a new side of ancient Russia would be portrayed: petty, wretched, dull-brained, envious, evil and malicious. (3) Don't forget, for God's sake, that after the *magnificent* scenes between Marfa and Golitzin in the 2nd act which you devised (her ridicule and *persiflage* about the "denunciation" and the unsuccessful attempt [at her assassination]) you should start a verbal skirmish between old Khovansky and Golitzin *immediately after that*. Khovansky, it seems to me, must be overjoyed at the now-revealed nastiness of Golitzin and must leap on him for all his *innovations,* for his "betrayal of ancient Russia" such as: the abolition of precedence, the leveling of the old families with some foul new upstarts (with whom it's shameful to sit at the same table), for his dealings with foreigners, his half-European life, etc. Gradually their quarrel should grow more heated as they frankly declare their mortal hatred of each other and their willingness to fight to the death—and here Shaklovity should appear with the news of the denunciation being nailed to the gate, just as *you* devised it. And meanwhile, during the entire scene, let Dosifei (as you have very well thought it out) look *contemptuously* upon these Russian *princes* and "statesmen," who, assembled for the direction and guidance of the affairs of all Russia, have grappled about their personal affairs like two silly roosters, and have forgotten all else. (4) Please don't discard the possibility at the very end of the 5th act (this would be after the trial, if you accept this proposal) of having Prince Andrei, who had been absent since his scene with Marfa, suddenly run in, frightened and desperate, to reproach Dosifei for the death of his father, about which he has *just* learned, as well as for the loss of all the promised benefits, the Tzar's throne, the German girl, etc. Dosifei, although himself shocked by the death of the old Khovansky, manages to pacify him and call out on the stage the canary—Agathe [Emma]. This all will give you: a little more interest in and a nice warmth for the personality of Andrei, it will bring the German girl on the stage once more in an extremely interesting contrast with the poor-spirited but nice Andrei and the granite pillar of Dosifei. (5) Please consider how and with what the denunciation can be *tied into* the rest of the opera, otherwise it remains quite wasted with neither result nor conclusion for the remaining development of the opera—one might say that all this denunciation might be skipped because it's not at all needed by the opera and has been obviously *forced* in as an effect for the 1st act.— All this is presented for your perception as material, for I see that you're working very energetically and that every minute you are devising splendid artistic scenes and details. Yes, all these are *extremely good,* but you must not lose sight of the general relationship, and it is about this that I consider it my duty to remind you.—I don't know what is to happen later, but now the plot, the libretto, is worked out and is worked over in exactly the way I would like to see it done by *all* composers, not only Russian, but European in general, and less than 2 days ago I was telling Mitya how happy you make me with this severe weighing and working out of the content, first of all of the musical content, examples of which I don't know in previous music. (Even Serov couldn't be included, because in the last analysis his libretti are trivial and never step beyond *domestic* matters, as for instance in *The Power of Evil,* or become pompous and rather silly as in *Rogneda!*)

—Well, enough of you. Repin pleases me more than you can imagine. He is like an eagle in full flight, with such a viewpoint on art, on its problems and modern demands, on Italy, etc., as I have never encountered, either in books or in talks. I've always imagined that I was to remain alone with such thoughts, without meeting anyone's agreement or sympathy. And all of a sudden I hear *almost* the very same from an artist, full of power, who not only thinks of this as I do but will even portray it. His sympathies and his hates are exactly like *mine.* Imagine for yourself whether or not I am in ecstasy. Repin is new and powerful in painting, putting an end to old traditions—exactly as *you* have in music. And, I hope, no one will move you.

V. S.

112. *To VLADIMIR STASOV, Paris*

6th of September '73, Petrograd

I admit that I *made* myself find a free minute to talk things over with you, my dear *généralissime*, that I *made* myself answer immediately your powerful call to *Europe*—to *Liszt*. But at the same time I *made* myself realize that, after all, *Khovanshchina* has to be started, because its time has come.

Never before have I felt so strongly that peace is indispensable for *creative work*, that only in this condition is it possible to concentrate, to sit tight in one's own little box, and peer from there at the characters: of what sort are they? Thus, having put myself in my little box, I prepared the scene of Marfa with Mother Susanna, which (I mean the scene) along with the piano, I just delivered to Dimitri Vasilyevich: we are going to try out the said scene in the house of Tatishchev, on Malaya Morskaya.

So, we've started *Khovanshchina*, my dear. What will be? Reading these lines, you are thinking: that rascal Musoryanin, why does he remain silent about Liszt?

I M P O S S I B L E

Don't curse me, but give me a chance to share the prepared scene with you—give me this consolation. Contrasts: Marfa and Susanna—a complete, strong and loving woman and an aged spinster, whose whole delight in life is in spite, in a search for adulterous sin and in its persecution—an extremely sensual and passionate alto with a dry, screeching soprano. The scene has its origin in an apparently trifling accident. Susanna happens to overhear Marfa's song, or rather, the end of the song. Susanna watches Marfa with satisfaction as the latter sings:

> As God's candles we all—with thee—shall burn,
> All around our brethren will be in flames,
> All our souls floating upwards in smoke and fire.

But when, exhausted by her frustrated passion for Andrei Khovansky, she (on a trill) sings

> Thy dear girl has lost thy love
> Out of her sight thou hast deceived her,
> So in evil eternal captivity
> Thou shalt feel the bitter sting of the dissentress.

Then Mme. Susanna, inflamed with rage, flies downstage crying: "Sin! Hell!" and so on (the text has turned out well). Marfa calmly asks Susanna "to open her sorrow to her," but the irritated spinster will not be calmed and hints to the "prodigal daughter" about her "Satanic song." Marfa makes it clear that she understands what's up, and to spite Susanna she says, using a sensual theme with a real folk character,

> Many nights I've spent with him,
> With warmth I have kissed my beloved.
> How sweet it was when he whispered to me,
> When his hot lips burned me with flame.

Susanna all this time (*a parte*) shrieks, then whispers: "Lord!" . . . "away with the power of hell" . . . "this place is holy!" and, going quite crazy, she gasps:

> Lord! my eyes seem clouded with a mist!
> I see the whore seated on a cloud,
> Borne by six sphinxes.
> Over her a fiery serpent—with seven mouths,
> The serpent is seven-winged—the seven mortal sins.
> The mouths are black and gaping—greedy,
> There perish the souls of the cursed whores,
> Hosts of them perish—both beast and human
> And God has forsaken them! . . .
> (to Marfa) Away with thee, daughter of Baal, away! . . .

> *Marfa*
> If you could only perceive
> The love of a heart weary with pain,
> If you would have loved, as I have,
> Day and night you would have thought of him,
> Many, many sins would then be forgiven
> You, you poor sick mother,
> Much you yourself would then forgive,
> Understanding then the cruel grief of love.

In reply to this impertinence ("sluggish word, sinful speech") Susanna speaks: "Stay, enchantress!" and she places a curse on Marfa as a temptress. Marfa calmly (apparently) says: "Very well, Mother, very well. Just like an over-ripened pod, an over-driven horse, you've wasted your lifetime." But Marfa's temper can stand no more and, in reply to the curse and the accusation of adultery, she throws [these words] at Susanna:

> To tempt thee?
> There's not one tattered sot,
> Not one homeless scamp,
> Not one helpless loafer,
> Who'd be tempted by *thy beauties!*

(this is in folk, sharply dissolute colors).

The half-priestly, half-bookish stilts fly from under Susanna. The woman who has touched a *sensitive feminine spot* in Marfa is *herself injured* there. As if stunned, she murmurs: "Beauties? . . . beauties? . . . Lord! Has my mind grown weak, or is the sly devil whispering evil things to me? . . . Over-ripened pod, over-driven horse? . . . I?"

Marfa, quickly collecting herself, repeats the dissenters' speech: "As God's candles" etc., and Susanna (*a parte*), suffocated with fury, says—"God, my God, turn me from the wickedness of Satan, from the unquenchable thirst for revenge!" But now that this is the main point of the phrase, Susanna, now firm, because she's back on her hobby-horse—in a vile rage, says to Marfa:

> Thou hast seduced me,
> Thou hast tempted me,
> Thou has planted in me
> The spirit of hell's fury.*
> To justice, to fraternal justice,
> To the dread justice of the church!
> For thy witchery
> I will denounce thee there
> I'll build there for thee
> A blazing pyre.

Marfa, who started at the word "justice," recovers herself (she need regret nothing—she has lost all) and calmly stops Susanna.

> No, Mother!
> Before the Lord my love is pure.
> At judgment he will protect me,

* Musorgsky's note: With such old maids as Susanna, it's always the others who are guilty.

249

> God's own angels will shelter me,
> Covering me with their bright wings.

Fury, superstitious fear, an irresistible desire to destroy Marfa, all become so fused in Susanna that she, like the ancient Hebrews, tramps the stage shaking her fists over her head, and shouting with all her might:

> Hell thunders, the devils rejoice,
> Hell has risen, Hell has triumphed,
> Woe, woe to us!

and in this charming condition she stumbles into Dosifei, who almost indifferently asks the *sisters:* "What's this fuss!" (I should have liked to say "What's being dreamt here?" but that seems wrong—tell me).

Till here it's ready—yesterday, September 5, by 11:00 at night.

I'll go further, perhaps, by your arrival, perhaps not, but it's planned grandly: *Marfa leaves Susanna in a stupor before Dosifei and he exorcizes the devil from Susanna and after rebuking her, drives her home.*[93]

O, how exhausted I am, *généralissime!*

I'm glad your bag was found, I'm glad that you've rebuked Prakhov, I'd like to know how this "flute with faun" * went about the Exposition, in a Roman toga or in a Greek peplum, for they couldn't admit him nude to the Exposition. But our dear spiritual triangle, Mordukh [Antokolsky] strayed from the furrow! Won't the "troika" ever reach its destination!

Soon, soon we'll see each other, my dear; work on our *Khovanshchina* will start boiling even more energetically; and *how* I miss you. I've made all sorts of notes on various parts of the opera, and I agree fully with your remark about its "princeliness," although I wished to show one aspect of that period—that noble families ran away to the people.

* Musorgsky's note: To distinguish him from his brother, "faun with flute." [94]

---

[93] This is the beginning of Act III—in the *streltzi* quarter.

[94] Adrian Prakhov, an art historian from whose affection for Greek and Roman antiquities derives Musorgsky's epithet, "flute with faun." Stasov and Prakhov had run into each other at the Vienna Exposition and had begun an argument that lasted an entire day, or so Stasov reports in a letter to Dimitri. Prakhov's brother Mstislav published his Russian translations of Heine over the signature "Faun."

I am rereading Solovyov,[95] to become acquainted with this epoch, as I became acquainted during *Boris* with the source among vagabonds of the "troubled times," so that history is my nocturnal mate—I absorb it and more than enjoy it, despite my weariness and my dismal mornings at the office. I want to apply for a rest and use it for good purposes, rather than to bring foresters to trial, the longer this goes on, the less it is to my liking.—Well, till we meet, my dear *généralissime*, don't curse me and don't pity me. *Flagon* [Shcherbachov] has composed a splendid etude [in B major], hot, nervous and dashing.

Your
MUSORYANIN

The admiral has a son—Misha.[96]

". . . Our Poor Musoryanin!"

. . . V. V. Stasov was in an especially happy mood all this time there [in Paris]. Only one sorrow gnawed at his heart: he was often mentally desolate on Musorgsky's behalf: "Ah, what is going on with our poor Musoryanin!" More than once V. V. attempted to rescue his genius friend, who in *his absence* sank to the bottom. It was really incredible how that well-bred Guards officer, with his beautiful and polished manners, that witty conversationalist with the ladies, that inexhaustible punster, as soon as he was left without V. V., quickly sank, sold his belongings, even his elegant clothes, and soon descended to some cheap saloons where he personified the familiar type of "has-been," where this childishly happy chubby child, with a red potato-shaped nose, was already unrecognizable . . . Was it really he? The once impeccably dressed, heel-clicking society man, scented, dainty, fastidious. Oh, how many times V. V., on his return from abroad, was hardly able to dig him out of some basement establishment, nearly in rags, swollen with alcohol . . . He would sit with shady characters till 2 in the morning, sometimes till daybreak. While still abroad V. V. would bombard all his closest acquaintances with letters, asking for word of him, of this now mysterious stranger . . . for no one knew to where Musorgsky had vanished . . . —ILYA REPIN

113. *To VASILI BESSEL*

DEAREST VASILI VASILYEVICH:

The Director has sanctioned *Boris*. I beg you to get the *Klavieraus-*

---

[95] Sergei Solovyov's *History of Russia*.

[96] The first child of Nikolai and Nadezhda Rimsky-Korsakov was born on August 20—Mikhail Nikolayevich.

zug ready *by the end of November.* This is indispensable—or it'll be all up.

Your

MUSORGSKY

22 October '73

113a. *ALEXANDER BORODIN to YEKATERINA BORODINA, Moscow*
    [*Extract*]

[October 25, 1873]

. . . By the way, here's some news for you—*Boris* is to be given in its entirety. Gedeonov, when he returned from abroad to Petersburg, as soon as he got out of his railway-carriage, said in his first words to Lukashevich—"Stage *Boris* without fail and as quickly as possible; send the score to Ferrero, I will order it passed." Now they're already copying the parts. What is the meaning of this dream? Where does such an unexpected switch come from?—no one knows anything. In any case, the affair is fine. And here is pitiful and sorrowful news—of the author of *Boris.* He has been drinking heavily. Nearly every day he sits in the Maloyaroslavetz restaurant on Morskaya, often drinking himself stiff.[97] This summer the Sorokins saw him completely drunk in Pavlovsk; he caused a disturbance there; the affair reached the police.[98] I have been told that he has already drunk himself to a state of seeing hallucinations and all sorts of trash. Stasova, out of friendship (knowing while she was still abroad about Modeste's adventures) wrote him a letter [No. 105a] about this, in which, casually, she developed the idea that, is it really possible, that all talented Russian musicians must end as Glinka did. This is horribly sad! Such a talented man and sinking so low morally. Now he periodically disappears, then reappears morose, untalkative, which is contrary to his usual habit. After a little while he again comes to himself—sweet, gay, amiable and witty as ever. Devil knows what a pity! . . .

---

[97] The Maly-Yaroslavetz, so prominent in Musorgsky's more lurid biographies, is not the hell-hole described by Rimsky-Korsakov, but a social center for Petersburg's radical intelligentsia.

[98] See Letter 101a.

V

Entr'acte
1873 — 1874

Boris Advances toward the Footlights

. . . having for long had the idea of getting *Boris* produced, I decided on an extreme step. In the summer of 1873, when the director
of theaters, Gedeonov, was in Paris, my contract came up for renewal,
and I wrote him my conditions, the first of which was: I demand *Boris
Godunov* for my *bénéfice*—otherwise I'll not sign the contract and
I'll leave. There was no reply from him, but I knew very well that I
should get my way, as the Directorate could not do without me. In the
middle of August Gedeonov returned, and his first words to N. A.
Lukashevich (officially the head of the costume and set department,
but actually the Director's factotum, then a good friend of mine and
of Musorgsky's), were:—"Platonova demands *Boris* for her *bénéfice*,
what can I do now? She knows I have no right to stage this opera, as
it has been rejected. What can we do? There's this: we'll call the committee again, let them examine the opera (in its new form), just for
formality's sake; perhaps they'll agree to pass *Boris* now."—No sooner
said than done. The committee, summoned at the Director's orders,
meet for the second time, reject the opera. On receipt of this unwel-
come answer, Gedeonov sends for Ferrero (former double-bass
player), the president of the committee. Ferrero appears. Gedeonov
meets him in the anteroom, pale with rage.

"Why have you rejected the opera?"

"Have mercy, Your Excellency, the opera is not at all good."

"Why not? I've heard good reports of it!"

"Have mercy, Your Excellency, his friend, Cui, is always abusing
us in *Peterburgski Vedomosti.*—Why, only the day before yesterday . . ."—at which he pulls a newspaper out of his pocket.

"In that case, I don't want to know anything about your committee, you hear! I'll stage the opera without *your* approval!"—shouts
Gedeonov, beside himself.

And the opera was authorized for production by Gedeonov himself:—the first instance in which the Director had exceeded his authority in this respect. The next day Gedeonov sent for me. Angry
and excited, he came up to me and shouted:

"Well, milady, see what you've got me into! I run the risk of being·
removed from my post on account of you and your *Boris*. And what

good you see in it, I can't make out! I've no sympathy whatever with your innovators, and now I may have to suffer for them!"

"The more honor to you, Your Excellency," I replied: "that not having any personal sympathy for this opera, you so energetically protect the interests of Russian composers."

Everything was now arranged, apparently. But no, a new obstacle: Mr. Napravnik, shrinking and inwardly furious, represented to the Director that he had no time to take the rehearsals as he had so much to do otherwise. Then we arranged to have private rehearsals at my house, conducted by Musorgsky himself. The chorus, by order of the Director, was to be trained by Pomazansky. And thus it was. We set to work full of zeal, studying with love the music which had enraptured us, and in one month we were ready. We presented ourselves to our conductor Napravnik and demanded rehearsal with the orchestra. He scowled, but undertook the task and of course, with his usual conscientiousness did his duty admirably . . . —YULIA PLATONOVA [1]

114. *To FRANZ LISZT, Pesth (A Collective Telegram)*

[October 28, 1873]

A circle of Russians, devoted to art, believing in its eternal forward-moving activity and aspiring to participate in this activity, warmly greet you on the day of your jubilee.[2] As a genius composer and executant who has broadened the boundaries of art, as a great leader in the struggle against ancient routine, as an indefatigable artist before whose colossal and lasting activity we bow.

BALAKIREV, BESSEL, BORODIN, CUI, MUSORGSKY, RIMSKY-KORSAKOV, SHCHERBACHOV, STASOV.

115. *To LUBOV KARMALINA* [3]

In Petrograd, 5 December '73

MY DEAR LADY LUBOV IVANOVNA,

You flashed across our musical family. I understood you. You are leaving for afar. As a farewell, hear my request: in your leisure hours

---

[1] Platonova wrote this well-known account of *Boris's* authorization twelve years after the event (in a letter to Stasov, November 27, 1885), so we may excuse her slightly romanticized freedom of detail in its telling. Her letter to Gedeonov (April 11, 1873) did not actually demand *Boris Godunov* as she claims. She asked merely for "a new opera," and furthermore, her contract, as finally signed, omits this condition altogether.

[2] In November 1873 there were celebrations in Budapest on the fiftieth anniversary of Liszt's musical career.

[3] An intelligent soprano who had studied voice under Lomakin and Italian

remember that in Petrograd there lives a certain musician, waiting for an epistle from you in regard to the dissenters. This is audacious on the aforesaid musician's part, but what's to be done?—in professing a religion, audacity in the sphere of this religion is recognized as faith.

I warmly thank you, Lubov Ivanovna, for the discourses on art— they'll always be remembered by me. One more fine artistic personality is added to the small but rich number in the album of my sympathies. This is comforting. If possible, don't forget me.

MUSORGSKY

116. *To VLADIMIR STASOV*

In Petrograd, 6 Dec. '73

Here, *généralissime*, is a small part of our long-past dream that is realized.[4] Remembering that it was in your home that the attached little pieces were often played, I arranged some inscriptions on that account. If it's not too difficult for you, please deliver these according to the inscriptions. As for the library, I remembered it for the simple reason that this is a foreign publication and that it is more convenient for you, directly from Musoryanin's hands, to find a cozy spot for it in the library. I shall not hide the fact that it is pleasant to lie with good people, but I admit that such a pleasure (author's vanity) is just

---

teachers. After a series of successful concerts in Italy and France she returned to Russia and married, in 1860, an officer of the General Staff, Nikolai Karmalin. Though Karmalin was stationed at the Caucasian fortress of Zakatali, in remote Daghestan, Lubov Ivanovna managed to visit her musical friends in St. Petersburg and Moscow at two- or three-year intervals. She knew the Balakirev Circle well, and evidently had promised Musorgsky to do some musical research on the *Khovanshchina* dissenters.

[4] *Frühlingsblüten* (Album für Piano)
No. 1. M. v. Azanchevsky. *Allegro tranquillo.*
" 2. F. Czerny. *A la Mazurka.*
" 3. I. Iohannsen. *Am Meer.*
" 4. M. Musorgsky. *Ein Kinderscherz.*
" 5. M. Musorgsky. *Intermezzo.*
" 6. A. Reichhardt. *Walzer.*
" 7. A. Rubetz. *Kinderstückchen.*
" 8. H. Wölfl. *Energico.*
Verlag von A. Büttner, St. Petersburg; Moskau, A. Gutheil.
Musorgsky is the only contributor to this album who was not attached to the St. Petersburg Conservatory. Azanchevsky was the director, Wölfl, Czerny and Reichhardt taught piano, Rubetz taught *solfeggio* and elementary theory, and Iohannsen was professor of harmony.

like tickling the sole of the foot, or as Balakirev loved to confide (*du temps*), melted butter on the belly. This isn't the point. There, if only Avvakum would succeed!

Turn your attention to the cover: of all the composers only Azanchevsky has been written with a *von*, as he has the motto of *"Allegro tranquillo,"* but Mr. Wolflflflfl . . . and so on into infinity, preaches *"energico."* I think that any sort of movement might be described as *"energico,"* whether it's an andante or an allegro: so what sort of movement can be understood by the *"energico"* of Mr. H. Wolflflflf . . . and so on into infinity?

The publication is elegant, except for the ribbons at the top of the cover and the sprigs of *hemlock* in the center.

I can't refrain from returning to the calm speed of von Azanchevsky (*Allegro tranquillo*); if at least he would have peeked into Ishimova's history: [5] well what *vons* are we? After this it could be written von Skwoznik Dmuchanowsky, von Potchetchuy (which actually is a hemorrhoid), or von Swerbiguz.[6] It's a pity, but this recalls the visiting card of the State Secretary [a very low rank in the civil service] Vasili Yevdokimov: Mr. Basile de Eudoximoff (and underneath) *gouvernement Secrétaire* (I saw this with my own eyes). Till! *généralissime.*

Your

Musoryanin

117. *To VLADIMIR STASOV*

2 January 1874
The Day of Vladimir Stasov

You so desired, my dear *généralissime;* and I found the time. I embrace you firmly and I congratulate you. This second version of *Sennacherib* belongs to you by rights; take it.

Not in Beethoven, who wrote 4 overtures to Fidelio-Leonore, do I seek justification for my dedication. I do not wish to justify myself even by the examples of great men. I am myself—a man himself—as is, and here's my justification to myself and to you: you know that our dear Mili Balakirev was very amused by my *Sennacherib* in its first version and even placed Gashinka Lomakin in an awkward position

---

[5] Alexandra Ishimova was a writer for children; her *History of Russia in Tales for Children* occupies a place in Russian literary history chiefly by virtue of Pushkin's praise of it in the last letter written before his fatal duel.

[6] Characters in Gogol's *Revizor* and his story "Christmas Eve."

at a concert in 1867 when *Sennacherib* was performed in the Nobles' Hall.[7] In its first version I dedicated it to Mili Balakirev: *peace to the memory of the past.* You, my splendid one, have persistently hinted at the imperfection of the central episode in my chorus. I composed it in your presence, and thousands of times we have together reaped approbation before our audiences of all sorts; but most important— in its second version you fell powerfully in love with *Sennacherib.* Honor to me and glory for that and my justification is in this. I dedicate *Sennacherib* to you and I take pride in this dedication.

MUSORYANIN

To Vladimir Vasilyevich Stasov

On the 2nd of January 1874.

THE DESTRUCTION OF SENNACHERIB

(A transcription from the Hebrew Melodies of Byron.) [8]

1. Like a pack of hungry wolves, the enemy came down on us. His cohorts, with gold and purple gleaming in the sun, oppressed and blinded the sons of Israel.

2. Their steel spears shone, like stars on the surging surf. Like a forest splendid and mighty was raised, with the rising of the sun, the enemy host. Obscured was the sun, perished was the dawn before the Assyrian horde—the heathen.

3. 'Tis not the waves of the sea that roar in the deep, 'tis not the wind of the desert that moans in the gorge—that is the enemy horde thirsting with wild laughter for the blood of Israel.

4. The shadows of sunset have already run over the distant hills; in tearful prayer, in wailing mourning, Israel is prostrate before the face of Jehovah, calling on Him to save the children of Canaan.

5. And there, on sable wings, rushing o'er the camp of the frenzied foe, is the Angel of Death—Asrael, touching with chilling breath the mouth of the heathen.

6. The children of Baal trembled, their hearts hammered with fear . . . and grew silent.

7. Along with the withered leaves, driven by the storm, the bodies

---

[7] See pp. 82–83.

[8] The reader may be interested in comparing Musorgsky's last version of the text with the quite different structure of Byron's original.

of the foe, at the setting of the sun, cover the plain; because the angel of the Lord did smite the enemy.

MUSORGSKY

117a. *FRANZ LISZT to VASILI BESSEL, St. Petersburg*

Horpacs (Chez le Comte Szechenyi)
February 2, 1874

DEAR SIR,

Pray excuse me for being so late in thanking you, you and all those who signed the telegram sent to Pesth on the occasion of my Jubilee fete. I am deeply touched with the most noble sentiments it expresses with chivalrous eloquence, and beg you to convey the tribute of my most sincere gratitude to Messrs. Balakirev, Borodin, Cui, Musorgsky, Rimsky-Korsakov, Shcherbachov, and Stasov.

You were kind enough, Sir, to let me see several of their works at Weimar; I appreciate and esteem them highly, and as far as it depends on myself I will do all I can to make them known, and shall feel honored thus to respond to sympathetic kindness which splendid colleagues such as these accord to

Their very devoted
F. LISZT [9]

118. *To VASILI BESSEL*

Herewith I send you, Vasili Vasilyevich, the last bit of proof on *Boris*. I ask you to send to Röder one of the dedications (selected by you). I should like the whole dedication engraved *in facsimile,* and I believe you will carry out my wish. But in any case I ask you to retain my name *in facsimile.*

M. MUSORGSKY

4 Jan. '74.

119. *A Dedication*

I comprehend the people as a great personality, inspired by a "single idea." This is my task. I have attempted to resolve it in opera.

[9] No. 140 in Vol. II, *Letters of Franz Liszt,* collected and edited by La Mara, translated by Constance Bache. (New York, Scribners, 1894).

To you, who with good advice and with sympathetic action, gave me the possibility to test myself on the stage, I dedicate my work.[10]

M. MUSORGSKY

21 January, 1874

120. *An Inscription on a Photograph*

To Polyxena Stepanovna Stasova. This is how I've looked ever since the first rehearsal of *Boris;* [11] so take me not as No. 6280, but as Musoryanin.

10 January 74.

—and that wreath you gave me pushes me on: do it, then, do what you must do. Thank you, little dove.

EVER THE SAME MUSORYANIN

121. *To STEPAN GEDEONOV (A Petition)* [12]

[18–20 January, 1874]

To His Excellency the Director of the Imp[erial] Theaters, Stepan Alexandrovich Gedeonov.

I have the honor most humbly to petition Your Excellency for the acceptance by the Directorate of the Imperial Theaters of *Boris Godunov,* an opera of my composition in 5 acts, subject to royalty for each performance.

M. MUSORGSKY

121a. *PAVEL FYODOROV to STEPAN GEDEONOV (A Memo)*

M. Musorgsky petitions for the acceptance by the Directorate of the Imperial Theatres of an opera in five Acts composed by him and entitled *Boris Godunov,* subject to payment for each performance. Mme. Platonova, a singer belonging to the troupe of the Russian Opera, asks permission to give the first performance of this opera for her *bénéfice.*

---

[10] The version of this dedication finally used: "To all of you, who with good advice and with sympathetic action gave me the possibility of realizing the task that lies at the base of the opera *Boris Godunov,* I dedicate my work. M. MUSORGSKY."

[11] According to Stasov, the first rehearsal at the theater took place on January 9, after which Musorgsky had his photograph taken at Lorens'.

[12] Another, similarly formal petition was sent to Gedeonov by Yulia Platonova.

In presenting this for Your Excellency's favorable consideration and decision I have the honor to inform you that the libretto of the aforesaid opera has been approved for the stage by the committee of Theatrical Literature and by the Censor [13] and that, in accordance with the Regulations for the remuneration of authors and translators, this opera appertains to the first class, entitling M. Musorgsky to receive for each performance a tenth share of two-thirds of the receipts.

20 January, 1874

On the Eve

. . . The rehearsals of *Boris Godunov* at the Marinsky Theatre went on speedily and well. Musorgsky attended each of them and always returned happy and full of hope for its success. He could not find sufficient praise for the attitude of all the artists in general, and especially that of the conductor Napravnik, who gave at these rehearsals, according to Musorgsky, many good suggestions, and it was on his insistence that many lengthy things were omitted, things that didn't really belong, or which didn't seem successful, or which spoiled the general theatrical impression. Such as: the scene in Pimen's cell, the tale of the parrot in the scene between the Tzarevich and Boris [actually omitted in subsequent performances], the clock with chimes and several others. Musorgsky fully and sincerely agreed with Napravnik's opinion and argued heatedly with those who accused him of weak character and compliance.

"All this is quite impossible on the stage," he used to say to me after such arguments, "and these gentlemen don't care to listen. They don't require quality of impression, only quantity. They say I have a weak character, but they don't understand that no author, before his opera reaches theatrical production, can possibly judge the impression a scene may make on the audience. Meyerbeer struck out entire pages without mercy—he knew what he was doing, and he was right!" . . .

On the eve of the première Musorgsky dropped in on me in the evening, sat down as usual at the piano, but, touching only a few chords, rose, shut the lid and said, with vexation:

—No, I can't. I know it's very silly, but what can I do? I can't get my tomorrow's examination out of my mind—what will it be?

. . . Musorgsky stayed with me for the night, but apparently he spent the entire night without sleep, for I woke several times and

---

[13] Was it the censor or the theater directorate who ordered the omission of four scenes from *Boris Godunov?* Or were there physical and economical motives for the omissions? As Shishkov's sets for the 1870 production of Pushkin's *Boris* were to be used now, and as that production had omitted 16 scenes of Pushkin's 23 (including the censored scene in Pimen's cell), did this determine the cuts in the opera made at this time—for example, the cell scene?

saw him pacing up and down the room with his hands clenched behind his back, deep in thought . . . —ARSENI GOLENISHCHEV-
KUTUZOV

122. *A program* [14]

Boris Godunov	Melnikov [15]
Fyodor ⎫ the children of Boris	Krutikova
Xenia ⎭	Raab
Xenia's nurse	Schroeder-Napravnik
Prince Vasili Ivanovich Shuisky	Vasilyev 2.
Andrei Shchelkalov, scribe of the council	Sobolev
Pimen, a chronicler (hermit)	Vasilyev 1.
The Pretender under the name of Gregori	Kommissarzhevsky
Maryna Mniszech, daughter of the Sando- mierz Voyevoda	Platonova
Rangoni, a secret Jesuit	Paleček
Varlaam ⎫ tramps	Petrov
Misail ⎭	Dyuzhikov
The hostess of the Inn	Abarinova
A simpleton	Bulakhov
Nikitich, a bailiff	Sariotti
Mityuka, a peasant	Lyadov
First boyar	Sobolev
The boyar Khrushchov	Matveyev
Lawicki and Czernikowski	Vasilyev 1 & Sobolev

Boyars, boyar children, *streltzi,* marketers, bailiffs, Polish nobles and
ladies, Sandomierz maidens, pilgrims, people of Moscow.

1598–1605

Performed on the stage of the Marinsky Theatre in
Petrograd, January 27, 1874, under the direction
of Napravnik, with Kondratyev as régisseur, and
Morozov as assistant, at the *bénéfice* of Yu. F.
Platonova.

---

[14] This cast and the performance note below it were written by Musorgsky on
a copy of the freshly printed piano score.
[15] Ivan Alexandrovich Melnikov, a pupil of Lomakin's, had made his debut in
I Puritani in 1867.

First-Night Audience

The opera *Boris Godunov* made a strong impression on the audience, and aroused talk, although opinions were varied. The majority agreed on one thing, that there was in the new opera very little music in the usual sense, and any success was due to the artists: their splendid acting, it was said, had rescued the composer. I recall that [at the première], after the scene of the inn, I stopped in at the loge of some friends whom I had interested in the new opera. The atmosphere in the loge was full of excitement: buzzing, laughter, analysis of the tramps' characters, enthusiasm for the acting of Petrov, Kommissarzhevsky, Leonova [Abarinova], and even of Dyuzhikov, a quite poor artist (who played Misail). After Scene 1 of Act IV (the Granovitaya Palata) I stopped in at another loge: there an elderly lady still held a handkerchief to her eyes. "I am very glad," I said, "that the opera has made such a strong impression on you."—"What sort of opera is this," objected the lady, "there's no music in it; but I must confess that I never took my eyes from the stage. How splendidly Melnikov acts, every word of his still rings in my ears! That's a genius, no actor!"—NIKOLAI KOMPANEISKY

123. *To YULIA MAKHINA* [16] (*An Inscription on a Photograph*)

[January 27–28, 1874]

On my return from the première of the opera *Boris Godunov*, I found your elegant gift. I accept it with an open heart, delighted by the sincere impulse of your pure and artistic soul.

MUSORGSKY

124. *To VLADIMIR STASOV*

My dear *généralissime,* I implore you: don't give any publicity in the press to the story of the wreath. Something might happen which you least of all would desire. *Boris* might not be kept on the stage. I implore you with all the strength of your love for me.

MUSORYANIN

28 January '74.

---

[16] Yulia Nikolayevna Makhina, a graduate of the Conservatory, had recently made her first public appearance at a Pomazansky concert in which she made a success with Musorgsky's song, "The Little Orphan Girl."

124a. *To the Editor of the* Peterburgski Vedomosti *(A Collective Letter)*
[*Extracts*]

. . . Astonished at such high-handed treatment of the audience, we asked one of our acquaintances [Vladimir Stasov] to make both a written and an oral statement . . . We were told verbally that Mr. Conductor [Napravnik] of the Marinsky Theatre never accepts wreaths brought to him from the box-office and refused to deliver this one because the usher who brought it to him told him that "it was ordered to be handed over to the composer," and he doesn't take orders, and furthermore doesn't know the names of the donors . . . Is it really required for wreaths to be presented only after submitting a request on stamped legal paper, properly numbered . . . ?

N[adezha Petrovna] D[utour]
N[atalia Fyodorovna] P[ivovarova]
Z[oya Mikhailovna] Ch[arukhina]

[Printed in the issue of February 2, 1874]

125. *To EDUARD NAPRAVNIK*

Saturday, 2 February '74

DEAREST EDUARD FRANTZOVICH,

I have been outraged by today's correspondence in the *Peterburgski Vedomosti.* The tactless affair of the wreath according to those who wished its public presentation to the composer at the *first* performance of this composer's *first* opera caused the good feelings, established in me during the rehearsals with my dear comrades in the performance of the opera to the conclusion of its première to be transformed to a painful feeling, oppressing me to this moment, because henceforth I cannot calmly await a single performance of the opera. I know with what sympathy you approached my *first* large work.

I know you as an artist of the highest caliber and I warmly thank you for *Boris.* I implore you not to think of me as holding common interests with such donors and such statements—they only oppress me.

I am answering today's correspondence in the same columns of the *Peterburgski Vedomosti.* This is a risk but I am not afraid of any possible consequences: let them chatter that it is indecent for the composer to meddle in *these affairs.*

Devotedly yours,
M. MUSORGSKY

126. *To the Editor of the* St. Peterburgski Vedomosti

[February 2?, 1874]
DEAR SIR,

In No. 33 of your esteemed newspaper of February 2, under the heading: "Correspondence," a statement was printed to the effect that a laurel wreath, submitted for presentation to the composer of the opera *Boris Godunov* at its première, was not turned over to the composer, and that the persons wishing to present the wreath "didn't even know where it was taken."

I read these last words with regret, the more so as on Wednesday, January 30, the composer had the occasion to thank personally two of the ladies participating in the presentation of the wreath, for their kind attention to his humble work.

But more regrettable is the accident that the statement mentions obscurely—a person [Napravnik] who commands the fullest respect and sympathy for his artistic activity on the opera stage.

Therefore I consider myself obliged to clarify the affair.

At the première of the opera *Boris Godunov,* before the 4th act began, the composer was informed by certain individuals *from the audience* of the intended public presentation of a laurel wreath to him: The composer lacked the courage to accept a wreath publicly on the first performance of his *first* opera. The composer started to leave the theater, but he was stopped and he requested that the wreath not be presented to him before the departure of the audience. At the close of the performance, the elegant wreath was gratefully received by the composer in one of the theater's dressing-rooms.

I appeal to you to spare space for this clarification in the earliest possible number of your esteemed newspaper, and please be assured, dear sir, of my respect and devotion.

M. MUSORGSKY

[Printed in the issue of February 5, 1874]

Backstage

. . . At the second performance [on February 3], after the fountain scene, K.N., sincerely devoted to me, as a friend, but, by the slander of the Conservatory people, a mortal enemy of Musorgsky, came up to me in the entr'acte with the words:

"And you like this music so much that you took this opera for your *bénéfice?*"

"Yes, I like it . . . ," I answered.

"So I say to you, that this is a *disgrace* to *all Russia*, this opera!" he screeched, almost frothing at the mouth, and turned and left me.—
YULIA PLATONOVA

An Article by ✱ ✱ [*CESAR CUI*]

BORIS GODUNOV, AN OPERA BY MR. MUSORGSKY,
TWICE REJECTED BY THE VAUDEVILLE COMMITTEE

in the *S.-Peterburgski Vedomosti*
(February 6, 1874)

[Extracts]

. . . The remainder of this scene [in the cell] is weak not because it was incorrectly or irrationally managed, not because the declamation was unsatisfactory—on the contrary, this as well as others was irreproachable—but because there is little music in it and its recitatives are not melodic . . . It is impossible to accept as a musical idea the device of taking continually repeated notes that enter into the content of some chord, but, regrettably, this scene consists exactly of such recitatives. No inspiration is needed to create such recitatives, only routine, practice. Concerning the routine narratives of Pimen about Ivan the Terrible and Tzar Fyodor, they are sharp in color, but dull in musical content. They consist of just such insignificant recitatives, and the orchestration aspires, for the most part, toward crude, decorative onomatopoeia and the portrayal of trifles, to which Mr. Musorgsky is so addicted . . . The Pretender is especially unsuccessful in the hands of Mr. Musorgsky . . . The entire role of the Pretender is noisy, difficult, fatiguing and ungrateful . . .

The two chief faults of *Boris* are: the choppy recitative and the disconnectedness of the musical thought, making the opera rather like a potpourri. These faults are by no means due to Mr. Musorgsky's creative impotence, not at all. Let us recall the two people's scenes and the inn scene: what melodic character the recitatives have in them; what a smooth and natural flow of music. Besides, Mr. Musorgsky is capable of striking, graceful prettiness: let us recall Fyodor's story of the parrot, the Tzar's reply and the end of the love duet. The defects derive directly from immaturity, from the fact that the composer is insufficiently self-critical, from that unfastidious, self-satisfied, hasty writing which has led to such lamentable results in the cases of Messrs. Rubinstein and Tchaikovsky.

In conclusion I want to drop a few sympathetic tears in behalf of those "few ladies" who, in their six initials, personifying the public, became "victims" of the non-presentation of the wreath to Mr. Musorgsky at the première of his opera, but alas! I haven't the strength to do it. On the contrary, I am very glad that it turned out exactly as it did, that the wreath was not presented and this is why. In the first place lavish public presentations to all kinds of performers have become so vulgarized that it would be delicate to release at least the composers from these. In the second place, a beginning composer, to whom such a presentation is made at the première of his first work, not knowing what his work is like as a whole, not knowing how it will look to a real audience, rather than to six initials—such a composer, if only he would not be blinded by himself finally, in the moment of presentation must sustain only one passionate, uncertain [irresistible?—R.-K.] desire to sink through the earth. I am very glad that Mr. Musorgsky did not have to undergo this desire, the more so that if this had happened, we would have been deprived of a very talented composer with an enormous future, to which the path through wreaths is as inconvenient, as in the circus where riders also have to jump through wreaths.

127. *To VLADIMIR STASOV*

My dear and *ever dear généralissime in spite of everything and everybody*. I was angry, as a loving woman is angry; I fumed and raged . . . now I am grieved and indignant, indignant and grieved. What a horror that article of Cui's is! To begin at the end: no well-bred man would dare to refer to women as Cui has done in his inconsiderate witticisms. *But shame on him* who in print, publicly, makes fun of women who deserve nothing but sympathy (as I heard) for their brave and fearless conduct. (As to me personally—that's another story, but I remain silent and will not forget a good deed.) In anger at you, my dear, at your rejection of my plea [to suppress the wreath story], I was rough—to the devil with tenderness! . . . *I was nasty to you* at the theater, *my anger nauseates me*. I dare to confess proudly, that neither at dinner at Dimitri's, nor even at the theater, *was I contemptible* nor did I belie your love. I repeat: no matter what would have happened—I could not part from you, I love you passionately and in your blanched face I read just as strong a love for me. I am happy about our quarrel, it has strengthened and heartened me;—it is good, it is *important* when people clash *thus*. I've said everything, I am whole before you, as I am.

Thus, it seems, it was necessary for *Boris* to appear for people to show their true selves. The tone of Cui's article is odious: what childish nonsense about the peasant women! [17] And this reckless assault on the *self-satisfaction* of the composer! The brainless ones are not satisfied with that modesty and humility, which has never left me and

---

[17] Cui said in his review, "In our choral dances the peasant women scream almost continually."

never will leave, as long as my brain and head are not altogether burnt out. Behind this insane attack, behind this deliberate lie, I see nothing, exactly as if soapy water had been spilt through the air dimming all objects.—*Self-satisfaction!!! Hasty composition! Immaturity!* . . . whose? . . . whose? . . . I'd like to know.

The thing is this: a loving woman can perceive, by various indications, that something menaces her beloved. You have often slipped and said: "I am afraid of Cui in regard to *Boris.*" You were justified in your loving foreboding. And after such a *thundering* indication of your love, how could I cease loving you?!! *Vade retro Satanas!*

MUSORYANIN

6 February '74, in Petrograd

An Article by HERMAN LAROCHE

AN INTELLECTUAL REALIST IN RUSSIAN OPERA

in the St. Petersburg *Golos*
(February 13, 1874)

[Extracts]

. . . When the three ladies had delivered their wreath to the box-office in the regular way, they waited to see what would happen next. Nothing happened: the wreath was not handed up. The ladies were furious, and the pages of the *S.-P.V.* were adorned with a beautiful correspondence, adorned with six initials. Someone had told the ladies that Mr. Napravnik was to blame for everything, whereupon they hastened to inform the public of the fact in the press, but with this reservation: "All this does not concern us. The truth is only that we became victims."

Three days later the composer himself enters the arena, hastily, excited, still glowing from his recent triumph, courteously disposed towards the ladies, full of respect for Napravnik, and—most important of all—highly delighted both with the wreath, and with its non-delivery: opening an opportunity to enable him to talk about himself in an important newspaper and thus to add the laurels of a publicist to those of a poet and composer . . .

When Mr. Musorgsky heard of the honor that was proposed for him, he decided to decline the gift; his nerves gave way, and he implored them not to show him the wreath. Later he became so frightened at the thought of the laurels, ribbons, inscriptions, to say nothing of the three masked beauties, that like the bride[groom] in Gogol's story he resolved on flight; someone brought him back, however, and embarrassed, yet happy, the composer wrote an article in which he announced what an honor had been bestowed on him on the occasion of the first performance of his first opera, *quod erat demonstrandum.*

127a.   *MARK ANTOKOLSKY to VLADIMIR STASOV, St. Petersburg*

Rome, 6 (18) Feb. 1874

I hasten to express to you from afar my joy, greetings and my congratulations to our Musorgsky. This morning I read in *Golos* of the performance of *Boris Godunov*. And in spite of all the critic's desire not to speak the truth, it is nevertheless obvious that the opera has had a tremendous success. I've just read the same thing in *S.-Peterburgski Vedomosti*, that the opera is definitely a success and that its gifted composer was called several times after each act.

From my own side I also call him to stand on guard before the art of truth and of the people, that which is based on the finest human feelings—on truth and on beauty. Once more I repeat your words: "And with new strength, let us continue our mutual, though diverse, work." [18] Once more greetings to the conqueror, I am very, very happy for him and for all new art!

Rome, 16/28 February, 1874
[extract]

. . . I am sorry, very sorry for Musorgsky. Recently I wrote exactly what you have now said: "Why do talents fade away so quickly?" I don't know.—Perhaps it is that only empty hearts beat evenly? Perhaps because consciousness comes to us before knowledge? The soul strains towards freedom, but where is it?—Well, an artist often comes upon a thorny path, first he moves forward, then he grows weary, then he stumbles, grows faint, and falls. Ekh, Russia! it needs so many more victims before it will begin to lead a normal life. Such victims will serve as a platform for the people of the future. This, in my opinion, is the truth, and therefore all the more saddening.

I read the analysis of the opera *Boris Godunov* in *Golos*. I think I have never encountered anything more stupid and trivial than this. It is stupid in that the one [Laroche] analyzing the opera nags pettishly at petty things and doesn't realize at all the essence of the opera. It is stupid mainly because he drags in personalities: this is unforgivable, this means that he has no respect for the printed word; and finally, this isn't fair. However, his trivial attitude that "nothingness is realism," and that realism is liberalism and both "try to break the chains of the times"—all this sufficiently proves that it's no use talking about such

---

[18] In Stasov's dedication of his book on *Modern Art in Europe* "To Ilya Repin, to Mordukh Antokolsky and to the memory of Hartmann."

people. This is some sort of an artistic denunciation. Honor and glory to *Golos!* It's making this a habit! . . .

128. *To ARSENI GOLENISHCHEV-KUTUZOV*

Petrograd, Shpalernaya No. 6. 2nd of March, '74

MY DEAR ARSENI,

Forgive me for this long silence: the thing is, that without you I've strayed from the furrow. The folk scene sent by you [19] delights me in the main, and this delight is the more significant as I begin to be feel calm in a bit of my conscience in regard to your creativeness. Yes, dear friend, this, exactly this, is the attitude one must have toward historical drama. To read penetratingly, to nose out, to dig into all the details, to shuffle your brains, not once, not twice, but a hundred times— if one is able to do it. This must be one's attitude towards historical drama; but is this the only way, i.e., by the above-mentioned means, that historical drama is to be created? Hats off, chests bared and let's speak:

People grow, consequently human society grows also; the correspondence between the demands of developed (according to the times) man and his demands on the developed (also according to the times) human society is the harmony that is sought for, and the path to the achievement of this sought-for harmony is a violent struggle, in whatever way it be manifested.[20]

For a modern artist, the abstracting of an ideal is only half of the artist's own task, and that but a particle of the labor as far as creation is concerned; he is involuntarily overtaken by this abstracting as a means of orientation—that same forced need that is in the instinct of self-preservation. The rebellious, the searching spirit of the genuine artist must not and cannot be appeased only by the integrity of abstracting one's task into an ideal, even though the creation, under such

---

[19] For *Shuisky.* Musorgsky was correcting these scenes in careful detail, with both poetic and dramatic purposes, before returning them to Golenishchev-Kutuzov. A study of the poet's manuscript and Musorgsky's corrections can be found in the appendix to *Letters to A. A. Golenishchev-Kutuzov* (1939).

[20] "Man, like every other animal, has no doubt advanced to his present high condition through a struggle for existence consequent on his rapid multiplication; and if he is to advance still higher, it is to be feared that he must remain subject to a severe struggle. Otherwise he would sink into indolence, and the more gifted men would not be more successful in the battle of life than the less gifted."— Charles Darwin, *The Descent of Man,* Chap. 21.

circumstances, would grow from firm ground. The ideal must be embodied in the spirit of the time chosen by the artist, and the artist must so command society, that society would not sense it, painlessly, nonviolently, fully grasping the event he has chosen, being inspired by it, and he must command with love, as does a passionately adored woman.

The artistic revelation of the spirit of the times demands that society be reminded as rarely as possible of turns and character of speech and methods of expression, contemporary to the interests of society—the more concealed and clear is the *real*, and not merely *visible* horizon—the more easily and integrally will society accept it and become inspired by it.

Arseni, you are strong, but not zealous enough: read, penetrate into that which reveals your Achilles heel. Kenevich [21] promised to write you about books useful to you (Book of insurrections and a narrative of how it happened [22]): precious books, my dear friend. I believe you have understood me. Let us put on our hats, button up our coats and say good-by.

If you don't mind—remind your *maman* once in a while that I, from afar, feel close to her good, illumined soul, because I adored my forever lost, my dear *maman*.

Your

MODESTE MUSORGSKY

129. *To VLADIMIR STASOV*

DEAR *généralissime*,

Greeting. I didn't go to Dimitri's because I fell into conversation with a gentleman both of whose sons are trying to fight off the measles. So I was afraid to go where there are little young ladies and masters.

Till Sunday.

MUSORYANIN

We are, finally, boiling with *Khovanshchina. Vale!*

9 March '74.

---

[21] Vladislav Kenevich, a literary scholar respected by Musorgsky.

[22] The full title of this work which Kenevich recommends for Golenishchev-Kutuzov's research on Shuisky is *The Relation and Story of How the Unfrocked Monk Grishka Otrepiev Conquered the Capital City of Moscow and of His Adventures.*

129a. *SERGEI TANEYEV*[23] *to PIOTR TCHAIKOVSKY, St. Petersburg*
[*Extract*]

March 24, 1874, Moscow

. . . I asked Nikolai Albertovich [Hubert] [24] for *Pskovityanka, The Nursery* and several songs by Musorgsky to show Fyodor Ivanovich [Maslov].[25] This music gave the Maslovs a headache: on another day they hid the score. However Fyodor Ivanovich liked "With the Doll" from *The Nursery*. But in general they say this is no better than Johann Sebastian Bach . . .

130. *To VLADIMIR STASOV*

Wednesday, some day or other [the 12th?] in
June '74

MY DEAR *généralissime*.

Hartmann [26] is boiling as *Boris* boiled—the sounds and the idea hung in the air, and now I am gulping and overeating, I can hardly manage to scribble it down on paper. Am writing 4 numbers—with good transitions (on "promenade"). I want to do it as quickly and steadily as possible. My physiognomy can be seen in the intermezzi. I consider it successful so far. I embrace you and I take it that you bless me—so give me your blessing!

MUSORYANIN

V[*otre*] *S*[*erviteur*]

Curious nomination [nomenclature]: "*Promenade (in modo russico)*"

No. 1. "*Gnomus*"—intermezzo (there's no name for the intermezzo);

No. 2. "*Il vecchio castello*"—intermezzo (also unnamed);

No. 3. "*Tuileries (dispute d'enfants après jeux)*";

---

[23] Sergei Taneyev, then a student at the Moscow Conservatory and the favorite pupil in Professor Tchaikovsky's harmony class.

[24] Director of the Moscow Conservatory since Nikolai Rubinstein's resignation.

[25] A friend of Tchaikovsky and Taneyev.

[26] In January 1874, Vladimir Stasov and Count Paul Suzor, president of the Architects' Society, organized a memorial exhibition of the works (water colors, drawings, projects) of Victor Hartmann, in the galleries of the Academy of Arts. Musorgsky was moved by the exhibition of his dead friend's career, but found no channel for his emotion until after the excitement of *Boris's* staging had passed. Then he began a piano suite in memory of Hartmann, based largely on particular items in the memorial show.

No. 4. Right between the eyes *"Sandomirzsko bydlo"* (*le télégue*)
it stands to reason that *le télégue* isn't named, but this is
between us).[27]

How well it works out!

MUSORYANIN

I should like to add Vityushka's Jews.[28]

[In the upper left-hand corner, Musorgsky has added:] Can't be at
your place.

131. *A Dedication*

Dedicated to Vladimir Vasilyevich Stasov.

PICTURES AT AN EXHIBITION.

M. Musorgsky's souvenir of Victor Hartmann, 1874.

To you, *généralissime,* the organizer of

the Hartmann exhibition in memory of

our dear Victor,

27 July '74

[Following is the full suite, with titles as in the manuscript]

Promenade
No. 1. *Gnomus*
No. 2. *Il vecchio castello*
No. 3. *Tuileries (Dispute d'enfants après jeux)*
No. 4. *Bydlo*
No. 5. Ballet of the Unhatched Chicks
No. 6. [Two Jews, one rich and one poor]
Promenade
No. 7. *Limoges. Le marché*

[Professor Lamm has deciphered two fragments of prose-pictures that

---

[27] *"Bydlo"* are Polish oxen. *"Le télégue"* is a typically Musorgskian Frenchification of *telega,* a Russian cart.

[28] In Alfred Frankenstein's exhaustive study of Victor Hartmann's works in relation to Musorgsky's memorial (*Musical Quarterly,* July 1939) he tells of two pencil drawings in the memorial show that were catalogued as belonging to Musorgsky: "A rich Jew wearing a fur hat: Sandomierz," and "A poor Sandomierz Jew." These may be "Vityushka's Jews."

Musorgsky had noted as a preface (?) to this episode, and then effaced with ink:]

La grande nouvelle: M. Pimpant de Pante Pantaléon vient de re-trouver sa vache: La Fugitive. "Oui, Maàme, c'était hier.—Non, Maàme, c'était avant-hier. Eh bien, oui, Maàme, la bête rôdait dans le voisinage.—Eh bien, non, Maàme, la bête ne rôdait pas du tout." —etc.

La grande nouvelle: M. de Puissangeout vient de retrouver sa vache "La Fugitive." Mais les bonnes dames de Limoges ne sont pas tout à fait d'accord sur ce sujet, parce que Mme. de Remboursac s'est ap-proprié une belle denture en porcelaine, tandis que M. de Panta-Pantaléon garde toujours son nez gênant—couleur pivoine.

No. 8. *Catacombae. Sepulcrum romanum.*

Con mortuis in lingua mortua.

[A marginal note:]

A Latin text: with the dead in a dead language. It should be a Latin text. The creative spirit of the departed Hartmann leads me toward the skulls and invokes them—the skulls begin to glow faintly.

No. 9. "The Little Hut on Chicken's Legs" ("Baba-Yaga")

No. 10. "The Bogatyrs' Gate (in the Ancient Capital of Kiev)"

22 June, 1874, in Petrograd

M. MUSORGSKY [29]

---

[29] Mr. Frankenstein establishes as the sources for the numbers in the suite the following Hartmann works, so far as he has located them:

No. 1. A design for a toy nutcracker made for the Christmas tree at the St. Petersburg Artists' Club in 1869.

No. 2. ?

No. 3. A watercolor, *Jardin des Tuileries.*

No. 4. ?

No. 5. Costume design for a ballet, *Trilbi,* "Canary-chicks, enclosed in eggs as in suits of armor."

No. 6. See footnote 28 above.

No. 7. ?

No. 8. "Interior of Paris catacombs with figures of Hartmann, the architect Kenel, and the guide holding a lamp."

No. 9. "Baba Yaga's hut on fowl's legs. Clock, Russian style of the 14th cen-tury. Bronze and enamel."

No. 10. "Stone city-gates for Kiev, Russian style, with a small church inside; the city council had planned to build these in 1869, in place of the wooden gates, to commemorate the event of April 4, 1866 [an unsuccessful attempt on Alexander II's life] . . ."

132.   *To VLADIMIR STASOV*

                                                         20 June '74
MY DEAR *généralissime,*

"*Crab & Co.*" [30] *ought to be thought about;* the crab's "anathema"
on the tramp is particularly amusing. I suppose it is possible *to concoct*
it and soon, too. But what a marvelous man you are—what a pusher!
Yes, if only there were free time—it wouldn't be necessary for me to
work this way; I myself feel that it wouldn't be necessary thus; anyway,
the crab affair can be pictured. I thank you. Therefore till Saturday
or Sunday in *"Pärgala."*

                                                         MUSORYANIN

132a.   *ARSENI GOLENISHCHEV-KUTUZOV to VLADIMIR STASOV*
        [*Extract from a draft*]

                                                         [Undated]
. . . Here, Vladimir Vasilyevich, is the form in which your
splendid idea for the "Hill of Nettles" has been dressed by me. If it's
not suitable—throw it away, if it is—deliver it to Modeste, the sound-
creator. I'm afraid he has forgotten the "Crab's" theme, which he
found at Dmitri V[asilyevich's] at Pargolovo . . .

132b.   *VLADIMIR STASOV to NIKOLAI RIMSKY-KORSAKOV, Nikolayev*
        [*Extracts*]

                                                         Spb. July 1, 1874
. . . Musoryanin has positively completed and written the last
stroke of his piece on Hartmann. The *second part* you don't know at
all, and there, I think, are the very best things. "The Limoges Gossips at the Market"—an enchanting Scherzino and very pianistic.
Then comes "Baba-Yaga"—excellent and powerful, and in conclusion—"The Kiev Bogatyrs' Gate"—in the manner of a hymn or a finale *à la* "Slavsiya" [31]—of course a million times worse and weaker,
but all the same a lovely, mighty and original thing. There is a particularly lovely church motif: "As you are baptized in Christ," and the
ringing bells—are in a completely new style. In this second part are
a few unusually poetic lines. This [musical quotation] is the music for

---

[30] See Stasov's letter to Rimsky-Korsakov (132b).
[31] In Glinka's *A Life for the Tzar.*

                            274

Hartmann's picture of the "Catacombs of Paris" all made of skulls. Musoryanin has begun with a depiction of a gloomy vault (long stretched chords, purely orchestral, with great ⌢). Then tremolando comes in a minor key the theme of the first *promenade,*—these are faint lights glimmering in the skulls, and here suddenly is sounded the magic, poetic appeal of Hartmann to Musorgsky . . .

But don't imagine, Admiral, that Musoryanin is readying himself only for this: now all of a sudden there has awakened in him such a desire for composition, that apparently not one day passes without it. He's beginning a new opera [*Fair at Sorochintzi*], and meanwhile he has planned, as an entr'acte, a new musical satire, in the manner of *Penny Paradise.* The new thing will be entitled *The Hill of Nettles* and the whole affair consists of this, that "Crab" (i.e., Laroche) convokes on this hill the whole Sanhedrin of animals, in order to give an account to them of the bad situation of present musical affairs, and complains here of the *Rooster* (i.e., Musorgsky), because he only screams all the time and shouts without sense, eternally scratching only in "dung-heaps," and God knows what they attribute to him, since once in a century he has found there some two or three tiny seeds!! [82] They listen to the sermon and say yes to him, *various* animals, for example, the old blind *Bear* (Maurer), *Rhinoceros* (Ferrero), *Marmoset* (Rybasov) [88] and so on, and also *Sloth* (Azanchevsky), *Sea-Cow* (Fyodorov), *Sheep* (Famintzin), *Bedbug* (Soloviov—with this significance, that he bites less than he stinks) and so on and so on. All this company say yes to everything the *Crab* says, promising to follow his example and his advice to go backwards and then to wring the neck of Rooster, and in conclusion the whole chorus yells and sings: *"Anathema, anathema on Rooster!"* There's already material for all this. Aside from this, Musoryanin has written a song on Kutuzov's poem "Longing," [84] and although this is not a first-rate song, it is all the same one of his *good* songs . . .

---

[82] A Krylov fable—"The Rooster and the Seed-Pearl."

[88] Ivan Osipovich Rybasov, conductor at the Alexandrinsky Theater. We don't know how he happened to incur Musorgsky's dislike.

[84] The manuscript is dated "2 June, year 1874. Petrograd." This is No. 4 of the new song cycle, *Sunless,* composed to texts by Golenishchev-Kutuzov.

132c. *NIKOLAI RIMSKY-KORSAKOV to VLADIMIR STASOV*, *St. Petersburg* [*Extract*]

Nikolayev, 26 July '74

. . . I am thoroughly happy for Modeste, that he has worked such a lot; the place from the "Catacombs" which you describe is beautiful, but it is taken out of the middle and thus is not very clear to me; how this appeal happens to be made by Hartmann to Musorgsky—I don't understand this at all. I absolutely do not agree with his intention to write *Hill of Nettles*. I have come to the conclusion that things like *Penny Paradise* are essentially things for a single day and for a very limited circle, they require explanations, commentaries, etc., and, chiefly, an acquaintance with the depicted personalities. How could an audience, unprepared in this way, seriously like, for example, "O, Patti, Patti!" Besides, if these things were to be composed quickly, easily, in some unpretentious form, with some cursory and perfunctory, but telling strokes, as caricatures are drawn or epigrams are written, then, maybe, I dare say . . . but I don't know of such a thing. The ponderous and massively constructed *Penny Paradise,* in my opinion, is far from satisfactory in this respect. I am afraid that *The Hill of Nettles* will turn out the same way . . .[85]

133. *To NADEZHDA OPOCHININA*[36]

CRUEL DEATH

An epitaph-letter [in song]
dedicated to N. P. O . . chi . . . a

Lento lamentabile

Cruel death, like a ravenous vulture, thrust her talons into your heart and killed you; this executioner, cursed throughout the ages, has carried you, too, away.

O, if only all those for whom I know my maddened cry sounds wild, could comprehend the power of grief!

O, if only it could give me tears, bitter and comforting tears—then, perhaps, in a luminous thought, I could portray for people

---

[85] Musorgsky left *The Hill of Nettles* unfinished.
[36] Nadezhda Opochinina died on June 29, 1874, at the age of fifty-three. This "epitaph-letter" was left unfinished.

Con delicatezza

Your shining image, glowing with the love of truth, your spirit that gazed upon people so calmly.

In good time you broke the "link of habit" with the glamour of society, you parted from it without wrath, and with tireless thought, you learned of this life.

Moderato

When, cast from my own hearth by the death of my beloved mother, and by the various misfortunes of life, I, crushed, angry, tormented, shy, alarmed, like a frightened child, knocked at your holy soul . . . seeking rescue . . .

No, I have not the strength to go on . . .
[Beginning of July, 1874]

134. *To LUBOV KARMALINA, Fortress Zakatali*

Petersburg, Shpalernaya No. 6
23 July '74

MY DEAR LADY
LUBOV IVANOVNA.

I don't wish to justify myself; I can't pretend to you. Accept me "with my guilt." You are an artist and you will be able to do this because of your heart's thought. But I can thank you warmly, and I do so want to discuss with you our art so close to us.

That which you were pleased to inform me of in such a comradely-artistic fashion, back in December, gave me joy and justifies my aspiration toward a historical musical drama. I particularly want to discuss the dissenters' song with you. There is so much suffering in it, so much unflinching readiness to accept all blows, that without the slightest fear I am going to give it in unison at the end of *Khovanshchina,* in the self-immolation scene. The *melismata* * (in the nature of *gruppetti*) I fully understand, and in octaves *unissono* the melismatic tune will waft old times and truth; the very pseudo-ecclesiastical text of the song will be very relevant. Bless you, Lubov Ivanovna!

But in the air sounds the command "draw in the reins" and *Khovanshchina* will appear (if it is destined to) later, and before it a comic

* Musorgsky's note: *Melismata,* when a syllable of the text is sung in many keys [?].

opera *"Fair at Sorochintzi,"* after Gogol, will be done.[37] This is good as an economy of creative strength. Two heavyweights, *Boris* and *Khovanshchina* in succession, might be crushing, but here already, that is, in the comic opera, there is that advantageous benefit, that the characters and surroundings depend on a different locality, of a different historical way of life, and a nationality that is new for me. The materials of Ukrainian folk-song are so little known, that incompetent experts consider them adulterations (of what?), and a considerable number of them have been collected. In a word, my work is well in hand: if only I will have enough strength and brain. But in the meantime *Khovanshchina* does not doze, either. Creative moods are as elusive as and more capricious than the most capricious coquette; thus one must catch them as they come and yield completely to their capricious commands. And how can you not catch them, when just as I was dreaming that the dissenters' song must contain *melismata*, you, Lubov Ivanovna, proved this to me definitely. As I am afraid of boring even an enemy, I close this epistle with a request to look over your song and when ready, to turn it over to Jurgenson, and to preserve your dear autograph for me.[38] Many good and sincere greetings to your esteemed husband.

MUSORGSKY THE GUILTY

135. *A Catalogue to VLADIMIR VASILYEVICH STASOV as a Memorandum from MUSORYANIN* [39]

26 August '74. In Petrograd

Opus—1

Kinderscherz (1859)
Scherzo in B minor for orchestra (1859)
Intermezzo (1861)
Scherzino (1872)

---

[37] This is the first reference to an opera that Musorgsky worked on, simultaneously with *Khovanshchina*, till his death seven years later. The story is one of the tales in *Evenings on a Farm near Dikanka.*

[38] An unknown (and unpublished?) song by Karmalina, possibly dedicated to Musorgsky.

[39] Given to Stasov for a planned article on modern Russian composers, intended for the *Vsemirni Illustratzi.* Instead of Stasov's piece, an article signed M.S. appeared in this magazine in December of this year: "Russian Composers (Borodin, Cui, Musorgsky, Rimsky-Korsakov and Tchaikovsky)."

Opus—2

The Destruction of Sennacherib (1867)
Re Jesus Navinus [Joshua] (1866) } choruses

Opus—3

Gopak (1866)
Gathering Mushrooms (1867)
Yeremushka's Cradle-Song (1868)
Sleep, Sleep, Peasant's Son (1865)
The Little Orphan Girl (1868)
The Goat (1867)

Opus—4

The Naughty Boy (1868)
The Seminarist (1866)
Savishna (1866)

Opus—5

Night (1864)
King Saul (1863)
The Feast (1867)
Jewish Song (1867)
The Magpie (1867)
Child's Song (1868)

Opus—6

(Album "The Nursery")
With Nursie
In the Corner
The Beetle } (1868–1869)
Going to Sleep
With the Doll

Opus—7

An Act of "Marriage" by Gogol (1868)

279

Opus—8

The Classicist (1867)
Penny Paradise (1869)

Opus—9

Opera "Boris Godunov" (1868–1872)

Opus—10

Fragments of the opera "Mlada" (not mine). } Festival of the "Black God" (1873)
Procession of the Princes and the Priests (1873)
The Market-Place

Opus—11

Pictures at an Exhibition (1874)
(in memory of Hartmann)

Opus—12

"Sunless"
(Album of poems by Count Golen[ishchev]-Kutuzov)
Within Four Walls
You Didn't Recognize Me in the Crowd
The Festive, Noisy Day Has Ended } (1874)
Longing
Elegy
By the River

Separately:

Studies for an opera "Salammbô"—by Flaubert (1864–65)
Journey to Yukki [40] (1873)
Song of the Dissentress [Marfa] (1874)

---

[40] This song (published as "Riding on a Stick" and also known as "By Hobby-Horse to Yukki") is dated "14 September 1872, in Petrograd," and, along with " 'Sailor' the Cat" (dated "15 August, year 1872 in Petrograd") is dedicated to Dimitri and Polyxena Stasov. Both songs were later added to the original five songs of *The Nursery*.

Forgotten (after [a painting by] Vereshchagin) [41] (1874)
The Hill of Nettles (1874)
Materials for the opera "Khovanshchina" (a people's musical drama) (1873–1874)
Further, I don't know.

M. MUSORYANIN

---

[41] This year, when Vasili Vereshchagin exhibited his paintings of General Kaufman's victorious Russian campaign in Turkestan, one canvas, "Forgotten," of a single Russian corpse, roused the displeasure of Alexander II and was removed from the walls. This only served to give added interest in this painting to all who had seen it before its removal. The painting was described by the artist as "a picture of a Russian soldier who had been left on the field to die, and the wild birds were hovering over him, while underneath was the one word, 'Forgotten.'" Golenishchev-Kutuzov and Musorgsky wrote one of their finest dramatic songs on the subject of this painting. Shcherbachov also attempted a poem inspired by the painting, and the manuscript, with ironic marginal notes by Musorgsky, has been found among the Golenishchev-Kutuzov papers. The publication (by Bessel) of Musorgsky's "ballad" was approved by the censors on November 23, 1874, but Stasov says that it was not distributed for the same reasons that induced the removal of the painting from the exhibition.

V I

Khovanshchina: Half-realized
1874 — 1875

An Apartment for Composer and Poet

In the autumn of 1874 Musorgsky and I decided to share quarters. He lived at that time on Shpalernaya. I took with him two rooms next to each other; the doors that divided our lodgings were left open, forming a small apartment, in which we organized a mutual house-keeping. All morning till 12 noon (when Musorgsky left for his office) and all evening we passed the time together in the larger room of our home. For the rest of the winter Musorgsky went ahead with his *Khovanshchina.* In addition to this, he wrote another song, "Forgotten," to my words, and a collection of songs entitled *Sunless*—also to my words, which had been written a year or two before . . .

"Many prattle," he once said to me, "that the only good things in me are my plasticity and sense of humor. Let's see what they'll pronounce now, when I hand them your verses. Here is nothing more than feeling, and I consider that it came out pretty well."—ARSENI GOLENISHCHEV-KUTUZOV

135a. *ALEXANDER BORODIN to YEKATERINA BORODINA,* Moscow [Extract]

S. Peterburg. 25 September 1874

. . . I was at Korsinka's on Sunday; there was a gathering. Cui is making progress in *Tisbé.* They played the 1st and 2nd acts in their entirety. (He worked on them all summer.) What loveliness, what beauty! Modeste performed 5 songs [*Sunless*] but they all remind one of *Boris,* or are the fruit of a purely intellectual invention, and produce a very unsatisfactory impression.

135b. *MODESTE TCHAIKOVSKY to PIOTR TCHAIKOVSKY, Moscow*

15 October 1874

. . . At last I've heard *Boris Godunov*. The auditorium was not quite full, although it was the first performance of the season. After the first scene, the Summons to the Throne, there was some hissing, whereas it impressed me. The second tableau, The Inn, was accompanied by vigorous applause and calls for the composer, though in my opinion this scene is horribly ugly in a musical respect and is far more deserving of hisses than its predecessor; its success was entirely due to the really artistic acting of Petrov and Kommissarzhevsky. All the rest, except the scene of the "Death of Boris," which produces a powerful impression, is revolting. The performance was excellent . . .

136. *To LUDMILA SHESTAKOVA*

27 October '74
in Peter

I hardly had time to eat and to rest a little, when I sped toward our dear *généralissime,* and all of a sudden, without rhyme or reason, I remembered this morning at your home, little dove Ludmila Ivanovna. This musical morning was arranged so simply, without hesitation or empty-headed conceit, but with this peculiarity, that again everyone acted without any conceit, just as God's spirit sent into his heart—*just like the good old days.* Musical ranks *as well as* their braidings, shoulder-straps and facings,[1] do not belong in such discussions as took place at your home today; the distribution of rewards and the awarding of ranks do not even crawl into one's head.

Almost all that has been thought out in *Khovanshchina* was shown: no one was asked, no one was commanded *to jibe;* the discussion went on in a free and easy way, went on lovingly, without frightening anyone, or nagging anyone. And we felt good—*just like the good old days.* Why did this happen and why at your home in particular? This is the reason for my epistle. In you lives the genius of Glinka; you yourself, perhaps, may not know, but, almost without your being aware of it, there comes out that of which we today were eye-witnesses. And I myself don't know—why, to what purpose I did what I did today; there's only one explanation—*it did itself.* No, we live on, little dove Lud-

---

[1] In *Gore ot Uma*, Skalozub says, "But men are different—in the braiding, shoulder-straps, and the facing of their uniforms."

mila Ivanovna, we live on in defiance of the deadening ferrule of musical officials and loafers. And we will live—the Lord keep you.
Viviam!

MUSORGSKY

The fool wished people to remember his foolishness. I want you to
save this letter.

MUSORGSKY

Written on Sunday

136a. *PIOTR TCHAIKOVSKY to MODESTE TCHAIKOVSKY, St. Petersburg*

Moscow. October 29, 1874

. . . Have been thoroughly studying [in score] *Boris Godunov* [by
Musorgsky] and *Demon* [by Anton Rubinstein]. With all my soul I
send Musorgsky's music to the devil; this is the most vulgar and vile
parody on music; there are lovely things in *Demon,* but a lot of ballast,
as well . . .

137. *To ARSENI GOLENISCHCHEV-KUTUZOV*

Thursday–Friday, 7–8 November '74

DEAR FRIEND ARSENI,

I should like to be called a friend, but I *must* remain a bureaucrat.
I couldn't accept your invitation for today, because the investigation
business won't let me go. There's *urgent work* tomorrow from morning on. And I'll come to you about the money tomorrow (that is, today,
as it's 3 hours after midnight), but I can, owing to my disorderliness,
provide extremely little. After this, they say, my own, that people are
brothers: "A fig for that." Provided your bones don't bother you—
what a misfortune! However, as long as the brain remains whole, one
can stay whole.

Your

MODESTE

A Lampoon by Mikhail Saltykov-Shchedrin [2]

ON THE SIDE

Notes, sketches, stories, etc. (II)

in *Otechestvennya Zapiski*, No. 11, November 1874.

[The author and his friend Glumov are calling upon the musical authority, Neuvazhai-Koryto.[3]]

"You've come at a very happy moment. Vasili Ivanych is here."

"Vasili Ivanych? Who's Vasili Ivanych?" I thoughtlessly asked.

Neuvazhai-Koryto was at first so astonished that he took a step backwards, but then recalling something, he slapped his forehead and smiled indulgently.

"How stupid of me!" he exclaimed, "I had forgotten that you're a new convert. You know of Musorgsky, Rimsky-Korsakov, Cui—and you imagine that that is sufficient! But we, batinka, we're not so easily satisfied! We never rest! We search, and we find! And we have found —Vasili Ivanych!"

Saying this, he shivered three times ecstatically, and paced the long study with his long legs, repeatedly throwing back his long hair with his long hands.

"Yes," he went on, "Vasili Ivanych is, in his own way, a meteorite! Such things can happen! The most complete and odious quiet may be reigning around one—and then—wham!—a rock hits your forehead! That—that is Vasili Ivanych!"

"But who is this Vasili Ivanych? Where did you dig him up?" Glumov asked with interest.

"Ah! That's still a secret! So far we're hiding him under a bushel! First we'll put him into storage, and then polish him, and then we'll give him to Laroche to be abused!"

"Won't you at least let us see him?"

"No, you can't see him. You may hear him, but you can't see him— no, no. He's right in the next room. He had lunch half an hour ago, and now he's asleep. He leads quite a regular life: half the day he eats and sleeps, the other half—he plays the piano. Can you imagine, he's

---

[2] This most bitter of all Russian satirists came from Musorgsky's own class—a noble family in reduced circumstances. This piece, signed "M.M.," has not been reprinted in Russian editions of Saltykov's works—perhaps because Musorgsky was one of his few undeserved targets. In a lengthy study of this satire, "Shchedrin, Musorgsky, Stasov," (*Krasnaya Nov*, No. 11–12, 1940) David Zaslavsky identifies the target as the whole Balakirev Circle, with a more profound target hidden behind the musicians; Zaslavsky speaks of Musorgsky's projected *Hill of Nettles* as a satirical response to Shchedrin's satire without noting that the "reply" is dated "10 August, '74" and that Shchedrin's piece was published in the issue of November 1874.

[3] The name "Neuvazhai-Koryto" (Do-Not-Respect-the-Pig's-Trough) appears on Korobochka's list of dead souls that she sells to Chichikov. Saltykov employs this thin disguise for his caricature of Stasov, while Musorgsky can be found in the unseen presence of "Vasili Ivanych."

never read a single book except my critical essays, and a collection of libretti published by Wolf!"

"But if he doesn't read anything, his mental horizon . . ."

"Must be limited, you were going to say? I completely agree with you. But we found him so recently that we haven't had time yet to do anything for his mental development." [. . .]

. . . Then we heard such a monstrous yawn that my imagination transported me at once to the Marinsky Theatre during a performance of *Pskovityanka.*

"What an amazing yawn!" exclaimed Neuvazhai-Koryto, and then he suddenly slapped his forehead. "Ha! an idea!"

He ran to his desk and hastily scribbled something on a piece of paper. Then he thrust the paper before my eyes. I read: *"A Symphonic Rhapsody (A major): a civil servant of the department of various taxes and collections yawns over his perusal of a musical criticism by Mr. Laroche."*

"But a department of various taxes and collections no longer exists as such," I remarked. "It has been subdivided into two sections: taxable and non-taxable collections."

"I sincerely thank you! Your remark has more significance than you realize! We are obliged to portray in combinations of sounds not only thoughts and feelings, but also the surroundings in which these occur, not excluding the color and form of the full-dress uniform. Everything must be in such order that nobody can sue you for libel."

At this moment a new sound came from the next room: Vasili Ivanych was wheezing.

"Another idea!" exclaimed Neuvazhai-Koryto, again rushing to his desk.

This time I read: *"A Symphonic Idyll (F minor): after his well-known abuse of the grape, Noah wakes and can't make out what's going on around him."*

"Is this for Vasili Ivanych?"

"Yes, of course [. . .] That reminds me! I mustn't forget to buy a Holy Bible for Vasili Ivanych."

"Be sure to get one with pictures," suggested Glumov.

"Lord! Forgive us our sins!" suddenly came from the next room.

"Did you hear that! [. . .] He never—never—speaks! This is something new! Vasili Ivanych! batushka! what's happening?"

"Moo-oo-oo!"

"You see! He always expresses his feelings in simple sounds! Sometimes something very original comes of them. Once he suddenly yelled: Ee!—and what do you think! He immediately sat down at the piano and improvised his immortal *bouffonade: The Izvoshchik Searching for His Whip on a Dark Night!"* [Vasili Ivanych, remaining invisible, was prevailed upon to play his dramatic étude, *Polenka,* and an extraordinary piece of program music, *A Symphonic Tableau de Genre: Triumph of the Section Chief of the Investigating Police Department on the Occasion of His Receipt of the Rank of State Counsellor,* with explanations by Neuvazhai-Koryto.]

138. *To LUDMILA SHESTAKOVA*

Saturday, 16 November, 1874
in Peter

LITTLE DOVE OF MINE, LUDMILA IVANOVNA,

I've remembered tomorrow's holiday [Shestakova's birthday] and I'll be there, but on the Molas's account I tell you, my dear, that tomorrow evening will be inconvenient in all respects: there are ladies, agreeable in all respects,[4] but this situation is inconvenient in all respects (perhaps agreeable ladies can be inconvenient).

The point is this, my little dove, that for tomorrow evening, especially for my sake, Bach is gathering Mordovtzov and Pavlov [5] for a discussion on the creative work of Count Arseni Kutuzov, and I can't refuse this business, which will begin at 10 o'clock in the evening;— and the Molas's go to their uncle's on Sundays and they are very strict in honoring domestic gatherings at the old man's.

As for the little evening at your place with the colleague-artists, we'll talk this over tomorrow; this can always be arranged.

I firmly kiss your little hand, little dove of mine.

MODESTE, ALSO MUSINKA

139. *To LUDMILA SHESTAKOVA*

27 November 1874
Venus is strolling by the sun [6]

LITTLE DOVE LUDMILA IVANOVNA,

I didn't give your little note to Petrov, for this reason, the Petrovs aren't free at present: they're fitting out Yekaterina Osipovna [Petrova] for permanent residence in Moscow, where she has been engaged by the Court of Justice, in the capacity of crown's stenographer. I've written Molas; I wanted to go to Bach today to rehearse with Alexandra Nikolayevna [Purgold-Molas]. I got terribly tired at the office (I'm now without an assistant). Some day soon I'll look in on you, my own.

Your

MUSORYANIN

---

[4] From *Dead Souls*.

[5] Daniel Mordovtzov, a writer of historical novels; Platon Pavlov, a professor of history who had recently returned from a long exile in Vyatka.

[6] One of the rare passages of the planet Venus across the sun occurred in November of 1874.

Khovanshchina is going well, but there's little time for it, and I get very tired.

140. *To LUDMILA SHESTAKOVA*

6 December, 1874

MY DEAR LITTLE DOVE,

LUDMILA IVANOVNA!

I have started a treatment for the throat—*had to,* am growing inaudible. Allow me to drop in on you tomorrow, little dove. Today, I'm taking advantage of the holiday and playing dumb.

I was at our splendid Petrovs on Monday, as I wanted to see Yekaterina Osipovna before her departure,—she's a fine and clever girl,—I showed them a bit of *Khovanshchina:* it seemed to have their blessing. —I kiss your little hand warmly, little dove of mine.

Your

MUSINKA

141. *To ARSENI GOLENISHCHEV-KUTUZOV, Tver*

Peter, 29 December, '74

MY DEAR ARSENI,

I *promptly* inform you that "Hashish" has been very warmly accepted by the editor of *Delo,* and Blagosvetlov impatiently awaits your return, and I am 1500 puds joyful and also await you. Give your *maman* my most sincere greetings. In *Khovanshchina,* the further into the forest, the more firewood; but what about *Shuisky?* The proofs on our album [7] will soon be sent.

Am writing to Miller [8]—but without being sure [of his address].

Warmly embrace you.

That's all.

MODESTE MUSORGSKY

---

[7] "Our album" is *Sunless,* which received the censor's permit on November 23, and was on Bessel's presses.

[8] Oreste Miller, a great authority on Russian literature, knew Golenishchev-Kutuzov at the Petersburg University. Musorgsky must have been seeking Miller's advice in behalf of his *Khovanshchina* or his friend's *Shuisky.*

142. *To VLADIMIR STASOV*

Wednesday, 5 March, '75

Généralissime,

I'll be at your place this evening. It is despicable and beneath contempt for us to live as we do—as if one of us were on the Cape of Finland and the other on the Cape of Good Hope. I'll be there, I'll be there—positively.

MUSORYANIN

143. *To ARSENI GOLENISHCHEV-KUTUZOV, Tver*

TO SIR MOST HIGH COUNT OF THE RUSSIAN EMPIRE
ARSENI ARKADYEVICH GOLENISHCHEV-KUTUZOV
FROM A MEMBER OF THE UNKNOWN MINISTRY OF SIMPLE AFFAIRS [9]

REPORT

We are informed, Your Highness, of the capture in the State of Tver of a certain person, dangerous and highly troublesome to the Chancery of Detective Affairs, an escaped man, unusually audacious, calling himself Arseni Kutuzov. This aforesaid dangerous man has been apprehended in the very city of Tver. And with the aid of some questioning and some gentle torture, it came to light that the said dangerous man, in his extreme arrogance feared neither the proximity of the Governor's seat nor the Detection. Overflowing with such audacity, the aforementioned dangerous individual strove also to remain invisible to the all-seeing eye. And he was caught in the act of harmful and crafty peotic licenses and all sorts of laws contrary to those established by Sir Sumarokov for dramatic statutes and comedies, as well as rules for all Russian writing.[10] And furthermore, he confessed to thieving relations, for these as well as for even more dangerous purposes, together with the already caught and published musician-compositor, passing himself off as Musorgsky. This latter, in fraudulent dreams, maliciously repudiating the codified musical laws,

---

[9] Musorgsky assumes the comic mask of a stupid eighteenth-century police investigator inditing a misspelled report.

[10] Alexander Petrovich Sumarokov was an eighteenth-century arbiter of literary style. Not only did he publish "Instructions to those wishing to become writers," but he also presented his translations of *Hamlet* and plays by Corneille and Racine as their co-author.

established throughout the centuries by the activity and labors of highly honorable and respected men and, furthermore, regulated by the centuries, opines that any kind of human speech can be brought into mussical harmony and by that, bearing malice in his obvious impotence of mussicianship, snares people for the sake of his evil and most dangerous purposes, and mournful this is: he has caught a great number of gullible and ignorant souls in mussical matters and worst of all—he continues to snare them.

Taking into consideration all the above-mentioned, the Unknown Ministry of Simple Affairs has the honor to apply to the wise assistance of Your Highness, if you will be gracious enough, Sir Count, to authorize the above-mentioned man who was questioned in the city of Tver, and calling himself Arseni Kutuzov—to be sent to S. Petersburg for confrontation of the afore-mentioned Kutuzov with the man mentioned in this report and to act thereafter with those dangerous persons, as is required by statute.

With the greatest happiness,
I have the honor to call myself
Your Highness's
most humble servant
A Member of the Ministry of Simple Affairs

This 7th Day of March, 1775
S. Petersburg

144. *To ARSENI GOLENISHCHEV-KUTUZOV, Tver*

My very dear Arsenius,
E'en though I am no genius
Neither evil, nor good,
I wish that you could fly to us
Our very dear Arsenius,
Our own melodious genius,—
Either at night, or at morn.

MODESTE

7 March, '75.
From Peter

144a. *ARSENI GOLENISHCHEV-KUTUZOV to MODESTE MUSORGSKY,*
St. Petersburg [A Draft]

[Tver—February–March 1875]

GOOD FRIEND, MODESTE PETROVICH.

I am again in Tver and again I feel a need to talk with you. You need have no apprehensions about Mother's health. She simply longed for me and resorted to the telegraph, in order to start the lazybones more quickly from his den . . .

Therefore I'm not worried.

What do I do? Absolutely nothing. I rise early, drink coffee, go out of town for a breath of fresh air, return to the hotel, eat, read Alfred de Musset, go to the club to talk politics with the appearance of a Petersburg savant and finally go to bed—but I don't sleep, instead I customarily busy myself with fruitless meditation or even more fruitless writing. Speaking of writing. Yesterday I was at the Tver theatre —saw a comedy by Dyachenko: *A Brilliant Connection,*—a comedy that is, as you know, not among the best. All the situations are false, the monologues are tiresome, the idea is petty and not particularly true to life; but what is one to say of the performance? The actors and actresses, with one exception (Miss Metallova), could successfully take on the jobs of lackeys and chambermaids in inelegant houses,—there's no use speaking of them. But this Miss Metallova is a real artist, *oblivious during the performance,* that before her sits a crowd of fools and ignoramuses who have no idea what's going on (she's an inspired artist). It's pitiful to watch her when in her mad scene she reached a point of ecstasy, and my neighbor calmly munched a Crimean apple and behind me there was some drunk shouting unreasonably:

"Bravo! Swell! How amusing! . . ." I couldn't stand this and before the end I ran home and wrote a poem "To a provincial actress." Here it is:

> Blinded by the magic of inspiration
> In the dark loneliness of dream
> With the flight of thought, the courage of oblivion,
> With the fire of speech, you were beautiful.
> Thus the nightingale in the walls of his prison,
> Closing his tired eyes at night,
> Starts his song, recalling another darkness,
> Another stillness . . . And it seems
> That near him trembles a birch leaf,
> That a brooklet babbles over the stones,

That through the air of spring fly dreams,
And that the sky glows throughout the night.
Alas! I did not have the strength to share
The comfort of your delusions!
Listening to you, I could not forget
The foolish crowd, their blind judgment,
I was thinking,—for what is your art,
For what is this impulse of raptured speech,
For what are these feelings recognized by none,
For what does this fire burn on the empty steppe?
God alone knows by whom kindled and forgotten,
Unshielded from storm and foul weather,
In the darkness this fire cannot long burn,
In your breast it will soon expire . . .[11]

145. *To ARSENI GOLENISHCHEV-KUTUZOV, Tver*

Peter, 18 March, '75

Well you'd never have guessed, my dear Arseni! and here I am:
I've sat down and shall write to you. Doing the trio [12] is not so easy as
it seems. To give each of the three participants movement deriving
from the difficult situation into which they have unwittingly fallen,
and not to disentangle them from this situation, for it is not I who
must disentangle them from this situation, nor themselves, but the
Babbler Khovansky,—that's my task, made more complicated in addition by the relationship of Andrei Khovansky to Marfa, considering
the violent and wild breed of the Khovanskys.—As God wills!

Kenevich willingly fusses with the Cossacks, but upon talking with
one of them I got an impression, very much like talking with the
Ukrainians: they know their own history, but they behave independently (!); I don't know if this will make any sense, aside from officialdom—of the most formal kind. I understand Kenevich. Before him
stands the job of writing the history of the whole land of the Don
army: this is good for him both on the face and on the reverse, yes,
and good in general, too; and in that event I should be willing to edit

---

[11] This drafted beginning of a letter is the only extant fragment of Golenishchev-Kutuzov's letters to Musorgsky. Its date is established by the reference to
Metallova, about whom her admirer had written to Vladimir Stasov, to use his
influence to have her shown at a St. Petersburg theater during the coming Lenten
season.

[12] Andrei Khovansky, Emma and Marfa in Act I of *Khovanshchina*.

the Don song.[13] But somehow, I might be taken for an upstart. Saw *Judic* [14] in the offenbachic *Mme. l'Archiduc.* In a tiny world—an attractive and cultured artist; I saw no unnecessary gestures, I heard no senseless intensification of the voice, I observed no unpleasant flavor of the guards or the bourse, no twitching or grimaces—a complete absence of cancan. Went to watch this a second time with old grandpa, and grandpa Petrov approved; she is indeed attractive. The bouffe audience, for this reason, does very little snickering. If some great upheaval does not arise in the structure of European life, the bouffe will enter into a legal relationship with the cancan and will smother *nous autres.* The methods of making easy profits and, of course, easy ruin (the bourse) live in very warm relationship with the methods of easy composition (the bouffe) and easy debauchery (the cancan). Our auditoriums are *les derniers des Mohickans;* it may be that we must close ourselves in our wigwams, smoke the council-pipe, face towards the setting of the great light and await judgment.—But, my God, how boring this is for everyone! How barbarously crammed everyone is with some killing, asphyxiating gas! A barrack-like hospital, a huge raft with the gloomy, greedy victims of shipwreck, frightened of each bit delivered to the stomach from the mutual meal. Soulless formal drifting (one must move)!—Lord, how many victims, how many pained victims are devoured by this monstrous shark—civilization! *Après nous le déluge* . . . dreadful! Thus I drag out my supply of impressions of the bouffe public: bourse—cancan, mostly; ach, what faces, what terrifying human envelopes! I don't know which mutilates worst: hashish, opium, vodka or greed for money? Shcherbachov (*Au rouet* and *Papillons*) was played by Yesipova in the Bolshoi Theatre (*Papillons* was very elegantly and brilliantly conveyed); I sat next to

---

[13] In preparation for the three hundredth anniversary of the settlement of the Cossacks on the Don, several activities were under way. Besides Kenevich's scholarly history, Musorgsky was to fit a Cossack melody to a sixteenth-century text, "How the men of Saratov were on the splendid steppe." Musorgsky has attached this undated note to his manuscript: "A Don song of the 16th century. Supplement to *Russkaya Starina,* interesting for lovers of native material. Published in 1825 by A Kornilovich. Printed by the Press of the Department of Public Enlightenment. . . Only one copy, in the Imperial Academy of Science, exists. Arranged for the jubilee of the glorious Don armies by Musorgsky. And orchestrated by Professor Rimsky-Korsakov for military band. The score, attached to my letter, is at the Ataman's. Musorgsky."

[14] The great Anna Judic, who helped Offenbach's international fame as much as he helped hers, brought his *Madame l'Archiduc* to St. Petersburg on March 11.

Shcherbachov; Shcherbachov hasn't changed;—this is good. *Tanéef fait de la musique chez Mme. la Grande Duchesse Cathérine de Meklenbourg Strelitz.*[15] The Gaul Brédif is summoning spiritualist miracles; an eyewitness assures me. And in general they say that one table left the house altogether and came to Brédif at his apartment. This, of course, is all nonsense; but nevertheless he does summon something (I'm not laughing—remember our talks).

I may see this at Dimitri's—interesting.[16] In the "Novosti" I read the following [feuilleton]:

Many Entertainers for Lenten Fasters

"Number the sands, Count the rays of the planets"[17] and so on. "Mr. Shinek—plays. Mr. *Melnikov*—sings. Mmes. Kamenskaya and Kosetzkaya—play and sing. Mr. Musorgsky—plays. Mr. Bekker—does magic tricks. Mr. Pomazansky plays . . . etc."

My immediate superior has left for 3 weeks;—my mornings are devoted to my own thoughts, and I go to the Department at noon. Traveling in Peter is becoming unpleasant for my "unbalancedness" —the droshkies over what's left of the ice. Today I go to Vanlyarsky[18] —for a meeting with my dearest A. Opochinin.

19 March—the taking of Paris[19]—an Invalids' concert! By the way, they are giving Berlioz's *Francs-Juges*—I fully agree: *rien de plus franc, que la guerre; point de juge plus compétent, qu'un guerrier victorieux.*

[Unsigned]

---

[15] Alexander Taneyev, a composer and high government official under whose papers and decrees was always hidden a beloved score, which he would work on between appointments. Sergei Taneyev, six years younger, was a relative. Musorgsky must have been personally acquainted with Alexander Taneyev, for there is a "Cradle-Song," inscribed to Vladimir Stasov, "arranged by Musorgsky from a sketch by A. S. Taneyev" (June 28, 1874).

[16] Both Dimitri Stasov and Golenishchev-Kutuzov took an interest in spiritualism—and Musorgsky had shown his interest as far back as 1858, when he was translating Lavater's letters (see p. 13).

[17] Derzhavin's *Ode to the Deity* (Catherine).

[18] Fyodor Ardalionovich Vanlyarsky is an old friend from Preobrazhensky days. In his "autobiographical note" Musorgsky says, "In the regiment his comrade Vanlyarsky introduced Musorgsky to the genius Dargomizhsky."

[19] On March 19, 1813, the Russian army had triumphantly entered Paris.

145a. *ALEXANDER BORODIN to LUBOV KARMALINA, Fortress Zakatali* [*Extract*]

S. Peterburg 15 April, 1875

. . . You've probably heard somewhat of our musical affairs from our musical friends and so on. Cui is active—has done a lot of work on his *Tisbé*. Modeste writes *Khovanshchina* and has done quite a bit, too. Korsinka is fussing around the Free School, writing all sorts of counterpoint, learning and teaching all sorts of musical cleverness. Writing a textbook on instrumentation—a phenomenal thing, there is and never has been anything like it.[20] But meanwhile he has no time and has put aside work [composition] for his leisure time. During Lent he conducted a Free School concert [21] as you undoubtedly have been informed. Meanwhile, he doesn't compose music. Undoubtedly, you've heard a lot about discord and disintegration and the like in our circle. I don't look on this exactly as Ludmila Ivanovna and many others do. So far I see nothing in this but a natural situation. As long as all were in the position of eggs under a setting hen (—thinking of Balakirev as the latter), we all were more or less alike. As soon as the fledglings broke out of their shells—they grew feathers. Each of them had to have different feathers; and when their wings grew—each flew to wherever his nature drew him. Lack of resemblance in tendency, aspiration, tastes, character of creative power, etc. is, in my opinion, exactly what is good and not at all sad about this affair. It must be thus when an artistic individuality is already built, ripened and strengthened. (Balakirev somehow never understood this and still doesn't.) Many now regret that Korsakov turned backward and launched himself into a study of musical antiquity. I don't mourn over this. This is quite understandable: Korsakov has grown in an opposite direction to, for example, mine. He started out with Glinka, Liszt, Berlioz, and of course grew dissatisfied with these and thereupon launched himself in that region unknown to him which has the interest of novelty. I began with the old masters and only finally moved over to the new ones . . .

---

[20] In his *Chronicle* Rimsky-Korsakov tells the whole story of the conception and death of this project.

[21] This unexpectedly "classic" program took place on March 27, in the City Hall, and included excerpts from Handel's *Israel in Egypt* and from Robert Franz's arrangement of Bach's *St. Matthew Passion* (sung by Kamenskaya and Kosetzkaya, mentioned in Musorgsky's letter of March 18), and works by Haydn, Palestrina, and Allegri.

146. *To LUBOV KARMALINA, Fortress Zakatali*

Peterburg, Shpalernaya No. 6
20 April, '75

My dear Lady

Lubov Ivanovna.

It seems to be my fate—to go on asking your pardon. More than one person would be broken by such a command [as yours]. I am fearful but not afraid. Your unceasing artistic participation in the affairs of art encourages me and reconciles me to myself—and, I dare say, convinces me of the strength and might of true friends of art.—All that you send me, Lubov Ivanovna, "will not die as long as I live," but will be turned over to the people.

Afraid to thank you: for what? for your artistic vocation? for your incessant thought to preserve the people's creativeness? That, which you do, loving art, will be beloved by history, and it is not for me, Musorgsky, to thank you, but for *someone* greater and more important than myself. Honor to you and glory, Lubov Ivanovna!

The songs of the Volyn region, from the 11 you sent, carry an impression of history in the majority: No. 1 ("I Shall Sow the Sage-Grass"), 3 ("Along the Shores, the Sweet Shores"), 4 ("I Stood under the Hazel-Tree"), 5 ("Wave, Dry Oak-Tree"), 9 ("Oh, What a Little Garden"), 10 ("Rustle Not, O Meadow") and 11 ("The Mother Made Ready Her Son for the Journey").[22]

And in respect to my musical raids—for the sake of discovery I am firmly standing by *Khovanshchina*. Many questions have already cropped up; not a few of the questions show themselves, like tiny buds hidden in a mass of foliage; but these must be nourished, in order for the tree to become more beautiful, and to give shelter to a greater number of people. It is difficult, but it has to be thus! I have given up the Little-Russian opera: the reason for this renunciation—the impossibility of a Great-Russian to pose as a Little-Russian, and therefore the impossibility of mastering the Little-Russian recitative, that is, all the shades and peculiarities of musical contours in Little-Russian speech. I prefer to lie less and speak truth the more. In genre opera the recitatives must be approached even more severely than in historical opera, for in the former there is no large historical event, covering, like a curtain, whatever inaccuracies and faults there may be; for this reason masters who don't sufficiently command recitative

---

[22] The use planned for these songs is obscure. No traces of them have appeared among Musorgsky's papers. Were they "turned over to the people"?

avoid genre scenes in historical opera. I know the Great-Russian to some extent, and for me his sleepy cunning under a haze of goodheartedness is not foreign to me, just as his sorrow which is a real burden to him is not foreign to me.—At present Count Kutuzov and I are constructing a *Danse macabre*—so far two scenes are ready, a third is in work, and there behind it is a fourth! [23] In *Khovanshchina* I am bringing the 1st act to its conclusion.

That's all my business, highly esteemed Lubov Ivanovna. I await some little missive from you.

Devotedly yours,
MUSORGSKY

147. *To ARSENI GOLENISHCHEV-KUTUZOV, Tver*

11 May, 1875
Petrograd

MY DEAR FRIEND ARSENI,

Our first installment of the *Macabres* is finished, for today the "Serenade" is written, which is why I did not show up at your dearest *maman's*. I think you will agree on the simplest of titles, one worthy of our new album—together we continue to overcome men with our albums: immodestly, but honorably. I have named the new child-album *She*. The first installment will be published (I hope) in this order: (1) "Cradle-Song," (2) "Serenade" and (3) "Trepak." [24]

---

[23] The song cycle, *Songs and Dances of Death*, whose first title, according to the following letter, was *She* (the Russian word for death is in the feminine gender).

[24] "Cradle-Song" is dedicated to Anna Vorobyova-Petrova, and is dated "14 April, year 1875"; "Serenade" is dedicated to Shestakova, and is dated "Petrograd, 11 May, year 1875"; "Trepak" is dedicated to Petrov and is dated "17 February, year 1875."

Several additions were considered at various times for this new album and a pencil sketch by Golenishchev-Kutuzov for an enormous cycle has been found among his papers:

1. *Rich Man*
2. *Proletarian*
3. Great Lady
4. Statesman
5. Tzar
6. Young Girl [*Serenade?*]
7. *Peasant* [*Trepak*]
8. Monk [see p. 340]
9. Child [*Cradle-Song*]
10. Merchant
11. Priest
12. Poet

Consequently, Your Highness, we together "plowed" the Album *Sunless* and our Album *She;* the first installment of the second album is ready, at which I have the honor to congratulate Your Highness. And only do not forget my testament, I beg you: as soon as you notice with your mind's eye that I've gone off the rails, at that moment take any measures you wish, provided the calamity can be avoided; in such a matter, that is, by my going off the rails, you are guilty, because you are the switchman, so now you have to take the consequences for your sins. You are terribly difficult.

Your

MODESTE

Don't forget to deliver to *maman* the full weight of my excuse and chagrin. I'll try my best to appear.

148. *To ARSENI GOLENISHCHEV-KUTUZOV, Tver*

22 May year 1875 in the city of Saint-Petersburg

I have the honor to congratulate Your Highness on the public appearance of your work bearing the title "Hashish." At the same time I take the liberty to report to Your Highness: do not deign to be distressed by our critics, because they—these critics—mostly abuse, I swear to God, they abuse, Your Highness; and to say something relevant—this just doesn't happen among them. Clever people say that one cannot, supposedly, demand that our critics do not abuse, because in the 1st place, it gives them pleasure to fool the "novices" and to do harm to the "novices" to the full strength of the critical little souls of those critics, and therefore, in the 2nd place, those critics have no interest at all in art, but in payment by the line, and in showing their fervor, they leap at it, Your Highness. And truly: these critics breed their stuff, just as civil servants' wives bear children, and they are as gluttonous as wolverines,—they also love to drink. But in general they're kind, *until they see a morsel.* And a few among them are decent, so to say—with dignity: one or two such may be found—and that's all. They mostly drive to oppress—such has become their habit. And those that do not oppress—those with dignity, they are not wolverines and they drink within reason. Do not deign to fear these last, Your Highness, the good ones are inclined to approve. I dare to be of the opinion, Your Highness, that you will mostly deign to come across the wrath of scribblers, and above all—compilers of poetical works.

In all this, I count as my obligation and even make it a joy for myself to bring to Your Highness my most tender congratulations and I have the pleasure to call myself

Your Highness's
most humble servant,
AULIC COUNCILOR MODESTE,
SON OF PIOTR, MUSORGSKY

149. To ARSENI GOLENISHCHEV-KUTUZOV, Tver

Petrograd, 22 May, '75

MY BELOVED ARSENI,

I was sure it would happen. You reminded me by your friendly confession of "the holy minute," when, discreet and silent, I understood your artistic soul. This minute shines brightly through the swampy darkness of official ink.

You are mistaken in one thing only: what do you thank me for? Did I ever dare to show you anything? I was fond of you and I am fond of you—and that's all. Why am I so fond—ask your artistic soul: you will find the answer.

Now about this: whatever obscure hole-in-the-corner critics say—I guarantee that "Hashish" will do its work, that you, in time, will be able to score off your critics, *hashished* (!) as they are and, consequently, not having understood the tragic quality and strength of the subject. Do not hold it against them, *create, as the spirit commands and forgive the judges.*

If *Shuisky* is demanded—print it; do not fear; the printed word is reliable. But *Shuisky* must be *understood* on the stage, so that "the descendants of the orthodox may know the past fate of their own land." [25] You are severe towards yourself—be more severe: you stand before society and before the people. Do get *Shuisky* printed.

Do not deprive society of the "trifles" either. Poetic works in compact form, with a sincere relationship between the author and his subject, remain behind in the reader's memory imperceptible to him, and make him the author's friend. This is the best path to intimate acquaintance with a poet, always valuable for the poet if such ac-

---

[25] From Pimen's monologue, opening the cell-scene in *Boris*—in both Pushkin's play and Musorgsky's opera.

quaintance succeeds. In my opinion—these should be printed: "The Little Room," "Elegy," "Longing," "By the River" (from our album [*Sunless*]); and then let us discuss those of your tales so negligently and easily strewn through the pages of your innumerable notebooks, aimlessly and without reason, just because of the laziness and heedlessness of *these tales (Dixi!)*.

Well, I send a greeting to you with a free heart, beloved Arseni mine, and long life to your glory!—*It's been begun*, there is no longer any turning aside, nor any subterfuge; now for great, restless work— God give you strength!

MODESTE MUSORGSKY

Enclosing in this letter to you one from someone with my name, evidently proud of the rank of Aulic Councilor. The letter is not too stupid although its form is horrible—"simply stinking of ink." You need not answer him, the more so as the Aulic Councilor did not indicate his address.[26]

MODESTE MUSORGSKY

Summer Laughter

. . . I remember the hot summer of 1875, when my mother went off for a while to visit a friend in Revel, and we were left behind with Father—Musorgsky and [Uncle] Vladimir Vasilyevich [Stasov], visited us especially often that summer, and they had the idea of rereading all of Gogol; after lunch, in the terrible heat, we all would gather in the study, seat ourselves on the sofa, and, taking turns, father, Vlad. Vas. and Musorgsky read aloud *May Night, The Carriage, The Nose* and *Dead Souls,* while we all nearly expired with laughter . . . — VARVARA STASOVA-KOMAROVA

150. *To VLADIMIR STASOV, Paris* [27]

Petrograd. Vas[ilyevsky] Ostrov, 5th
line, opposite the garden of the
Acad[emy] of Arts, No. 10
7 August, '75

In place of an epigraph:
"The first act of *our*
Khovanshchina is finished."

---

[26] This is a Musorgskian joke, relating to Letter 148.
[27] Stasov had been sent to Paris by the Public Library to attend the Geographic Congress.

At last, dear *généralissime,* I send you greetings to universal Paris!
You'll find out how *Khovanshchina* is getting along when you return to us. How I—your *modest* Musoryanin—am getting along you
can see by the address written above on this bit of paper: a simple
matter—Arseni took the apartment key with him, and I, because of
this, am boarding at the expense of Naumov, my very kind friend,[28]
where I finished the 1st act of *Khovanshchina,* in spite of my office
obstacles. I'm starting on the 2nd act: what a hard task you've set me
in *all this!*

Well, "in for a penny [in for a pound]" etc. It has to be done. It
has been spoken: "Towards new shores," and there's no turning back;
—I've put to sea—I must not fail! But how I should like to pass it *all*
on to you; *all* that's been done; *all* that in which faith has not yet
grown poor. How many unknown, unheard-of worlds and lives reveal
themselves! How enticing they all are, how they attract comprehension and possession! Achievements are difficult, fearful to approach;
but when you do approach them—where does the courage come from!
—*and how good one then feels.*

If a few minutes can be spared, write me, my dear: how you found
Ilya Repin (my hearty greetings to him); what Bogoliubov [29] is doing;
aren't there any "eminent" Russians besides Turgenev and A. Tolstoy
giving more than 1000 rubles for the people of Morshansk [30] (judging
by the papers) to prove the long since proven truth, that if the authorities and *zemstvos* are inactive, then society, which they're supposed
to be guarding, has to reach into *its own pockets.* In Petrograd, in the
park dedicated to the family of Mr. Yegarov and therefore bearing

---

[28] Naumov's niece gives this account of how Musorgsky moved in with the
Naumovs: "Musorgsky, hopelessly in arrears in his rent, came home to find his
suitcase and things piled beside the outer door, which was locked. With this suitcase and empty pockets, he wandered for long at night through the Petersburg
streets, finally sitting down to rest on one of the stone lions decorating some important building on the Neva embankment. Here, meditating despondently on
his situation, an idea suddenly came to him: 'What am I thinking of? Why, there
on the other side is my dear friend Naumov! To him!!' In the middle of the
night the Naumov door was opened for the homeless M.P."

[29] Alexei Bogoliubov, a marine painter who had made Paris his permanent
home.

[30] On May 25 fire had wiped out the community of Morshansk (province of
Tambov). When Turgenev and Alexei Tolstoy, then summering in Karlsbad,
heard of the tragedy, they arranged a literary evening in a Karlsbad restaurant
and collected more than a thousand rubles for the stricken inhabitants of Morshansk.

the discreet designation of a *family* park, the same righteous story took place: before my eyes, one titled person bought [lottery] tickets—*allegri* for 250 rubles—the tickets were distributed by *Alphonsine* and another something like *Alphonsine*—a little younger, but a little less classy. And then may come: Bryansk, Pultusk and many, many others, "their names you know, Lord!" [31]

— — and this
happens almost every summer!

How do you like universal [Paris]?

Par parenthèse: I am sprinkling the little monologue of V. Golitzin with some Latin maxims—from among the best-known, of course, at the time of Kolpakov's scholasticism, but in regard to the princess's *superstitions,* "*d'abord* that thesis," that one mustn't neglect incomprehensible things—"because not to any man is it given to understand all." Ai, ai—why are you not with us here "this very *second!*" Well, let's prepare and judge. Not once have I seen Platon [Pavlov], he is in great ecstasy over my communication (only in story) of the conclusion of the 1st act of *Khovanshchina;* [32] and he deigned to express himself: "There is nothing to be added or subtracted; this is just as it should be, those times were exactly like this: this is just as it should be."

How I have wished for a missive from you, how much sooner it would have brought you back from your temporary remoteness! Arseni tells me of corrections in *Shuisky,* but he tells this so lazily somehow; strange man! Here he writes how he eats (*read:* sleeps) a lot in the country. A dreamy lazy-bones! but if this belly could only grasp how beloved he is by me—and there is no anger in my heart,—truly. I met the Roman [Rimsky-Korsakov]. We both jumped down from our drozhkies and embraced heartily. Then I learn—that he has written 16 fugues, each more complicated than the last, and nothing more.

Oh that his ink had dried up quite,
Before it helped the quill to write!

Cesar, they say, has finished the 3rd act of *Angelo.* I haven't been to see him—I couldn't, I'm afraid; that is, I'm afraid of his 3rd act.

[31] From the mass for the dead, Russian orthodox liturgy.

[32] Act I ends on Prince Ivan Khovansky ordering the rebel *streltzi* to surround the Kremlin, as Dosifei prays.

I did not bother the Roman about Cesar. (Again we bump into Rome!)

When will these people, instead of their *fugues and obligatory* 3rd acts, glance into sensible books and converse in their pages with sensible people? or is it already too late? . . .

It isn't this sort of art that a modern *person* needs, it's not in this that will be found the justification of an artist's task. *Life,* wherever it shows itself; *truth,* no matter how bitter; bold, sincere speaking to people *à bout portant,* this is what ferments me, that's what I want—and that's where I'm afraid of missing the mark. *So* somebody pushes me and *so* I stick.

I embrace you, my dear, heartily.

MUSORYANIN

Send me a missive.

151. *To ARSENI GOLENISHCHEV-KUTUZOV, Altynovo*

Petrograd, Vas. Ostrov, 5th line, No. 10
17 August, '75

DEAR ARSENI, Greetings. The first act of *Khovanshchina* is finished: work is boiling on the 2nd. How are you, what have you been doing, has everything worked out? Piotr [Golenishchev-Kutuzov] was here, couldn't find the key (just like me), committed a violence and lodged himself in your apartment; I, great sinner, at 5 o'clock in the morning on the day of your departure, dragged my feet to Naumov, where I found refuge, thanks to having warned Naumov for, as you know, I am afraid to stay *alone.* Of the city's news there is one thing: I am definitely returning to the goose-quill—the steel pen-points begin to look to me like bayoneted guns *à la Bismarck.* Thanks for the two letters. You haven't heard from me till now, for lack of interesting information. By the peculiarity of human self-love, I consider news of work on *Khovanshchina* interesting. I wait for you and I wait to hear from you: I hope that this will come *at last?* But will this come at last from you? This year's October can not be referred to that period when the human brain grows to triple strength (Darwin):—in the meantime, artistic works are necessary for us. What a spacious rich world art is, if one would only take man as one's aim! One flies on uncommonly and entirely unforeseen tasks, and not forcibly, but so—as if it all happened accidentally. The understanding of such flights in musical

drama is more integral and is easier in the listening, and if these flights
are described, then, I dare say, one becomes verbose. Consequently,
I believe, you will hear first and then we shall talk it over. Do me the
kindness, Your Highness, not to forget and push aside your artistic
matters. Of course, to kill a defenseless and absolutely harmless snipe
—is commendable, because the snipe is a tasty bird, but why not leave
the accomplishment of these great deeds to people dealing in and living on killed snipe, not eating said bird at the same time.

I like very much being at Naumov's, especially in the summer: the
garden, the broad street, the near-by Neva. Visitors: Kolyush [Nikolai
Konstantinovich] Larin, Zhemchuzhnikov (Kuzma Prutkov); good
talks; occasional music; all sorts of news, chatter and rechatter—one
lives, breathes and works. I await you as long as my strength holds out
and I wait with a key, and meanwhile, I kiss you warmly.

Your

MODESTE MUSORGSKY

Naumov sends greetings, Larin and Voyeikov also. [Platon] Pavlov
has left for Kiev. Vl[adimir] Stasov is expected from Paris at the end
of August.

151a.   *ANDREI KATENIN to ARSENI GOLENISHCHEV-KUTUZOV, Alty-*
nova [Extract]

S.-Petersburg. 4 September, 1875

You can't imagine, dear friend Arseni, how much your letter has
astonished and alarmed me with its news about your wrenched foot.
There, I was right, you should have come with us to Peter and let the
woodcocks be shot (as Musorgsky says) by those who deal in them.
And too, I was very sorry that the pain prevented you from writing
me in detail about your illness, about how you are passing the time
at Altynova and whether you are working.—I've long meant to write
you, but wanted to have something interesting to tell you, but encountered no one in that time.

Stasov hasn't arrived yet, but I managed to grab Musorgsky only
the day before yesterday, he dined at our place and stayed all evening.
I'd like to write you in detail about what we did that evening, but
if it's boring for you to read—then skip this. After dinner I showed
him my things: firstly, a song which you don't know, a *pendant* to the
one I wrote in Yakovlevo, which he sufficiently approved, then a sec-

304

ond song which you know and which he liked *very* much; and finally we got around to *Shuisky*.[33] My wife and I played it in 4 hands and we earned his complete approval and he often patted our heads. *Shuisky* seems to have completely satisfied him, he doesn't demand any changes except some most insignificant ones, for instance to repeat two bars of the *Adagio religioso,* where the bells are.

Musorgsky promised to come again in order to play over *Shuisky* a couple of times with me and definitely give his opinion of some changes then, which I repeat are of the most trifling sort (in one place to insert a pause and in another place to remove one).

I've kept aside the most interesting news for you till the end. Musorgsky has finished the 1st act of *Khovanshchina* and has begun the second and, to be exact, has written two scenes of it and prepared material for further work. What he has just written is indeed marvelous and I like it unreservedly. The entrance of Dosifei and the chorus of dissenters turned out extremely successfully. Golitzin's theme in the second act in the generally European mood is terribly beautiful and melodic. God grant that he continue thus. He is now living at Naumov's, but absolutely plans to move in with you as soon as you return. He seems in good health and his stay with us left us with the most cheering impression.

That, it seems, is all our news.

I almost forgot to tell you the *most* interesting of all: Petrov is taking *The Stone Guest* for his *bénéfice* and it seems he wants to maneuver a production of the *1st act of Khovanshchina*.[34] How's that! I am in ecstasy . . .

151b. *ALEXANDER BORODIN to YEKATERINA BORODINA, Moscow* [*Extracts*]

S. Peterburg 19 September, 1875

. . . News of my musical activity in Moscow has spread with the speed of lightning since my first day here: Stasov Vladimir, with the Shcherbachovs, flew to me the next day and, of course, didn't find me home. Close upon this I received a whole series of floods of words from Vladimir Vasilyevich [Stasov] who, by the way, hasn't yet heard my music and won't until Sunday. I must admit I never expected my

---

[33] Possibly Katenin was composing incidental music for Golenishchev-Kutuzov's drama.

[34] A good idea that did not materialize.

Moscow products to create such a furore—Korsinka is in ecstasy, Modeste too, Ludmila Ivanovna has invited the Petrovs to listen to the products. I am particularly astonished by their sympathy for the first chorus [in Act I of *Prince Igor*], which we tried out with voices and—without bragging, I can say—they found it extremely effective, bold and cleverly handled theatrically speaking. Konchak has obviously made the impression I wanted; except for a few awkwardnesses, purely vocal ones (which will have to be corrected), he comes out quite well in the singing. Korsinka particularly likes him. He, as well as Modeste, terribly likes that wild oriental ballet, which I composed last of all in Moscow; remember? the lively one, in 6/8? Of course all, in chorus, say that I should write the remainder quickly, without putting it in the bottom drawer . . . Cui has completed *Angelo* and has given it to the printer; the opera will be given sometime in December for Melnikov's *bénéfice*. Korsinka has composed 36 fugues and 16 canons; Modeste has finished the first act of *Khovanshchina,* and has done some work on the other acts. That's all for you about music . . .

Prince Igor

. . . And hearing separate numbers and scenes from this opera [*Prince Igor*] we children were already discriminating in what we especially liked and we would even venture to beg "Musoryanin" or Alexander Porfiryevich to play this or that scene. I remember how Borodin once, at my humble request—I was already 13—played over the Polovetzky choruses and dances from the 2nd act of *Igor*—special favorites of mine since childhood—while Musorgsky would repeatedly say: "Now, do let me play for you, *professore!* Well, what can you do with those fat little pullets of yours?" (This expression referred to Borodin's hands, which were plump and white, but by no means wanting in agility, so that this friendly jest never evoked anything but laughter.) Musorgsky then sang Konchak's aria. He sang this absolutely incomparably, with special emphasis given by him to particular phrases or words. For instance, he gave the line:

To you *I will give* . . .

with a curiously exaggerated expression, accompanying it with a broad gesture of the hand. I still remember how he conveyed a lofty, truly oriental dignity:

All here is subject to the Khan
All are afraid of me
All around me trrremble . . .

And then the following, with incomparable tenderness:

> But you did not fear me
> You never begged mercy, Prince.

And with a sort of passionate melancholy:

> Ah, your enemy I would not be . . .

VARVARA STASOVA-KOMAROVA

152. *To ARSENI GOLENISHCHEV-KUTUZOV, Altynova*

Petrograd, Vas. Ostr. 5th line,
house No. 10, apt. of Naumov
Approximately [35]
6 September, '75

MY DEAR SUFFERING FRIEND ARSENI.

I hear from Katenin that you are still laid up. I've long wanted to have a talk with you—but it couldn't be managed. Don't be angry, friend, I've been in a complete whirl. You wrote me that I've scribbled too little news and you demand more. I should love to enter paradise but my sins will not admit me.

Where can I get them from? I mean news items, not sins. The eternal struggle of the Slavs with Islam [36]—is an old song; all sorts of tightenings, even to *extremes*—this also is an old song; general madness while being penniless; general omniscience while being ignorant; a raising of the level of the public masses with some rights for something while being without rights; unconscious inertia . . . *Viel Lärm um Nichts.*[37] Let us speak of our modest world of art, and let's lock ourselves for a little while in some cozy little corner and from there, close to life and people, but far from the blathering tirades on rights, freedom, protests, let's look life boldly in the eye. This is necessary, because one must speak truth to the people, not blather, but genuine truth. Humanity has hidden itself behind the blather of conventional, quasi-artistic methods, categorical and consequently not at all artistic forms, has hidden itself willingly, and even with delight, probably irrevocably hidden itself because "the sun never rises in the west." It seems to me that with rare exceptions people cannot bear to see themselves as they actually are; the desire of people to appear better even to themselves is natural. But this is deliberate idiocy, that both past

---

[35] This and the closing date are in imitation of Gogol's *Diary of a Madman.*

[36] A peaceless intermission between the conquest of Turkestan and the opening of war with Turkey.

[37] *Much Ado About Nothing.* Most of Musorgsky's knowledge of Shakespeare was through German translation.

and present—modern artists, showing people to people as better than
they are, actually picture life worse than it is. The irreconcilable Old
Believers snuffle that it is necessary for the sharpness of colors; the
transigents, swinging like a pendulum, whisper that the tasks of art
are as yet insufficiently clarified; the radicals wail that only a scoundrel
can create artistically the figure of a scoundrel (and other parallels
that are in harmony with such a conception). All three factions could
easily be reconciled, and such a reconciliation would be incomparably
more useful than fighting in airy space, as long as nature has not given
them wings to hold them there. The thing is simple: the artist cannot
run from the external world, and even in the tints of subjective creation there is a reflection of an impression of the external world. Only
don't lie—speak the truth. But this simple thing is a heavy thing to
lift. Artistic truth cannot stand preconceived forms; life is many-sided
and often capricious; it is tempting, but very seldom can one create
a living phenomenon or a figure in a form inherent to this figure,
which has never before been used by any artist. Here the old nurse
will not help one to stand on one's feet, will not say "sturdy oak;" no,
let the artist himself stand on his feet, let me tell myself "sturdy oak."
That is what I am pregnant with at present, dear friend Arseni, and
how I am to be delivered of this child—I don't know, only the birth is
sure to be a difficult one.

All this was written, my friend, back in September and was intended
to be sent to the village of Altynova care of Skripitzin. Today *at the
office* I heard from Katenin, that you have deigned, with the assistance
of your cousin, to occupy yourself with the moving to *"maman"* in
Tver. I find myself at a loss and this is why: the sufferings of bronchitis
make enough fun of my patience; it's hard to speak, I can't smoke, it's
hard to move my feet, I can't compose, O unknown, unexpected acci-
dents!!—and only one consolation—I have only myself to blame, but
why or for what I don't know, but only, as does every human being, I
feel—*guilty, and that's all.* There is some mysterious, evil *gluttony*
(pareo) in nature. What causes her to suddenly break the thread and
settle accounts—*henbane* alone knows. Just as the people gathered in
Petrograd, just as we *began our talks* with these people,—here, as if
purposely, this gluttony appears and gives me bronchitis. It's even
hard to write.

Yes, I almost forgot, I was at L. I. Shestakova's. Cui was amiable
and showed his 3rd act [of *Angelo*]: it's all right, it will do. Borodin

showed fragments of *Igor*—much of it is genuine. You, they say, will soon come here, it will be better to explain everything when we meet, but all joking aside, *one must joke,* seriously: *one must joke*—that's the thing! In the amalgam of Borodin's dramatic creative power, and it's a very attractive one, too, sits a *lecturing* tendency: you, as an artist, can sense this in a twinkling. I hope you have understood me: Borodin commands his heroes to draw conclusions from a collision of facts and casual incidents—as you wish, it's all the same. With all the attractiveness of the composition the hearer has no way out, and there is only one: "Draw closer, gentlemen, look at the wild beast" and so on.

Well, when you come—you'll hear.

O, bronchitis!

Your

MODESTE

I beg you to give your dearest Countess-mamá my sincere greeting.

THE SAME MODESTE

They say, 3 October, '75.

153. *To VLADIMIR STASOV*

Vas. Ostr. 5th line, No. 10
14 October, '75

MY DEAR *généralissime,*

It's a nasty business. Bronchitis is winning. I've swallowed powders, and today I had a talk with Doctor Carrick. I'll have to swallow *calomel*—brrr!—this means it's an inflammation. Bronchitis has so choked me and continues to choke me, that all our affairs have come to a standstill, and I'm in some sort of struggle, between drowsiness and vitality; it's a pity *Heil Dir im Siegerkranz, o Calomel mit Eulapa vermischt!* [38]

How marvelous, I feel a little easier. The calomel has worked. I started this letter with a vile, melancholy feeling of some sort of long separation from you, my dear, and it looks as though you, *généralissime,* are the one who understands me. And then in this very minute

---

[38]   *Heil Dir im Siegerkranz,*
         Herrscher des Vaterlands,
            Heil König Dir!
A German hymn with a melody borrowed from "God Save the King!"—a melody that also served as the Russian national anthem before Lvov's *God Save the Tzar.*

started dreams about the *dispute* of the Russian men [Khovansky and Golitzin]—just as I felt easier. Man has always been a *big belly*, man is a *belly* and always will be a *belly*, so what's the use. Well, therefore, Musoryanin, to work!

154. *To LUDMILA SHESTAKOVA*

14 October, 1875

Little dove of mine, a really serious thing has happened,—I was all but choked with a bronchitis. I bore it stoically, took all kinds of palliatives, but today I called Doctor Carrick. Calomel and digitalis,— this means it's serious. Now I'm a little better, thank God. As soon as I'm well—I shall show myself to you, little dove of mine. Oy-oy, it was pretty bad. For more than a fortnight! I sent a report to the office. Music—nothing doing—is silenced. Carrick, however, calmed me. He is a specialist in respiratory organs. *Yes, my own, in all respects it's too bad about October 10.* My kindest thanks to you, little dove. With all my might I kiss your little hand for the *portrait*.[39] Ach you, my own.

MUSORYANIN

155. *To MALVINA CUI*

[October? 1875]

MY DEAR LADY,

I thank you from my heart for your kind concern. I hope to be well soon and to see your dearest family; but only the phrase, *to cease loving*, is not in my disposition, and there is, fortunately, no reason for this.[40] This is what happened to me: I was running in circles; as I ran in circles I caught cold; catching cold I got sick, and getting sick I imagined that I could fight it with natural methods—it didn't work out; well, it resulted in calomel and digitalis. Now it's better. I kiss your little hand and I beg you to caress the children for me. I send my sincere greetings to Cesare and to Yuli Yuliyevich [Hubner]. *Once more "hearty thanks."*

MODESTE

---

[39] Shestakova had sent two photographic reproductions that she had had made of daguerreotypes (taken on May 18, 1852), the first, of Glinka, with this inscription: "The year 1875, 10th of October, with this dear day today I congratulate our splendid Musinka. Lud. Shestakova"; the second, of Glinka and Shestakova together, inscribed: "To dear Musinka from his truly devoted L. I. Shestakova."

[40] The old quarrel with Cui (see pp. 266–267) had been patched up.

156. *To VLADIMIR STASOV*

Vas. Ostr. 5th line, house 10, apt. of Naumov
19 October, '75

My dear *généralissime*.

You cannot doubt how much your energetic and distantly gazing face, now residing on my work table,[41] pushes me towards all sorts of good things. Enormous thanks to you, my dear. I often look upon you: all *concentrated*, looking into the distance, as though you sensed something ahead of you; power and the knowledge of truth are engraved in each wrinkle—good work, Ilya Repin! Enormous thanks to you! It is this fine, living gaze into the distance, into the future, that pushes me on. When I think of certain artists "behind the barrier [*Schlagbaum*]," I feel not merely anguish, but some sort of *slushy sorcery*. All they long to do—is to *drizzle* drop by drop, and all in such equal precious little drops; it amuses them, but to a man it's distressing and boring; break through, my good man, as living people break through, show whether you have claws or web-feet; whether you're a beast or some sort of amphibian. You can't!—and how about the *barrier?* Without reason, without will, they've chained themselves—these artists, fettered by tradition, imagine they're doing something important, but they're merely proving the law of inertia.

All this wouldn't be so bad, though rather antipathetic, if only they—these artists, would never before have seized the staff of a different sort of banner and had never tried *"to raise it proudly before humanity."* As long as they were held in Balakirev's iron grip, they breathed deep breaths with his powerful lungs (though not quite as his heroic breast did), setting themselves tasks that would have worried even great men. As soon as Balakirev's iron grip was relaxed they felt tired and in need of rest; where to find this rest?—in tradition, of course, "as our forefathers did, so will we." They have put away the glorious banner of battle in some secret hiding-place, *hiding* it carefully and locking it behind seven locks and seven doors.—They have rested and relaxed. *Without a banner*, without desire, neither seeing nor wishing to see into the distance, they plod away at things already done long before and which no one summons them to do again. And there, from time to time, the croaking frogs [critics], tenderly puffing in their inherited swamp, pass out to them—these artists—their little

---

[41] Stasov had sent Musorgsky a photograph of his 1873 Repin portrait.

approvals. And why shouldn't they approve! The "mighty heap" have degenerated into soulless traitors; the "lash" has become a child's toy whip. I don't believe you'd find people *anywhere under the skies* more indifferent to the essence of life, more useless to modern creativeness —than these artists.

20 October, '75

Yesterday I didn't dare come to you, for fear of ignoring the doctor's advice and I wanted *to get repaired properly*. I've begun to write the dispute of the Russian men—oy, how difficult! Well, the more difficult, the more tempting—that's my way. I've just seen a handbill: the "Mus[ical] Soc[iety]" intends to give us a treat. From [Rimsky-Korsakov's] *Antar*, [Liszt's] *Divina Comedia* [*Dante*], to Schumann's *Faust* (3rd part), which means—a mystic two-part chorus; a double portion of Sadyk-Pasha (Tchaikovsky),[42] but why a *piano* concerto! The Schumann 3rd [Symphony], [excerpts from] *Les Troyens* by the great Hector [Berlioz]—how appetizing; and finally Saint-Saëns (what's this, who's this?). *Antar!* is it possible that the memory *of the past* won't rouse him [Rimsky-Korsakov] from his woodchuck's sleep; if at least a single living thought would slide over the brain tissues (of the one who required it), would pierce the one (who should be pierced). Penance is a great thing. The calamity is that penance is inaccessible to the Talmudists, they cling too tightly to the dead letter of the law, they are too soulless slaves. And, perhaps, beneath the rustle of dry whispers from his spouse, (he who is concerned) will feel an accumulation of penance for the *broken discipline* of *Antar*,—and will turn back again. When a man with a strong soul, but who is falling, is shown who and what he was, then this man is overcome with fever; and such a man is ready to cry "help!" for having stolen from himself. In an artist who has dozed off such an awakening has to be a hundred times stronger. We shall see.—Ach, you stuffed animals: "What ever will the Princess Maria Alexeyevna say!" [43] What business can you have with the Maria Alexeyevnas; art does not and never has lived through their care; this carrion is only for wandering jackals, yes, for cowardly hyenas to feast upon, but for people, fresh food is more pleasing. Give it to the people—the people ask you for fresh

---

[42] The "double portion": Tchaikovsky's first piano concerto (première) and his Third Symphony.
[43] Famusov's famous curtain line at the end of *Woe from Wit*.

food. Grave-robbers! everything was necessary in its time, this was the growth of art. Thus let it grow; hinder it as you may—it still will grow. Why do you stand on the tail-board?—it's more comfortable in the master's seat; try it!

I feel better, my dear; so therefore—till our approaching long-desired meeting. And your mighty image is ever before me. I thank you heartily.

MUSORYANIN

156a. *VLADIMIR STASOV to MODESTE MUSORGSKY*

Thursday (23 October, 1875)

Five hundred million *hurrahs* to you, Musoryanin!!!

It's only people of this sort whom I can love and understand, from them alone can I expect truly great and lasting things. You wrote me just as Repin or Antokolya would have written,—that's why you three are my trinity.

A *great* artist is not one who only knows and practices fugues, hands and feet—but he in whom truth grows and ripens, who has in him a jealous, restless and never silent feeling of truth in everything, everything.

Cui's behavior yesterday nauseated me and I disliked it very much. After closing the door after him, I said to Meyer: "This whole business is nasty!!" And Meyer answered: "Yes, it comes from cowardice!" . . .

Till later, or till tomorrow.

I would have flown quickly to embrace you heartily, heartily—but it's time for me to go.

Your
V. S.

The only change that may injure you is my determination on completely upsetting this vile meeting [Cui and Korsov] without waiting for the first reverence or request from Korsov.[44]

---

[44] Cui had written one of his vitriolic articles about the singer Korsov, and Korsov had threatened him. A crisis was finally avoided by Cui, who apologized.

157. *To LUDMILA SHESTAKOVA*

Extremely important
The same place
'74 [1875?], 29 October at night

My little dove, my dear, what a wonderful epistle you sent me. *On Saturday I'll be with you, my own, as you command:* yes, time doesn't wait. A great Russian festival, a great sermon *to all Russians,* on whom the Lord has bestowed a love of art, no matter in what sphere—this is what pleases my modest soul at the imminent, half-century jubilee of Osip Afanasyevich Petrov, my priceless grandpa.[45] I can understand how joyful it must be for you, little dove, when an affair thought up long ago, by *you alone,* is now boiling and overflowing, and "adding flesh and strength" to every good Russian. Why linger! Let each do what he can.—Were your brother-genius Glinka now alive, what would he be feeling in these approaching blessed moments, when Petrov, in his declining days, full of strength and inspiration, a Susanin [in *A Life for the Tzar*]—no ordinary peasant, no: *an idea, a legend,* a mighty creation of inevitability (perhaps historical *at that time*)—would suddenly appear before the spectators and by the sheer strength of his inspiration would turn our present miserable world *head over heels,* which is not only unable to prevent the Turk from strangling those *who wear the cross,* but is even unconscious of itself. The entrance of grandpa Petrov as Susanin is, to my mind, the entrance of Susanin (the idea) in Petrov. *Once more we shall hear and see our ever-beloved Glinka—the great teacher-founder (in time to come) of the great school of Russian music.* Bearing on his Homeric shoulders almost all that has been composed in [Russian] dramatic music from the 30's of the nineteenth century, Petrov, the titan, must not dare to doubt that if the ancient Greeks knew how to adorn their *great men* with the chaplet of victory, the Russians (no matter how servile they have become) will also know how to discern and recognize a master. Forgive this ferment of anger, forgive it with good humor: it applies to the miserable ones who are going to declare in all the cafés, restaurants, at the crossroads, at every spot where the impudent devil pokes them: Haven't you been at the festival in honor of Petrov?

---

[45] This jubilee, which was planned for April 21 of the following year, was the fiftieth anniversary of Petrov's career, which he had begun four years previous to his debut in 1830 at the Marinsky Opera as Sarastro in *Die Zauberflöte.* His first great Russian role was that of Susanin in Glinka's *Life for the Tzar,* which was staged on November 27, 1836.

—"*Qu'est ce que c'est?*" "*Enfin, vous devinez bien, le fameux Petrow.*"
"*Ça a eu lieu?*" "*Le 26 décembre.*" "*Oh, mais certainement*" . . .
"But do you know how fine Nordet is in *Indigo?*" [46] "*Mais c'est mira-
culeux, mon très cher: je l'idolâtre, moi, cette petite là.*" The devil
take them,—these financiers, these *unenigmatic sphinxes* of the nineteenth century. This is what Russia, beloved by me, sinner that I am,
has stumbled against! Lord! . . .

Yours, my dear,

MUSINKA

So on Saturday I am yours.

158. *To ARSENI GOLENISHCHEV-KUTUZOV*

[1 November, 1875]

MY DEAR FRIEND ARSENI,

What have you done with yourself! You little dove, coming across
the whole yard with your bad leg, coming to me, at the same time that
I was climbing the stairs from the main entrance, asking about you.
"He just left." Lord, what a calamity! I dreamt about and prepared
to absorb the *Shuisky* that is a million thousand times dear to me, and
I did not absorb it. I dreamt about and imagined hearing "In
Ruins" [47]—it didn't turn out that way. After what you have done with
yourself, tell me, friend: *what have you done with me?* My nerves are
in shreds. *All that is written here is the truth.* I've questioned everyone at home except the *Naumin* (my host) who has gone to the *Hugue-
nots.*

And how could you, friend, have felt misgivings and run from the
lady of the house! [48] I'm surprised you didn't trust *me:* she had been
prepared by me for you, she waited (for she told me that you are nice);
I assure you that she is a perfect lady, as shy as you are, but affection-

---

[46] Blanche Nordet in Johann Strauss' first operetta, *Indigo und die Vierzig
Raüber* (1871), which reached Russian audiences in 1875.

[47] Among Golenishchev-Kutuzov's papers a curious history was revealed for
this poem. Begun in the spring of 1875 as a large-scale picture of conflict between
peasant and landlord, it was later revised around more cautious images: a long-
awaited thunderstorm, rain, and the agony of an abandoned girl.

[48] This is Maria Izmailovna Fyodorova, sister-in-law and now common-law wife
of Pavel Naumov. Musorgsky lived in their apartment for more than four years,
beginning that July. This Christmas Musorgsky dedicated a song to her (undoubtedly *about* her, too)—to "the little lady under the Christmas tree"—*The
Incomprehensible* (dated "21 December, year '75").

ate, good, a reader and *an intelligent reader,* at that, only she's a little unsociable until she's had time to know you better. How many good minutes on artistic affairs we might have caught, my dear Arseni! *E basta, per pietà.*

The thing is this: following you, dear, Katenin Andrei dropped in on me at the Department. In the expectation of great blessings out of our awkwardly collapsed meeting today, I arranged an appointment, begging leave of the aforesaid and dearest Katenin Andrei, to break bread at their place with his wife on Monday (this will be on November third) with you (*bien entendu*) and the permission is granted. *Dixi.* Now today I bumped into Kenevich and immediately questioned him about Pushkin. The basis of his forthcoming paper (that is, Kenevich's paper) is served by some authentic documents, in addition to which * he will receive more: manuscript verses for Terpigorev, a casual acquaintance of Pushkin's. I, backed by Mey's research in Pskov antiquities of Ivan the Terrible's time, hinted to Kenevich the possibility of the escape of the Terpigorevs (the descendants of tradespeople) to the "Cossacks" on the Don (soon to be recognized by the Terrible), the expulsion of the Terpigorevs to Tambov from the Don was later, but it was a Tambov Terpigorev that Pushkin met. Kenevich denies this as apocryphal. Vouched for by the style of Pushkin's writing (abbreviations—i.e., *on* instead of *only,* etc.), he attests the *wretchedness* of the verses, and without equivocation—intends to prove this and present these to posterity, because of Pushkin's genius. Meanwhile, people are already raging about this: some curse him, others treat Kenevich justly—all as usual. Friend, I embrace you; console me with an answer or otherwise it is *as though darkness overshadows me.* Yesterday I worked. To your Countess-*maman,* my childishly warm greeting and good wishes.

Your

MODESTE

* Musorgsky's note: "Which"—my hate—you know.

159. *To the ELDERS of the ARTISTS' CIRCLE of MOSCOW* [49]

[Petrograd, 1 November, '75]

To the Gentlemen Elders of the Artists' Circle of Moscow.

DEAR SIRS,

Thank you for the sympathy expressed in your kind letter of October 11, '75, towards the opera, *Boris Godunov*. It is thought, Dear Sirs, that a production of the complete opera of *Boris Godunov* on your esteemed stage would demand too great an expenditure of money as well as of important orchestral and choral powers: this was made clear to me in discussions with the highly esteemed worker in Russian opera affairs, Gennadi Petrovich Kondratyev.

[Unsigned]

The Bookkeeper's Page for Musorgsky's Account with Vasili Bessel

Amounts received by Mr. Musorgsky.

1/IX	71	77 r. 90 k.
1/X	71	75 r. –
1/XI	71	10 r. –
1/II	72	23 r. 60 k.
1/I	74	100 r. –
1/II	74	150 r. –
1/II	75	100 r. –
1/II	75	50 r. –
1/XI	75	100 r. –
1/XI	75	15 r. –

Total— 701 rubles, 50 kopeks.

At the Malo Yaroslavetz

. . . Whenever the [Malo Yaroslavetz] restaurant was full, we landed in the rooms where the habitués of the restaurant lunched or, rather, emptied bottles of wine and beer. I can't mention the names of all these, because I didn't know many of them. I remember meeting Musorgsky there, sitting at a table loaded with bottles, and Sergei Vasilyevich Maximov, telling stories in his hoarse voice about the hills, forests and convicts of Siberia, and the actor Pavel Vasilyevich Vasilyev, also industriously emptying wine and beer bottles, and another Vasilyev, the opera-basso Vladimir Ivanovich . . . I didn't see this last there very often, but I met Maximov, Gor-

[49] Organized in 1865 by Ostrovsky and Nikolai Rubinstein.

bunov and other partisans of alcoholic liquids, many times at the Malo Yaroslavetz.

I recall one scene. Musorgsky sits on a chair near the bottle-laden table and holds an open newspaper in both hands. I cannot say he sits very steadily on his chair, but his back is pressed quite firmly against the back of his chair, and though he sways a little, he doesn't lose his balance. The opened sheet of newspaper apparently proves that Musorgsky has the intention of occupying himself with reading. However, if you should carefully examine his face, swollen from excessive wine-bibbing, and his eyes, which wander wildly over the surface of the newspaper, you will come unmistakably to the conclusion that he would be barely able to decipher even one line of the paper by syllables. It is quiet in the room. Gorbunov is telling something about A. N. Ostrovsky, something about their trip to London together,—everyone roars with laughter, but Musorgsky sits there wheezing through his nose . . . Pavel Vasilyev has gotten up from the bottle-laden table, wanting to go over to Musorgsky. Maximov hastily rises and clutches Vasilyev's hand.—"Don't touch him, don't touch: he'll fall!" he says hoarsely, wagging his beard . . . —DMITRI STAKHEYEV

160. *To VLADIMIR STASOV*

23 November, '75

Saint-Saëns.[50] Aida (Verdi).[51] Sardanapalus (Famintzin).[52] 15, 19 and 20 *November '75* in Petrograd.

When they name the author but not his works, then (as the old nurses of art used to say) that author is a somebody—worth something. Well, let's be kind: let's not start a dispute about the opinion of the old nurses of art! Who's this M. de Saint-Saëns?—one knows of him, partly from the papers, partly from conversations. What does M. de Saint-Saëns do?—he utilizes a miniature chamber orchestra and attains with it such solidity that he shows in rich orchestral powers tiny little thoughts inspired by a tiny versifier, and calls this crumb *Danse macabre*. The trend of M. de Saint-Saëns' mind was capable of digesting such an indigestible thought (a deliberation, perhaps?), and confronts the oppressive and aching *"Dies irae—Danse macabre"* of the Abbé Liszt with a sentimental miniature *"Violino solo danse macabre*

---

[50] November 15—the second concert of the Imperial Russian Musical Society, at which Camille Saint-Saëns conducted the first Russian performance of his *Danse macabre*.

[51] November 19—the Russian première (in Italian) of Verdi's Egyptian commission.

[52] November 20—the première of the newest opera of Musorgsky's old antagonist.

M. de Saint-Saëns." This is no matter for brains. And why did these brains throw themselves into symphonic program music? One hears that the brains have brewed an opera entitled *Samson:* evidently propaganda for female labor *(coupe de cheveux)*—and will have to be forbidden in Russia. I don't trust M. de Saint-Saëns' *Samson* any more than I do *his innovator's toys.* It's not merely music, words, palette and chisel that we need—no, devil take you, you liars and dissemblers *e tutti quanti,*—give us living thoughts, have living talks with people, whatever *subject* you've chosen! You can't fool us with sweetish sounds: the lady luxuriously passes the box of bonbons to her *dear friend,* and that's all. You, master of orchestral powers, M. de Saint-Saëns, you—creative crumb, you are so omnivorous that you derive pleasure from various trios, quartetti, quintetti, etc., arithmetically. M. de Saint-Saëns, innovator! With every brain in my skull —I deny him; with all the strength in the beating of my heart—I push him aside! A utilizer of miniatures, what business of ours is he!

But *maestro Senatòre Verdi* is quite another matter! This one pushes ahead on a grand scale, this innovator doesn't feel shy. All his *Aida*—ai–da!—outdistancing everything, outdistancing everyone, even himself. He has knocked over *Trovatore,* Mendelssohn, Wagner —and almost Amerigo Vespucci, too. The spectacle is wonderful, but demonstrates a fabulous impotence in personifying (with reminiscences!) the teeth-champing, hot African blood.

Sardanapalus by Famintzin: heard it twice. I beg the pardon of all *office supplies,* a substitution in our time for mediaeval pages and messengers, for being compelled to write about the opera *Famintzin,* composed by Sardanapalus, just as Sardanapalus fell. *Total madness.*

I am very pleased by the jolt given the public by you in *"Golos"* in regard to the production of *Aida.* I am sending you, my dear, an epistle for Borodin.[53] If only you could help drag out of that teacup or samovar his arrangement of the ace [second] symphony. *The dispute at Golitzin's is ripening.*

I embrace you,
MUSORYANIN

---

[53] Not extant.

Déclamateur

. . . In 1874 [1875], being one evening at Camille Saint-Saëns's, who had just returned from a tour to Moscow, I happened to lay hands on a score of *Boris Godunov*. As I leafed through it, reading with increasing interest the pages of a composer unknown to me, Saint-Saëns uttered the pronouncement that "all the ridiculous criticisms usually addressed to Wagner could be applied exactly to Musorgsky."

The rapid reading that I was able to make prevented me from concurring with this opinion; and two or three weeks later, having gone again to Camille Saint-Saëns's, I took away the score to study it at leisure. Later I attempted, on several occasions, to share with my friends this admiration of mine, which grew endlessly for this music, whose formula was so strangely new. But everywhere I met nothing but scorn, sneers and indifference. Decidedly, Saint-Saëns was not the only one of his opinion, and quantities of "the musically eminent," whose authority is law, agreed with him on this point: "Musorgsky is nothing but a fool, an obscure and grotesque *déclamateur*." . . .—
JULES DE BRAYER

161. *To ARSENI GOLENISHCHEV-KUTUZOV*

My dear friend Arseni, whatever happens, my own, we *absolutely must* meet, drag yourself along with your little children [poems], "it is not for me to be a stranger—it is nothing but the lure of loving hearts." How much business, how much disgust and dissipation, and hopes—great desires (terrible to utter!)—and you, my own, you haven't acted properly. What happened to you? Shall I open myself? All right—listen: you are loved by me, with you I feel at ease; do not bow to the Prince of the Earth, but hold your head higher and remember: *verily*, is it so? This day Wednesday (December 10) we await you—when you will grant us your presence, and kindly bring your good offspring; how fond I am of talking with them.

Come when you wish: come, if you wish and we love you—*I repeat this.*

Yours, without any doubt,
MODESTE MUSORGSKY

9–10 December, Night, '75

Under the impression of your first verses for the subject *"Danse macabre"* there is something,—I speak of the theme of "The Exile." [54]
MUSORGSKY

[54] A draft of these verses for an unused subject in *Songs and Dances of Death* was found among the poet's papers—the ship bringing a political exile home

10–11 December—night again.

Here is what has happened, dear friend Arseni: it appears to me now that I was not myself, I didn't have the nerve to send you this letter and I received a ferocious reprimand from my dearest hosts. I entreat you: understand, and if you can, with the heart (how could you not!)—*you are the chosen one, one can't help loving you*—what is this that you're doing? This week has a Friday—we await you, friend.

Yours, forever, without doubt, your

MODESTE

162. *To LUDMILA SHESTAKOVA*

Dear one of mine, little dove, I was scared by the frost and didn't venture to go out to the Stasovs in the evening, especially as they sit up late at the General's. My kindest thanks to you, dear, for having written when occasion arose the name "Musinka": it wafts to me a feeling of warmth and love and to no one but you, shall I give it up.

Listen to me quietly: a wretched little intrigue has been started against me at the Ministry; either by rinsing—or rubbing, they want to stick me. Well, they did stick me. But somehow the result was that I, the tormented one, have thought of something really delightful for *Khovanshchina*. I'll tell you about it in person this week. It is *so* untried, and effective, and historically plausible—it should be worked out this very minute. And here is the moral of this. All people—are human beings; a human being loves a *solid base*. A push is needed, or else the yeast will not work, let it ferment and fulfill its purpose. It's too soon yet to write to F. F.[55] I kiss your little hand, my little dove.

THE SAME MUSINKA

17 December, 1875

---

founders and sinks in sight of the exile's home. The poet Yakov Polonsky has told Lapshin that he had heard Musorgsky play a piano piece (?) portraying the mental state of a dying political prisoner in the fortress of Peter and Paul, while in the background, out of tune, chimes play Bortnyansky's hymn, "How Glorious Is Our Lord in Zion."

[55] Fyodor Fyodorovich Trepov, military police-master of St. Petersburg, whose permission was required for part of the festivities in honor of Petrov's approaching jubilee.

163. *To ARSENI GOLENISHCHEV-KUTUZOV*

My friend Arseni, it is quiet in the warm, cozy home, at the writing-table—only the fireplace sputters. Sleep is a great wonder-worker for those who have tasted the affliction of this earth, thus sleep reigns—powerful, tranquil, loving. In this silence, in the peace of all minds, all consciences and all desires—I, adoring you, I alone threaten you. My threat has no anger: it is as calm as sleep without nightmares. Neither goblin, nor ghost, I stood before you. I should like to stay a simple, artless, unfortunate friend to you. You have chosen your path —go! You disdained all; an empty intimation, the joking sorrow of friendship, the assurance in you and in your thoughts—*in your creations,* you disdained the cry of the heart—and you do disdain it! It's not for me to judge; I am no augur, no oracle. But, at leisure from the anxieties that are coming for you *alone,* do not forget

"The narrow, tranquil, peaceful room,[56]
And me, my friend,
do not curse."

Forever your
MODESTE

23–24 December, '75.
At night, "sunless."

164. *To VLADIMIR STASOV*

My good *généralissime,* perhaps you have become doubtful about Musoryanin. The second act of our *Khovanshchina* is ready—I wrote it during the holidays, right through the night.—It seems to have turned out well. Well, I will certainly drag it to you on Sunday (you have graciously decreed that the 2nd of January [Stasov's birthday] is not to be observed: God will judge you, but *as you wish*—"the beloved must be obeyed"). The thing is this, my dear, a lad has gone astray, drawn by various desires. And he who has strayed is none other than M. Arseni Kutuzov-Golenishchev-Count—and this is the way it is: he has decided to get married! and this is no joke, he says it's *the real thing.* So yet another "takes leave, to go to his native village," never to return. God! here one succumbs to the stagnation of a little clerk, stabbing after any little idea that appears (and one is glad to stab it!), but there people, who don't succumb to this civil stagnation, get mar-

---

[56] The opening phrase of No. 1 of the *Sunless* cycle.

ried without even being properly tempted. I frankly scolded Arseni and was extremely rude to the aforesaid Arseni. But lying is not for me. He asked me to come to his fiancée [57] (whom I don't know)—but *I'm not going;* I would have to lie. I don't want him to do what he's doing—and I won't go, that's all. He says that he fell in love with her —all the same *I won't go.* It's not necessary.

Such things make me want to work more than ever. And I am left alone—so, I'll be alone. You have to die alone anyway; not everyone will follow me there. It's a pity, *généralissime,* about Arseni.

And the third act is all mapped out. It will be easy now.

Of course and eternally,
MUSORYANIN

Night. 29–30 December, '75. Petrograd.

165. *To DIMITRI STASOV*

1 January, 1876

DEAREST DIMITRI VASILYEVICH,

Your friendly invitation did not find the *civil servant Musorgsky* at home, as he had already left for the office. From this occurred the calamity that I, Musoryanin, could not come to your dearest family to greet the New Year. But the entire 2nd act of *Khovanshchina* was and is at hand. I took up the 3rd act at night and I am writing it zealously. Great gratitude to your little dove of a lady for her kind feelings toward Musoryanin. Unless you send me some message, dearest Dimitri Vasilyevich, allow me to count on your permission to be at your house *in the very near future* with *Khovanshchina.* A hearty bow to your dearest lady and to the kiddies.

Your
MUSORYANIN

166. *To DIMITRI STASOV*

DEAREST DIMITRI VASILYEVICH,

Tomorrow, Sunday, at 9:00 P.M., I intend to come to Nadezhdin-skaya St. [Vladimir Stasov's], *at my fullest speed,* and with *Khovan-*

---

[57] The seventeen-year-old Olga Andreyevna Gulevich.

shchina. I should like to reach the middle of the 3rd act today. I bow many times to the lady and to the kiddies.

Your

MUSORYANIN

Saturday 3 January, '76.

I'm writing you from my civil service career.

VII

Last Songs
1876 — 1879

A Poem by Alexei Apukhtin [1]

A MINSTREL IN THE CAMP OF RUSSIAN MUSICIANS
[extract]

. . . .

Hail, O offspring of the new age,
  Bards of your native land,
For wisely making minuets
  A means of propaganda!
Whom do I see? Is that really
  The great Stasov who has
Fully grasped the style Byzantine,
  Expert on iconstasis?
You—a general of music,
  Man of words and councils,
You don't plan to compose yourself . . . ?
  O, hail to thee for that!

And Korsakov, so says the press,
  You're a famous maestro,
You're a real Sadko: in each bowl
  Leading marine orchestras!
You, Musorgsky, by means of notes
  Can show us anything:
To sew a seam and grow mushrooms,
  How children laugh and cry.
You've killed off Boris Godunov—
  Serves him right, the villain!
Did he have to murder the child!
  I can't really blame you.

---

[1] Apukhtin, a minor poet and friend of Tchaikovsky, writes a parody on Zhukovsky's famous *Minstrel in the Russian Camp*.

But who's this Caesar, this Cui,
  Who has turned columnist,
In order to throw burning words
  To delight novices?
Like William Ratcliff, he spreads fear:
  For even ancient Bach
And Beethoven, nothing to him,
  Stand in the prisoners' dock.
He wastes little love on Russians:
  O, how many he's worsted!
Why, Edwards, your sword's all gory,
  For famous blood thirsted? . . .

[1875]

167. *To LUDMILA SHESTAKOVA*

17 January, 1876 [Saturday]

Little dove Ludmila Ivanovna, here's what I ask you. Borodin and I should like to come to you on Thursday 22 January at 8:00 P.M., with the object of seeing you and of examining Borodin's heroic [second] symphony. If this is not inconvenient for you, little dove, do allow us—you see, all good musical matters start at your home and are done there: like a tomcat, I'm getting used to the house. Borodin will submit a petition to you on his own.

I saw grandpa [Petrov] at the beginning of the week—everything's all right. I expect he'll be on his feet in a few days, and then I'll go directly to place the letter in the petition box.[2] I think that if our Thursday date holds, I'll report on everything to you in person. Only, if possible, no one on Thursday besides the two of us. I feel sorry for people who are leaving "this vale of tears and sorrow," [3] but if they find this necessary, there's nothing to be said, nothing I can do. Of that *terrible thing* [?] of which you write, little dove, no one knows anything, so thinking about it is quite unnecessary—and to no purpose. Guard yourself from individuals—society needs you, do not yield to exhausting feelings; flap your little wings like a bold little birdie and cry: "We won't allow it." [4] This is how it is, my dear little dove; remember, you are needed by our art, you are thrice dear to us. Take care of yourself.

MUSINKA

---

[2] Asking Trepov to approve the planned festivities for Petrov.
[3] From the mass for the dead.
[4] Varlaam's words in the Kromy scene of *Boris.*

168. *An Inscription on a Photograph* [*See Frontispiece*]

To Ludmila Ivanovna Glinka-Shestakova.

MUSINKA. 1 February, '76

Be patient, little dove, love as you have loved and everything you've passed through will pass.

Khovanshchina, 3rd act. MODESTE MUSORGSKY

169. *To VLADIMIR STASOV*

My dear *généralissime,* thank you for the wonderful letter in regard to "the quarrel of the princes in *Khovanshchina.*" This is a rare hour in my life. Frankly and with complete sincerity: I am *grateful* for that great word—*respected!*—which rings in the speech of people greater and better than I. You, perhaps, cannot entirely know of my stimulation from *that word,* said by an *unchangeable* man, a mighty fighter for independence of thought and problems in art, for the eternity * of art. Remember how your Musor [5] was delighted by the article about your impressions of the London universal exposition (the 1st) in *Sovremennik.*[6]—Thank you, my dear! and our aims and tasks in "the quarrel of Princes" are very similar, except in Marfa's entrance (I am doing a lot of thinking now)—[more] of this when we meet on Sunday.

This is what, my splendid one; I have just come from O. A. Petrov. If the sculptor Laveretzky is still willing—he may present himself to Osip Afanasyevich (he's always at home) in Malaya Podyacheskaya—house of Berte, No. 10, and model the artist who has returned to life, *who on his death-bed reviewed his roles,* of which this writer was a witness. Let Laveretzky gather all his strength and hand down our dear Osip Afanasyevich to posterity.

How have society's demands on modern Russian artists grown! A great proof of the discontent in these terrible times throughout all classes. And how intolerable are the *old-believer* artists, stagnating in their closet labor and their four-walled dreams. O *Angelo!* [7]—*Dixi.*

* Musorgsky's note: I'm entangled in the dirtiest gossip.

---

[5] This humblest of Musorgsky's nicknames means "sweepings."

[6] This article, on the London Exhibition of 1862, is the one to which Musorgsky referred in Letter 31, to Cui.

[7] *Angelo* had finally reached the Marinsky stage on February 1, at a *bénéfice* for Melnikov.

I heartily embrace you, my dear, and the 3rd act is also being thought over—the regeneration of the 2nd act will not hinder it.

Your
MUSOR

12 February '76

[Written across the top of this letter:]

My host Naumov greets you zealously. He is in ecstasy over your letter: I could not help reading it aloud to him; and his ecstasy derives from *your notice and care* for us little ones.

170. *To LUDMILA SHESTAKOVA*

Little dove Ludmila Ivanovna, you have so consoled me with your energetic, splendid letters. You are right, little dove! Among people there *must* still be *real people,* when "playing false" depresses us and makes us suffer. All (almost all) "play us false" in our enlightened age in which everything you could wish progresses, except *humanness.* Not behind one's back, but right before one's eyes has been perpetrated an impertinent treason *à bout portant* of the best, vital, omnipotent conceptions of art in that very home, where, *once upon a time,* boiled new life, where new powers of thought were united, where new tasks of art were discussed and evaluated. But let's not bother about C. Cui and N. Rimsky-Korsakov: "there is no shame for the dead." [8] All that is here written was felt and *realized in your home,* my dear. "Truth loves not a lying atmosphere." Then there were no lies at your house, neither by us nor by them—the very walls told no *lies on that* memorable evening: all was *truth,* and such *truth!*—the aforesaid gentlemen (Cui and Korsakov) have abjured the *covenant of art—to speak "truthfully" with the people.*

I am yours irrevocably for Friday, March 5, little dove; it looks as though Borodin will not betray us: it's too late and it would be aimless. *O, if only Borodin could lose his temper!*

P. A. Naumov is grateful to you, my own, from the bottom of his heart, and wanted to visit you himself, but *caught the grippe*—now he's gradually getting rid of it. And as I read him your letter, he flushed and paced up and down the room: what a one—he said—how lovely and good Ludmila Ivanovna is! Ach, you, little dove (this is he speaking to himself). But I am as ever: your Musinka, yes and only that.

---

[8] From the mass for the dead.

An architectural project by Victor Hartmann: "City-Gate of Kiev"
(No. 10 of "Pictures at an Exhibition")

From *Annals of the Imperial Theaters*

Ludmila Shestakova
An engraving by Matte

Count Arseni Golenishchev-Kutuzov
A photograph of the early '80's

28–29 [February] night, 1876. Peter

On Friday, March 5, [I'll come] to you straight from my duties, little dove, meaning—at 5 o'clock.

Your

MUSINKA

171. *To NIKOLAI MOLAS*

DEAR FRIEND NIKOLAI PAVLOVICH,

For Thursday, March 11, they've harnessed me to a student concert,[9] so this time I can't, as I should wish, respond to your friendly summons. This means [waiting] till some occasion in the near future. And to that dearest lady [Alexandra Nikolayevna] a kiss on her little hand nevertheless, yes, and a little pat for Boris.

Your

MODESTE MUSORGSKY

9 March, '76

172. *To OLGA GOLENISHCHEVA-KUTUZOVA*

Our shining friend, Countess Olga Andreyevna, bless this "young Persian girl" [10] with your pure heart, and allow me to inscribe your shining name on this musical caprice. With its just-written notes scarcely cooled, this "Persian girl" was performed by me on Easter eve at grandpa O. A. Petrov's, who for the first time in his life was forced to remain at home alone, while all his family greeted Easter at church. Lonely as I am, I understood this and did what was necessary. For you, Countess, there is no doubt that the "young Persian girl" appeared in the world, as yet noticed only by few, on the 4th of April, 1876. I heard that 17 years ago, also on April 4, there appeared in the world of men a shining being, but at that time for very few observers.

I'm afraid, have I been understood?

Devotedly yours,

MODESTE MUSORGSKY

9 April, '76. P-bg.

---

[9] At the Petersburg Hall of Artists, in aid of needy students of the medical-surgery academy. Musorgsky was the accompanist.

[10] In a gesture of apology and reconciliation Musorgsky dedicates to Golenishchev-Kutuzov's young wife on her birthday the "Dance of the Persian Slaves" from *Khovanshchina*.

173. *To LUDMILA SHESTAKOVA*

Little dove of mine, dear Ludmila Ivanovna, this is the thing, my own: (1) the gendarmes are the police's affair, not ours, as the police themselves recognize the need: (2) I've not done any of your dearest commissions (in this final stage), it was impossible because the illnesses (real ones) of MM. the artists hindered grandpa's tryout for his jubilee performance.[11] However, our opinion remains *intacto:* after such heroic illness it would be heroic activity indeed—for dear grandpa to appear, fully armed, from his sickbed, *straight* into his 50-year jubilee. In regard to *the time for the ovation* during the performance we'll speak further: of course—best of all would be after the 4th act, and particularly in the first scene of the epilogue, as you and I have already discussed. Today and tomorrow I shall see Kondratyev Gennadi, and we'll talk it over further and further. Little dove of mine, how well yesterday's concert matinée for aid to student technologists turned out! I've decided not to go any more to grandpa's until the very day of the jubilee. To you, my own, great *remerciement for the announcement of the loge;* I'll remember, little dove, and I consider it an honor to present myself to you. This whole week was devoted to my little brother,[12]—that's why I haven't stopped in on you.

Devoted
MUSINKA

19 April, 1876

174. *To LUDMILA SHESTAKOVA*

Little dove of ours, dear and splendid Ludmila Ivanovna, your letter of April 27 was a stunning blow and left me *in a rage.* You, the good and loving one, who in former times gathered beneath your warm wings a musical family of powerful young Russians, for communion in art, *for study*—you, incessant and steadfast herald of the national, historical merits of your genius brother who gave musical *revelation* to the Russian soil—you, the *inviolable,* are disturbed in

[11] The festivities of Petrov's jubilee were to begin with his participation (in the role of Susanin) in a performance of Glinka's *Life for the Tzar* on April 21. He was to be brought home and surprised by a large shield hanging in front of his house on which his initials were outlined in a gas illumination. The police not only permitted this surprise illumination but, in their zeal, also notified Petrov of their permission—somewhat spoiling Shestakova's grand surprise, though Petrov concealed the mistake from her until after the festivities.

[12] Philarète has reappeared.

these bright days when the people's art triumphs, and you are en-tangled in trashy trifles—because of the solemn adoration of M. I. Glinka's glorious fellow-champion planned *a year ago* by you alone, now so gloriously and valuably carried out;—because glorious O. A. Petrov, so dear to all Russia, is now honored as no one before in Russia in the field of art has ever been honored;—because fate entrusted to you alone, the wreath with which you openly, before a solemn assem-bly of representatives of Russian musical affairs, crowned with im-mortality the bust of the glorious Petrov, who has been consecrated *by the people's will.*[13]—Honor to you and glory! Disavow the petty idle talkers, the staled self-lovers, no room for them here. Your con-solation and holy justification *in the people* who consecrated on the 21st day of April 1876 the dear and glorious personality of grandpa O. A. Petrov and *reminded* the petty idle talkers of the other glorious fellow-champion of M. I. Glinka—Anna Yakovlevna Vorobiova-Petrova, has been *by right* consecrated by that same *people.* The truth came out: the people thus wished, recognized and did.

Your bright name, already inscribed in the chronicles of art, now shines there forever with a worthy, heartfelt acknowledgment. Forget the petty gossips—they are unworthy of you and your holy cause! But, may your bright love bless my heart and my mind, which trembled when those lines appeared in your letter of April 27: "More than once have I read the inscription on your portrait [see 168]."

Tomorrow, Wednesday, my own, I shall drop in to see you—I am going to *dyainka* Nikolsky. For God's sake—take care of your heart and may your thought be calm and bright.

Ever the same
MUSINKA

27 April, 1876

175. *To LUDMILA SHESTAKOVA*

[1876]

Our dear little dove, Ludmila Ivanovna, I am not master where you are mistress. In you, little dove, lives for all of us, dearly holy to all of us, your brother Mikhail Ivanovich. The business is about the

---

[13] The festivities were concluded on April 24 in the Hall of the Conservatory, where testimonials were presented to Petrov, and Shestakova presented to Petrov the bust made by Nikolai Laveretzky, crowned with a laurel wreath.

monument to the great creator—*read the enclosed,*[14] *and it would be good if Dyainka would also read it, and would correct it where necessary. About these corrections,* I ask you to give me an answer *right away.* (What an audacious one I am!) This is a historical article.

Your soul's
MUSINKA

Here in all his true self is Grandpa [Petrov], forever *unofficial,* but intimate so that he can speak about art with human society.

Declares MUSINKA

176. *To NIKOLAI RIMSKY-KORSAKOV*

Friend Nikolai Andreyevich, on *Monday (May 17) I will be at your place at 8:00 P.M.* We must see each other—this is such nonsense! Your task, friend, to communicate the Russian song to the Russian people and to *others,* is a great consolation to me.[15]—A blessed, historical service. This beloved thing might be lost, *might be lost com-*

---

[14] This may be a lost article by Musorgsky, about the relations between Petrov and Glinka, written on the occasion of Petrov's jubilee. Its aim was to enlist sympathy for Shestakova's project to erect a monument to Glinka in his home town of Smolensk.

[15] Rimsky-Korsakov's collection was completed the following year: *100 Russian Folk-Songs* (Op. 24), collected and harmonized by N. Rimsky-Korsakov; dedicated to V. V. Stasov (who had located rare volumes for it—Prach, Yakushkin, etc.). The preface is dated St. Petersburg, November 1877. Four songs in the volume were recorded by Musorgsky: 1. "Within the Walls of Kiev," communicated by M. P. Musorgsky, who heard it from Ryabinin; 2. "Volga and Mikula," communicated by M. P. Musorgsky, to whom Ryabinin sang it [used by Musorgsky in the Kromy scene of *Boris,* sung by Misail and Varlaam]; 11. "There Passed a Maiden," communicated by M. P. Musorgsky, who recorded it as sung by I. F. Gorbunov [used by Musorgsky as Marfa's divination aria in *Khovanshchina*]; 92. "Oh, Bridal Gifts so Splendid, La-du, La-du," communicated by M. P. Musorgsky, who recorded it as sung by M. F. Shishko [used by Musorgsky for the chorus in Act IV, Scene I, of *Khovanshchina*].

Other songs in this volume that Musorgsky had used in *Boris:* 18. "See the Proud Eagle Swiftly Soaring," arranged by Balakirev, after P. Yakushkin (Vol. III, 1815) [used by Musorgsky in the Kromy scene]; 45. "Glory Be to God in Heaven," from Johann Pratsch [Jan Prach] (Vol. II, 1815) [used first by Beethoven for the Trio of the scherzo in his E minor quartet, Op. 59, by Musorgsky for the chorus in the coronation scene and later by Rimsky-Korsakov in *The Tzar's Bride* and the cantata, *Slava*]; 71. "Pealing Are the Bells in Novgorod," communicated by S. V. Rimskaya-Korsakova [used by Musorgsky for drunken Varlaam's song in the inn scene].

pletely; but when one thinks that a competent Russian has undertaken such a blessed matter, then one becomes joyful and consoled. Don't forget, that in scientific matters, the bringing together of nationalities is an axiom, their mutual cognition is also an axiom. In the civilized family of nations it is impossible to be *naked*—one must be clothed. If each one brings a tiny thread for his necessary clothing, thanks to him; but you, friend, are contributing an entire *costume*. That's so. You have no time, yes and it's time for me to sleep. I embrace you, friend.

To your dearest lady and to the kiddies, my cordial greeting.

MODESTE

15–16 May—night
1876

176a. *VLADIMIR STASOV to MODESTE MUSORGSKY*

Tuesday, 18 May, '76

Mu-sya-lya-nin, yesterday I was disturbed first by the "second advent" of the admiral [Rimsky-Korsakov] and then by the "first" of A. N. Engelhardt, and I didn't have time to express even a quarter of what I intended to say. So I shut up at once and in my heart decided: to put it all on paper at a time when no one would interrupt by bowing himself into the room or by sitting silently in the corner like our spectacled commodore.

So, sir, this is what I must tell you; but only remember, for God's sake, that all this is neither a *demand* nor an *admonition* (which you, least of all, need), but simply question-marks placed here by a man from the public, madly devoted to you and to your affairs.

I repeat: in its present form your opera has too many choruses and too little activity of individual personalities, characters. I dare say that your warmest partisans (not to mention your opponents), hearing your opera on the stage, admiring the gifts and originality of the music, would ask: "But why are the characters of *Golitzin, Marfa, etc.* in the opera! Throw them out and the opera would lose nothing— these characters are purely *inserted ones,* superfluous to all the action, and not in the least interwoven into either the motivation or the denouement of the plot." I also am ready to ask this question, but at the same time I realize how this jerkiness and external episodic quality happened: because the previous plan had to be slightly changed be-

333

cause Sofia and Peter had to be eliminated—meaning that the rest
was immediately damaged to some extent (as far as the libretto was
concerned); the former continuity was broken and scenes, details and
even entire characters now exist without means to stand firmly on the
ground, but are left strangely suspended between ceiling and floor.

So I decided to scribble you a few suggestions, by which might be
achieved a stronger continuity, a greater solidity and in consequence
a greater interest in the action.

(1) I find everything in the 1st act *ready and completed* from every
viewpoint and I have no objection to make.

(2) But I have plenty of objections to make in the 2nd act. Marfa's
sorcery is splendid musically, but purposeless; her return to Golitzin
after the attempt on her life—is also purposeless, it has no motivation
and comes to no conclusion. The dispute and quarrel between Golitzin and Khovansky are purposeless, as this isn't followed up further
in the opera, so that, truly, this entire act (*as libretto*) may as well be
thrown out, and the opera would lose nothing by this as far as the plot
is concerned. Besides, Dosifei for the 2nd time "stops" someone; they
might say that he must be some sort of *policeman,* a seeker of order
and silence—and nothing more!! In a way he has no character or
physiognomy of his own whatever.

In order to change all this chaos I would suggest the following:
would it be impossible for Marfa to be not only a dissenter and an
accomplice of Golitzin,—but also a young widow, afire with life, and
—Golitzin's *mistress?* Would it be impossible in this 2nd act for her
to come to him, in answer to his summons, to tell his fortune and to
tease him ironically as well as his correspondent, the amorous Princess
Sofia, and then suddenly transform her mood from pensiveness and
irony to *resolution,* telling Golitzin that she no longer wishes to have
any relationship with him, that all this has become repulsive to her,
that sin is frightful, that their "true faith" forbids such a thing, that
she doesn't want to take any part in their political affairs, retreats from
everything, and departs. Golitzin doesn't want to believe her, suspects
some other motive, pesters her, pursues her with requests and threats,
now ridiculing Sofia and assuring Marfa that he wouldn't give a copper for Sofia, and then attempting to fan the political-religious flame
in Marfa again. But all is in vain. Marfa pays no attention to anything;
but when Golitzin approaches her with even greater force, she finally

recovers herself, and admits passionately: "Well, yes, I am in love with a man, with all the power of passion, like a madwoman, like a lost woman, but I know that this will certainly ruin me, as well as others,—and so I want to put an end to all this, I want to leave it all, and hide myself somewhere, in order to live only for the sake of the true faith and for God . . ." This would seem to me to be a worthy motif for a composer. Golitzin, all the while pretending, now feels genuinely sorry for the loss of this beautiful, passionate woman,—he comes suddenly to a decision and with an icy appearance lets her go. "Ah, I am abandoned, despised!" he says to himself, now alone,—"I am Golitzin the all-powerful, who runs his country and holds in his hand the heart of Sofia and the destinies of Russia. All right, let it be as you wish. Only you can no longer remain alive—you will denounce me and spill out the whole story. This would be too injurious to me, all my plans would collapse,"—so he calls a trusted man and orders Marfa to be drowned in the marsh, and himself coldly speaks to Khovansky who at this minute comes in for the general council meeting. Khovansky has come, however, not only for the council—he also wants to settle his own accounts: he accuses Golitzin of Europeanism, of selfish and simulated amorous intrigues with Sofia, of desertion from their chief cause, of *"separate scheming"* for personal ends. A quarrel flares up (at the same time Golitzin's mind and speech returns, instantaneously and briefly, *a parte*, to Marfa: he is torn between two feelings). Dosifei, like an autocrat, tries to quench this quite untimely flare, which hinders their cause, just as Marfa runs in and with wails and tears complains to the entire "council" of true-believers about the attempt that had been made on her life and goes to Dosifei for protection, declaring that henceforth she is devoting her life to nothing but faith and penitence. All—each in his own way—strive to *persuade* her to remain as before their loyal ally, a mighty spring of action in their camp—she remains inflexible: meanwhile the quarrel between Golitzin and Khovansky reaches a state of definite hostility and hate, and each *swears* to the other—to wipe out his enemy or perish. And with this—Shaklovity appears, and the chorus of dissenters is heard in the distance.

In a word, I would entitle this entire act:

"Schism within the schism."

(3) In the 3rd act (the *streltzi* settlement) I must also object to many

335

things. There are choruses and songs (male and female) and beautiful music, but neither action nor interest of any sort. There is also no connection of any kind with the rest of the opera.

Therefore, this is what I suggest:

Wouldn't it be possible to leave all that has been composed so far (and it is *magnificent* in the extreme), but to add the following scene. After Marfa's song, the awakening of the *streltzi* and the lynching of the scribe, young Andrei Khovansky comes to the settlement and starts to incite the *streltzi,* the greatest hot-heads and fire-brands among them, promising them money, wine and bold glory, something better than the lynching of the scribe,—he incites them to go with him to kidnap the German beauty, a heretic and an unholy person. The *streltzi* delightedly go to arm themselves and get their horses and carts ready; but just as Andrei, pleased with his success, is about to follow them—Marfa, who has heard and discovered all, rushes to him; her resolution to retreat from all worldly things is broken, she is suffocating with jealousy, with fury and lust for this young, handsome hussar of the seventeenth century—she flings and tosses herself about like a real Potiphar's wife, the voice of the dissenter and of "the true faith" has left her and is silenced, leaving only a furiously amorous and jealous woman. But Andrei manages to free himself from her and declares that he doesn't love her and never will love another man's slave, Golitzin's mistress! . . . She is left alone, crushed and beaten, she looks about her in dismay at her solitude, and just then, from the background of the street (or from a window) Susanna, who has silently witnessed the whole scene, sneaks up to her; Susanna, yellowed, parchment-like, withered and envious, expresses all her hatred towards Marfa, expresses all her triumph over her because she now knows her *secret,* and announces that she will summon her to *trial* by their entire community of true-believers in their forest retreat.—I hope that in this way both movement and interest can be put into this act, and that it will give the composer the richest of problems.

(4) In Act IV (the German settlement), I should again suggest agreement with what we were able to discuss yesterday: to make the entire scene a *"Scène d'intérieur,"* i.e., auntie, niece, an unclouded henlike life, peaceful conversation, etc. Enter Andrei, a-courting, he is given a cold shoulder, he calls in his assistants, and they forcibly remove Emma, the little canary.

(5) For the scene in the anciently regulated household of Khovan-

sky you already have made an important addition: the conversation between father and son is splendid. The father's reproaches, his wish to incite his son's ambition, the son's indifference to all this, intercut with returns to thoughts of Emma—all this is quite good and rich. But, before the dinner and the harem chorus and the "Persian girls" I should suggest bringing in Golitzin here, also. In the 2nd act Khovansky was at Golitzin's; now let Golitzin be at Khovansky's: a counter-visit, the obverse side of the medal. Horrified, Golitzin enters to say that all is lost, and implores Khovansky to forget the squabble and join forces, to take measures, to call out the *streltzi* against Peter and even against Sofia (the *half-European* has passed beyond the *full-European* and has arrived at the Asiatic); but Khovansky the booby is blinded by this unexpected triumph, he's all conceit and pomp; he exults, he is prouder than the silliest of peacocks, and when Shaklovity and the others sent by Sofia enter the room, Khovansky, far from feeling his ruin, grows even more conceited and exults before Golitzin: "You see, what did I tell you!! Things have gone bad, not for *us*, but for them! Now they need *me*, and they send for *me*; now they perceive their ruin, and my power!" He declares this, then goes through the ceremony of donning his most glorious golden robe—and goes . . . to his death! Golitzin drops his head, and they will at once arrest him.

(6) I have nothing to say about the last scene (the retreat). Everything here is fine. Dosifei settles his life's accounts, Andrei gallops in at full speed from Moscow, his scene with Dosifei, then with Emma, his efforts to arm the entire retreat to repulse Peter's troopers, Dosifei's refusal (he feels that all is now lost), the trial of Marfa, her acquittal and glorification by Dosifei as the *purest being among them all,* the fanaticism of all and the self-immolation of ancient, perishing Russia —all this is rich, lively, full of action, interest and the most splendid of motifs.

That's what I want to suggest to you. Here *all the characters* take on outlines, reveal themselves, and receive definition and action. Think this over for God's sake and consider all this within yourself. Perhaps it will be of some use to you. You will find here new materials for your talent. And let's talk it all over on Thursday. Perhaps even better tomorrow (Wednesday), at our house on Nadezhdinskaya. But perhaps this is impossible! Haven't you crossed off this street from your memory?

V. S.

177. *To VLADIMIR STASOV*

My dear *généralissime*, for the first time you've taken the trouble to frighten Musoryanin, and to do it by appearing to get angry. Musoryanin hardly called forth your wrath, but if it's thus—believe me, my dear, that Musoryanin will accept and endure this wrath with love. For some little time, but long enough, Musoryanin has been subject to doubts, misgivings, conjectures and all these *tutti quanti* of leisure in the country. Musoryanin is working—but only, *for work* he needs peace. *Khovanshchina* is too big, too extraordinary a task. You, *généralissime*, I am sure, did not suppose that your remarks and suggestions had been taken by me in any other manner than Musoryanin's usual one. *I have halted work—I have fallen into thought*, and now, and yesterday, and weeks ago, and tomorrow are all spent in thought —the one thought to go forth as a conqueror and speak to people *a new word* of friendship and love, *a frank word, one as broad as the Russian plains*, the true-sounding word of a modest musician, but a fighter for the true concept of art. And here's your last letter: I have again fallen into thought. Your proposal *screams* of something good; the idea must be given a lot of thought, and already there is a program in regard to Marfa. By the way, it's thanks to you that we understood Marfa and that we are doing this Russian woman *purely*. But the pathos is good, and is well placed in the tragic quality of Marfa and why try to conceal its usefulness for the musician. I thank you. Thus or otherwise, but I have fallen into thought and if you're still the same (for you to change would be a crime), our business will move more speedily, and it already goes speedily. After our long separation, that's what I wanted to tell you; here's the present, and not the former

MUSORYANIN

Another by the way: so far fate has taken care of me. In the present *general* state of affairs, one can expect anything. During this time, working a great deal at the piano, I'm coming to the conviction that if I am destined to earn my daily bread by *clattering*—we'll be able to do this. Another by the way (*passez-moi ça*) I, during this time of *thinking*, shall rest in the folk scenes—I am very much in the mood for this. Well, and in order for there to be no doubt, *généralissime*, what disorderly nonsense!

Ever your
MUSORYANIN

'76. 15 June. Day of St. Modestus

178. *To LUDMILA SHESTAKOVA*

15 June, 1876

Dear little dove of mine, Ludmila Ivanovna, my hearty thanks to you for your message. I have, recently, secluded myself,—I had to, nature itself willed it. In seclusion I have pondered a great deal over *Khovanshchina*, and found much that was not as it should be. When we meet I'll explain everything. I am almost never satisfied with myself, but now, more than ever, I am inclined to think that my role lies more in seclusion and concentration for the sake of art. The old boy has quite exhausted himself during the winter and spring. This is, of course, no reason to seclude myself from you, my own, and from good people. On the contrary, I'll present myself with all due freshness and vigor—the executant of your ever good and friendly purposes, and we shall call on the most splendid grandpa [Petrov], as you are pleased to command. All good health to you, my own, little dove. I shall drop in on you one of these days.

Your

MUSINKA

178a. *ALEXANDER BORODIN to LUBOV KARMALINA, Fortress Zakatali* [*Extract*]

Moscow. June 1, 1876

. . . To what degree I'll be able to realize my intentions—of this I'm no judge, of course, but the *tendency* of my opera will be closer to *Ruslan* than to *The Stone Guest*, this I can vouch for. So far it is curious that all the members of our circle are united about *Igor*: the ultra-innovator-realist Modeste Petrovich, the innovator in the field of lyrical-dramatic music Cesar Antonovich, the severe one in regard to external form and musical tradition Nikolai Andreyevich, and the passionate champion of novelty and power in everything, Vladimir Vasilyevich Stasov. Thus far all are pleased with *Igor*, although they are, in other things, widely divergent . . .

179. *To VLADIMIR STASOV*

Dear *généralissime*, Ludmila Ivanovna has written you that she wishes to receive you and me at a repast on the 14th or 15th of July, and asks me to tell you that the 16th of July is also at your dearest command.

339

Remembering that July 15 is YOUR DAY and being happy that on one of these three proposed days you and I shall have a *fine* talk about good things, I dare to dream—that the day selected by you would be YOUR DAY; and how many lovely, lively memories are associated with this good day!

Notify Ludmila Ivanovna and Musoryanin, dearest *généralissime,* about which of the three days you choose, and as soon as you can.

Your

MUSORYANIN

For me all three days are at your disposal—I am free. Wednesday, July 14, 10:00 A.M.—I've just remembered that Wednesday is impossible for you.

179a. *VLADIMIR STASOV to NIKOLAI RIMSKY-KORSAKOV,* Pargolovo
[*Extract*]

17 July, 1876, Spb.

. . . I see only Musoryanin, now and then: he works *more than a little,* and furthermore, not only on *Khovanshchina,* but also on *Fair at Sorochintzi*—two operas at once! And here and there he has produced splendid things that would indeed please you. But this is not all: in his *Danse macabre* (three numbers of which you know) he has begun a 4th: "Monk"—very good—and is starting a 5th: "Anika the Warrior and Death." [16] A hundred times I've asked Musoryanin and Kutuzov to go to you, all three of us together, but both are such sluggards, and went on planning this so long, that Kutuzov has left for the country . . . and now it won't be possible to move Musorgsky . . .

180. *To LUDMILA SHESTAKOVA*

Dear little dove of mine, Ludmila Ivanovna, Musinka asks you to count on him as yours and the Petrovs' for July 28 (Wednesday). This gray-haired young man, so spoiled by you, little dove, is all this while

---

[16] Anika the Warrior was a *bylini* figure who destroyed towns and churches, committing sacrilegious acts towards holy ikons, and Latinizing the Holy Faith. The *bylina* about him that may have interested Musorgsky is "The Struggle between Life and Death."

blazing with musical work: for he has further acquired a little chorus of girls for *Sorochintzi*, and in *Khovanshchina* it has become apparent how all should be in the scene of the scribe's story to the *streltzi* about the troopers. Well and good! Yesterday I dined and spent the evening at the *Généralissime's*, Repin was there and we were glad to see each other. It was delightful. Yes, I nearly forgot, I have invented something extremely physiognomical for the pastor in *Khovanshchina*.[17] Really! Till our meeting in the very near future, my dear little dove; be well, and your Musinka greets you heartily; on Wednesday it shall be done as you have deigned to command.

Your

Musinka

24 July, 1876

180a. *VLADIMIR STASOV to DIMITRI STASOV [Extract]*

July 31, 1876

. . . Last Friday I invited Musorgsky over with Repin, and the latter was in great ecstasy over all that Musorgsky had composed in the 3 years that he [Repin] had been away. Yes, I give you my word, all this time Musorgsky has gone ahead in my esteem so enormously that mere "Musicians"—Rimsky-Korsakov, Cui and the like—simply cannot see or understand this situation . . .

181. *To LUDMILA SHESTAKOVA*

Tzarskoye Selo, New Places
Zhukovsky's *dacha*, No. 7
2 August, 1876

Dear little dove of mine, Ludmila Ivanovna, you see I have moved. The *dacha* is so excellent that the trees creep into the window and whisper, what exactly—I don't know, but they seem to be whispering something nice. With these good and peaceful friends, although they are a little noisy at times, God help us accomplish our strong desires, to achieve "those" deeds—of which one only dreams. Possessed of a strong body and, if God so grants, peace of mind, perhaps *Khovanshchina* will not reject me. Last night I hardly slept in the "new place";

---

[17] A satirical scene in Act II: the German pastor comes to Prince Golitzin requesting permission to build a second church in the German quarter of Moscow.

in the evening N[aumov?] and I took a long walk—5 or 6 versts, all through the best spots. Both of us were overjoyed, neither of us could get to sleep: stillness; in the distance a signaler on the railway blows his horn, there the watchdogs bark dutifully; and here, like a harp glissando, the leaves start and dreamily rustle, no wonder we couldn't sleep. And more! On top of all this, the "invisible moon" creeps through the leaves directly over the head of my bed, gently, softly it creeps along. After the "businesslike" Petersburg noise, after the reckless bustle of the capital, one doesn't rest at first, one only feels irritated: why don't I hear this noise, whither has it fled. Yesterday, sitting under the boughs on the balcony, I was consoled by a playful song of the passing holiday crowd. The song was over an accordion accompaniment: I remembered it, but hesitated to stop the passers-by and ask them for the story of the song, and now I'm sorry. I was sitting on the balcony, pondering over *Khovanshchina*—and I thought something out. If only they would give me a leave—we would go prancing off across the music paper. It's time! Almost everything is composed, now one has to write and write. It's only this dragging of oneself to the office that stands in the way.

My own little dove, I've wanted to talk with you, just as I feel in my soul—now I've done it. Till the next letter, very soon. Keep well, my dear little dove.

Your

MUSINKA

Spare me some news of yourself, my own. Musinka would so appreciate it.

6 August, 1876

The scene with the pastor is written, and we go ahead.

Little dove, Ludmila Ivanovna, I've received your letter, and on August 18 (on Wednesday) I'll fly straight to you from the office, our dear one. And let this letter be proof that I am not forgetful of those who love me. I moved on August 1 and wrote on August 2. Didn't send the letter because of my sinful whims. *Khovanshchina* makes good progress. I feel content, and we have a piano.

Ever devotedly your

MUSINKA

So, till August 18 (Wednesday), little dove.

182. *To VLADIMIR STASOV*, *St. Petersburg*

[Postmarked: August 16 1876]
Tzarskoye Selo. New Places
Zhukovsky's *dacha*, No. 7

My dear *généralissime*, such adventures happen only to me: imagine, I had written you two letters about my musical affairs—and
yesterday, in the storm,[18] they were both whirled away to some unknown place along with a stack of envelopes! What's to be done? I
wrote you (on August 2) that I'm working zealously, and (on August 6)
that the scene with the pastor is done, and that it is absolutely necessary to outline the portrait of Golitzin as history indicates, in the 2nd
scene [act] of *Khovanshchina* so that one could use it in the episode
at Iv[an] Khov[ansky's] in the 5th scene, during the "old-fashioned"
repast. I think you will be satisfied with the scene with the pastor, my
dear. As soon as the scene in Golitzin's study gets to the quintet, i.e.,
the finale of the scene, at that moment I will take up the completion
of the 3rd scene (the *streltzi* quarter), and I will write the quintet in
Peter under R. Korsakov's supervision, for its technical requirements
are mischievous: alto, tenor and 3 basses.

On Wednesday, Aug. 18, at the summons of Ludmila Ivanovna, I
hope to see you and discuss things *heartily*. Yes, and perhaps I'll also
bring the 2nd scene of *Khovanshchina*—you can judge the pastor's interview and all that is written beyond it. Today, very likely, Dosifei
will come into the meeting, and material is ready for that. But about
the meeting, we'll talk it over together: it must be done very com-
pactly, but *substantially,* and in asking for your kindest help, Musoryanin has never yet been refused, and, spoiled by you, he again applies
to you. Oh, if I could only master this 2nd scene of our *Khovanshchina,* and the rest would go along successfully, I hope. It is now
clear that the 2nd scene is a lever for turning all the fussing factions
in the whole drama.

The *dacha* is excellent: the air is wonderful, we go walking for 5 or
6 versts; but my nerves torment me now and then. However, I suppose
I must resign myself to this for the rest of my life. All the same, work
goes on and on with progress—in other words, as real work ought to

---

[18] This storm left its musical mark. On the cover of the manuscript of the
2nd act of *Khovanshchina*, Musorgsky has scribbled six measures of an idea: "Allegro. The winds blow at Tzarskoye Selo on Aug. 12, '76," and below: "All in D
major. 7:00 P.M."

go, and not some sort of concoction. Till we meet soon, my dear, send me some little message—you know how your talks strengthen me in the struggle and in work.

Your

MUSORYANIN

My greeting to all of yours and to A. V. Meyer.

182a.　*VLADIMIR STASOV to MODESTE MUSORGSKY, Tzarskoye Selo*

Nadezhd[inskaya St.] 9, August 16, '76

How altogether happy you made me today, Mu-sa-lya-nin—Horsie!!! You are truly sitting in "new places." And hiking for 100 versts, and writing such nice letters to me, and to Ludmila Ivanovna, about the things that you're again cooking up for your opera. Let's hold off your starting lessons in *polyphony* with Rimsky, and meanwhile, how like a lion you move ahead! I had a real holiday reading how you are now peering at your 2nd scene, and how you seek there not *technique,* not music, but a profound inner structure, historical painting of this sort must be on fresco imperishable from any fire, and each brushstroke must smell of the eagle's talon. You've again gladdened me, and I'll wait even more impatiently than before for that minute when, after finishing off the rich pie and the fish-soup, we shall start our pacing up and down on Ludm. Ivan.'s parquet floor, attending to our business. Perhaps I can then succeed in offering you this or that of some use to you, but meanwhile listen to some of my preliminary considerations:

There is *everything* in abundance in your opera so far—nationality, and genuine historical coloring ("Is it so, children," [19] etc.), and opposed factions, and contrasting nations and peoples and opposed characters and tendencies, mean and good people, clean and dirty, serious and funny—everything, everything in abundance, only one thing is lacking: an active political element, *undertaking* something, *aimed at some purpose.* But your letter today seems to show me that you have felt this shortcoming and this lack of an important feature. If this is so, I implore you even more than before, and I would stretch out a hundred hands if, like some Indian god, I had them, to help. Yes, yes, I too always found a great gap here in the opera: it always seemed to me that despite all the perfection and unprecedented novelty of the por-

---

[19] From Prince Ivan Khovansky's demagogic speech to the *streltzi* in Act I.

trayal of the dissenters, a thoughtful man could still ask you: "Well, all right, all your dissenters exist entirely through their desire to preserve their ancestors' Russian antiquity, and for this they did away with everyone (or many) harmful to them—perfect! But all this took place before the rising of the curtain, before the start of your act: so what does their activity, their enterprise, their undertaking consist of during your 5 acts?" So far your opera has no answer to this—but now it has, I see this, because today you yourself bumped into this with a bang.

In my opinion the main sense of the 2nd act must be the color of a

c o n s p i r a c y

political, national, and social. After all the executions, alarums, and murders, all the principals assemble to discuss and to decide: "What are we to do now? What must we undertake in order to reduce our enemies to ashes, and to seat in *their* places, *our* people."

Perhaps, to embody this, it would be good to give the following shape to the 2nd scene, from the moment of Khovansky's arrival at Golitzin's: at first the princes stupidly and absurdly fly at each other and quarrel: then, in the presence of Dosifei (who has also appeared in the meantime) Marfa runs in, complaining that she had almost been done to death by the treacherous command of Golitzin (because in her love for Andrei she had told Golitzin that she is giving up their cause and everything secular and was going to dedicate herself to God till the end of her days)—after the exposure of all of Golitzin's abominations, both princes are ready to grapple with each other, but now, in all the grandeur of apostle and prophet—Dosifei comes forward. With thundering power he forces them to make peace, and compels them to *hold a council* on what they need. At first both princes, even unwillingly, *almost snarling* (an even *comical* motif), answer Dosifei's questions: "How many warriors have we altogether? On whom can we depend? Who should attack first? On what day will all be ready?" etc., but gradually all comic elements disappear and they decide, united, *how and when* they are to capture the two Tzareviches and the Tzarevna [Sofia], how they will lock them up, and how in their place is to be seated—Prince Andrei. All this has been a swift, *pathetic* recitative, and the following *morceau d'ensemble* would be an expression of the feelings of each of all four characters, present here and each pulling *in his own direction* (The Swan, the Pike and the Crab [20]):

---

[20] A Krylov fable.

this is the sort of ensemble that would be heretofore unheard any-where. And at this very moment, after this ensemble, would be heard the chorus of dissenters in the distance, celebrating their first victory (far from completed). This might not be bad!!!

Throughout this entire act or scene Golitzin, in my opinion, must be knavish, foxy and cowardly, but he still counts on success, *but behind the backs* of the others, the strong ones.

Till Wednesday.

                                                          Your

                                                          V. S.

183. *To LUDMILA SHESTAKOVA, St. Petersburg*

Tzarskoye Selo. New Places
Zhukovsky's *dacha* No. 7.
31 August, 1876

My dear little dove, Ludmila Ivanovna, just as I was going to have a little chat with you, you already scold me, my own, for my silence. And I wanted to write, not an ordinary letter, but one with a little surprise, that the infinitely disorderly Musinka has finished the 2nd act of *Khovanshchina*. Well, there's nothing to be done about it. To-day I will complete the act, while my heart, or as much as I have left of it, tells me that only those who love can scold. Why should I conceal it from you, little dove? In each of your letters there is so much bright and invigorating sentiment, that with such moral support one would not mind acquiescing in the inhuman excrescences of modern society. How invariably good you are, little dove. Now I will tackle the completion of the third act of *Khovanshchina*. I have composed a gypsy for *The Fair at Sorochintzi*—and I am able to report to you that this gypsy is quite a dashing fellow and rogue. I've been dreaming about certain scenes at the fair, half graceful, half comic. Something hovers before me for the love scene between Parasya and the young peasants. And how much more I dream of doing! In music, my "eyes are bigger than my stomach." [21]

What is this perpetual mourning that pursues N. V. Stasov? [22] Like a real beast, fate claws his heart to shreds. Horrible. And while you, little dove, with your loving soul, bring comfort to the wounded man, fate plagues you with the petty squabbles of petty people. Dear little

---

[21] The Russian figure of speech is "priest's eyes."
[22] Nikolai Stasov's family has suffered a series of illnesses and deaths.

dove of mine, let them buzz—let them do what they were created for. There is no escape from mosquitoes and gnats. Let the swarms swarm. Nothing one can do about it, anyway. Keep well, my dear little dove. Musinka's hearty thanks ever belong to you. Till we meet very soon, my dear little dove, Ludmila Ivanovna.

Your

MUSINKA

I don't believe and I don't want to think that we could do without Napravnik.[23] *There must be Russian opera in Russia—there must be —a Napravnik,* no matter how the pens of the bureaucrats scratch. What madness! I don't want to think of it.

MUSINKA

184. *To LUDMILA SHESTAKOVA, St. Petersburg*

Tzarskoye Selo, New Places
Zhukovsky's *dacha,* No. 7
10 September, 1876

Dear little dove of mine, Ludmila Ivanovna, just as I left you today, my own, I heard for a fact that Napravnik has won and, thank God, the cause of Russian opera is safe. I hasten to share with you, little dove, this happy news; even if you should have learned this before my letter gets to you, my heart is greatly concerned that it should be from Musinka, apart from all others, that you, my own, should receive this news. Before I could continue this letter, I received yours, little dove. I really don't know how to praise you enough, our own; you are truly an extraordinary little dove; aren't you? With such all-powerful

---

[23] "Napravnik's three-year contract with the Directorate of the Imperial Theaters terminated in 1876. In April of that year Napravnik sent a notification to Baron Kister [Director] that he was ready to sign a new contract, provided that the chorus and orchestra would be given a full *bénéfice.* This was not answered, and after May 1, E. F. Napravnik's salary was stopped. Under the direction of the 2nd conductor, Vojaček, rehearsals were begun on August 1. Vojaček also conducted the first five performances at the Opera. According to notes in E. F. Napravnik's diary, kindly communicated to us by [his son] V. E. Napravnik, on September 5 at the request of Baron Kister, N. A. Lukashevich called upon Eduard Franzovich. On September 7 Eduard Franzovich was asked to see Baron Kister, who gave his consent to a full *bénéfice* for the orchestra and chorus, in addition to the usual concert for the orchestra's benefit, and a bonus of 25 rubles to Vojaček for each performance. On both September 6 and 8 (during a rehearsal and a performance) the chorus and orchestra honored Eduard Franzovich for his unselfish assistance."—Andrei Rimsky-Korsakov.

matters surrounding you, you've remembered about Musinka the tru-
ant! My very own, little dove, only with the heart can one fathom the
invincible and indestructible power of your love for people, though
many (and I among them) are not entirely worthy of it.

The mailman has just brought your two letters, little dove. I am
giving you what you required, my own.

I am working a lot. The people's scene (among the *streltzi*) in *Khovanshchina* (Scene 3) has cooked up very successfully. I'll bring in on
the train everything I've written when I come on September 16 [her
name-day].

Your soul's and heart's
MUSINKA

Little dove, forget, if you can, but I implore you: forget all these
human inhumanities and, for the Lord's sake, take care of yourself, I
implore you.

184à. *VLADIMIR STASOV to ARSENI GOLENISHCHEV-KUTUZOV* [*Extract*]

October 2, 1876

. . . . Musoryanin has composed a lot of wonderful stuff this summer
and, besides, has lost all his fat and his red nose—and walks whole
versts . . .

185. *To ARSENI GOLENISHCHEV-KUTUZOV* 24

[Autumn? 1876]

My dear friend Arseni, I'll absolutely be there. How could I not be!

All yours,
MODESTE

When Boris Godunov *appeared on the Marinsky stage this season* 25
(*October 20—the thirteenth performance of* Boris), *brutal cuts made it
almost unrecognizable. Stasov lost no time in submitting an angry letter
of protest to the press.*

---

24 The quarrel over Golenishchev-Kutuzov's marriage is now past and forgotten.
25 Fyodor Stravinsky replaced Petrov in the role of Varlaam, and Leonova, returned from her world tour, sang the Hostess of the Inn.

185a. *VLADIMIR STASOV to the EDITOR of* Novoye Vremya *[Extract]*

. . . Our operas resemble chickens that can't defend themselves against a powerful cook. At any day and hour of his choice some Terenti or Pakhom has the right to catch the most talented Russian opera by the wings, chop off its legs or tail, cut its throat and cook a fricassee of his own invention. When Musorgsky's *Boris* was being considered, I remember hearing some profound connoisseurs saying with an important mien and with their customary aplomb, that the entire 5th act was quite superfluous, that it simply had to be cut off, or, at least, that it should be transposed, and played before the 4th act. O God, it was just like being in the kitchen! . . . Poor Glinka paid bitterly all his life for the famous "experience" of those who surrounded him. "Count Vielgorsky," says Glinka in his *Memoirs,* "made merciless cuts in *Ruslan* (after its first performances) and often in its best parts, saying with a self-satisfied air: Am I not a master at making *coupures!*" This self-satisfied air and merciless barbarity continue to this day . . . The other day all Petersburg saw with amazement that the entire 5th act of *Boris* had been discarded, and this without consulting or notifying anybody. One goes to hear an opera as it has been conceived and created by its author, and not as some manager thinks it should be! It may be objected: "Yes, but we have the author's consent, he himself approved the cut." Ah, don't speak to me of "consent!" While you hold the author in your claws, he'll consent to anything. He can't defend himself or protest, and when his entire opera may be removed from the calendar, he has no alternative but to consent. Not everyone has the fortitude of a Beethoven or a Schubert, not everyone is big enough to withdraw his work rather than have it mutilated . . .
[Printed in the issue of October 27, 1876]

Lies and Apologies

Later, when (I don't know by whose initiative) they began to omit the last act from performances of *Boris*—Musorgsky not only approved this cut, but was especially pleased with it. Agreeing with him that this last act was obviously superfluous in the development of the drama and that it had the appearance of something hastily pasted on at the end (as it actually was) I nevertheless regretted its complete omission because I found much that was good musically in it, and therefore I told Musorgsky that I would prefer to see this act moved forward, so that the arrival of the Pretender would precede Boris's death. Musorgsky argued against this opinion of mine and once said heatedly that a complete omission of this scene is required, not only by dramatic development and by theatrical conditions, but also by his—Musorgsky's—author's conscience. I was surprised and asked for an explanation.

"In this act," Musorgsky answered me, "and for the only time in my life, I lied about the Russian people. The mocking of the boyar by the Russian people—this is untrue, this is un-Russian. Infuriated people kill and execute, but they don't mock their victims."

I had to agree . . .[26]—ARSENI GOLENISHCHEV-KUTUZOV

186. *To ALEXANDER and MARIA MOROZOV,[27] Karevo*

KIND ALEXANDER STEPANICH AND MARIA MIKHAILOVNA,

For nearly a year now I've not pestered you to send me money but, on the strength of your last letter, I now ask you not to forget about me and to send me as much money as possible by December at the usual address: St. Petersburg, at the Sini Most, Forestry Department, Modeste Petrovich Musorsky.[28] Along with this tell me how the farming arrangement goes, in general, and why you are concerned about the land sales, for there's no reason for you to be disturbed about the land; if you see such reasons, let me know how you deduce them. Thus I bow to you and ask for the most detailed reply.

MODESTE MUSORSKY

26 November '76. St. Petersburg

186a. *ALEXANDER BORODIN to MODESTE MUSORGSKY*

[November 29, 1876]

Little dove, Modeste Petrovich, you were so kind to accept our invitation to participate in the concert of the 2nd of December for the benefit of our student body.

The bearer of this note—a deputy from the student body—will give you, together with mine, a request not to refuse your participation.

---

[26] "It is difficult to ascertain whether these or similar words were ever said by Musorgsky. But even if they were said, they do not express the genuine relation of the author toward this scene. From statements by Golenishchev-Kutuzov and others we know the softness, the instability of Musorgsky, who often fell under the influence of the person he happened to be speaking with, readily giving in to him. Accidentally, under the influence of a passing mood, he could throw out a phrase for which he would not hold himself responsible."—Yuri Keldysh.

[27] The Morozovs had rented the Karevo farm from the Musorgsky brothers.

[28] A relapse to Musorgsky's elegant version of his name.

The singers will be Menshikova, Kamenskaya, Paleček, Ende, Bichurina. A Schroeder piano. I press your hand. If necessary—dash off a word right away.

Your

A. BORODIN

Benefit Concert

. . . Without Musorgsky no charity concert, generally speaking, could take place. In the 70's the musical soirées organized each year by the student bodies of colleges and institutes for the benefit of their needy comrades were unthinkable without his participation.

Modeste Petrovich accompanied singers splendidly. He was himself as poor as Job, yet he never took any money for his work when charity was the object.

One winter I had to organize a concert for the benefit of medical students. Three weeks before the concert I flew about, the whole day, from one artist to another . . .

Though I boldly declared to all participants that their accompanist would be M. P. Musorgsky, which at once effected their consent, I must confess that unwillingly I was forced to lie to them.

The fact is that the author of *Boris Godunov* . . . was drinking heavily, so that asking him to assist in a concert three weeks ahead of its date, without knowing whether or not he would be in shape at that time, was useless. Although I knew he would consent I couldn't be sure that on the day of the concert he would not be so drunk that he couldn't recognize his own father.

Besides artists of the Russian Opera I was fortunate in obtaining, as a special favor, the splendid tenor of the Italian Opera, Ravelli, who was then singing at the Bolshoi Theater . . .

On the day before the concert Ravelli told me that he wished to meet his accompanist and asked me to bring him around next day for an early rehearsal,

Having gotten Musorgsky's consent the day before, happily finding him in a lucid period, I went to him once more to carry out Ravelli's commission.

But, to my horror, I found Musorgsky drunker than wine! In a mumbling voice he tried to assure me, speaking in French, for some reason, that it was no use going to the Italian, that he would manage everything, etc.

No persuasions or pleas of mine had any effect, and with the stubbornness of the drunken he went on saying: *"Non, monsieur, non; maintenant c'est impossible. Ce soir je serai exacte."*

At that time Musorgsky lived in a small, slovenly room. On the dirty table stood some vodka and some scraps of miserable food.

In saying good-by to me he got up with difficulty, but saw me to the door and bowed me out in a manner which, though not quite worthy of Louis XIV, was quite amazing for anyone so completely "tight," saying: *"Donc à ce soir!"*

351

So I went back to my tenor and told him that I hadn't found Musorgsky at home . . .

In the meantime I located one of my colleagues who agreed to stand guard over Musorgsky and bring him to the concert in plenty of time.

Sure enough, Modeste Petrovich showed up promptly at 7 at Kononov's hall where the concert was to take place.

Musorgsky, unfortunately, remained long enough in the greenroom to sample all the drinks on the table there, growing drunker and drunker. Suddenly my Italian tenor, after trying some runs, decided that his voice was a little strained and would therefore be compelled to sing his entire program a half or even a whole tone lower than usual.

This was all we needed.

I rushed to Musorgsky to ask him whether he could do this *Kunststück* for Ravelli. Rising from his chair with a certain gallantry, Musorgsky calmed me with the words: *"Pourquoi pas?"* (apparently Musorgsky spoke only French with cultured people, even when he was drunk).

To prove his assuring words he suggested that the tenor at once run through his whole program *mezza-voce*.

Musorgsky, who was probably hearing all Ravelli's Italian stuff for the first time, so charmed the Italian with his refined performance and his ability to transpose to any key that the tenor embraced him, saying repeatedly: *"Che artista!"* . . . —VASILI BERTENSSON

187. *To VLADIMIR STASOV*

Vas. Ostr. 5th line, No. 10
[December 25, 1876]

MY DEAR *généralissime*,

I have a petition to place before you. On the corner of Nevsky Prospect and that square where the Mikeshin bell [29] is always about to fall, there is a building [the Public Library], and on the roof of that building sits Minerva. Good friends of mine wish to get inside that building and furthermore, into that very department where Your Grace holds sway. I have the honor to introduce my friends: Maria Izmailovna Fyodorova (it is under this lady's hospitable roof that Musoryanin lives), Pavel Alexandrovich Naumov, little Sergei Naumov —in other words, the family where this sinner is cherished. As you, my dear, have never denied people your shining love and keen knowledge, I, Musoryanin, ask you, but only if it doesn't in the least inconvenience you, to arrange this visit to you at the Library on Monday, December 27. I should like to be with my friends when they come to

[29] Mikeshin's monument to Catherine the Great.

you; without you, it's always so cold and not quite the same under Minerva. If possible, write me two lines [about this].

And now: I begin to feel rested and, consequently, work is boiling.

You know that before *Boris* I did some folk scenes. My present desire—is to make a prognostication, and here it is—this prognostication: *true to life* and not melodic in the classical sense. I'm working with human speech; I've arrived at a sort of melody created by this speech, I've arrived at an embodiment of recitative into melody (aside from dramatic movements, *bien entendu,* where one may even make interjections possible) I should like to call it intelligently justified melody. And this work pleases me; suddenly, unexpectedly and ineffably, something different from classic melody (so beloved) but at once understandable by everyone and everybody, will be sung. If I achieve this—I will consider it a conquest in art, and it must be achieved. I should like to do a few scenes as a test. However, there are already some examples of this in embryo in *Khovanshchina* (Marfa's grief before Dosifei) and in *Sorochintzi*—both are mapped out.` *V[otre]. S[erviteur].*

I bow to you, *généralissime.*

Your

MUSORYANIN

A few more words. During this time, willed by motives that were inexplicable to me, I have acted in our way, *dans les plus hauts rangs* and I have conquered a good field of battle for art. The position is entrenched. I've become tired, but my work is *irrevocable,* this I guarantee.

THE SAME MUSORYANIN

188. *To LUDMILA SHESTAKOVA*

Little dove of mine, dear Ludmila Ivanovna, you alone with your wonderfully loving heart have recognized what your Musinka has succeeded in doing in art during the past season. To what extent I have done any real service for art, I don't know; I haven't rested yet and my ideas are all wandering; but I feel that I have done something righteous, and irrevocable. You alone, and only you, little dove, have given me the consolation of completely understanding me. I have only just realized that I was tired to death. My kindest thanks to

you, dear, for the announcement of the concert of Yu. F. Platonova.[30]
How good you are, little dove of ours, Ludmila Ivanovna. Very soon
I'll come around to look upon you, dear.

Your
MUSINKA

December 25, 1876

Pugachovshchina

. . . How curious it would be to find out that Musorgsky intended
to write, after *Khovanshchina* was completed, an opera on "Pugachov's Men." We had many discussions about this and traces of these
intentions remain in our correspondence.[31] Musorgsky planned, to a
certain extent, to base this on Pushkin's story "The Captain's Daughter," but later to add to his creation many other new elements. In
one of the acts of the opera the following scene was to appear: Pugachov on the porch, surrounded by his comrades, aides and a whole
pack of wild, unruly freebooters, Asiatic and Russian, and alongside, Father Gerasim (from Pushkin's story) standing with crucifix
in hand, in poor country vestments, barefoot and shivering with
fright . . .[32]—VLADIMIR STASOV

189. *A Sketch [A Folk-Melody Transcribed by Musorgsky, with This Inscription:]*

Pashino, 17 April '77. For the last opera, Pugachov's Men.

190. *A Scenario for* Fair at Sorochintzi [33]

Orchestral prelude. A hot day in Little Russia.

Act 1.

1. Fair (chorus)
2. Entrance of the Lad [Gritzko] with his comrades (allusion to Parasya and Khivrya).
3. The Carter [Cherevik] and Parasya (details—wheat—beads).

[30] Platonova's farewell concert on February 17, 1877.
[31] Not in Musorgsky's—perhaps in Stasov's lost letters to Musorgsky.
[32] This is an unaltered description of Vasili Perov's painting, *Pugachov's Justice*, painted in 1873.
[33] Compare Musorgsky's scenario with Gogol's story.

4. Choral scene of peddlers about the Red Jacket—out of this must come a scene of the 4: the Godfather and the Carter, *Parasya and the Lad.*
5. A little later, Cherevik interferes in the matter between Parasya and the Lad. Recitative scene of recognition between the Lad and Cherevik (tavern). N.B. From the opposite side the gypsy watches the scene.
6. Entrance of Khivrya—scene with Cherevik (the Lad witnesses this scene). Khivrya leads her husband away.
7. The Lad in grief. Appearance of the gypsy (terms for the *oxen* on Parasya's account).
8. Hopak.

Act 2. N.B. Intermezzo?
(the Godfather's hut)

1. Cherevik sleeps. Khivrya wakes him. (Conversation on domestic affairs, but this is mostly to drive her spouse out of the house.)
2. Khivrya's recitatives—*cooking*—appearance of Afanasy Ivanovich. *Duettino.*
3. All come in from the fair. Tale of the Red Jacket. *Grande scène comique.*

Act 3.

1. Night. Rumpus (with a *Präludium*—maybe the gypsy)—after running away from the Red Jacket, the Godfather and Cherevik fall down in exhaustion—screams about theft of the horse and oxen. Arrest of the pair. Comic conversation of the arrested pair. The Lad saves them.
2. The Lad sings a dumka.
3. Nearly dawn. Parasya comes out into the garden. Dumka. Thought of Khivrya—independence—triumph—stomping.
4. Cherevik and Parasya—a dance.
5. The Godfather and the Lad roar with laughter—the wedding is arranged. (Talk of Khivrya's greediness.)
6. Finale.

19 May 1877, at the home of A. Y. and O. A. Petrov in Petrograd.

191. *To ARSENI GOLENISHCHEV-KUTUZOV*

[5–6 June, 1877]

DEAR FRIEND ARSENI,

I can't come today, but tomorrow I'll come straight from the office, and not alone, but with our "field marshal." [84]

Your

MUSORGSKY

192. *To DIMITRI STASOV, St. Petersburg*

Tzarskoye Selo. New Places
Zhukovsky's *dacha*, No. 7
14–15 June, '77

Dearest Dimitri Vasilyevich, from the core of my brain to the ventricle of my heart am I grateful to you for your most kind sympathy for Modestus Musoryanin. And I, in order not to waste valuable time, armed myself with my pen and wrote No. 4 of the macabres, i.e., death as a field-marshal, and that's how I entitled it—"Field Marshal." And now, torn by the office, I gather my shreds together in the evening and write a Jewish chorus *Jesus Navinus* [*Joshua*],[85] which if you recall—at one of the art soirées in your home, was acknowledged by the wonderful Mme. la Baronne Anna Hinzbourg [Gunzbourg] as *authentique*. And then my opera will also spring up. We shall fly to Zamaniłovka; how could it be otherwise? God knows what would have happened if Musoryanin had not suddenly seen your dearest family in the dearest little nest and had not breathed, nor talked with you on fine topics in the Zamanilovka garden. By the end of June I will present the 4th macabre and perhaps by that time *Jesus Navinus* will have completely conquered the Canaanite so hated by him, and will also present himself for your judgment: *si vous voulez bien me donner la permission.*

---

[84] A fourth number for the cycle, *Songs and Dances of Death*—dated "Tzarskoe Selo, 5 June, year 1877," the date of this letter, and dedicated to its author. Musorgsky had composed another song to a poem by him, "The Vision," dated "6 April, year 1877. S. Petersburg," and dedicated to Yelizaveta Andreyevna Gulevich, sister of Countess Golenishcheva-Kutuzova.

[85] The chorus of *Joshua* is largely a reworking of the "War-Song of the Lybians" from *Salammbô*, with additions, chiefly a new middle section, based on Mâtho's lament in Act IV of *Salammbô*. This reworking was done in 1874–75 but the manuscript is dated "Tzarskoe Selo, 2 July 1877," and is dedicated to Nadezhda Rimskaya-Korsakova.

In regard to publishing my little musical sins, I would evaluate the rights on this edition in this manner: for the macabres—150 rubles and for the three by Count Tolstoy,[36] 50 rubles—making a total of 200 rubles.

Once more I thank you from the soul, dearest Dimitri Vasilyevich. I ask you to proffer my sincere greetings to the little dove of a lady and don't forget to tell the children that Musoryanin loves them very much.

Your

MUSORYANIN

P.S. If it's difficult to add the 4th macabre—as you have written Jurgenson [37] about the 3 macabres that you know, and you haven't mentioned a fourth, of which you've heard only hints, then you may leave it as 3 macabres without the "Field Marshal" and in that case the price would be 120 rubles for the 3 macabres and for Count Tolstoy's 3—50 rubles = 170 rubles. But I should like to have all 4 macabres published: the "Field Marshal," in my opinion, is not worse than the "Peasant" ["Trepak"]. In any case I completely submit to your view on this matter and once more I thank you heartily, dearest Dimitri Vasilyevich.

All yours,

MUSORYANIN

193. *To LUDMILA SHESTAKOVA*

14–15 June, 1877. Tzarskoye Selo

Little dove, my dear Ludmila Ivanovna, each line of your wonderful letter has the sound of a dear friend, of a kindred heart. You care for and caress your Musinka a little, perhaps, not quite according to his deserts; but all the more strongly will Musinka approach his beloved, his chosen cause of Russian music, in order to master this cause

---

[36] Musorgsky's songs to poems by Alexei Tolstoy have always been a group of *five*, unless Musorgsky intended to omit two for publication. They are all dated within a single month, 1877—(1) March 4–5, (2) March 9, (3) March 15–16, (4) March 20, and (5) March 21. The first is dedicated to Fyodor Ardalionovich Vanlyarsky, the third to Anatoli Yevgrafovich Palchikov, and the fifth to Olga Andreyevna Golenishcheva-Kutuzova. See full listing in Appendix.

[37] Dimitri Stasov was acquainted with Josif Jurgenson, head of the Petersburg branch of this music publishing house, but it was with Piotr Jurgenson, in Moscow, that these abortive negotiations were being conducted.

and not live uninvited in the world of light. The most precious to me—is your visit tomorrow to A[nna] I[vanovna] Gr[omov]a at her *dacha:* a better greeting, dear little dove of mine, I not only could not wish for, but with all my powers I should have forbidden you to act otherwise—how many times have I begged you to take care of yourself for us, for the cause of music, for you yourself—in other words, for everything that is precious and near to me. And there, fortunately, on this day (of which you deigned to remind me) I am happy that my ardent wishes are realized and that my little dove Ludmila Ivanovna will breathe a little good fresh air and, perhaps, or surely, this will benefit her. There in this "with benefit to myself, for my health" is the substance of everything, as Tredyakovsky is ready to exclaim: "Let's gaily dance with our feet and link our arms!" Good little dove of mine, get into the open air more often, more often, as often as you can—further away from Peter: I implore you, don't be afraid of returning to the capital's air. The more you store up your forces in the clean air, the more good you'll do yourself. Get into the open air more often—once again I implore you. And on June 22 I am yours, straight from the office, without the slightest doubt, and I am so happy that I shall be talking things over with Dyainka. Perhaps P. A. Lodi [38] may also come (*si vous souffrez la musique, Madame*); and then I would bring with me, *just now composed by me,* "Field Marshal" (for tenor), and under your warm wings we would see: "What sort of thing is this?"

Your devoted
MUSINKA

P.S. May I ask you, little dove, to give Dimitri Vasilyevich Stasov the [enclosed] letter [No. 192] about my musical affairs.

In addition: I wrote Dimitri Vasilyevich about the price for my music pieces after receiving from him a very kind letter along with yours, little dove. Making use of the information supplied by you, that you are seeing Dimitri Vasilyevich on Thursday, I ask you, little dove, to give him the letter addressed to him, for this means will be faster and surer than postal delivery. I'm leaving both letters to you and to Dimitri Vasilyevich at your home personally. If P. A. Lodi would tire you, little dove, on June 22, then I beg you to cancel this

---

[38] Piotr Alexeyevich Lodi, tenor, was to join the staff of the Marinsky Theater in the following year. His father, also a tenor, had been a friend of Glinka.

business. You and Dyainka and I will ourselves try out the "Field Marshal."

Your
MUSINKA

193a. *VLADIMIR STASOV to ARSENI GOLENISHCHEV-KUTUZOV, Shubino [Extract]*

July 31, 1877

. . . Have heard hardly anything of Musarion, except certain scraps, and even they are rare, rumors from the "wretched old woman" (in the words of Brédif's friend): [39] yet it is said that he has composed and even has written out an excellent scene for Khivra [in *Fair at Sorochintzi*]. True or not—I don't know a thing . . .

194. *To ARSENI GOLENISHCHEV-KUTUZOV, Shubino*

Dear friend Arseni, you've sent me a little more, so therefore until our first meeting I am your debtor for this bit.[40] And I, dear friend, have so plunged into *Sorochintzi*, that if the Lord would help me to carry on this matter further under the same conditions, then I should think that season after next we'll both be able to decide: is this *Fair at Sorochintzi* a good or a bad opera? I started right off, not with the 1st act, whose scenic structure requires more concentration and freedom (I haven't gotten my leave yet), but with the 2nd act, i.e., with the kernel of the whole opera. This act (2nd), as you'll remember, follows hard upon the *Intermezzo* (Witches' Sabbat on Bald Mountain;—which will be called "Dream of the Young Peasant Lad"). The scenes of Khivra and Cherevik, of Khivra and the Priest's Son are already written, and I've even had time to bring in the godfather with Cherevik and the guests—this is all written; now I advance towards the kernel: the tale of the Red Jacket.[41] The problem is an excessively difficult one. You know, friend, that your modest Modeste cannot help seeking out in the author whom he dares to reproduce musically, that which may elude the feeling and attention of a less modest musician. This isn't my first encounter with Gogol (*Marriage*) and, therefore,

---

[39] It is Shestakova who is characterized as the "wretched old woman" by Shcherbachov, also, apparently, interested in Brédif's spiritualist manifestations.

[40] This may be a new poem by Golenishchev-Kutuzov, or some of his work on the text of the "Tale of the Red Jacket," for *Sorochintzi*.

[41] See Scenario on pp. 354-355.

359

his capricious prose frightens me no longer; but *Marriage* is only the humble exercise of a musician, or rather, a non-musician, who wishes to study and grasp the twistings of human speech in that spontaneous true exposition which is the means used by that greatest genius Gogol. *Marriage* was an étude for a chamber trial. With a large stage it is necessary for the speeches of the *characters,* each according to his nature, habits and "dramatic inevitability," to be conveyed to the audience in bold relief,—it is necessary to construct so that the audience will easily sense all the artless peripeteia of urgent human affairs, at the same time making these artistically interesting. Imagine, my dear friend, that what you read in the speeches of Gogol's *characters,* must be delivered from the stage to us in musical speech by my *characters, without any alterations* contrary to Gogol's intention. Many ordeals are required, many wearisome thirstings to take by storm a citadel which has scared off, apparently, all musicians; but when one is able to capture even the smallest lunette of this impregnable citadel—one somehow takes wing and the soul grows joyful: one wants so much to disclose truth to people—if only one had the time to disclose the tiniest fragment of this truth! And how great Gogol is! The delight I experienced during the musical exposition of Pushkin (in *Boris*) is reborn during the musical exposition of Gogol (in *Sorochintzi*). Pushkin wrote *Boris* in dramatic form, but not for the stage; Gogol wrote "The Fair at Sorochintzi" in the form of a story—and, of course, not for the stage. But both giants with their creative power projected so subtly the contours of scenic action that all one has to do is to apply the colors. But woe to him whose whim it is to use Pushkin or Gogol for his only text. You know me, friend, by those artistic works of yours over which your modest Modeste labored; your modest friend hasn't changed in his relations with Gogol. As only the *genuine, sensitive* nature of an artist can create in the realm of the word, the musician must maintain a very "polite" attitude towards the creation, in order to penetrate into its very substance, into the very *essence* of that which the musician intends to embody in musical form. *The genuine, truly artistic* cannot be anything but capricious, because *independently* it cannot easily be embodied in another artistic form, because it is *independent* and demands profound study and sacred love. But when artistic kinship between workers in different fields of art does work out— it's a fine trip! You know this, Your Highness—do not deign to be angry.

Musorgsky
A drawing by Alexandrovsky, made in 1876

Musorgsky

A portrait by Ilya Repin, painted on March 2, 3, 4, and 5, 1881, at the Military Hospital

There you have, dear friend of mine Arseni, my present affairs! In regard to publication in Mother Russia, there's something peculiar. At first Mr. Jurgenson *expressed pleasure* in the proposition of publishing the Macabres, and then became stubbornly silent. But here is something pleasant for us, friend: at L. I. Shestakova's, Lodi twice sang your most marvelous "Field Marshal." (I am obliged to report to Your Highness that *everyone* to whom I read it *palpitates with rapture* over the "Field Marshal"). You can't possibly clearly imagine, dear friend, the amazing distinction of your scene when it is rendered by a tenor! You hear in it some transfixion, some inexorable, death-like love! To be more exact: death, coldly passionately in love with death, enjoys death. The novelty of its impression is heretofore unheard! And with what talent P. A. Lodi was able to feel your wonderful scene!—he is a real artist-singer. Yes, after the war! . . .

I forgot to inform you, friend, that I've written a Biblical scene *Jesus Navinus [Joshua]*, entirely according to the Bible and even following the route of the victorious marches of Navinus through Canaan. This little piece is based on themes which you already know, but you won't recognize it, that is, you will recognize that your modest Modeste has approached the work with the intention of mastering its content.

So here in all my entirety I stand before you, my dear friend. I further add, that in *Sorochintzi* the tale of the red jacket is the finale of the 2nd act; meaning that shortly, with the help of the Lord, one act of *Sorochintzi* will be done; and the scenario of the whole is ready—this is important and, extremely important—with the kindest help of the genius of A. Ya. Vorobiova-Petrova.

My dear friend, kindly give my heartfelt greeting to the Countess Olga Andreyevna and to Countess *maman:* from all my soul I thank them for their kind remembrance of me. How are the colts belonging to the little dove of a Countess? Are the tiny ones well?—I've fallen in love with them just from your reports of them. I don't dare guarantee—whether I can visit you, dear friend of mine, and your dearest family, in Shubino. As soon as they grant me a leave, I'll write you immediately, How and What.

I embrace you heartily, friend Arseni.

Your

MODESTE

Aug. 15, '77. Tzarskoye Selo

194a. *VLADIMIR STASOV to ARSENI GOLENISHCHEV-KUTUZOV, Shubino [Extracts]*

August 22, 1877

. . . It's sometimes dangerous to tell people the truth!! Perhaps some day you also will tear me to shreds! What's strange about it: there was a time when Musarion entirely broke with me, and for what reason?— . . . And besides, I've heard absolutely nothing of Musarion this whole summer: only once Shcherbachov's "wretched old woman" said that he [Musorgsky] has written some scene for Khivrya and something else, but that all this was *terribly mediocre and pale*, like this whole unfortunate Little-Russian undertaking so far, incited by the foolishness of Anna and Osip [the Petrovs], Russia's Rosciuses . . .

November 7, 1877

. . . You are imagining things in vain about Musarion, he holds absolutely nothing against you, and he doesn't reply because he has the usual laziness and slovenliness of an artist. He has written a lot of *rubbish* for *The Fair at Soroch.* this summer, but after everyone's attacks (especially mine), has now decided to throw it all away, leaving only the good stuff. But now during the last few weeks he has written 2 splendid gypsy choruses (also for it), and one of them is a women's chorus "with clapping and whistling"—simply a *chef d'oeuvre* . . .

195. *To ARSENI GOLENISHCHEV-KUTUZOV, Shubino*

MY DEAR FRIEND ARSENI,

You may be quite angry with me; change your wrath to mercy. I have been thoroughly upset by a nervous fever, for almost 20 days and nights I didn't close my eyes and I was in such gloom that it would have been sinful to write you then, especially after your last letter about rural affairs and about what one has to live through in this endlessly transient situation of Russian economy. And too, friend, you made me hesitate slightly in having this chat with you by the news of your plans to go to Moscow late in the fall to arrange for *Shuisky*. But now I've learned from Katenin and Stasov that one can and should address you at Shubino. So I've taken paper and pen to talk with you, friend. I'll start from the fact that during the first display of the 2nd act of *Sorochintzi* I became convinced of the basic lack of understanding of Little-Russian humor by the musical sages of the disintegrated "heap": such a frost exuded from their opinions and demands, that "the heart did freeze," as Archpriest Avvakum says. Nevertheless I have stopped, fallen into thought and more than once I've tested myself. After resting from this hard work over myself I will resume work on *Sorochintzi*. It cannot be that I have been wholly wrong in my intentions, it cannot be so. But it's too bad that one is obliged to talk with the musical sages of the disintegrated "heap," over the "barrier" behind which they remain. However, the Little-Russians fervently beg me to bring *Sorochintzi* quickly to the stage; I am nearly certain that my novelty is close to their hearts. No matter what has happened I haven't been dozing and I've prepared some decent materials for further along; and it looks as though the best thing is to go on working and writing. If you'd like a sample of the many pronouncements of the aforesaid musical sages, here's one: "The text uses a common, everyday prose, so insignificant that it's almost laughable, but in the music all these people are very serious—attaching some sort of importance to their speeches." Curious, isn't it? Gogol's humor consists in embodying the insignificant—for us—interests of the [Ukrainian] carters and village shopkeepers in fully sincere truth. *Sorochintzi* is no bouffonade, but a genuine comic opera based on Russian music and is, chronologically, the first of its kind. How well these musical sages understand the substance of comedy! It wasn't so very long ago that "Savishna" and the "Seminarist" evoked laughter until a certain person explained to the musical sages that both these little scenes have a tragic base. "Varlaam and Misail" (in *Boris*) evoke laughter until they appear in the "tramps" scene [Kromy]; it then is realized what dangerous beasts these seemingly funny people are. I am sure that you, friend, will see praise in the quoted pronouncement of the "heap-ist," but believe me, friend, that this pronouncement was uttered as a harsh remark about basic faults in the opera. Someone said: what luck Musorgsky always has—no matter what musical enterprise he undertakes, wild disputes immediately begin. All the better; life is given to us to be lived, and art lives and grows only in struggle with the Sadducees who plan to make of it something like a 2nd edition of the Talmud,—high priests of fallen idols! renowned Sisyphi!

My dear, don't punish me, but console me with a missive about yourself and how you're getting on, about your works and your artistic dreams, about everything. I have, as you see, moved on with my pen to another sheet of paper; meaning—that I'm not lazy, friend. See how I boast. Are we going to see each other this winter season? How fine it would be to go, if not to "the chilly Finnish rocks," then at least to the coast of Ingermanland; perhaps the Muse herself will agree to such an excursion; she is a rather capricious lady and her shrewish nature shows itself occasionally. However, you are on splendid terms with Lady Muse and consequently you yourself will agree to her favorite request if such a request does come from her. But truly, it would be fine if we could see each other. Everything can't be written in a letter: according to Tredyakovsky—"This is no work for mere men"; talking face to face is quite a different matter. Aside from talking, haven't we sinners the right to be introduced to your new works? I even dare to be sure that the Countess Olga Andreyevna will also not complain because of my good wish to see you this winter in the northern capital. New grass has appeared here, and there are new buds on the trees; it seems that the gap left by the continuous cold of the summer is being filled, according to the law of averages, by a warmish and intolerable November; this dusky warmth treads on the nerves. Bruce's calendar stubbornly goes on predicting a bitter winter; how good that would be, it's about time to get out the sleighs.

I beg you, friend, to deliver my soul's greetings to the Countess Olga Andreyevna and to Countess *maman*.

In the absolute expectation of a meeting, I firmly embrace you, dear friend. Send me a missive.

Your

MODESTE MUSORGSKY

November 10, 1877. P-bg.

195a. *PIOTR TCHAIKOVSKY to NADEZHDA VON MECK, Moscow* [42]

San Remo
24 December, 1877—5 January, 1878

. . . All the new Petersburg composers are very talented, but they are all permeated by horrible presumptuousness and a wholly amateur conviction of superiority to all other musicians in the universe.

---

[42] Madame von Meck has written Tchaikovsky for his opinion of the "nationalist" group of Petersburg composers. This extract from his reply is translated by Sonya Volochova.

The sole exception is Rimsky-Korsakov. Like the others, he is self-taught. Recently, however, he has undergone a sharp turn. By nature he is very earnest, very honest, and conscientious. As a mere youth he fell into society that first convinced him that he was a genius and then told him that *study* isn't necessary, that schools kill inspiration and dry up creative power, etc. At first he believed it. His earliest compositions showed a striking ability and a lack of theoretical training. In his circle they were all in love with themselves and with each other. Each attempted to imitate one or another composition which came from the circle, proclaimed by them to be a masterpiece. As a result the whole group soon sank into a dull mire of uniformity of method, affectation, and lack of distinction. Korsakov is the only one among them who discovered, five years ago, that the doctrines propagated by his circle were without reasonable basis, and its contempt of the schools, of classical music, its hatred of authority and of models, were just ignorance. I have kept a letter of his written during this period. It both agitated and moved me deeply. He was in despair at the sudden realization of the many years he had wasted, the many years during which he had followed a path that led nowhere. What shall I do? he asked himself. The obvious answer was that one must study, and he began to study with such zeal that academic technique soon became indispensable to him. In one single summer he wrote sixty-four fugues in addition to an incredible number of contrapuntal exercises. Ten of the fugues he sent to me for approval. Though faultless in their way, the fugues showed me that the transition from one type of writing to its opposite had been too violent. From contempt of the schools, he went over abruptly to the cult of musical technique. Shortly after that, his symphony and quartet appeared. Though both works are full of tricks, they bear the stamp, as you so justly observe, of dry pedantry. At present he appears to be passing through a crisis, and it is difficult to foresee how this crisis will end. Either he will turn out a great master or he will be completely swallowed up in contrapuntal complexities. *Cui* is a talented dilettante. His music is graceful and elegant, but lacks originality. It is too coquettish, too smooth, and therefore it pleases at first hearing, then one tires of it. The reason for this is to be found in the fact that Cui is a musician only by avocation. Professionally he is a professor of fortification and is very busy lecturing in practically every military school in Petersburg. He has himself confessed to me that he cannot compose without first picking out little melodies on the keys, accompanied by little chords. Once he comes across a pretty little idea, he fusses with it a long time, embellishes and adorns and greases it in every way, and all this takes a lot of time. It took him ten years, for instance, to write his opera *Ratcliff*. Nevertheless, I repeat, he undoubtedly has talent; at least he has taste and foresight. *Borodin* is a fifty-year-old professor of chemistry at the Academy of Medicine. He, too, has talent, great talent even, but a talent that has perished because of lack of knowledge and a blind *fate* which led him to the lecture platform of a chemistry class instead of to a living musical activity. He has not so much taste as *Cui* and his technique is so poor that he cannot compose a single measure without help. *Musorgsky* you are quite correct in characterizing as hopeless. His talent is perhaps the most remarkable of all these. But he has a narrow nature, is totally devoid of desire for self-improvement, and is deluded by a blind faith in the absurd theories of his circle and in his own genius. In addition he has some sort of low nature which loves all that is coarse, crude, and rough. He is, in short, the direct antithesis of his friend *Cui*, who, though he swims in the shallows, is at any rate always decorous and graceful, whereas Musorgsky coquets with his illiteracy and takes pride in his ignorance, rolling along, blindly believing in the infallibility of his genius. But he has a real, and even original, talent which flashes out now and then. The most important personality of the circle is *Balakirev*. But he has become silent, after having done very little. The great talent of this man has perished because of some fatal circumstances which have turned him to extreme piety after long having taken pride in complete atheism. Today Balakirev practically lives in church. He is continually fasting, preparing himself for the sacrament, and genuflecting to the relics of the saints, and nothing more. His great talent notwithstanding, he has been the cause of much harm. For example, he ruined Korsakov by convincing him that study is harmful. In fact, he is the inventor of all the theories of this strange circle, which contains in its midst so many undeveloped, misdirected, or prematurely decayed forces.

This then is my frank opinion of this group. What a sad phenomenon! So many talented men from whom, except for Korsakov, we hardly dare expect anything serious. But is it not always thus in Russia? Vast forces impeded by the fatal shadow of a Plevna [43] from taking

---

[43] Plevna was a Bulgarian town held by the Turks and taken by the Russians, after a prolonged siege, on the night of November 27, 1877.

the open field and fighting as they should. All the same, however, the forces exist. A Musorgsky, for all his ugliness, speaks a new language. Beautiful it may not be, but it is fresh. So this is why we may expect Russia some day to produce a whole Pleiad of forceful talents who will open up new paths for art. Our ugliness is, at any rate, better than the pitiful impotence, masked as serious creative power, of Brahms and other Germans. They are irreparably evaporated. With us, one must hope that *Plevna* will fall and our strength will make itself felt. So far, however, very little has been accomplished. In France, on the other hand, there are strong progressive forces. Berlioz, it is true, is only now, ten years after his death, beginning to be performed. Nevertheless, many a new talent and many an energetic warrior has entered the fight against *routine*. It is difficult to wage such a fight in France, for in art the French are terribly conservative. They were the last of all to recognize *Beethoven*. As late as the forties he was still considered a hare-brained eccentric, no more, and only twenty-five years ago, Fétis, the foremost French critic of the time, regretted that Beethoven made errors (?) against the rules of harmony and never failed to correct Beethoven's mistakes. Among contemporary French composers my favorites are Bizet and Delibes. I am not acquainted with the *Patrie* overture about which you write, but Bizet's *Carmen* I know well. The music does not pretend to be profound, but it is so charming in its simplicity, so vital, so spontaneous and sincere, that I have practically memorized every note of it from beginning to end. Concerning Delibes I have already written you. In their aspirations toward novelty, the French are not as daring as our innovators. But they don't transcend the limits of the possible as Borodin and Musorgsky do . . .

Grandpa Petrov

. . . We sat with him [Musorgsky] on a little green divan opposite the coffin of the dearly beloved "grandpa," O. A. Petrov [who died on March 2, 1878], and talked in whispers about the terrible grief that had overtaken his friends, and about the inevitable consequences. Only then did I understand what a wonderful, gentle and loving soul Musorgsky had, how warmly he had loved Osip Afanasyevich and how crushed he was by his end. He sobbed inconsolably, convulsively and loudly over the coffin as only children can cry. After drinking a glass of water he recovered a little from his hysterics, sat down on the green divan and said in a voice broken with tears: "With the end of grandpa I have lost all. I have lost the support of my whole bitter life. Lately in this house I have felt like one of the family. I have lost an irreplaceable guide. He nourished me with artistic truth and inspired me to creativeness. Know—that in that coffin lies the fate of the whole scarcely blossomed Russian opera. From now on it will again be overgrown by foreign weeds, and for a long time they will stifle our green shoots. So it will be." These last words of M. P. were pronounced between clenched teeth in a deafening voice and again he broke into sobs . . . —NIKOLAI KOMPANEISKY

196. *To VLADIMIR STASOV*

March 22, 1878

MY DEAR *généralissime,*

I *have seen* the Archdeacon [44] whom our splendid Ilya Repin created. Yes, this is a whole fire-breathing mountain! and those Varlaam-like eyes seem to follow the spectator. What terrific-sized brush-strokes, what an abundant breadth! And that one—"From the Shy Ones"—a rascal, a peasant-bandit: the turned head and the in-human glance, guarantee that when he gets a chance, he'd wipe out ten human souls.

Your

MUSORYANIN

196a. *VLADIMIR STASOV to ARSENI GOLENISHCHEV-KUTUZOV* [*Extract*]

April 1, 1878

. . . The "wretched old woman" tells me that Musoryanin was at her home a few days ago, completely recovered and looking almost like a respectable person. God grant this, for I had already placed a cross over him and expected nothing more of him . . .

197. *To LUDMILA SHESTAKOVA*

Dear little dove of mine, Ludmila Ivanovna, on July 28, Friday, I will come straight from my duties to you, with a great desire to talk

---

[44] This painting and Repin's "From the Shy Ones" were in the sixth Itinerant Exhibition of the realist group of painters. On November 9, 1863, thirteen students of the Academy of Arts, headed by Kramskoy, refused to accept the mythological theme ("A Feast in Valhalla") offered by the Academy. These thirteen left the Academy and in 1870 formed the Society of Itinerant Exhibitions, to show their works throughout Russia.

with you, dear, about the many things bequeathed to us by the humble, truly great and glorious grandpa. How much was bequeathed, how many unforgettable and profoundly artistic things were taught us by dear grandpa!

Ever your
MUSINKA

I was at Mili's and I am in ecstasy; it's too bad that this week isn't convenient—I will write to dearest Mili, but on July 25, the day I received your letter, little dove, a nervous fever shook me—so I stayed in Peterhof and couldn't answer you, my own, immediately.

Once again thus your
MUSINKA

26 July, 1878

198. *To VLADIMIR STASOV, Paris* [45] *(A Collective Letter)*

28 July
1878

[from Modeste Musorgsky]

B e g i n n i n g

My dear *généralissime*, I have seen Mili and I am in ecstasy. Many good things were talked about, we went over many good things and above all the great artistic memory of our former affairs.

Meanwhile I can write only this, truthfully.

Your
MUSORYANIN

The 28th, 5 o'clock in the afternoon
  the day of the first appearance of
  Osip Afanasyevich Petrov on the stage [in 1830]

Turn over!

[from Mili Balakirev]

It so happened that today I too am at Ludm[ila] Iv[anovna's], who only recently told me of the receipt of your letter. I await impatiently your letter with the news of what has happened to my arrangement of *Harold*. Ludm. Iv. told me that Modinka had been at her place and even showed me his note to you. I will also tell you that I was pleasantly surprised by him as a person. No swagger or anything in the way

---

[45] There to see the *Exposition Universelle*. Among other errands, he had promised to arrange for the printing (at Brandus) of Balakirev's piano arrangement (four hands) of Berlioz's *Harold en Italie*.

of self-adoration; on the contrary he was very modest, listened seriously to what was said to him and didn't protest at all against the need for *knowing harmony*, didn't even jib at the suggestion that he should work at it with Korsinka. All this pleasantly—even *very, very pleasantly*—surprised me, and of course I was very delighted.—For the present (before autumn) I've set him to a good piece of work; he has taken from me the score of his *witches' sabbat* to revise and rewrite. There are such powerful and beautiful things in it that it would be a pity to leave it in its present disorder.

I will write after our 2nd meeting with him, and once more I give you my great thanks for the promise to stop in at Brandus and I firmly embrace you.

Your

M. BALAKIREV

July 28, 1878. 8:00 P.M.
at Ludm. Ivan.

[from Ludmila Shestakova]

July 28

I am sure you will be pleased to receive this letter, Musoryanin and Mili have written you, and what more could there be! Now to business:

(1) Thanks for the missive.

(2) And for the prompt mailing of the proofs to Röder, only I don't understand why you had the idea of writing to him, I'm afraid that Balakirev thought the whole thing up.[46] Please, if there's something to be written to Röder, better send it to me (Röder won't mind), and it will be better if he receives all letters from one place and *from me alone*. Yesterday I wrote him at Mili's request. I imagine you'll find this suitable. Mili promises to apply all his strength to get everything finished by my name-day, i.e., by September 16. Only I doubt this, even though Mili is working very diligently.

I often see Sonya [Medvedeva [47]] these days. She is happy about the

---

[46] Shestakova's dream of printing a true edition of *Ruslan and Ludmila* was finally being realized. Balakirev, Rimsky-Korsakov, and Lyadov had prepared the full score for publication by Röder, in Leipzig. Shestakova, however, had no intention of dividing authority in this matter with the recently resurrected Balakirev.

[47] The first husband of Stasov's illegitimate daughter, Sofia Vladimirovna, was Vasili Medvedev.

recuperation of her husband and she wanted to write to you today. I await your articles impatiently. I went in to the business-office of *Novoye Vremya*, took those issues that were on hand with articles of yours and requested that each issue in which an article of yours appears would be put aside for me. For now this *seems to be all*.[48]

Your

L. SHEST[AKOVA]

198a. *LUDMILA SHESTAKOVA to VLADIMIR STASOV, Paris [Extract]*

August 9, 1878

. . . In conclusion let us speak of a man close to you—that is, Musorgsky. All this while I was silent about him—because I did not want to distress you. For several days last week, almost continuously, he appeared at my house looking dreadful and stayed quite a long while; seeing that things were getting worse, I felt I had to do something, and in order to save him and to protect myself, I wrote him a letter, asking him not to call on me when suffering from his nervous irritation (as he calls it); I wrote him everything in the letter, but of course I put it as gently as I could, and so, yesterday evening, my dear Musinka appeared in *complete* order, and gave me his word never to distress me again. We shall see how things go, but for some time at least, I am certain that he will keep himself in hand. He asked me to tell you that he has composed a small scene in *Khovanshchina* between Marfa and Andrei which, he reckons, will satisfy you. It's too bad about Musorgsky, he's such a wonderful person! If there were only some way to pull him away from Naumov, I think he might be rescued definitely . . .

A Servant of Artists

A close friend of Balakirev's, Government Comptroller T[erti] I. Filippov, formerly a great expert on Russian folk-songs,[49] saved Musorgsky from starvation by getting him a post [on October 1, 1878] in the Government Control,[50] at which he [Filippov] became indulgent to the point of being unfair and even compromising himself, and as

---

[48] The close of Fyodor's parrot story in *Boris*.

[49] Forty Russian folk-songs recorded by Rimsky-Korsakov from Filippov's memory were harmonized by Rimsky-Korsakov and published in 1882.

[50] On the notice of Musorgsky's transfer from the Forestry Department to Government Control, there is a scribbled remark by his former chief: "Very glad!"

371

his superior, he forgave Musorgsky absolutely anything, though the latter did no work and very often arrived in a state of intoxication after sleepless nights. Terti Ivanovich never reprimanded him for it, and admitting his indulgent attitude, said: "I am the servant of artists."—NIKOLAI LAVROV

198b. *MILI BALAKIREV to VLADIMIR STASOV* [Extract]

October 13, 1878

. . . Musorgsky is such a physical wreck that he can hardly become more of a corpse than he is at present . . .

199. *To ARSENI GOLENISHCHEV-KUTUZOV*

to Count Arseni Golenishchev-Kutuzov
from Modeste Musorgsky.

Coming just as your drama *Tzar Vasili Shuisky* is to be artistically embodied [in print], your friendly thought to dedicate this work of art *to me, sinner that I am,* caressed me. I now pester as I've never pestered before. Yesterday's séance has confirmed me in the justice of the cause. Your sincere relationship to historical events, your insight into the old chronicles, your sincerity, and the warmth and vitality that comes from this, embodying historical figures and events—all this moves me with great love for your powers.—It seems to me that your field for artistic work is—history, the chronicles of Russia. It looks as though, "in our time, when and so forth," as Dobroliubov loved to jest, the study of history, and its communication in artistic forms are jobs required both by the creative instinct of an artist and by Russian society. Understand: *contemporary novels* were written in a period when *nothing was being undertaken,* but we sinners *live in the interval* between the undertaking of certain measures and their repression. Is a modern novel possible where the relation of an individual towards human society *et vice versa* is one way today, and tomorrow—as They may decree? Only something permanent (to a certain time) can give an artist *a certain figure out of a total of events;* otherwise—this artistic figure, in order to be artistic, must portray something like a *"tour de Babel."*—If you, dear friend, should take up a new drama, a hitherto *unheard-of subject—the life-campaign-*

ers! [51] There's plenty of material—plenty to work with. Do it—talk it over and discuss it with Stasov Vladimir, and I (if I'm still alive) will do an opera [of it]. Only don't think that I'm pushing you toward history on this account; No! but it would be pleasant and fine to go to work on the basis of your creative ideas. Let's hope so!!—Only do it quite independently, *as it should be done,* and don't think of me.

Your

MOD. MUSORGSKY

Come to us today, November 14—whenever you wish.

200. *To LUDMILA SHESTAKOVA*

Dear little dove of mine, Ludmila Ivanovna, yes, I was very ill; only now am I beginning to get well. I'm afraid that the doctor [52] will not let me out on Friday—however, I feel a great deal better today. *Who could dare forget the 8th of this month?* [53]

Your

MUSINKA

November 24, '78

200a. *ARSENI GOLENISHCHEV-KUTUZOV to VLADIMIR STASOV*
[Extract]

December 19, 1878

. . . Thanks to you, *Unrest* has been printed quite satisfactorily,[54] as I already wrote you, but what distresses me is that Blagosvetlov did not carry out my request to print on the title page that it is dedicated to Musorgsky! This is positively shameful. How many years I sweated over this drama based on Modeste Petrovich's idea with the hope of

---

[51] The "life-campaigners" were a company of grenadiers in the Preobrazhensky Regiment, formed by the Empress Elizabeth on her ascension to the throne. This company was put into the field by Catherine against Pugachov's rebellion—and this may account for Musorgsky's special interest in this subject at this time.

[52] It is assumed that this doctor was Lev Bertensson, as Shestakova later presented this letter to him. Dr. Bertensson was also the personal physician of Piotr Tchaikovsky and Lev Tolstoy.

[53] Day of the Archangel Michael—Glinka's name-day.

[54] *Unrest* is the final title for Golenishchev-Kutuzov's "dramatic chronicle in five acts," formerly called *Tzar Vasili Ivanovich Shuisky.* Its publication was passed by the censor on January 9, 1879.

someday bringing it to him as a gift—and all this was prevented thanks to a journalist's negligence! If possible, order at least the reprints to have the imprint "Dedicated to M. P. Musorgsky." Better late than never . . .

In January, 1879, Rimsky-Korsakov conducted, at a concert of the Free Music School, the first performance of the scene in Pimen's cell, which had always been omitted from the productions of Boris Godunov.

Rehearsal

At the rehearsal of the scene Musorgsky behaved queerly. Under the influence of wine, or simply for the sake of showing off, of which he had become increasingly fond at that time, he behaved queerly; his conversation was frequently unclear and muddled. At that rehearsal he lent an ear with great significance to what was played, constantly going into raptures over the playing of individual instruments, often in the most commonplace and indifferent passages, sometimes bowing his head pensively, sometimes haughtily raising it and shaking his hair, sometimes throwing up his hand with a theatrical gesture—which he had often done. When at the end of the scene the gong was struck *pianissimo,* imitating the monastery bell, Musorgsky made the player a deep and respectful bow, crossing his hands on his breast. That rehearsal was preceded by a home rehearsal at the house of the singer Vasilyev I, who sang Pimen. I was coaching and accompanying. After the rehearsal, a supper was served; the host got quite drunk and talked much bosh. Musorgsky kept himself well in hand . . . —NIKOLAI RIMSKY-KORSAKOV

201. *To VLADIMIR STASOV*

My dear *généralissime,* I approach the wished-for talk. The Empress Regent Sofia could and was able to do that which I did not see in our friend's painting: [55] my dream summoned to me a plump little woman, who had not once experienced life without copybook virtue, and instead of this I saw an evil woman resembling Peter but not an angry one, a huge woman, not a tiny one, not a plump little woman, but instead one all spread out so that with her enormous size (in the painting) there would be little room for spectators—so it seems to me.

And meanwhile, thanks to you and to other important friends of

---

[55] In the seventh annual exhibition of the Itinerants. This painting by Repin is entitled "The Tzarevna Sofia on the Day of the Execution of the *Streltzi.*"

mine, I dared, nevertheless, to recognize this Regent Sofia. Why did our friend, *first-class* artist that he is, why did he not want to be taught by Sofia's contemporaries before tackling his painting? If she, that is, Sofia, would go from her bed-chamber to the prayer-cell and, seeing her brother's monstrosities, like a tigress first throw herself at the window and then turn away, and her eyes would become fixed on the very bridge of her nose, freeze there and she would herself freeze with *cast-iron fists*—I would have understood the artist, I would have recognized Sofia.

Passing on to the portrait of Litovchenko [by Kramskoy], I jumped back: I saw him and met him, even though we are personally unacquainted. What a wonder-worker Kramskoy is! This is not canvas—this is life, art, the sought-for might in creativeness.

From the "Condemned" [56] I went downstairs, sat down near some good old woman, custodian of the overcoats, smoked recklessly, and didn't care to see any more paintings.

Your
MUSORYANIN

The fuller the recognition of the amazing brush-work of our artist-friend—the sorrier I feel about his Regent Sofia.

THE SAME MUSORYANIN

Wednesday, March 7, '79

[56] A painting by Vladimir Makovsky—bought from this exhibition by Dimitri Stasov. His interest in this particular painting was more than casual; he had volunteered the defense of several arrested revolutionaries.

V I I I

Russia
1879 — 1881

202. *To LUDMILA SHESTAKOVA*

Dear little dove of ours, Ludmila Ivanovna, believe this cry from my heart: take care of yourself for us—to us artists you are beloved, you are a blessed nest. About himself your Musinka cannot speak, and on this is his signature, your Musinka. June 16, 1879: yesterday at your home it was June 15, the day of St. Modestus.

202a. *VLADIMIR STASOV to MILI BALAKIREV [Extract]*

June 17, 1879

. . . Musorgsky himself is in raptures about his proposed tour, because he expects to make from it about 1,000 rubles (!!!) . . .

202b. *MILI BALAKIREV to LUDMILA SHESTAKOVA [Extract]*

June 17, 1879

. . . What's happening to Modeste is terrible. If you could only upset this tour with Leonova, you would be doing a good deed. On the one hand you would release him from the shameful role he wishes to assume, and, besides, Modeste and Leonova are running a big risk. Well, suppose his blood should flow from someplace, as once happened at your home, will it be pleasant for her to fuss over him; and his ruin is probable, because Leonova, naturally, will not fail to exploit him—and it's cheaper for her this way!—Simply shameful for him.

Your

BALAKIREV

A Handbill

POLTAVA

with the permission of the authorities

in the Hall of the
NOBLES' CLUB
on Sunday, July 29

SECOND CONCERT

of the artists of the Imperial theaters

D. M. Leonova and M. P. Musorgsky

Program:

Part I.

(1) "The Wanderer," a song .... Schubert
                      perf. by D. M. Leonova.
(2) "The Little Orphan Girl" .... Musorgsky
                      perf. by D. M. Leonova.
(3) Scene from the opera *Boris Godunov* .... Musorgsky
    (Coronation of Boris as Tzar, with a
    great pealing of bells and the Tzar's
    march during the acclamation by the people)
                perf. at the piano by the Composer
(4) "It Happened on Our Street," song of Olga
    from the opera *Rusalka* .... A. S. Dargomizhsky
                perf. by D. M. Leonova.
(5) "The Blue Sea Moaned," Varangian ballad
    from the opera *Rogneda* .... A. N. Serov
                perf. by D. M. Leonova.
(6) "Past the Rivulet, past the Bridge,"
    a grand fantasy on a folk theme .... Vitelyaro
                perf. by D. M. Leonova.
(7) Musical scene from
    Byron's *Hebrew Melodies,*
    The Destruction of Sennacherib .... Musorgsky
                perf. at the piano by the Composer

(8) "Just One Moment"   ⎫   songs by
(9) "In the Blood Flames the Fire of Desire"   ⎬   M. I. Glinka
                                     perf. by D. M. Leonova.
(10) "The Little Birds Sing On and On," a song . . . . Gumbert
                                     perf. by D. M. Leonova.
(11) *The Seamstress,* scherzino . . . . Musorgsky
                                     perf. at the piano by the Composer
(12) "Ah, Those Merchant Fellows Are All Clothiers!" song of
     Spiridonovna from the opera, *The Power of Evil* [by Serov]
                                     perf. by D. M. Leonova.

The accompaniments at the piano will be by
M. P. Musorgsky.

Beginning at 8:00 P.M.

Prices for seats: reserved: 3 rubles, 2 rubles

and 1 ruble. 50 kop.

Unreserved: at the door 1 ruble, gallery 50 kop. . . .

---

203. *To MARIA FYODOROVA, to PAVEL and SERGEI NAUMOV, St. Peters-*
      burg

                                     Poltava, July 30, '79

Dear Auntie, dearest Papchen and lovely Sergushok, greetings, from
the handbills you'll see what interesting music has kept us busy in
Poltava. The receipts were good, but less than we expected * but we
had an *unquestionable* artistic triumph. A blessed destiny brought
us into contact with the splendid families of Miloradovich, Mosolov
and Schroeder. To our regret we had no opportunity to meet the Ta-
mara and Khristianovich families—these two families were away with
their children, on their estates, far from Poltava. Daria Mikhailovna
has been, is and will be beyond all comparison. What an extraordinary
person! Such energy, power, genuine depth of feeling, everything—
ever captivating and attractive. And there were tears aplenty, and rapture too—we were covered with flowers, and such flowers! On the
estate of Ye[lizaveta] I[vanovna] Miloradovich, in Guzhuli near Pol-

* Musorgsky's note: The fair was moved up from the 20th to the 10th, so we
were late.

tava, we were enchanted by the exquisitely artistic site, with its luxurious parterre (*tapis*), its pink acacias (all in blossom) and its charming
hostess. Highly cultured, lovable, a European to the tips of her fingers
and a calm, elegant and really clever woman. In expressing my rapture over the site, I noticed a peasant's home, pointed out by Fyodor
Dimitriyevich [Gridnin], where Parasya might well live, and therefore I dedicated Parasya['s song], which was written in Petersburg,[1] to
the dearest Ye. I. Miloradovich. Well, as the distance between man
and nature isn't too great, I can tell you that in Poltava and its sub-
urbs the air is so soft that one might well become reconciled to any
evil and forgetful of it. The beauty of Poltava—pyramidal poplars
like giant sentries guard the homes, hills and valleys, and in the gentle
moonlight reflected from the white peasant homes in an air like *"vert
de lumière"* these giant poplars seem almost black: a magic picture.
The green and yellow roofs of the homes and huts peep delicately
from the rich, luxurious verdure, scattered all over the hills and valleys as by the hand of a master artist. The stillness, the calm, vast,
luxurious fields, the wonderful sky and air, bewitching both in its
color, especially towards evening, and in its taste—what a tasty, life-
giving air.[2]

Dear Papchen, tell our scholar-friends that I've noticed one peculiarity in Little Russia: they don't curse at all, you never hear a swear-
word, and the saloons tempt good travelers with original little lan-
terns: square vodka-bottles of white glass have candles stuck in them
and are hung over the entrances; very subtle and yet impossibly
frank.

Dear Auntie, if you could only see the rustic picture of Little Russia, if you could breathe its life-giving air and hear the song that floats
across the fields, you'd throw away even your Count Matei.[3] I've often
thought of you as I was enchanted by this gentle and elegant nature,
and it would be a sin to hide the fact that I've terribly wanted to see
you among us and to enjoy your enjoyment of the charming Little-

---

[1] Dated: "Peterhof. July 9, 1879."

[2] In this passage and in subsequent descriptive passages on the Ukrainian and
South Russian landscape, there is a remarkable resemblance to the style and
flavor of the landscape descriptions in Gogol's Ukrainian tales; Musorgsky may
have been under the influence of these at this period of his work on *Fair at Sorochintzi*, as well as enchanted by his first sight of southern Russia.

[3] A patent medicine known as "liquid electricity," absorbed through the skin
by the application of varicolored papers!

Russian evening. To complete the delight given us in Guzhuli by the hospitable Ye. I. Miloradovich, Daria Mikhailovna, like a real ace, sang the "Little Orphan Girl," "Forgotten" and Marfa['s song] before the self-immolation. Daria Mikhailovna was nearly suffocated with kisses, and even ladies kissed her hands, and on the following day they declared that they hadn't been able to sleep, that they couldn't forget this gift from God. [. . .] Papchen, when the occasion arises, you must speak about this son-of-a-bitch railroad of the Actual State Councilor Polyakov, it's beyond belief, the rails are worn to shreds, the cars rattle and are suffused with a foul stench, unbearably stifling.

We're off to Yelizavetgrad—we all greet you heartily, and do accept a friendly kiss from me.

Your
M. MUSORGSKY

Papchen, embrace our friends, including Prokofi Gerasimovich [?], for me—I'll write.

204. *To MARIA FYODOROVA, to PAVEL and SERGEI NAUMOV, St. Petersburg*

Near the Dnieper Estuary.   Nikolayev
   (Bug-Ingul.)
                                          August 3, 1879

Dear Auntie of mine, Papchen and Sergushok, greetings. We've just arrived from Yelizavetgrad, where Daria Mikhailovna had a fresh triumph amidst a select society. It's impossible to convey the vital interest which overtook the auditors as the concert began, growing into complete rapture, without exclamations, but that kind of rapture which is the affirmation of genuine artistic delight. Among those who honored us with their presence were naturally a few who had heard Daria Mikhailovna 18 or 20 years ago; their amazement was unbounded and they told each other and their acquaintances, with real heartfelt joy, that Daria Mikhailovna sings even better than then and that her voice not only has lost none of its force and freshness, but has gained in power. And I can confirm this with delight, because Daria Mikhailovna sounded indeed extremely fresh and powerful, and as for expression, she has enough and to spare. The Nobles' Club in Yelizavetgrad is charming, and, although all the great landowners were away on their estates, the hospitable gentlemen commanders of regiments and divisions, along with their amiable spouses, supported us as well as they were able, and we are very grateful to the kind regimental ladies for the attention they've shown us. Complete artistic delight was expressed by a deputation that came to invite Daria Mikhailovna to give another concert; the tone and character of this invitation touched me deeply: such sincere, good feeling rang in it. But it was impossible to alter our schedule and straight from the concert we rolled on by train to Nikolayev. Papchen, I could discover nothing in Yelizavetgrad about Sasha [Naumov], because the person from whom I might have gotten the information poured such official chill over Daria Mikhailovna and myself that I was awestruck. I saw the birthplace of grandpa Petrov in Yelizavetgrad, among the interminable steppes, infinitely free and rich, like grandpa's broad mighty soul.

It was in Yelizavetgrad that Daria Mikhailovna gave us a chance for the first time to hear her own composition directly from the platform (*en forme d'une lettre, dite: "Après le bal"*). A very graceful, nice little piece on a valse motif,—the accompaniment portrays the distant sound of a recollected valse and on this musical background the following is sung: ("Letter after the Ball") "In the whirlwind of the valse, you whispered the golden dreams of your youthful love. And I listened to you, as I turned with you, and these whispers of youthful love were rapture to me. But in these golden dreams, my young friend, and in the impulse of passion, you've forgotten your secret oath, forever forswearing the ecstasies of love. And believe me, my young friend—love will cheat you and cheat you badly . . . I await an answer, an answer to me, without reproach for my having disturbed you. Answer at once, without simulation or falsehood, whether I have engendered hatred in you toward me: or when and where I am to see you and where I may reveal the mystery of my oath.")

Daria Mikhailovna has more than once been pleased to declare— that this letter was supposedly written by me to her musical composition;[4] be that as it may, such a letter is better than that doggerel which I've noticed in the graceful and very nice society valse. It produced a full effect and we encored it.—If God keeps us alive—we all shall hear it. [. . .]

---

[4] Although Musorgsky refuses to take credit for more than the text of Leonova's song, the song, as published by Bernard on the tour's return from the South, shows many evidences of an experienced hand. Did Leonova hum her waltz tune to Musorgsky?

Today, in Nikolayev, we visited the commander-in-chief [of the Black Sea Fleet]. We were given a charming, cordial reception, he [Bazhenov] has great knowledge, great wit and frank, warm feelings, and what a fine, staunch love for art! We visited the honored gentlemen admirals: real gentlemen and human beings, and extremely nice —here is something truly genuine, without any *bonbonisms,* and glory to them, the dear ones. Our repertoire constantly adds new musical things to itself: "The King of Thule" by Liszt, "The Sea" by Borodin and "My Petted One" (a romance-mazurka) by Chopin [5] are already mapped out. Daria Mikhailovna is zealously introducing these welcome guests into her artistic memory. And there's more to come.

Nikolayev has been built up on a grand scale. True, the streets are unpaved except for two or three whose paving has just begun, but the boulevard has tall bushy acacias; lots of gardens, the steep bank of the Bug, the hills and at their top, on the horizon, is a row of windmills, all making Nikolayev, with its extremely fragrant air, a very attractive place. The Hall of the Winter Naval Club is very elegant in its mixed Moorish style (like Naina's castle in *Ruslan* except for the colors). The boulevard runs along the steep bank of the Bug and this place, covered with greenery, looking over charming little bays and capes, is the favorite evening promenade for the townspeople. In the light of the setting sun the colors of the Bug waters and of the surrounding hills and slopes are enchanting when one looks down from the height of the boulevard. The buildings have a character all their own and are blended sometimes with gardens and sometimes with low stone walls: this is very appropriate for the expansive layout of Nikolayev. Old residents say that in a hot, dry summer Nikolayev is so covered with dust that one can't distinguish objects; on the other hand—in rainy weather the mud becomes such a morass that sometimes a horse with its wagonload goes completely under and must be given up as drowned. This is probably true as long as the very broad streets are left unpaved. And speaking of horses: Sergushok, I've watched Ukrainian riders on the steppes both close and at a distance; they seem part of their steeds and look exactly like centaurs, riding with unbelievable calmness and alertness, it's a real joy to watch them; these riders of the steppe show us something powerful. Dear Auntie, what is little "Bronzik" doing, is he able to run up and down the

---

[5] From the six mazurkas arranged for voice by Pauline Garcia-Viardot, with words by Louis Pomey.

stairs, does he growl enough and is he as amusing as little puppies of his age should be? I imagine he *is*. And what about Little Devil? He must be a very amusing little devil now that he has recovered under your kind care. If you could only see the infinite remoteness of the Ukrainian steppe, if you could only see the starry sky all spangled with points of light, a sky that in the transparent air is both as bright and as dark as a sapphire, if you could only inhale this south Russian air which calls out the lungs and heart from your very chest, an air so tender that one wants to live and go on living as long as possible! Apropos or not, I can't be silent any longer about one comical episode of our art tour: no sooner were we seated in the omnibus of the *Grand Hôtel Rainaud* in Nikolayev, going from the train to a few days of stationary existence, than I heard from the lips of the *concièrge-conducteur à l'hôtel* that in Nikolayev a Princess Menshikova along with other aristocratic people in the field of art is giving concerts. Upon making inquiries it turns out that this aristocratic lady is a fellow godparent of mine, A. G. Menshova-Menshikova, General Menshov's wife, who never in her life has been a Princess, not even on the stage. As soon as this aristocratic lady heard of the arrival of Daria Mikhailovna and of her aforesaid fellow godparent, she scrupulously avoided them both and on the following day appeared to be "in hiding." Fyodor Dimitriyevich [Gridnin] discovered some hand-bills of my renowned fellow godparent and ah, what horror overcame me to see what my respected fellow godparent has invented for Her Highness: Judith *in the costume of Judith* (this is what the handbill says), and Prindik [Pribik], a *pianist from the Prague Conservatory*, playing a *Hungarian* rhapsody, and Mr. Lavrov (bass—as the handbill says), "sensing the truth" in M. I. Glinka's opera, *A Life for the Tzar*, through his beard (they told me this about Lavrov and I myself heard him in Peter and begged him not to yell, because the Poles, before falling asleep, might hear him and kill him ahead of time, but Mister Lavrovbass didn't care to sense my truth but measured Glinka in the Lavrov manner). I said: "in the Lavrov manner." I repeat because I completely forgot to tell you in my letter from Poltava about Ye[lizaveta] A[ndreyevna] Lavrovskaya—an attractive singer with a charming voice, as you know, but without the slightest dramatic feeling, as you also know. The truth is that when Daria Mikhailovna sang Dargomizhsky's song: "I Loved and Shall Forever Love," in Poltava (where Ye. A. Lavrovskaya's estate is), those ladies unanimously declared to Daria Mikhailovna that, very likely, the attractive Ye. A. Lavrovskaya "has not loved." *Je ne dis que ça!* The splendid, courteous, profoundly cultured and profoundly sensitive Ye. I. Miloradovich, at her luxurious Poltava residence, presented Daria Mikhailovna with a great many magnificent Ukrainian embroideries on linen, the most varied and *tasteful* ones in various applications to everyday household use: a blouse, pillow slips, sheets, various "plateaux" etc., and Ye. I. Miloradovich gave Fyodor Dimitriyevich and me, each, a towel with marvelous designs and embroidered inscriptions; I forgot to tell you about this, so I tell it now, as this was done by great admirers of Ye. A. Lavrovskaya—this is what vital artistic power does to vital and truly vital people!

Nikolayev, 7 August

Today was D. M. Leonova's first concert, she sang masterfully, there was not a very large audience, but it was a very representative one; the artistic success was tremendous! What harm touring artists have done to art, Daria Mikhailovna has had to repair this harm, and not for the first time on our tour.—Honor and glory to her, who proudly lifts the banner of Russian musical art! Captain Golenishchev has charmed us with his courtesy, his attentions and kind, unforgettable aid in everything; a reserved gentleman but passionately fond of art. —We were at the Observatory. From the top balcony the view over Nikolayev surpasses all charms—I can't describe it. Amidst the family of Captain Yurkovsky, where we were received with sincere cordiality, Daria Mikhailovna asked me to introduce Yurkovsky's children to my scenes from child life [*The Nursery*], and I, the sinner, surrounded by the dear little kiddies, fulfilled her request, and Daria Mikhailovna, seated at a great table (I was at the piano), sang the *"Erlkönig"* like an ace of aces.—Colonel Karatazzi, the director of the Observatory, toasted Daria Mikhailovna with a fine champagne, and the Yurkovsky kiddies, entirely of their own accord, presented Daria Mikhailovna with a bouquet of rare flowers which they themselves picked in our presence. In the evening heaven breathed fire and by night a thunderstorm, with a shower and a squall, broke over us. Yesterday Captain Brovtzin, commander of the Floating Dock at Nikolayev, showed us over the Popovka: [6] O wonder of wonders! I'll tell you all about it

---

[6] An armored ship constructed by Vice-Admiral Popov, modeled after John Ericsson's *Monitor* (1862).

when we meet, as we were all over the Popovka, inside and out. Daria Mikhailovna was presented with a photograph of the Popovka at anchor. We spent a most charming evening at the house of that dearest admiral, A. I. Bazhenov, who gave a reception for Daria Mikhailovna in the garden of his hospitable home with a splendid illumination. What a lovely, splendid and extremely nice gentleman Admiral Bazhenov is; I grew quite fond of him. We played a lot of music.

Nikolayev, 10 August

Today is to be our second concert, at D. I. Russinov's theater. I'll wait and write afterwards.

The concert has taken place. Russinov speeded up the redecoration of his theater, which is now very good-looking. I enclose, dear friends, a clipping from No. 88 of the *Nikolayevsky Vestnik,* where they speak of our musical affairs.[7] On Sunday, August 12, our third concert will take place; I'll send you its program.

Kherson, 15 August

Today is our first concert here. It will determine our further musical excursions. Along the road I'll capture more musical pieces of importance, and Daria Mikhailovna will deliver these novelties to the auditors. So far—we've had a firm, unbroken artistic success. Without any doubt, our artistic tour must have and already has significance as a good art service for the good Russian people. But what charm the approach to Kherson along the Dnieper has! Magic of magics! In this watery avenue of historic reeds (sometimes as high as 2 or 3 men), from which bold Zaporozhtzi [Cossacks], in carven log boats, raided the Turks, and where in the crystal surface of the azure Dnieper great trees look down on reflections of their full height, not only along the bank, but across the broadest, most luxurious stretches of water, all this is lit by a lavender-pink sunset, by the moon and by Jupiter. An enchanting impression. Apropos and very apropos of Jupiter. At the Nikolayev Observatory its director Karatazzi kindly gave us the opportunity of looking at Jupiter and Saturn through the splendid telescopic apparatus. I nearly lost my senses with delight.

There are the impressions of the journey so far. I'll write more and

---

[7] The anonymous critic of the first two Nikolayev concerts has particular praise for Leonova's rendition of Schubert's *Erlkönig* and Musorgsky's *Gopak,* and for Leonova's new song.

more, but I'd like to hear about you, friends; I'll ask you to write at least a few lines as soon as I make sure which address can be used with certainty. I terribly want to get at least a few lines from you, you fine and good people. We travelers greet you heartily and I send you a hearty, friendly kiss.

Please give my greetings to the whole household. I send friendly greeting to all our friends and I firmly embrace them and Prokofi Gerasimovich.

Your

M. MUSORGSKY

A Poster

KHERSON

On Saturday, August 18, 1879.

in the Salle of the City Club.

L A S T   C O N C E R T

by the artists of the Imperial Theaters

D. M. Leonova and M. P. Musorgsky

Program:

Part I.

(1)   "The Wanderer, a song .... Schubert
perf. by D. M. Leonova.

(2)   "Dawn over the Moscow River," introduction to
the people's musical drama *Khovanshchina* ... Musorgsky
perf. at the piano by the Composer.

(3)   "Forgotten," a ballad .... Musorgsky
perf. by D. M. Leonova.

(4)   "Southern Night," a song .... Rimsky-Korsakov
perf. by D. M. Leonova.

(5)   "Coronation of Tzar Boris with the Great Pealing
of Bells during the People's Acclamation," a scene
from the opera *Boris Godunov* .... Musorgsky
perf. at the piano by the Composer.

386

(6)   "Ah, Tell Me, Flowers," Siebel's aria
      from the opera *Faust* .... Gounod
perf. by D. M. Leonova.

(7)   "As Free as Freedom"   } Russian songs by Kashperov
(8)   "How Healthy and Young" }
perf. by D. M. Leonova.

Part II

(9)   "My Soul Is Dark," a Hebrew melody
      (King Saul) .... Rubinstein
perf. by D. M. Leonova.

(10)   A musical scene, *"Jesus Navinus,"*
      on ancient Israelite themes .... Musorgsky
perf. at the piano by the Composer.

(11)   "I Beg You, Little Birds, for One Thing," song ... Gumbert
perf. by D. M. Leonova.

(12) a. "Evening Promenade of the Guests in the
       Gardens of the Sandomierz Voyevoda Mnis-
       zech" (Polonaise), a scene from the opera
       Boris Godunov
    b. "Gopak of the Merry Peasant Lads" from the   Musorgsky
       new opera *Fair at Sorochintzi*
    c. "Triumphal march of the Preobrazhensky
       Company of Tzar Peter's bodyguard" from
       the new opera *Khovanshchina*
perf. at the piano by the Composer.

(13)   "Ah, Those Merchant Fellows—They're All
      Clothiers," song of Spiridonovna, from the
      opera *The Power of Evil* .... A. N. Serov
perf. by D. M. Leonova.

(14)   "Remember, My Good Man"   } Russian folk-songs
      "Ah, You, Pantry of Mine, My Pantry" }
[arranged by K. Lyadov]

perf. by D. M. Leonova.

The piano accompaniment will be by
M. P. Musorgsky.

Begins at 8:30 P.M.

387

Rescued in Yalta

. . . At that time I lived in Yalta, where I managed a large hotel, the Russia . . . you may imagine what delight I felt when I saw notices of a concert by Musorgsky and Leonova . . . The concert was to be in the building of an old club . . .

When I came to the concert I was distressed to see the very small attendance, although at that time high society, so to say, came from both the capitals and from other cities to Yalta . . .

In the first intermission I rushed to the greenroom. There in an armchair sat M. P., with arms drooping like a wounded bird. The absence of an audience, the failure of the concert were obviously having a depressing effect on him. It seems that, having arrived on the eve of their concert in Yalta, which was jammed with people, as August was nearly the height of the season, they could find no place to stay and were forced into some private house, absolutely disorganized, and dirty and disgusting besides. And this had to happen to the adored Musoryanin, to be in such surroundings! Of course I arranged for them to move the following day to the Russia, which was provided with great comforts, and had an excellent large salle with a fine piano, and furthermore was filled with the sort of people who could be interested in the next concert . . . —SOFIA STASOVA-FORTUNATO [8]

205.   *To LUDMILA SHESTAKOVA, St. Petersburg*

Yalta, Hotel Russia
September 9, 1879

Dear little dove of ours, Ludmila Ivanovna, the decisive step, taken by me in my art life, is justified: Poltava, Yelizavetgrad, Nikolayev, Kherson, Odessa, Sevastopol, Yalta all have rung, *in a real way*, with the sounds of the creative thought of the immortal founder of the Russian school of music, Glinka, and of his fine fellow-champions; for the first time in these places has been heard and, I hope, has been realized all the mighty power of that immortal who bequeathed to posterity the true unshaken testament to Russia's musical creative spirit. Glory to Glinka, who pointed out the road to truth! Of those stops on our tour mentioned by me, Odessa and Sevastopol have proved to be comparatively less musical, but even in these two cities the cause of Russian music was recognized and those who must be left behind the barrier, were left behind irrevocably. I am enclosing in this epistle to you, dear little dove of mine, the piece by the Kherson

[8] Sofia Vladimirovna had married a second husband, Mikhail Fortunato, and was managing Yalta's best hotel.

correspondent of the newspaper *Odessky Vestnik*.[9] In the list of our musical sages not mentioned in this piece are Borodin and An[atoli] Lyadov; but in the Odessa paper *Pravda* I read with great consolation about *Prince Igor* by Borodin and about an opera by An. Lyadov: [10] this is expressed in the newspaper *Pravda* with full sympathy. Up to this minute we have been received on our artistic tour by the best families and by the best representatives of local centers of culture. The earnestness of their relations to art, and, consequently, of their demands, astonished me, although I had prepared myself for all kinds of encounters. We found a particularly exacting attitude in Kherson, where there is no lack of well-grounded musical circles, acquainted with musical literature and following the development of the cause of music with love. Our repertoire includes, with preponderance, Glinka, Dargomizhsky, Serov, Balakirev, Cui, Borodin, R.-Korsakov, Fr. Schubert, Chopin, Liszt, Schumann. With such levers one might move the whole wide world. And how many new, delightful, and restoring things nature gives! How many new and sometimes highly substantial encounters with new people, who feel art a good deal more sensitively than certain unrecognized heralds of the All-Russian press! This renewing and refreshing tour has been a great education for me. Many years off my shoulders! Life calls for new musical labors, broad musical work; further, still further on the good road; what I am doing is understood; with great vigor *towards the new shores* of art, which so far is limitless! To search for these shores, to search untiringly, fearlessly and without confusion, and *to tread with firm step on the promised land*—there's a great and captivating task! Assuming that my epistle, which I am sending by registered mail, will reach you, my dear little dove, before the day that is most dear to us of all holidays, your name-day, September 16, imagine your Musinka being present at your home on the fine morn of that day, warmly kissing your grace-

---

[9] An article on Musorgsky and his principles: ". . . in the Pleiad of Russian realists, which includes Tchaikovsky, Musorgsky, Rimsky-Korsakov, Cui, Balakirev and a few others, the first two occupy the most prominent position . . ."

[10] "They say that Mr. Borodin, author of two symphonies and songs, is finishing an opera *Prince Igor*. A. Lyadov is actively working on his opera, of which two acts are already composed—an opera from ancient Russian times entitled *Princess Zorka*. Mr. Cui and Mr. Solovyov have begun 2 operas. Mr. Balakirev has begun an opera on a Russian historical subject. And Mr. Musorgsky (who is at present giving concerts in Odessa) has nearly completed the operas *Fair at Sorochintzi* and *Khovanshchina*." (August 22.)

ful little hands, with the heartiest of congratulations. Do this, dear little dove, and the heart of your Musinka will rejoice greatly.

We have magnificent quarters in Yalta, thanks to the wonderful, loving heart and the whole sympathetic being of Sofia Vladimirovna, in spite of the absolute impossibility of putting up anywhere, except on the open rocky ground, under the open sky. It's true that we were chased into some sort of mud-hut on our arrival, but the wonderful Sofia Vladimirovna promptly extracted us from thence and gave us shelter in her magnificent hotel with its magnificent arrangements, select society and on the very shore of the sea. Great and cordial thanks to the truly good and most splendid Sofia Vladimirovna, and how solicitous she is about us, God! as if we were relatives; and what a charming and delightful gentleman her husband is, and how passionately he loves music! I am writing at once to my *Généralissime*, with greetings to Nadezhda Vasilyevna, and on the way toward the Don and the Volga I will not be slow in writing again and again, dear little dove of mine. When you see Mili tell him that I firmly embrace him and kiss him many times: a splendid gentleman he is, my dear Mili. When you see dearest *dyainka,* tell him that I nearly lost my senses at the sight of Baidari and the Black Sea, that in Yelizavetgrad I visited the birthplace of our dear grandpa Petrov and that I've seen the interminable steppes, broad and free, like grandpa's mighty soul; I embrace and kiss dear, good *dyainka* ever so firmly. *Dyainka* has been in grandpa's birthplace, and so have I—so I boast. Till my next epistle, little dove of mine, keep in good health, take care of yourself for our sakes. I kiss your little hands firmly.

Your

MUSINKA

Daria Mikhailovna Leonova, on hearing that I am writing to you, dear little dove, has asked me to give you her soul's sincere greetings on your dear holiday.

To use up the free space on this sheet, I'll do a little postscript, *like a regular boarding-school girl.* First and *for me, foremost,* is the following: probably you, little dove, will soon see our splendid Anna Yakovlevna [Vorobiova-Petrova] (I presume on September 16); tell the splendid Anna Yakovlevna from me that in the birthplace of dear grandpa his whole mighty and loving image appeared before me as if alive, and that in feeling and thought I conversed with him at length, as if he had never left us; indeed, everything returned, awoke and touched me to the very core. Secondly—there is a grave error in the enclosed clipping from Kherson, as if Glinka had written his contralto roles for Leonova; the whole world knows that they were created for the splendid Anna Yakovlevna Vorobiova-Petrova, first and genius interpreter of Glinka's genius. With all my heart I kiss the little hands of splendid Anna Yakovlevna.

MUSINKA

206. *To VLADIMIR STASOV, St. Petersburg*

Yalta. Hotel Russia
(Grand Hôtel de Russie)
September 10, 1879

My splendid and dear *généralissime,* greeting! "The runaway from the blessed native land" finds himself in Yalta in a magnificent hotel overlooking the Black Sea itself, with its wonderful aquamarine color and luxuriously breaking surf, under the patronage of the lovely, lovable Sofia Vladimirovna and her dearest, nicest husband, Mikhail Antonovich. A team of four quadrupeds with extremely long manes and tails brought us here to Yalta, through the Baidari valley up the Baidari approach, through its pass, and along its slopes, which seem to dive into the very depths of the sea, from scorching vertical cliffs, and here they put us down in some mud-hut along with centipedes that bite and a kind of snapping beetle, which also bites, and other insects that justify their earthly existence by an ideal of making life nasty for people; but the magic hand of lovely Sofia Vladimirovna extracted us in a twinkling from the aforesaid bug-infested place in the Vereshchagin manner,[11] and transplanted us into Europe. Furthermore: Sofia Vladimirovna, like a kinswoman, looks after us and cherishes us even in the extraordinary orderliness, the astonishing cleanliness, comfort and luxury of this hotel. This is what I must tell you: I could not have wished for a better administrator, not for myself alone, but for all the world of good people. And this is a fact, that everyone is hurrying and rushing to the *Grand Hôtel de Russie à Jalta,* under the patronage of the dearest Sofia Vladimirovna; and they hurry and rush because everyone, without exception, including the scullery maid, feels good, comfortable and peaceful under the magic wand of the magic regent Sofia, yes and this time, happily for the

---

[11] Referring to Vereshchagin's ultrarealist painting of the romantically filthy Samarkand bazaar.

people, it is not Sofia Alexeyevna [Tzarevna] but Sofia Vladimirovna. The wonderful, attractive, dear human heart that is in the being of your and our Sofia Vladimirovna! And what a splendid, kind, nice (and how handsome!) husband she has, Mikhail Antonovich; he loves music passionately, and has at his disposal a varied and rich musical repertoire and, in it, has significant musical novelties. It is with great joy that I can tell you that Mikhail Antonovich introduced us to his nice voice (a *baritenore*) and his fully attractive, artistically intelligent manner of singing. A sensitivity, understanding and immediate grasp of the requirements of new music struck me in Mikhail Antonovich and, you will readily realize, my dear *généralissime*, how much closer this brought me to his nice personality. "And our suit is trump."

I turn to my travel *diary*.

Here this very second I have written Ludmila Ivanovna, and to you, my dear, I shall say that Peter[sburg] is not such a wonderful connoisseur of the Russian provinces. What I intend to tell you *is in the following points.*

The cities of Russia, particularly those frequented by artistes and artists, are not only not musical but are in general little concerned with art (Odessa, Nikolayev, Sevastopol); but on the other hand the Russian cities that are rarely or not at all frequented by artistes and artists, are very musical and in general provide for art (Yelizavetgrad, Kherson, Poltava).

In Yelizavetgrad and Kherson (an unheard-of business even in Peter) after the *"Erlkönig"* even I, sinner that I am, was loudly called and had to take a bow. By good fortune at the time of our arrival in Yelizavetgrad, V. I. Anastasyev came in from his estate, and musical matters quickly took on the finest shape; there was no end to our mutual happiness and rapture; not without, of course, a display of novelties from Musoryanin's doings—in other words, all was done worthily. And in Yelizavetgrad I met the very nice Blumenfeld family,[12] highly advanced in musical matters and vigilantly following musical literature; all our musical sages are well known there, and our conversation flowed as easily as in Peter itself. In Kherson I was enchanted by the sensitive understanding of new musical creations and new artistic requirements, especially in the splendid families of Pashchenko and De-Lazari; A. M. De-Lazari, an excellent pianist and a very solid

---

[12] The Blumenfeld brothers, Sigismund, Stanislav and Felix. Felix had married Anastasyev's daughter, Maria.

musical expert, takes an unusually sane and genuine attitude to musical matters and with great critical tact, besides; the Pashchenko home is the music center of Kherson with selected and quite varied programs. In Poltava the art center is the home of Y. I. Miloradovich, an attractive beauty, and in a European way, a highly cultured and advanced woman. *Khovanshchina* made an irresistible impression there, and the concluding scene of Marfa and Andrei Khovansky, in the capital performance of D. M. Leonova, had a stunning effect on the auditors. *Sorochintzi* aroused the greatest sympathy there and everywhere in the Ukraine; Ukrainian men and women recognized that the character of the *Sorochintzi* music was thoroughly national, as I became convinced, verifying myself on Ukrainian soil.—I saw our M. A. Miloradovich in Poltava; oh, how glad we were to see each other! he is zealously working on music and is considering coming to Peter this winter. But Odessa! O "southern beauty"! She has nothing to do with art; she's interested in nothing but corn and silver rubles. Dry, cold, unfriendly, with a heat of almost 40° [Reaumur]! In Odessa I attended the Itinerant Exhibition of paintings, and looked with even more pleasure at things I had already seen in Peter, and joyfully embraced G. G. Myasoyedov; his "Peasant with a Crowbar" I liked terribly: in attitude and veracity of expression it has much in common with I. Ye. Repin's Archdeacon. With the Myasoyedovs I visited the museum of history and antiquities (not at all frequented by the Odessians); there I was pleasantly surprised by Ukrainian portrait painting, up till now unseen by me anywhere. We signed the visitors' book (how few there have been), and I also took away a catalogue. In Sevastopol, or more accurately, in the ruins of Sevastopol, I was fascinated by the memorial to Admiral Lazarev, untouched by enemy shells, but surrounded by frightful ruins of the formerly magnificent buildings of the admiralty and docks. The monument-master Mikeshin should learn how to erect memorials to good Russian people, if he himself (ai, ai!) had not erected a memorial to Admiral Greig in Nikolayev. Aside from among the dearest family of the Makukhins, one hardly dares to utter a word about art in Sevastopol. We have visited the Makukhins quite frequently and have made good music there: there were no limits to their rapture, and their sincere enthusiasm. Yes, I almost forgot,—D. M. Leonova at Nikolayev in the very nice home of the Yurkovskys, got me to show my *Nursery* to the Yurkovsky kiddies. How those kiddies did enjoy it, and the mothers quite overpraised me; the same thing happened at Kherson in the Boshnyak family, with the same effect, the same raptures. O Laroche! O Solovyov! O Laroche and Solovyov and Ivanov, along with Haller! [13] On the steamer from Odessa to Sevastopol, near the Tarkhankhut lighthouse (where the [imperial] yacht *Livadia* was wrecked), when most of the passengers had begun to be seasick, I wrote down Greek and Jewish songs, as sung by some women, and I sang the latter with them myself, and they were very pleased and among themselves they referred to me as *Meister*.—By the way, in Odessa, I went to holy services at two synagogues, and was in raptures. I have clearly remembered two Israelite themes: one sung by the cantor, the other by the temple choir—the latter in unison; I shall never forget these!

Now along the Don and the Volga towards home.

There you have, my dear *généralissime,* my little narrative. I heartily embrace you and congratulate you along with your splendid family on the family's holiday on September 17. I bow to all the nice Stasovs and send them my cordial greeting. Please embrace my dear Alexander Vasilyevich Meyer for me. And please give this little note (enclosed herewith) to the little dove Nadezhda Vasilyevna.

Your

MUSORYANIN

If you wish, my dear, to make me, like a fine elastic substance, leap with joy to the very ceiling, do write me at Samara in care of general delivery. Well, dearest, do this, to make your Musoryanin happy.

207. *To NADEZHDA STASOVA, St. Petersburg*

DEAR LITTLE DOVE,

NADEZHDA VASILYEVNA,

On your holiday, September 17, allow yourself the thought that your devoted Musoryanin is bringing you in person his soul's congratulation and is present in the midst of your dearest family, ever so affable and affectionate to Musoryanin and, though I know not why, loving Musoryanin. And I, like cheese melting in butter, am luxuriating in Yalta under the patronage of the enchantress Sofia Vladimirovna and her enchanting husband Mikhail Antonovich. What air, what surroundings, what sea, what marvelous walks in the vicinity! How is it,

---

[13] Critics who wrote ill of *The Nursery.*

Lord, that so much charm and inspiration can be given at the same time? I've written of everything to my dear *généralissime,* and I'll write further and further, my soul and hand are in the proper mood— I'll write lots and lots.

From all my heart I kiss your little hands.

Devotedly your

MUSORYANIN

Yalta *"Grand Hôtel de Russie,"* September 11, 1879

After Yalta, Musorgsky and Leonova performed in Rostov, Novocherkassk, and Voronezh. The three concerts in Voronezh were diluted with dramatic sketches and vaudevilles given by a touring troupe. At the first concert, the obstacles were entitled A Female Othello *and* In the Dust; *at the second,* A Strange Concurrence of Circumstances *and* On Bread and Water; *at the last,* As You Winnow, So You Grind *and* The Bengal Tiger, or, Jealous Husband and Brave Lover. *Following Voronezh, they stopped at Tambov and Tver before returning to St. Petersburg at the end of October.*

Leonova's Maestro

. . . Leonova, who had left the Imperial stage several years before, and had made a tour to Japan,[14] now lived in St. Petersburg, giving singing lessons. She organized these lessons on a grand scale, and founded something like a small music school. Leonova was a talented artist who had had, some time before, a good contralto voice, but who had actually gone through no school, and I doubt whether she was capable of teaching the technique of singing. There was sometimes something of the gypsy in her singing. But in dramatic and comic pieces she was often inimitable . . . So her lessons consisted mainly in coaching of songs and opera excerpts. An accompanist and musician was needed who could watch over the correct practice of the pieces, which Leonova couldn't do herself. It was in the position of such a maestro that Musorgsky found himself. By that time he was long retired [from the civil service] and was in need of means. Leonova's classes furnished some support for him. He spent considerable time in these classes, teaching even elementary theory and composing exercises for Leonova's pupils, some trios and quartets with horrible vocal part-writing . . .

This association with Musorgsky served Leonova, to a certain extent, for publicity. His function in her classes was, of course, unenviable, but either he didn't realize this or he tried not to. His work on the composition of *Khovanshchina* and *Fair at Sorochintzi* went on somewhat lifelessly in those days . . . —NIKOLAI RIMSKY-KORSAKOV

---

[14] This tour, made in 1876, also included China, the United States, and Europe.

Pianist

. . . "The Song of the Flea" [15] created a sensation in the circle and brought an uproar of applause from the audience. Here Musorgsky's skill in picturesque accompaniment was vividly demonstrated, and at times one could almost hear the flea jump. The arpeggios in the middle of the song resounded splendidly, smacking of something positively Rubinsteinesque. [Nikolai] Lavrov had never before and has never since heard such a performance of arpeggios: during the terrific fortissimo of the piano, Leonova's voice was not obscured for a second, each word of the song was audible.

At one of the soirées in which Musorgsky and Leonova took part the audience became so enthusiastic that they all crowded up to the platform and begged Musorgsky to play something of his own. Leonova prompted the audience to ask Musorgsky to play his *Storm [on the Black Sea]*.[16] At that time Lavrov didn't realize that Musorgsky could play solo, and was amazed when he saw the latter sit down at the piano and begin his *Storm*. By the performance of this composition Musorgsky greatly puzzled not only Lavrov, who was comparatively unacquainted with new music and unaccustomed to it, but even [Anatoli] Lyadov as well. Lavrov was in complete perplexity because he could find no music in the *Storm*. But what he could not deny in it was its amazing perfection of onomatopoeia. When in the pealing passages Musorgsky reached the highest notes on the keyboard the complete illusion of waves breaking against a cliff was achieved.

Neither Lavrov nor Lyadov ever again heard this piece, nor did they know if it had been written down, even in sketches. With all their amazement at this piece they still didn't know what attitude to take towards it. Lyadov's face, at least, always showed some perplexity whenever he mentioned the *Storm* . . . —VICTOR BELAYEV

207a. *VLADIMIR STASOV to NIKOLAI RIMSKY-KORSAKOV [Extract]*

November 25, 1879

. . . After the rehearsal today I was at Musarion's and found him in perfect order. The orchestration of "Marfa" was already finished, and he was expecting the arrival of Gridnin (Leonova's husband), who was to come, take away the score and give it to be copied in a day (as he assured me). Musorgsky asked me to tell you, in addition, that all

[15] Composed on the tour. The Russian translation of Goethe's text (*Faust*, Part I, Scene 5) is by Strugovshchikov.

[16] No sketches of this work have been discovered, unless we can assume that Musorgsky used the idea given him by the storm at Tzarskoye Selo (see p. 343). The storm itself is probably that reported by him from Nikolayev in Letter 204.

this had been arranged with Leonova and Gridnin, and he hopes that "Marfa" will go perfectly with one rehearsal (the 2nd) . . .[17]

The Persian Dances Orchestrated

. . . The Persian dances were already listed on the programme, but there was no sign of a score. What was to be done! Musorgsky wasn't around—so Nikolai Andreyevich [Rimsky-Korsakov], without any lengthy meditation, sat down and orchestrated this number. The piece had a great success at the concert: Musorgsky was called out several times; he was extraordinarily happy and, when he finally returned from the platform, more than once repeated, with positively childish naïveté, that *he was very happy that everything had gone off as well as it had and that he himself would have orchestrated it* "exactly" *as Korsakov had done;* and that he was simply amazed with what finesse Rimsky had *guessed* all his intentions, while Musorgsky took *absolutely* no notice of the harmonic changes that Nikolai Andreyevich had made in the orchestration [18] . . . —VASILI YASTREB-TZEV

208. *To LUDMILA SHESTAKOVA*

Dear little dove of mine, Ludmila Ivanovna, with your good words and your frank talk to me, involving matters of worldly vanities, you have blessed my feeling as an artist and as a human being. Yes, little dove, dear Ludmila Ivanovna, if I should dare to betray, to surrender, *to treat art* and myself lightly, I should not have in my consciousness those profoundly heartfelt words—those with which you have blessed me. What has been received from you—is holy. Once more you stood at the fountainhead of *genuine* feeling, and not *dim consciousness,* regardless of present-day warriors for art and well-wishers for its blessedness. Glinka was saved by you and you alone, in the tiniest gleams of his artistic doings; Glinka, through the power of your activity, was made clear in the development of his creative power; Glinka was given by you to all the world's knowledge in the greatest creation of his genius *Ruslan and Ludmila*—honor and pride of the Russian

---

[17] On November 27, at a concert of the Free Music School, three excerpts from *Khovanshchina* were to be presented under the direction of Rimsky-Korsakov: Awakening and Exit of the *Streltzi*, Marfa's song (sung by Leonova), and the Dance of the Persian Maidens.

[18] As Rimsky-Korsakov's adoring Boswell, Yastrebtzev's impartiality on this point is open to doubt.

soil and of the whole Slavic world. And amidst your cares for that Great Russian worker, you have found in your lovely heart the possibility of giving me your good word and frank speech! I repeat: you have blessed me, dear little dove Ludmila Ivanovna, blessed me as artist and as human being.

With my whole soul devoted to you,

MUSINKA

December 19, 1879

209. *To ARSENI GOLENISHCHEV-KUTUZOV*

S.P-bg. Vas. Ostr. 5th l. No. 10
[December, 1879]

MY DEAR FRIEND ARSENI,

Don't be displeased with me; since spring some strange illness has overtaken me, breaking out in November with such force that my doctor, who knows me well, gave me only 2 more hours to live. Now I'm a little better, but just a little. So I use this more or less satisfactory condition of my brain to talk with you.

I was extremely delighted about the publication of your poetic works and about the printing of *Shuisky*. In regard to the former I was very caressed by the sympathetic and occasionally clever reviews about the nature of your creative powers. The form is unanimously declared faultless; consequently the question of your problems and their realization arose: in this case you well know, dear friend, to what extent the benevolence of men is parceled out in relation to this or that creative problem, and you further very well know that almost always the inner, indefinable demand screens the accuracy of the criterion: as I'm not fond of such and such a subject—*ergo:* this poetic work leaves me unsatisfied, and vice versa. But aside from this inevitability, the reviews are led to an acknowledgement of that force that produces the flesh and blood of a genuine artistic work. And as for *Shuisky!* here's where some of them are caught. Not being able to stand resolutely in the realm of history, these few start a dispute about theatricality or non-theatricality, forgetting that the most common work can be fitted for the stage as far as the merely hollow external effect is concerned, and, vice versa, a drama that has been profoundly thought out and felt by a poet, without any pranking or screening itself behind good looks, carries within itself the very laws of the stage and cannot fail to find a response in the spectator who is even slightly receptive. Your *Shuisky* is not for actors who distinguish themselves in *Little Sparrows, Fly Not around the Flame,* or *Under Siege,*[19] and this very *Shuisky* of yours is not for the general public, but for the particular public. For that tendency towards contradiction, common to mankind, ensnares even decent people, who thirst for something to criticize, without being able to grasp the most substantial, the most important features of drama. However, "grind away the chaff [and the flour remains]," and I, with my opinion of *Shuisky,* shall sit triumphant on the peak and, as modestly as ever, say: "Now you've become more acquainted with the drama." If you only knew, friend, how people have to be hammered for the sake of the movement and growth of art! Just doze off a moment and such a pile of idle opinions will be born that you have to watch out.—At the same time I should stand guilty before you and before the opponents of my love for *Shuisky* if I didn't declare to you that the huge majority of scenes alarm (to my advantage) the aforesaid opponents. And thus it must be. Profound creations do not take possession of people at one stroke.

And now this, friend: I've become acquainted with V. V. Vereshchagin, who came to us together with Vl. Vas. Stasov, and "Forgotten," by V. V. Vereshchagin, by you and by me, was performed.[20] You were absent, but you were felt by us as closely—as if you had been present among us. This was one of the most wonderful of art matinées. Of course V. S. arranged at his home two days later a grand musical soirée on the eve of V. V. Vereshchagin's departure for Bulgaria: Vereshchagin was highly enthusiastic. "Forgotten"—its text and music touched him to the soul, and even more deeply: he said that in places he was overtaken by a nervous emotion. I hope to meet V. V. Vereshchagin's brother soon—you've spoken about him to me.—V. V. Vereshchagin made the most comforting and attractive impression on me; strength, might, delicacy, receptivity—a born artist-giant. It's too bad, friend, that you weren't present at these meetings, so unforgettable to me.

[19] Musorgsky may not have chosen these plays by chance, for he may well have entertained a grudge against each of their authors: *Little Sparrows* (1878) is by Tarnovsky, the author of a play (*As You Winnow, So You Grind*) that was thrust into one of the Voronezh programs; *Fly Not Around the Flame* (1879) is by Averkiev, author of the libretto for Serov's *Rogneda; Under Siege* is by Victor Krylov, author of the unfortunate *Mlada* libretto (as well as for Cui's *The Mandarin's Son*)!

[20] See pp. 280–281.

I have neither much nor little to say of myself. For the summer I lived in Peterhof; 3 months were spent in music with D. M. Leonova [on tour] and I, great sinner, was crowned with a wreath. I wrote a quite decent scene between Marfa and Andrei Khovansky before the self-immolation—in this scene Leonova brought tears to the eyes of the listeners; it is an entirely unusual and unprecedented scenic situation, you'll hear it, friend, when we meet.

And we waited for you and the Countess in Peter, but we've stopped waiting. I for one have become completely stale with expectation during these 3 months. Well, what's to be done? At a distance of several hundred versts from stories and surmises, one can't determine how it's to be done and what is possible. And it would be desirable for us to see each other: there are so many things that one can't remember to say in a letter, there's nothing like talk—face to face.

I beg you, dear friend, to give my greeting to the Countess Olga Andreyevna and to Countess *maman*. I embrace you firmly.

Your
MODESTE MUSORGSKY

May one expect your arrival in Peter?

Credo

. . . I met M. P. at the end of 1879, when he still had a respectable appearance, his dress was not immaculate but it was neat, and he walked with a proudly held head, which, with his characteristically arranged hair, gave him a cocky air. It was from this time on that he sank rapidly, appearing not always in very good order and, for the most part, talking about himself, attacking us—the youth. "You young ones," he said on one of our strolls, "sitting in the Conservatory, not wishing to know anything beyond your *cantus firmus*, do you think that the Zaremba formula 'the minor key—is our original sin, but the major key—is our sin's redemption,' or this 'rest, movement, and rest again' [21]—do you think this exhausts everything? No, little doves, to my way of thinking, if you want to sin, then go ahead and sin, if you want movement, there's no return to rest, but forward, smashing everything." While saying this he shook his head proudly . . . —MIKHAIL IPPOLITOV-IVANOV [22]

---

[21] Musorgsky is still laughing at the Zaremba formula he satirized in *Penny Paradise*.

[22] At this time a promising, twenty-year-old music student.

209a. *VLADIMIR STASOV to MILI BALAKIREV [Extract]*

January 3, 1880

. . . I want without fail . . . to attempt to do something for Musorgsky. He is sinking—since January 1 he is left without a post and without means of any sort. It would be no wonder if he should drink more! Won't you do something for him—quickly, if possible. Time won't wait. And just because I know and see your fatherly and protecting nature, more and more do I feel that you need some active, extremely active field of action . . .

210. *To IVAN GORBUNOV*

Welcome friend Ivan Fyodorovich, greeting!

I will open myself to you; and about what, that will be dictated by my heart and by my thought. On the night from the 4th to the 5th of January, 1880, in the brightly shining family of him who is dear to the Russian people, that of Terti Ivanovich Filippov, you, good friend of mine, for the first time in my presence were forced to act as you, a Russian *elder*, should have acted long ago. Gorbunov—not recited by "himself," but Gorbunov—a creator, with all the strength of truth, love and spontaneity.[23]

Go further, go forward, on that creative path; further, forward, with that strength of truth, love and spontaneity!—Gorbunov, who has recited on a stage a scene from the people's life, *written* by "*himself*," will die, for we all are mortal; but Gorbunov-creator will not die, but will live for eternity on Russian soil.

If you have understood me, then you will understand this friendly epistle.

Your

MODESTE MUSORGSKY

Night, from the 4th to the 5th of January
1880, in Peter

211. *To VLADIMIR STASOV*

Cordial thanks, *généralissime*, for your good news.[24] In spite of small misfortunes, I have not and will not give way to fainthearted-

---

[23] Apparently Gorbunov departed from his set repertoire of recitations, and improvised something that especially impressed Musorgsky.

[24] In Musorgsky's emergency Balakirev had suggested a concert in his aid, but

ness. You know my motto: "Dare! Forward to new shores!"—it has remained unchanged. If fate allows me to widen the beaten path toward the vital aims of art, I shall rejoice and exult; the demands that art makes upon modern workers are so huge that they are capable of swallowing up the whole man. The time has passed for writing *at leisure;* one must give one's whole self to the people—that's what is now needed in art.—Once more thanks to you.

Your

MUSORYANIN

16 January 1880

211a. *VLADIMIR STASOV to MILI BALAKIREV [Extract]*

February 17, 1880

Mili, it appears that some other people are helping Musorgsky at the rate of 80 rubles a month on the sole condition that he finish his opera *Fair at Sorochintzi* within a year or thereabouts. That is why he resists so sedulously the writing of *Khovanshchina* now . . .

212. *To NIKOLAI BERNARD*

HIGHLY ESTEEMED

NIKOLAI MATVEYEVICH

I beg you to rush the publication of the excerpts from my opera *Fair at Sorochintzi;* this will greatly oblige me.

Tomorrow I shall be at your place. Hearty greetings to your good family.

Devoted to you,

M. MUSORGSKY

May 1, 1880

Bonfire

. . . Musorgsky spent the last summer before his death at the [Bobrovo] estate of my aunt, the Princess Anna Vasilyevna Shakhovskaya, *née* Golenishcheva-Kutuzova, in the Province of Pskov. On leaving, he left a heap of papers and music manuscripts in his rooms. The next year, during the repairs of the house and the sum-

---

Stasov, Filippov and others (including Alexei Zhemchuzhnikov and a certain Neronov) decided on a surer method, to pool their finances and pay Musorgsky one hundred rubles a month on the condition that he was to finish *Khovanshchina.* This may be Musorgsky's reply to Stasov's notification of the pension.

mer cleaning of all rooms, the housekeeper, without consulting my
aunt, decided to burn all the papers which she found in Musorgsky's
old rooms. As he had left them without any word as to their disposition, and as no one after his death inquired about them, she attached no importance to them, and added them to the bonfire of
the house-trash . . . —YELENA ROERICH

212a. *NIKOLAI RIMSKY-KORSAKOV to VLADIMIR STASOV, Rome*
    [Extract]

[May 11, 1880]

I am very delinquent, Vladimir Vasilyevich, in not answering you
at once; my excuse is Musoryanin, whom I wanted to visit before
writing you. Well, I was at his place. He is *terribly busy,* exhausted
by a ceaseless *writing of music,* exhausted by the 2 concerts he gave
with Leonova (the Japanese) in Tver. However, he has written, apparently, the fifth (?) scene of *Khovanshchina,* where Golitzin is taken
away to exile. He also says that he's almost finished the intermezzo
(scene on Bald Mountain or "Dream of the Peasant Lad") in *Sorochintzi* up to the pedaling (the bells) in C-sharp; though when I asked
him to show me the score, it turned out to be all old stuff, left over
from *Mlada* and, except for two or three pages, not even copied out
afresh. He is considering living this summer at the Jap's house in
Oranienbaum, but the Jap is going away somewhere. He has printed
his *Seamstress* at Bernard's. I learned from him that Bernard has lost
2 or 3 numbers of the manuscript of *Fair at Sorochintzi,* which he had
taken away to print, so Musorgsky was obliged to write them out all
over again. He is also publishing the fair scene from *Sorochintzi* for
2 hands. It seems to me that ZZ & Co., who are paying Musorgsky for
Sorochintzi, are behaving mistakenly, by forcing him to print separate numbers from it at Bernard's, for he has to prepare these for the
press; and, by the way, Bernard loses them, so Musorgsky is distracted
from the completion of the opera which, he says, he is obliged to
finish by November, thus putting aside the completion of *Khovanshchina* till next year. I strongly urged him to come to our *dacha* for the
summer and to be our guest there; at first he was evasive, and then
he began to surrender. Perhaps we'll succeed yet in luring him. For
the concerts of the Free School he promises to instrument the intermezzo from *Sorochintzi,* which would be good. But this intermezzo
doesn't have much to do with *Fair at Sorochintzi.* I went to him in

the morning, at about noon, he was still in bed and vomiting nearly every minute; but he seems little disturbed by this, as if it were the most ordinary thing, and he says, indeed, that this is very good . . .

213. *To VLADIMIR STASOV, St. Petersburg* [25]

Rambov,[26] Aug. 5, '80, house of Leonova

Why has Your Excellency showered me with such severe epithets such as even the shark, who appeared in the vision of Pythagoras, could not have swallowed? But, all joking aside, I am happy about your return, and all that's left to be written of *Khovanshchina* is a little bit of the self-immolation scene, and then all is ready. I'll write you in detail about *Fair at Sorochintzi;* there's a great deal done and the Black God is all ready. I am undertaking a suite for orchestra with harps and piano on motifs I've collected from various good pilgrims of this world: its program is from the shores of Bulgaria, through the Black Sea, the Caucasus, the Caspian, Ferghana to Burma. The suite is already somewhat begun.

My hand has become terribly tired writing. I greet the two Alexander Vasilyeviches [Stasov and Meyer] and I embrace you.

A FRIEND

Soirée

In the year 1880 I was living with my parents at Oranienbaum, in the *dacha* of D. M. Leonova. I was 11 years old. I saw M. P. Musorgsky every day in the garden and the courtyard. He looked remarkably like his celebrated portrait by Repin. His costume was always somewhat shabby, and Mr. Drury told me later that he had often bought second-hand clothing for the unfortunate musician . . . Once a week D. M. Leonova gave a musical soirée, with a supper, which was usually managed by "Musinka." From the room in the rear, you could hear the clatter of plates and the uncorking of bottles. Every time he came out of that room, Musorgsky became more and more "tight." After supper the concert began, where Musorgsky, (who was already quite "full") acted as accompanist and as soloist. He played his own pieces with amazing perfection and with "thrilling effect" upon his audience . . . —S. V. ROZHDESTVENSKY

[25] Just returned from a tour of several months through the Balkans, Austria, Poland, Germany, Italy and France, examining the archives of monasteries and libraries in preparation for his monumental work, *Slavic and Eastern Ornament.*

[26] The peasants' name for Oranienbaum, which they found too difficult to pronounce.

214. *To VLADIMIR STASOV, St. Petersburg*

Rambov, house of Leonova
Aug. 22, '80

Dear *généralissime*, our *Khovanshchina* is finished, except for a little piece in the final scene of the self-immolation: we must talk this over together, for this *"schelm"* is completely dependent on scenic technique. I was overjoyed to see Terti Ivanovich Filippov in Rambov and I showed him (my voice has returned) the act of the death of Prince Ivan Andr[eyevich] Khovansky. Terti Ivanovich was satisfied. But tell me, what should I do with my devils in *Sorochintzi,*—what should they look like and, in general, how should their appearance be managed? I might find out from Michelet,[27] but I value your directions more. What would a drunken Ukrainian village lad see in his dream? Gogol, it seems, asked exactly this same question. I beg your good help. The scene of the Black God is turning out well, but . . . but with new and lively means of portraying devils on the stage. A senseless setting is an abomination to me, and a senseless portrayal of a human dream fantasy, furthermore, that of a drunken fantasy— all the more so. Help me.

I firmly embrace you,
MUSORYANIN

[Enclosed with this letter is the following program, in red pencil:]

Dream Vision of the Peasant Lad

The Lad sleeps at the foot of a hillock, far from the hut where he has to go. *And he dreams:*

(1) An underground rumble of inhuman voices, pronouncing inhuman words.
(2) The underground kingdom of darkness asserts its rights,—jeering over the sleeping Lad.
(3) Portents of the appearance of the Black God and Satan.
(4) The spirits of darkness leave the Lad. Appearance of the Black God.
(5) Glorification of the Black God and the black mass.
(6) *Witches' Sabbat.*
(7) At the very climax of the *Sabbat* the bell in the village church strikes. The Black God vanishes instantly.
(8) Suffering of the demons.
(9) Voices of the church choir.
(10) Disappearance of the demons and the awakening of the Lad.

---

[27] *La Sorcière* (1862), by Jules Michelet.

215. *To VLADIMIR STASOV, St. Petersburg*

Oranienbaum, house of Leonova
27–28 Aug. '80

My dear *généralissime,* with all my heart and all my understanding I am glad about the return of dearest Dimitri Vasilyevich: [28] Glory be to God! the good, hospitable family can be at peace (that family so beloved by me). I am completely overjoyed. As for the sinful Musoryanin I can only say that at this very second, at night, he has done the fair scene of *Sorochintzi*—as for *Khovanshchina* it is *on the eve* of completion: but the instrumentation—O gods!—time . . . !

Perhaps Musoryanin will be faithful to that of which he always spoke: a new, untrodden path, and he stops before it? Not so. *Dare!*

Ever, with all my soul,
Your
MUSORYANIN

Green Soap

. . . The last time I saw him before his illness was at the "Maly Yaroslavetz" restaurant, where I, Laroche and Glazunov [29] had gone in order to see him. We found him in a completely irresponsible condition. As soon as he saw me he immediately, as if habitually, burst out against Rubinstein, Balakirev, and Rimsky-Korsakov for their erudition and repeated several times: "Must create, create" and then became silent. Then he raised his sleepy eyes to me and asked unexpectedly: "And with what do you remove spots from your cutaway?"—"I try not to make any, M.P.," I answered. "And you know, I do it with green soap," said he, "it takes them out very nicely, very nicely." And he became completely silent. On this our conversation with him ended . . . —MIKHAIL IPPOLITOV-IVANOV

215a. *NIKOLAI RIMSKY-KORSAKOV to SEMYON KRUGLIKOV, Moscow*
[Extract]

November 9, 1880

. . . One can learn by oneself; sometimes one needs advice, but one has to learn, that is, one must not neglect harmony and counterpoint

---

[28] Dimitri Stasov must have defended one revolutionary too many, for he himself was "restricted" to Tula in March, being allowed to return to St. Petersburg at the end of August.

[29] The fifteen-year-old Alexander Glazunov had begun private lessons in elementary theory of composition with Rimsky-Korsakov in December, 1879.

and the development of a good technique and a clean leading subject. All of us, that is, myself and Borodin, and Balakirev, and Blaramberg,[30] but especially Cui and Musorgsky, neglected this. I consider that I caught myself in time and made myself get down to work. Owing to such deficiencies in technique Balakirev writes little, Borodin—with difficulty, Cui—sloppily, and Musorgsky—messily and often nonsensically; Blaramberg suffers from all these deficiencies to a greater or lesser degree, and all this constitutes the very regrettable specialty of the Russian school . . .

216. *To IVAN GORBUNOV*

[a musical greeting card]

In memory of the 16th of November, 1880—
jubilee of the 25th anniversary of the *people's*
Russian artist Ivan Fyodorovich Gorbunov,
     written for him by one who is deeply devoted
to him, so dear to the Russian people
                                    MODESTE MUSORGSKY

217. *To NIKOLAI RIMSKY-KORSAKOV*

[December 1880]

MY DEAR NIKOLAI ANDREYEVICH,
    With all my soul I trust you to take away from the Conservatory of the Imperial Russian Musical Society my score of the march (*The Capture of Kars*) with the orchestral parts.[31]
                                    Your soul's
                                    M. MUSORGSKY

---

[30] P. I. Blaramberg had frequented the Balakirev Circle in the past. He was now an instructor at Shostakovsky's music school.

[31] This is the former March of the Princes from the ruins of *Mlada*, refurbished with a new trio and submitted as *The Capture of Kars* for another unrealized project—a series of allegorical *tableaux vivants* in honor of the twenty-fifth anniversary of Alexander II's reign. Other products of this plan were Borodin's *On the Steppes of Central Asia* and Rimsky-Korsakov's *Slava*. All these found their way to the public ear, however, *Kars* being conducted by Napravnik at the second concert in the season of the Imperial Russian Musical Society, on October 18. This is Musorgsky's last extant letter.

A Book by CESAR CUI [Extracts]

(*La Musique en Russie*, published in Paris, 1880 [32])

M. Musorgsky has a melodic faculty of great richness and remarkable abundance. The harmonies which he finds are almost always quite striking and new. This highly gifted nature appears at times, however odd it may seem to say so, not to be altogether musical, or, at any rate, not to belong to the category of *sensitive* musical beings. In fact, very wide gaps are to be found in him, side by side with a number of fine qualities. Symphonic form is altogether alien to Musorgsky, and the working out or development of a musical situation is not his domain. His modulations are too free, and sometimes one might say that they only proceed along lines of pure chance. When he harmonizes a melody, he cannot give the requisite continuity to the laying out of the parts, and these parts, as he writes them, often look quite impossible and unnatural, and produce harmonies which only fall to pieces, and lengths of an intolerable duration. Critical instinct and the sense of beauty were not always revealed to his understanding, and his gifts assume a character of astounding wildness, which brooks no kind of restraint. And yet all these impetuous digressions and disordered outbursts are the signs of an abundant and vigorous vitality, and give Musorgsky an entirely individual and original physiognomy of his own . . .

M. Musorgsky is a recognized master of declamation. In this he holds first place after Dargomizhsky. But his immoderate abuse of imitative accents unfortunately denotes too great a tendency to grasp and to produce external effects, to the detriment of musical sense . . .

Farewell to Dostoyevsky

. . . The well-known archeologist V. G. Druzhinin kindly informed me that a few days after the death of Dostoyevsky (on January 28, 1881), at an evening devoted to his memory at a literary club, when they brought in the portrait of the deceased writer framed in black crepe, Musorgsky sat down at the piano and improvised a funeral knell, similar to that heard in the last scene of *Boris*. This was the next to the last public appearance of Musorgsky,[33] and this musical improvisation was his farewell, not only to the deceased singer of the "insulted and injured," but to all the living . . . —IVAN LAPSHIN

---

[32] Cui's book had first appeared as a series of articles in *Revue et Gazette Musical de Paris*, between 1878 and 1880. It is not known whether Musorgsky read it in either form.

[33] Grigorovich also participated in this evening, reciting the story of the boy and Christ under the Christmas tree, *The Heavenly Christmas Tree*. Musorgsky took part in one more public concert, as an accompanist on February 9.

217b. *NIKOLAI RIMSKY-KORSAKOV to SEMYON KRUGLIKOV, Moscow*

Petersburg. 4 February 1881

Yesterday the first concert of the Free School was given. The program was the following: (1) *Antar*—it went all right and was well received; (2) the chorus *Destruction of Sennacherib* by Musorgsky—it went well, but there wasn't a very satisfactory balance between chorus and orchestra, Musorgsky took a bow . . .

217c. *MILI BALAKIREV to NIKOLAI RIMSKY-KORSAKOV [Extract]*

February 10, 1881

. . . Send me Musorgsky's song [from *The Fair at Sorochintzi*], I'll orchestrate it soon, so that you won't be torn away from your work . . .

217d. *NIKOLAI RIMSKY-KORSAKOV to MILI BALAKIREV [Extract]*

. . . am sending you [the song from] *Fair at Sorochintzi;* Musorgsky orchestrated it up to the Allegro. If you have time, complete it. He used 4 horns in E-flat, 2 trombones in E-flat and tympani in G-flat and D-flat. In the Allegro he wants a tambourine and a triangle . . .

Farewell to Music

. . . It is very probable that everything was weighing on him—his spiritual excitements as well as his material privations. He was living in terrible poverty. One day [February 11, 1881] he called on me in an extremely nervous, excited state, and said that he had no place to go, that nothing was left for him but to walk the streets, that he had no further resources and saw no way out of his situation. What was I to do? I tried to console him, saying that although I didn't have much, I would share what I had with him. This calmed him somewhat. On this very evening we were going together to General Sokhansky, whose daughter, our pupil, was to sing for the first time in her home to a large gathering. She sang very well and this, apparently, made an impression on Musorgsky. I noticed that his accompaniment was nervous. Everyone remarked that she was singing very well for such a short period of study. Everyone was pleased and her mother and father were very grateful to us. After the singing, dancing began, and I was invited to play cards. Suddenly Sokhansky's son rushed to me and asked me if Musorgsky suffered from fits. I assured him that as long as I had known him I had never heard of anything of the sort. Apparently he had just had a stroke. A doctor who was there attended to him; when the time came to go, Musorgsky was quite restored, and on his feet. We rode away together. Arriving at my apartment, he earnestly begged me to allow him to stay there, on account of some condition of nerves and fear. I readily consented, knowing that if anything further was to happen to him he could get no help in his lonely lodging. I got the little study ready for him and posted my maid there to watch him all night, telling her to wake me the moment anything happened to him. He slept in a sitting position the whole night. When I came into the dining-room in the morning to have my tea, he also came in, quite gay. I asked him about his health. He thanked me and said that he felt well. With these words he turned to the right and suddenly fell full length on the floor. My precautions had not been in vain—if he had been alone, he would certainly have choked to death; but we turned him over, gave him immediate help and sent for a doctor. Before evening he had two more such fits. By evening I sent for all his friends who had previously shown their sympathy, including Vladimir Vasilyevich Stasov and Terti Ivanovich Filippov, and others who loved him. We held a consultation: as we anticipated a complicated treatment, requiring constant attention, we decided to persuade him to enter a hospital, explaining the importance and usefulness of this to him. We promised to arrange for a fine private room. He resisted for a long time and declared that he definitely wished to stay at my place. At last we persuaded him. Next day we took him in a carriage to the hospital . . . —DARIA LEONOVA

Admitting Office

. . . When Musorgsky, then retired, having no means of existence, living in the most dreadful, pitiful conditions, fell seriously ill, his most intimate friends: V. V. Stasov, C. A. Cui, N. A. Rimsky-Korsakov and A. P. Borodin, separately and in a body, applied to me— "a doctor who loved and respected musicians and writers,"—with a request to find a good place for Musorgsky in this or that hospital. This request greatly disturbed and alarmed me for I saw no possibility for my carrying it out properly. At that time I worked in 2 hospitals: the Rozhdestvenskaya City Hospital for common laborers with general wards only, and Nikolayevsky Military Hospital for soldiers and officers. At both these institutions I was then only a junior staff physician, that is, "small fry" with no executive powers, and could act only in the capacity of a humble petitioner, delivering the request of such aces as Rimsky-Korsakov, Stasov and the others. But in the City Hospital nothing could be done, not even by the Lord Mayor himself, and the Nikolayevsky Military Hospital, as its name indicates, served the army and army offices exclusively,—and as Musorgsky at that time was registered in his passport as a retired civil servant of the State Control, there was no hope for successfully entering him in this hospital. However, having promised my petitioning friends, not without some embarrassment, to do my best for the great man, I hastened to the chief surgeon [at the Nikolayevsky]. The first attack on my superior was not only unsuccessful, but even brought down on me the irritated remark that I was begging the impossible; but as I was about to leave in a grieved and depressed state, my severe superior, suddenly thinking of an unusual solution to the hopeless situation, stopped me and proposed that Musorgsky be entered in the hospital as the "hired orderly of Dr. Bertensson"— providing, of course, that both Musorgsky and his friends would consent to this high rank being bestowed on him . . . Needless to say, I was overjoyed at this unexpected and happy answer to my request and, receiving the consent of the aforesaid friends (the consent of the patient was unnecessary as in consequence of his high fever he was still unconscious), I immediately moved Musorgsky into the hospital. With the benevolent attitude of the chief surgeon I was able to make arrangements better than "good" for the patient: he was provided with a spacious, high-ceilinged, sunny room, equipped with all necessary furniture (not stylish, naturally), in the most quiet and isolated part of the hospital. As for his attendants, nothing better could possibly have been desired, for he was put in the charge of two Red Cross nurses, two male nurses and an interne. The diet was more than satisfactory, for, in addition to officers' rations, the patient was brought an abundance of various foods by acquaintances and friends who constantly showed him their heartfelt attention . . . — DR. LEV BERTENSSON

217e. *MILI BALAKIREV to VLADIMIR STASOV [Extract]*

February 14, 1881

. . . Honor and glory to Leonova. She must have a good heart if she can take such disinterested care of such a person as Modeste Petrovich, and without any hope for his improvement . . .

217f. *VLADIMIR STASOV to MILI BALAKIREV [Extract]*

. . . The doctors [Bertensson] now say that these were not paralytic strokes, but the beginning of epilepsy. I've been with him [Musorgsky] today and yesterday (Borodin and Korsakov were there yesterday and the day before, many other friends as well); he looks as if nothing were the matter with him and now recognizes everybody, but he talks the devil knows what gibberish and tells lots of impossible stories. They say that besides the epilepsy and the strokes he is also a bit mad. He is done for, though he may linger on (the doctors say) for a year, or only for a day . . .

". . . Something Important"

. . . On his deathbed a few days before the end, he told me, hoping that he would recover, of his wish to begin something important and big.

"And you know," he added, "I should like something entirely new, something I've never touched. I'd like to get away from history, and in general from all this *prose,* which in life as well doesn't give one a chance to breathe . . . And I'll tell you something else—up to now, we've busied ourselves only with trifles. Let's get to work on something important—you write a fantastic drama, and I'll clothe it in sounds; yes, and so that not a word would be changed, just as Dargomizhsky did with *The Stone Guest.* But listen, not a word about this to anyone, let it be a secret for a while."—ARSENI GOLEN-ISHCHEV-KUTUZOV

Last Portrait

. . . I. Ye. Repin had a chance to see Musorgsky for the last time at the beginning of Lent. He came here from Moscow for the Itinerant Exhibition; he found Musorgsky already at the Nikolayevsky Military Hospital. Judging by all indications, Repin saw that he would have to hurry with his portrait of the beloved man: it was clear that they would never again see each other. Here fortune came to the assistance of the portrait: at the beginning of Lent, Musorgsky's illness entered a stage when he looked fresher, cheered, even becoming gay, believing in his rapid recovery and dreaming of new musical works, even within the walls of his military hospital. It is with profound gratitude that one must say—that he owed all this to Dr. L. B. Bertensson, who considered him not only as one of his patients, but as a close friend and as a person of historical significance. The place, the atmosphere, the endless watchfulness and care —all this acted upon Musorgsky to such an extent that he often repeated to many of his visitors (and to me) that it was so fine that it was just as if he were in his own home, surrounded by his own family and by the fondest of attention. It was at this time that Repin saw Musorgsky. In addition to this good mood the weather was lovely and Musorgsky's big room was bathed in sunlight from the high windows. Repin managed to do his portrait in four days altogether: the 2nd, 3rd, 4th and 5th of March; after this began the last fatal period of his illness. The portrait was painted despite all sorts of obstacles: the artist didn't even have an easel, and had to arrange himself at a small table before which Musorgsky was seated in a hospital armchair . . . —VLADIMIR STASOV

. . . When I painted M. P.'s portrait in the Nikolayevsky Hospital, it was just as a *terrible event* had occurred: the death of Alexander II,[34] and in the intermissions between sittings we read a mass of newspapers, all on one and the same terrible topic. The birthday of Modeste Petrovich was approaching. He lived under a severe regimen

---

[34] A bomb ended the life and reign of Alexander II on March 1 (March 13).

of *sobriety* and he was in an especially healthy, sober condition . . . But, as always, alcoholics are gnawed inside by the worm of Bacchus; and M.P. was already dreaming about compensating himself for his long patience. In spite of the rigid orders given to the attendants forbidding cognac, after all, "the heart is not a stone," and for the birthday an attendant obtained for M.P. (he was so loved by all) a whole bottle of cognac [35] . . . —ILYA REPIN

218. *To TERTI FILIPPOV (A Deed)*

In the year one thousand eight hundred and eighty-one, on the fourteenth day of March, I the undersigned, Collegiate Councilor Modeste Petrovich Musorgsky, have drawn up this deed for Privy Councilor Terti Ivanovich Filippov in order to turn over to him for his full and sole possession all my appertaining author's rights on all my musical compositions, both published and unpublished, evaluating these rights at two thousand silver rubles. Excluded from this deed are those compositions already sold to other persons. Collegiate Councilor Modeste Petrovich Musorgsky's signature, because of his illness and at his personal request, is herewith made by Count Arseni Arkadyevich Golenishchev-Kutuzov. At the drawing of this deed we were present and we testify the presence of Modeste Petrovich Musorgsky and his legal capacity to draw deeds. Actual State Councilor Vladimir Vasilyevich Stasov, Aulic Councilor Nikolai Andreyevich Rimsky-Korsakov, Citizen of the Great Principality of Finland Fyodor Dmitriyevich Gridnin. In the year one thousand eight hundred and eighty-one, on the fourteenth day of March this deed was presented to me, Mikhail Ivanovich Uspensky, St. Petersburg notary whose office is in the Moskovskaya City District at Nevsky Prospect, No. 51, by the Collegiate Councilor Modeste Petrovich Musorgsky at the place of his treatment, Rozhdestvenskaya City District, Konnogvardeiskaya Street, in the Nikolayevsky Military Hospital, the personality and legal capacity of whom to draw legal deeds have been witnessed by the present and personally known to me witnesses, Actual State Councilor Vladimir Vasilyevich Stasov, Aulic Councilor Nikolai Andreyevich Rimsky-Korsakov and Citizen of the Great Principality of Finland Fyodor Dmitriyevich Gridnin, the former two living in the Liteinaya City District at Sergiyevskaya No. 79 and Furshtadtskaya No. 21, the last

[35] This bottle of cognac has been inflated by legend to the dimensions of the immediate cause of Musorgsky's death.

in the Spasskaya City District at Alexandrovskaya Square No. 3. Signing because of the illness and at the personal request of Musorgsky is Count Arseni Arkadyevich Golenishchev-Kutuzov, living in the Liteinaya City District at Mokhovaya No. 29, personally known to me. Stamp-duty and city tax of ten rubles collected. Registered as No. 2742. Signed by Notary Uspensky.

Last Words

Intrigues and unpleasantnesses affected Musorgsky terribly, he became ill more and more often, and his nerves were completely upset. Falling ill in 1881 . . . his weakened, exhausted organism was unable to resist the illness and he passed away in a hospital, surrounded by his intimate friends, on his birthday, March 16/28, 1881, at the age of 42.[36] M.P. died at night. The nurse then in attendance told us that he suddenly screamed loudly—"All is ended. Ah, how miserable I am!"—ALEXANDRA PURGOLD (MOLAS)

Thirty-second Generation from Rurik [37]

23. Modeste Petrovich, born 9 March 1839; on leaving the school of Guards-Ensigns and Cavalry Cadets was promoted Ensign in the Reserve Regiment of the Preobrazhensky Life Guards, 23 June 1856; received his discharge, 5 June 1858; appointed to the Chief Engineering Board, with the rank of Collegiate Secretary, 1 December 1863; Assistant to the Chief Clerk, 20 January 1864; Titular Councilor, 1 December 1866; struck off the rolls, 1 May 1867; Assistant to Chief Clerk of the Forestry Department, 21 December 1868; Collegiate Assessor, 1 December 1869; Junior Chief Clerk, 11 March 1872; Aulic Councilor, 1 December 1872; Senior Chief Clerk, 1 March 1875; Honorary Justice of the Peace for Toropetz County, 21 June 1876; Collegiate Councilor, 1 December 1877; transferred as Junior Director of the Temporary Inspection Committee of the State Control, 1 October 1878; appointed to the State Control, 15 February 1879; died [of erysipelas of the leg] in the Nikolayevsky Military Hospital, 16 March 1881 . . .

The Dead

. . . At 10 A.M. I went to visit him at the Nikolayevsky Hospital. His ward was pointed out to me, and at its door I collided with Count Golenishchev-Kutuzov. "You want to see Musorgsky?—He's dead."

Today was his birthday. I entered the ward. Involuntarily my heart constricted. The conditions in which Musorgsky had died,—

---

[36] See note 86, p. 42.

[37] From a family tree prepared by S. V. Lyubimov, in *The Princes Kostrov; Materials for a Genealogy of the Musorgskys.* Pskov, 1916.

the complete solitude, the hospital atmosphere in which this great talent was extinguished, made a depressing impression on me. The large room with its white plastered walls looked unfriendly, despite its cleanliness. Aside from the absolutely necessary—there was nothing. It was evident that a bohemian had died here. Half the room was partitioned off with gray screens, behind which stood several beds; directly before the door stood a closet, a lectern, two chairs, two small tables with newspapers and five or six books, among them Berlioz's treatise "On Orchestration": he had died like a soldier, with weapons in his hands. At the right of the door—a small bed on which lay the body of Musorgsky, covered by a gray hospital blanket. How greatly he had changed! His face and hands, as white as wax, made a queer impression,—exactly as if some stranger lay there. The expression on his face was, however, peaceful; one might even think that he was sleeping, if it had not been for that deathly pallor. Involuntarily a bitter feeling stirred in me, involuntarily I thought of the strange fate of our Russian people. To be as talented as was Musorgsky (a talent recognized by all, even by those who didn't agree with the tendencies of the deceased), to possess all this, to stand aloft and to live—and instead of this to die in a hospital among strangers, without friend or kin to close his eyes. What a fate haunts our gifts . . .

Several close friends of the deceased soon arrived: Vladimir Vasilyevich Stasov, his brother D. V. Stasov, N. A. Rimsky-Korsakov, an Uhlan officer, Mr. Kelchevsky, who had formerly shared an apartment with the deceased, several other persons, among them two ladies (one, apparently, was the wife of Mr. Rimsky-Korsakov) . . . — MIKHAIL IVANOV

218a. *LUDMILA SHESTAKOVA to VLADIMIR STASOV*

I am sending you, Vladimir Vasilyevich, the letters of our dear Musinka. You cannot imagine how saddened I am that I did not see him during his illness; I was prevented from doing this by a letter that I received from him, in which he told me that he was feeling so well that he expected to leave the hospital in a few days and would then come to see me. I am consoled only by the fact that in all the years of our friendly acquaintance he received from me, neither in word nor in deed, one shadow of displeasure; yes, I can call it friendly, for he never hid from me his feelings and his relationships with his brother and other people. This is an irreplaceable loss for art and for his friends, but for his own future there was nothing better in view; with his self-love, breeding and education, you must agree it can't have been easy to be under the patronage of D. M. L[eonova] and her gentleman (I can't recall his name [Gridnin]). Although I have read

everything and heard a great deal [about the death and funeral] I wish
to hear full details from you; Bach, you are no mere man, you are
more than a man, or I should say, in you alone is all that is best in
everyone else, collected together. And I will say that for me Musorgsky
will live forever, not only as the author of *Boris,* but as a rare, kind,
honest and gentle man.

Your
L. Shestakova

I am ill and cannot leave the house, but of course the first time I
go out it will be to Musorgsky's grave.

*Soon after Musorgsky's death Stasov organized a campaign to erect a
monument over the grave in Alexander Nevsky cemetery. To defray the
expenses of this, Repin turned over the amount paid by Tretyakov for his
portrait of Musorgsky, Rimsky-Korsakov gave the receipts from the first
performance of* Khovanshchina *(which had been edited and orchestrated
by him), Lyadov turned over the receipts of a Musorgsky concert given by
him, Glazunov gave the prize money awarded him for his first symphony,
and both the architect Bogomolov and the sculptor Ginsburg refused all
remuneration for their work.*

*The monument was erected. Under a bas-relief portrait of Musorgsky,
Vladimir Stasov ordered this inscription, from Pimen's monologue in*
Boris Godunov:

> *"So that the descendants of the orthodox*
> *may know the past fate of their own land."*

*At the unveiling ceremony in 1885 the four corners of the veil were
lifted by Borodin, Balakirev, Rimsky-Korsakov and Cui.*

219. *Autobiographical Note* [38]

[June 1880]

Modeste <Piotr> Musorgsky. Russian composer. Born in 1839, the
16th of March, province of Pskov, county of Toropetz. Son of an
ancient Russian family. Under the direct influence of his nurse, he

---

[38] This note was prepared for Hugo Riemann's music dictionary, and as Musorgsky knew that at least a year would pass before its publication, he felt safe in
going a little beyond the present, such as imagining both *Khovanshchina* and
Fair at Sorochintzi on the press! The other weakness of this note has been excused
by Dr. Samuel Johnson: ". . . he that speaks of himself has no motive to falsehood or partiality except self-love by which all have so often been betrayed that
all are on the watch against its artifices."

416

became familiar with Russian fairy tales. This acquaintance with the spirit of the folk-life was the main impulse of musical improvisations before he had learned even the elementary rules of piano-playing. His mother gave him his first piano lessons and he made such progress that at the age of seven he played small pieces by Liszt, and at nine played a grand concerto by Field before a large audience in his parents' house. His father, who worshiped music, decided to develop the child's ability—and entrusted his further musical education to An[ton] Herke in Petersburg. The professor was so satisfied with his pupil that when he was twelve he had him play a Concerto Rondo by Herz at a private charity concert in the home of the Court Lady-of-Honor, Ryumina. The success and impression made by the young musician's performance was such that Professor Herke, ever a severe critic of his pupils, presented him with a copy of Beethoven's Sonata in A-flat. At thirteen young Musorgsky entered the Cadet School of the Guards and was honored by the particularly kind attention of the late Emperor Nikolai. It was then that Musorgsky composed a little piano piece and dedicated it to his comrades. This piece was published by his father with the help of An. Herke. This was the first work of the young <talented> musician to appear in print. In school he visited a great deal with the religious instructor, Father Krupsky, thanks to whom he acquired a profound knowledge of the very essence of ancient Greek and Catholic church music.[39] At the age of 17 he entered the Preobrazhensky regiment. In the regiment his comrade Vanlyarsky introduced Musorgsky to the genius Dargomizhsky. In the home of Dargomizhsky Musorgsky became friendly with the prominent workers of musical art in Russia: C. Cui and M. Balakirev. With the latter the young 19-year-old composer studied the whole history of the development of musical art,—with examples, with severe systematic analysis of all the most important musical creations by the *composers of European art* in their historical sequence, this study proceeded during regular readings together of the musical works on two

---

[39] Kompaneisky, who was studying music with Father Krupsky at the time of his acquaintance with Musorgsky, claims that Musorgsky could not possibly have learned more than "a rudimentary knowledge of ancient church music," Krupsky having little interest or information in this field. According to an anonymous correspondent (signed M.P.), Father Krupsky, when asked about Musorgsky's statement, smiled and said that his role in Musorgsky's musical education was far more modest. He said that Musorgsky was at that time singing in the school choir and that his only contact with Musorgsky was in the choir's work on choruses by Bortnyansky and other modern masters of church music.

pianos. Balakirev brought Musorgsky close to the family of one of the most important connoisseurs of arts in Russia, the well-known art critic Stasov, and with the sister of the genius-creator of Russian music Glinka. On his part Cui introduced Musorgsky to the famous Polish composer Moniuszko. Shortly thereafter the composer came close and became friendly with other such talented composers, such as the present well-known professor of the Petersburg conservatory, N. A. Rimsky-Korsakov. This closeness to a talented circle of musicians, regular discussions and the establishment of firm contacts with a wide circle of Russian scholars and writers, such as Vladimir Lamansky, Turgenev, Kostomarov, Grigorovich, Kavelin, Pisemsky, Shevchenko <Dostoyevsky> and others, particularly stimulated the mental activity of the young composer and gave it a serious, strictly scientific direction. The result of this fortunate closeness was a whole series of musical compositions on Russian folk life, and the friendly companionship in the home of Shestakova with Professor V. Nikolsky caused the creation of the grand opera *Boris Godunov,* based on a subject by the great Pushkin. In the family circle of Privy Councilor Purgold, a great lover of art, and with the collaboration of his nieces A. and N. Purgold, serious and talented interpreters of music, *Boris Godunov* was performed for a large gathering, in the presence of the distinguished Petrov, Platonova, Kommissarzhevsky and Associate-Director Lukashevich. Directly thereupon it was decided to stage 3 scenes of this opera, although this very opera not long before had been rejected by the theater Directorate. With the participation of the distinguished artist D. Leonova, the opera, supported on the shoulders of the above-named artists, was staged, finally, in its entirety with stupendous success. The impression it made on the audience, the artists and the orchestra was astonishing. The success of the opera was a complete triumph for its author. Following this opera there were planned, with the assistance of the critic Stasov, Professors Nikolsky and Kostomarov, two more operas simultaneously: *Khovanshchina* and *The Fair at Sorochintzi,* based on Gogol. As a relaxation from this work there were composed the *Album Series* on the exhibition of the works of the genius architect Hartmann, *Danse macabre* (5 scenes) on a text by the author's friend Count Golenishchev-Kutuzov and several songs with text by Count Al[exei] Tolstoy. In 1879 the distinguished Russian dramatic singer Leonova invited Musorgsky to undertake a grand artistic tour of Russia and Little Russia, the Crimea and along the Don and the Volga. This journey, taking 3 months, was a genuine triumphal procession for the two important Russian artists: the talented composer and the well-known singer. On tour the author conceived the idea of transposing into music one of the as yet untouched, from the musical point of view, creations of the great Goethe: Song of Mephistopheles in Auerbach's Cellar about the Flea. As an impression of the tour through the Crimea Musorgsky published two caprices for piano: *Baidari* and *Gursuf;* then there was composed and played by the author himself at several concerts a large musical picture, *"Storm on the Black Sea."* He is bringing to completion both grand operas—*Khovanshchina* and *Fair at Sorochintzi,* which are on the press, as well as a large suite on themes of the Trans-Caspian region. Several of the most sharply original pictures for singing—"Savishna," "The Orphan Girl," "The Naughty Boy," "Gopak" (Shevchenko), struck the author's friend von Madeweiss, who handed them over for safekeeping to the Strasburg library with explanatory letters on these pieces by the author.

Two scherzi: B-flat major and C-sharp minor; the former was performed by an orchestra under the direction of A. Rubinstein, which was the first opportunity the author had to hear his work played by an orchestra, *Impromptu, Prelude and Menuet monstre,* "Savishna," "Gopak," "Gathering Mushrooms" (Mey), "Jewish Song" for chorus and orchestra, *The Destruction of Sennacherib* (Byron), *Jesus Navinus [Joshua]* (on ancient Israelite themes. recorded by the author), "The Naughty Boy," "The Magpie" (Pushkin), *Intermezzo symphonique, Kinderscherz, La Fileuse,* "King Saul" (after an Israelite text), "Jewish Song," "The Nurse's Child's Song," *Album from Childhood,* "Forgotten" (from the Central Asiatic war), "Night—A Fantasy" (from Pushkin), "Yeremushka" (Nekrasov), the polemical pieces: "The Classicist," *Penny Paradise,* "The Seminarist"—prohibited and circulated in a mass of hand-written copies, published abroad.

Musorgsky cannot be classed with any existing group of musicians, either by the character of his compositions or by his musical views. The formula of his artistic *profession de foi* may be explained by his view, as a composer, of the task of art: art is a means of communicating with people, not an aim in itself. This guiding principle has defined the whole of his creative activity. Proceeding from the conviction that human speech is strictly controlled by musical laws (Virchow, Gervinus [40]) he considers the task of musical art to be the reproduction in musical sounds not merely of the mood of the feeling, but chiefly of the mood of human speech. Acknowledging that in the realm of art only artist-reformers such as Palestrina, Bach, Gluck, Beethoven, Berlioz and Liszt have created the laws of art, he considers these laws as not immutable but liable to change and progress, like the entire spiritual world of man.

Under the influence of such developed artistic views of the composer on the tasks and character of his creative work—was a whole . . . [The manuscript breaks off.]

---

[40] The names of Rudolf Virchow, scientist, and Georg Gervinus, Shakespearean scholar, are curiously juxtaposed here. No one has ventured a guess on what work of Virchow's may have impressed Musorgsky, but the Gervinus work in question certainly seems to have been his *Handel und Shakespeare,* with its very thoughtful exposition of relations between word and music. Another factor bringing these two German names together may have been Chernyshevsky's admiration for both these men: he pulls both names into his didactic novel, well known to Musorgsky: *What Is to Be Done?*

Appendix

Chronology

1839   Modeste Petrovich Musorgsky was born in the village of Karevo, Pskov province.

1852   Moved to St. Petersburg with his family and entered the Cadet School with his brother Filaret; his interest in music produced his first published composition: *Porte-Enseigne Polka.*

1856   Graduated from the school and entered the Preobrazhensky regiment.

1857   Came into contact with Dargomizhsky, Balakirev, Cui, and Stasov.

1858   Began composition lessons with Balakirev and resigned his Army commission.

1859   Composed a choral scene for *Oedipus in Athens.*

1861   Financial state of the Musorgsky family seriously affected by liberation of the serfs.

1863   Musorgsky took a civil service job, lived in a communal apartment and began work on an opera, *Salammbô.*

1867   First songs, *Gopak* and *Savishna,* published.

1868   First act of an opera, *Marriage,* composed and composition of *Boris Godunov* begun.

1872   Second version of *Boris Godunov* and song cycle, *The Nursery,* completed; *Khovanshchina* planned.

1874   *Boris Godunov* published and staged; piano suite, *Pictures at an Exhibition,* composed.

1875   *Khovanshchina* in progress; comic opera, *Fair at Sorochintzi,* begun.

1877   Cycle, *Songs and Dances of Death,* completed.

1879   Musorgsky undertook a concert tour in the Ukraine, Crimea, and Volga region, as soloist and accompanist for Daria Leonova.

1880   Did further work on both *Khovanshchina* and *Fair at Sorochintzi,* without completing either opera.

1881   Collapsed and was taken to the Military Hospital, where he died.

Musorgsky's Works

The semitragic postscript to Musorgsky's tragic end is the fact that his music has become familiar in forms other than those in which he composed it. Outside of Russia his greatest opera has never been heard (except on the radio) as its composer wrote it, published it, and saw it staged. His most important piano work is played in many editions and arrangements, but rarely in Musorgsky's own version. His songs, though universally recognized as a turning point in the history of modern music, have gone through every mill known to publishers and performers. Audiences are never informed that they are hearing a collaboration between an editor and a composer who was unable to protect his work.

Fortunately it is no longer required critical practice to shake one's fist at Musorgsky's first and most valuable "arranger." Nikolai Rimsky-Korsakov maintained Musorgsky's name and basic musical contributions in public circulation during a period in which we might have lost sight of this genius-ahead-of-his-time. Rimsky-Korsakov has himself given the clearest definition of his function in relation to Musorgsky's music:

> . . . If Musorgsky's compositions are destined to live unfaded for fifty years after their author's death, (when all his works will become the property of any and every publisher) such a musicologically accurate edition will always be possible, as the manuscripts went to the Public Library on leaving me. For the present, though, there was need of an edition for performances, for practical artistic purposes, for making his colossal talent known. . .[1]

Those fifty years have passed and the world of music is now highly in debt to Professor Pavel Lamm, for providing Musorgsky's history with a happier post-postscript: a complete edition of Musorgsky's works based on all the existing original manuscripts, including those in the archives of the Leningrad Public Library. This so-called

---

[1] Rimsky-Korsakov, *Chronicle.*

424

"academic" edition has become Professor Lamm's lifework, and he has been somewhat rewarded by the scattered cries of astonishment that have been heard at the appearance of each volume of this edition, since the first, *Boris Godunov*, was published jointly by the Musical Section of the State Publishing House, Moscow, and the Oxford University Press, London, in 1928. But this definitive academic edition is yet too little known; too few libraries outside the Soviet Union have felt obliged to replace or supplement the older, familiar "arrangements."

The only reliable modern listing of Musorgsky's works must be drawn from the Lamm volumes, and the following list (by volume) has been thus compiled, in consultation with Professor Lamm, and with the co-operation of the reference library in the Leeds Music Corporation, New York, American agency for the State Music Publishing House, Moscow. It is hoped that this will direct the attention of musicians and music libraries to the necessity for consulting this edition for all purposes, practical or scholarly.

OPERAS

Boris Godunov, an opera in four acts with prologue, based on the play by Pushkin. Printed (Vol. I, 1928) in orchestral score (25 autographs), piano and vocal score (35 autographs), and libretto (17 autographs). Since this publication enough additional autograph material has been discovered to warrant a new edition, which has not yet appeared, except for the separate publication of the orchestral scores for the inn scene (in 1932), and the scene near Kromy (in 1933). [125–131, 147, 148, 150, 155, 157–159, 163, 166–180, 183–184, 188–189, 194, 197, 201–203, 205–207, 211–212, 216, 226, 236, 251–254, 258–269, 271, 280, 283, 284, 299, 317, 319, 326, 332, 348–350, 360, 363, 374, 377, 386–387, 416, 418][2]

Khovanshchina, a people's musical drama in five acts and six scenes. Printed (Vol. II, 1931) in piano and vocal score (26 autographs). Only portions orchestrated by the composer: Marfa's Song (Vol. VII, No. 2, 1931), and Chorus of the *streltzi* (unpublished). Boris Asafeyev (Igor Glebov) has prepared an orchestration of the entire opera, based on the composer's piano score, but this orchestration is not yet published (1947). [135, 151, 185–190, 194–195, 197, 219–220, 223–251, 255, 270, 277–278, 281, 282, 283, 288, 292, 295–297, 300–306, 309–310, 312, 319, 321–324, 327–329, 332, 333–348, 353–354, 371, 380, 386, 387, 389, 393, 396–397, 400, 402–406, 416, 418–419]

---

[2] The numbers in brackets indicate the pages in this volume containing references to the composition.

Fair at Sorochintzi, an unfinished comic opera in three acts, based on the story by Gogol. Printed (Vol. III, 1933) in piano and vocal score (43 autographs). Only portions orchestrated by the composer: Prelude (unpublished), and Parasya's dumka (incomplete, unpublished). Complete orchestration prepared by Visarion Shebalin, based on the piano score (published in 1934). [176, 181–182, 275, 278, 340, 346, 353–355, 359–363, 379, 387, 389, 393, 402–406, 409, 416, 418–419]

Salammbô (or *The Lybian*), an unfinished opera, based on the novel by Flaubert. Printed (Vol. IV, No. 1, 1939) in piano and vocal score (10 autographs). Only portions orchestrated by the composer: War Song of the Libyans (chorus, unpublished), and Act IV, Scene 1 (the Acropolis dungeon, unpublished). [58–61, 66–67, 76, 165, 167, 280, 356]

Marriage, an experiment in dramatic music in prose, based on the play by Gogol. Only one act composed. Printed (Vol. IV, No. 2, 1933) in piano and vocal score (first version—six autographs). Opera completed (Acts II, III, IV) by Mikhail Ippolitov-Ivanov (published in piano score, 1934). An orchestration of all four acts, by Ippolitov-Ivanov, is not yet published (1947). [107–115, 117–119, 122–125, 166, 203–204, 279, 359–360]

Mlada, excerpts from a collectively composed opera-ballet. Printed (Vol. IV, No. 3–4, 1931) in piano and vocal score: Market Scene and March of the Priests. [181–182, 184, 280]

ROMANCES AND SONGS

YEARS OF YOUTH (VOL. V, NO. 1, 1931)

1. "Where Art Thou, Little Star?" (text by Nikolai Grekov).
   Dated: Begun 3 June at 1 o'clock at night; completed 4 June at 6 o'clock in the afternoon, 1858. Orchestration (unpublished) inscribed: My little song, arranged by me for orchestra (first experience in orchestration).

2. "Happy Hour," a drinking song (text by Alexei Koltzov). [12]
   Dated: April 28, 1859. St. Petersburg. Dedicated to Vasili Vasilyevich Zakharin.

3. "Sadly Rustle the Leaves," a musical story (text by Alexei Pleshcheyev). [12]
   Dated: S.P-bg, year 1859. Dedicated to Mikhail Osipovich Mikeshin.

4. "Many Chambers and Gardens Have I" (text by Alexei Koltzov). [165]
   Dated: Petersburg, year 1863. Dedicated to Platon Timofeyevich Borispoletz.

5. "Prayer" (text by Mikhail Lermontov). [165]

Dated: 2 February, year 1865. Dedicated to Yulia Ivanovna Musorgskaya.

6. "Tell Me Why, Dearest Maiden" (author of text unknown). [12, 165]

   Dated: 13 July, year 1858. St. Petersburg. Dedicated to Zinaida Afanasyevna Burtzova.

7. "What Are the Words of Love to You?" (text by A. Ammosov).

   Dated: 1860 Sp.-bg. Dedicated to Maria Vasilyevna Shilovskaya.

8. "Blow Winds, Wild Winds" (text by Alexei Koltzov). [64, 165]

   Dated: 28 March, year 1864. St. Petersburg. Dedicated to Vyacheslav Alexeyevich Loginov.

9. "If I Could But Meet You" (text by Vasili Kurochkin). [165]

   Dated: 15 August, year 1863. Village of Volok. Dedicated to Nadezhda Petrovna Opochinina.

YEARS OF YOUTH (VOL. V, NO. 2, 1931)

10. "Malyutka," a romance (text by Alexei Pleshcheyev).

    Dated: 7th of January, 1866, Peter. Dedicated to L. V. Azaryeva.

11. "Old Man's Song" (text by Goethe, from *Wilhelm Meister*). [56, 165]

    Dated: 13 Aug., 1863. Village of Kanishchevo. Dedicated to Alexander Petrovich Opochinin.

12. "King Saul" (text by Byron—*Hebrew Melodies*, translated by Pavel Kozlov). [165, 216, 279, 419]

    Dated: Year 1863. Village of Volok. Dedicated to Alexander Petrovich Opochinin.

13. "Night," a fantasy (text by Alexander Pushkin). [64, 165, 216, 279, 419]

    Dated: 10 April, year 1864. St. Petersburg. Dedicated to Nadezhda Petrovna Opochinina. Orchestrated by composer (published in Vol. VII, No. 3, 1931).

14. "Kalistrat," an étude in the folk manner: a lullaby (text by Nikolai Nekrasov). [64, 68, 165]

    Dated: 22 May, 1864. St. Petersburg. Dedicated to Alexander Petrovich Opochinin.

15. "The Outcast," an experiment in recitative (text by Ivan Goltz-Miller). [165]

    Dated: 5 June, 1865. S-Pbg.

16. "Sleep, Sleep, Peasant's Son," a cradle-song (text by Alexander Ostrovsky—*Voyevoda*). [65, 149, 166, 216, 279]

    Dated: Year 1865. Dedicated to the memory of Yulia Ivanovna Musorgskaya.

17. "Song of the Balearic Islander," from the opera *The Libyan* (*Salammbô*) (text by composer?). [58, 166]

Dated: Novaya Derevnya. August, year 1864.
18. *"Ogni sabato avrete il lume accesso,"* canto popolare toscano. Musica di Gordigiani. L'arrangemento a due voci di Modesto Mussorgski. [166]
Dated: Anno 1864. San-Pietroburgo. L'arrangemento e dedicato al signor Vold. Grodskii.

SEVEN ROMANCES AND SONGS (VOL. V, NO. 3, 1933)

1. *"Meines Herzens Sehnsucht"* (German text by ?). [12]
Dated: Den 6-ten September, 1858. Dedicated: An Fräulein Malwina Bamberg. Published without consultation of the original manuscript. The source used was the Kiev magazine, *V mirye iskusstvo*, April 15, 1907, which had been furnished the manuscript by Cui.
2. "Desire" (text by Heine, translated by Mikhail Mikhailov). [66]
Dated: From the 15th to the 16th of April, 1866. Peter. (2 o'clock in the morning). Dedicated to Nadezhda Petrovna Opochinina. In memory of her judgment upon me.
3. "Gopak" (text by Taras Shevchenko—*The Haidamaks,* translated by Lyov Mey). Inscribed: Lute player. The old man sings and dances. [75, 166, 279, 385, 419]
Dated: Pavlovsk, 31 Aug., year 1866. Dedicated to Nikolai Andreyevich Rimsky-Korsakov. Orchestrated by composer (published in Vol. VII, No. 6, 1931).
4. "There Is Much That Grows from My Tears" (text by Heine, translator unknown).
Dated: Pavlovsk. 1 Sept., '66. Dedicated to Vladimir Petrovich Opochinin.
5. "Lovely Savishna" (text by composer). [65, 68, 75, 90, 100–102, 112, 166, 279, 363, 419]
Dated: Pavlovsk. 2 Sept., '66. Dedicated to Cesar Antonovich Cui.
6. "Ach, You Drunken Woodcock," from the adventures of Pakhomich (text by composer). [72]
Dated: 22 Sept., '66. Dedicated to Vladimir Vasilyevich Nikolsky.
7. "The Seminarist" (text by the composer). [136, 146, 149, 151–153, 166, 197, 279, 363, 419]
Dated: 22 Sept., '66. Dedicated to Ludmila Ivanovna Shestakova.

THIRTEEN ROMANCES AND SONGS (VOL. V, NO. 4, 1931)

1. "Hebraic Song" (text from the Song of Solomon, translated by Lyov Mey). [166, 279, 419]
Dated: Minkino Farm. 12 June, year 1867. Dedicated to Philarète Petrovich and Tatyana Pavlovna Musorgsky.

2. "The White-Flanked Magpie," a joke (text by Alexander Pushkin).
[166, 168, 279, 419]
Dated: 26 Aug., '67. Peter (also: Minkino Farm. September 67).
Dedicated to Alexander Petrovich and Nadezhda Petrovna Opochinina.

3. "Gathering Mushrooms," a little song (text by Lyov Mey). [166, 279, 325, 419]
Dated: Peter. August. Dedicated to Vladimir Vasilyevich Nikolsky.

4. "The Feast," a tale (text by Alexei Koltzov). [102, 103, 166, 279]
Dated: year 1867. Dedicated to Ludmila Ivanovna Shestakova.

5. "The Naughty Boy" (text by the composer). [166, 279, 419]
Dated: Petrograd, 19 December, year 1867. Dedicated to Vladimir
Vasilyevich Stasov.

6. "The He-Goat," a worldly fable (text by the composer). [149, 166, 168, 279]
Dated: Petrograd, 23 December, 1867. Dedicated to Alexander
Porfiryevich Borodin.

7. "The Classicist," in answer to Famintzin's notice on the heresies of
the Russian school of music (text by the composer). [104, 138, 166, 280, 419]
Dated: Petrograd, 30 December, year 1867. Dedicated to Nadezhda
Petrovna Opochinina.

8. "On the Don the Gardens Bloom" (text by Alexei Koltzov).
Dated: December, year 1867. Petrograd.

9. "The Little Orphan Girl" (text by the composer). [112, 149, 166, 262, 279, 377, 380, 419]
Dated: 13 January, year 1868. Petrograd. Dedicated to Yekaterina
Sergeyevna Borodina.

10. "Yeremushka's Cradle-Song" (text by Nikolai Nekrasov). [105, 112, 149, 166, 279, 419]
Dated: 16 March, year 1867. Petrograd. Dedicated: To the great
teacher of musical truth, Alexander Sergeyevich Dargomizhsky.

11. "Child's Song" (text by Lyov Mey). [149, 279, 419]
Dated: April, year 1868. Petrograd.

12. "Evening Song" (text by Alexei Pleshcheyev).
Dated: 15 March, year 1871. Dedicated to Sofia Vladimirovna Serbina.

13. "Forgotten," a ballad (text by Arseni Golenishchev-Kutuzov). [281, 282, 380, 386, 399, 419]
Undated. Dedicated to Vasili Vasilyevich Vereshchagin.

VOL. V, NO. 5, 1931:

Penny Paradise (text by the composer). [137, 139–146, 148–149, 166, 215–216, 276, 280, 400, 419]
Dated: 15 June, 1870. Petrograd. Dedicated to Vladimir Vasilyevich Stasov.

VOL. V, NO. 6, 1931:

The Nursery, episodes from child life (text by the composer). [164, 184, 201, 210, 213, 225, 226, 236, 271, 279–280, 384, 393–394, 419; *see also* individual songs]

1. "With Nursie." Dated: 26 April, 1868, in Petrograd. Dedicated: To the great teacher of musical truth, Alexander Sergeyevich Dargomizhsky. [105, 112, 166, 210]
2. "In the Corner." Dated: 30 September, 1870. Dedicated to Victor Alexandrovich Hartmann. [166]
3. "The Beetle." Dated: 18 October, year 1870 in Petrograd. Dedicated to Vladimir Vasilyevich Stasov. [166, 168]
4. "With the Doll." Dated: 18 December, year 1870. Dedicated to Tanyushka and Goga Musorgsky. [166]
5. "Going to Sleep." Undated (composed in 1870). Dedicated to Sasha Cui. [164, 166]
6. " 'Sailor' the Cat." Dated: 15 August, year 1872 in Petrograd. Dedicated to Dimitri Vasilyevich and Polyxena Stepanovna Stasov. [134, 280]
7. "Riding on a Stick." Dated: 14 September 1872, in Petrograd. Dedicated to Dimitri Vasilyevich and Polyxena Stepanovna Stasov. [134, 280]

VOL. V, NO. 7, 1929:

Sunless, an album of poetic works by A. A. Golenishchev-Kutuzov. [275, 280, 282, 288, 298, 300, 322]

1. "Within Four Walls." Dated: 7 May, year 1874 in Petrograd.
2. "You Didn't Recognize Me in the Crowd." Dated: 19 May, year 1874. The manuscript indicates an earlier title: "Forgotten."
3. "The Festive, Noisy Day Has Ended." Dated: 19/20 May, year 1874. The manuscript indicates an earlier title: "Shadow."
4. "Longing." Dated: 2 June, year 1874. The manuscript indicates an earlier title: "In the Album of a Society Lady."
5. "Elegy." Dated: 19 August, 1874.
6. "By the River." Dated: 25 August, year 1874.

TEN ROMANCES AND SONGS (VOL. V, NO. 8, 1934).

1. "Incomprehensible" (text by the composer). [315]
   Dated: 21 December, 1875. Dedicated: To Maria Izmailovna Fyodorovna. The little lady under the Christmas tree.

2. "Grief Does Not Crash like God's Thunder" (text by Alexei Tolstoy).
   [357]
   Dated: 4–5 March, 1877, Petrograd. Dedicated to Fyodor Ardalionovich Vanlyarsky.

3. "The Soul Calmly Floated through the Heavenly Empyrean" (text
   by Alexei Tolstoy). [357]
   Dated: 9 March, 1877 in SPB.

4. "Pride Passes by, Puffed Up" (text by Alexei Tolstoy). [357]
   Dated: 15–16 March, 1877. Dedicated to Anatoli Yevgrafovich
   Palchikov.

5. "Ah, Is It an Honor for a Young Man to Weave Flax?" (text by
   Alexei Tolstoy). [357]
   Dated: 20 March, 1877.

6. "Grief Disperses and Gives Way" (text by Alexei Tolstoy). [357]
   Dated: S.Pbg. 21 March, 1877. Dedicated to Olga Andreyevna
   Golenishcheva-Kutuzova.

7. "The Vision" (text by Arseni Golenishchev-Kutuzov). [356]
   Dated: 6 April, year 1877. Dedicated to Yelizaveta Andreyevna
   Gulevich.

8. "The Wanderer" (text by Fr. Rückert, translated by Alexei Pleshcheyev).
   Undated. No autograph—printed from the posthumous edition
   (1883) edited by Karatygin.

9. Mephistopheles' Song in Auerbach's Cellar (text by Goethe—*Faust*,
   translated by A. Strugovshchikov). [396, 419]
   Undated (composed August–September, 1879). No autograph—
   printed from a copy made by Vladimir Stasov. Dedicated to Daria
   Mikhailovna Leonova.

10. "On the Dnieper," my travels through Russia (text by Taras Shev-
    chenko). [68, 166]
    Dated: 23 December, 1879. Dedicated to Sergei Pavlovich Naumov.

VOL. V, NO. 9, 1928:

Songs and Dances of Death, a song cycle for voice and piano on a text by
A. A. Golenishchev-Kutuzov. [297–298, 320–321, 340, 356–359, 361, 418]

1. "Cradle-Song." Dated: 14 April, year 1875. Dedicated to Anna
   Yakovlevna Vorobyova-Petrova.

2. "Serenade." Dated: Petrograd, 11 May, year 1875. Dedicated to Ludmila Ivanovna Glinka-Shestakova.

3. "Trepak." Dated: 17 February, year 1875. Dedicated to Osip Afanasyevich Petrov.

4. "Field Marshal." Dated: Tzarskoye Selo, 5 June, year 1877. Dedicated to Arseni Arkadyevich Golenishchev-Kutuzov.

NOTATIONS OF FOLK SONGS, ROUGH DRAFTS, AND OTHER MATERIALS

This collection (Vol. V, No. 10) is sometimes referred to as "Musorgsky's notebook," but it actually consists of all miscellaneous autograph materials of Musorgsky found by Professor Lamm before the year of its publication, 1939. It contains the following classifications:

I. Russian Folk Songs, for male chorus unaccompanied.
These five arrangements were probably written in 1880, for Daria Leonova's voice classes.

II. Three-Part Vocalises.
Three vocalises for Leonova's pupils.

III. Notations of Folk Songs with Texts.
Two communicated by A. I. Zinoviev (December, 1876), four dissenters' hymns communicated by Lubov Karmalina, one hymn communicated by Terti Filippov, and four Caucasian and Asiatic folk songs (dated 17 Apr., '77).

IV. Ukrainian Folk Songs.
Notations of twenty-seven songs, most of which were used by Musorgsky in *Fair at Sorochintzi*.

V. Notations of Themes for the Opera *Fair at Sorochintzi*.
Six themes, three of which were not developed or incorporated by Musorgsky into the opera.

VI. Notations of Songs without Text.
Eight notations, including a song communicated by "A. M. Zhemchuzhnin in Uralsk, in the '50's" (on which Musorgsky has noted: "Nonsense! Here is Rossini and Verdi, but not Russia."), a song "From M. O. Shishko heard in Byeloruss," a Don song of the sixteenth century (see p. 293), a Turkish song, a Persian song, and "Greetings to Gorbunov" (see p. 407).

VII. Notations of Themes.
Five themes, including "The Winds Blow in Tzarskoye Selo" (see p. 343), and *"Romance sans paroles (de ménestrel)."*

VIII. Musical Autographs in Letters.
These passages, quoted by Musorgsky in ten different letters, are printed in facsimile, above, in the text of this volume.

IX. Songs from the Opera *Fair at Sorochintzi*.

The first versions, not used in the 1933 piano and vocal score of this opera (Vol. III), of Khivrya's song and Parasya's dumka.

X. Unfinished Works.

1. *An Epitaph-Letter.* Dedicated to Nadezhda Petrovna Opochinina, who had recently died—on June 29, 1874. The composer's text for this unfinished song appears on pp. 276–277.

2. *The Hill of Nettles* (text by the composer). Dated: 10 August, '74. The idea for this unfinished satire is described on pp. 274–276.

CHORAL WORKS (Vol. VI, 1939)

1. Chorus of the People from the tragedy of *Oedipus.* [10, 12, 25–27, 36, 165]

The only extant portion of Musorgsky's project for incidental music for *Oedipus.* Left unpublished during Musorgsky's life, the material of this chorus was reworked for *Salammbô* (Act II, finale of Scene 2), and later for the fist fight in *Mlada.*

First version dated: 23 January, year 1859. Inscribed: "To dear Mili Modeste dedicates Scene in the Temple from the tragedy *Oedipus in Athens,* year 1859."

Second version (orchestral score) dated: 1st March year 1860. Inscribed: "Dedicated to Mili Alexeyevich Balakirev Scene in the Temple from the tragedy *Oedipus* (Sophocles) Chorus, year 1860."

Third version undated. Inscribed: "Chorus of the People from the tragedy *Oedipus,* 1861."

2. *The Destruction of Sennacherib* (text adapted by the composer from Byron's *Hebrew Melodies*). [77, 82–83, 166, 256–258, 279, 377, 409, 419]

First version (orchestral score) dated: 29 January, year 1867. Dedicated to Mili Alexeyevich Balakirev.

Second version dated: 2nd January, year 1874. Dedicated to Vladimir Vasilyevich Stasov.

3. *Jesus Navinus* [*Joshua*]. Dated: Tzarskoye Selo, 2 July, 1877. Dedicated to Nadezhda Nikolayevna Rimskaya-Korsakova. [279, 356, 361, 387, 419]

ORCHESTRAL WORKS

1. March *The Capture of Kars* (Vol. VII, No. 1, 1931). Composed on order during the winter of 1879–80 (see p. 407).

2. The Song of Marfa from the opera *Khovanshchina* (Vol. VII, No. 2, 1931).

3. *Night* (Vol. VII, No. 3, 1931). Orchestrated in 1868.

4. Scherzo in B-flat (Vol. VII, No. 4, 1931). Dated: year 1858, November 19th. Dedicated to A. S. Gussakovsky. [20, 23, 165, 278]

5. Intermezzo (Vol. VII, No. 5, 1931). Orchestration dated: At night from the 11th to the 12th of July, 1867, at Minkino Farm. Dedicated to Alexander Porfiryevich Borodin. [93, 165, 419]

6. *Gopak* (Vol. VII, No. 6, 1931). Orchestration inscribed: composed in 1866 in Pavlovsk. Instrumented in 1868 in Petrograd.

7. *Where Art Thou, Little Star?* (This and following orchestral scores yet unpublished [1947].)

8. Chorus from *Oedipus* (first version).

9. *The Destruction of Sennacherib* (first version).

10. *Night on Bald Mountain.* [25, 67, 85–91, 96, 99–101, 166, 359, 370, 405]

11. March—Nocturne.

12. War Song of the Libyans (from *Salammbô*).

13. Act IV, Scene 1 of *Salammbô*.

14. Chorus from *Oedipus* (second version).

15. *The Destruction of Sennacherib* (second version).

WORKS FOR PIANO (Vol. VIII, 1939)

This volume contains a complete chronological listing of Musorgsky's piano works, including those known, but destroyed or lost:

1. *Porte-Enseigne Polka.* Dedicated: To the Comrades of the Junker School. Published by Matvei Bernard in 1852, but neither autograph nor copy of this edition has been discovered. [4, 14, 164, 417]

2. *Souvenir d'enfance.* Dated: 16 October, year 1857. Dedicated: *A son ami, Nicolas Obolensky.* [4]

3. Sonata in E-Flat Major. Not extant; themes cited in letter to Balakirev, August 13, 1858. [6, 9, 11]

4. Scherzo in C-Sharp Minor. First version dated: 25 November, 1858. Dedicated to Lubov Mikhailovna Buba. Second version (undated) dedicated to A. Izvolskaya. [9, 165]

5. Arrangement of works by Glinka (for 4 hands):
   a. Persian chorus from the opera *Ruslan and Ludmila.* Dated: Begun May 23. Completed May 27, 1858. Unpublished. [14]
   b. *Night in Madrid.* Second Spanish Overture. Dated: Began arrangement October 28. Completed it November 11, year 1858. On the eve of the production of *Ruslan and Ludmila* in the year 1858, November 12. Unpublished. [28]

6. Arrangement of works by Beethoven (for 2 hands): Andante of the String Quartet in C Major (Opus 59, No. 3). Dated: Apr. 9, 1859. Dedicated to A. S. Gussakovsky. [41]

7. *Ein Kinderscherz;* known also as *Puss-in-the-Corner.* First version dated: 1859. Dedicated to Nikolai Alexandrovich Levashov. Second version dated: Village of Glebovo, May 28, 1860. Same dedication. [26, 154, 165, 255, 278, 419]

8. *Impromptu Passionné.* First version undated. Second version dated: 1st of October, year 1859. Both versions dedicated to Nadezhda Petrovna Opochinina. Second version inscribed: To the memory of Beltov and Lyuba. [19]

9. Sonata in C major (for 4 hands). Dated: 8 December, 1860. Inscribed (at conclusion of first movement): *Sonata.* allegro assai—C major, andante—D flat major, scherzo—F major [this key had been crossed out], allegro con brio—C major; A symphonic exercise for orchestra. *Dixi.* [25, 30, 33, 34]

10. Arrangement of works by Balakirev (for 4 hands). [18, 28, 30]
    a. Entr'acte before the Second Act of *King Lear.* Dated: December 11, 1860. Unpublished.
    b. Entr'acte before the Fourth Act of *King Lear.* Dated: November 23 [1860]. Unpublished.
    c. Entr'acte before the Fifth Act of *King Lear.* Dated: November 25 [1860]. Unpublished.
    d. Overture on Three Russian Themes. Undated. Unpublished.

11. *Menuetto, or Menuet Monstre* (for orchestra or piano). Not extant.

12. *Preludio in modo classico* (for orchestra or piano). Not extant.

13. Arrangement of works by Berlioz (for 8 hands): Excerpts from the *Romeo and Juliet* Symphony (Opus 17). (a) *Grande fête chez Capulet,* (b) *La reine Mab.* Undated, but possibly composed at the beginning of 1862. Unpublished.

14. Sonata in D Major. Not extant. [40–41]

15. Arrangement of works by Beethoven (for 4 hands): String quartet in B-Flat Major (Opus 130). Allegro dated: March 27, 1862. Presto dated: March 28, 1862. Cavatina dated: April 25, 1862. Scherzo dated: April 27, 1862, Village of Volok. Finale Allegro unfinished. Unpublished. [41, 45]

16. Arrangement of works by Balakirev:
    "Sing Not, Beauty, in My Presence." Published in 1862 by Fyodor Stellovsky.

17. "Nurse and I." Dated: April 22, 1865. Inscribed: "I dedicate this to the memory of my mother; *From Memories of Childhood* No. 1. 'Nurse and I.'" [65]

18. "First Punishment." Inscribed: "I dedicate this to the memory of my mother; *From Memories of Childhood* No. 2. 'First Punishment (Nurse Shuts Me in a Dark Room).'" [65]

19. *Reverie,* based on a theme by Loginov. Dated: July 22, 1865. Dedicated to Vyacheslav Alexeyevich Loginov.

20. *La Capricieuse,* based on a theme by Count L. Heyden. Dated: July 26, 1865. Dedicated to Nadezhda Petrovna Opochinina.

21. Intermezzo, or *Intermezzo in modo classico.* First version undated. Second version dated: July, '67, Minkino Farm. Dedicated to Alexander Porfiryevich Borodin. [38–39, 54, 93, 165, 255, 278]

22. Work on the opera *The Stone Guest* by Dargomizhsky. Musorgsky prepared a printed copy of the piano score with a German text for Franz Liszt, to be delivered by Vasili Bessel. Inscribed: German text after Bodenstadt was done by me in June, 1872. M. Musorgsky.

23. *Pictures at an Exhibition,* a collection of pieces for 2 hands. Dated: July 26, '74. Dedicated to Vladimir Vasilyevich Stasov. [271–276, 280, 418]

24. Work on a composition by Nikolai Lodyzhensky:
Oriental Lullaby for Voice and Piano. Dated: June 26, 1874, in Petrograd. Dedicated to Arseni Golenishchev-Kutuzov. Inscribed: For Vladimir Vasilyevich Stasov, taken from a pencil sketch by N. Lodyzhensky, with a few simplifications. Unpublished.

25. Work on a composition by Giuseppe Sarti:
The First Government of Oleg. Excerpts prepared for chorus and piano. Unpublished.

26. *On the Southern Shore of the Crimea. Gurzuf at Ayu-Dagh:* From the travel notes of M. Musorgsky. Published in 1880 by Nikolai Bernard in his magazine, *Nuvellist.* Dedicated to Daria Mikhailovna Leonova. [419]

27. *Meditation. Feuillet d'album.* Published in 1880 in *Nuvellist.*

28. *Une larme.* Published in 1880 by Piotr Jurgenson.

29. *The Seamstress,* Scherzino. Published in 1880 in *Nuvellist.* Dedicated to Piotr Adamovich Shestakovsky. [156, 166, 278, 325, 378, 419]

30. *Near the Southern Shore of the Crimea. Baidarki. Capriccio. Gurzuf at Ayu-Dagh:* From travel notes. Dated: January, 1880. Published in 1880 in *Nuvellist.* [419]

31. *In the Village,* or *Au village. Quasi fantasia.* Published in 1880 in *Nuvellist.* Dedicated to Ivan Fyodorovich Gorbunov.

32. *Grand Suite,* a project. Not extant. [404, 419]

33. *Storm on the Black Sea.* Not extant. [396, 419]

34. The Fair Scene, from the opera *Fair at Sorochintzi* transcribed for 2 hands by the composer.

35. *Gopak of the Merry Peasant Lads,* from the opera *Fair at Sorochintzi,* transcribed for 2 hands by the composer.

VOL. VIII, NO. 3:

Scherzo for orchestra, arranged for piano by Dmitri Kabalevsky.

VOL. VIII, NO. 4:

Intermezzo for orchestra, arranged for piano by Dmitri Kabalevsky.

VOL. VIII, NO. 5:

March, *The Capture of Kars,* arranged for piano by Pavel Lamm.

A List of Musorgsky Letters

KEY TO LIST OF MUSORGSKY'S LETTERS

BE	Estate of Yasha Bunchuk, Hollywood, California
BM	Collection of Boris Molas, Leningrad
BTM	Bakhrushin Theater Museum, Moscow
CHA	Central Historical Archives, Leningrad
CML	Central Music Library, Leningrad
DC	Collection of Sergei Dianin, Moscow
DU	Drama Union, Leningrad
HM	State Historical Museum, Moscow
LPL	Leningrad Public Library in the name of Saltykov-Shchedrin
LSC	Leningrad State Conservatory
MAG	Music Archives of Gosizdat (State Publishers)
MLP	Museum of the Leningrad Philharmonic Orchestra
NE	Estate of Eduard Napravnik, Leningrad
PH	Pushkin House, Leningrad
TM	Tchaikovsky Home-Museum, Klin

The first column shows the numbering of documents contained in this volume; the second records the numbering used in the Russian editions of Musorgsky's letters. The contents of all omitted letters are indicated briefly. The bracketed numbers are those of other Russian letter collections.

1857

1	1	Dec. 16	to M. Balakirev	LPL
2	2	Dec. 17	to M. Balakirev	LPL

1858

3	3	Jan. 7	to M. Balakirev	LPL
	4	Jan. 13	to M. Balakirev	LPL
			"I've been assigned to the guard."	
4	5	Jan. 24	to M. Balakirev	LPL
5	6	Feb. 25	to M. Balakirev	LPL
5A	[19]	July 5	from M. Balakirev to V. Stasov	
6	7	July 12	to M. Balakirev	LPL
7	8	Aug. 13	to M. Balakirev	LPL

1859

8	9	Jan. 7	to M. Balakirev	LPL
	10	Jan. 25	to M. Balakirev	LPL
			Cancellation of date at Shilovskaya's	
	11	Feb. 7	to M. Balakirev	LPL
			"Please let us know if you are quite well."	
	12	May 2	to M. Balakirev	LPL
			"Tell Vasenka that Kitosha and I are dining with him."	
9	13	June 18	to M. Balakirev	LPL
10	14	June 23	to M. Balakirev	LPL
11	15	Sept. 20	to M. Balakirev	LPL
12	—	Oct. 1	Dedication to N. Opochinina (*Impromptu passionné*)	LPL
	16	Oct. 4	to M. Balakirev	LPL
			An invitation for the evening	
13	17	Oct. 8	to M. Balakirev	LPL
14	18	Oct. 18	to M. Balakirev	LPL
15	19	Oct. 19	to M. Balakirev	LPL

1860

16	20	Feb. 10	to M. Balakirev	LPL
	21	Feb. 14	to M. Balakirev	LPL
			An invitation to Cui's	
		Apr. 1	to A. Zakharina	
			"The banker who sends money abroad is Gunzbourg."	
17	22	Sept. 26	to M. Balakirev	LPL
	23	Nov. 5	to M. Balakirev	LPL
			"We'll expect you on Monday."	
18	24	Nov. 9	to M. Balakirev	LPL
19	25	Dec. 25	to M. Balakirev	LPL
	26	Dec. 27	to M. Balakirev	LPL
			An errand for Levashov, a piano student.	
20	27	Dec. ?	to M. Balakirev	LPL
20A		Dec. 31	from M. Balakirev to A. Zakharina	LSC

1861

21	28	Jan. 13	to M. Balakirev	LPL
22	29	Jan. 16	to M. Balakirev	LPL
23	30	Jan. 19	to M. Balakirev	LPL
	31	Feb. 6	to M. Balakirev	LPL
			"Levashov . . . will be well by Carnival week."	

23A	[66]	Feb. 13	from V. Stasov to M. Balakirev	
24	32	Mar. 24	to M. Balakirev	LPL
25	33	May 1	to M. Balakirev	LPL
	34	May 3	to M. Balakirev	LPL

". . . must clean up our matter before we leave."

26	35	Oct. 14	to M. Balakirev	LPL
26A		Nov. 26	from N. Rimsky-Korsakov to his mother	
	36	Winter	to M. Balakirev	LPL

". . . my stomach will not allow me to come to you."

1862

27	37	Mar. 11	to M. Balakirev	LPL
28	38	Mar. 31	to M. Balakirev	LPL
29	39	Apr. 28	to M. Balakirev	LPL
	40	Oct. 22	to M. Balakirev	LPL

". . . Selivachev . . . planning to go to Moscow . . ."

1863

| 29A | — | Feb. 26 | from C. Cui to M. Balakirev | LSC |
| | 41 | Mar. 14 | to M. Balakirev | LPL |

A rehearsal date

29B	—	Apr. 22	from C. Cui to N. Rimsky-Korsakov	LPL
29C	[137]	May 17	from V. Stasov to M. Balakirev	
29D	[138]	June 3	from M. Balakirev to V. Stasov	
30	42	June 10	to M. Balakirev	LPL
31	43	June 22	to C. Cui	LPL
32			Inscriptions on *Salammbô* MSS	LPL

1864

| 33 | 44 | Jan. 16 | to M. Balakirev | LPL |
| | 45 | Mar. ? | to M. Balakirev | LPL |

"The department has some matters that must get out."

| | 46 | Apr. ? | to M. Balakirev | LPL |

"Thanks . . . for the tickets . . . Dargun's father."

| 34 | 47 | May 3 | to M. Balakirev | LPL |
| | 48 | ? | to M. Balakirev | LPL |

"The Caucasian lady has bought a piano."

| 34A | | June 14 | from C. Cui to M. Balakirev | LSC |

1865

	49	Feb. ?	to M. Balakirev	LPL
			"We are to be treated to the deep-sea chords of Mendel."	
35	50	Feb. ?	to M. Balakirev	LPL

1866

36	51	Jan. 27	to M. Balakirev	LPL
37		Apr. 15	Dedication to N. Opochinina (*Desire*)	
38	52	Apr. 20	to M. Balakirev	LPL
39	53	Aug. 14	to M. Balakirev	LPL
40A		Dec. 28	from M. Balakirev to L. Shestakova	LSC

1867

40	54	Jan. 5	to L. Shestakova	LPL
41	55	Jan. 9	to M. Balakirev (in a collective letter)	LPL
41A		Jan. 11	from M. Balakirev to M. Musorgsky	
41B		Jan. 18	from C. Cui to M. Balakirev	LSC
41C		Jan. 23	from M. Balakirev to C. Cui	
42	56	Jan. 23	to M. Balakirev	LPL
43	57	Jan. 26	to M. Balakirev	LPL
44	58	Apr. ?	to L. Shestakova	LPL
45	59	July 5	to N. Rimsky-Korsakov	LPL
46	60	July 12	to V. Nikolsky	LPL
46A		July 10	from N. Rimsky-Korsakov to M. Musorgsky	
47	61	July 15	to N. Rimsky-Korsakov	LPL
47A		Aug. 1	from N. Rimsky-Korsakov to M. Musorgsky	
48	62	Sept. 24	to M. Balakirev	LPL
49	63	Sept. ?	to N. Rimsky-Korsakov	LPL
49A		Oct. 8	from N. Rimsky-Korsakov to M. Musorgsky	
	64	Winter	to M. Balakirev	LPL
			"We can still talk over the *witches*."	
50		Dec. 30	A satire by Musorgsky (*The Classicist*)	LPL
50A		?	from A. Dargomizhsky to M. Musorgsky	

1868

51		May 4	An inscription (*Yeremushka's Lullaby*)	MLP
52	65	July 3	to C. Cui	LPL
53	66	July 30	to L. Shestakova	LPL
54	67	July 30	to N. Rimsky-Korsakov	LPL
54A		July 27	from C. Cui to M. Musorgsky	PH
54B		Aug. 7	from N. Rimsky-Korsakov to M. Musorgsky	
55	69	Aug. 15	to C. Cui	LPL

441

56	70	Aug. 15	to N. Rimsky-Korsakov	LPL
57	68	Aug. 15	to V. Nikolsky	LPL
57A	[45]	Sept. 25	from A. Borodin to his wife	DC
58			Title page and scenario of *Boris Godunov*	LPL
58A		Oct. 4	from V. Stasov to H. Berlioz	

1869

58B		July 18	from V. Stasov to D. Stasov	PH
59	71	Sept. 27	to M. Balakirev	LPL
60		Dec. ?	to K. Albrecht	HM

1870

60A		Feb. 13	from N. Rimsky-Korsakov to M. Musorgsky	
61	72	May 19	to V. Nikolsky	LPL
61A		June 1	from L. Shestakova to V. Nikolsky	LPL
62	73	June 18	to A. and N. Purgold	LPL
63	74	June 24	to A. and N. Purgold	LPL
64	75	June 28	to V. Nikolsky	LPL
64A		July 9	from V. Stasov to N. Purgold	
65	76	July 13	to A. and N. Purgold	LPL
	77	July 14	to V. Stasov	LPL
			". . . would very much like to spend a day with you."	
66	78	July 23	to N. Rimsky-Korsakov	LPL
66A		July 26	from V. Stasov to M. Musorgsky	LPL
66B		July 29	from V. Stasov to D. and P. Stasov	PH
67	79	Aug. 18	to V. Stasov	LPL
68	80	Aug. 22	to V. Stasov	LPL
		Oct. ?	from C. Cui to M. Musorgsky	PH

1871

68B		Jan. 7	from N. Rimsky-Korsakov to M. Musorgsky	
69	81	Jan. 8	to N. Rimsky-Korsakov	LPL
	82	Jan. 21	to D. Stasov	PH
			Acceptance of an invitation	
69A		Feb. 10	from G. Ferrero to S. Gedeonov	CHA
69B		Feb. 17	from P. Fyodorov to M. Musorgsky	CHA
70	83	Mar. 27	to N. Rimsky-Korsakov	LPL
70A		May 9	from N. Rimsky-Korsakov to M. Musorgsky	
71	84	Apr. 18	to V. Stasov	LPL
72	85	July 1	to M. Cui	LSC
73	86	July–Aug.	to L. Shestakova (a list of works)	PH

	87		to L. Shestakova	PH
			A list of Cui's works	
74	88	Aug. 10	to V. Stasov	LPL
75	89	Aug. 17	to N. Rimsky-Korsakov	LPL
76	90	Sept. 11	to V. Stasov	LPL
76A [142]		Sept. 20	from A. Borodin to his wife	DC
	91	Dec. 10	to V. Nikolsky	LPL
			An invitation to the Purgolds'	
76B		Dec. 14	from N. Purgold to N. Rimsky-Korsakov	
77	92	Dec. 14	to V. Stasov	LPL
	93	?	to A. Purgold	LPL
			Cancellation of a date	

1872

78	94	Jan. 3	to A. Purgold	LPL
79	95	Jan. 7	to V. Stasov	LPL
80	96	Feb. ?	to V. Nikolsky	LPL
81	97	Feb. ?	to A. and N. Purgold (original missing; printed from copy found among N. Rimskaya-Korsakova's papers)	
82	98	Mar. 22	to M. Balakirev	LPL
83	99	Mar. 31	to V. Stasov	LPL
84	100	Apr. 7	to V. Nikolsky	LPL
85	101	Apr. 24	to M. Balakirev	LPL
86	102	May 1	to V. Stasov	LPL
		May 6	to V. Bessel	DU
			"A meeting about 'Boris' this evening . . ."	
87	103	June 22	to V. Stasov	LPL
88	104	July 11	to L. Shestakova	LPL
89	105	July 13	to V. Stasov	LPL
90	106	July 15	to V. Stasov	LPL
91	107	Sept. 13	to V. Stasov	LPL
92	108	Sept. 29	to V. Stasov	LPL
93	109	Oct. 18	to V. Stasov	LPL
94	110	Dec. 26	to V. Stasov	LPL

1873

95	111	Jan. 2	to V. Stasov	LPL
96	112	Jan. 30	to V. Stasov	LPL
97	113	Feb. 6	to E. Napravnik	NE
98	114	May 3	to V. Stasov	LPL
99	115	May 14	to V. Bessel	MAG
100	116	May 16	to V. Stasov	LPL

100A		May 21	from V. Stasov to Z. Stasova	PH
	117	May ?	to V. Bessel	MAG
			An appointment	
101	118	June 1	to V. Stasov	LPL
101A		June 6	from D. Stasov to P. Stasova	PH
102	119	June 13	to I. Repin	LPL
103	120	June 19	to V. Stasov	LPL
104	I	June 29	to A. Golenishchev-Kutuzov	HM
105	II	July 22	to A. Golenishchev-Kutuzov	HM
105A		July ?	from P. Stasova to M. Musorgsky (a draft)	PH
106	121	July 23	to P. Stasova	PH
107	122	July 23	to V. Stasov	LPL
108	123	July 26	to P. Stasova	LPL
109	124	Aug. 2	to V. Stasov	LPL
110	125	Aug. 2	to N. Stasova	LPL
111	126	Aug. 6	to V. Stasov	LPL
111A		Aug. 15	from V. Stasov to M. Musorgsky	LPL
112	127	Sept. 6	to V. Stasov	LPL
	128	Sept. 21	to M. Cui	BTM
			Two tickets for Cui at *The Stone Guest.*	
113	129	Oct. 22	to V. Bessel	MAG
113A [214]		Oct. 25	from A. Borodin to his wife	DC
114		Oct. 28	A collective telegram to F. Liszt	
	130	Dec. 1	to V. Stasov	LPL
			"Katenin (the musician) thirsts to be introduced."	
115	131	Dec. 5	to L. Karmalina (original missing; printed from copy made by Karmalina for Stasov) [1]	
116	132	Dec. 6	to V. Stasov	LPL

1874

117	133	Jan. 2	to V. Stasov	LPL
117A [140]		Feb. 2	from F. Liszt to V. Bessel	
118	134	Jan. 4	to V. Bessel	MAG
119		Jan. 21	A dedication (*Boris Godunov*)	LPL
	135	Jan. ?	to V. Bessel	MAG
			Reminder of the facsimile dedication	
120		Jan. 10	An inscription on a photograph (to P. Stasova)	PH
121	136	Jan. 18?	to S. Gedeonov	CHA

[1] Sergei Dianin, editor of Borodin's correspondence, assumes that the original letters from Borodin and Musorgsky, from which Karmalina made the copies now in the Stasov papers, were destroyed when the Karmalin estate was burned in 1917 or 1918.

121A		Jan. 20	from P. Fyodorov to S. Gedeonov	CHA
122		Jan. 27	A program	
123		Jan. 27	to Y. Makhina (an inscription on a piano score)	
124	137	Jan. 28	to V. Stasov	LPL
		Jan. 31	Contract with V. Bessel	DU
125	138	Feb. 2	to E. Napravnik	NE
126	139	Feb. ?	to Editor of *St. Peterburgski Vedomosti* (original missing; printed from text published on Feb. 5)	
127	140	Feb. 6	to V. Stasov	LPL
127B		Feb. 6	from M. Antokolsky to V. Stasov	
	141	Feb. 26	to V. Bessel	MAG
			A rendezvous	
128	III	Mar. 2	to A. Golenishchev-Kutuzov	HM
129	142	Mar. 9	to V. Stasov	LPL
129A		Mar. 24	from S. Taneyev to P. Tchaikovsky	TM
130	143	June 12?	to V. Stasov	LPL
131		July 27	a dedication (to V. Stasov—*Pictures at an Exhibition*)	LPL
132	144	June 20	to V. Stasov	LPL
132A		June ?	from A. Golenishchev-Kutuzov to V. Stasov (draft)	
132B		July 1	from V. Stasov to N. Rimsky-Korsakov	
132C		July 26	from N. Rimsky-Korsakov to V. Stasov	
133		July ?	An "epitaph-letter" to N. Opochinina	LPL
134	145	July 23	to L. Karmalina (original missing; see 115)	
135	212	Aug. 26	to V. Stasov (a catalogue)	LPL
		Sept. ?	to A. Golenishchev-Kutuzov	HM
			"Here's the key to our apartment."	
135A		Oct. 15	from M. Tchaikovsky to P. Tchaikovsky	TM
136	146	Oct. 27	to L. Shestakova	LPL
136A		Oct. 29	from P. Tchaikovsky to M. Tchaikovsky	TM
137	IV	Nov. 7	to A. Golenishchev-Kutuzov	HM
138	148	Nov. 16	to L. Shestakova (original missing; printed from text published in *Muzikalni Sovremennik*, 5–6, 1917)	
139	149	Nov. 27	to L. Shestakova (original missing; see above)	
140	150	Dec. 6	to L. Shestakova (original missing; see above)	
141	V	Dec. 29	to A. Golenishchev-Kutuzov	HM

1875

	151	Jan. 13	to P. Stasova	PH
			Instructions to find Platonova	
	152	Feb. 28	to P. Stasova	PH
			Arrangements to help in a benefit concert	

142	153	Mar. 5	to V. Stasov	LPL
143	VI	Mar. 7	to A. Golenishchev-Kutuzov	HM
144	VII	Mar. 7	to A. Golenishchev-Kutuzov	HM
144A		Mar. ?	from A. Golenishchev-Kutuzov to M. Musorgsky (A draft)	HM
145	VIII	Mar. 18	to A. Golenishchev-Kutuzov	HM
145A [279]		Apr. 15	from A. Borodin to L. Karmalina (original missing; see above—115)	
146	154	Apr. 20	to L. Karmalina (original missing; see above—115)	
147	IX	May 11	to A. Golenishchev-Kutuzov	HM
148	X	May 22	to A. Golenishchev-Kutuzov	HM
149	XI	May 22	to A. Golenishchev-Kutuzov	HM
	XII	May 25	to A. Golenishchev-Kutuzov	HM
			A favor for Petrova, going to Tver.	
	155	June 13	to V. Stasov	LPL
			Going to the country on Sunday	
	156	June 27	to L. Shestakova (original missing; see above—138)	
			Books for Nikolsky, a score for Shestakova	
	157	Aug. 2	to L. Shestakova (original missing; see above—138)	
			Act I of Khovanshchina is finished	
150	158	Aug. 7	to V. Stasov	LPL
151	XIII	Aug. 17	to A. Golenishchev-Kutuzov	HM
151A		Sept. 4	from A. Katenin to A. Golenishchev-Kutuzov	HM
151B [285]		Sept. 19	from A. Borodin to his wife	LPL
152	XIV	Sept. 6	to A. Golenishchev-Kutuzov	HM
	159	Sept. 16	to L. Shestakova (original missing; see above—138)	
			Congratulations on her name-day	
153	160	Oct. 14	to V. Stasov	LPL
154	161	Oct. 14	to L. Shestakova (original missing; see above—138)	
155	162	Oct. ?	to M. Cui	LA
156	163	Oct. 19	to V. Stasov	LPL
156A		Oct. 23	from V. Stasov to M. Musorgsky	LPL
157	147	Oct. 29	to L. Shestakova (original missing; see above—138)	
158	164	Nov. 1	to the Artists' Circle	LPL
159	XV	Nov. 1	to A. Golenishchev-Kutuzov	HM
	165	Nov. 7	to L. Shestakova (original missing; see above—138)	
	XVI	Nov. 9	to A. Golenishchev-Kutuzov	HM
			Two dates for tomorrow	
	166	Nov. 22	to L. Shestakova (original missing; see above—138)	
			Preparations for the Petrov jubilee	
160	167	Nov. 23	to V. Stasov	LPL
	168	Nov. 24	to P. Stasova	PH

			Cancellation of an appointment	
161	XVII	Dec. 9	to A. Golenishchev-Kutuzov	HM
162	169	Dec. 17	to L. Shestakova (original missing; see above—138)	
163	XVIII	Dec. 23	to A. Golenishchev-Kutuzov	HM
164	170	Dec. 29	to V. Stasov	LPL

1876

165	171	Jan. 1	to D. Stasov	PH
	172	Jan. ?	to Y. Albrecht	CML
			Acknowledgement of reports from the Quartet Society	
166	173	Jan. 3	to D. Stasov	PH
167	174	Jan. 17	to L. Shestakova (original missing; see above—138)	
168		Feb. 1	An inscription on a photograph (to L. Shestakova)	
169	175	Feb. 12	to V. Stasov	LPL
170	176	Feb. 28	to L. Shestakova (original missing; see above—138)	
171	177	Mar. 9	to N. Molas	BM
	178	Mar. 14	to N. Molas	BM
			Acceptance of invitation	
	179	Mar. 27	to L. Shestakova (original missing; see above—138)	
			Arrangements for Petrov's piano	
172		Apr. 9	to O. Golenishcheva-Kutuzova	HM
	180	Apr. 12	to N. Molas	BM
			Acknowledgement	
173	181	Apr. 19	to L. Shestakova (original missing; see above—138)	
174	182	Apr. 27	to L. Shestakova (original missing; see above—138)	
175	183	May ?	to L. Shestakova (original missing; see above—138)	
176	184	May 15	to N. Rimsky-Korsakov	LPL
176A		May 18	from V. Stasov to M. Musorgsky	LPL
177	185	June 15	to V. Stasov	LPL
178	186	June 15	to L. Shestakova (original missing; see above—138)	
178A	[308]	June 1	from A. Borodin to L. Karmalina (original missing; see above—115)	
	187	June 18	to L. Shestakova (original missing; see above—138)	
			A response	
179	188	July 14	to V. Stasov	LPL
179A		July 17	from V. Stasov to N. Rimsky-Korsakov	
180	189	July 24	to L. Shestakova (original missing; see above—138)	
180A		July 31	from V. Stasov to D. Stasov	PH
181	190	Aug. 2	to L. Shestakova (original missing; see above—138)	
182	191	Aug. 16	to V. Stasov	LPL
182A		Aug. 16	from V. Stasov to M. Musorgsky	LPL

183	192	Aug. 31	to L. Shestakova (original missing; see above—138)	
184	193	Sept. 10	to L. Shestakova (original missing; see above—138)	
184A		Oct. 2	from V. Stasov to A. Golenishchev-Kutuzov	
	XIX	Nov. 20	to A. Golenishchev-Kutuzov	HM
			"I promised to dine with Molas . . ."	
185	XX	Nov. ?	to A. Golenishchev-Kutuzov	HM
186	194	Nov. 26	to A. and M. Morozov	LPL
186A	[323]	Nov. 29	from A. Borodin to M. Musorgsky	LPL
187	195	Dec. 25	to V. Stasov	LPL
188	196	Dec. 25	to L. Shestakova (original missing; see above—138)	

1877

	197	Jan. 11	to P. Stasova	PH
			". . . from 7 to 9 must take part in literary work."	
189		Apr. 17	A sketch "for the last opera, *Pugachov's Men*."	
190		May 19	A scenario for *Fair at Sorochintzi*	
191	XXI	June 5?	to A. Golenishchev-Kutuzov	HM
192	198	June 14	to D. Stasov	PH
193	199	June 14	to L. Shestakova (original missing; see above—138)	
	200	June 18	to L. Shestakova (original missing; see above—138)	
			Appointments with the Petrovs and Nikolsky	
193A		July 31	from V. Stasov to A. Golenishchev-Kutuzov	
194	XXII	Aug. 15	to A. Golenishchev-Kutuzov	HM
194A		Aug. 22	from V. Stasov to A. Golenishchev-Kutuzov	
	201	Sept. 22	to L. Shestakova (original missing; see above—138)	
			A choice of dates	
	202	Oct. 31	to N. Molas	BM
			Confirmation of an appointment	
195	XXIII	Nov. 10	to A. Golenishchev-Kutuzov	HM
	203	Nov. 11	to N. Molas	BM
			". . . they won't let me go for anything on earth."	
	204	Nov. 12	to A. and N. Molas	BM
			Greetings on their wedding anniversary	
	205	Dec. 5	to N. Molas	BM
			Arranging an appointment	
195A	[71]	Dec. 24	from P. Tchaikovsky to N. von Meck	TM
	206	Dec. 26	to N. Molas	BM
			A concert to aid the Society for Cheap Apartments	

1878

	207	Jan. 9	to N. Molas	BM
			Confirmation of appointment	

	208	Feb. 7	to V. Stasov	LPL
			Arrangements to see *The Wedding of Belugin*	
196	209	Mar. 22	to V. Stasov	LPL
196A		Apr. 1	from V. Stasov to A. Golenishchev-Kutuzov	
197	210	July 26	to L. Shestakova (original missing; see above—138)	
198	211	July 28	to V. Stasov (in a collective letter)	LPL
198A		Aug. 9	from L. Shestakova to V. Stasov	
198B		Oct. 13	from M. Balakirev to V. Stasov	
199	XXIV	Nov. 14	to A. Golenishchev-Kutuzov	HM
200	213	Nov. 24	to L. Shestakova	PH
200A		Dec. 19	from A. Golenishchev-Kutuzov to V. Stasov	

1879

201	214	Mar. 7	to V. Stasov	LPL
202	215	June 16	to L. Shestakova (original missing; see above—138)	
202A		June 17	from V. Stasov to M. Balakirev	LPL
202B		June 17	from M. Balakirev to L. Shestakova	LSC
203	216	July 30	to M. Fyodorova and P. and S. Naumov (original missing)	
204	217	Aug. 3	to M. Fyodorova and P. and S. Naumov	BE
205	218	Sept. 9	to L. Shestakova (original missing; see above—138)	
206	219	Sept. 10	to V. Stasov	LPL
207	220	Sept. 11	to N. Stasova	LPL
207A		Nov. 25	from V. Stasov to N. Rimsky-Korsakov	
208	221	Dec. 19	to L. Shestakova (original missing; see above—138)	
209	XXV	Dec. ?	to A. Golenishchev-Kutuzov	HM
	222	?	to A. Molas	BM
			A projected concert programme	

1880

209A		Jan. 3	from V. Stasov to M. Balakirev	LPL
210	223	Jan. 4	to I. Gorbunov	LPL
211	224	Jan. 16	to V. Stasov	LPL
	225	Feb. 9	to V. Stasov	LPL
			A projected program for Fortunato	
211A		Feb. 17	from V. Stasov to M. Balakirev	LPL
212	226	May 1	to N. Bernard	CML
212A		May 11	from N. Rimsky-Korsakov to V. Stasov	
213	227	Aug. 5	to V. Stasov	LPL
214	228	Aug. 22	to V. Stasov	LPL
215	229	Aug. 27	to V. Stasov	LPL
215A		Nov. 9	from N. Rimsky-Korsakov to S. Kruglikov	

216		Nov. 16	An inscription to I: Gorbunov	BTM
217	230	Dec. ?	to N. Rimsky-Korsakov	LSC

1881

217B	Feb. 4	from N. Rimsky-Korsakov to S. Kruglikov	
217C	Feb. 10	from M. Balakirev to N. Rimsky-Korsakov	
217D	Feb. ?	from N. Rimsky-Korsakov to M. Balakirev	
217E	Feb. 14	from M. Balakirev to V. Stasov	
217F	Feb. 16	from V. Stasov to M. Balakirev	LPL
218	Mar. 14	to T. Filippov (a deed)	
219	231	June ('80) to H. Riemann (an autobiographical note)

Musorgsky's Works on Records

Compiled by Philip L. Miller

NOTE: The aim of this diskography is to list all important recordings whether or not they are to be had on the regular market today. It is not always possible to give dependable information at the present time as to the availability even of domestic records. However, wherever possible, dates of recording or release have been given (unless otherwise noted, all dates represent the year of publication). Some old records have been listed because no other version of the music presented has been traced; but in the matter of duplications it has been deemed advisable to limit the listings to disks of historical or personal interest. The titles have been standardized: they do not attempt to follow record labelings.

OPERAS

Boris Godunov

Unfortunately none of the *Boris* recordings presents Musorgsky's own version of the score. The Chaliapin records, however, are without exception to be treasured as remarkably vital souvenirs of one of the great performances of our day. He recorded most of the selections a number of times, but here in each case only the most modern recording has been listed, except for the historic set of disks made at an actual Covent Garden performance. Though none of the other singing actors has approached Chaliapin's Boris, several celebrated interpreters of the role are here represented. Of the two most recent sets of excerpts, the Kipnis album is recommended above the Italianate though popular performance of Pinza. In up-to-date recording these two albums head our list. The Riga performances were very good in their day, but the reproduction is no longer impressive. Several acoustic records have been included for historical reasons. Sobinov and Smirnov were among the great Russian tenors of their time. Ober and Althouse represent the early casts of the opera at the Metropolitan in New York, shortly after the American *première*. Ober's voice is particularly lovely in this music.

Abridged Recordings

Prologue; Coronation Scene (Prologue, Scene 2); In the Town of Kazan (Act 1, Scene 2); I Have Attained the Highest Power (Act 2); Dialogue between Prince Shuisky and Boris (Act 2); Clock Scene (Act 2); Farewell and Death of Boris (Act 4, Scene 1). Alexander Kipnis, basso (Boris and Varlaam); Ilya Tamarin, tenor (Shuisky); Victor Chorale, Robert Shaw, director; Victor Symphony Orchestra, Nicolai Berezowsky, conductor. (In Russian.) Victor M-1000. (1945)

Prologue; Coronation Scene (Prologue, Scene 2); I Have Attained the Highest Power (Act 2); Clock Scene (Act 2); Polonaise (Act 3, Scene 2); Pimen's Narrative (Act 4, Scene 1); Farewell and Death of Boris (Act 4, Scene 1). Ezio Pinza, basso; Metropolitan Opera Chorus and Orchestra, Emil Cooper, conductor. (In Italian.) Columbia M-563. (1945)

Prologue, Scene 1

Opening Chorus; Pilgrims' Chorus. Riga Opera Chorus and Orchestra, Emil Cooper, conductor; Jan Nedra, baritone. (In Russian.) Decca 25402. (Recorded 1929?)

Prologue, Scene 2

Coronation Scene. Feodor Chaliapin, basso; Chorus and Symphony Orchestra, Albert Coates, conductor. (In Russian and Italian.) Victor 11485. (Recorded 1927?)

Coronation Scene. Vanni-Marcoux, basso. (In French.) HMV DB 4950. (1935?)

Act 1, Scene 1

Scene in the Monastery Cell. Dmitri Smirnov, tenor; C. E. Kaidonoff, basso. (In Russian.) HMV DB 765. (Acoustic recording, 1925)

Pimen's Monologue. Feodor Chaliapin, basso, with orchestra. (In Russian.) Victor 6489. (Acoustic recording, 1925)

Act 1, Scene 2

In the Town of Kazan. Feodor Chaliapin, basso, with orchestra. (In Russian.) Victor 1237. (1927)

Act 2

I Have Attained the Highest Power. Feodor Chaliapin, basso; Royal Opera Orchestra, Covent Garden, Vincenzo Bellezza, conductor. (In Russian.) HMV DB 1181. (Recorded at an actual performance, July 4, 1928.)

I Have Attained the Highest Power. Feodor Chaliapin, basso, with Orchestra, M. Steinmann, conductor. (In Russian.) Victor 14517. (1937)

I Have Attained the Highest Power. Georges Baklanoff, baritone, with Orchestra. (In Russian.) Decca 25813 or 20415. (1929?)

I Have Attained the Highest Power. Vanni-Marcoux, basso, with Orchestra. (In French.) HMV DB 1112. (1930?)

Clock Scene. Feodor Chaliapin, basso; Royal Opera Orchestra, Covent Garden, Vincenzo Bellezza, conductor. (In Russian.) HMV DB 1182. (Recorded at an actual performance, July 4, 1928.)

Clock Scene. Feodor Chaliapin, basso; with orchestra, M. Steinmann, conductor. (In Russian.) Victor 14517. (1937)

Clock Scene. Vanni-Marcoux, basso, with orchestra. (In French.) HMV DB 1112. (1930?)

Act 3, Scene 1

Chorus of the Sandomierz Maidens. Riga Opera Chorus and Orchestra, Emil Cooper, conductor. (In Russian.) Decca 25403. (Recorded 1929?)

Act 3, Scene 2

Polonaise. Riga Opera Chorus and Orchestra, Emil Cooper, conductor. (In Russian.) Decca 25403. (Recorded 1929?)

Oh! Tzarevich, I Implore Thee. Maria Davidoff, mezzo-soprano; Dmitri Smirnov, tenor. (In Russian.) HMV DB 753. (Acoustic recording, 1923)

Oh! Tzarevich, I Implore Thee. Margarete Ober, contralto; Paul Althouse, tenor, with orchestra. (In Italian.) Victor 76031. (Acoustic recording, 1915)

Oh! Tzarevich, I Implore Thee. H. A. Sadoven, mezzo-soprano; N. I. Nagachevsky, tenor. (In Russian.) HMV EK 94.

Oh! Tzarevich, I Implore Thee (complete). Friedl Beckmann, contralto; Helge Roswaenge, tenor, with orchestra. (In German.) HMV DB 5593.

Act 4, Scene 1

Come, Let Us Vote, Boyars; It Is a Pity Prince Shuisky Is Absent; Farewell, My Son; Prayer of Boris; Death of Boris. Feodor Chaliapin, basso; Royal Opera Orchestra and Chorus, Covent Garden, Vincenzo Bellezza, conductor. (In Russian.) HMV DB 1182, DB 1183, DB 3464 (the last disk issued in this country as Victor 15177). (Recorded at an actual performance, July 4, 1928.)

Pimen's Narrative. Feodor Chaliapin, basso, with orchestra. (In Russian.) HMV 76446. (Acoustic recording)

Pimen's Narrative. Michael Gitovsky, basso, with orchestra, Felix Günther, conductor. Homocord 4-8959.

Farewell and Death of Boris. Feodor Chaliapin, basso, with orchestra and chorus, Eugene Goossens, conductor. (In Russian.) Victor 6724.

Farewell of Boris. Georges Baklanoff, baritone, with orchestra. (In Russian.) Decca 25813. (1929?)

Farewell and Death of Boris. Vanni-Marcoux, basso, with orchestra. (In French.) HMV DB 1114. (1930?)

Act 4, Scene 2

Scene Near Kromy. Walter Widdop, tenor; B. Mills; E. Halland; R. Gwynne; F. Kelsey; Orchestra and chorus, Albert Coates, conductor. (In English.) Victor 9507-8. (1929)

Scene Near Kromy. La Scala Chorus and Orchestra, Milan. (In Italian.) Columbia GQX 10264.

Khovanshchina

The outstanding record of this collection is Koussevitzky's performance of the *Prelude,* notable for some beautifully recorded soft playing. All but one of the vocal disks are from a series made by a Russian opera company at Harbin, Manchuria, in the late 1920's. These recordings were issued by Victor on their special export lists. The performances are generally competent. Albert Coates, of course, has long been famous for his interpretations of Russian music, though his recordings (outstanding in their day) are not of the newest.

Act 1

Prelude. Boston Symphony Orchestra, Serge Koussevitzky, conductor. Victor 14415. (1937)

Prelude. Cleveland Orchestra, Artur Rodzinski, conductor. Columbia 11657D (in M-478). (1941)

The Time of Darkness Came. V. Shushlin, basso, with orchestra. (In Russian.) Victor 4099.

Act 2

Marfa's Divination. A. A. Zelinskaya, mezzo-soprano, with orchestra. In Russian.) Victor 4090.

Act 3

Shaklovity's Aria. K. L. Knijnikoff, baritone, with orchestra. (In Russian.) Victor 4091.

Shaklovity's Aria. A. Ivanov, baritone, with orchestra. (In Russian.) Compass USSR–13202/3.

Chorus of Streltzi and Wives. Russian Opera Chorus (in Russian). Victor 4121.

Act 4

Dance of the Persian Maidens. Columbia Broadcasting Symphony Orchestra, Howard Barlow, conductor. Columbia 17286D. (1941)

Dance of the Persian Maidens. London Symphony Orchestra, Albert Coates, conductor. Victor 11135. (1931)

Act 5

Entr'acte. E.I.A.R. Symphony Orchestra, Willy Ferrero, conductor. Decca 25948. (1934)

Fair at Sorochintzi

The following list is a rather miscellaneous one. The rare Smirnov and Koshetz disks are of personal interest. There are many recordings of the popular *Gopak* in various transcriptions which are not listed here.

Act 1

Prelude. Opéra-Comique Orchestra, Paris, G. Cloëz, conductor. Decca 20116.

Reverie of the Young Peasant. Igor Gorin, baritone; Max Rabinowitsch, piano. (In Russian.) Victor 2038 (in M-634). (1940)

Reverie of the Young Peasant. Vladimir Rosing, tenor; Myers Foggin, piano. (In Russian.) Decca 29022 (in D-1). (1938)

Reverie of the Young Peasant. Dmitri Smirnov, tenor. (In French.) HMV DB 753. (Acoustic recording, 1924)

Act 3, Scene 2

Parasya's Reverie and Dance. Xenia Belmas, soprano, with orchestra. (In Russian.) Polydor 66748. (1928?)

Parasya's Reverie and Dance. Nina Koshetz, soprano, with orchestra. (In Russian.) Brunswick 30106. (Acoustic recording, 1924)

Parasya's Reverie and Dance. Ada Slobodskaya, soprano. (In Russian.) HMV EK 113.

Gopak. Opéra-Comique Orchestra, Paris, G. Cloëz, conductor. Decca 20117.

Gopak. London Symphony Orchestra, Albert Coates, conductor. Victor 11443. (1933)

Gopak. London Philharmonic Orchestra, Walter Goehr, conductor. Columbia 69154D. (1938)

Gopak. Lamoureux Orchestra, Albert Wolff, conductor. Polydor 66968.

ROMANCES AND SONGS

Most of the following songs are included in collections made by three singers. Of these three Gorin is generally the most attractive vocally, Rosing the most temperamental and Rudinow the most authentic. Only the last-named has made a point of using Musorgsky's original and unedited scores.

Where Art Thou, Little Star? (edited by Olin Downes). Igor Gorin, baritone; Max Rabinowitsch, piano. (In Russian.) Victor 2038 (in M-634). (1940)

455

Where Art Thou, Little Star? Vladimir Rosing, tenor; Myers Foggin, piano. (In Russian.) Decca 29021 (in D-1). (1938)

Song of the Old Man. Jacques Bastard, baritone, with piano. (In French.) Pathé PG 53. (1935)

King Saul. Moshe Rudinow, baritone; Esther Elkin, piano. (In Russian.) Gamut 10.106 (in MS-4). (1937)

Gopak. Igor Gorin, baritone, with orchestra, Wilfred Pelletier, conductor. (In Russian.) Victor 4414. (1939)

Gopak. Vladimir Rosing, tenor; Myers Foggin, piano. (In Russian.) Decca 29020 (in D-1). (1938)

Lovely Savishna. Vladimir Rosing, tenor; Myers Foggin, piano. (In Russian.) Decca 29025 (in D-1). (1938)

Hebraic Song. Sophie Braslau, contralto. (In Russian.) Victor 64478. (Acoustic recording, 1915)

The White-Flanked Magpie. Nina Koshetz, soprano, with orchestra. (In Russian.) Brunswick 10138. (Acoustic recording, 1924)

Gathering Mushrooms. Vladimir Rosing, tenor; Myers Foggin, piano. (In Russian.) Decca 29022 (in D-1). (1938)

The He-Goat. Vladimir Rosing, tenor; Myers Foggin, piano. (In Russian.) Decca 29025 (in D-1). (1938)

On the Don the Gardens Bloom. Igor Gorin, baritone; Max Rabinowitsch, piano. (In Russian.) Victor 2039 (in M-634). (1940)

The Little Orphan Girl. Vladimir Rosing, tenor; Myers Foggin, piano. (In Russian.) Decca 29022 (in D-1). (1938)

Yeremushka's Cradle-Song. Vladimir Rosing, tenor; Myers Foggin, piano. (In Russian.) Decca 29020 (in D-1). (1938)

Forgotten. Igor Gorin, baritone; Max Rabinowitsch, piano. (In Russian.) Victor 2039 (in M-634). (1940)

Forgotten. Paul Robeson, basso; Lawrence Brown. HMV B 9149. (1941)

Forgotten. Vladimir Rosing, tenor; Myers Foggin, piano. (In Russian.) Decca 29025 (in D-1). (1938)

Forgotten. Moshe Rudinow, baritone; Esther Elkin, piano. (In Russian.) Gamut 10.106 (in MS-4). (1937)

The Nursery (Cycle of seven songs: No. 2 omitted). Igor Gorin, baritone; Adolf Baller, piano (in English: translation of M. H. C. Collet). Victor M-686. (1940)

The Nursery (Cycle of seven songs: No. 4 omitted). Betty Martin, soprano. (In English.) Columbia J-14. (1940)

Sunless (Cycle of six songs). Moshe Rudinow, baritone; Esther Elkin, piano. (In Russian.) Gamut 10.103-5 (in MS-4). (1937)

Sunless: No. 1, Within Four Walls. Paul Robeson, basso; Lawrence

Brown, piano. (In English and Russian.) Columbia 71367D. (1942)

Pride Passes By, Puffed Up. Moshe Rudinow, baritone; Esther Elkin, piano. (In Russian.) Gamut 10.105 (in MS-4). (1937)

Mephistopheles' Song in Auerbach's Cellar. Feodor Chaliapin, basso; G. Godzinski, piano. (In Russian.) Victor 14901. (Recorded Feb. 3, 1936)

Mephistopheles' Song in Auerbach's Cellar. Feodor Chaliapin, basso, with orchestra. (In Russian.) Victor 6783.

Mephistopheles' Song in Auerbach's Cellar. Vladimir Rosing, tenor, with piano. (In Russian.) Decca 25197.

Mephistopheles' Song in Auerbach's Cellar. Lawrence Tibbett, baritone, with orchestra. (In English.) Victor 7779.

On the Dnieper. Vladimir Rosing, tenor; Myers Foggin, piano. (In Russian.) Decca 29021 (in D-1). (1938)

Songs and Dances of Death (Cycle of four songs). Igor Gorin, baritone; Max Rabinowitsch, piano. (In Russian). Victor 2036-37 (in M-634). (1940)

Songs and Dances of Death (Cycle of four songs). Vladimir Rosing, tenor; Myers Foggin, piano. (In Russian.) Decca 29023-24 (in D-1). (1938)

Songs and Dances of Death (Cycle of four songs). Marko Rothmueller, baritone; Suzanne Gyr, piano. HMV DB 10062-63. (1945)

Songs and Dances of Death (Cycle of four songs). Moshe Rudinow, baritone; Esther Elkin, piano. (In Russian.) Gamut MS-5. (1940)

Songs and Dances of Death: No. 3, Trepak. Feodor Chaliapin, basso, with orchestra, Laurence Collingwood, conductor. (In Russian.) HMV DB 1511.

ORCHESTRAL WORKS

Night on Bald Mountain. London Symphony Orchestra; Albert Coates, conductor. Victor 11448. (1933)

Night on Bald Mountain. Berlin Philharmonic Orchestra; Viscount Hidemaro Konoye, conductor. Polydor 67259. (1939)

Night on Bald Mountain. Colonne Orchestra, Paul Paray, conductor. Columbia 68305D. (1935)

Night on Bald Mountain. Pittsburgh Symphony Orchestra; Fritz Reiner, conductor. Columbia 12470D. (1947)

WORKS FOR PIANO

Une Larme. Anna Antoniades, piano. Polydor 47369. (1940)
Pictures at an Exhibition. Alexander Brailowsky, piano. Victor M-861. (1942)
Pictures at an Exhibition. Benno Moiseiwitsch, piano. HMV C3576-9. (1947)
Pictures at an Exhibition (orchestrated by Maurice Ravel). Boston Symphony Orchestra, Serge Koussevitzky, conductor. Victor M-102.
Pictures at an Exhibition (orchestrated by Maurice Ravel). Philharmonic-Symphony Orchestra of New York; Artur Rodzinski, conductor. Columbia M-641. (1946)

RUSSIAN FOLK SONGS ARRANGED FOR MALE CHORUS

Arise, Beautiful Sun. Russian State Choir (formerly Russian Imperial Choir), Prof. M. Klimoff, conductor. (In Russian.) HMV EK 59. (1928)

Sources: The Testimony of Musorgsky's Contemporaries

Belayev, Victor (see Lavrov)

Bertensson, Lev

"For a Biography of M. P. Musorgsky," *Yezhenedelnik Petrogradskikh Akademicheskikh Teatrov*, No. 3, Oct. 1, 1922.

Bertensson, Vasili

For Thirty Years. St. Petersburg, 1914.

Bessel, Vasili

N. F. Findeisen, *V. V. Bessel, A Study of His Musical-Social Activity.* St. Petersburg, 1909.

Boborykin, P.

"For Half a Century," *Russkaya Starina*, February, 1913.

Borodin, Alexander

V. V. Stasov, *A. P. Borodin. His Life, Correspondence and Musical Articles.* St. Petersburg, 1889. (Includes the letter written in 1881 to Stasov, at the latter's request, on Borodin's encounters with Musorgsky.)

Brayer, Jules de

Pierre d'Alheim, *Moussorgsky.* Paris, 1896. (Includes Brayer's letter to d'Alheim on his introduction of Musorgsky's scores to French musical circles.)

Golenishchev-Kutuzov, Arseni

"Reminiscences of M. P. Musorgsky," *Muzikalnoye Nasledstvo*, 1935.

Ippolitov-Ivanov, Mikhail

50 Years of Russian Music in My Memories. Moscow, 1934.

Ivanov, Mikhail

"M. P. Musorgsky," *Novoye Vremya*, No. 1814, March 17, 1881.

Kompaneisky, Nikolai

"Towards New Shores. Modeste Petrovich Musorgsky (1839–1881)," *Russkaya Muzikalnaya Gazeta*, Nos. 11–12, 14–18, March 12, 19, April 2, 9, 16, 23, 30, 1906.

Krylov, Victor

"The Composer C. A. Cui, Fragment from My Memoirs," *Istoricheski*

Vestnik, No. 2, February, 1894. (Reprinted in Vol. II of Krylov's collected works.)

Lapshin, Ivan
Artistic Creation. Petrograd, 1923.

Lavrov, Nikolai
Yuri Keldysh and Vasili Yakovlev, *M. P. Musorgsky, On the Fiftieth Anniversary of His Death 1881–1931.* Moscow, 1932. (Includes this memoir, dictated by Lavrov to Victor Belayev.)

Leonova, Daria
"Reminiscences of D. M. Leonova," *Istoricheski Vestnik,* February–April, 1891.

Musorgsky, Filaret
V. V. Stasov, *Articles on M. Musorgsky and His Works.* Moscow, 1922. (Includes memorandum written in 1881 to Stasov at the latter's request, providing data on Musorgsky's early years.)

Platonova, Yulia
N. Findeisen, "New Material for M. P. Musorgsky's Biography," *Russkaya Muzikalnaya Gazeta,* No. 12, December, 1895. (Includes the complete text of Platonova's letter to Stasov of November 27, 1888.)

Purgold (Molas), Alexandra
Yuri Keldysh and Vasili Yakovlev, *M. P. Musorgsky, On the Fiftieth Anniversary of His Death, 1881–1931.* Moscow, 1932. (Includes this memoir by Mme. Molas.)

Purgold (Rimskaya-Korsakova), Nadezhda
"From My Reminiscences of A. S. Dargomizhsky," *Russkaya Molva,* No. 53, February 2, 1913. (Reprinted in *Muzika,* No. 116, 1913.)

Repin, Ilya
Igor Grabar, *Repin.* Moscow, 1937. (Includes material from Repin's manuscript memoirs.)

Rimsky-Korsakov, Nikolai
Chronicle of My Musical Life. Moscow, 1935 (fifth edition).

Roerich, Yelena
A letter written to the editors of *The Musorgsky Reader.*

Rozhdestvensky, S. V.
I. I. Lapshin, *Artistic Creation.* Petrograd, 1923. (Includes this interview with Rozhdestvensky.)

Shestakova, Ludmila
"My Evenings," *Yezhegodnik Imperatorskikh Teatrov,* Season 1893–94.

Stasov, Vladimir
Pp. 6, 38, 57, 65, 128, 155, 187, 354: *Articles on M. Musorgsky and His Works.* Moscow, 1922. (A collection of most of Stasov's published writings on Musorgsky.)

P. 83: "20 Letters from I. S. Turgenev," *Severnyi Vestnik*, No. 10, 1888.

P. 170: "Seventeen Letters to A. M. Kerzin," *Muzikalnyi Sovremennik*, No. 2, 1916.

P. 183: *Nikolai Nikolayevich Gay, His Life, Works and Correspondence*. Moscow, 1904.

P. 412: "Musorgsky's Portrait," *Golos*, No. 85, March 24, 1881. (Reprinted in Vol. I of Stasov's collected works.)

Stasova (Fortunato), Sofia
Yuri Keldysh and Vasili Yakovlev, *M. P. Musorgsky, On the Fiftieth Anniversary of His Death, 1881–1931*. Moscow, 1932. (Includes this memoir, written at the request of the editors.)

Stasova (Komarova), Varvara
"From Childhood Memories of Great Men: Musorgsky," *Muzikalnyi Sovremennik*, Nos. 5–6, 1917.

Stakheyev, Dmitri
"Groups and Portraits," *Istoricheski Vestnik*, February, 1907.

Yastrebtzev, Vasili
My Memories of N. A. Rimsky-Korsakov. Petrograd, 1917.

OTHER SOURCES USED IN THE PREPARATION OF THIS VOLUME

Apukhtin, Alexei. *Poetic Works.*

Belayev, Victor. *Musorgsky's Boris Godunov and Its New Version*, translated from the Russian by S. W. Pring. London, Oxford University Press, 1928.

Borodin, Alexander. *Letters*, edited by S. A. Dianin. Moscow, 1928, 1936.

Calvocoressi, M. D., and Abraham, Gerald. *Masters of Russian Music.* New York, Alfred A. Knopf, 1936.

"Correspondence of M. A. Balakirev and N. A. Rimsky-Korsakov (1862–1898)," *Muzikalnyi Sovremennik*, 1915–1917.

Correspondence of M. A. Balakirev and V. V. Stasov. Moscow, 1935.

Cui, Cesar. *La Musique en Russie.* Paris, 1880.

Dargomizhsky, Alexander. *Autobiography—Letters—Contemporaries' Reminiscences*, edited by N. F. Findeisen. Petrograd, 1921.

Frankenstein, Alfred. "Victor Hartmann and Modeste Musorgsky," *Musical Quarterly*, No. XXV, July, 1939.

Godet, Robert. *En marge de Boris Godounof.* Paris, 1926.

Karenin, Vladimir (Stasova). *Vladimir Stasov.* Leningrad, 1927.

Keldysh, Yuri, and Yakovlev, Vasili, editors. *M. P. Musorgsky, On the Fiftieth Anniversary of His Death (1881–1931); Articles and Materials.* Moscow, 1932.

Khotinsky, M. S. *Witchcraft and Mysterious Phenomena of Modern Times.* St. Petersburg, 1866.

Letters of Franz Liszt, collected and edited by La Mara, translated by Constance Bache. New York, Charles Scribner's Sons, 1893.

"Letters of V. V. Stasov and N. A. Rimsky-Korsakov," edited by V. Karenin (Stasova), *Russkaya Mysl,* Nos. VI–VIII, 1910.

Lyubimov, S. V. *The Princes Kostrov, Materials for a Genealogy of the Musorgskys.* Pskov, 1916.

Musorgsky, M. P. *Letters and Documents,* collected and arranged for publication by A. N. Rimsky-Korsakov, with the participation of V. D. Komarova-Stasova. Moscow-Leningrad, 1932.

Musorgsky, M. P. *Letters to A. A. Golenishchev-Kutuzov,* edited by Yuri Keldysh. Moscow-Leningrad, 1939.

Musorgsky, M. P. *Works,* edited by Pavel Lamm. Moscow-Leningrad, 1928–1939.

Musorgsky, M. P. *Boris Godounov.* London, 1926. (The illustrated Chester edition of the first edition of the piano score.)

Musorgsky's Boris Godunov (collection of articles and materials). Moscow, 1930.

Muzikalnyi Sovremennik, Nos. 5–6, 1917. A special issue devoted to Musorgsky studies and documents.

Orlov, Georgi. *Chronicle of the Life and Creative Work of M. P. Musorgsky.* Moscow-Leningrad, 1940.

Rimsky-Korsakov, A. N. *N. A. Rimsky-Korsakov, Life and Creative Work.* Moscow, 1933–1937.

Rimsky-Korsakov, Nikolai. *100 Russian Folk-Songs* (Op. 24). St. Petersburg, 1877?

Rubinstein, Anton. "Of Music in Russia," *Vek,* No. 1, 1861. (Reprinted in Glebov, *Anton Grigoryevich Rubinstein in His Musical Activity and in His Contemporaries' Views (1829–1929),* Moscow, 1929.)

(Saltykov-Shchedrin, Mikhail) "On the Side," *Otechestvennya Zapiski,* No. 11, November, 1874.

Stasov, Vladimir. *Collected Works.* St. Petersburg, 1894.

Stasov, Vladimir. *Mark Antokolsky, His Life, Creative Work, Letters and Articles.* Moscow, 1905.

Tchaikovsky, Modeste. *Letters of P. I. Tchaikovsky and S. I. Taneyev.* Moscow, n.d.

Tchaikovsky, Modeste. *The Life of P. I. Tchaikovsky.* Moscow, 1900–1902.

Tchaikovsky, P. I. *Correspondence with N. F. Von Meck.* Leningrad, 1934–1935.

Timofeyev, G. N. "Balakirev in Prague," *Sovremennyi Mir,* No. VI, 1911.

Index

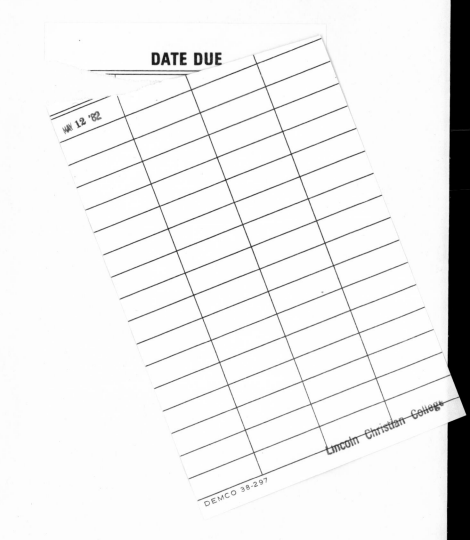

DATE DUE

MAY 12 '82

DEMCO 38-297

Lincoln Christian College